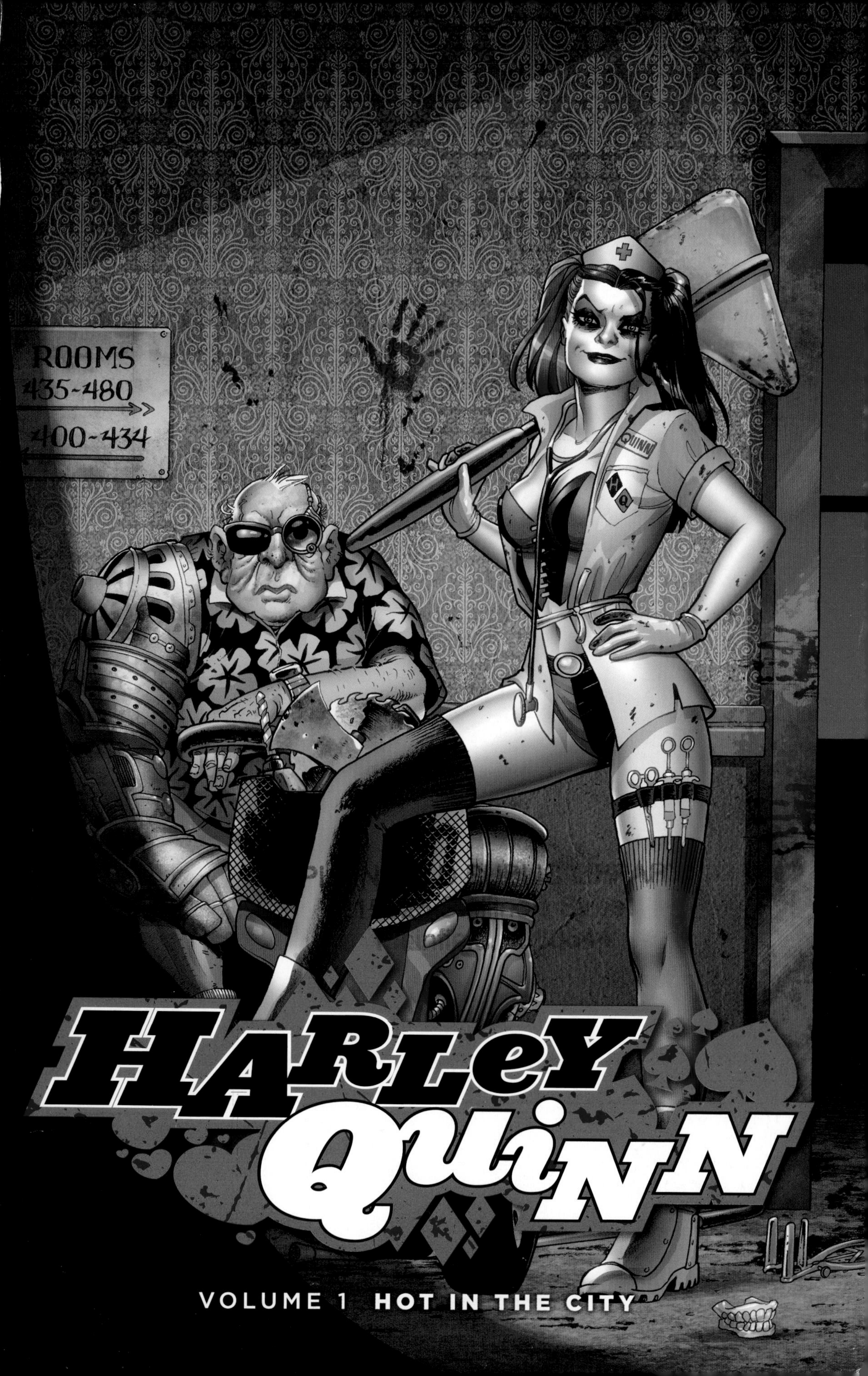
ROOMS
435-480
400-434
QUINN
HQ
HARLEY
QUINN
VOLUME 1 HOT IN THE CITY

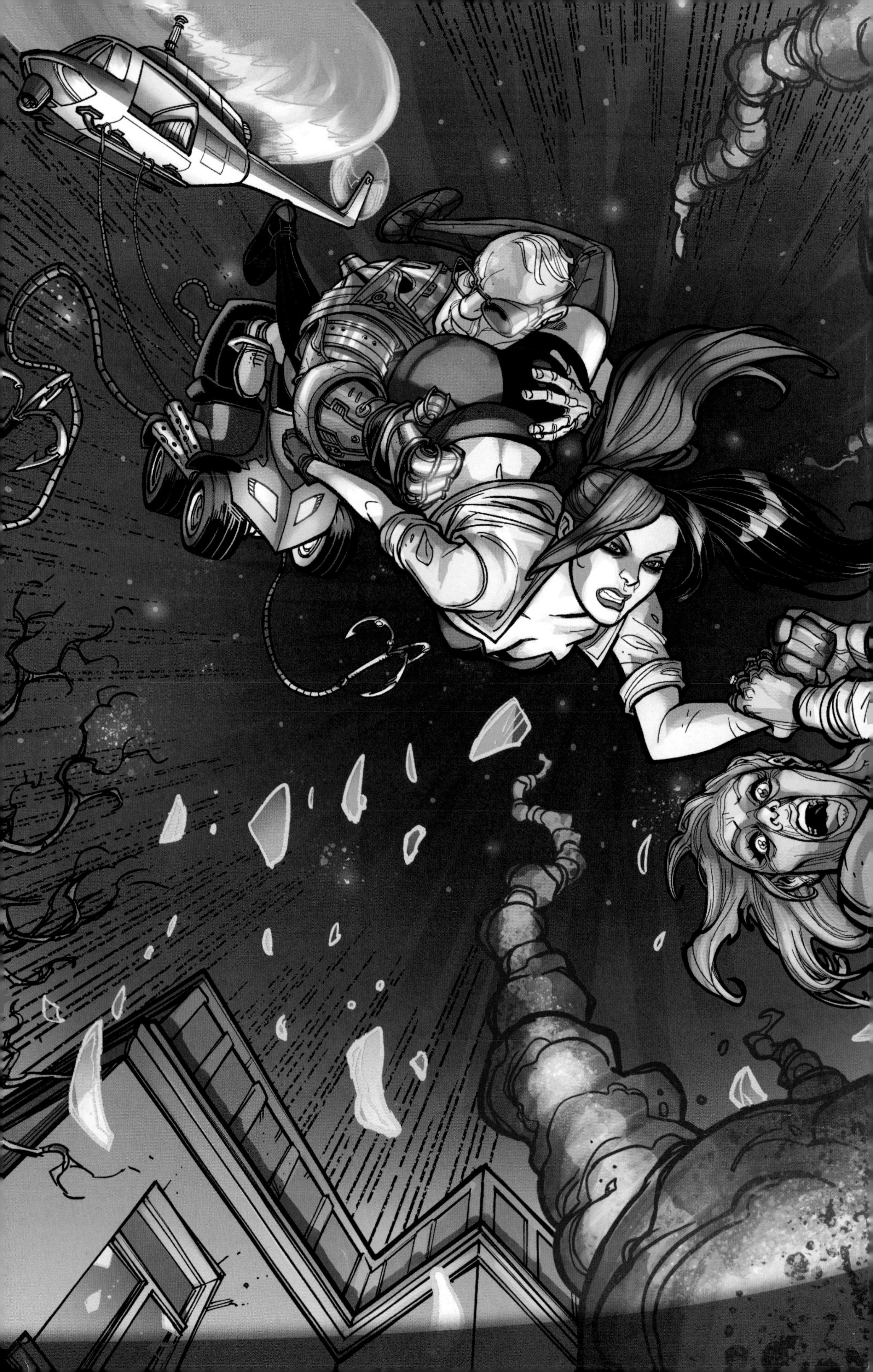

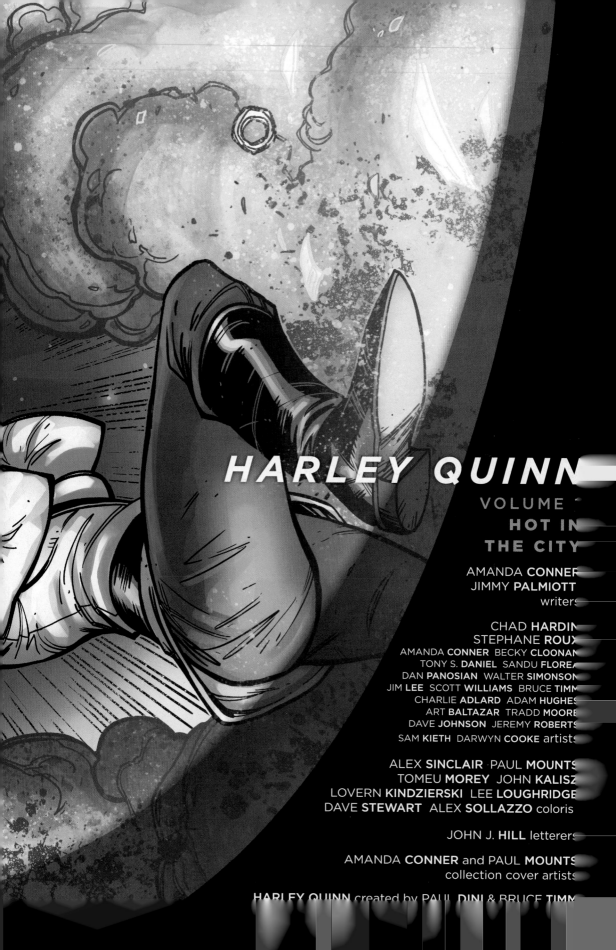

HARLEY QUINN

VOLUME 1
HOT IN
THE CITY

AMANDA **CONNER**
JIMMY **PALMIOTTI**
writers

CHAD **HARDIN**
STEPHANE **ROUX**
AMANDA **CONNER** BECKY **CLOONAN**
TONY S. **DANIEL** SANDU **FLOREA**
DAN **PANOSIAN** WALTER **SIMONSON**
JIM **LEE** SCOTT **WILLIAMS** BRUCE **TIMM**
CHARLIE **ADLARD** ADAM **HUGHES**
ART **BALTAZAR** TRADD **MOORE**
DAVE **JOHNSON** JEREMY **ROBERTS**
SAM **KIETH** DARWYN **COOKE** artists

ALEX **SINCLAIR** · PAUL **MOUNTS**
TOMEU **MOREY** JOHN **KALISZ**
LOVERN **KINDZIERSKI** LEE **LOUGHRIDGE**
DAVE **STEWART** ALEX **SOLLAZZO** colorists

JOHN J. **HILL** letterers

AMANDA **CONNER** and PAUL **MOUNTS**
collection cover artists

HARLEY QUINN created by PAUL **DINI** & BRUCE **TIMM**

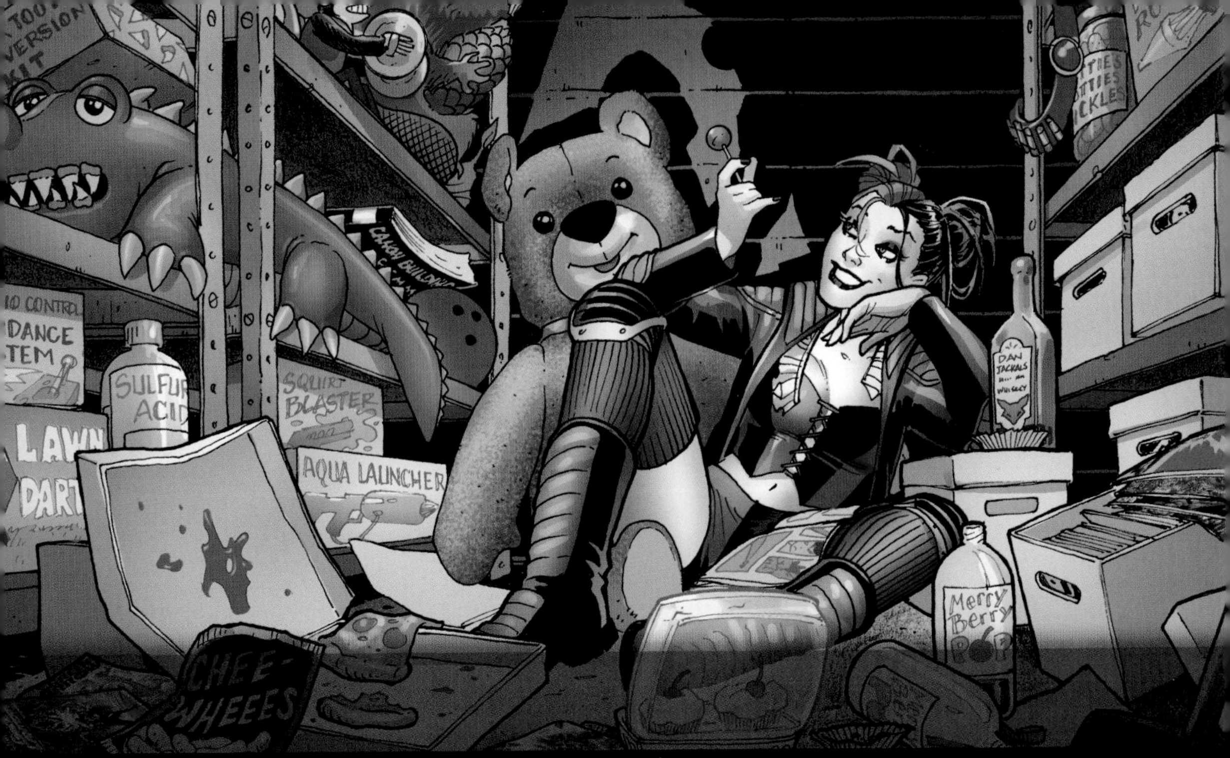
SQUIRT BLASTER
AQUA LAUNCHER
Merry Berry POP
CHEE-WHEEES

KATIE KUBERT CHRIS CONROY Editor – Original Series MATT HUMPHREYS Assistant Editor – Original Series
PETER HAMBOUSSI Editor ROBBIN BROSTERMAN Design Director – Books ROBBIE BIEDERMAN Publication Design

BOB HARRAS Senior VP – Editor-in-Chief, DC Comics

DIANE NELSON President DAN DIDIO and JIM LEE Co-Publishers GEOFF JOHNS Chief Creative Officer
AMIT DESAI Senior VP – Marketing and Franchise Management
AMY GENKINS Senior VP – Business and Legal Affairs NAIRI GARDINER Senior VP – Finance
JEFF BOISON VP – Publishing Planning MARK CHIARELLO VP – Art Direction and Design
JOHN CUNNINGHAM VP – Marketing TERRI CUNNINGHAM VP – Editorial Administration
LARRY GANEM VP – Talent Relations and Services ALISON GILL Senior VP – Manufacturing and Operations
HANK KANALZ Senior VP – Vertigo and Integrated Publishing JAY KOGAN VP – Business and Legal Affairs, Publishing
JACK MAHAN VP – Business Affairs, Talent NICK NAPOLITANO VP – Manufacturing Administration SUE POHJA VP – Book Sales
FRED RUIZ VP – Manufacturing Operations COURTNEY SIMMONS Senior VP – Publicity BOB WAYNE Senior VP – Sales

HARLEY QUINN VOLUME 1: HOT IN THE CITY

DC Comics, 1700 Broadway, New York, NY 10019
A Warner Bros. Entertainment Company.
Printed by RR Donnelley, Salem, VA, USA. 9/19/14. First Printing.
HC ISBN: 978-1-4012-4892-5
SC ISBN: 978-1-4012-5415-5

Library of Congress Cataloging-in-Publication Data

Palmiotti, Jimmy, author.
Harley Quinn. Volume 1, Hot in the city / Jimmy Palmiotti, Amanda Conner.
pages cm. — (The New 52!)
Includes bibliographical references and index.
ISBN 978-1-4012-4892-5 (hardback)
1. Graphic novels. I. Conner, Amanda, illustrator. II. Title. III. Title: Hot in the city.

PN6728.H367P35 2014
741.5'973—dc23

2014034093

SUSTAINABLE FORESTRY INITIATIVE
Certified Chain of Custody
20% Certified Forest Content,
80% Certified Sourcing
www.sfiprogram.org
SFI-01042
APPLIES TO TEXT STOCK ONLY

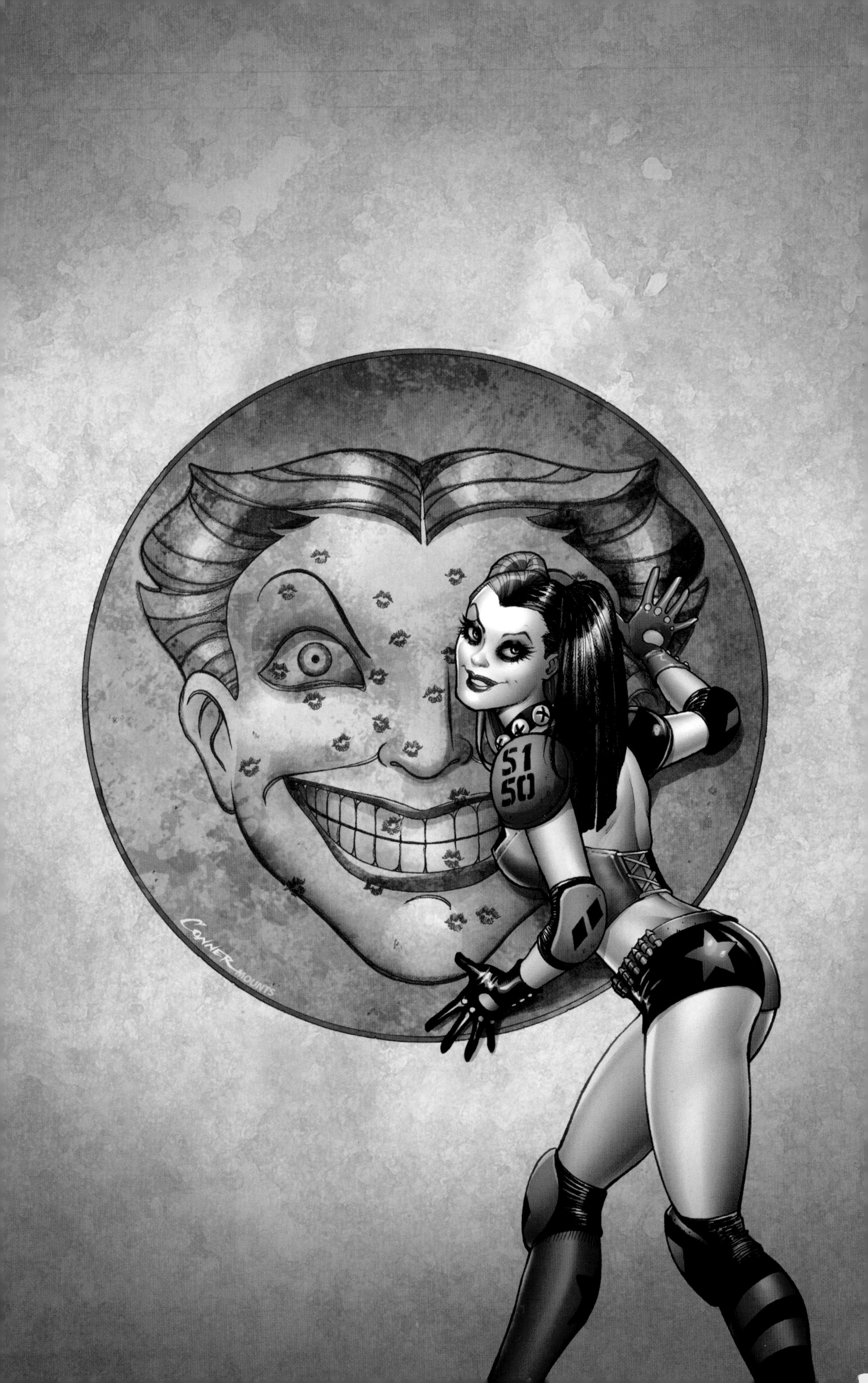
51
50
CONNER MOUNTS

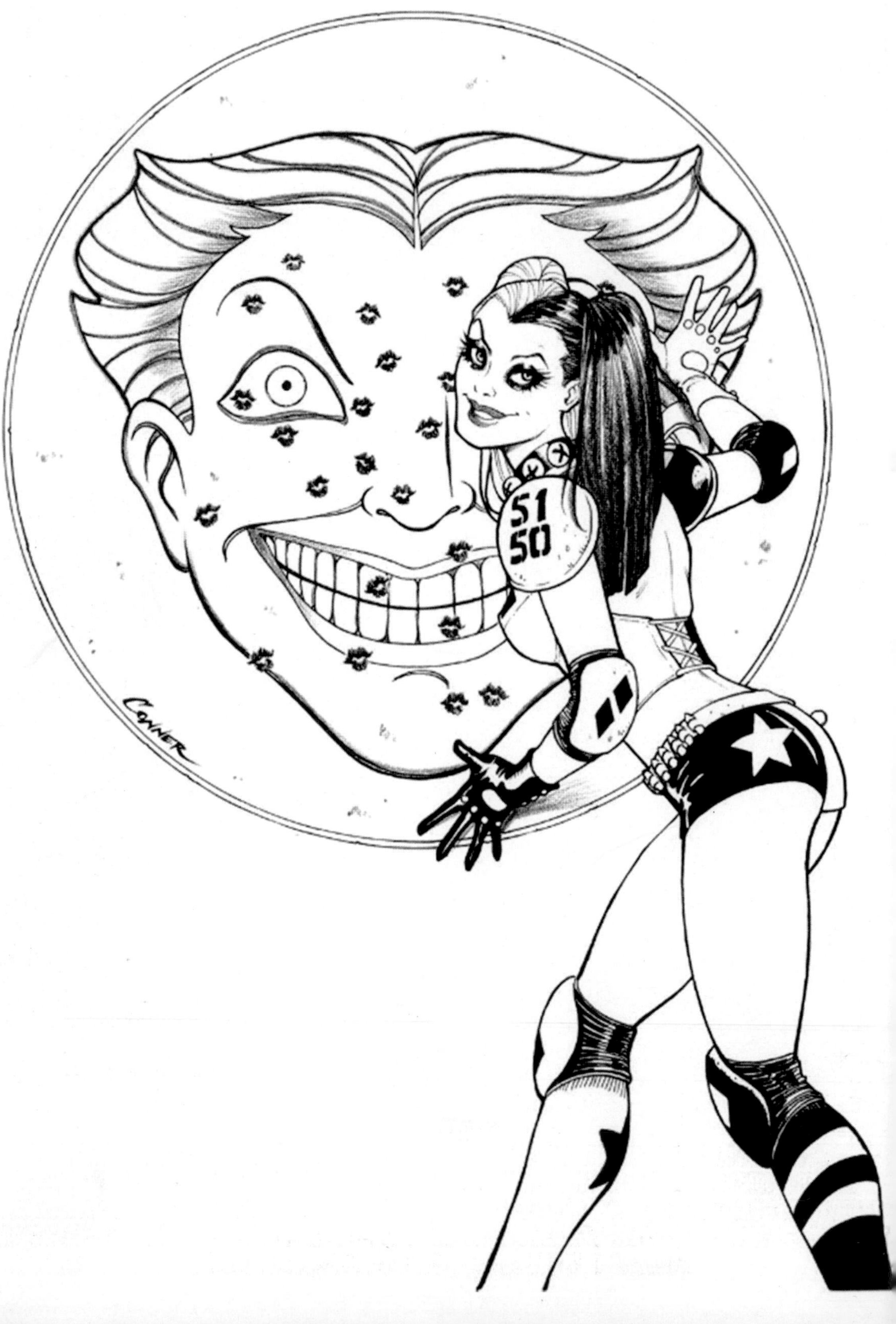
51
50
CONNER

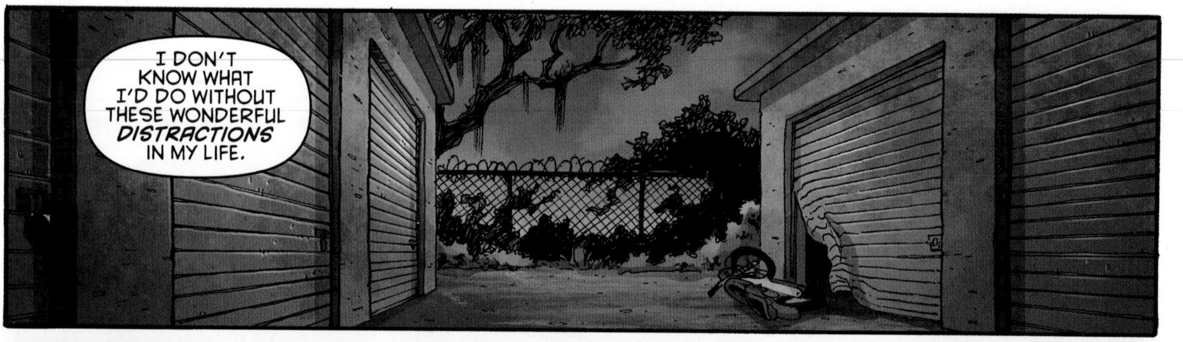
I DON'T KNOW WHAT I'D DO WITHOUT THESE WONDERFUL *DISTRACTIONS* IN MY LIFE.

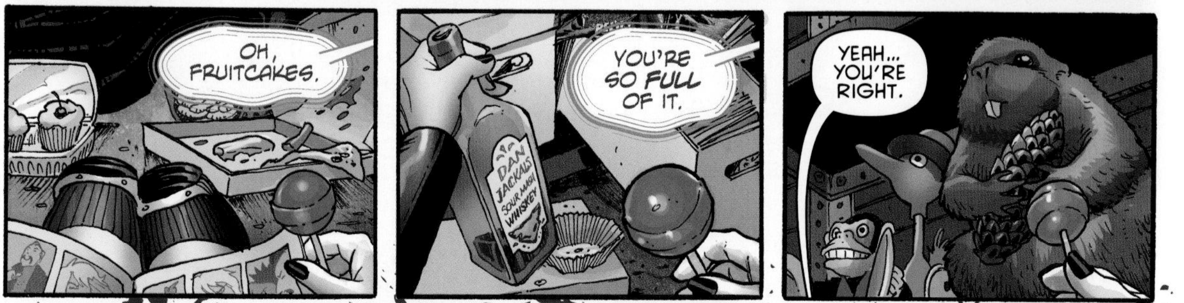
OH, FRUITCAKES.
YOU'RE SO *FULL* OF IT.
DAN JACKALS SOUR MASH WHISKEY
YEAH... YOU'RE RIGHT.

PICKY SICKY

written by AMANDA CONNER & JIMMY PALMIOTTI

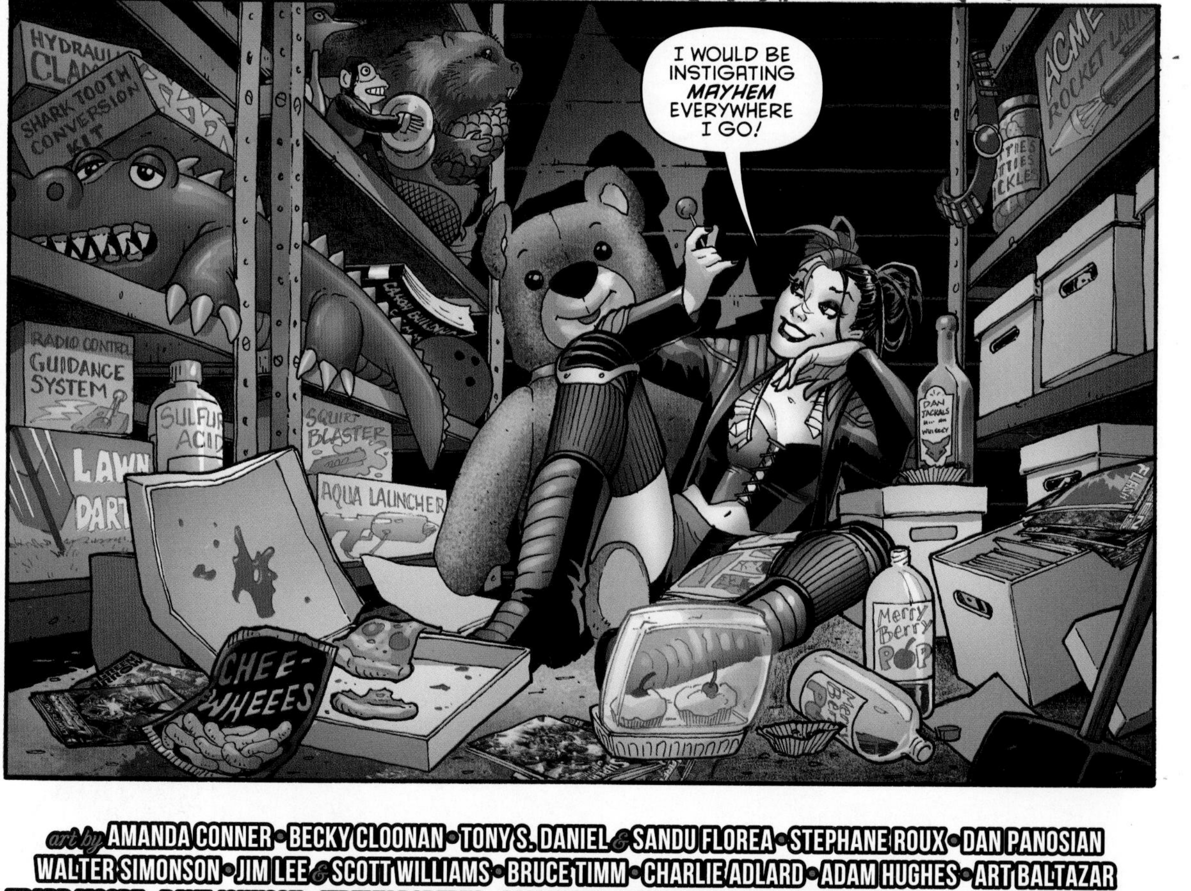
I WOULD BE INSTIGATING *MAYHEM* EVERYWHERE I GO!
SHARK TOOTH CONVERSION KIT
ACME
RADIO CONTROL GUIDANCE SYSTEM
SQUIRT BLASTER
AQUA LAUNCHER
DAN JACKALS WHISKEY
Merry Berry POP
CHEE-WHEEES

art by AMANDA CONNER • BECKY CLOONAN • TONY S. DANIEL & SANDU FLOREA • STEPHANE ROUX • DAN PANOSIAN
WALTER SIMONSON • JIM LEE & SCOTT WILLIAMS • BRUCE TIMM • CHARLIE ADLARD • ADAM HUGHES • ART BALTAZAR
TRADD MOORE • DAVE JOHNSON • JEREMY ROBERTS • SAM KIETH • DARWYN COOKE • CHAD HARDIN *colors by* PAUL MOUNTS
TOMEU MOREY • JOHN KALISZ • LOVERN KINDZIERSKI • ALEX SINCLAIR • LEE LOUGHRIDGE • DAVE STEWART • ALEX SOLLAZZO
letters by JOHN J. HILL *cover by* AMANDA CONNER & PAUL MOUNTS

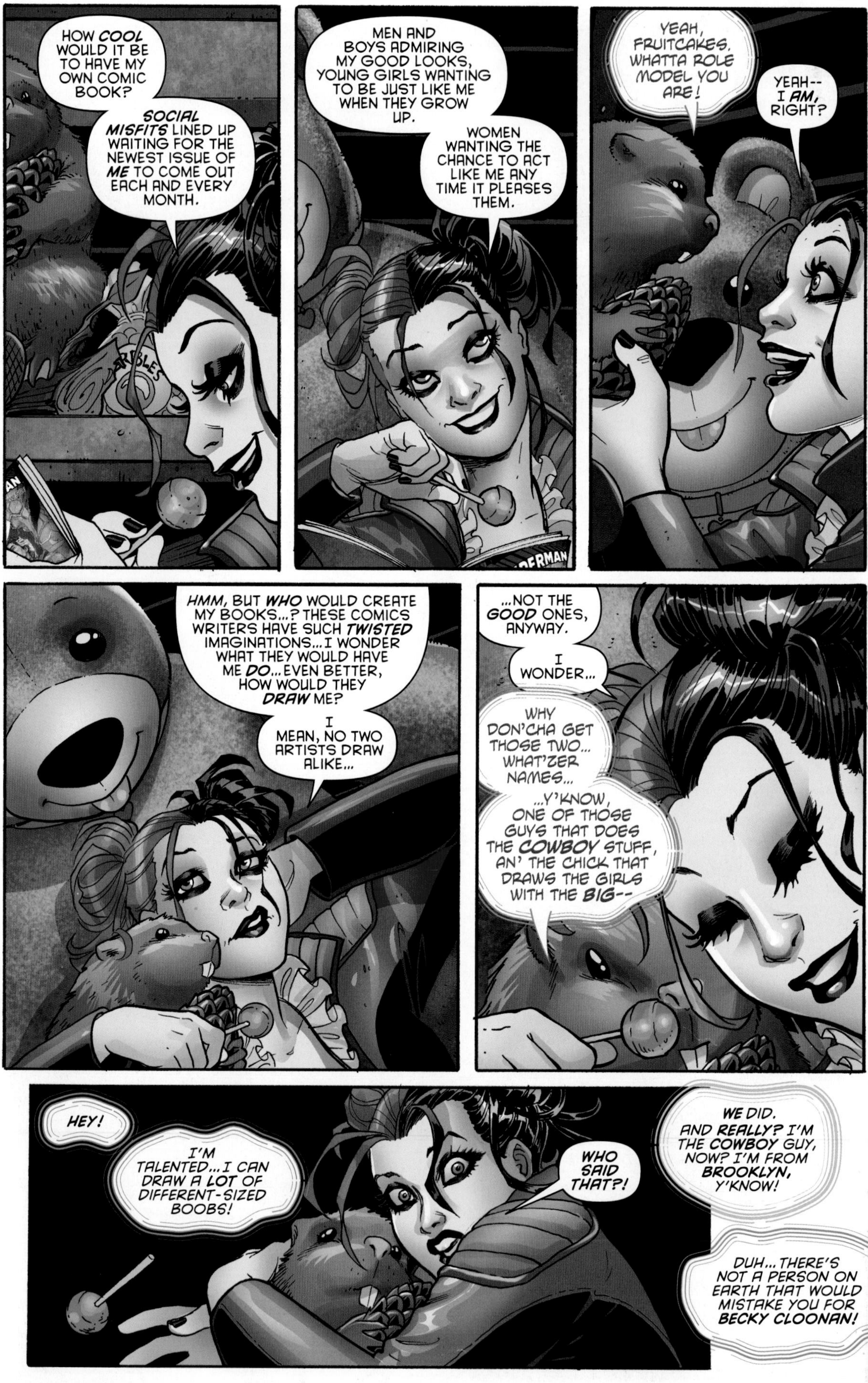

HOW COOL WOULD IT BE TO HAVE MY OWN COMIC BOOK?
SOCIAL MISFITS LINED UP WAITING FOR THE NEWEST ISSUE OF ME TO COME OUT EACH AND EVERY MONTH.
MEN AND BOYS ADMIRING MY GOOD LOOKS, YOUNG GIRLS WANTING TO BE JUST LIKE ME WHEN THEY GROW UP.
WOMEN WANTING THE CHANCE TO ACT LIKE ME ANY TIME IT PLEASES THEM.
YEAH, FRUITCAKES. WHATTA ROLE MODEL YOU ARE!
YEAH-- I AM, RIGHT?
HMM, BUT WHO WOULD CREATE MY BOOKS...? THESE COMICS WRITERS HAVE SUCH TWISTED IMAGINATIONS... I WONDER WHAT THEY WOULD HAVE ME DO... EVEN BETTER, HOW WOULD THEY DRAW ME?
I MEAN, NO TWO ARTISTS DRAW ALIKE...
...NOT THE GOOD ONES, ANYWAY.
I WONDER...
WHY DON'CHA GET THOSE TWO... WHAT'ZER NAMES...
...Y'KNOW, ONE OF THOSE GUYS THAT DOES THE COWBOY STUFF, AN' THE CHICK THAT DRAWS THE GIRLS WITH THE BIG--
HEY!
I'M TALENTED... I CAN DRAW A LOT OF DIFFERENT-SIZED BOOBS!
WHO SAID THAT?!
WE DID. AND REALLY? I'M THE COWBOY GUY, NOW? I'M FROM BROOKLYN, Y'KNOW!
DUH... THERE'S NOT A PERSON ON EARTH THAT WOULD MISTAKE YOU FOR BECKY CLOONAN!

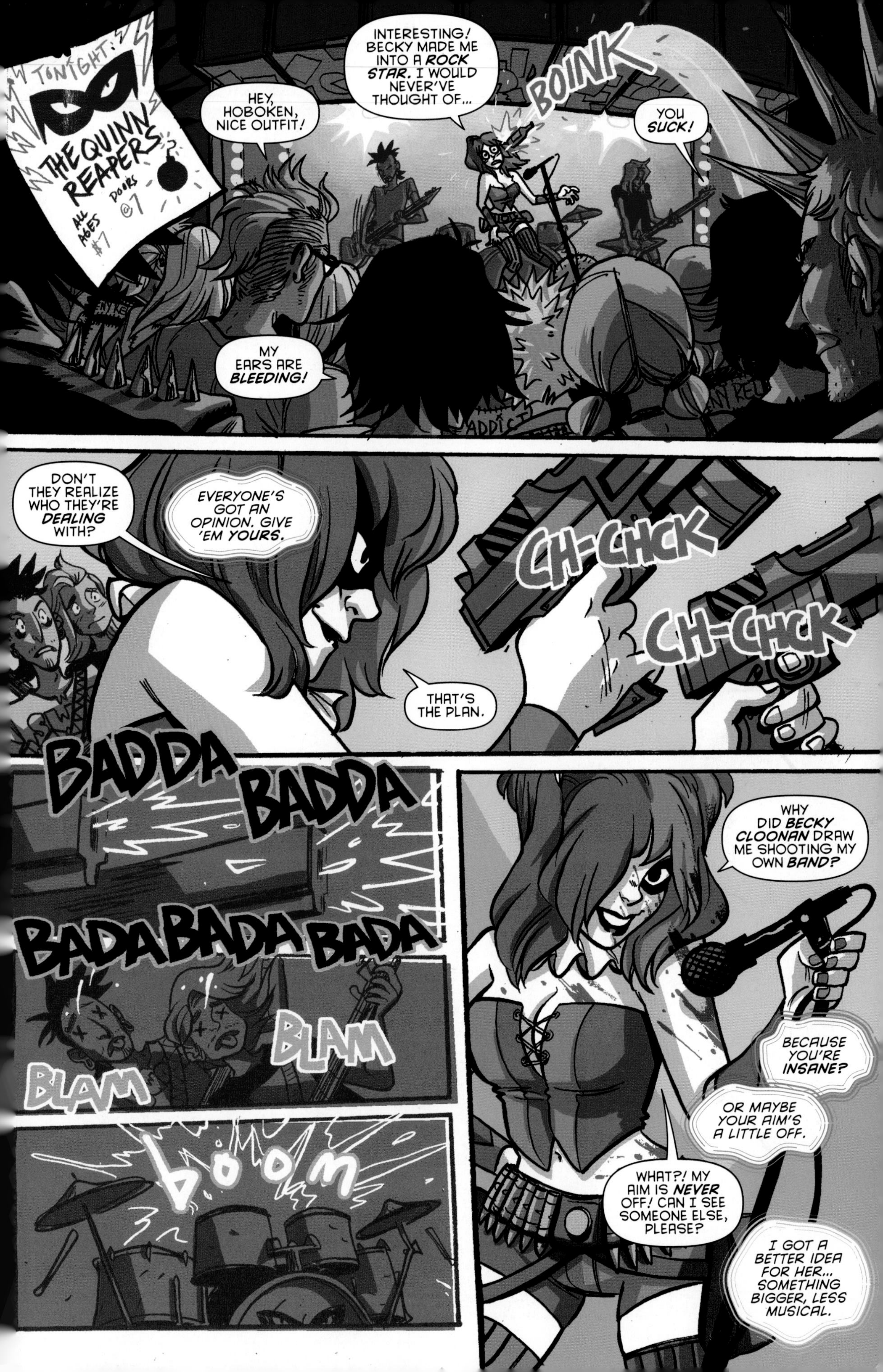
TONIGHT:
THE QUINN REAPERS
ALL AGES $7
DOORS @7
HEY, HOBOKEN, NICE OUTFIT!
INTERESTING! BECKY MADE ME INTO A ROCK STAR. I WOULD NEVER'VE THOUGHT OF...
BOINK
YOU SUCK!
MY EARS ARE BLEEDING!
DON'T THEY REALIZE WHO THEY'RE DEALING WITH?
EVERYONE'S GOT AN OPINION. GIVE 'EM YOURS.
CH-CHCK
CH-CHCK
THAT'S THE PLAN.
BADDA BADDA
BADA BADA BADA
BLAM
BLAM
BOOM
WHY DID BECKY CLOONAN DRAW ME SHOOTING MY OWN BAND?
BECAUSE YOU'RE INSANE?
OR MAYBE YOUR AIM'S A LITTLE OFF.
WHAT?! MY AIM IS NEVER OFF! CAN I SEE SOMEONE ELSE, PLEASE?
I GOT A BETTER IDEA FOR HER... SOMETHING BIGGER, LESS MUSICAL.

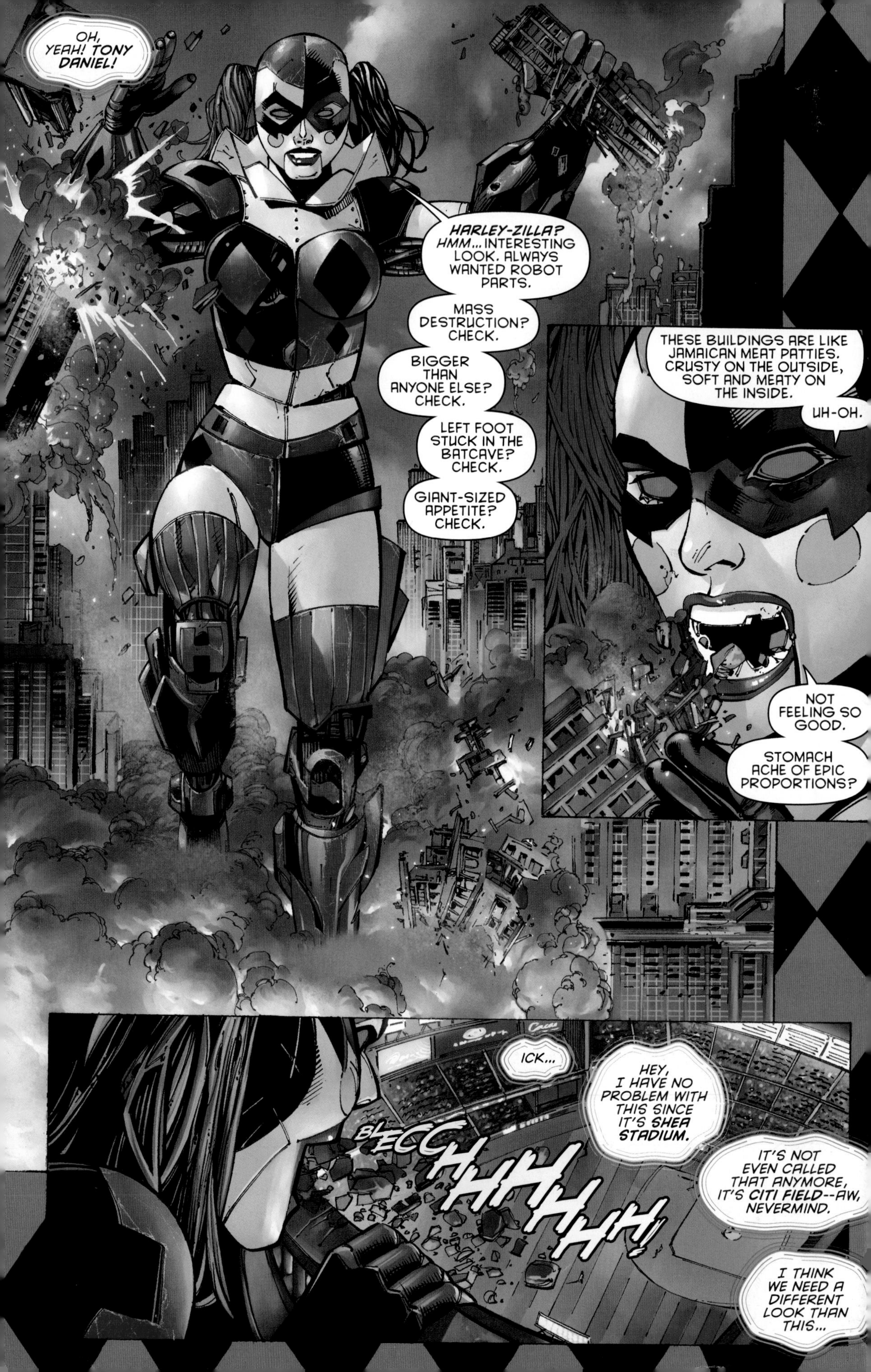
OH, YEAH! TONY DANIEL!
HARLEY-ZILLA? HMM... INTERESTING LOOK. ALWAYS WANTED ROBOT PARTS.
MASS DESTRUCTION? CHECK.
BIGGER THAN ANYONE ELSE? CHECK.
LEFT FOOT STUCK IN THE BATCAVE? CHECK.
GIANT-SIZED APPETITE? CHECK.
THESE BUILDINGS ARE LIKE JAMAICAN MEAT PATTIES. CRUSTY ON THE OUTSIDE, SOFT AND MEATY ON THE INSIDE.
UH-OH.
NOT FEELING SO GOOD.
STOMACH ACHE OF EPIC PROPORTIONS?
ICK...
HEY, I HAVE NO PROBLEM WITH THIS SINCE IT'S SHEA STADIUM.
BLECCHHHHHHH!
IT'S NOT EVEN CALLED THAT ANYMORE, IT'S CITI FIELD--AW, NEVERMIND.
I THINK WE NEED A DIFFERENT LOOK THAN THIS...

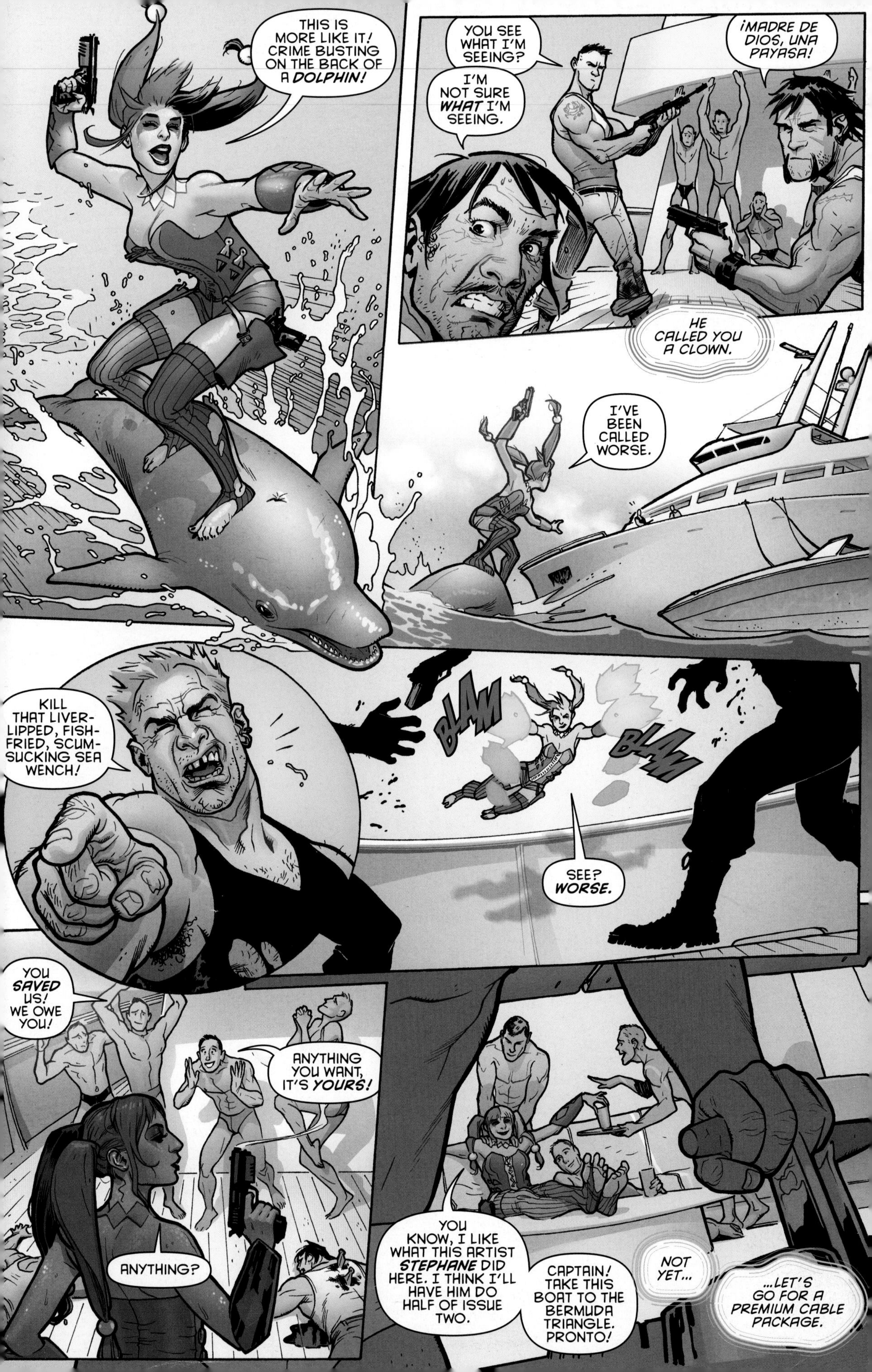

THIS IS MORE LIKE IT! CRIME BUSTING ON THE BACK OF A DOLPHIN!
YOU SEE WHAT I'M SEEING?
I'M NOT SURE WHAT I'M SEEING.
¡MADRE DE DIOS, UNA PAYASA!
HE CALLED YOU A CLOWN.
I'VE BEEN CALLED WORSE.
KILL THAT LIVER-LIPPED, FISH-FRIED, SCUM-SUCKING SEA WENCH!
BLAM
BLAM
SEE? WORSE.
YOU SAVED US! WE OWE YOU!
ANYTHING YOU WANT, IT'S YOURS!
ANYTHING?
YOU KNOW, I LIKE WHAT THIS ARTIST STEPHANE DID HERE. I THINK I'LL HAVE HIM DO HALF OF ISSUE TWO.
CAPTAIN! TAKE THIS BOAT TO THE BERMUDA TRIANGLE. PRONTO!
NOT YET...
...LET'S GO FOR A PREMIUM CABLE PACKAGE.

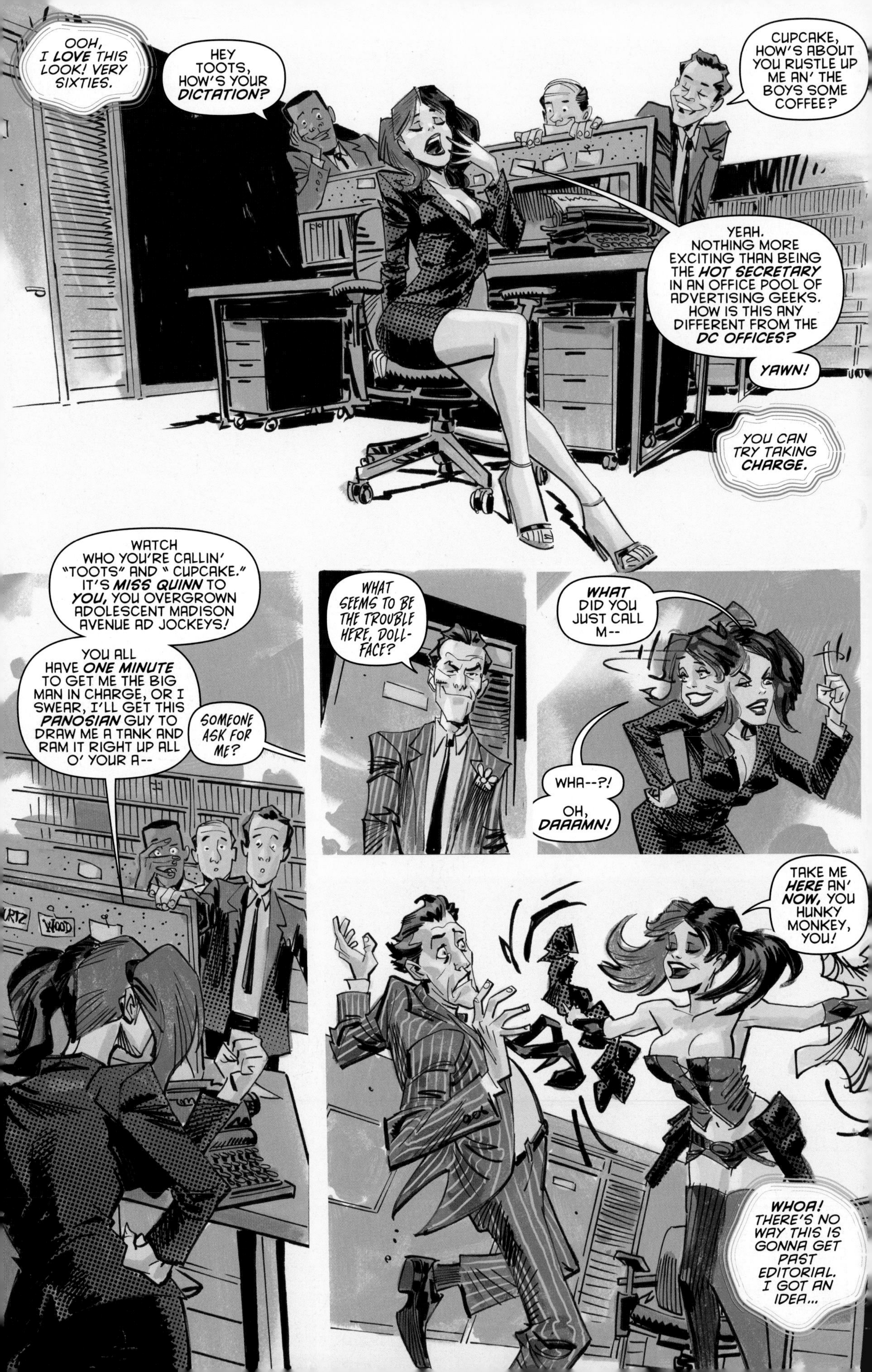
OOH, I LOVE THIS LOOK! VERY SIXTIES.
HEY TOOTS, HOW'S YOUR DICTATION?
CUPCAKE, HOW'S ABOUT YOU RUSTLE UP ME AN' THE BOYS SOME COFFEE?
YEAH. NOTHING MORE EXCITING THAN BEING THE HOT SECRETARY IN AN OFFICE POOL OF ADVERTISING GEEKS. HOW IS THIS ANY DIFFERENT FROM THE DC OFFICES?
YAWN!
YOU CAN TRY TAKING CHARGE.
WATCH WHO YOU'RE CALLIN' "TOOTS" AND "CUPCAKE." IT'S MISS QUINN TO YOU, YOU OVERGROWN ADOLESCENT MADISON AVENUE AD JOCKEYS!
YOU ALL HAVE ONE MINUTE TO GET ME THE BIG MAN IN CHARGE, OR I SWEAR, I'LL GET THIS PANOSIAN GUY TO DRAW ME A TANK AND RAM IT RIGHT UP ALL O' YOUR A--
SOMEONE ASK FOR ME?
WHAT SEEMS TO BE THE TROUBLE HERE, DOLL-FACE?
WHAT DID YOU JUST CALL M--
WHA--?!
OH, DAAAMN!
TAKE ME HERE AN' NOW, YOU HUNKY MONKEY, YOU!
WHOA! THERE'S NO WAY THIS IS GONNA GET PAST EDITORIAL. I GOT AN IDEA...

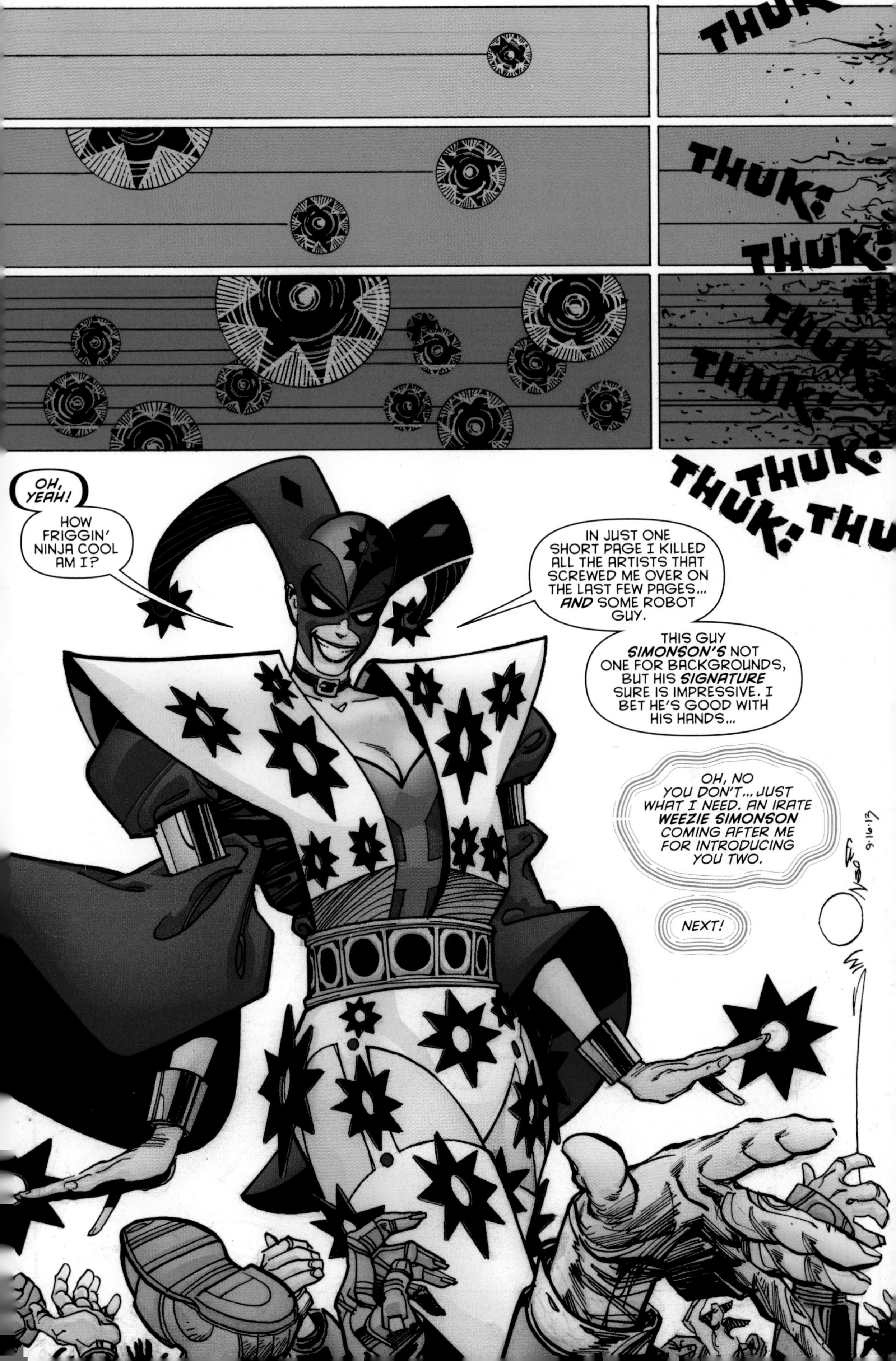
THUK!
THUK!
THUK!
THUK!
THUK!
THUK!
THUK! THUK!
THUK! THU
OH, YEAH!
HOW FRIGGIN' NINJA COOL AM I?
IN JUST ONE SHORT PAGE I KILLED ALL THE ARTISTS THAT SCREWED ME OVER ON THE LAST FEW PAGES... AND SOME ROBOT GUY.
THIS GUY SIMONSON'S NOT ONE FOR BACKGROUNDS, BUT HIS SIGNATURE SURE IS IMPRESSIVE. I BET HE'S GOOD WITH HIS HANDS...
OH, NO YOU DON'T... JUST WHAT I NEED. AN IRATE WEEZIE SIMONSON COMING AFTER ME FOR INTRODUCING YOU TWO.
NEXT!
9-16-13

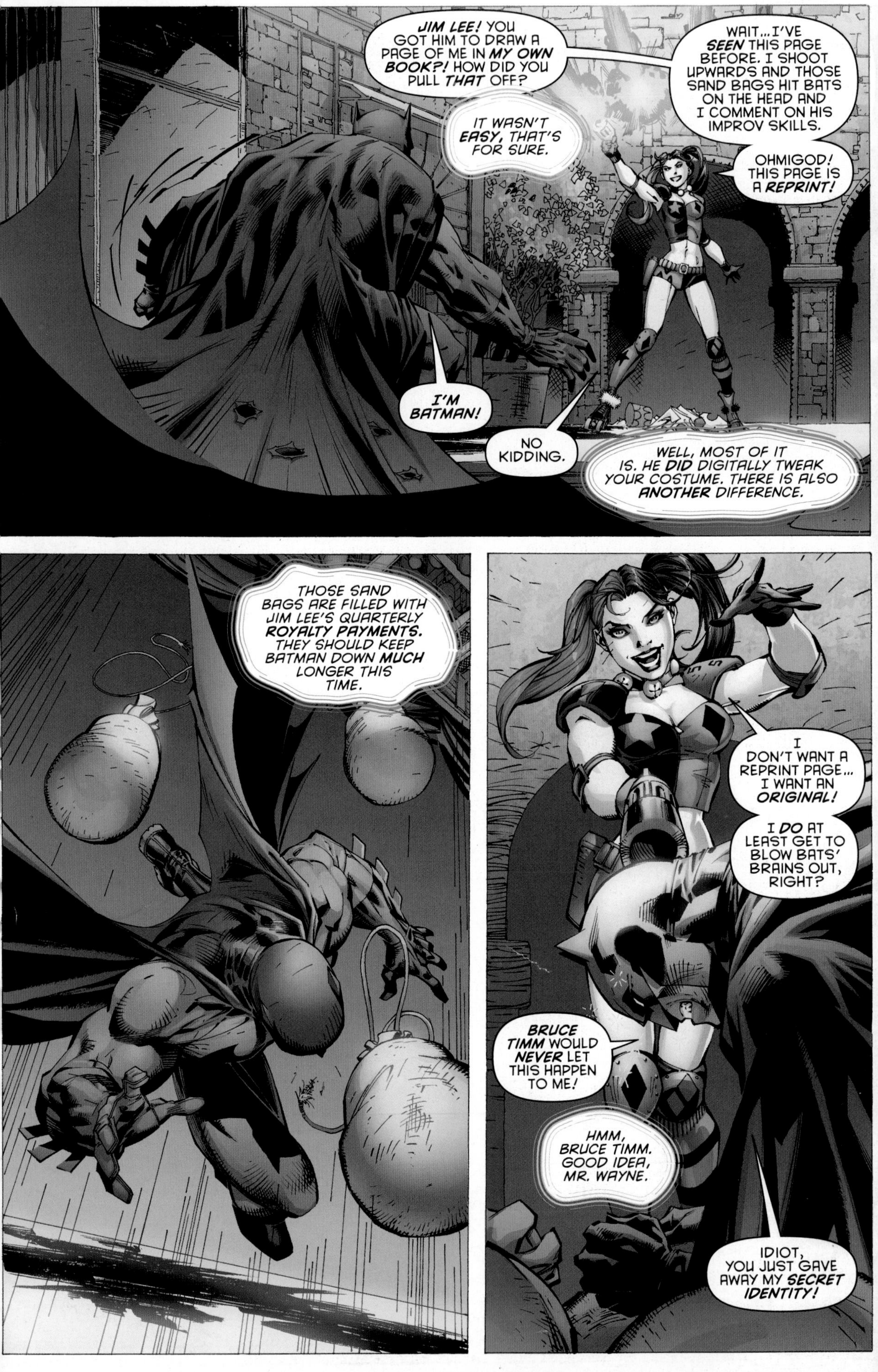
JIM LEE! YOU GOT HIM TO DRAW A PAGE OF ME IN MY OWN BOOK?! HOW DID YOU PULL THAT OFF?
IT WASN'T EASY, THAT'S FOR SURE.
WAIT...I'VE SEEN THIS PAGE BEFORE. I SHOOT UPWARDS AND THOSE SAND BAGS HIT BATS ON THE HEAD AND I COMMENT ON HIS IMPROV SKILLS.
OHMIGOD! THIS PAGE IS A REPRINT!
I'M BATMAN!
NO KIDDING.
WELL, MOST OF IT IS. HE DID DIGITALLY TWEAK YOUR COSTUME. THERE IS ALSO ANOTHER DIFFERENCE.
THOSE SAND BAGS ARE FILLED WITH JIM LEE'S QUARTERLY ROYALTY PAYMENTS. THEY SHOULD KEEP BATMAN DOWN MUCH LONGER THIS TIME.
I DON'T WANT A REPRINT PAGE... I WANT AN ORIGINAL!
I DO AT LEAST GET TO BLOW BATS' BRAINS OUT, RIGHT?
BRUCE TIMM WOULD NEVER LET THIS HAPPEN TO ME!
HMM, BRUCE TIMM. GOOD IDEA, MR. WAYNE.
IDIOT, YOU JUST GAVE AWAY MY SECRET IDENTITY!

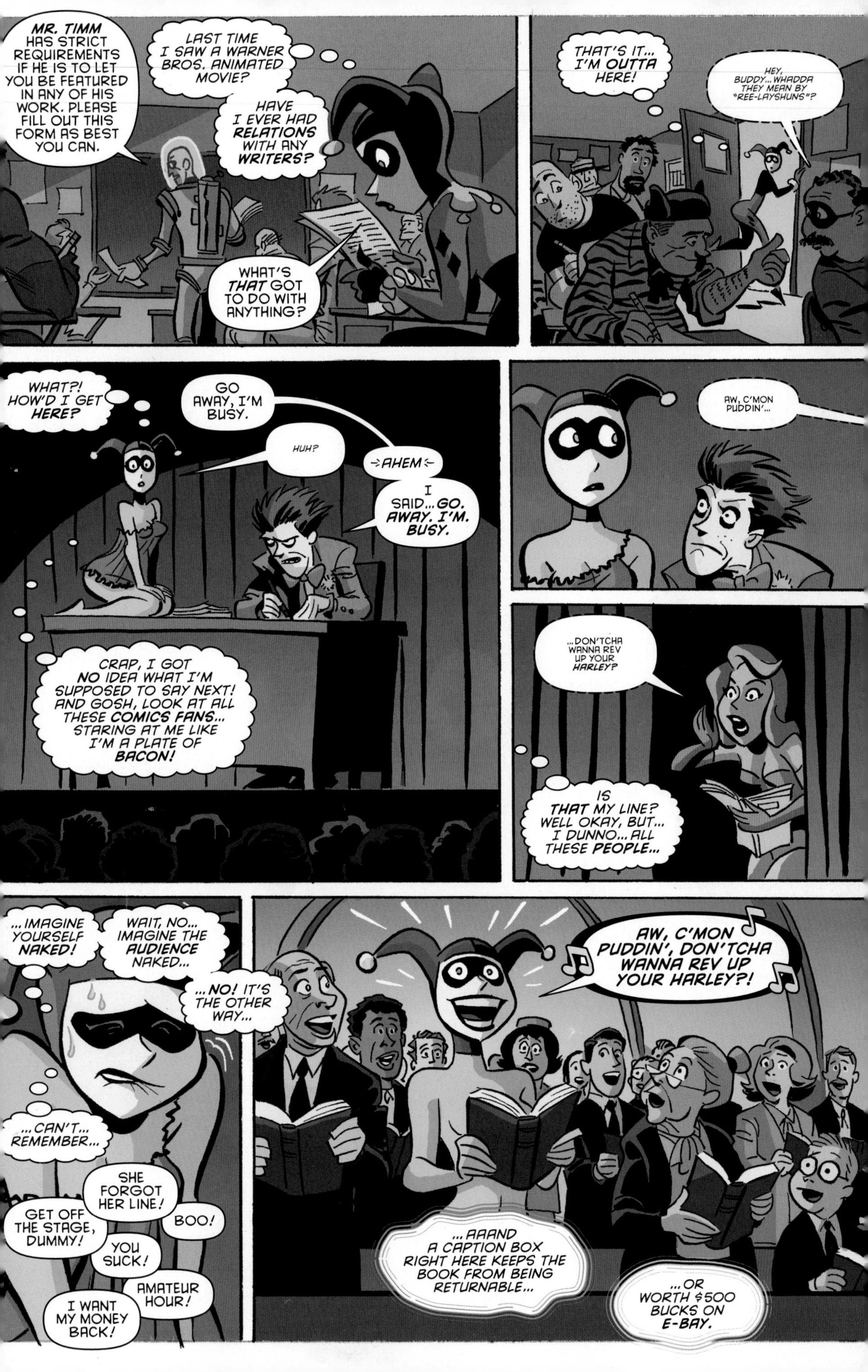
MR. TIMM HAS STRICT REQUIREMENTS IF HE IS TO LET YOU BE FEATURED IN ANY OF HIS WORK. PLEASE FILL OUT THIS FORM AS BEST YOU CAN.
LAST TIME I SAW A WARNER BROS. ANIMATED MOVIE?
HAVE I EVER HAD RELATIONS WITH ANY WRITERS?
WHAT'S THAT GOT TO DO WITH ANYTHING?
THAT'S IT... I'M OUTTA HERE!
HEY, BUDDY... WHADDA THEY MEAN BY "REE-LAYSHUNS"?
WHAT?! HOW'D I GET HERE?
GO AWAY, I'M BUSY.
HUH?
AHEM
I SAID... GO. AWAY. I'M. BUSY.
CRAP, I GOT NO IDEA WHAT I'M SUPPOSED TO SAY NEXT! AND GOSH, LOOK AT ALL THESE COMICS FANS... STARING AT ME LIKE I'M A PLATE OF BACON!
AW, C'MON PUDDIN'...
...DON'TCHA WANNA REV UP YOUR HARLEY?
IS THAT MY LINE? WELL OKAY, BUT... I DUNNO... ALL THESE PEOPLE...
...IMAGINE YOURSELF NAKED!
WAIT, NO... IMAGINE THE AUDIENCE NAKED...
...NO! IT'S THE OTHER WAY...
...CAN'T... REMEMBER...
SHE FORGOT HER LINE!
GET OFF THE STAGE, DUMMY!
BOO!
YOU SUCK!
AMATEUR HOUR!
I WANT MY MONEY BACK!
AW, C'MON PUDDIN', DON'TCHA WANNA REV UP YOUR HARLEY?!
...AAAND A CAPTION BOX RIGHT HERE KEEPS THE BOOK FROM BEING RETURNABLE...
...OR WORTH $500 BUCKS ON E-BAY.

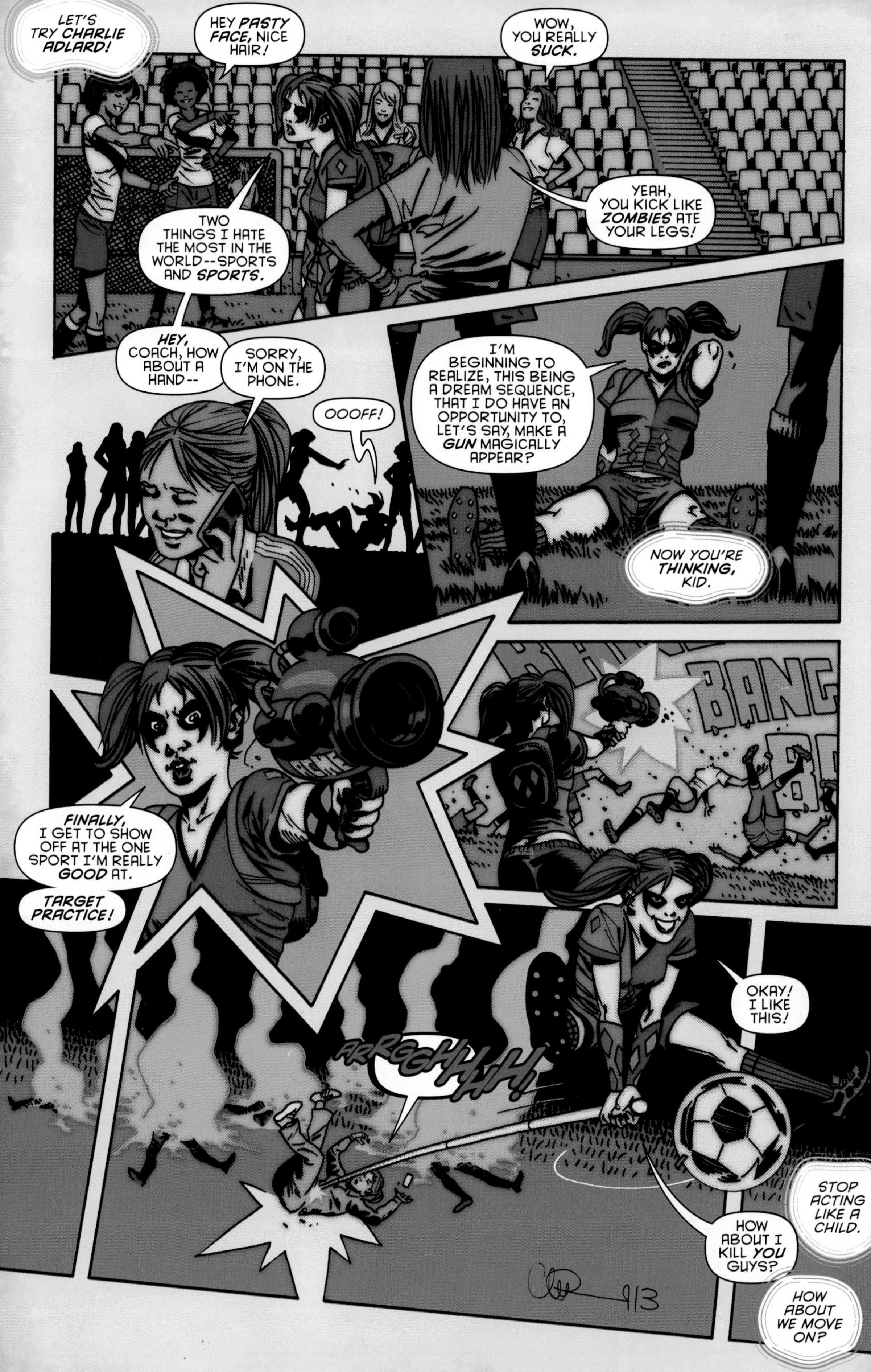
LET'S TRY CHARLIE ADLARD!
HEY PASTY FACE, NICE HAIR!
WOW, YOU REALLY SUCK.
TWO THINGS I HATE THE MOST IN THE WORLD--SPORTS AND SPORTS.
YEAH, YOU KICK LIKE ZOMBIES ATE YOUR LEGS!
HEY, COACH, HOW ABOUT A HAND--
SORRY, I'M ON THE PHONE.
OOOFF!
I'M BEGINNING TO REALIZE, THIS BEING A DREAM SEQUENCE, THAT I DO HAVE AN OPPORTUNITY TO, LET'S SAY, MAKE A GUN MAGICALLY APPEAR?
NOW YOU'RE THINKING, KID.
BANG
FINALLY, I GET TO SHOW OFF AT THE ONE SPORT I'M REALLY GOOD AT.
TARGET PRACTICE!
OKAY! I LIKE THIS!
ARRGGHHHHH!
HOW ABOUT I KILL YOU GUYS?
STOP ACTING LIKE A CHILD.
HOW ABOUT WE MOVE ON?

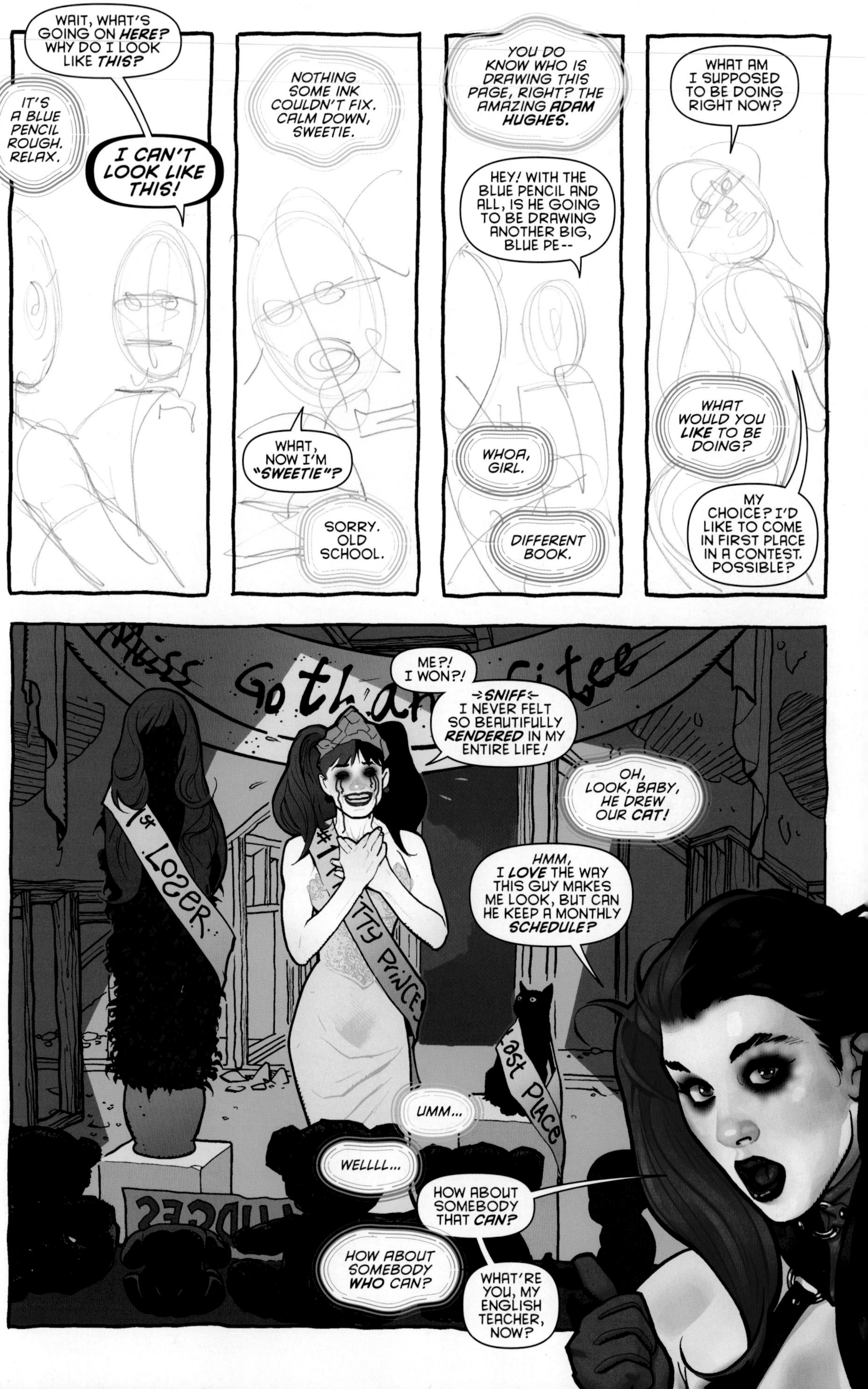
WAIT, WHAT'S GOING ON *HERE?* WHY DO I LOOK LIKE *THIS?*
IT'S A BLUE PENCIL ROUGH. RELAX.
I CAN'T LOOK LIKE THIS!
NOTHING SOME INK COULDN'T FIX. CALM DOWN, SWEETIE.
WHAT, NOW I'M *"SWEETIE"?*
SORRY. OLD SCHOOL.
YOU DO KNOW WHO IS DRAWING THIS PAGE, RIGHT? THE AMAZING *ADAM HUGHES.*
HEY! WITH THE BLUE PENCIL AND ALL, IS HE GOING TO BE DRAWING ANOTHER BIG, BLUE PE--
WHOA, GIRL.
DIFFERENT BOOK.
WHAT AM I SUPPOSED TO BE DOING RIGHT NOW?
WHAT WOULD YOU *LIKE* TO BE DOING?
MY CHOICE? I'D LIKE TO COME IN FIRST PLACE IN A CONTEST. POSSIBLE?
ME?! I WON?!
SNIFF I NEVER FELT SO BEAUTIFULLY *RENDERED* IN MY ENTIRE LIFE!
OH, LOOK, BABY, HE DREW OUR *CAT!*
HMM, I *LOVE* THE WAY THIS GUY MAKES ME LOOK, BUT CAN HE KEEP A MONTHLY *SCHEDULE?*
1st LOZER
Last Place
UMM...
WELLLL...
HOW ABOUT SOMEBODY THAT *CAN?*
HOW ABOUT SOMEBODY *WHO* CAN?
WHAT'RE YOU, MY ENGLISH TEACHER, NOW?

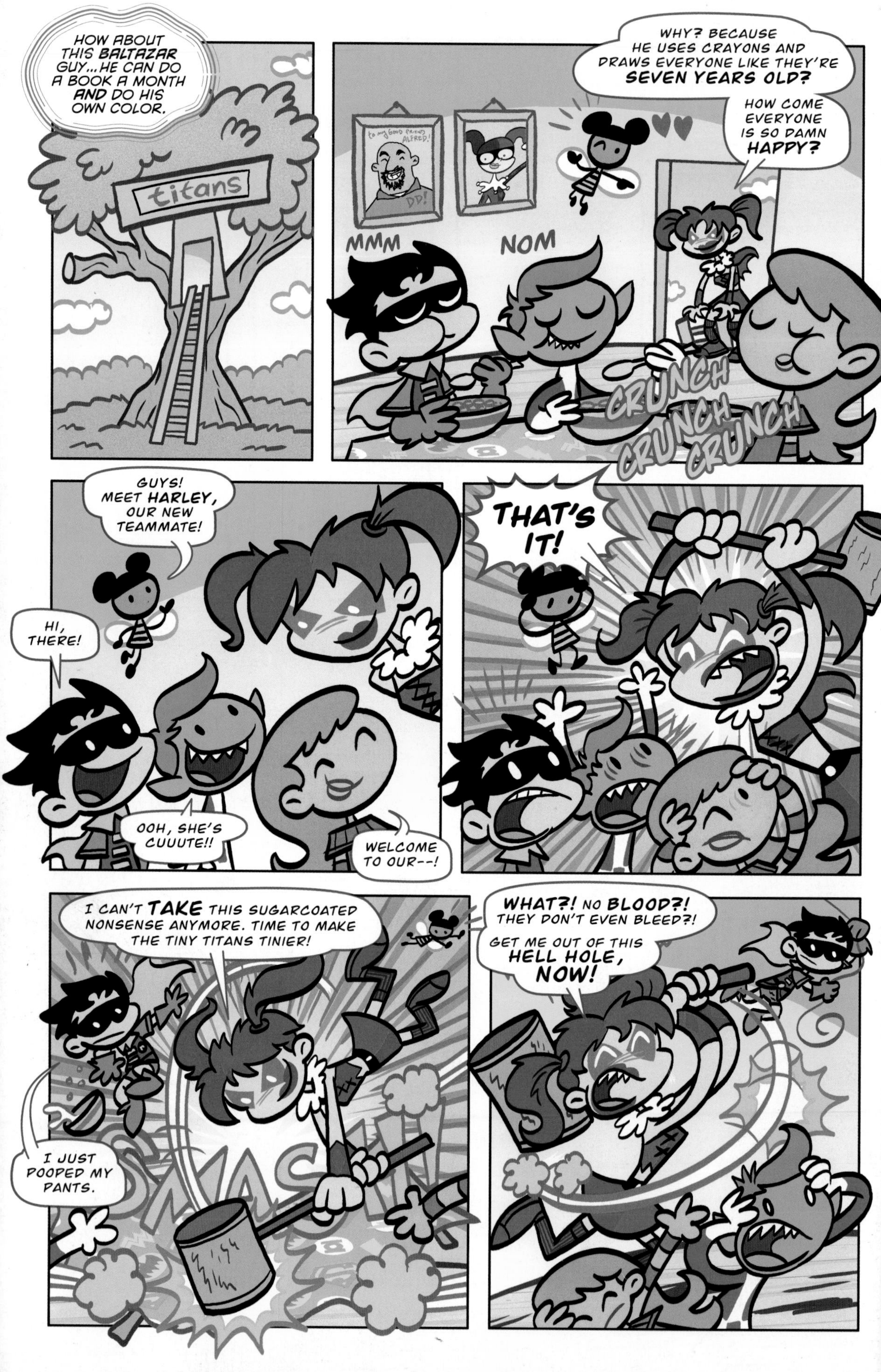

HOW ABOUT THIS BALTAZAR GUY... HE CAN DO A BOOK A MONTH AND DO HIS OWN COLOR.
titans
WHY? BECAUSE HE USES CRAYONS AND DRAWS EVERYONE LIKE THEY'RE SEVEN YEARS OLD?
HOW COME EVERYONE IS SO DAMN HAPPY?
MMM
NOM
CRUNCH
CRUNCH
CRUNCH
GUYS! MEET HARLEY, OUR NEW TEAMMATE!
HI, THERE!
OOH, SHE'S CUUUTE!!
WELCOME TO OUR--!
THAT'S IT!
I CAN'T TAKE THIS SUGARCOATED NONSENSE ANYMORE. TIME TO MAKE THE TINY TITANS TINIER!
I JUST POOPED MY PANTS.
WHAT?! NO BLOOD?! THEY DON'T EVEN BLEED?!
GET ME OUT OF THIS HELL HOLE, NOW!

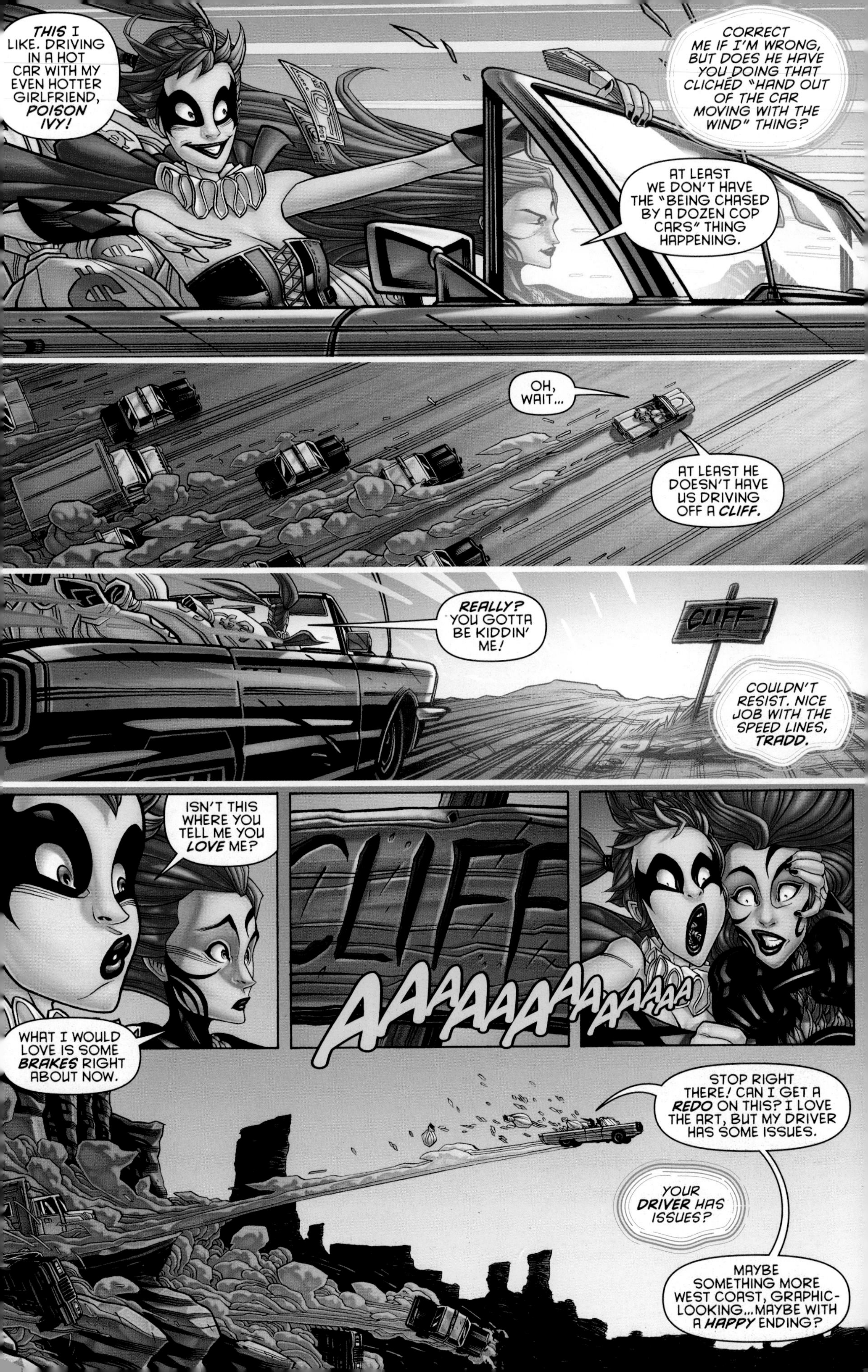
THIS I LIKE. DRIVING IN A HOT CAR WITH MY EVEN HOTTER GIRLFRIEND, POISON IVY!
CORRECT ME IF I'M WRONG, BUT DOES HE HAVE YOU DOING THAT CLICHÉD "HAND OUT OF THE CAR MOVING WITH THE WIND" THING?
AT LEAST WE DON'T HAVE THE "BEING CHASED BY A DOZEN COP CARS" THING HAPPENING.
OH, WAIT...
AT LEAST HE DOESN'T HAVE US DRIVING OFF A CLIFF.
REALLY? YOU GOTTA BE KIDDIN' ME!
CLIFF
COULDN'T RESIST. NICE JOB WITH THE SPEED LINES, TRADD.
ISN'T THIS WHERE YOU TELL ME YOU LOVE ME?
WHAT I WOULD LOVE IS SOME BRAKES RIGHT ABOUT NOW.
CLIFF
AAAAAAAAAAAAA
STOP RIGHT THERE! CAN I GET A REDO ON THIS? I LOVE THE ART, BUT MY DRIVER HAS SOME ISSUES.
YOUR DRIVER HAS ISSUES?
MAYBE SOMETHING MORE WEST COAST, GRAPHIC-LOOKING...MAYBE WITH A HAPPY ENDING?

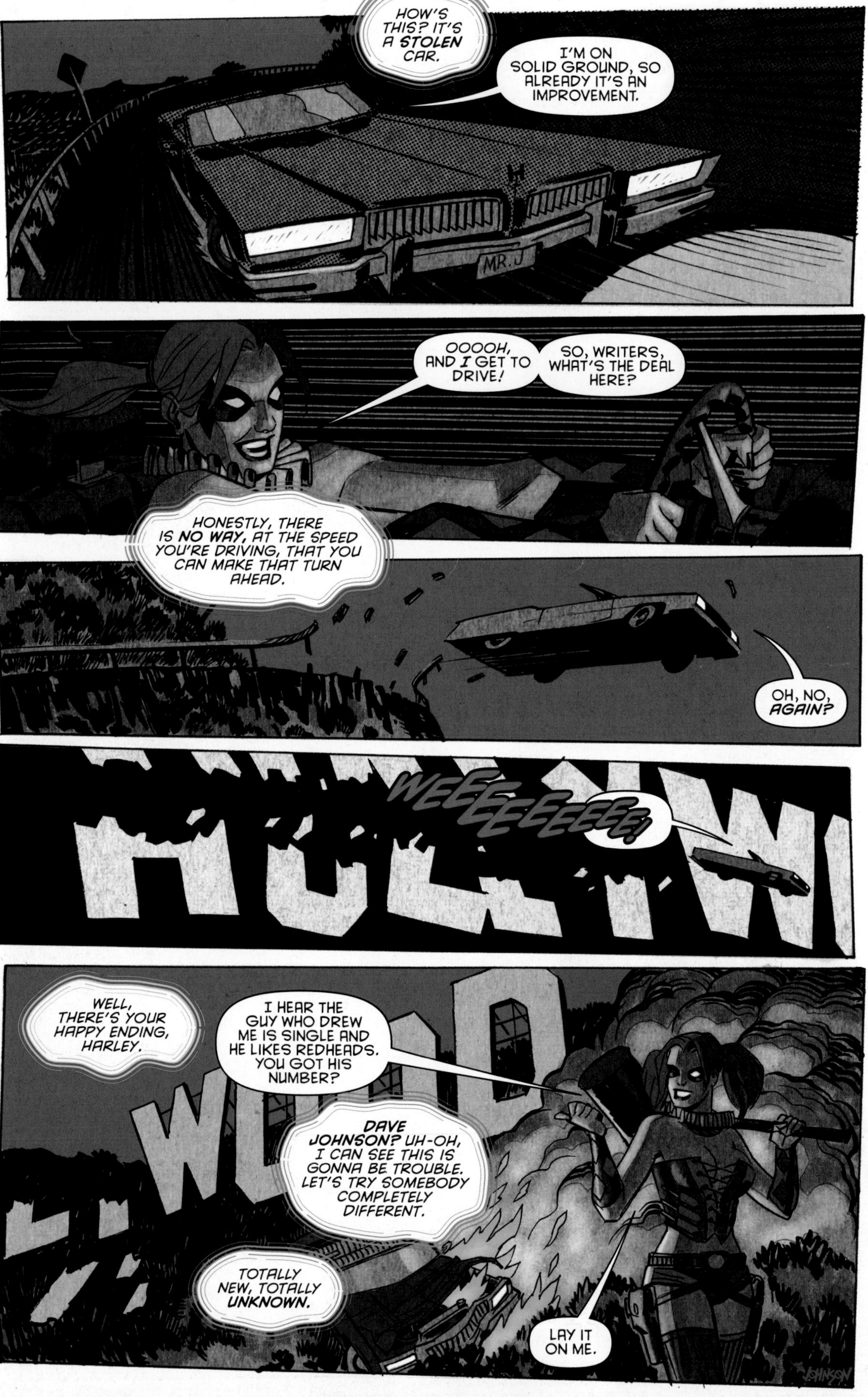
HOW'S THIS? IT'S A STOLEN CAR.
I'M ON SOLID GROUND, SO ALREADY IT'S AN IMPROVEMENT.
MR. J
OOOOH, AND I GET TO DRIVE!
SO, WRITERS, WHAT'S THE DEAL HERE?
HONESTLY, THERE IS NO WAY, AT THE SPEED YOU'RE DRIVING, THAT YOU CAN MAKE THAT TURN AHEAD.
OH, NO, AGAIN?
WEEEEEEEEEE!
WELL, THERE'S YOUR HAPPY ENDING, HARLEY.
I HEAR THE GUY WHO DREW ME IS SINGLE AND HE LIKES REDHEADS. YOU GOT HIS NUMBER?
DAVE JOHNSON? UH-OH, I CAN SEE THIS IS GONNA BE TROUBLE. LET'S TRY SOMEBODY COMPLETELY DIFFERENT.
TOTALLY NEW, TOTALLY UNKNOWN.
LAY IT ON ME.
JOHNSON

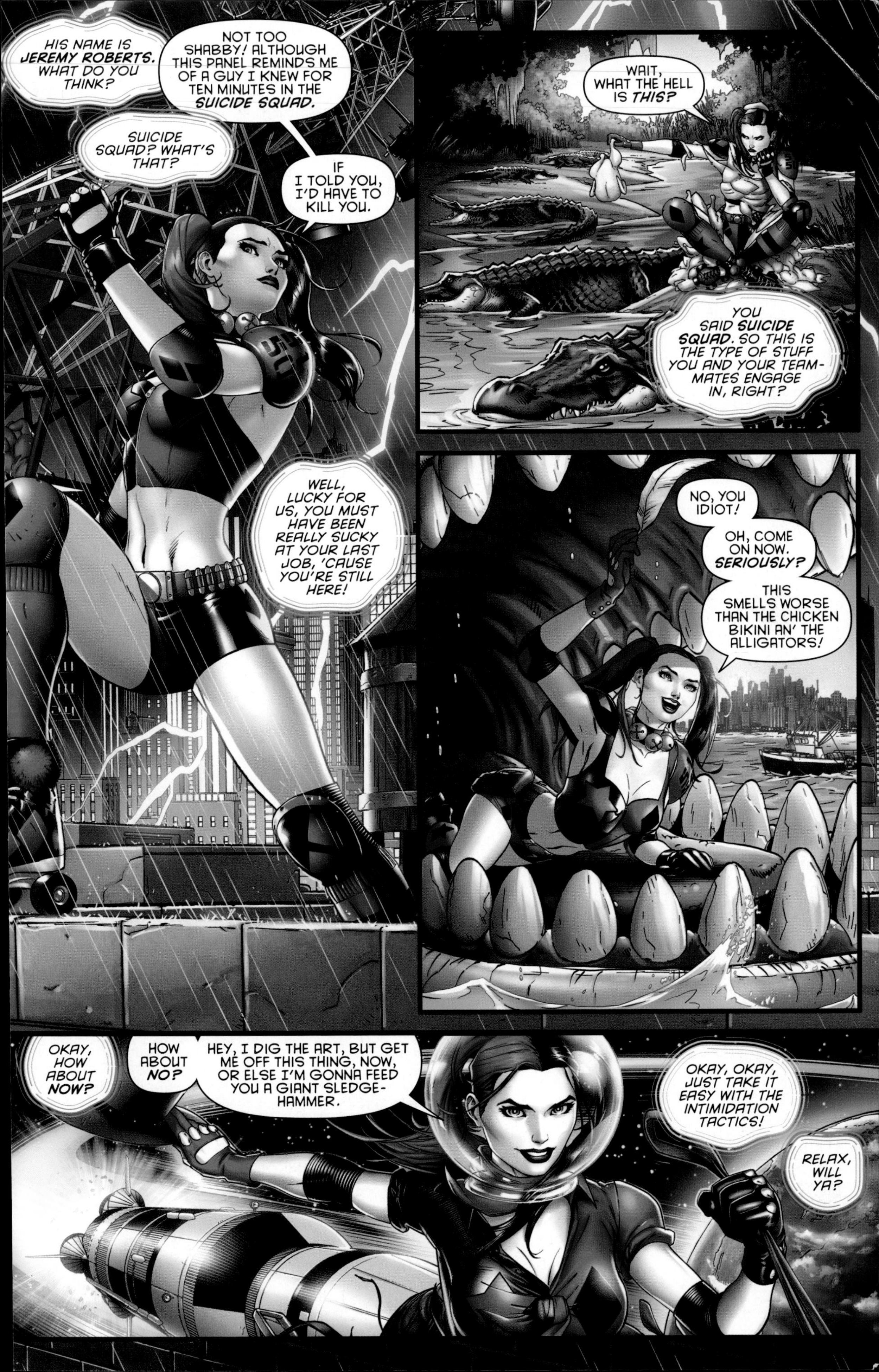
HIS NAME IS JEREMY ROBERTS. WHAT DO YOU THINK?
NOT TOO SHABBY! ALTHOUGH THIS PANEL REMINDS ME OF A GUY I KNEW FOR TEN MINUTES IN THE SUICIDE SQUAD.
SUICIDE SQUAD? WHAT'S THAT?
IF I TOLD YOU, I'D HAVE TO KILL YOU.
WELL, LUCKY FOR US, YOU MUST HAVE BEEN REALLY SUCKY AT YOUR LAST JOB, 'CAUSE YOU'RE STILL HERE!
WAIT, WHAT THE HELL IS THIS?
YOU SAID SUICIDE SQUAD. SO THIS IS THE TYPE OF STUFF YOU AND YOUR TEAM-MATES ENGAGE IN, RIGHT?
NO, YOU IDIOT!
OH, COME ON NOW. SERIOUSLY?
THIS SMELLS WORSE THAN THE CHICKEN BIKINI AN' THE ALLIGATORS!
OKAY, HOW ABOUT NOW?
HOW ABOUT NO?
HEY, I DIG THE ART, BUT GET ME OFF THIS THING, NOW, OR ELSE I'M GONNA FEED YOU A GIANT SLEDGE-HAMMER.
OKAY, OKAY, JUST TAKE IT EASY WITH THE INTIMIDATION TACTICS!
RELAX, WILL YA?

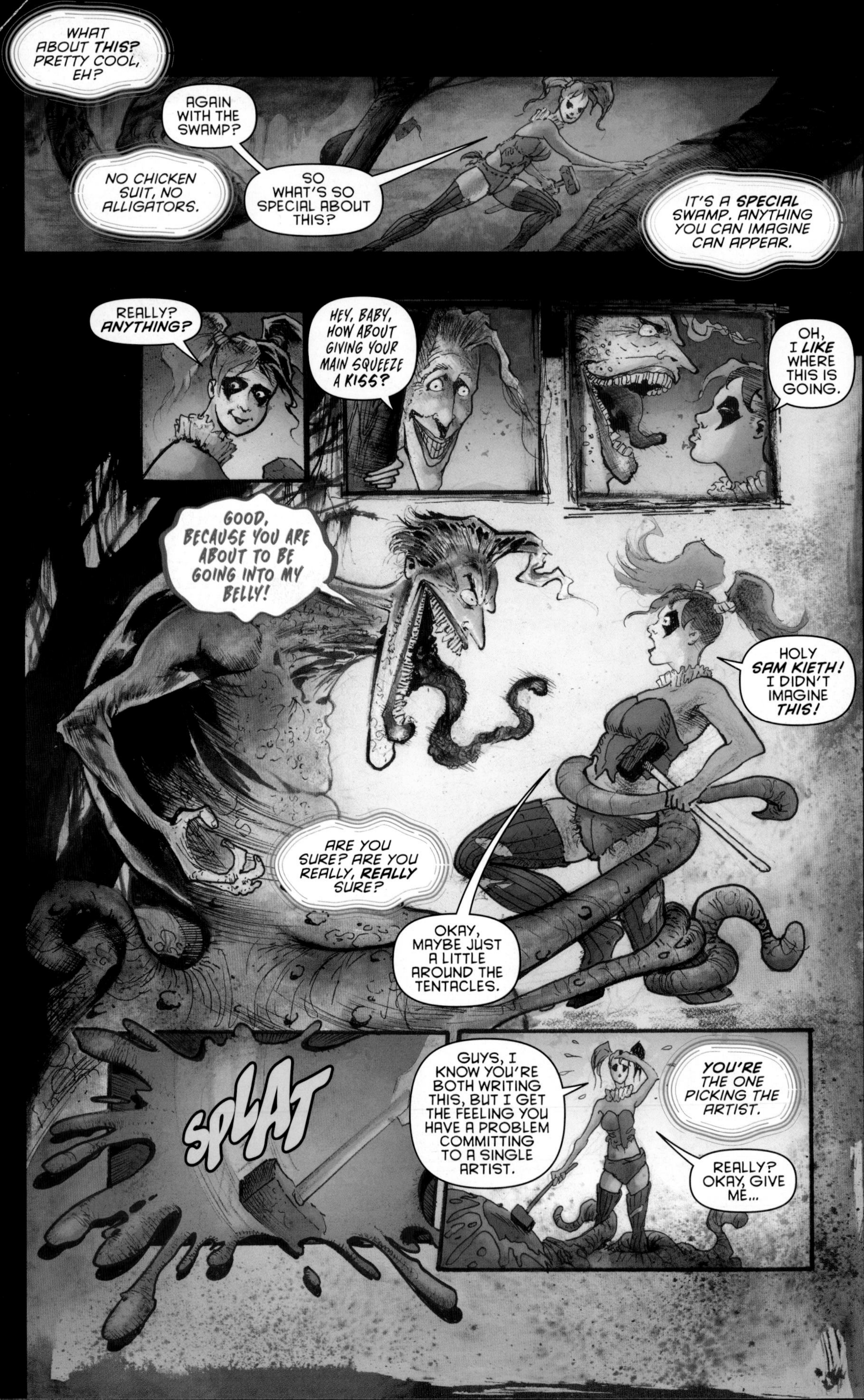
WHAT ABOUT THIS? PRETTY COOL, EH?
AGAIN WITH THE SWAMP?
NO CHICKEN SUIT, NO ALLIGATORS.
SO WHAT'S SO SPECIAL ABOUT THIS?
IT'S A SPECIAL SWAMP. ANYTHING YOU CAN IMAGINE CAN APPEAR.
REALLY? ANYTHING?
HEY, BABY, HOW ABOUT GIVING YOUR MAIN SQUEEZE A KISS?
OH, I LIKE WHERE THIS IS GOING.
GOOD, BECAUSE YOU ARE ABOUT TO BE GOING INTO MY BELLY!
HOLY SAM KIETH! I DIDN'T IMAGINE THIS!
ARE YOU SURE? ARE YOU REALLY, REALLY SURE?
OKAY, MAYBE JUST A LITTLE AROUND THE TENTACLES.
SPLAT
GUYS, I KNOW YOU'RE BOTH WRITING THIS, BUT I GET THE FEELING YOU HAVE A PROBLEM COMMITTING TO A SINGLE ARTIST.
YOU'RE THE ONE PICKING THE ARTIST.
REALLY? OKAY, GIVE ME...

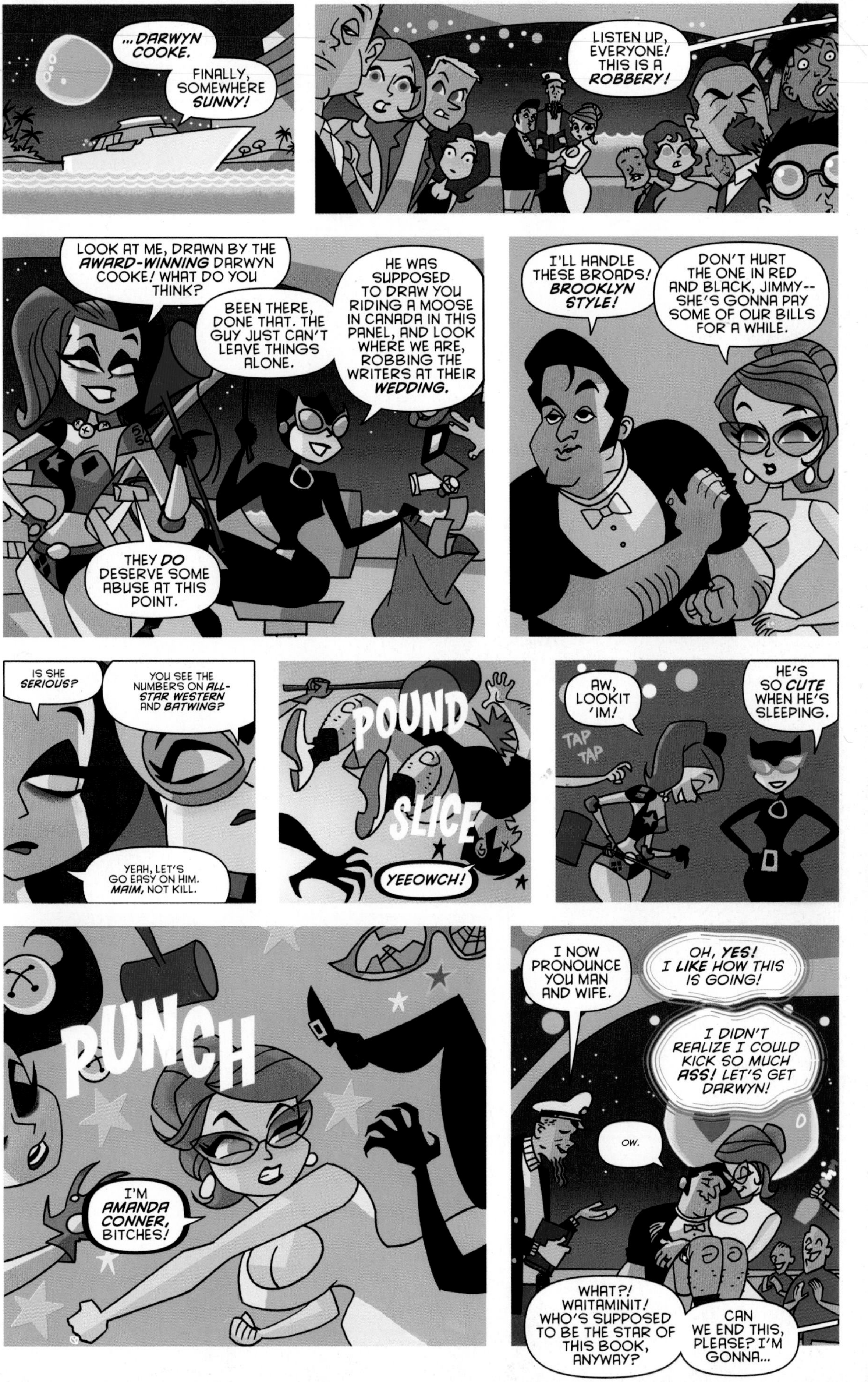
...DARWYN COOKE.
FINALLY, SOMEWHERE SUNNY!
LISTEN UP, EVERYONE! THIS IS A ROBBERY!
LOOK AT ME, DRAWN BY THE AWARD-WINNING DARWYN COOKE! WHAT DO YOU THINK?
BEEN THERE, DONE THAT. THE GUY JUST CAN'T LEAVE THINGS ALONE.
HE WAS SUPPOSED TO DRAW YOU RIDING A MOOSE IN CANADA IN THIS PANEL, AND LOOK WHERE WE ARE, ROBBING THE WRITERS AT THEIR WEDDING.
THEY DO DESERVE SOME ABUSE AT THIS POINT.
I'LL HANDLE THESE BROADS! BROOKLYN STYLE!
DON'T HURT THE ONE IN RED AND BLACK, JIMMY-- SHE'S GONNA PAY SOME OF OUR BILLS FOR A WHILE.
IS SHE SERIOUS?
YOU SEE THE NUMBERS ON ALL-STAR WESTERN AND BATWING?
YEAH, LET'S GO EASY ON HIM. MAIM, NOT KILL.
POUND
SLICE
YEEOWCH!
AW, LOOKIT 'IM!
TAP TAP
HE'S SO CUTE WHEN HE'S SLEEPING.
PUNCH
I'M AMANDA CONNER, BITCHES!
I NOW PRONOUNCE YOU MAN AND WIFE.
OH, YES! I LIKE HOW THIS IS GOING!
I DIDN'T REALIZE I COULD KICK SO MUCH ASS! LET'S GET DARWYN!
OW.
WHAT?! WAITAMINIT! WHO'S SUPPOSED TO BE THE STAR OF THIS BOOK, ANYWAY?
CAN WE END THIS, PLEASE? I'M GONNA...

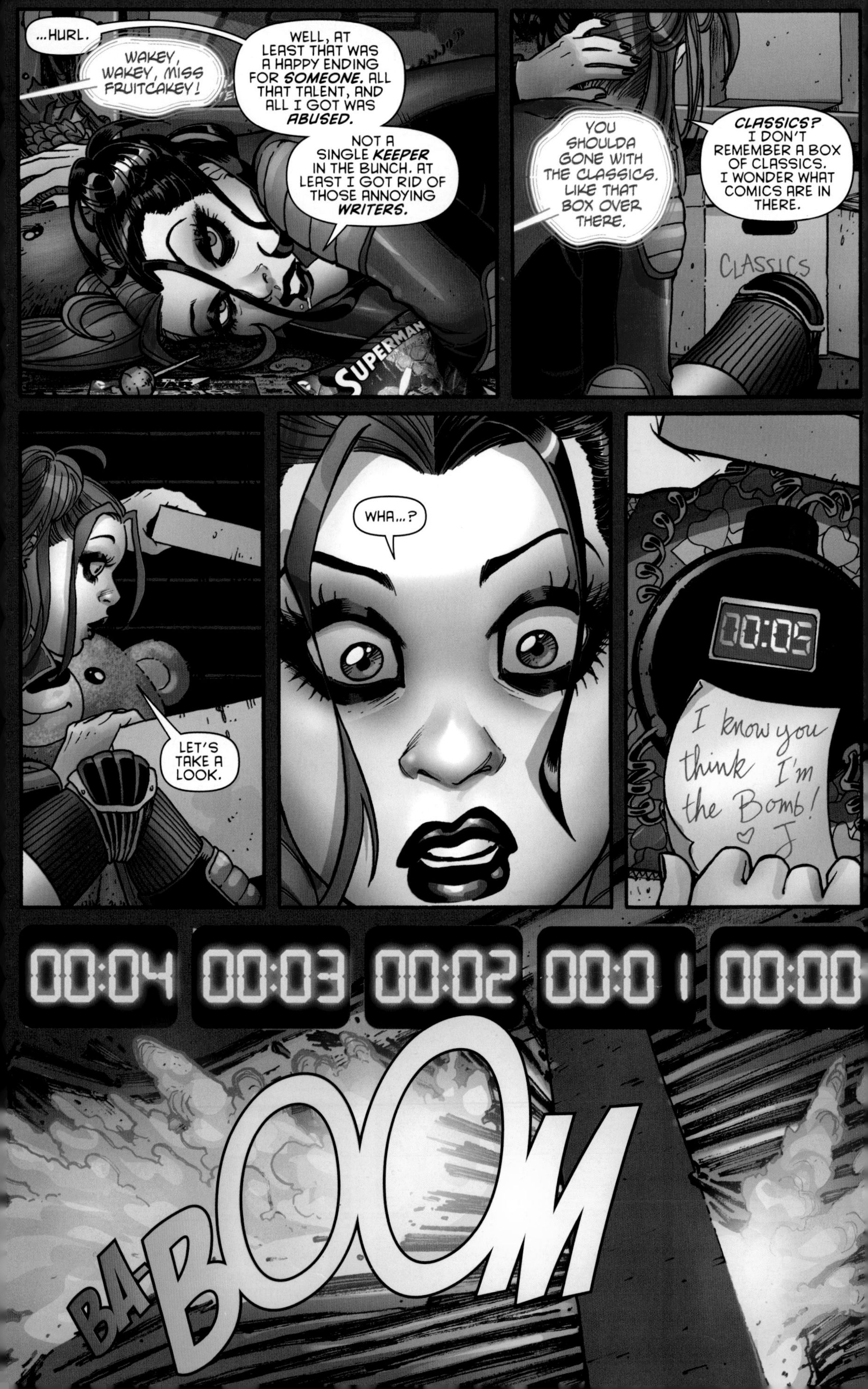

...HURL.
WAKEY, WAKEY, MISS FRUITCAKEY!
WELL, AT LEAST THAT WAS A HAPPY ENDING FOR SOMEONE. ALL THAT TALENT, AND ALL I GOT WAS ABUSED.
NOT A SINGLE KEEPER IN THE BUNCH. AT LEAST I GOT RID OF THOSE ANNOYING WRITERS.
SUPERMAN
YOU SHOULDA GONE WITH THE CLASSICS. LIKE THAT BOX OVER THERE.
CLASSICS? I DON'T REMEMBER A BOX OF CLASSICS. I WONDER WHAT COMICS ARE IN THERE.
CLASSICS
LET'S TAKE A LOOK.
WHA...?
00:05
I know you think I'm the Bomb! ♡ J
00:04
00:03
00:02
00:01
00:00
BA-BOOOM

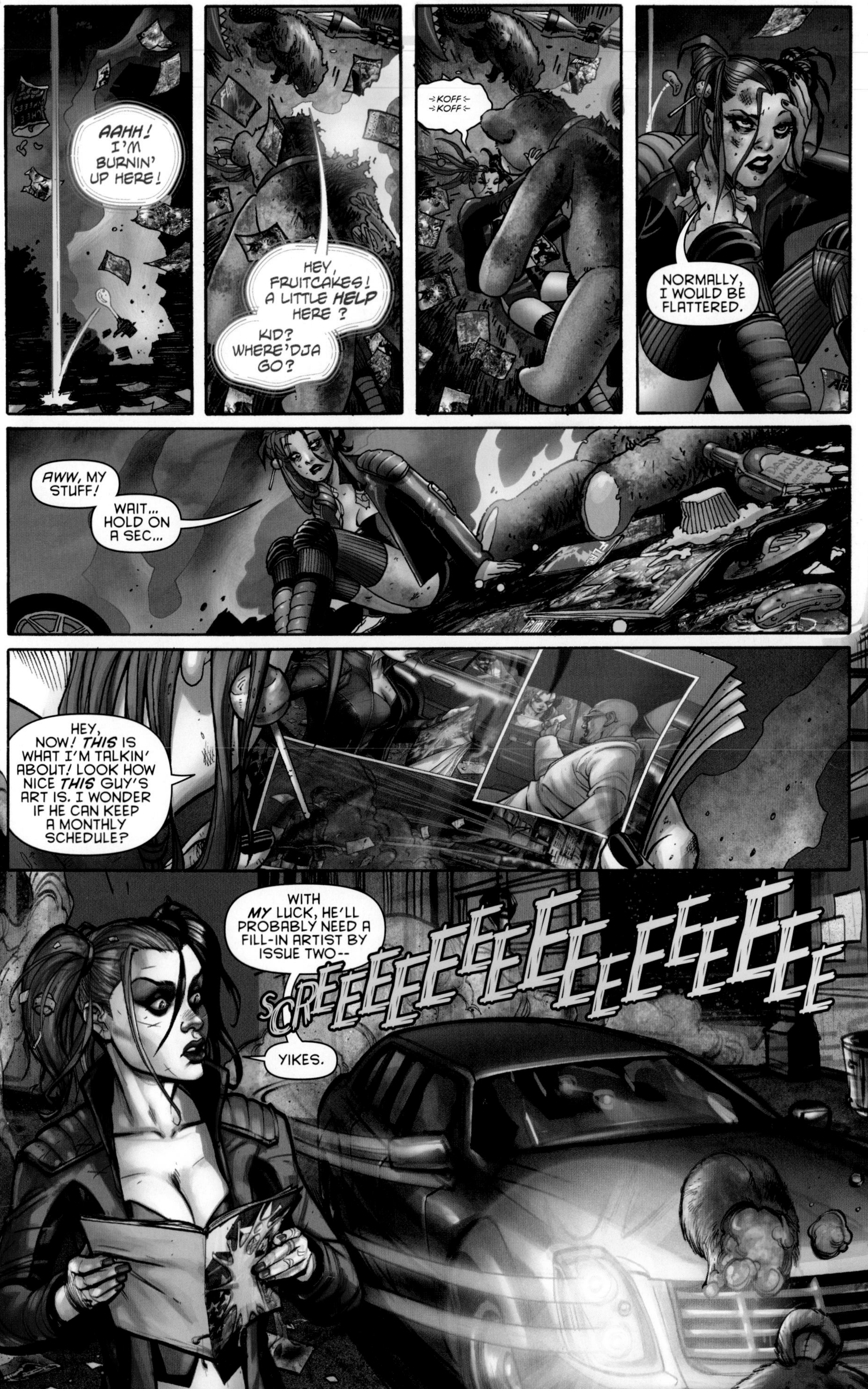
AAHH! I'M BURNIN' UP HERE!
HEY, FRUITCAKES! A LITTLE HELP HERE?
KID? WHERE'DJA GO?
KOFF KOFF
NORMALLY, I WOULD BE FLATTERED.
AWW, MY STUFF!
WAIT... HOLD ON A SEC...
HEY, NOW! THIS IS WHAT I'M TALKIN' ABOUT! LOOK HOW NICE THIS GUY'S ART IS. I WONDER IF HE CAN KEEP A MONTHLY SCHEDULE?
WITH MY LUCK, HE'LL PROBABLY NEED A FILL-IN ARTIST BY ISSUE TWO--
SCREEEEEEEEEEEEEEEEE
YIKES.

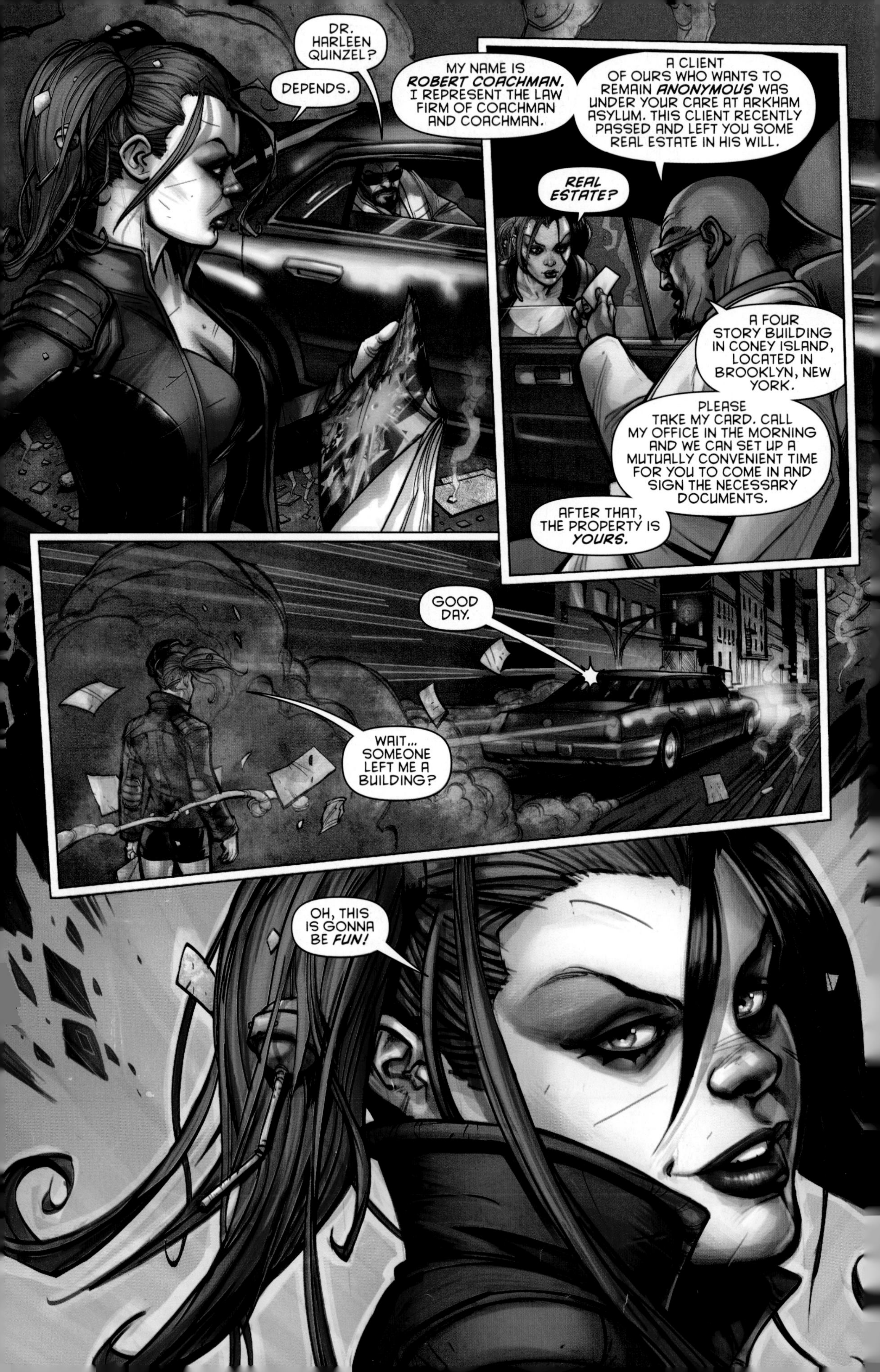

DR. HARLEEN QUINZEL?
DEPENDS.
MY NAME IS *ROBERT COACHMAN.* I REPRESENT THE LAW FIRM OF COACHMAN AND COACHMAN.
A CLIENT OF OURS WHO WANTS TO REMAIN *ANONYMOUS* WAS UNDER YOUR CARE AT ARKHAM ASYLUM. THIS CLIENT RECENTLY PASSED AND LEFT YOU SOME REAL ESTATE IN HIS WILL.
REAL ESTATE?
A FOUR STORY BUILDING IN CONEY ISLAND, LOCATED IN BROOKLYN, NEW YORK.
PLEASE TAKE MY CARD. CALL MY OFFICE IN THE MORNING AND WE CAN SET UP A MUTUALLY CONVENIENT TIME FOR YOU TO COME IN AND SIGN THE NECESSARY DOCUMENTS.
AFTER THAT, THE PROPERTY IS *YOURS.*
GOOD DAY.
WAIT... SOMEONE LEFT ME A BUILDING?
OH, THIS IS GONNA BE *FUN!*

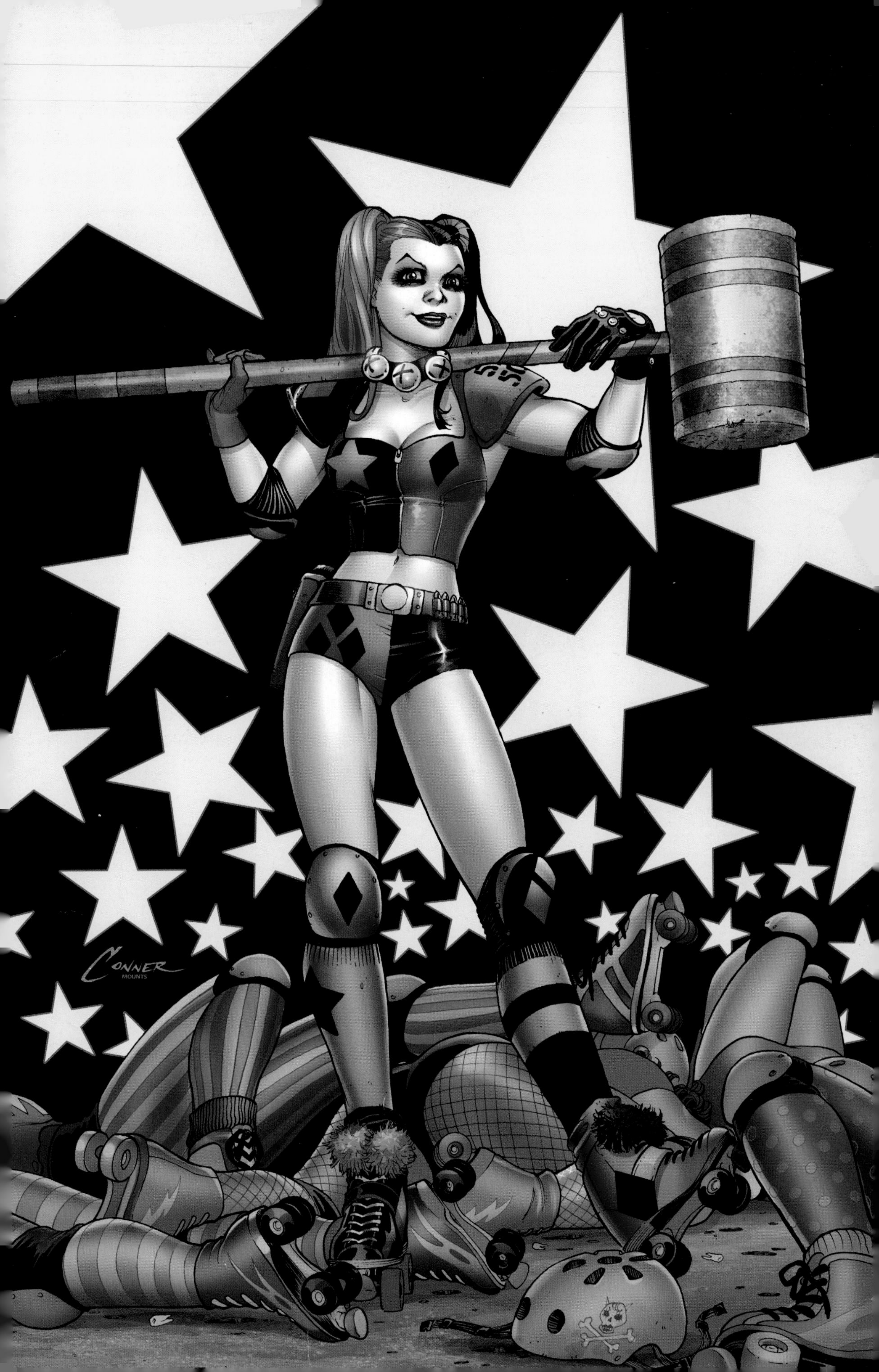
CONNER
MOUNTS

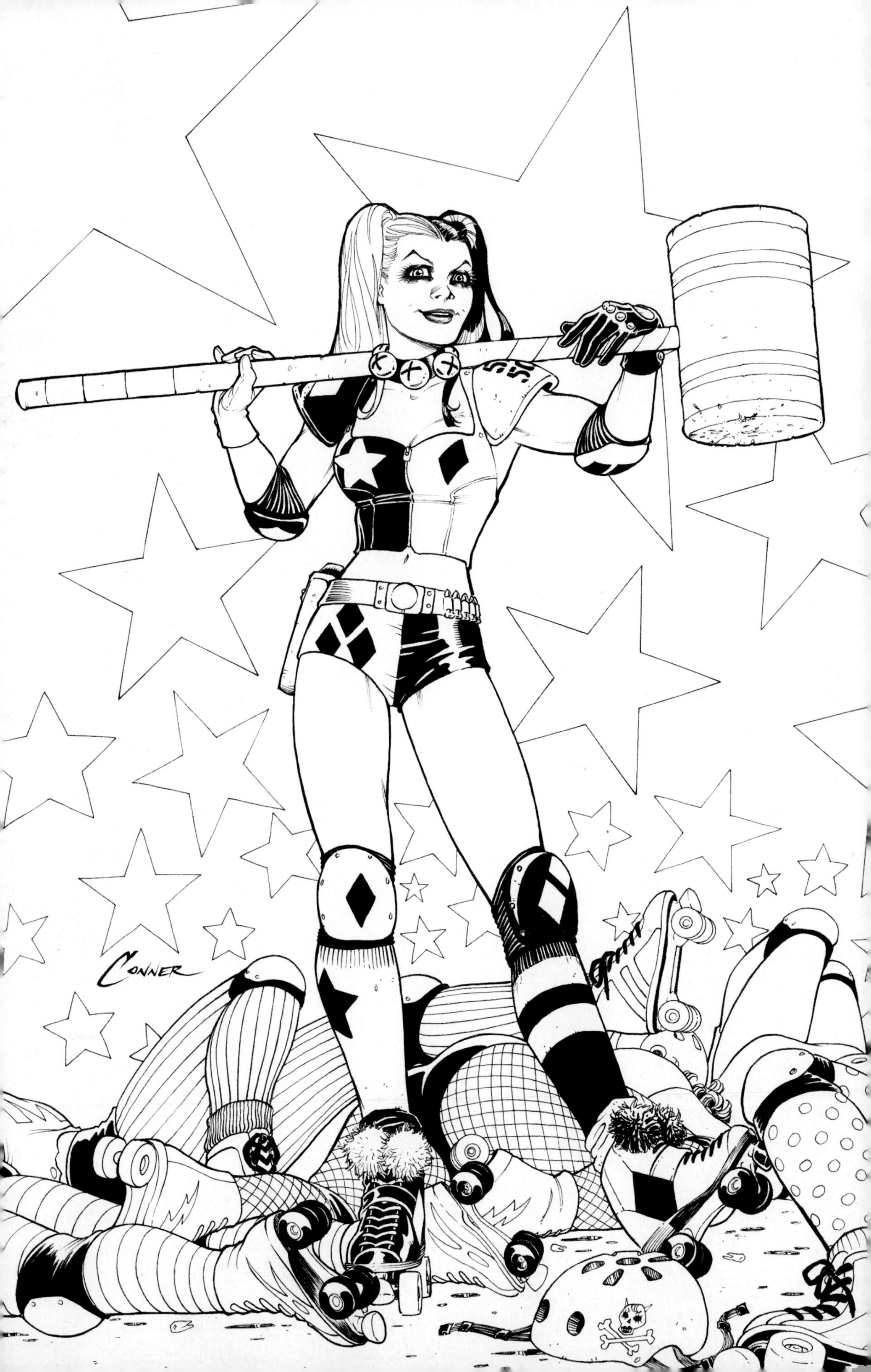
CONNER

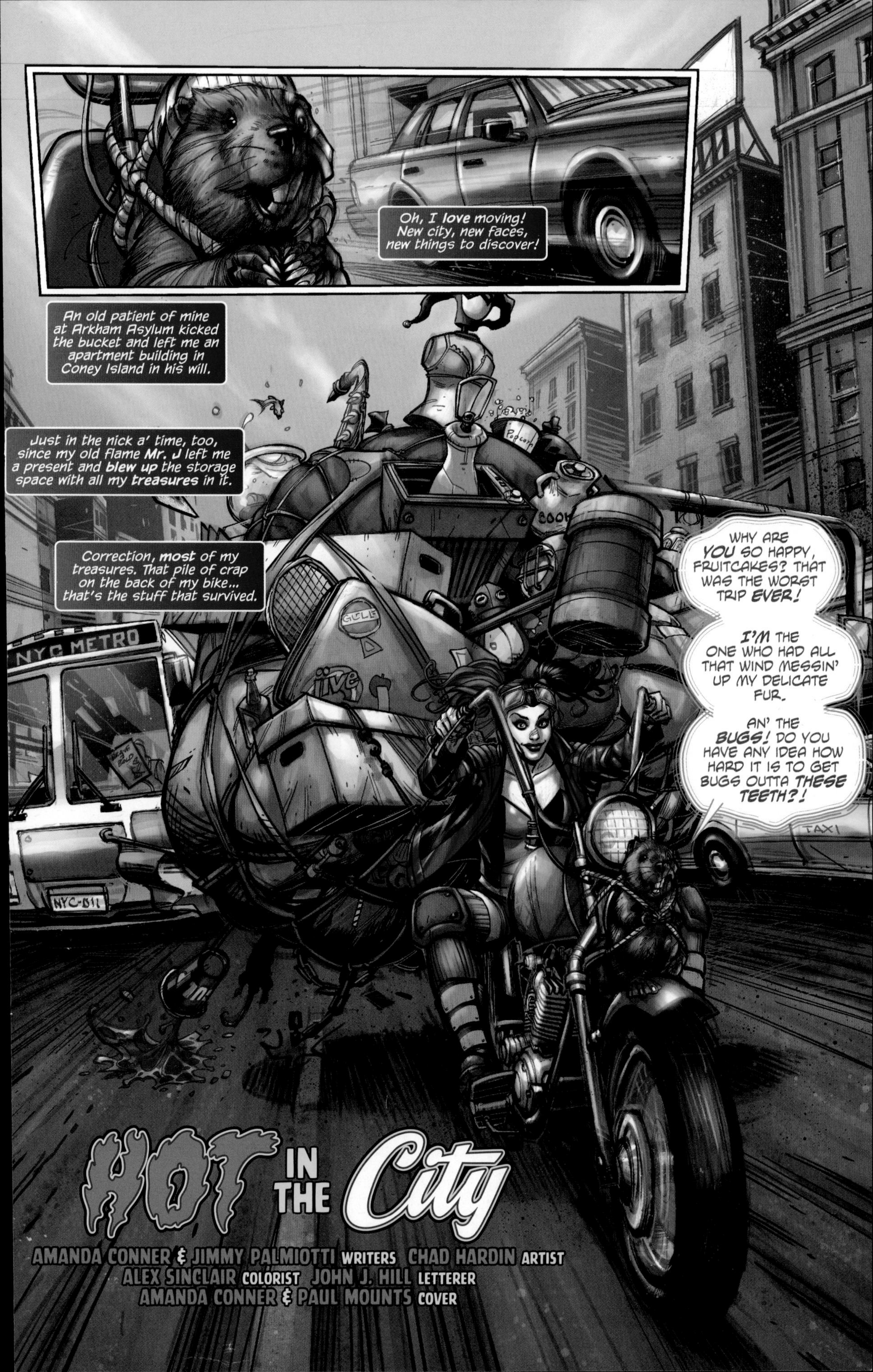
Oh, I love moving! New city, new faces, new things to discover!
An old patient of mine at Arkham Asylum kicked the bucket and left me an apartment building in Coney Island in his will.
Just in the nick a' time, too, since my old flame Mr. J left me a present and blew up the storage space with all my treasures in it.
Correction, most of my treasures. That pile of crap on the back of my bike... that's the stuff that survived.
WHY ARE YOU SO HAPPY, FRUITCAKES? THAT WAS THE WORST TRIP EVER!
I'M THE ONE WHO HAD ALL THAT WIND MESSIN' UP MY DELICATE FUR.
AN' THE BUGS! DO YOU HAVE ANY IDEA HOW HARD IT IS TO GET BUGS OUTTA THESE TEETH?!
NYC METRO
NYC-D11
TAXI
HOT IN THE City
AMANDA CONNER & JIMMY PALMIOTTI WRITERS CHAD HARDIN ARTIST
ALEX SINCLAIR COLORIST JOHN J. HILL LETTERER
AMANDA CONNER & PAUL MOUNTS COVER

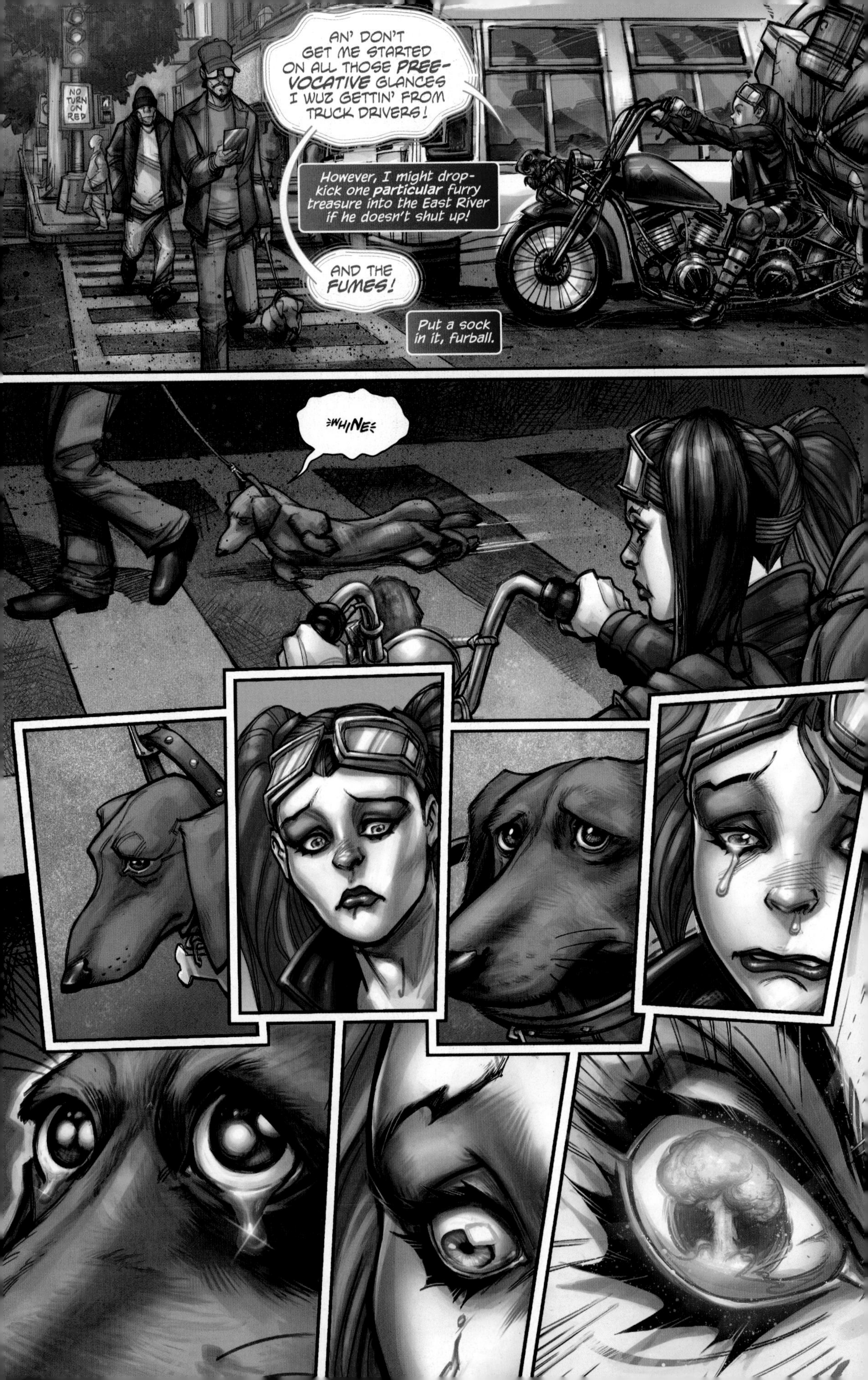
NO TURN ON RED
AN' DON'T GET ME STARTED ON ALL THOSE PREE-VOCATIVE GLANCES I WUZ GETTIN' FROM TRUCK DRIVERS!
However, I might drop-kick one particular furry treasure into the East River if he doesn't shut up!
AND THE FUMES!
Put a sock in it, furball.
WHINE

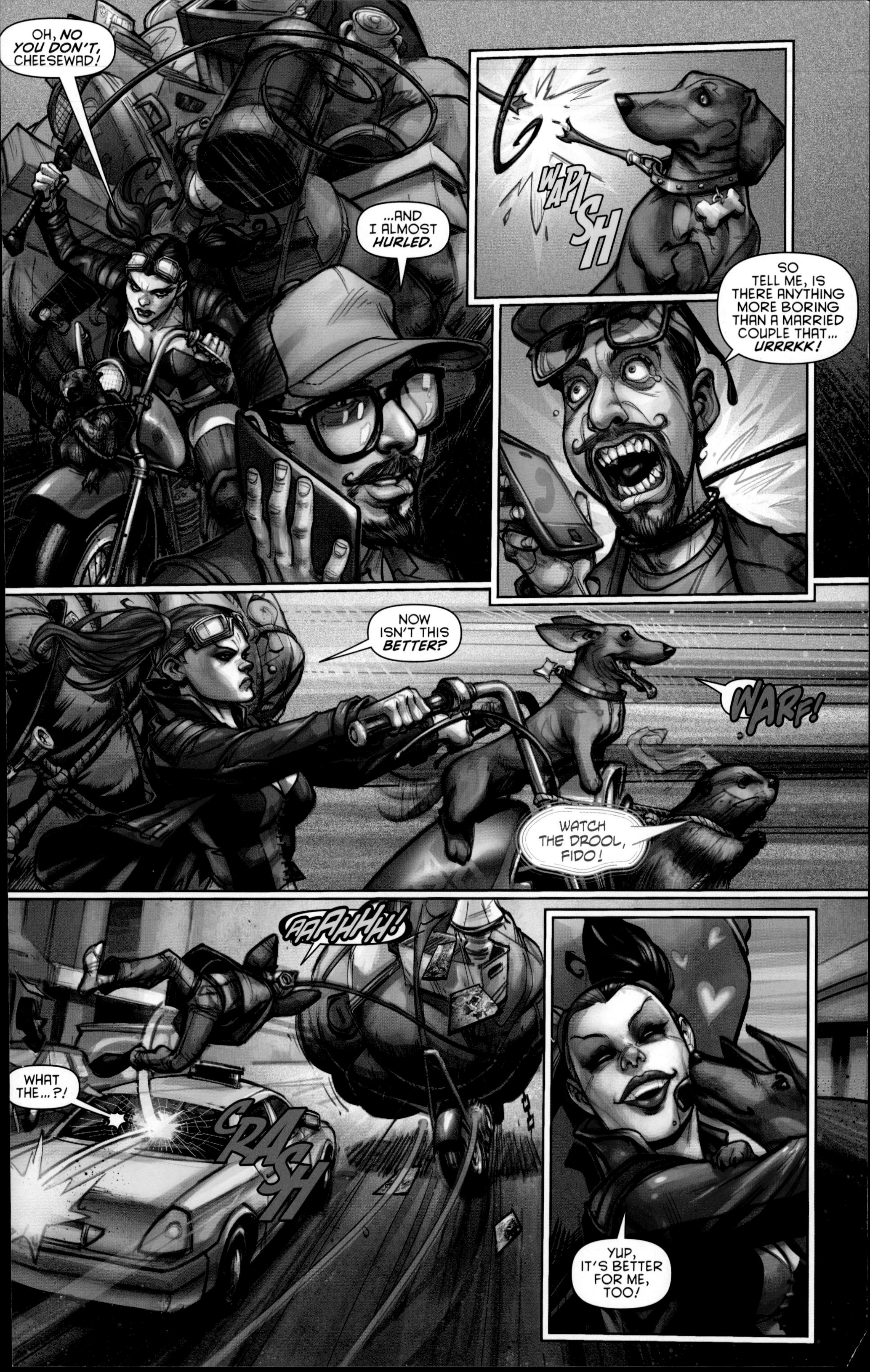
OH, NO YOU DON'T, CHEESEWAD!
...AND I ALMOST HURLED.
WAPISH
SO TELL ME, IS THERE ANYTHING MORE BORING THAN A MARRIED COUPLE THAT... URRRKK!
NOW ISN'T THIS BETTER?
WARF!
WATCH THE DROOL, FIDO!
AAAHHH!
WHAT THE...?!
CRASH
YUP, IT'S BETTER FOR ME, TOO!

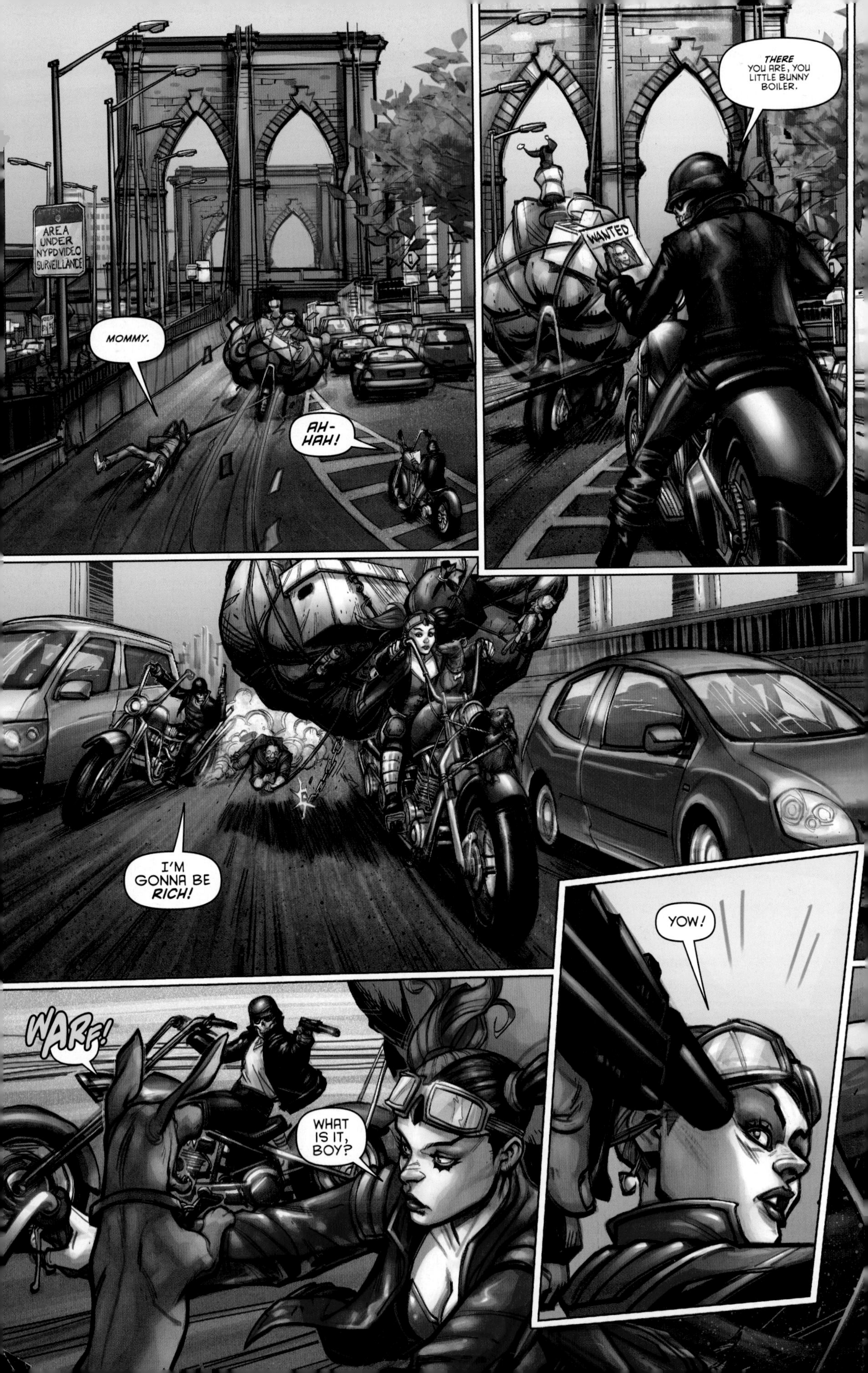
ATTENTION
AREA UNDER NYPD VIDEO SURVEILLANCE
MOMMY.
AH-HAH!
THERE YOU ARE, YOU LITTLE BUNNY BOILER.
WANTED
I'M GONNA BE RICH!
YOW!
WARF!
WHAT IS IT, BOY?

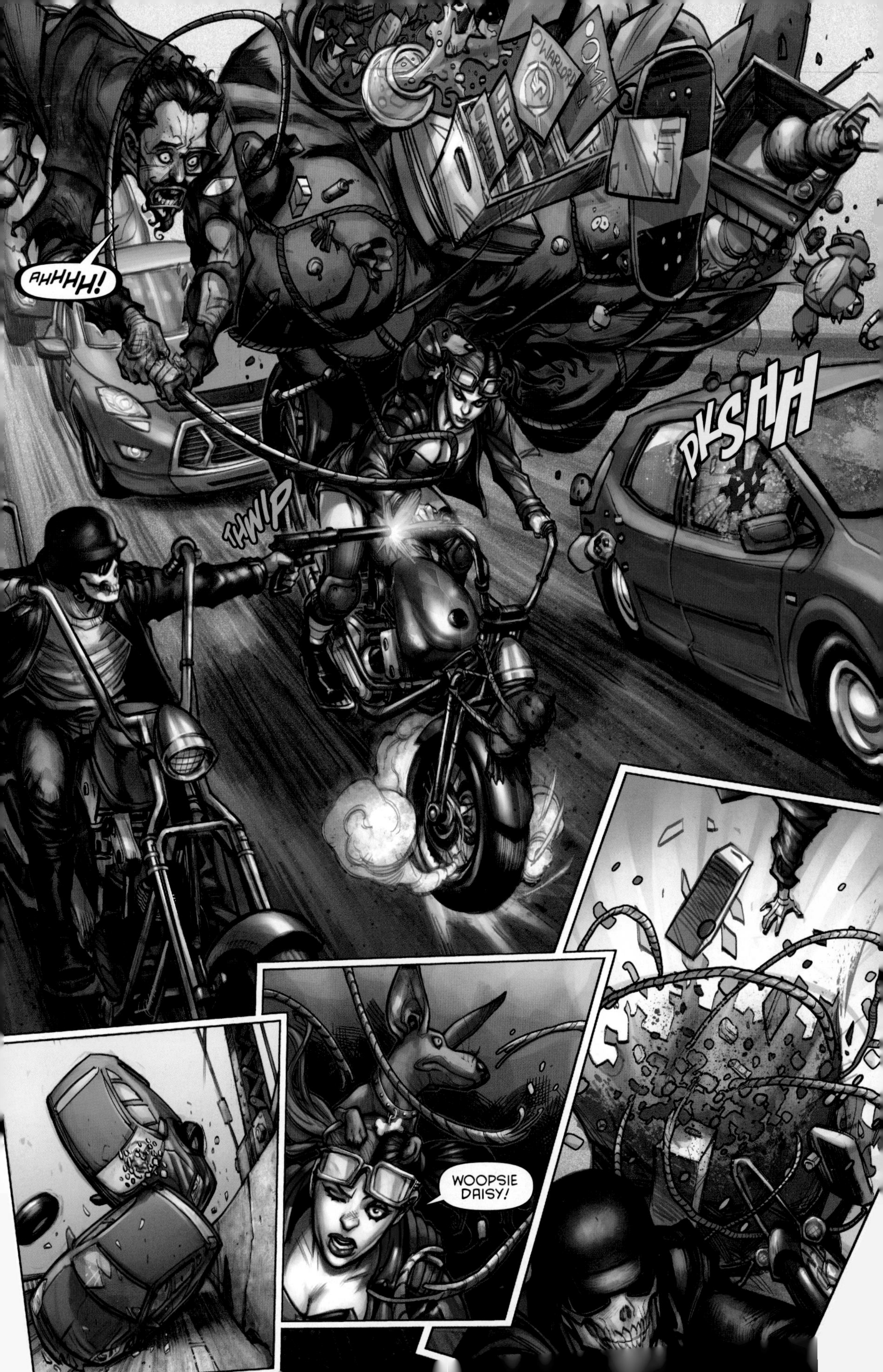
WARLORD
OMAK
AHHHH!
PKSHH
THWIP
WOOPSIE DAISY!

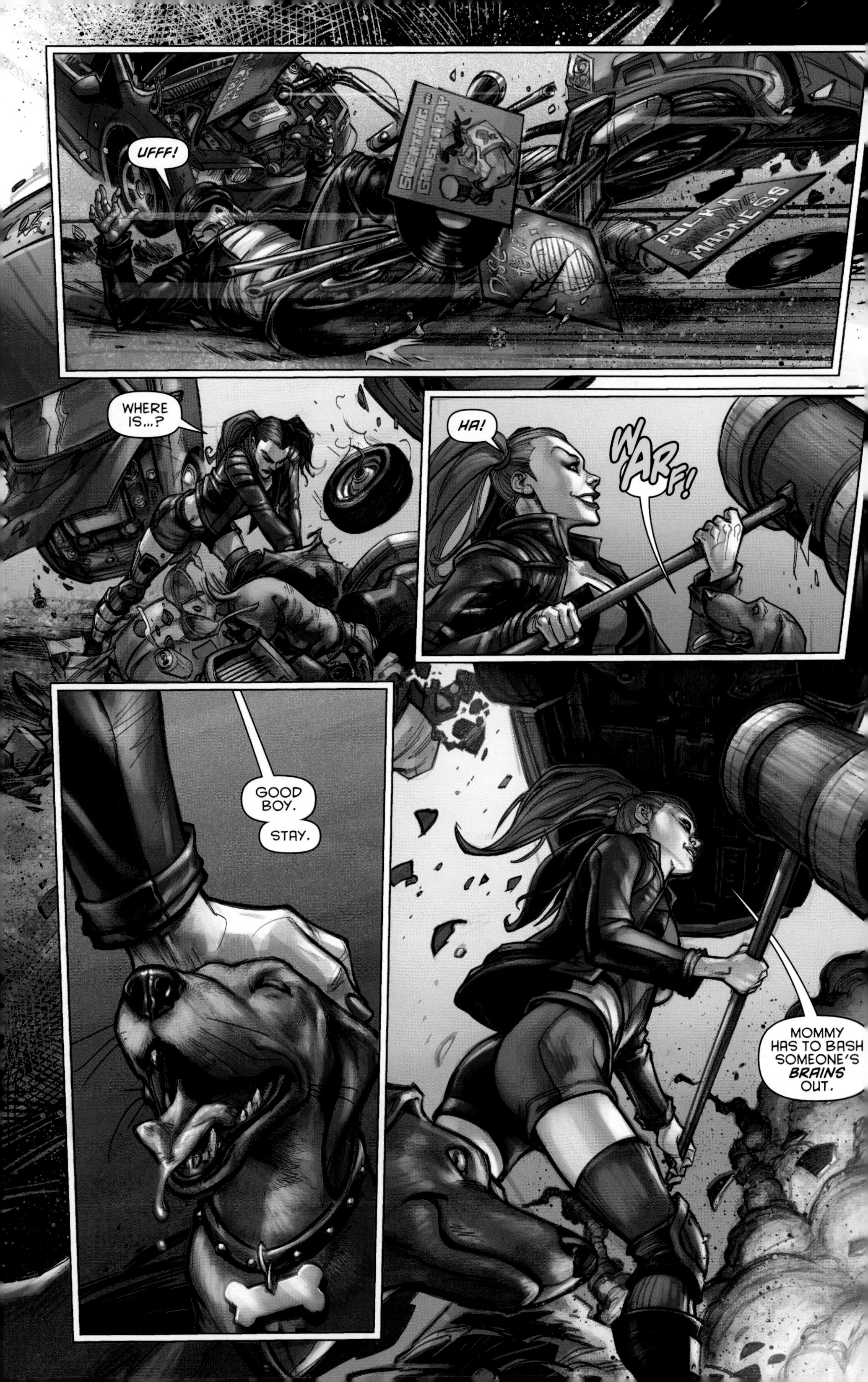
UFFF!
SWEATING TO GANSTA RAP
POLKA MADNESS
WHERE IS...?
HA!
WARF!
GOOD BOY.
STAY.
MOMMY HAS TO BASH SOMEONE'S *BRAINS* OUT.

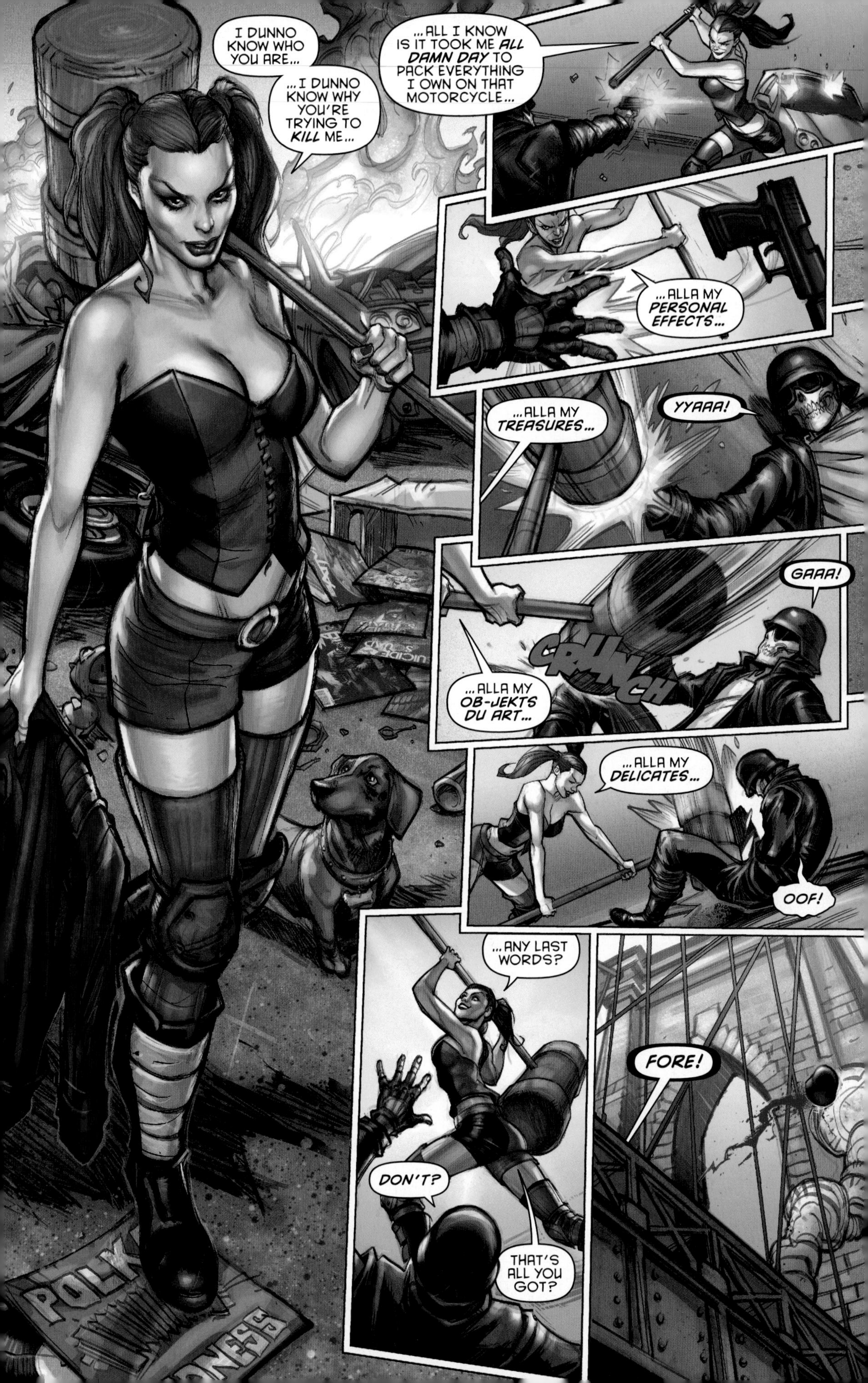
I DUNNO KNOW WHO YOU ARE...
...I DUNNO KNOW WHY YOU'RE TRYING TO KILL ME...
...ALL I KNOW IS IT TOOK ME ALL DAMN DAY TO PACK EVERYTHING I OWN ON THAT MOTORCYCLE...
...ALLA MY PERSONAL EFFECTS...
...ALLA MY TREASURES...
YYAAA!
GAAA!
CRUNCH
...ALLA MY OB-JEKTS DU ART...
...ALLA MY DELICATES...
OOF!
...ANY LAST WORDS?
DON'T?
THAT'S ALL YOU GOT?
FORE!

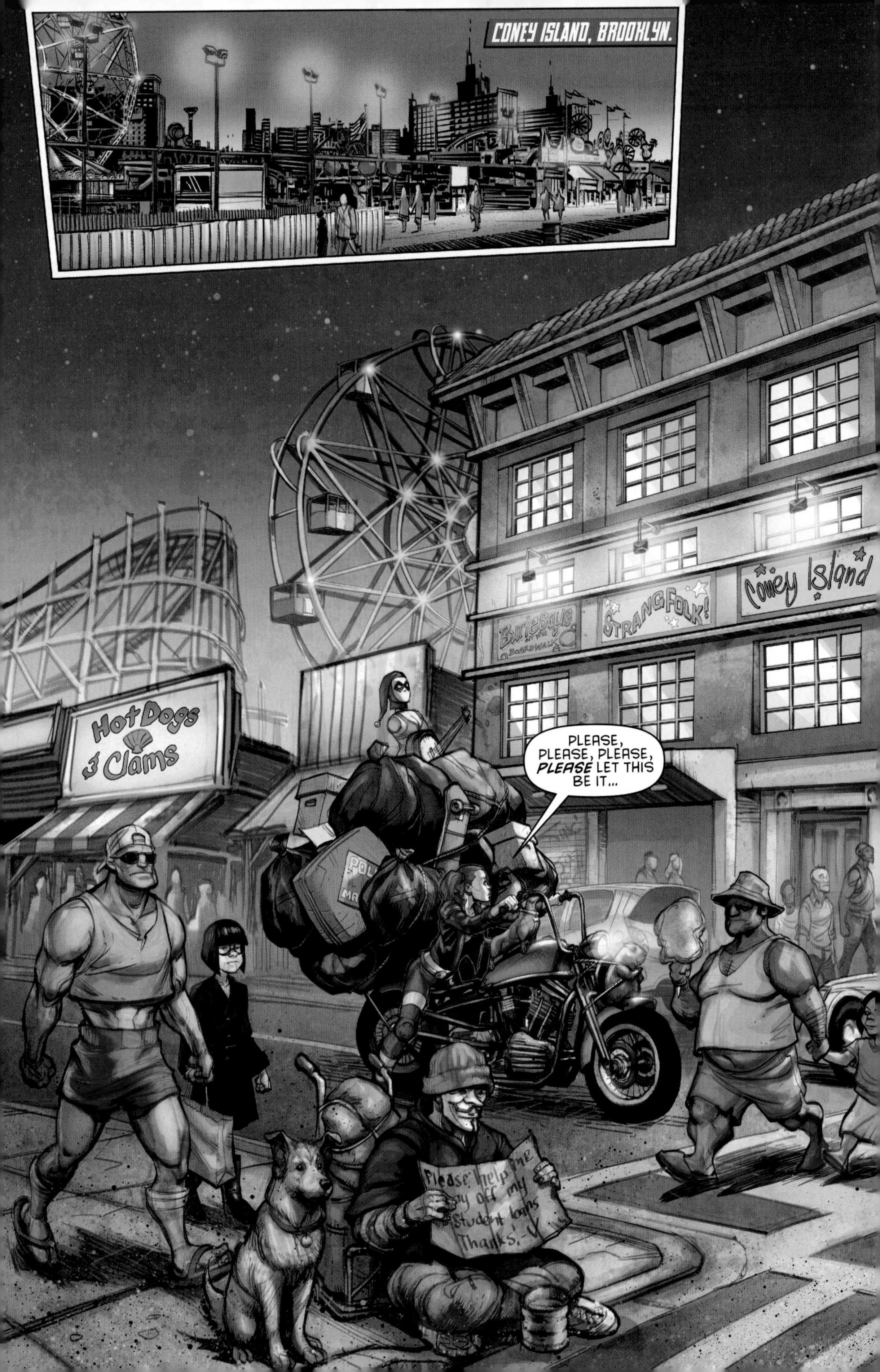
CONEY ISLAND, BROOKLYN.
Hot Dogs & Clams
STRANGFOLK!
Coney Island
PLEASE, PLEASE, PLEASE, *PLEASE* LET THIS BE IT...

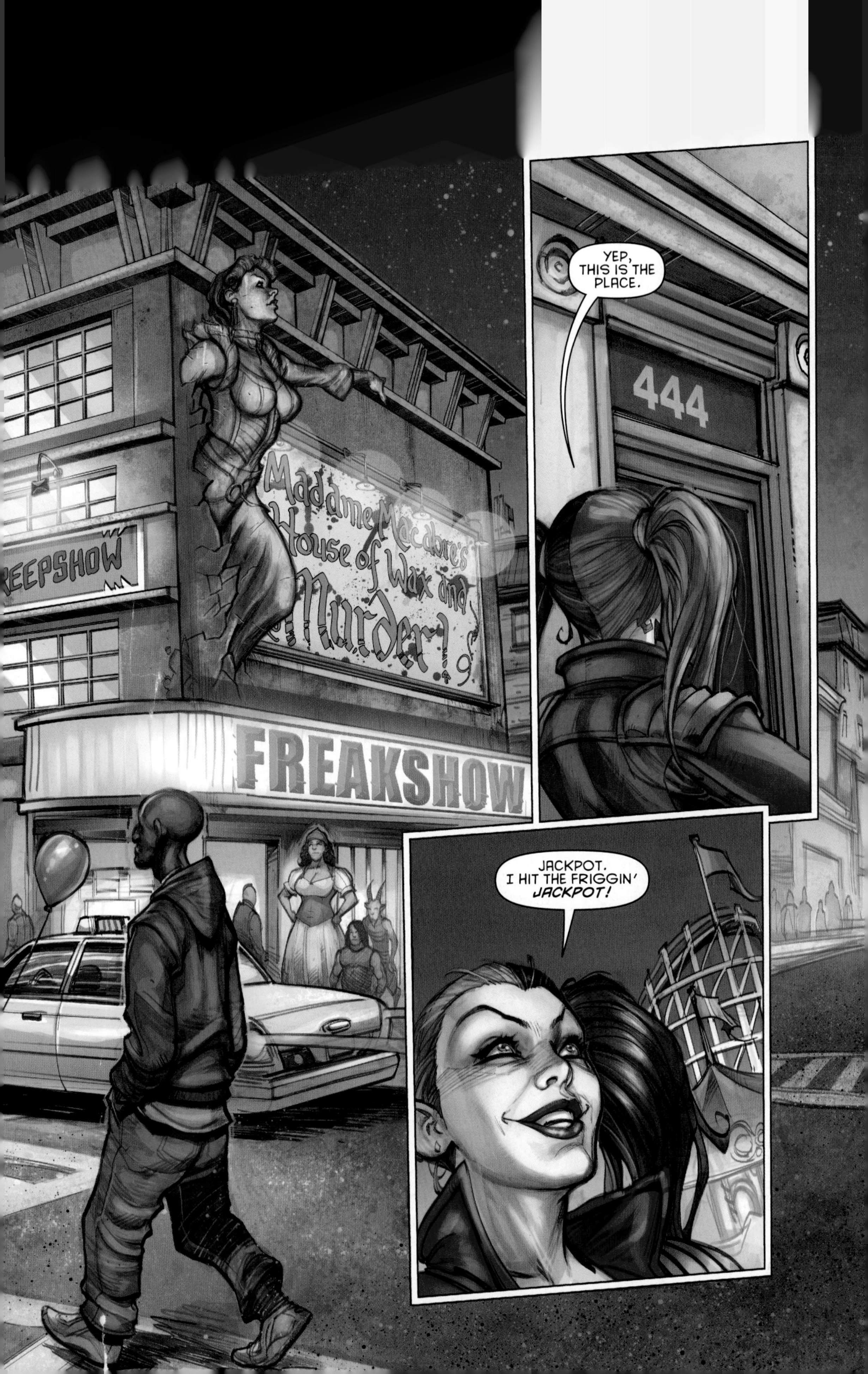

Madame Macabre's House of Wax and Murder!
REEPSHOW
FREAKSHOW
YEP, THIS IS THE PLACE.
444
JACKPOT. I HIT THE FRIGGIN' *JACKPOT!*

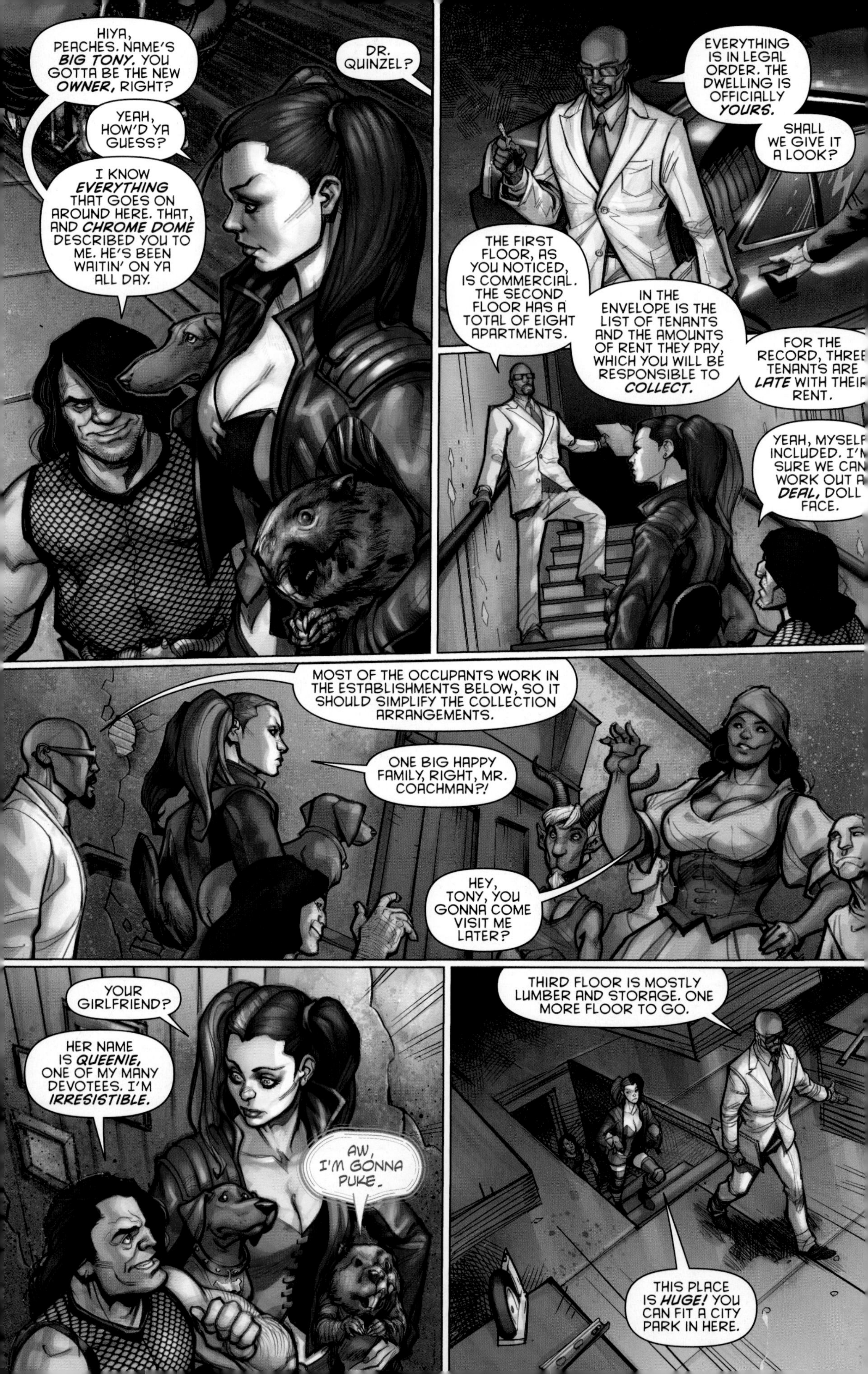
HIYA, PEACHES. NAME'S BIG TONY. YOU GOTTA BE THE NEW OWNER, RIGHT?
YEAH, HOW'D YA GUESS?
I KNOW EVERYTHING THAT GOES ON AROUND HERE. THAT, AND CHROME DOME DESCRIBED YOU TO ME. HE'S BEEN WAITIN' ON YA ALL DAY.
DR. QUINZEL?
EVERYTHING IS IN LEGAL ORDER. THE DWELLING IS OFFICIALLY YOURS.
SHALL WE GIVE IT A LOOK?
THE FIRST FLOOR, AS YOU NOTICED, IS COMMERCIAL. THE SECOND FLOOR HAS A TOTAL OF EIGHT APARTMENTS.
IN THE ENVELOPE IS THE LIST OF TENANTS AND THE AMOUNTS OF RENT THEY PAY, WHICH YOU WILL BE RESPONSIBLE TO COLLECT.
FOR THE RECORD, THREE TENANTS ARE LATE WITH THEIR RENT.
YEAH, MYSELF INCLUDED. I'M SURE WE CAN WORK OUT A DEAL, DOLL FACE.
MOST OF THE OCCUPANTS WORK IN THE ESTABLISHMENTS BELOW, SO IT SHOULD SIMPLIFY THE COLLECTION ARRANGEMENTS.
ONE BIG HAPPY FAMILY, RIGHT, MR. COACHMAN?!
HEY, TONY, YOU GONNA COME VISIT ME LATER?
YOUR GIRLFRIEND?
HER NAME IS QUEENIE, ONE OF MY MANY DEVOTEES. I'M IRRESISTIBLE.
AW, I'M GONNA PUKE.
THIRD FLOOR IS MOSTLY LUMBER AND STORAGE. ONE MORE FLOOR TO GO.
THIS PLACE IS HUGE! YOU CAN FIT A CITY PARK IN HERE.

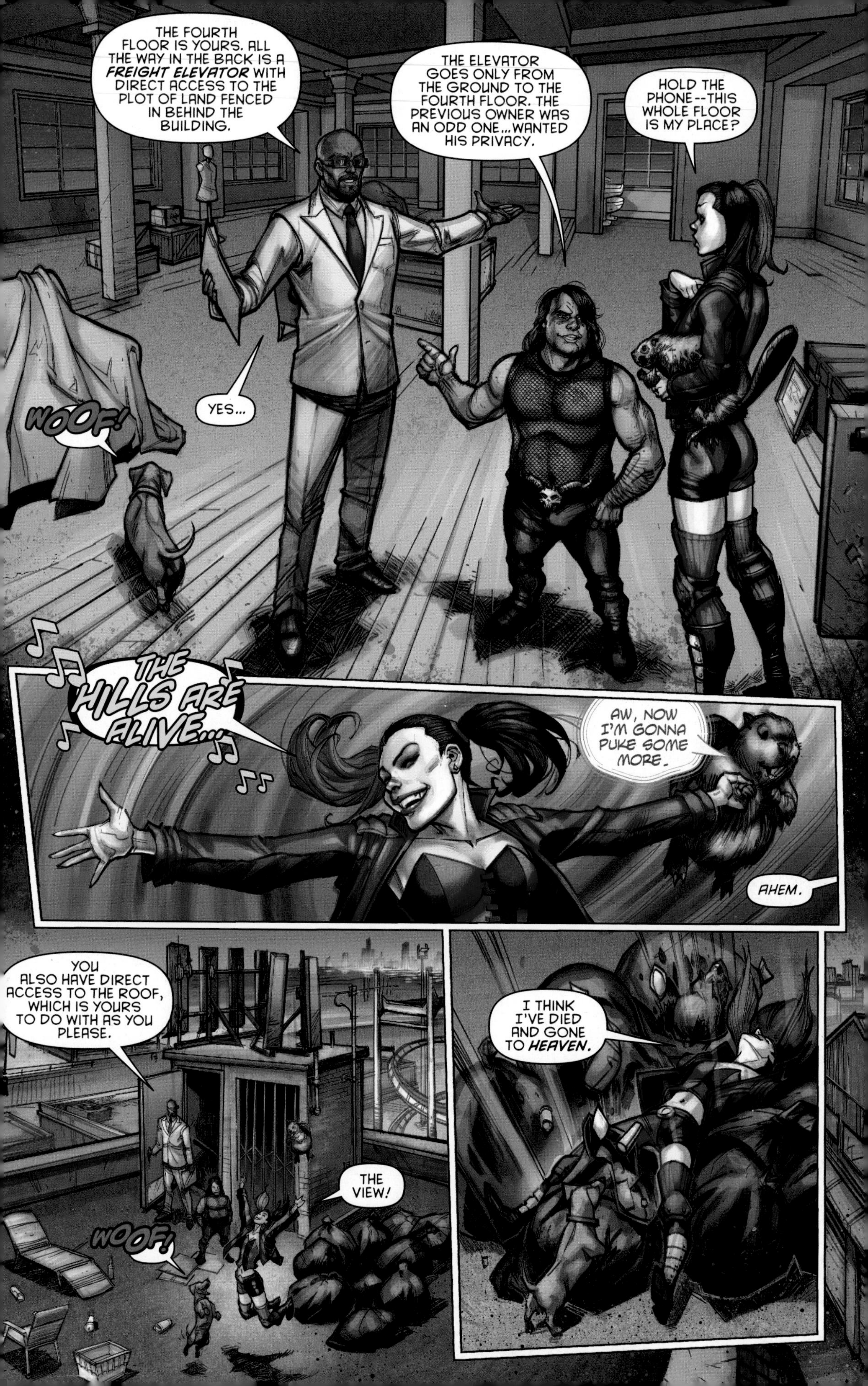
THE FOURTH FLOOR IS YOURS. ALL THE WAY IN THE BACK IS A **FREIGHT ELEVATOR** WITH DIRECT ACCESS TO THE PLOT OF LAND FENCED IN BEHIND THE BUILDING.
THE ELEVATOR GOES ONLY FROM THE GROUND TO THE FOURTH FLOOR. THE PREVIOUS OWNER WAS AN ODD ONE...WANTED HIS PRIVACY.
HOLD THE PHONE--THIS WHOLE FLOOR IS MY PLACE?
YES...
WOOF!
THE HILLS ARE ALIVE...
AW, NOW I'M GONNA PUKE SOME MORE.
AHEM.
YOU ALSO HAVE DIRECT ACCESS TO THE ROOF, WHICH IS YOURS TO DO WITH AS YOU PLEASE.
THE VIEW!
WOOF!
I THINK I'VE DIED AND GONE TO **HEAVEN**.

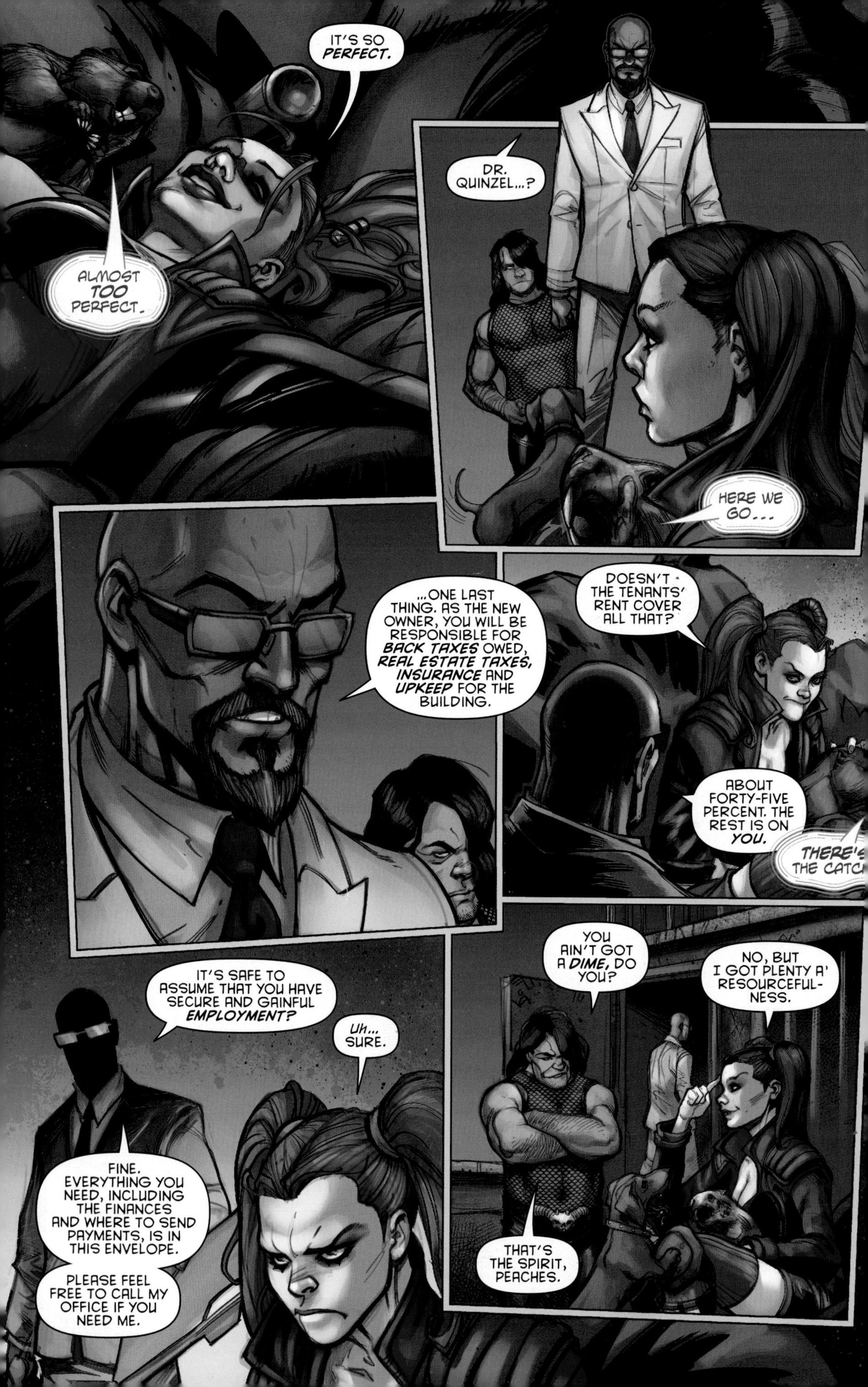
IT'S SO PERFECT.
ALMOST TOO PERFECT.
DR. QUINZEL...?
HERE WE GO...
...ONE LAST THING. AS THE NEW OWNER, YOU WILL BE RESPONSIBLE FOR BACK TAXES OWED, REAL ESTATE TAXES, INSURANCE AND UPKEEP FOR THE BUILDING.
DOESN'T THE TENANTS' RENT COVER ALL THAT?
ABOUT FORTY-FIVE PERCENT. THE REST IS ON YOU.
IT'S SAFE TO ASSUME THAT YOU HAVE SECURE AND GAINFUL EMPLOYMENT?
Uh... SURE.
FINE. EVERYTHING YOU NEED, INCLUDING THE FINANCES AND WHERE TO SEND PAYMENTS, IS IN THIS ENVELOPE.
PLEASE FEEL FREE TO CALL MY OFFICE IF YOU NEED ME.
YOU AIN'T GOT A DIME, DO YOU?
NO, BUT I GOT PLENTY A' RESOURCEFUL-NESS.
THAT'S THE SPIRIT, PEACHES.

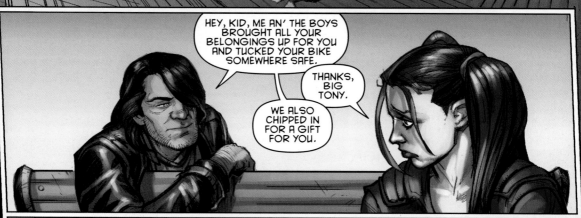

HEY, KID, ME AN' THE BOYS BROUGHT ALL YOUR BELONGINGS UP FOR YOU AND TUCKED YOUR BIKE SOMEWHERE SAFE.

THANKS, BIG TONY.

WE ALSO CHIPPED IN FOR A GIFT FOR YOU.

IN THIS MAGICAL BAG IS THE KEY TO YOUR SALVATION.

ONE LOCAL NEWSPAPER WITH HELP WANTED ADS, A HIGHLIGHT PEN TO CIRCLE THE LEADS, A GIANT COFFEE-- TWO SUGARS, NO MILK--

--AND ONE AUTHENTIC BROOKLYN EVERYTHING BAGEL, TOASTED, WITH CREAM CHEESE.

AWW, YOU GUYS!

HEY... YER KILLIN' ME.

SORRY.

Jonathan's
WORLD FAMOUS FRANKS

DAMN.

I'M TOO FAR, AN' THAT BIZZO WON'T SIT STILL.

I GUESS I HAVE TO GET MY HANDS DIRTY ON THIS ONE.

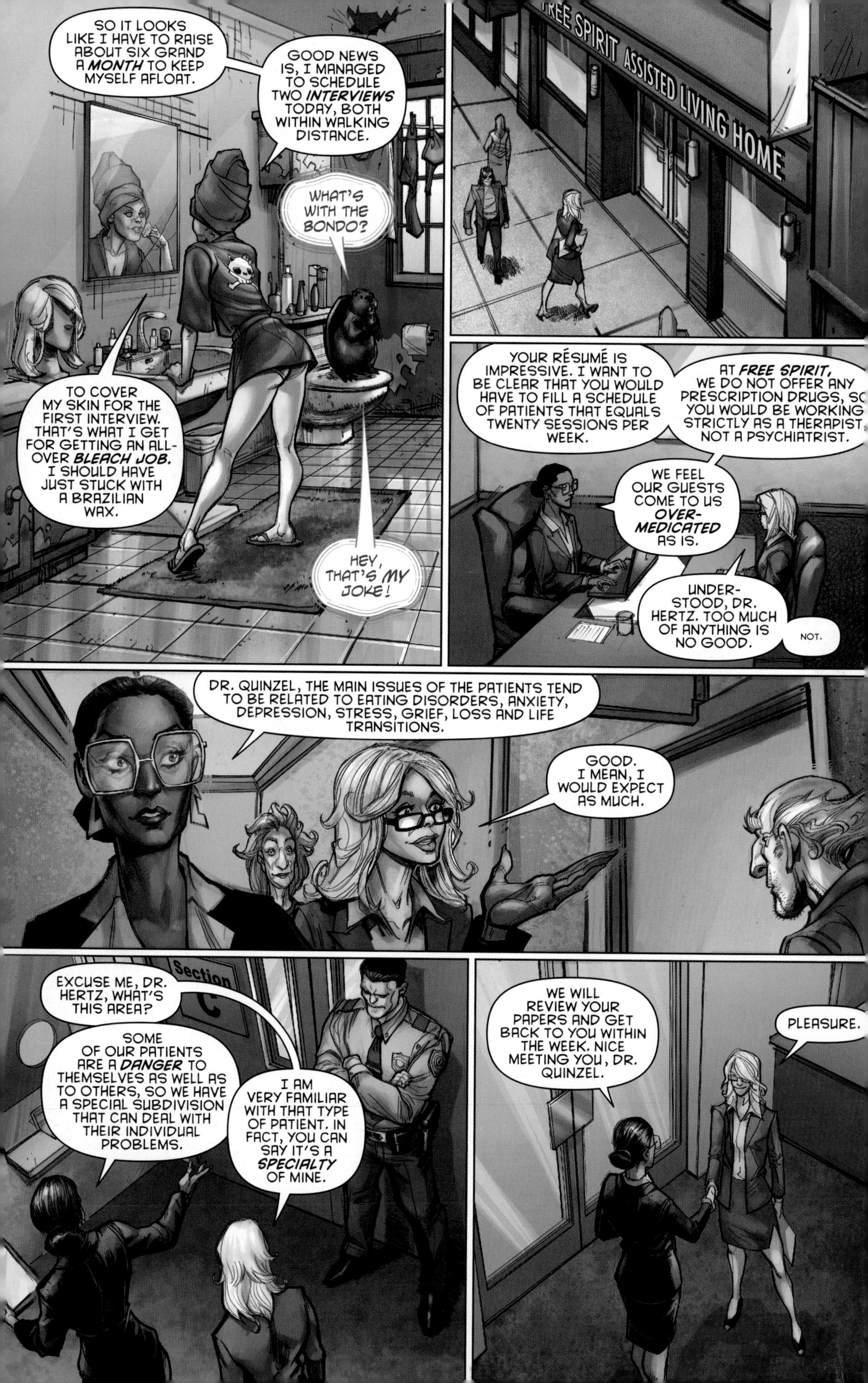
SO IT LOOKS LIKE I HAVE TO RAISE ABOUT SIX GRAND A MONTH TO KEEP MYSELF AFLOAT.
GOOD NEWS IS, I MANAGED TO SCHEDULE TWO INTERVIEWS TODAY, BOTH WITHIN WALKING DISTANCE.
WHAT'S WITH THE BONDO?
TO COVER MY SKIN FOR THE FIRST INTERVIEW. THAT'S WHAT I GET FOR GETTING AN ALL-OVER BLEACH JOB. I SHOULD HAVE JUST STUCK WITH A BRAZILIAN WAX.
HEY, THAT'S MY JOKE!
FREE SPIRIT ASSISTED LIVING HOME
YOUR RÉSUMÉ IS IMPRESSIVE. I WANT TO BE CLEAR THAT YOU WOULD HAVE TO FILL A SCHEDULE OF PATIENTS THAT EQUALS TWENTY SESSIONS PER WEEK.
AT FREE SPIRIT, WE DO NOT OFFER ANY PRESCRIPTION DRUGS, SO YOU WOULD BE WORKING STRICTLY AS A THERAPIST, NOT A PSYCHIATRIST.
WE FEEL OUR GUESTS COME TO US OVER-MEDICATED AS IS.
UNDER-STOOD, DR. HERTZ. TOO MUCH OF ANYTHING IS NO GOOD.
NOT.
DR. QUINZEL, THE MAIN ISSUES OF THE PATIENTS TEND TO BE RELATED TO EATING DISORDERS, ANXIETY, DEPRESSION, STRESS, GRIEF, LOSS AND LIFE TRANSITIONS.
GOOD. I MEAN, I WOULD EXPECT AS MUCH.
Section C
EXCUSE ME, DR. HERTZ, WHAT'S THIS AREA?
SOME OF OUR PATIENTS ARE A DANGER TO THEMSELVES AS WELL AS TO OTHERS, SO WE HAVE A SPECIAL SUBDIVISION THAT CAN DEAL WITH THEIR INDIVIDUAL PROBLEMS.
I AM VERY FAMILIAR WITH THAT TYPE OF PATIENT. IN FACT, YOU CAN SAY IT'S A SPECIALTY OF MINE.
WE WILL REVIEW YOUR PAPERS AND GET BACK TO YOU WITHIN THE WEEK. NICE MEETING YOU, DR. QUINZEL.
PLEASURE.

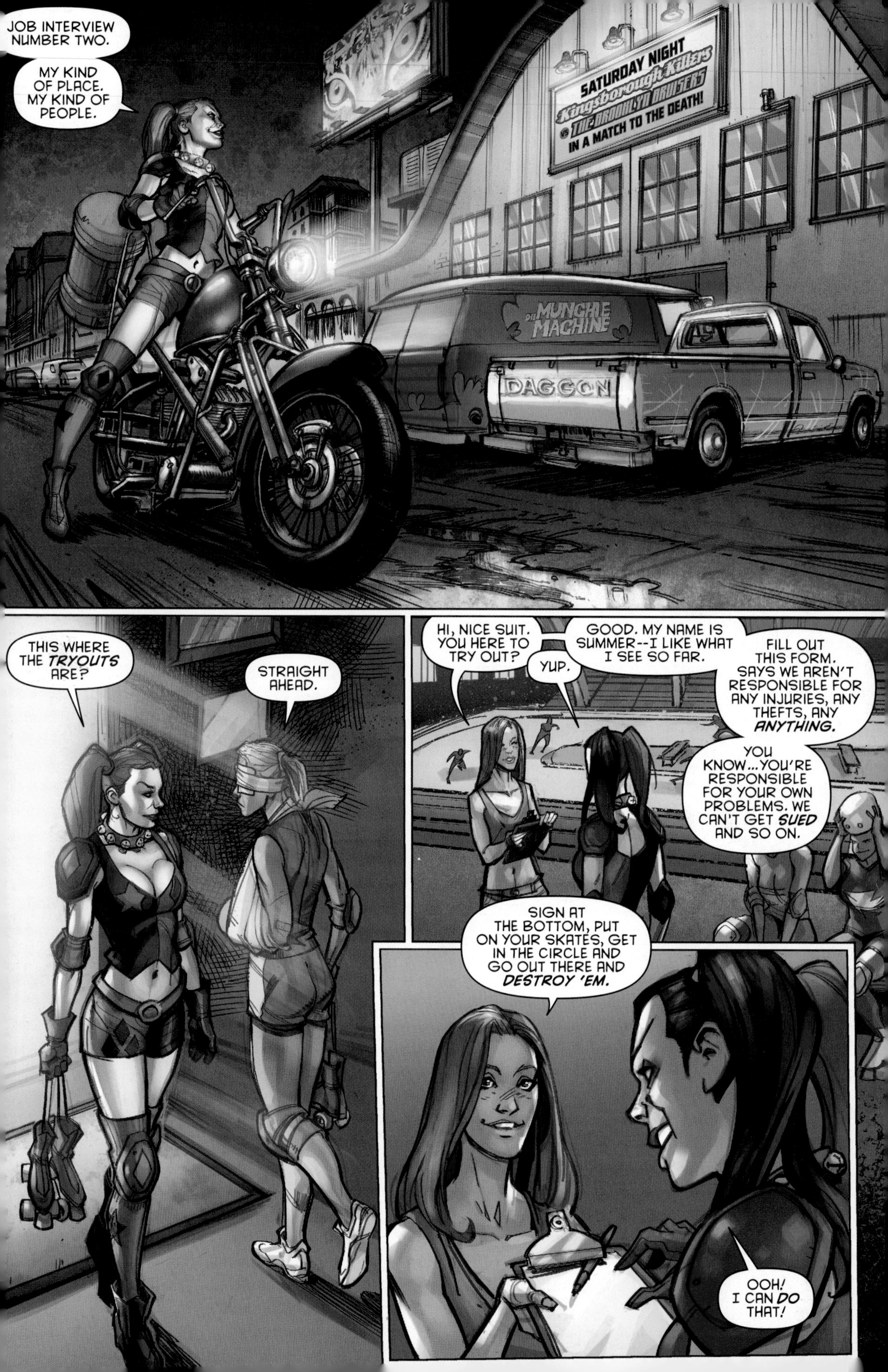
JOB INTERVIEW NUMBER TWO.
MY KIND OF PLACE. MY KIND OF PEOPLE.
SATURDAY NIGHT
Kingsborough Killers
VS
THE BROOKLYN BRUISERS
IN A MATCH TO THE DEATH!
MUNCHIE MACHINE
DAGGON
THIS WHERE THE TRYOUTS ARE?
STRAIGHT AHEAD.
HI, NICE SUIT. YOU HERE TO TRY OUT?
YUP.
GOOD. MY NAME IS SUMMER--I LIKE WHAT I SEE SO FAR.
FILL OUT THIS FORM. SAYS WE AREN'T RESPONSIBLE FOR ANY INJURIES, ANY THEFTS, ANY ANYTHING.
YOU KNOW...YOU'RE RESPONSIBLE FOR YOUR OWN PROBLEMS. WE CAN'T GET SUED AND SO ON.
SIGN AT THE BOTTOM, PUT ON YOUR SKATES, GET IN THE CIRCLE AND GO OUT THERE AND DESTROY 'EM.
OOH! I CAN DO THAT!

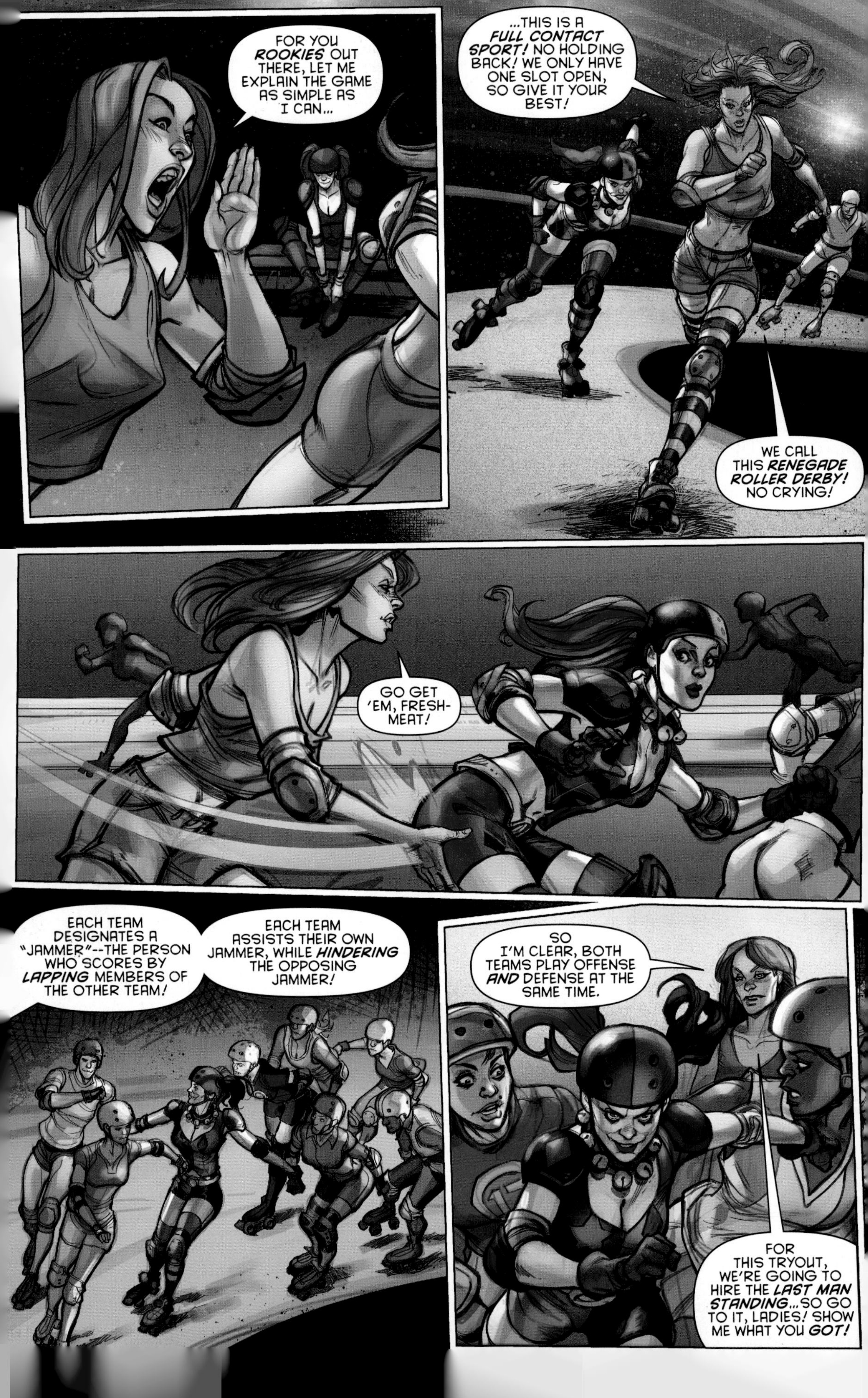

FOR YOU *ROOKIES* OUT THERE, LET ME EXPLAIN THE GAME AS SIMPLE AS I CAN...
...THIS IS A *FULL CONTACT SPORT!* NO HOLDING BACK! WE ONLY HAVE ONE SLOT OPEN, SO GIVE IT YOUR BEST!
WE CALL THIS *RENEGADE ROLLER DERBY!* NO CRYING!
GO GET 'EM, FRESH-MEAT!
EACH TEAM DESIGNATES A "JAMMER"--THE PERSON WHO SCORES BY *LAPPING* MEMBERS OF THE OTHER TEAM!
EACH TEAM ASSISTS THEIR OWN JAMMER, WHILE *HINDERING* THE OPPOSING JAMMER!
SO I'M CLEAR, BOTH TEAMS PLAY OFFENSE *AND* DEFENSE AT THE SAME TIME.
FOR THIS TRYOUT, WE'RE GOING TO HIRE THE *LAST MAN STANDING*...SO GO TO IT, LADIES! SHOW ME WHAT YOU *GOT!*

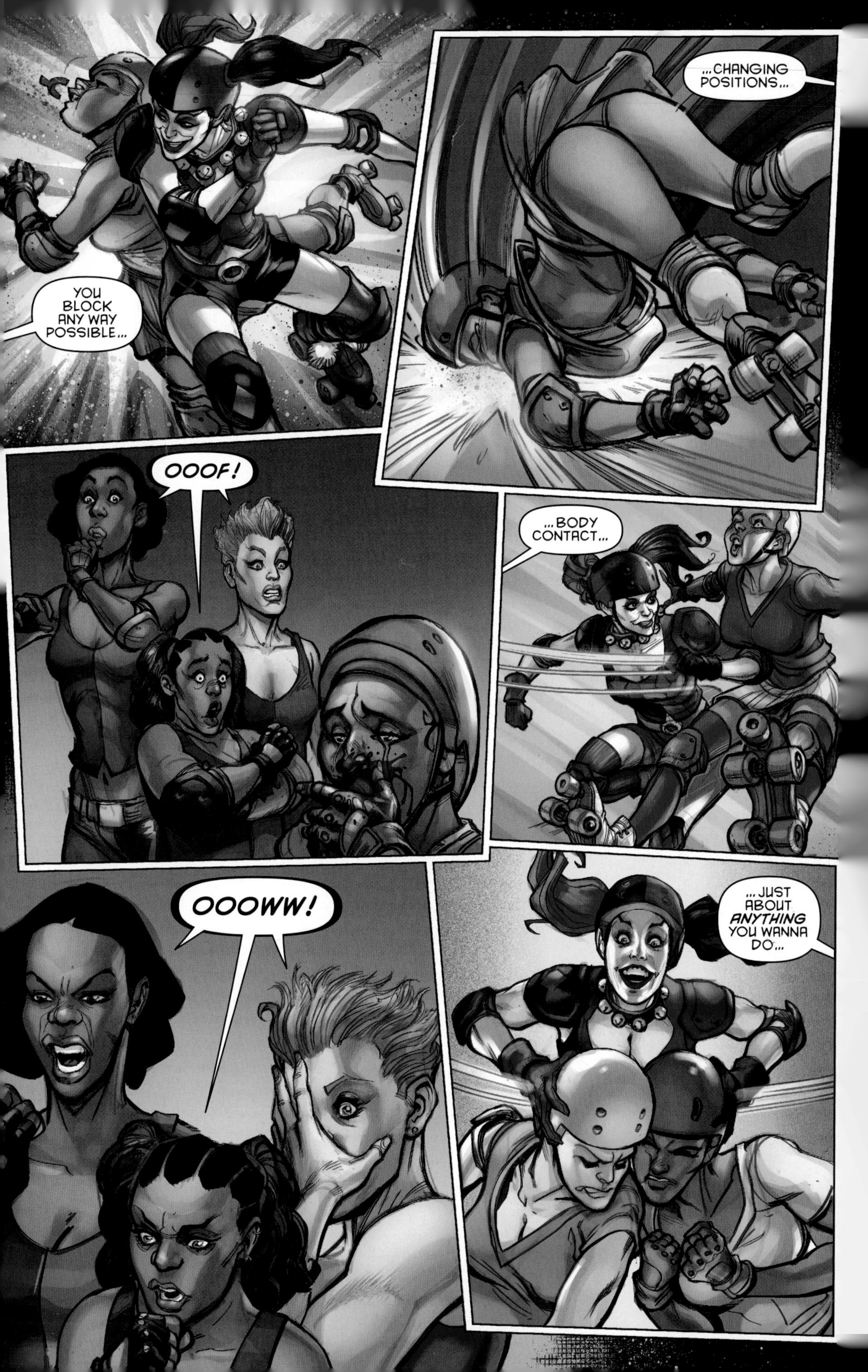
YOU BLOCK ANY WAY POSSIBLE...
...CHANGING POSITIONS...
OOOF!
...BODY CONTACT...
OOOWW!
...JUST ABOUT *ANYTHING* YOU WANNA DO...

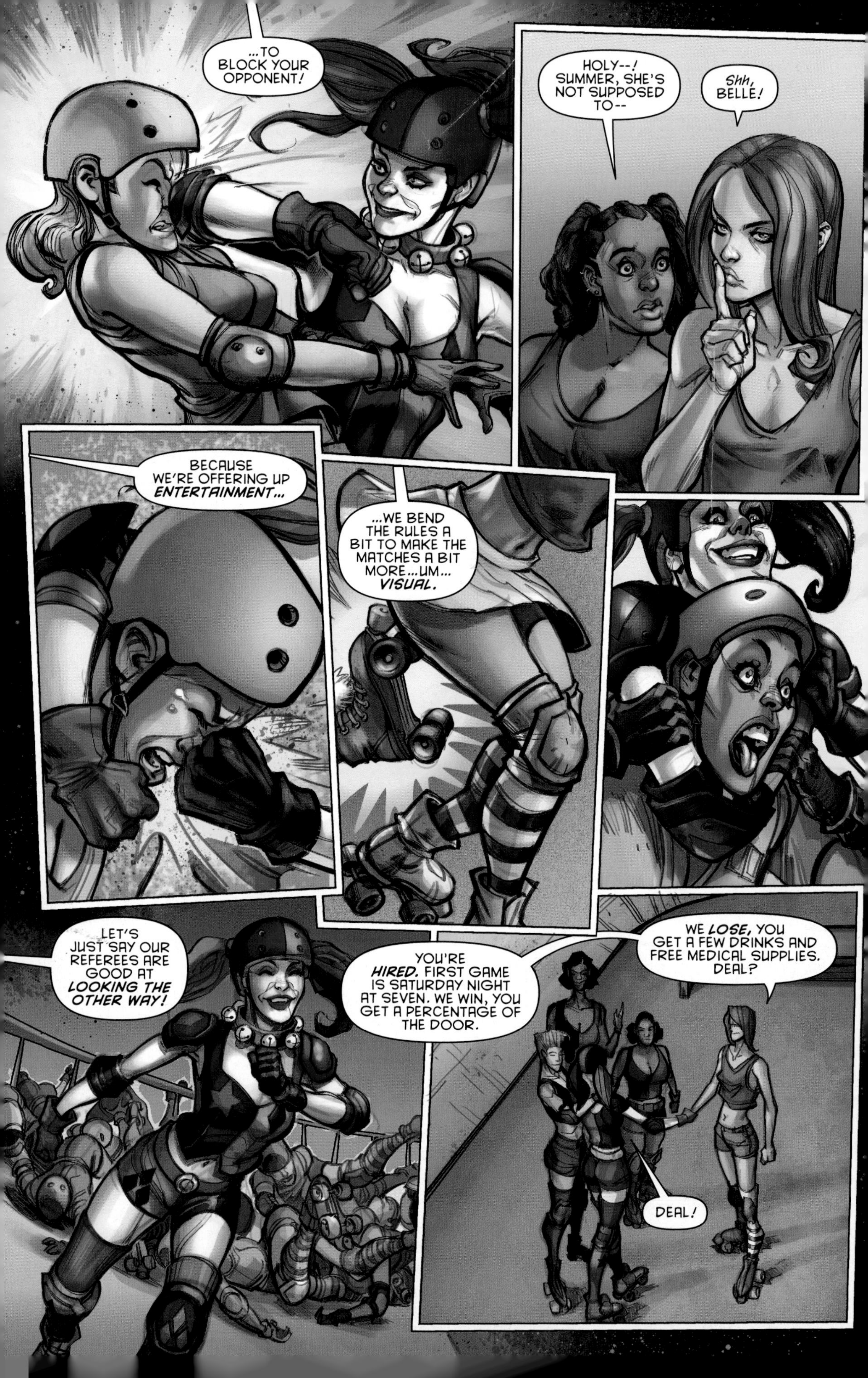
...TO BLOCK YOUR OPPONENT!
HOLY--! SUMMER, SHE'S NOT SUPPOSED TO--
SHH, BELLE!
BECAUSE WE'RE OFFERING UP ***ENTERTAINMENT...***
...WE BEND THE RULES A BIT TO MAKE THE MATCHES A BIT MORE...UM... ***VISUAL.***
LET'S JUST SAY OUR REFEREES ARE GOOD AT ***LOOKING THE OTHER WAY!***
YOU'RE ***HIRED.*** FIRST GAME IS SATURDAY NIGHT AT SEVEN. WE WIN, YOU GET A PERCENTAGE OF THE DOOR.
WE ***LOSE,*** YOU GET A FEW DRINKS AND FREE MEDICAL SUPPLIES. DEAL?
DEAL!

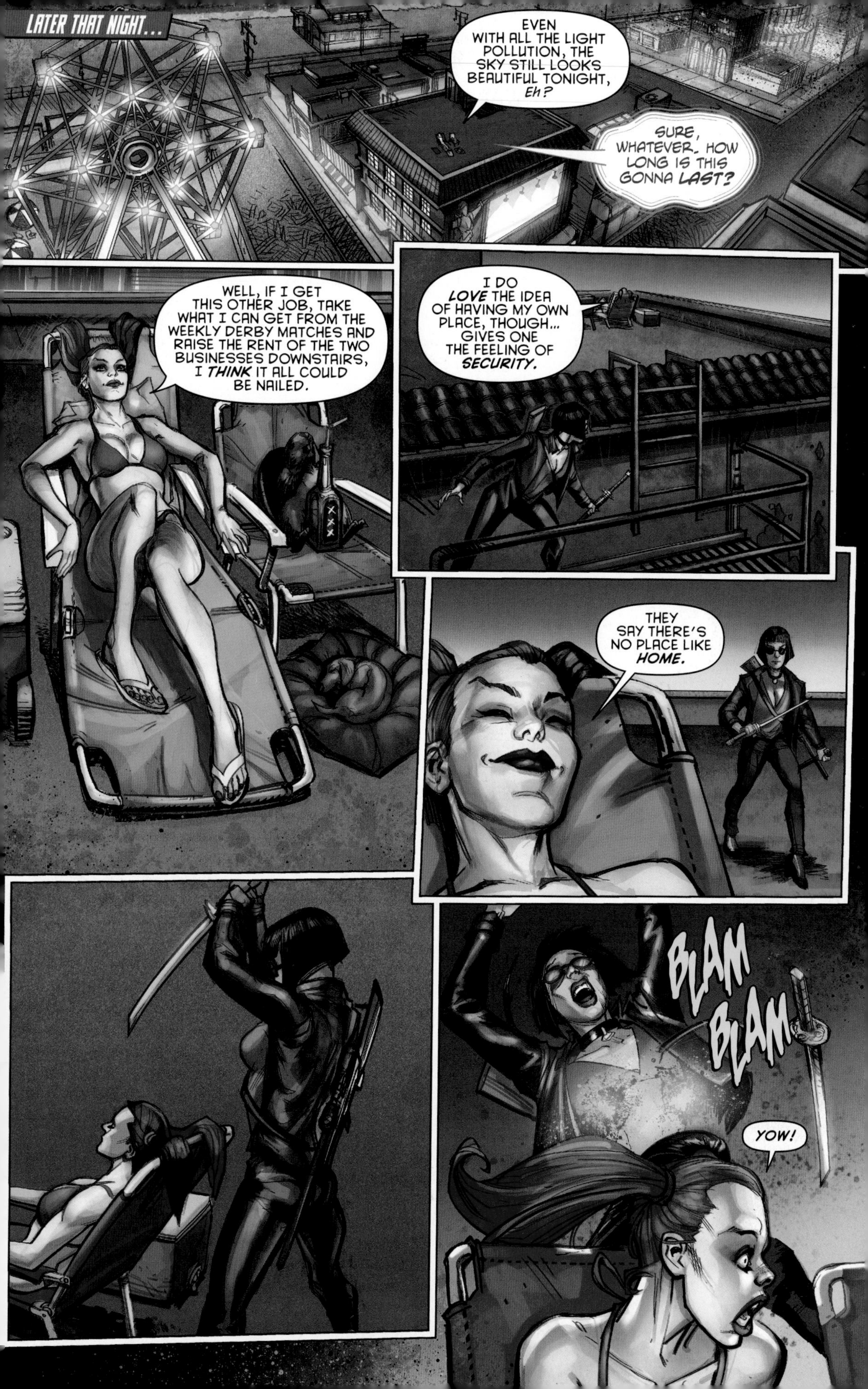
LATER THAT NIGHT...
EVEN WITH ALL THE LIGHT POLLUTION, THE SKY STILL LOOKS BEAUTIFUL TONIGHT, Eh?
SURE, WHATEVER. HOW LONG IS THIS GONNA LAST?
WELL, IF I GET THIS OTHER JOB, TAKE WHAT I CAN GET FROM THE WEEKLY DERBY MATCHES AND RAISE THE RENT OF THE TWO BUSINESSES DOWNSTAIRS, I THINK IT ALL COULD BE NAILED.
I DO LOVE THE IDEA OF HAVING MY OWN PLACE, THOUGH... GIVES ONE THE FEELING OF SECURITY.
THEY SAY THERE'S NO PLACE LIKE HOME.
BLAM
BLAM
YOW!

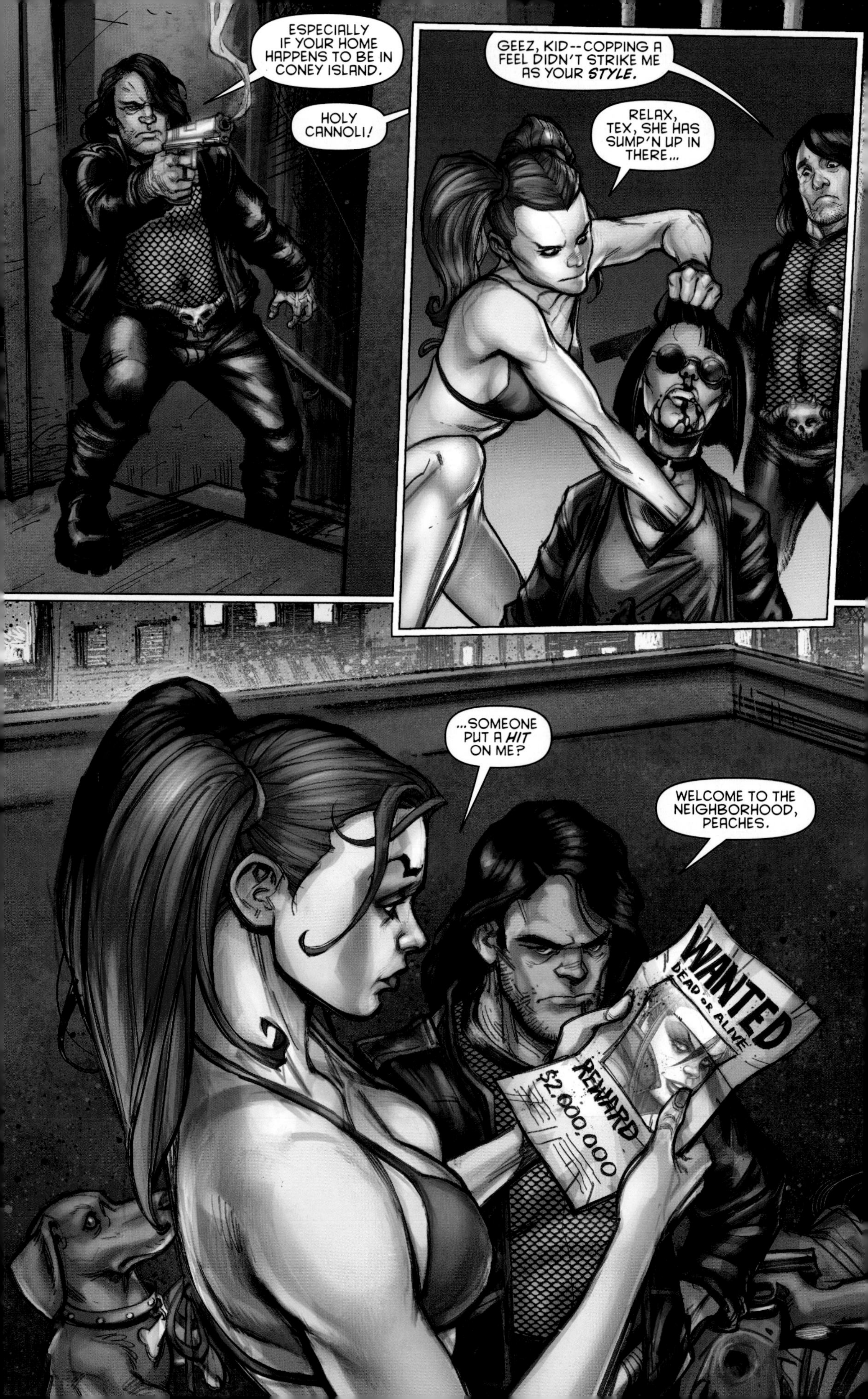
ESPECIALLY IF YOUR HOME HAPPENS TO BE IN CONEY ISLAND.
HOLY CANNOLI!
GEEZ, KID--COPPING A FEEL DIDN'T STRIKE ME AS YOUR *STYLE*.
RELAX, TEX, SHE HAS SUMP'N UP IN THERE...
...SOMEONE PUT A *HIT* ON ME?
WELCOME TO THE NEIGHBORHOOD, PEACHES.
WANTED
DEAD OR ALIVE
REWARD
$2,000,000

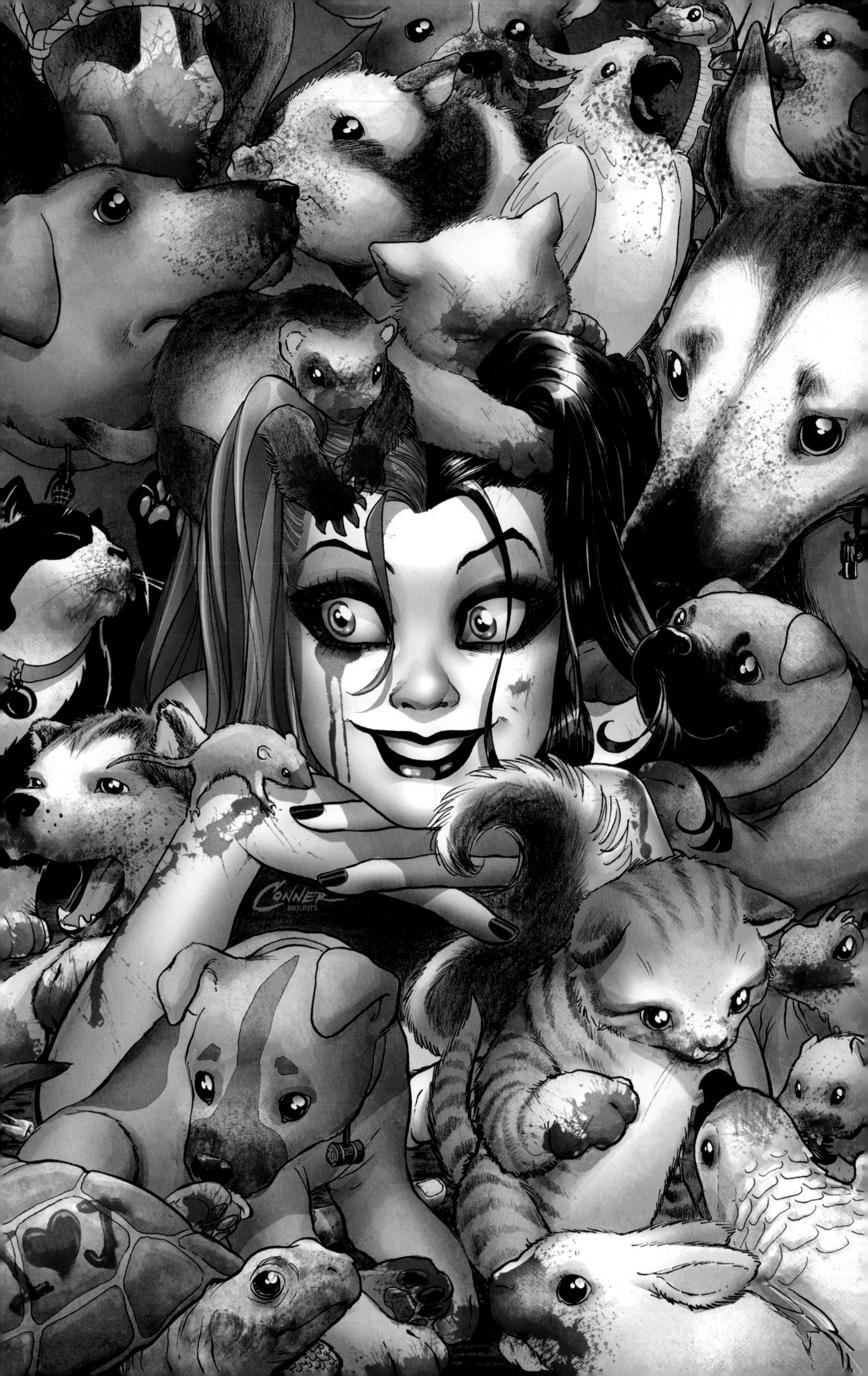
CONNER
MOUNTS

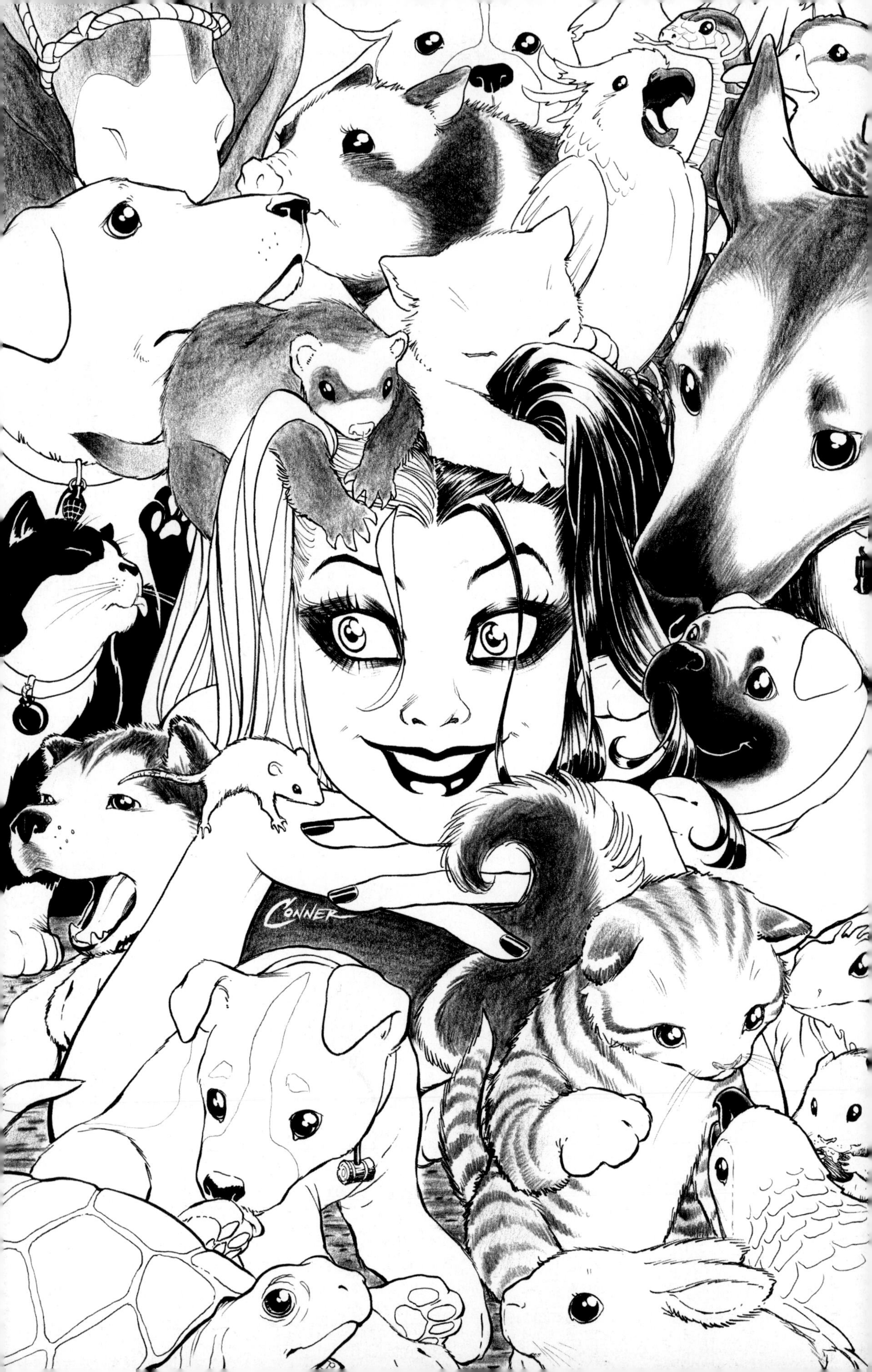
CONNER

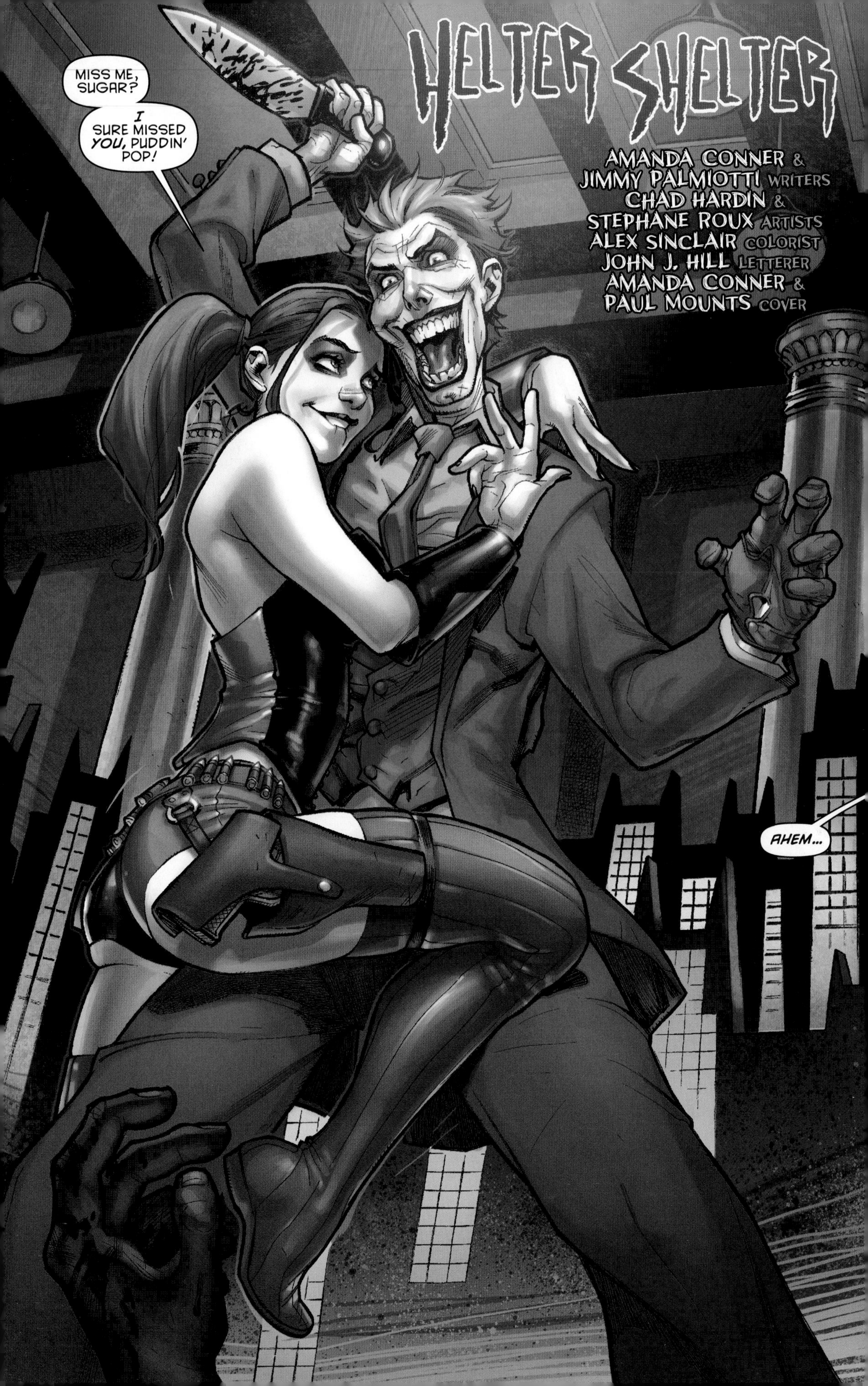

HELTER SHELTER
MISS ME, SUGAR?
I SURE MISSED YOU, PUDDIN' POP!
AMANDA CONNER & JIMMY PALMIOTTI WRITERS
CHAD HARDIN & STEPHANE ROUX ARTISTS
ALEX SINCLAIR COLORIST
JOHN J. HILL LETTERER
AMANDA CONNER & PAUL MOUNTS COVER
AHEM...

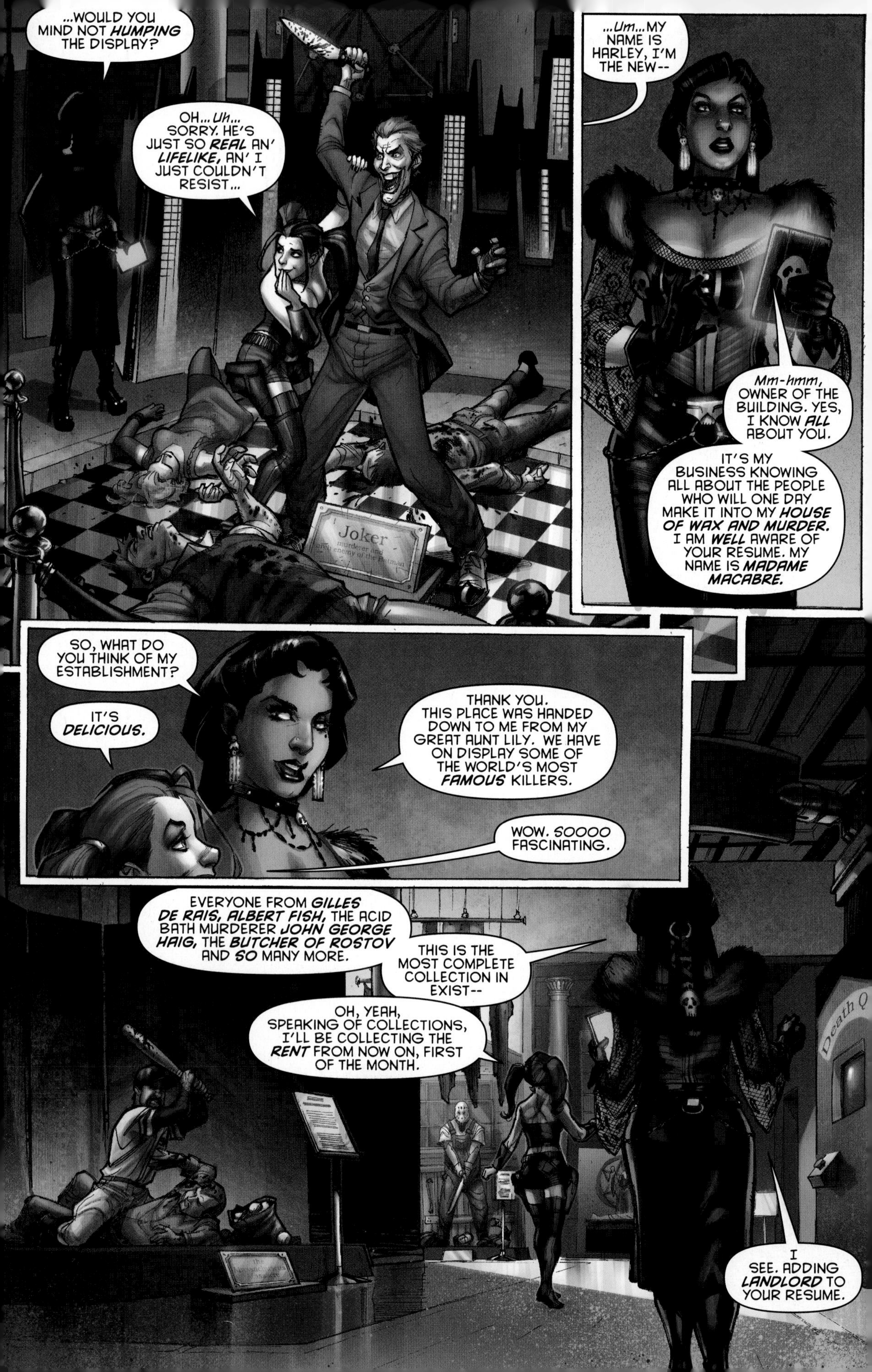

...WOULD YOU MIND NOT *HUMPING* THE DISPLAY?
OH... *Uh*... SORRY. HE'S JUST SO *REAL* AN' *LIFELIKE,* AN' I JUST COULDN'T RESIST...
Joker
...*Um*... MY NAME IS HARLEY, I'M THE NEW--
Mm-hmm, OWNER OF THE BUILDING. YES, I KNOW *ALL* ABOUT YOU.
IT'S MY BUSINESS KNOWING ALL ABOUT THE PEOPLE WHO WILL ONE DAY MAKE IT INTO MY *HOUSE OF WAX AND MURDER.* I AM *WELL* AWARE OF YOUR RESUME. MY NAME IS *MADAME MACABRE.*
SO, WHAT DO YOU THINK OF MY ESTABLISHMENT?
IT'S *DELICIOUS.*
THANK YOU. THIS PLACE WAS HANDED DOWN TO ME FROM MY GREAT AUNT LILY. WE HAVE ON DISPLAY SOME OF THE WORLD'S MOST *FAMOUS* KILLERS.
WOW. *SOOOO* FASCINATING.
EVERYONE FROM *GILLES DE RAIS, ALBERT FISH,* THE ACID BATH MURDERER *JOHN GEORGE HAIG,* THE *BUTCHER OF ROSTOV* AND *SO* MANY MORE.
THIS IS THE MOST COMPLETE COLLECTION IN EXIST--
OH, YEAH, SPEAKING OF COLLECTIONS, I'LL BE COLLECTING THE *RENT* FROM NOW ON, FIRST OF THE MONTH.
I SEE. ADDING *LANDLORD* TO YOUR RESUME.

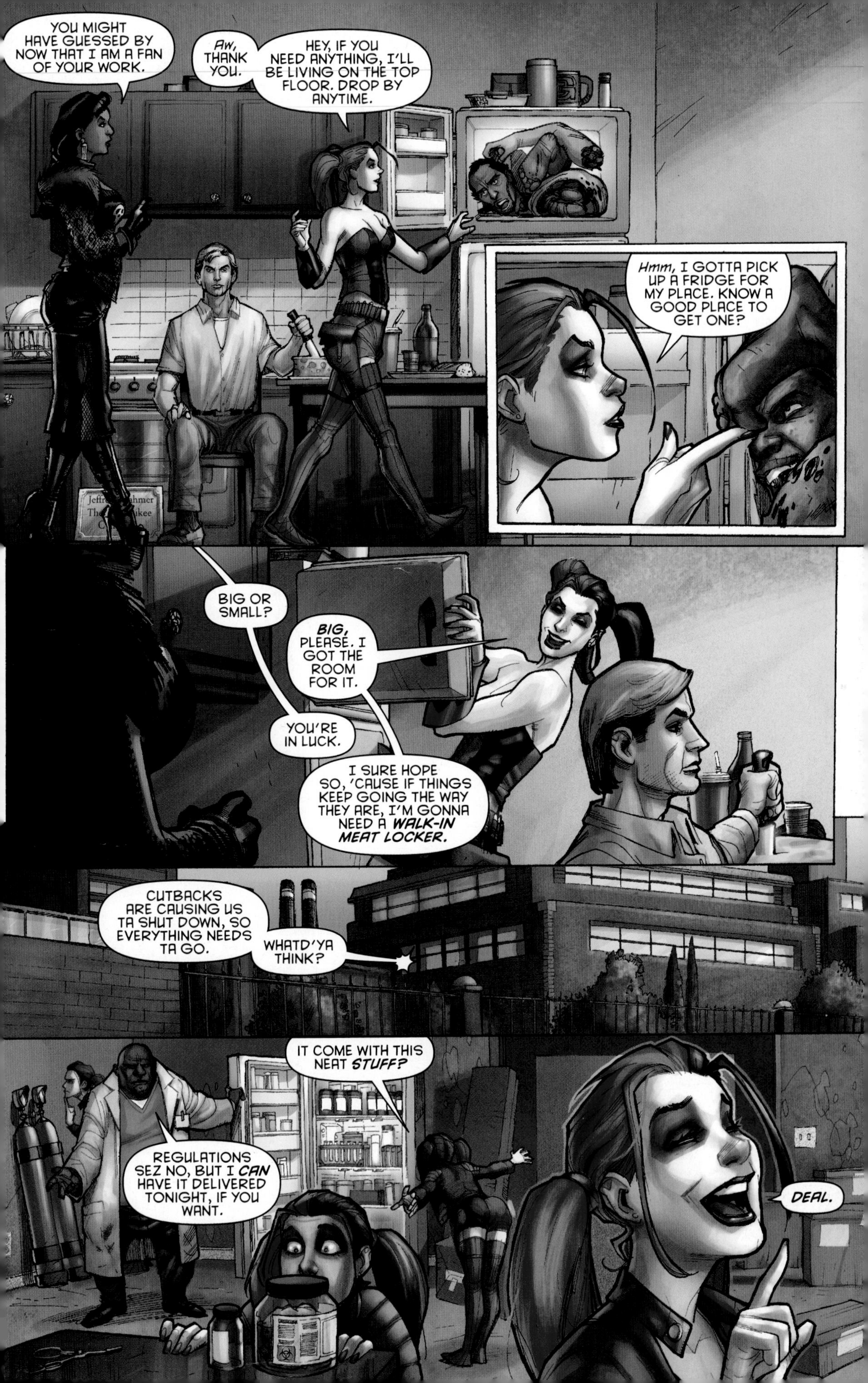
YOU MIGHT HAVE GUESSED BY NOW THAT I AM A FAN OF YOUR WORK.
AW, THANK YOU.
HEY, IF YOU NEED ANYTHING, I'LL BE LIVING ON THE TOP FLOOR. DROP BY ANYTIME.
HMM, I GOTTA PICK UP A FRIDGE FOR MY PLACE. KNOW A GOOD PLACE TO GET ONE?
BIG OR SMALL?
BIG, PLEASE. I GOT THE ROOM FOR IT.
YOU'RE IN LUCK.
I SURE HOPE SO, 'CAUSE IF THINGS KEEP GOING THE WAY THEY ARE, I'M GONNA NEED A WALK-IN MEAT LOCKER.
CUTBACKS ARE CAUSING US TA SHUT DOWN, SO EVERYTHING NEEDS TA GO.
WHATD'YA THINK?
IT COME WITH THIS NEAT STUFF?
REGULATIONS SEZ NO, BUT I CAN HAVE IT DELIVERED TONIGHT, IF YOU WANT.
DEAL.

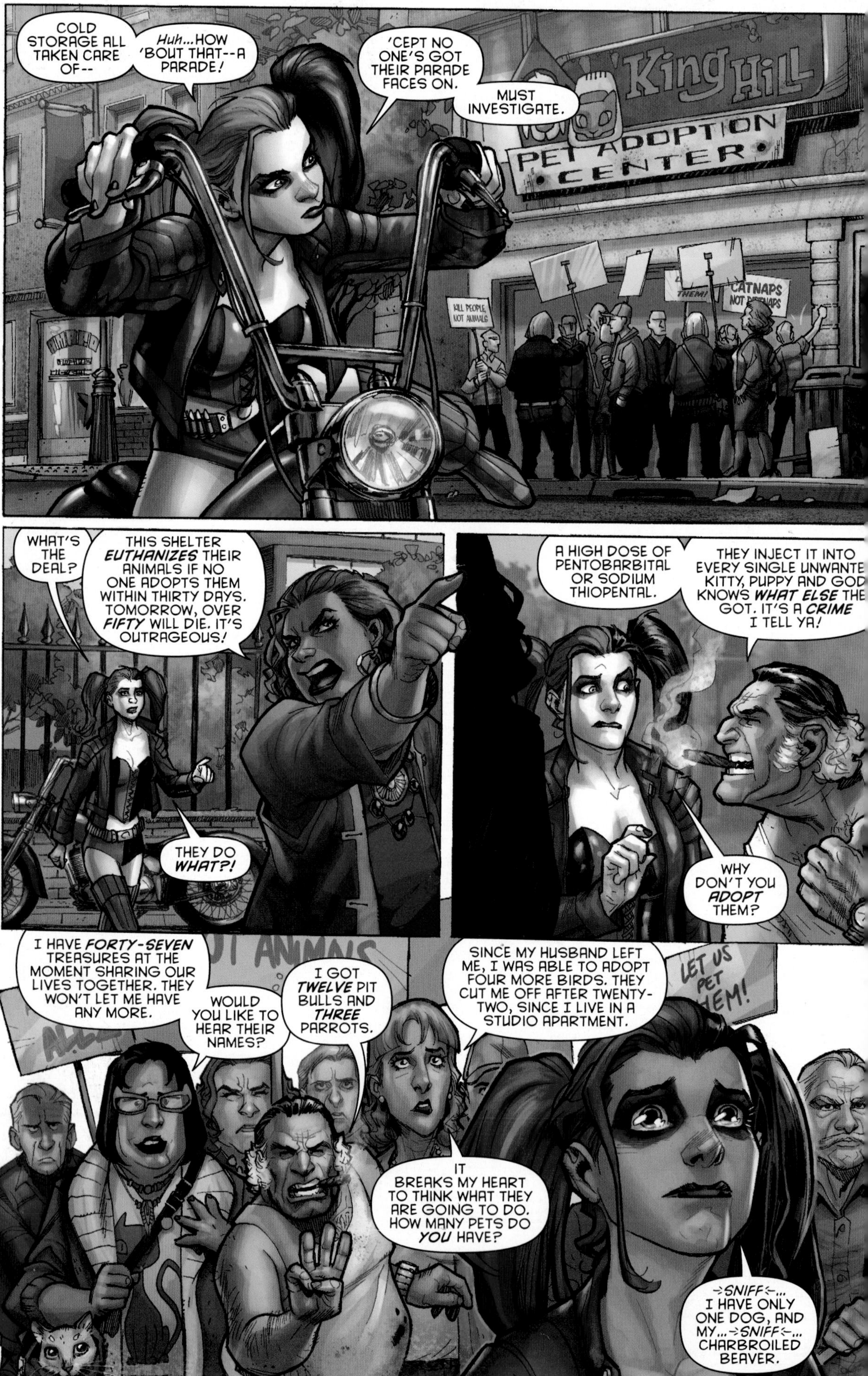
COLD STORAGE ALL TAKEN CARE OF--
Huh...HOW 'BOUT THAT--A PARADE!
'CEPT NO ONE'S GOT THEIR PARADE FACES ON.
MUST INVESTIGATE.
King Hill
PET ADOPTION CENTER
KILL PEOPLE, NOT ANIMALS
THEM!
CATNAPS NOT DIRTNAPS
WHAT'S THE DEAL?
THIS SHELTER EUTHANIZES THEIR ANIMALS IF NO ONE ADOPTS THEM WITHIN THIRTY DAYS. TOMORROW, OVER FIFTY WILL DIE. IT'S OUTRAGEOUS!
THEY DO WHAT?!
A HIGH DOSE OF PENTOBARBITAL OR SODIUM THIOPENTAL.
THEY INJECT IT INTO EVERY SINGLE UNWANTE KITTY, PUPPY AND GOD KNOWS WHAT ELSE THE GOT. IT'S A CRIME I TELL YA!
WHY DON'T YOU ADOPT THEM?
I HAVE FORTY-SEVEN TREASURES AT THE MOMENT SHARING OUR LIVES TOGETHER. THEY WON'T LET ME HAVE ANY MORE.
WOULD YOU LIKE TO HEAR THEIR NAMES?
I GOT TWELVE PIT BULLS AND THREE PARROTS.
SINCE MY HUSBAND LEFT ME, I WAS ABLE TO ADOPT FOUR MORE BIRDS. THEY CUT ME OFF AFTER TWENTY-TWO, SINCE I LIVE IN A STUDIO APARTMENT.
LET US PET THEM!
IT BREAKS MY HEART TO THINK WHAT THEY ARE GOING TO DO. HOW MANY PETS DO YOU HAVE?
>SNIFF<... I HAVE ONLY ONE DOG, AND MY...>SNIFF<... CHARBROILED BEAVER.

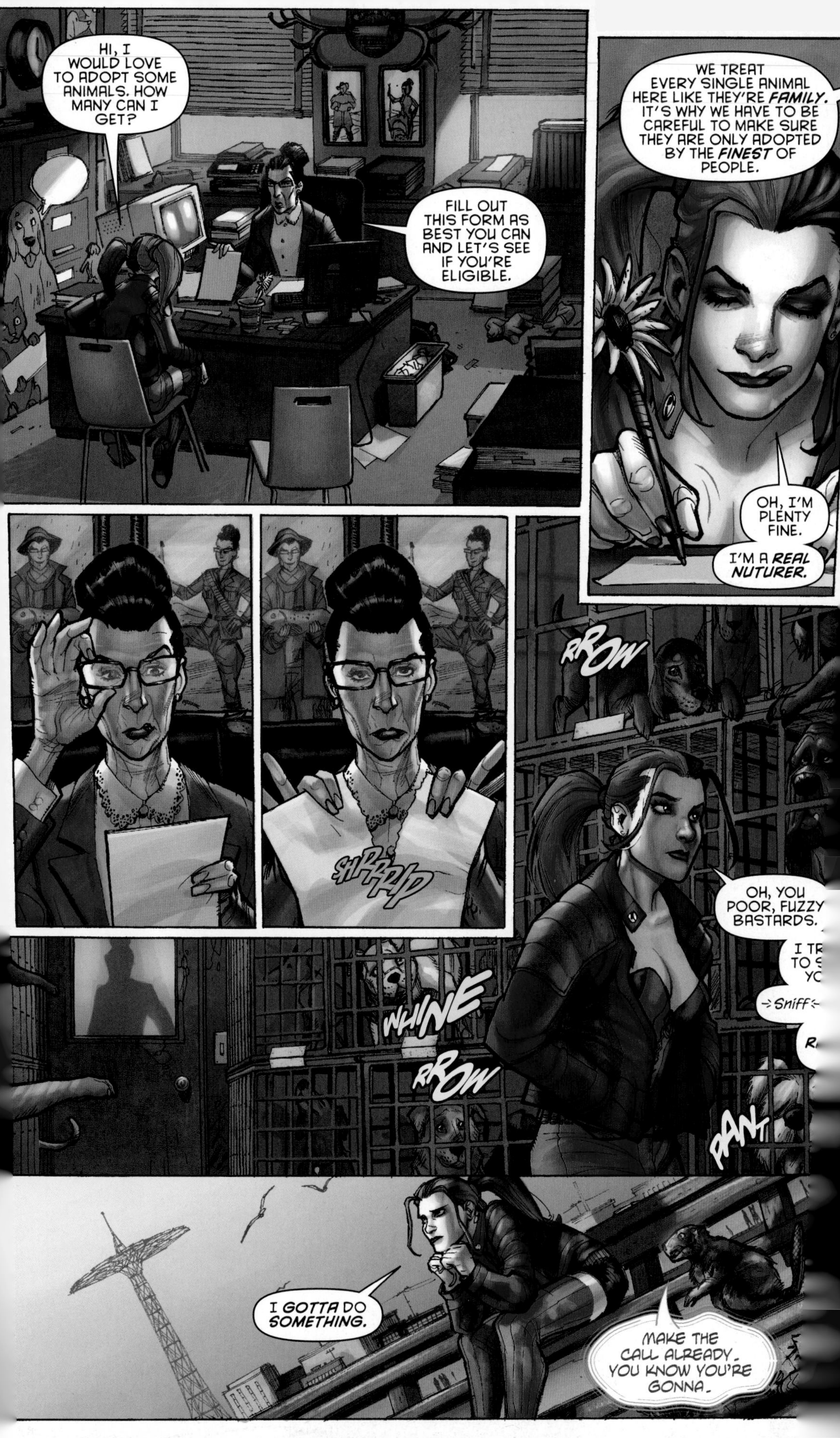
HI, I WOULD LOVE TO ADOPT SOME ANIMALS. HOW MANY CAN I GET?
FILL OUT THIS FORM AS BEST YOU CAN AND LET'S SEE IF YOU'RE ELIGIBLE.
WE TREAT EVERY SINGLE ANIMAL HERE LIKE THEY'RE *FAMILY.* IT'S WHY WE HAVE TO BE CAREFUL TO MAKE SURE THEY ARE ONLY ADOPTED BY THE *FINEST* OF PEOPLE.
OH, I'M PLENTY FINE.
I'M A ***REAL NUTURER.***
SHRRRIP
RROW
OH, YOU POOR, FUZZY BASTARDS.
-Sniff-
WHINE
RROW
PANT
I *GOTTA* DO *SOMETHING.*
MAKE THE CALL ALREADY. YOU KNOW YOU'RE GONNA.

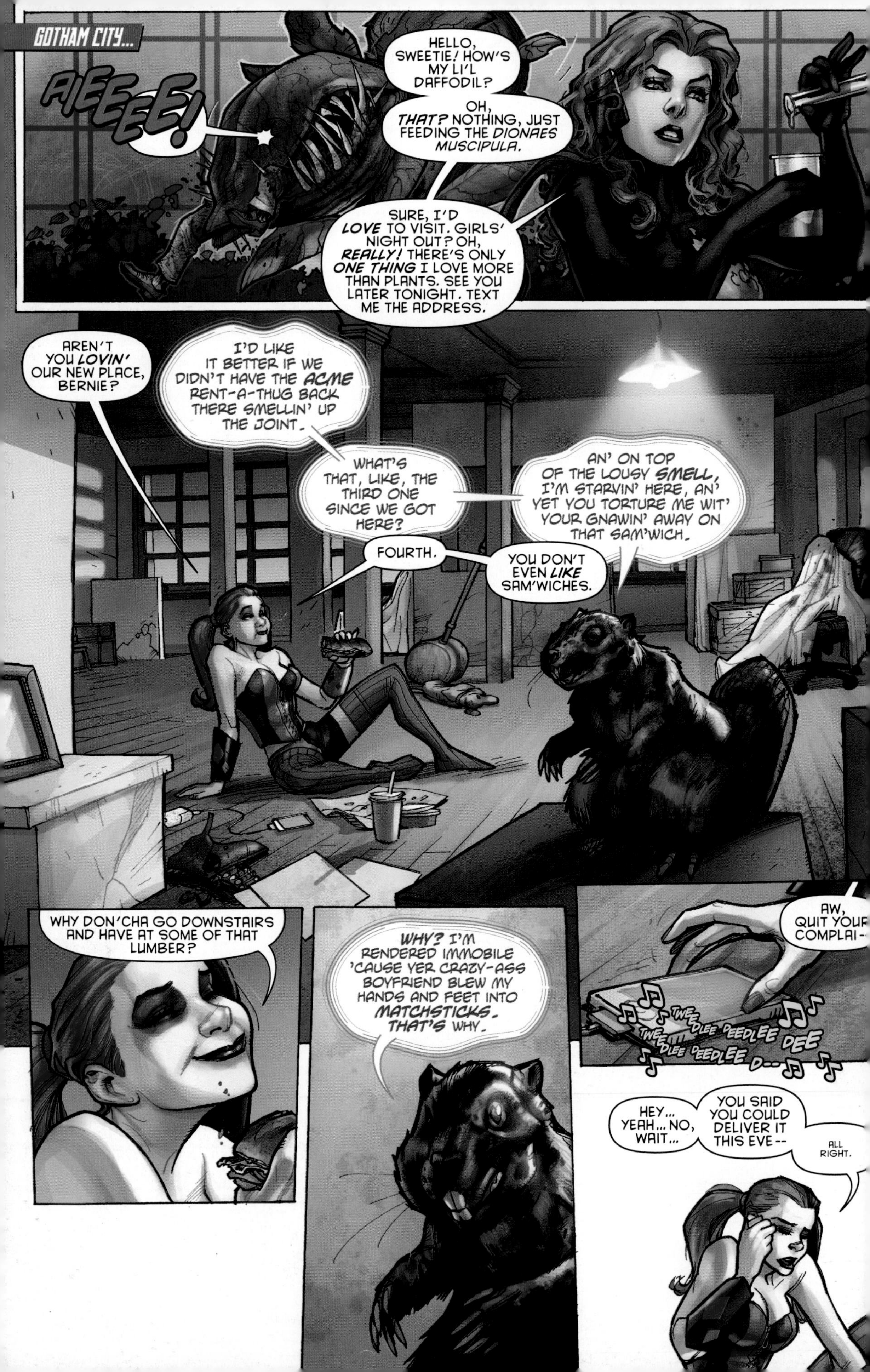
GOTHAM CITY...
AIEEEEE!
HELLO, SWEETIE! HOW'S MY LI'L DAFFODIL?
OH, THAT? NOTHING, JUST FEEDING THE DIONAES MUSCIPULA.
SURE, I'D LOVE TO VISIT. GIRLS' NIGHT OUT? OH, REALLY! THERE'S ONLY ONE THING I LOVE MORE THAN PLANTS. SEE YOU LATER TONIGHT. TEXT ME THE ADDRESS.
AREN'T YOU LOVIN' OUR NEW PLACE, BERNIE?
I'D LIKE IT BETTER IF WE DIDN'T HAVE THE ACME RENT-A-THUG BACK THERE SMELLIN' UP THE JOINT.
WHAT'S THAT, LIKE, THE THIRD ONE SINCE WE GOT HERE?
AN' ON TOP OF THE LOUSY SMELL, I'M STARVIN' HERE, AN' YET YOU TORTURE ME WIT' YOUR GNAWIN' AWAY ON THAT SAM'WICH.
FOURTH.
YOU DON'T EVEN LIKE SAM'WICHES.
WHY DON'CHA GO DOWNSTAIRS AND HAVE AT SOME OF THAT LUMBER?
WHY? I'M RENDERED IMMOBILE 'CAUSE YER CRAZY-ASS BOYFRIEND BLEW MY HANDS AND FEET INTO MATCHSTICKS. THAT'S WHY.
AW, QUIT YOUR COMPLAI--
TWEEDLEE DEEDLEE DEE
TWEEDLEE DEEDLEE D--
HEY... YEAH... NO, WAIT...
YOU SAID YOU COULD DELIVER IT THIS EVE--
ALL RIGHT.

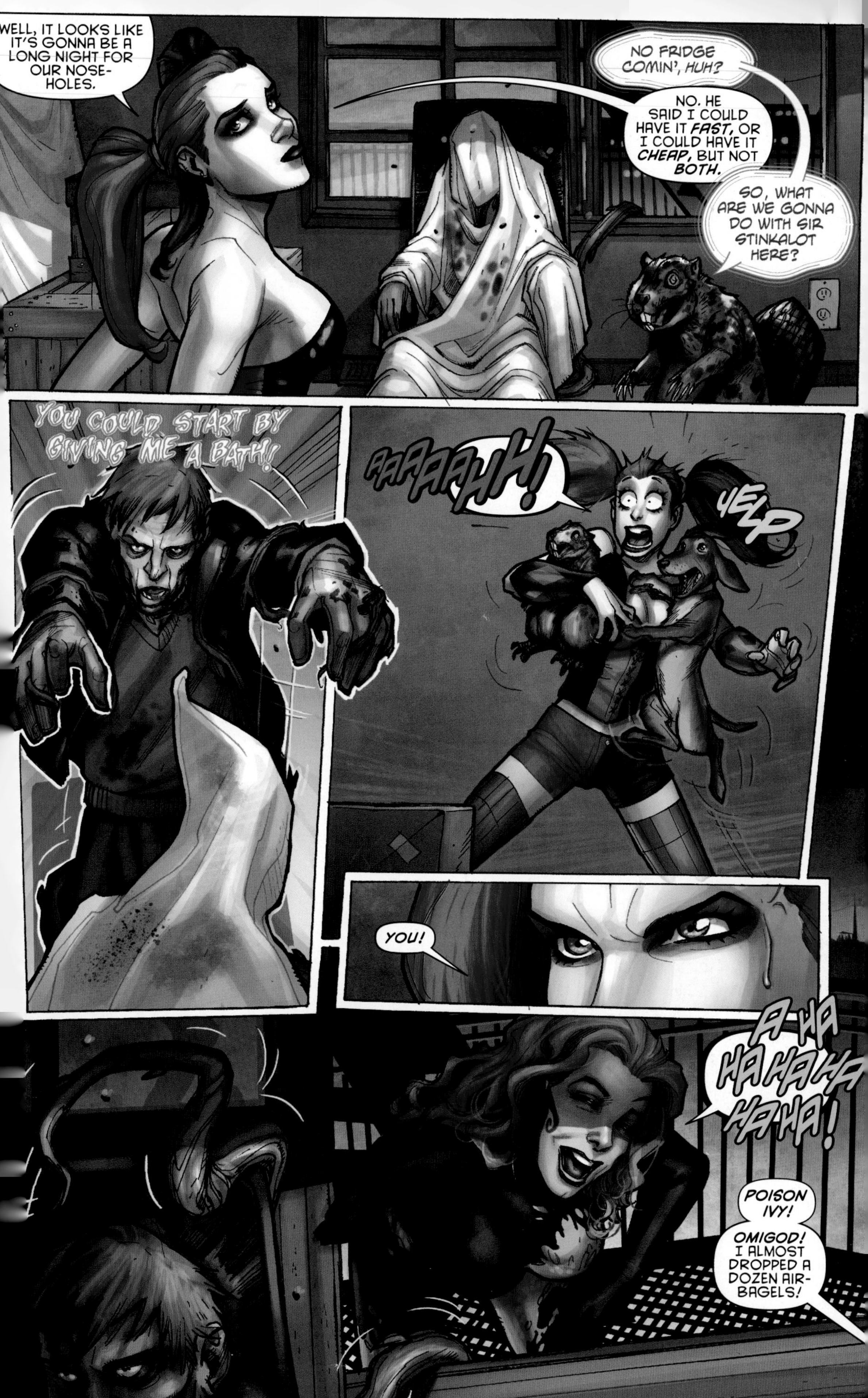

WELL, IT LOOKS LIKE IT'S GONNA BE A LONG NIGHT FOR OUR NOSE-HOLES.
NO FRIDGE COMIN', *HUH?*
NO. HE SAID I COULD HAVE IT *FAST*, OR I COULD HAVE IT *CHEAP*, BUT NOT *BOTH*.
SO, WHAT ARE WE GONNA DO WITH SIR STINKALOT HERE?
YOU COULD START BY GIVING ME A BATH!
AAAAAAUH!
YELP
YOU!
A HA HA HA HA HA HA HA!
POISON IVY!
OMIGOD! I ALMOST DROPPED A DOZEN AIR-BAGELS!

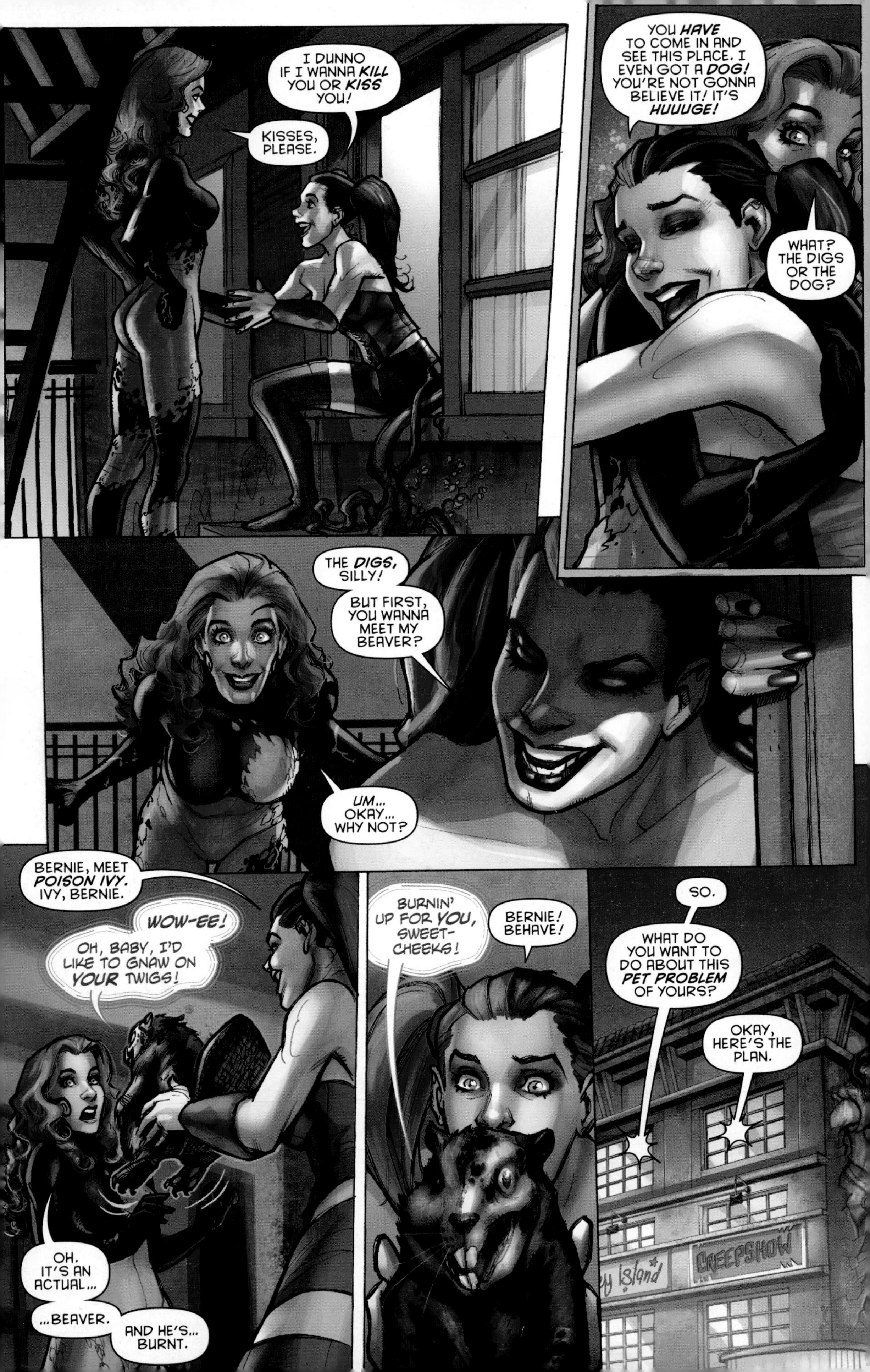
I DUNNO IF I WANNA *KILL* YOU OR *KISS* YOU!
KISSES, PLEASE.
YOU *HAVE* TO COME IN AND SEE THIS PLACE. I EVEN GOT A *DOG!* YOU'RE NOT GONNA BELIEVE IT! IT'S *HUUUGE!*
WHAT? THE DIGS OR THE DOG?
THE *DIGS,* SILLY!
BUT FIRST, YOU WANNA MEET MY BEAVER?
UM... OKAY... WHY NOT?
BERNIE, MEET *POISON IVY.* IVY, BERNIE.
WOW-EE!
OH, BABY, I'D LIKE TO GNAW ON *YOUR* TWIGS!
OH. IT'S AN ACTUAL...
...BEAVER.
AND HE'S... BURNT.
BURNIN' UP FOR *YOU,* SWEET-CHEEKS!
BERNIE! BEHAVE!
SO.
WHAT DO YOU WANT TO DO ABOUT THIS *PET PROBLEM* OF YOURS?
OKAY, HERE'S THE PLAN.
CREEPSHOW

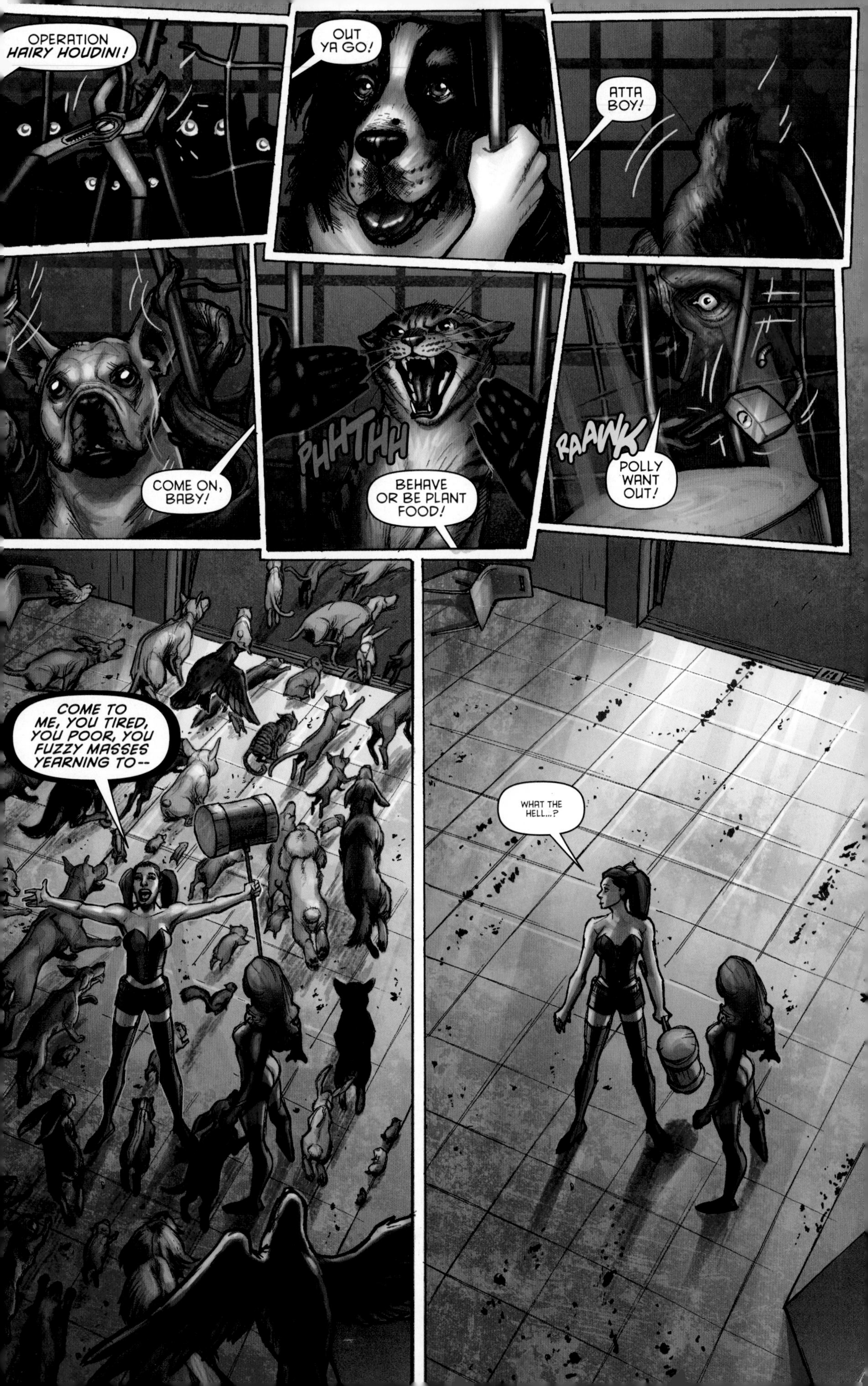
OPERATION HAIRY HOUDINI!
OUT YA GO!
ATTA BOY!
COME ON, BABY!
PHHTHH
BEHAVE OR BE PLANT FOOD!
RAAWK
POLLY WANT OUT!
COME TO ME, YOU TIRED, YOU POOR, YOU FUZZY MASSES YEARNING TO--
WHAT THE HELL...?

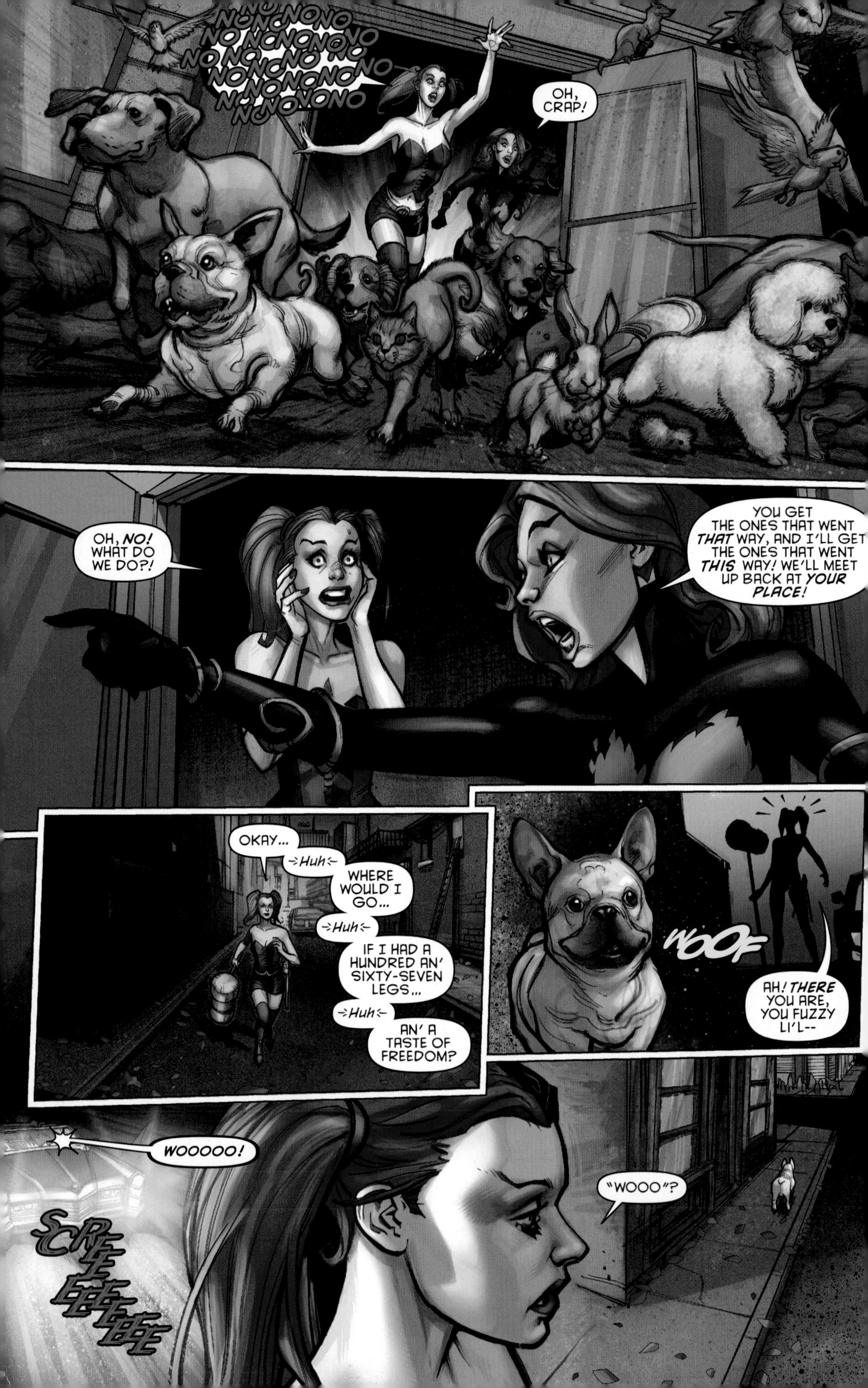
NONONONO NO NONONONO NO NONONONO NONONONO NONONONO NONONONO
OH, CRAP!
OH, *NO!* WHAT DO WE DO?!
YOU GET THE ONES THAT WENT *THAT* WAY, AND I'LL GET THE ONES THAT WENT *THIS* WAY! WE'LL MEET UP BACK AT *YOUR PLACE!*
OKAY...
Huh
WHERE WOULD I GO...
Huh
IF I HAD A HUNDRED AN' SIXTY-SEVEN LEGS...
Huh
AN' A TASTE OF FREEDOM?
WOOF
AH! *THERE* YOU ARE, YOU FUZZY LI'L--
WOOOOO!
SCREEEEEEEE
"WOOO"?

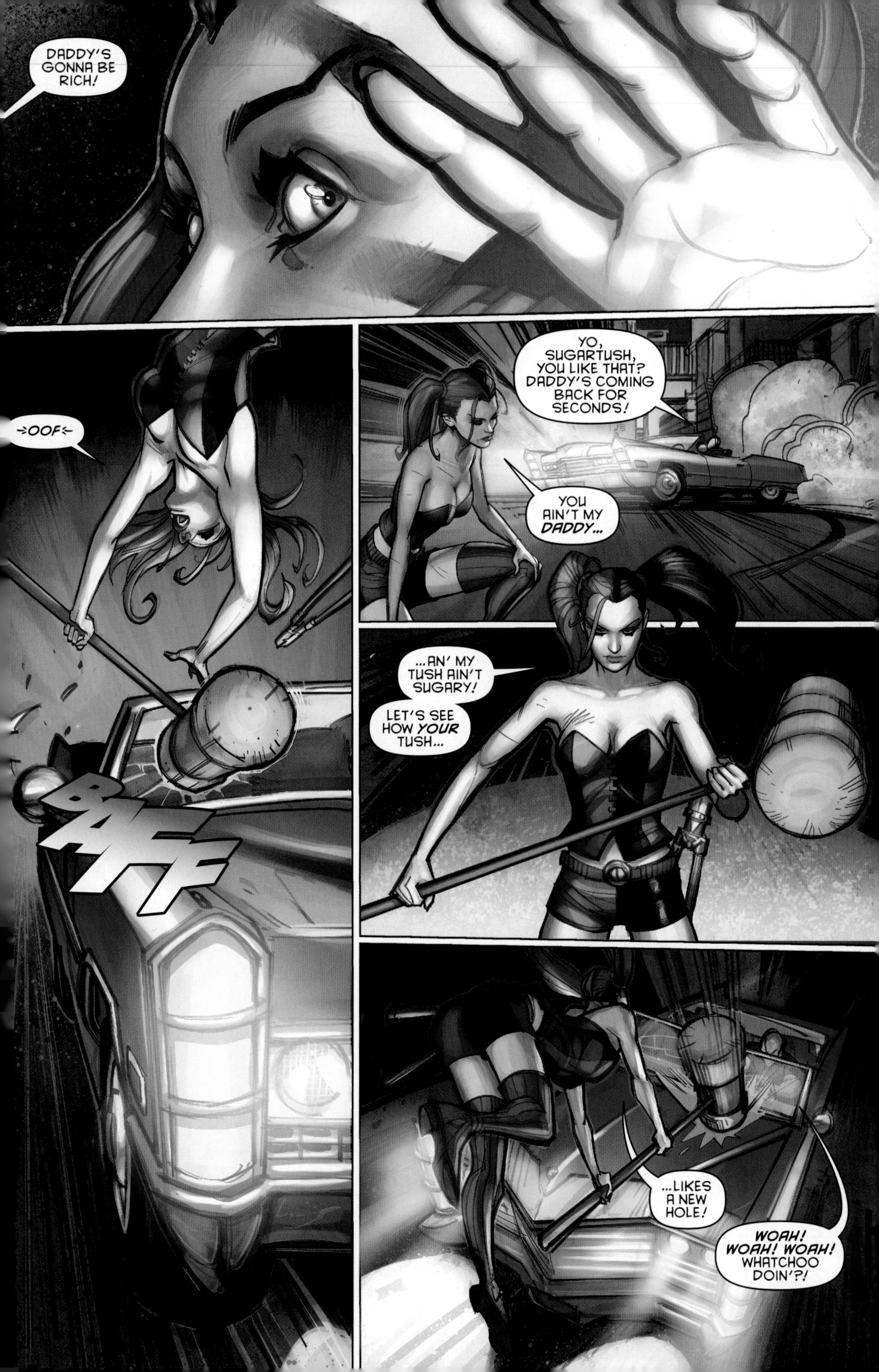
DADDY'S GONNA BE RICH!
OOF
BAFF
YO, SUGARTUSH, YOU LIKE THAT? DADDY'S COMING BACK FOR SECONDS!
YOU AIN'T MY DADDY...
...AN' MY TUSH AIN'T SUGARY!
LET'S SEE HOW YOUR TUSH...
...LIKES A NEW HOLE!
WOAH! WOAH! WOAH! WHATCHOO DOIN'?!

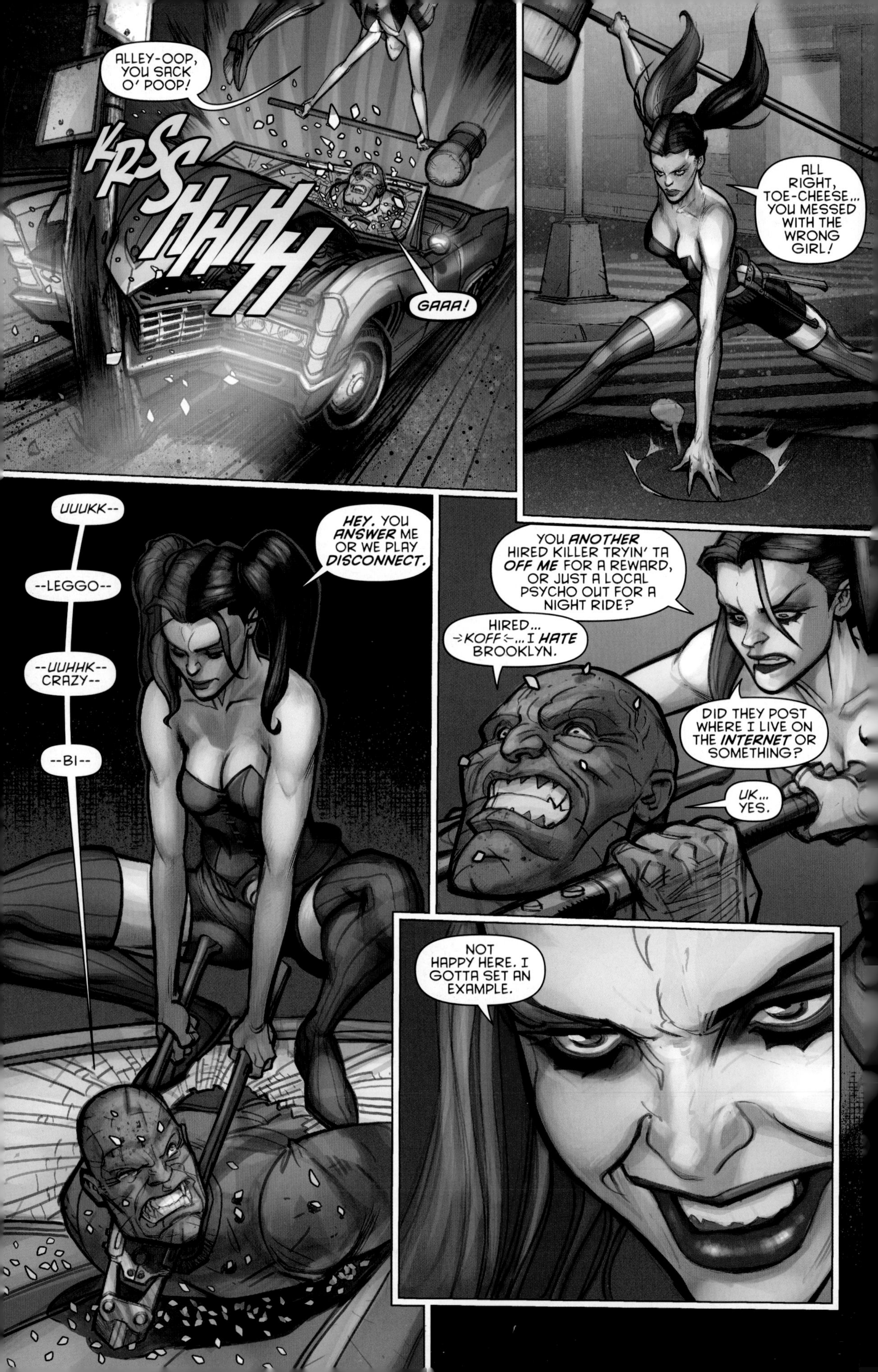
ALLEY-OOP, YOU SACK O' POOP!
KRSSHHHH
GAAA!
ALL RIGHT, TOE-CHEESE... YOU MESSED WITH THE WRONG GIRL!
UUUKK--
--LEGGO--
--UUHHK-- CRAZY--
--BI--
HEY. YOU ANSWER ME OR WE PLAY DISCONNECT.
YOU ANOTHER HIRED KILLER TRYIN' TA OFF ME FOR A REWARD, OR JUST A LOCAL PSYCHO OUT FOR A NIGHT RIDE?
HIRED... →KOFF←... I HATE BROOKLYN.
DID THEY POST WHERE I LIVE ON THE INTERNET OR SOMETHING?
UK... YES.
NOT HAPPY HERE. I GOTTA SET AN EXAMPLE.

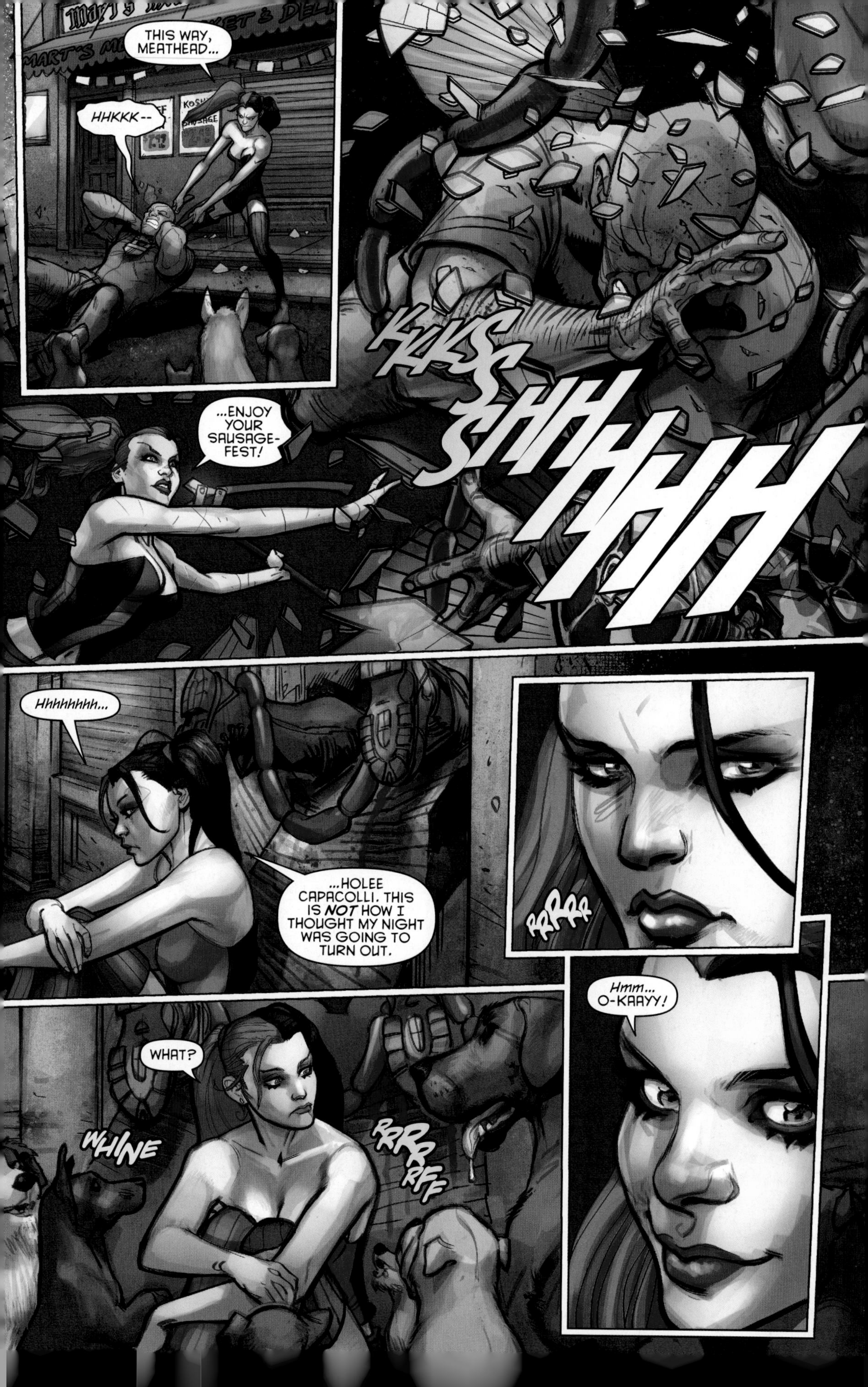

THIS WAY, MEATHEAD...
HHKKK--
...ENJOY YOUR SAUSAGE-FEST!
KKKS SHHHHHH
Hhhhhhhh...
...HOLEE CAPACOLLI. THIS IS *NOT* HOW I THOUGHT MY NIGHT WAS GOING TO TURN OUT.
RRRRR
WHAT?
WHINE
RRRRRFF
Hmm... O-KAAYY!

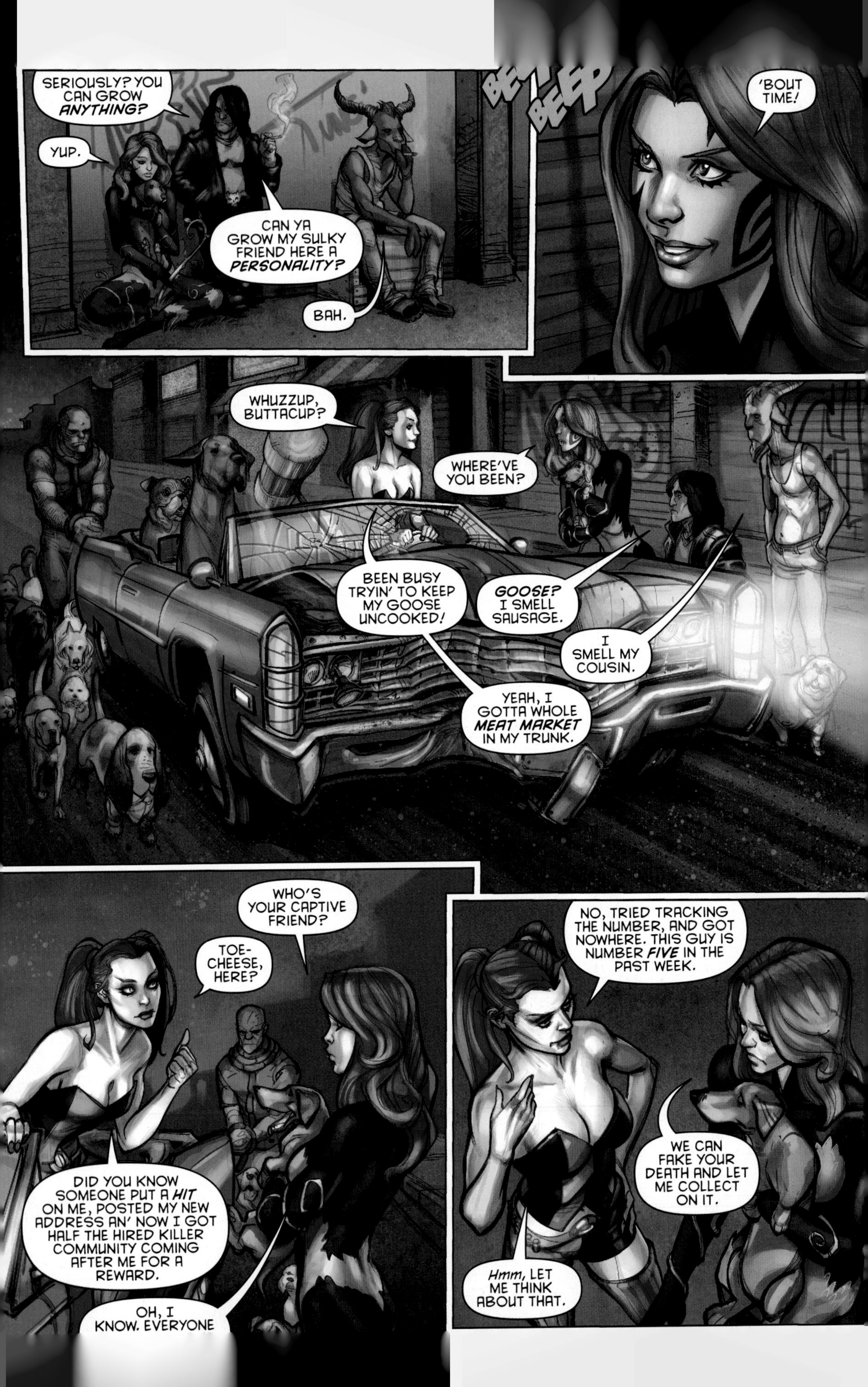
SERIOUSLY? YOU CAN GROW *ANYTHING?*
YUP.
CAN YA GROW MY SULKY FRIEND HERE A *PERSONALITY?*
BAH.
BEEP BEEP
'BOUT TIME!
WHUZZUP, BUTTACUP?
WHERE'VE YOU BEEN?
BEEN BUSY TRYIN' TO KEEP MY GOOSE UNCOOKED!
GOOSE? I SMELL SAUSAGE.
I SMELL MY COUSIN.
YEAH, I GOTTA WHOLE *MEAT MARKET* IN MY TRUNK.
WHO'S YOUR CAPTIVE FRIEND?
TOE-CHEESE, HERE?
DID YOU KNOW SOMEONE PUT A *HIT* ON ME, POSTED MY NEW ADDRESS AN' NOW I GOT HALF THE HIRED KILLER COMMUNITY COMING AFTER ME FOR A REWARD.
OH, I KNOW. EVERYONE
NO, TRIED TRACKING THE NUMBER, AND GOT NOWHERE. THIS GUY IS NUMBER *FIVE* IN THE PAST WEEK.
WE CAN FAKE YOUR DEATH AND LET ME COLLECT ON IT.
Hmm, LET ME THINK ABOUT THAT.

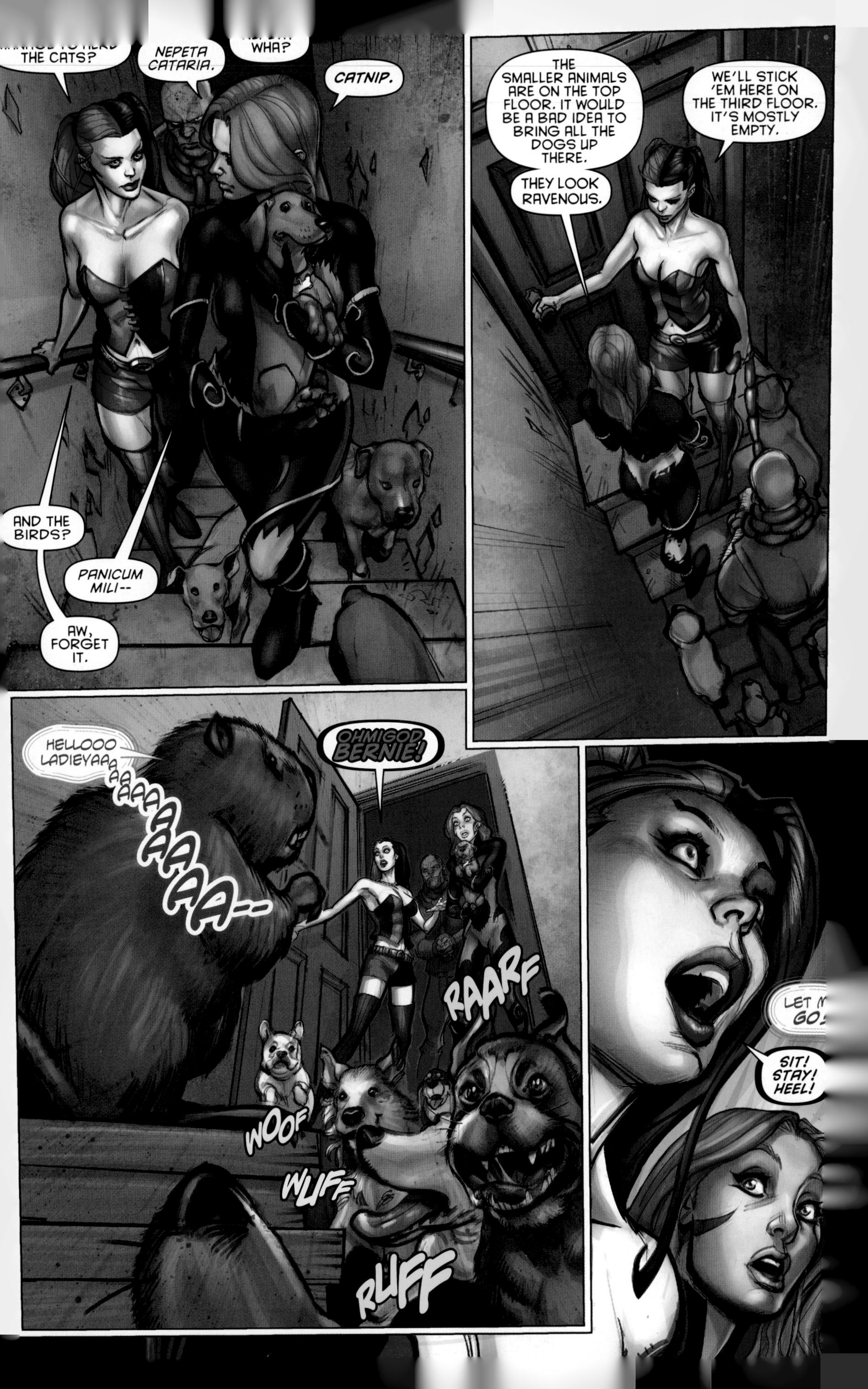
THE CATS?
NEPETA CATARIA.
WHA?
CATNIP.
AND THE BIRDS?
PANICUM MILI--
AW, FORGET IT.
THE SMALLER ANIMALS ARE ON THE TOP FLOOR. IT WOULD BE A BAD IDEA TO BRING ALL THE DOGS UP THERE.
THEY LOOK RAVENOUS.
WE'LL STICK 'EM HERE ON THE THIRD FLOOR. IT'S MOSTLY EMPTY.
HELLOOO LADIEYAAAAAAAAAAAAA--
OHMIGOD BERNIE!
RAARF
WOOF
WUFF
RUFF
LET M
GO
SIT! STAY! HEEL!

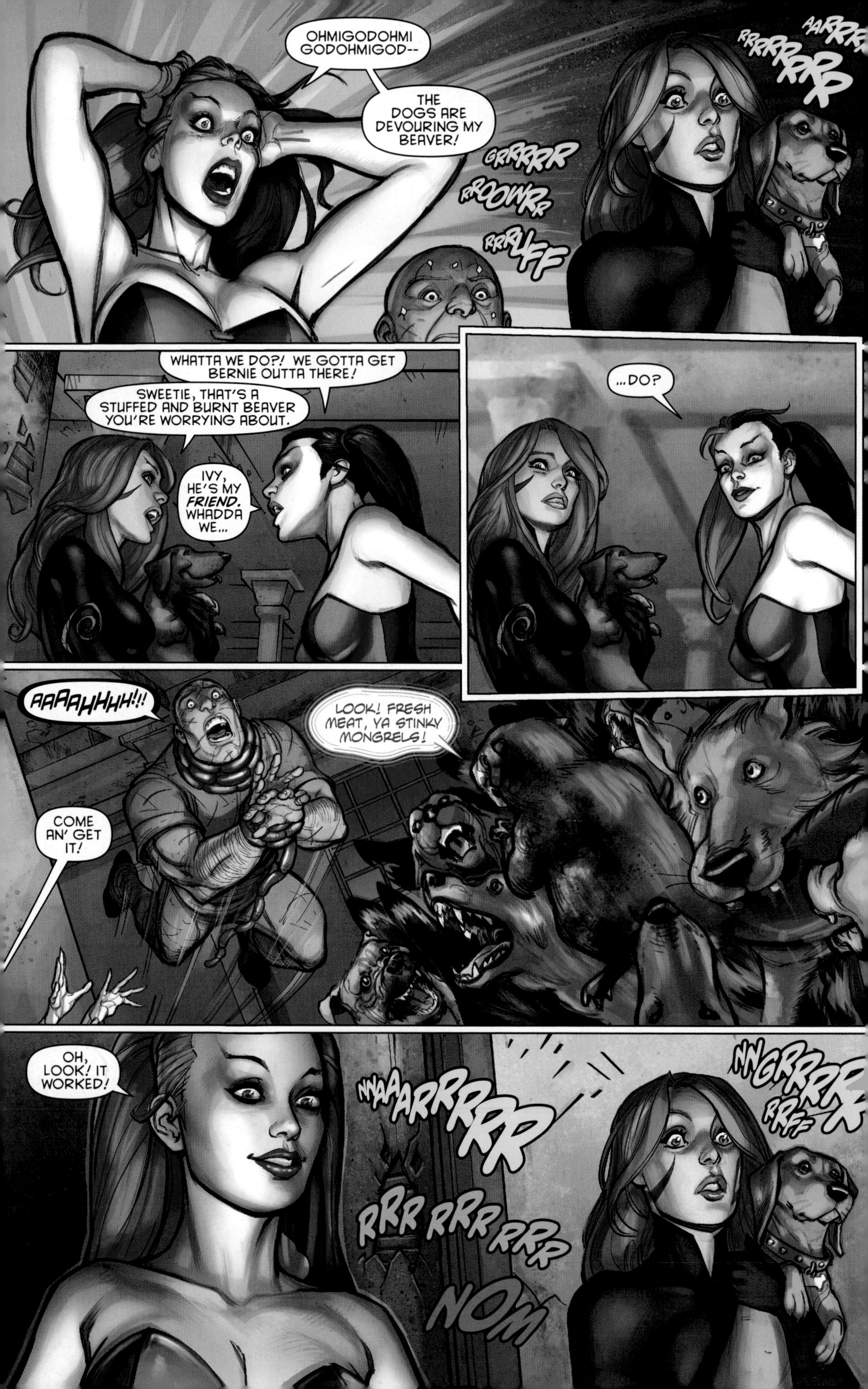
OHMIGODOHMI GODOHMIGOD--
THE DOGS ARE DEVOURING MY BEAVER!
GRRRRRR
RROOWRR
RRRUFF
AARRR RRRRRRRR
WHATTA WE DO?! WE GOTTA GET BERNIE OUTTA THERE!
SWEETIE, THAT'S A STUFFED AND BURNT BEAVER YOU'RE WORRYING ABOUT.
IVY, HE'S MY FRIEND. WHADDA WE...
...DO?
AAAAHHHH!!!
LOOK! FRESH MEAT, YA STINKY MONGRELS!
COME AN' GET IT!
OH, LOOK! IT WORKED!
NNAAARRRRR
RRR RRR RRRR
NOM
NNGRRRRRR RRFF

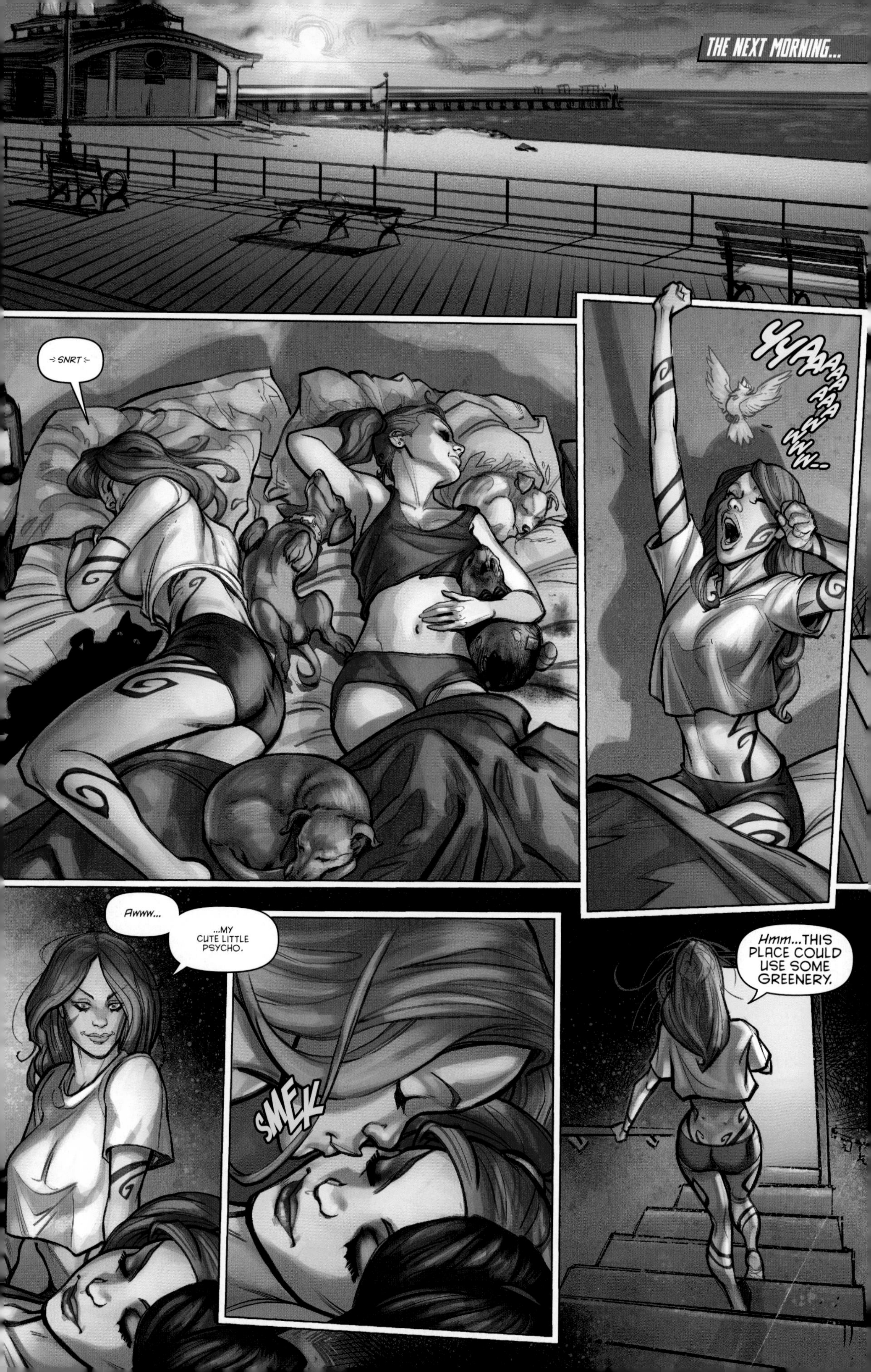
THE NEXT MORNING...
SNRT
YYAAAAAAAAWWWW--
Awww...
...MY CUTE LITTLE PSYCHO.
SMEK
Hmm...THIS PLACE COULD USE SOME GREENERY.

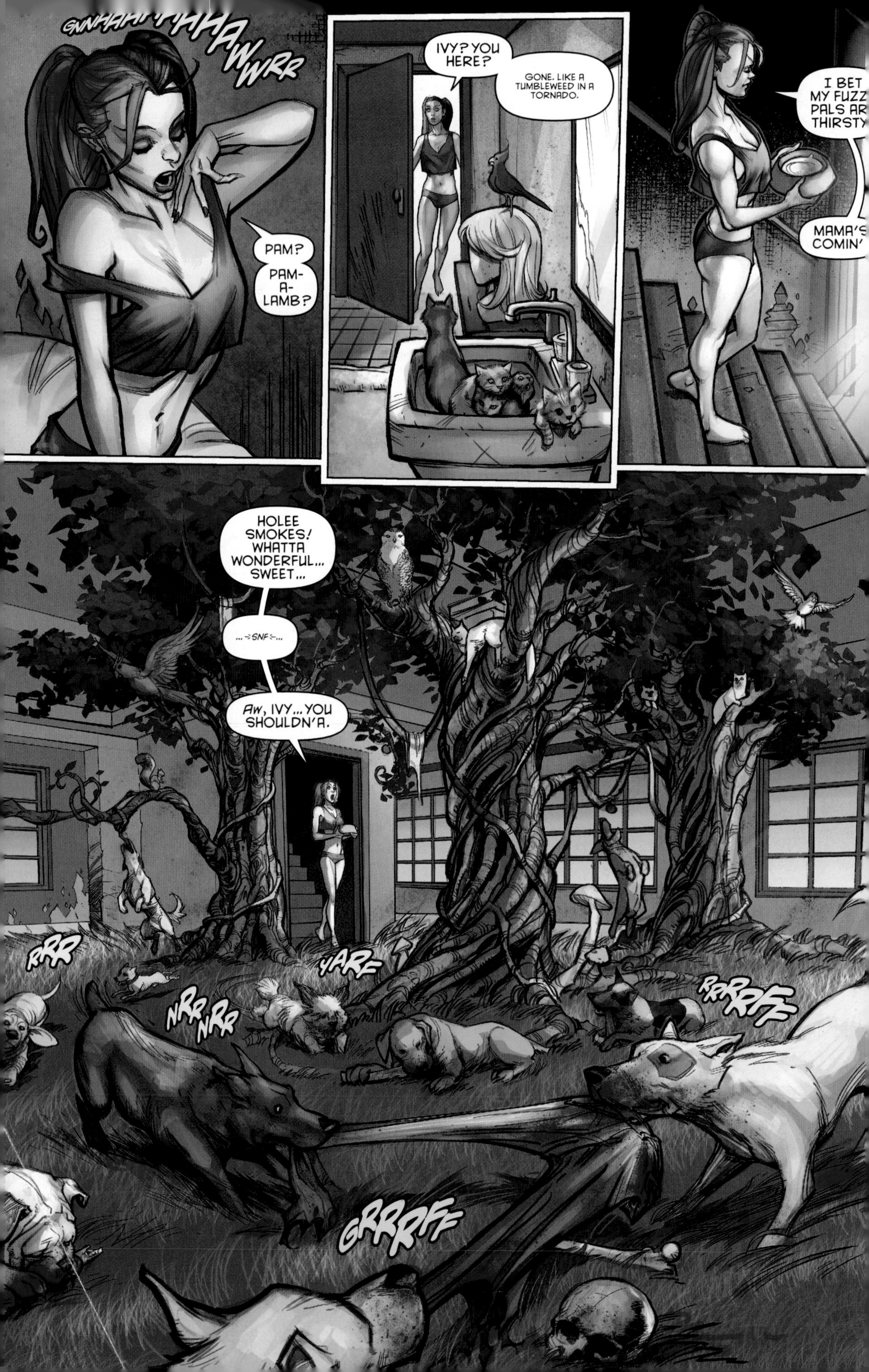
GNHAAHHHAAWWRR
PAM?
PAM-A-LAMB?
IVY? YOU HERE?
GONE. LIKE A TUMBLEWEED IN A TORNADO.
I BET MY FUZZ PALS AR THIRSTY
MAMA'S COMIN'
HOLEE SMOKES! WHATTA WONDERFUL... SWEET...
...SNF...
AW, IVY... YOU SHOULDN'A.
RRR
YARF
NRR NRR
RRRRFF
GRRRFF

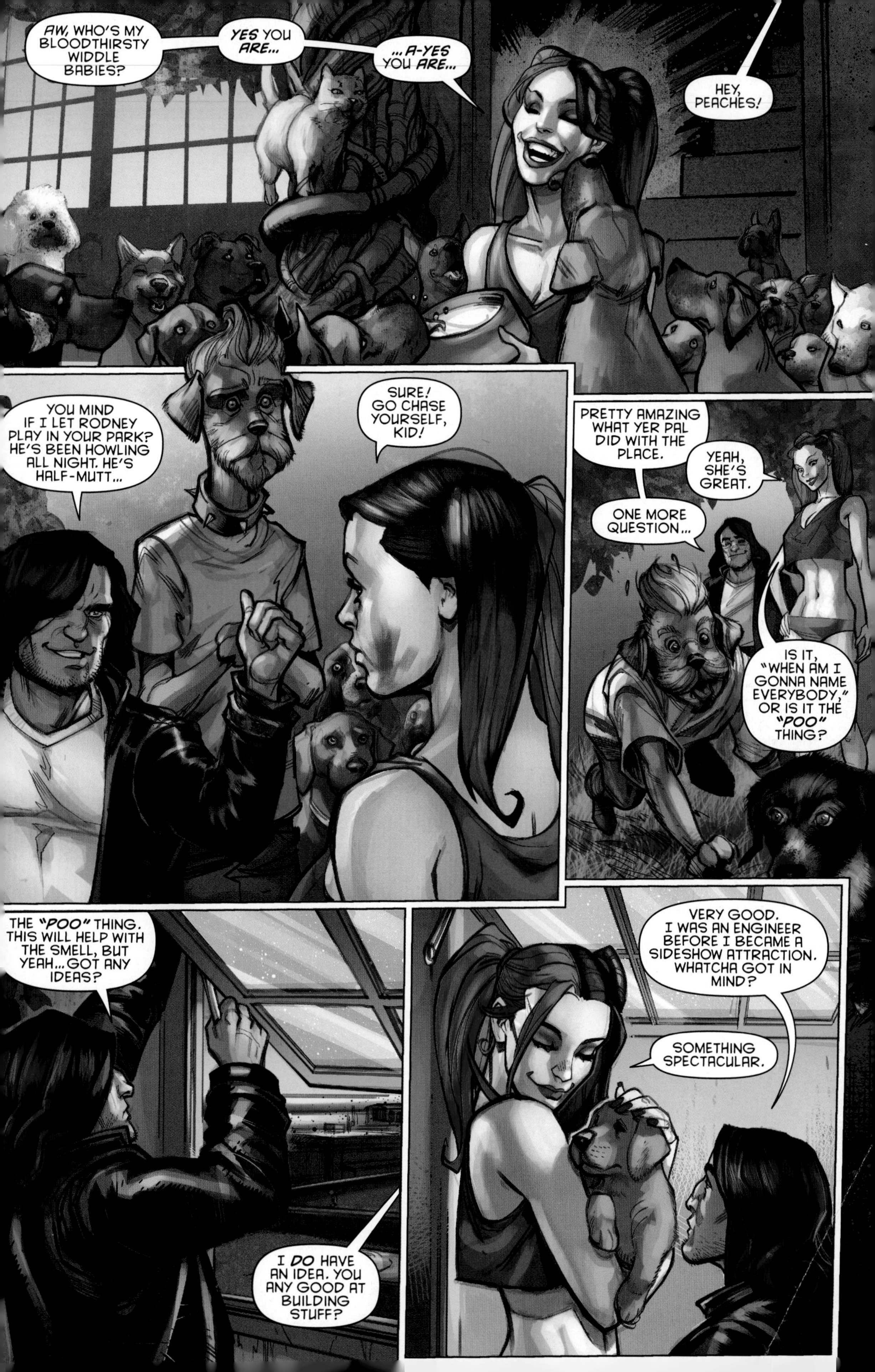

AW, WHO'S MY BLOODTHIRSTY WIDDLE BABIES?
YES YOU ARE...
...A-YES YOU ARE...
HEY, PEACHES!
YOU MIND IF I LET RODNEY PLAY IN YOUR PARK? HE'S BEEN HOWLING ALL NIGHT. HE'S HALF-MUTT...
SURE! GO CHASE YOURSELF, KID!
PRETTY AMAZING WHAT YER PAL DID WITH THE PLACE.
YEAH, SHE'S GREAT.
ONE MORE QUESTION...
IS IT, "WHEN AM I GONNA NAME EVERYBODY," OR IS IT THE "POO" THING?
THE "POO" THING. THIS WILL HELP WITH THE SMELL, BUT YEAH... GOT ANY IDEAS?
I DO HAVE AN IDEA. YOU ANY GOOD AT BUILDING STUFF?
VERY GOOD. I WAS AN ENGINEER BEFORE I BECAME A SIDESHOW ATTRACTION. WHATCHA GOT IN MIND?
SOMETHING SPECTACULAR.

I know who you *are*.

I know what you are **capable** of.

Fate has brought us together.

Within a week you will be mine to do with as I please.

SNACK TIME! YOU CAN PLAY WITH YOUR TOY LATER.

And soon after, with your help, my dear, all my enemies will be lying at my feet.

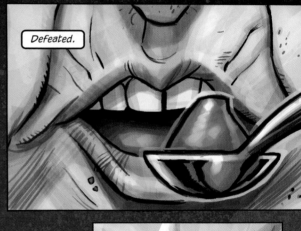

Defeated.

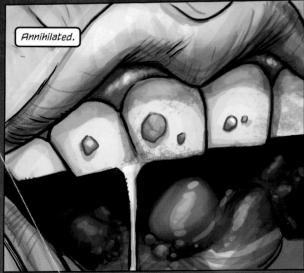

Annihilated.

Dead!

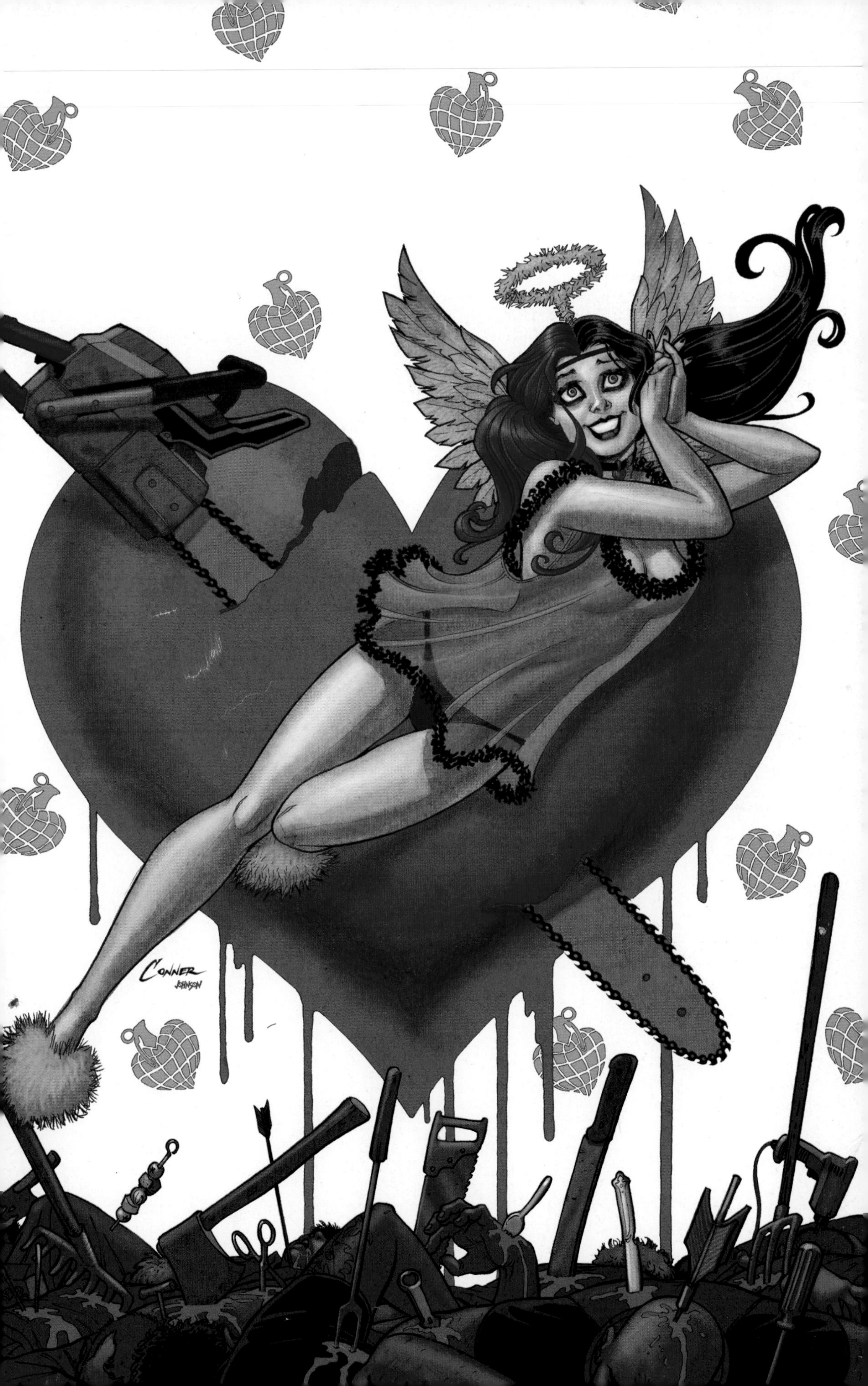
CONNER
JOHNSON

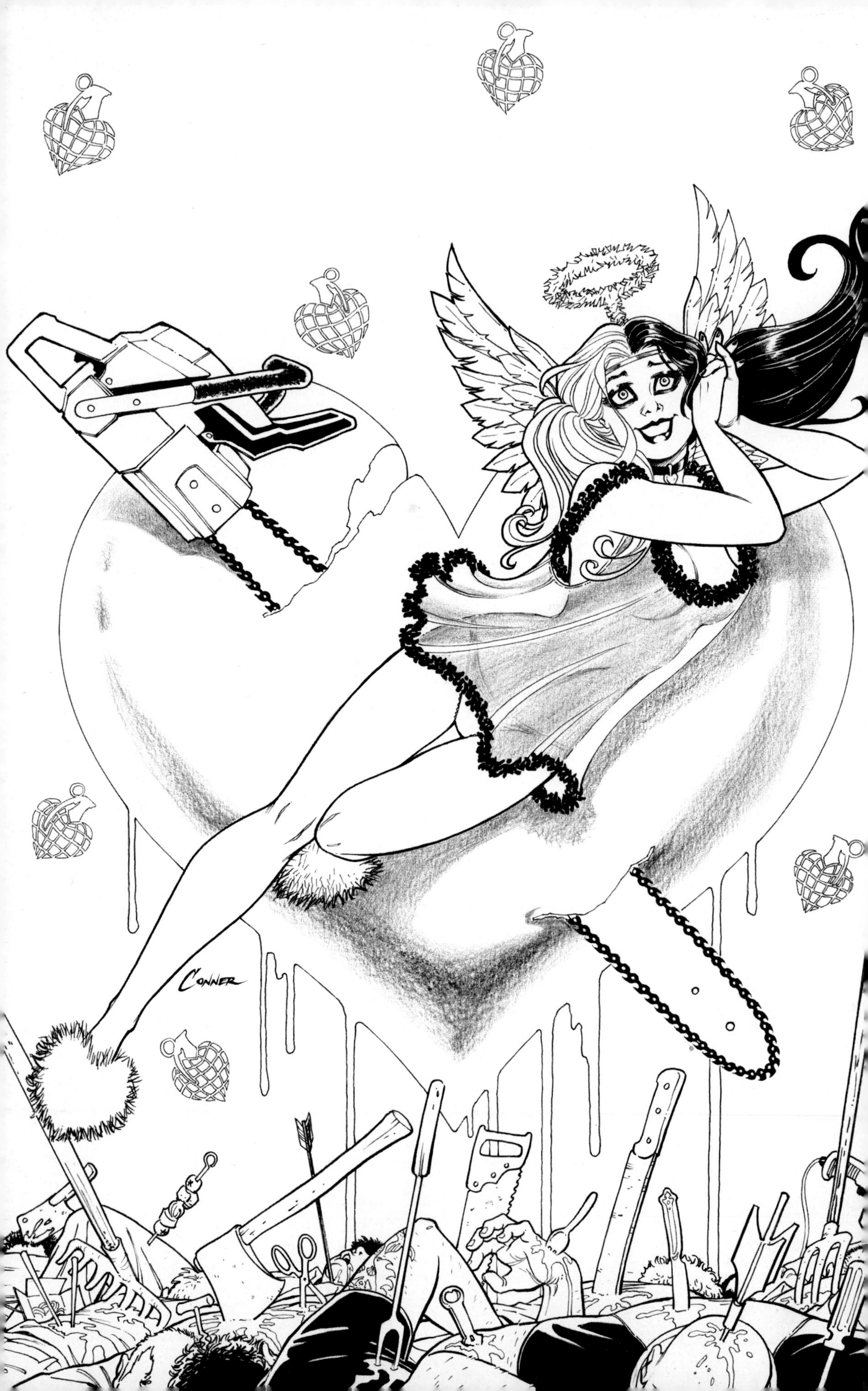
CONNER

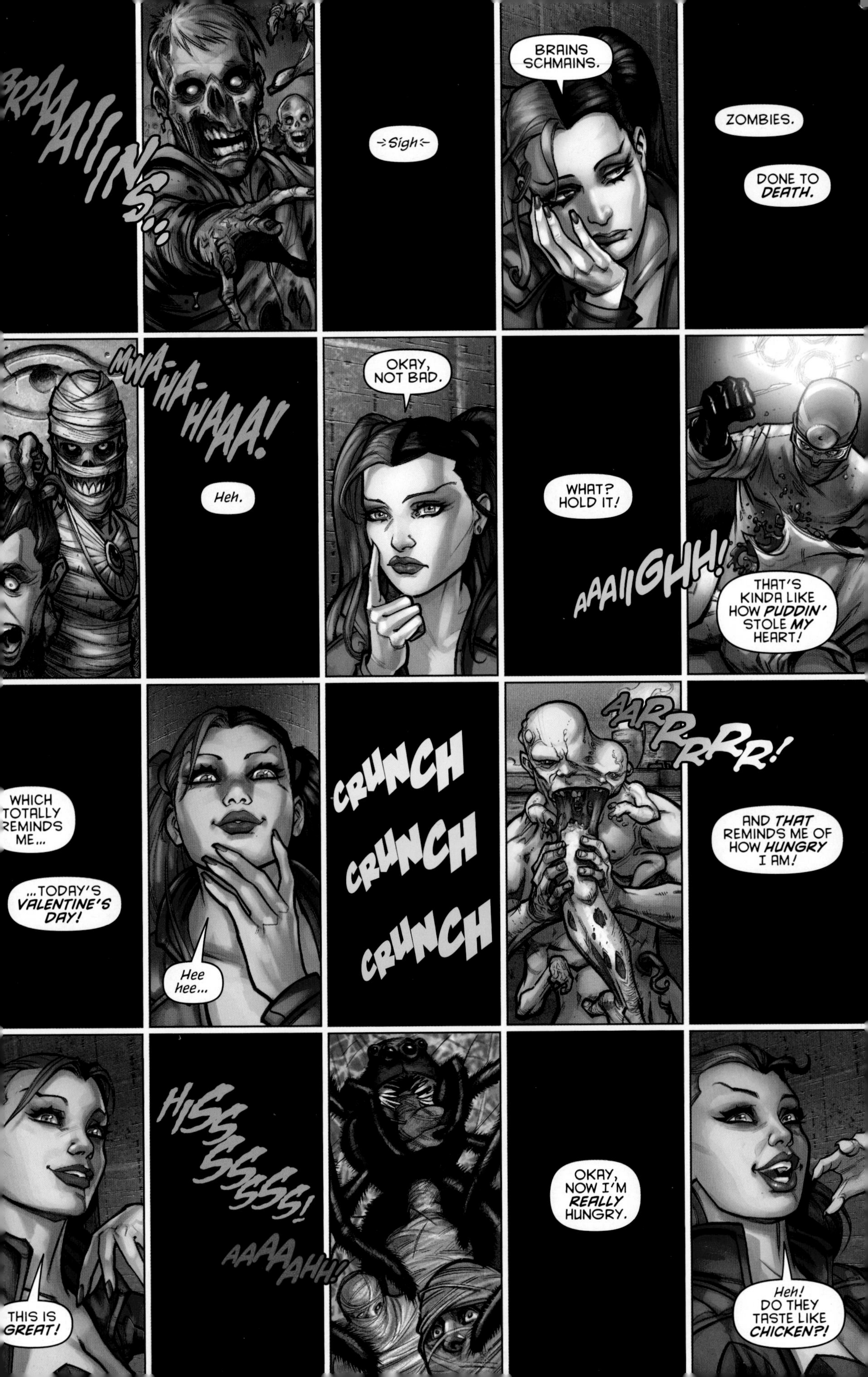
BRAAAIIINS...
-Sigh-
BRAINS SCHMAINS.
ZOMBIES.
DONE TO DEATH.
MWA-HA-HAAA!
Heh.
OKAY, NOT BAD.
WHAT? HOLD IT!
AAAIIGHH!
THAT'S KINDA LIKE HOW PUDDIN' STOLE MY HEART!
WHICH TOTALLY REMINDS ME...
...TODAY'S VALENTINE'S DAY!
Hee hee...
CRUNCH
CRUNCH
CRUNCH
AARRRRR!
AND THAT REMINDS ME OF HOW HUNGRY I AM!
THIS IS GREAT!
HISSSSSSS!
AAAAAHH!
OKAY, NOW I'M REALLY HUNGRY.
Heh! DO THEY TASTE LIKE CHICKEN?!

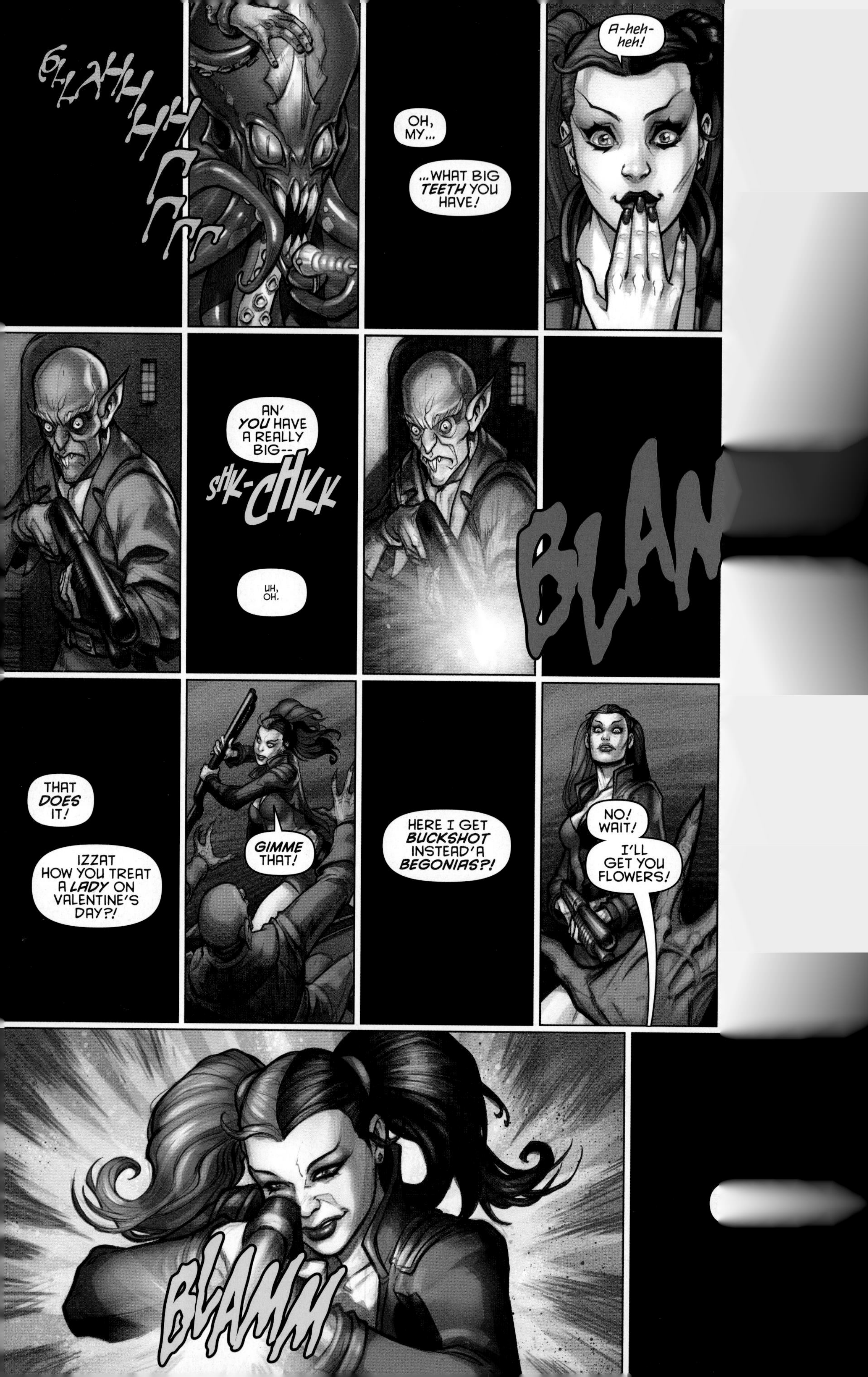

SHLAHHHHGGGG
OH, MY...
...WHAT BIG TEETH YOU HAVE!
A-heh-heh!
AN' YOU HAVE A REALLY BIG--
SHK-CHKK
UH, OH.
BLAM
THAT DOES IT!
IZZAT HOW YOU TREAT A LADY ON VALENTINE'S DAY?!
GIMME THAT!
HERE I GET BUCKSHOT INSTEAD'A BEGONIAS?!
NO! WAIT!
I'LL GET YOU FLOWERS!
BLAMM

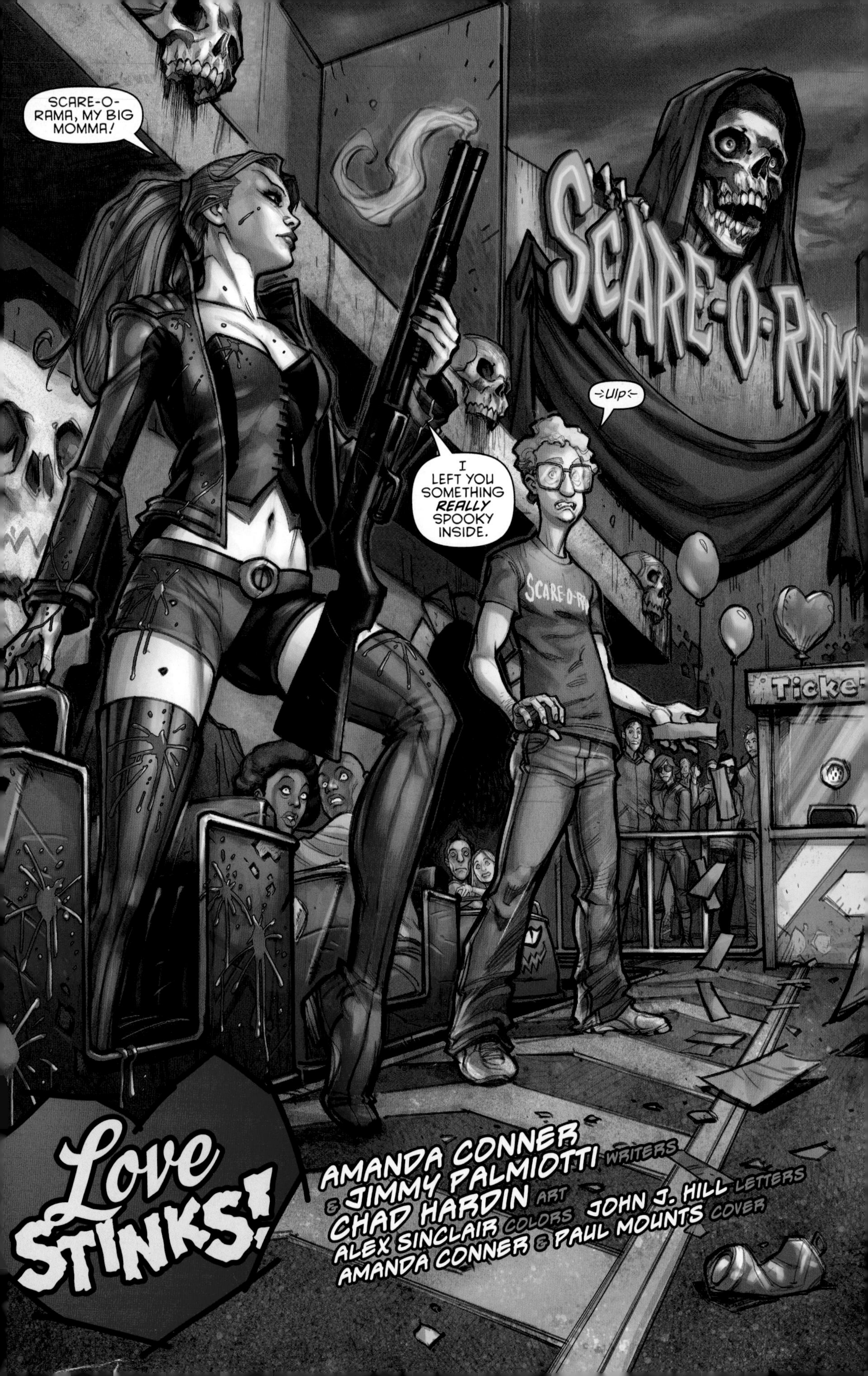
SCARE-O-RAMA, MY BIG MOMMA!
SCARE-O-RAMA
-ULP-
I LEFT YOU SOMETHING REALLY SPOOKY INSIDE.
SCARE-O-RA
Ticke
Love STINKS!
AMANDA CONNER & JIMMY PALMIOTTI WRITERS
CHAD HARDIN ART
ALEX SINCLAIR COLORS JOHN J. HILL LETTERS
AMANDA CONNER & PAUL MOUNTS COVER

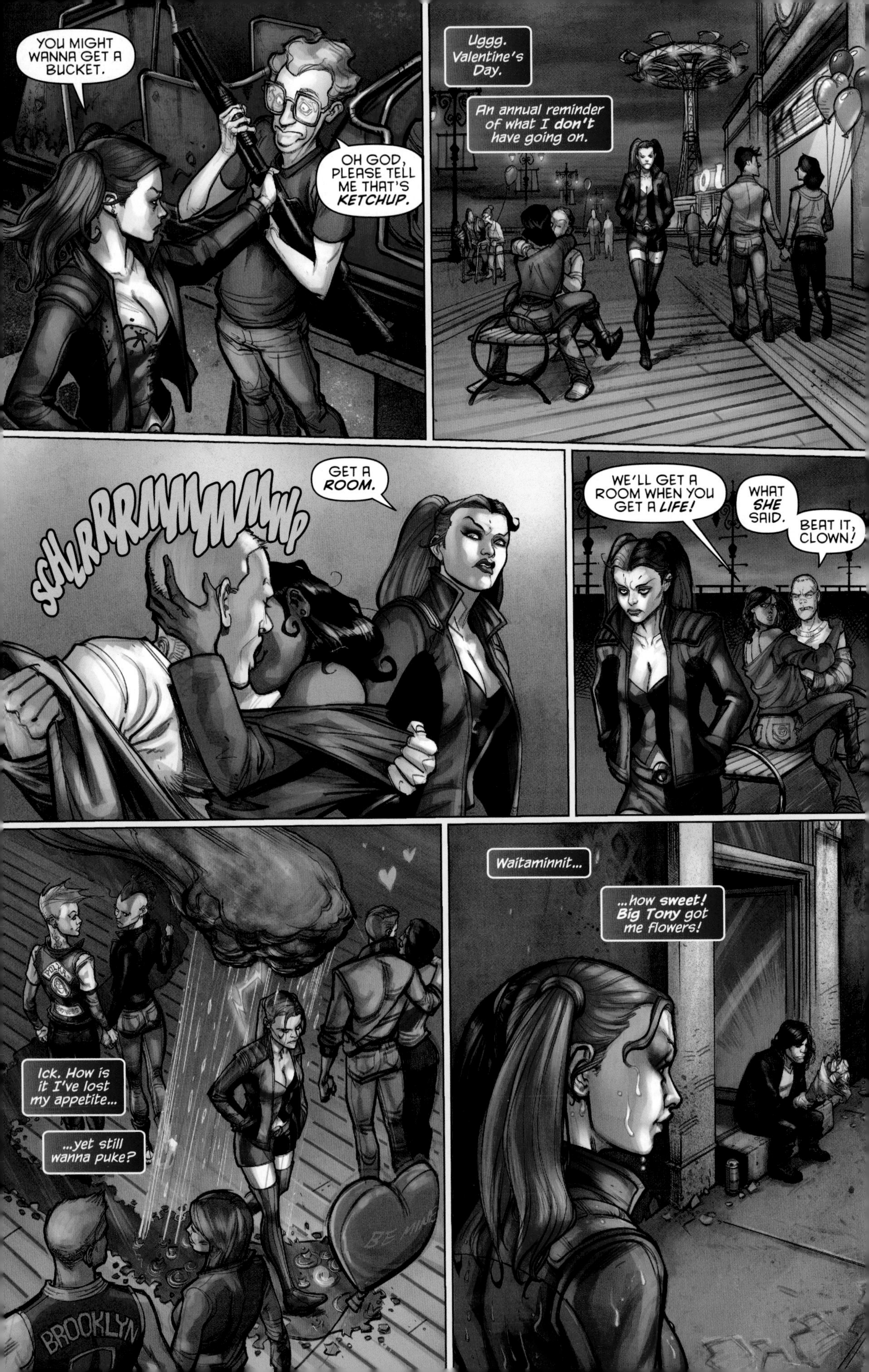
YOU MIGHT WANNA GET A BUCKET.
OH GOD, PLEASE TELL ME THAT'S *KETCHUP*.
Uggg. Valentine's Day.
An annual reminder of what I **don't** have going on.
GET A *ROOM*.
SCHLRRRMMMMMWP
WE'LL GET A ROOM WHEN YOU GET A *LIFE!*
WHAT *SHE* SAID.
BEAT IT, CLOWN!
Ick. How is it I've lost my appetite...
...yet still wanna puke?
BE MINE
BROOKLYN
Waitaminnit...
...how **sweet!** **Big Tony** got me flowers!

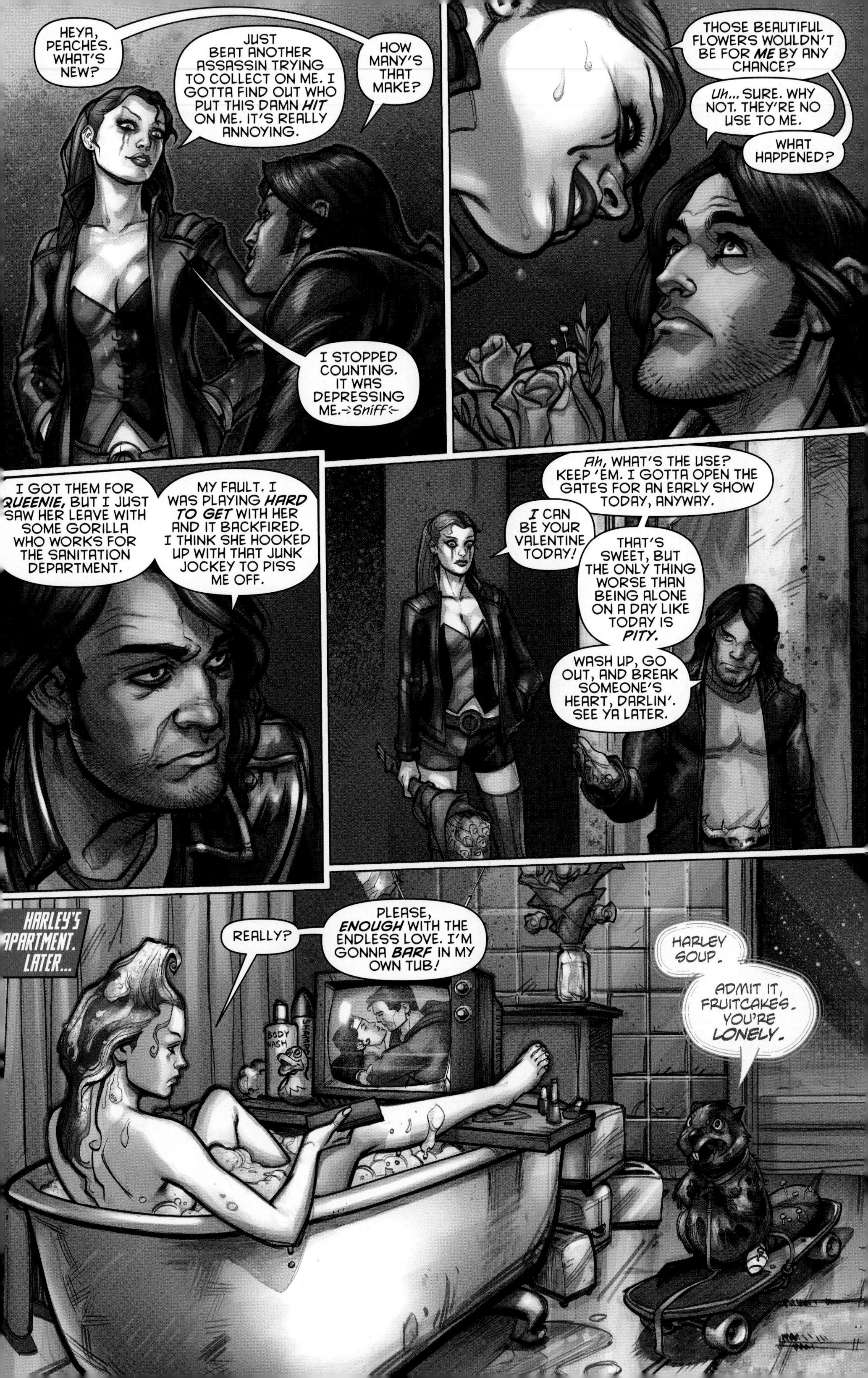

HEYA, PEACHES. WHAT'S NEW?
JUST BEAT ANOTHER ASSASSIN TRYING TO COLLECT ON ME. I GOTTA FIND OUT WHO PUT THIS DAMN *HIT* ON ME. IT'S REALLY ANNOYING.
HOW MANY'S THAT MAKE?
I STOPPED COUNTING. IT WAS DEPRESSING ME. ⇒*SNIFF*⇐
THOSE BEAUTIFUL FLOWERS WOULDN'T BE FOR *ME* BY ANY CHANCE?
UH... SURE. WHY NOT. THEY'RE NO USE TO ME.
WHAT HAPPENED?
I GOT THEM FOR *QUEENIE,* BUT I JUST SAW HER LEAVE WITH SOME GORILLA WHO WORKS FOR THE SANITATION DEPARTMENT.
MY FAULT. I WAS PLAYING *HARD TO GET* WITH HER AND IT BACKFIRED. I THINK SHE HOOKED UP WITH THAT JUNK JOCKEY TO PISS ME OFF.
I CAN BE YOUR VALENTINE TODAY!
AH, WHAT'S THE USE? KEEP 'EM. I GOTTA OPEN THE GATES FOR AN EARLY SHOW TODAY, ANYWAY.
THAT'S SWEET, BUT THE ONLY THING WORSE THAN BEING ALONE ON A DAY LIKE TODAY IS *PITY.*
WASH UP, GO OUT, AND BREAK SOMEONE'S HEART, DARLIN'. SEE YA LATER.
HARLEY'S APARTMENT. LATER...
REALLY?
PLEASE, *ENOUGH* WITH THE ENDLESS LOVE. I'M GONNA *BARF* IN MY OWN TUB!
HARLEY SOUP.
ADMIT IT, FRUITCAKES. YOU'RE *LONELY.*
BODY WASH
SHAMPOO

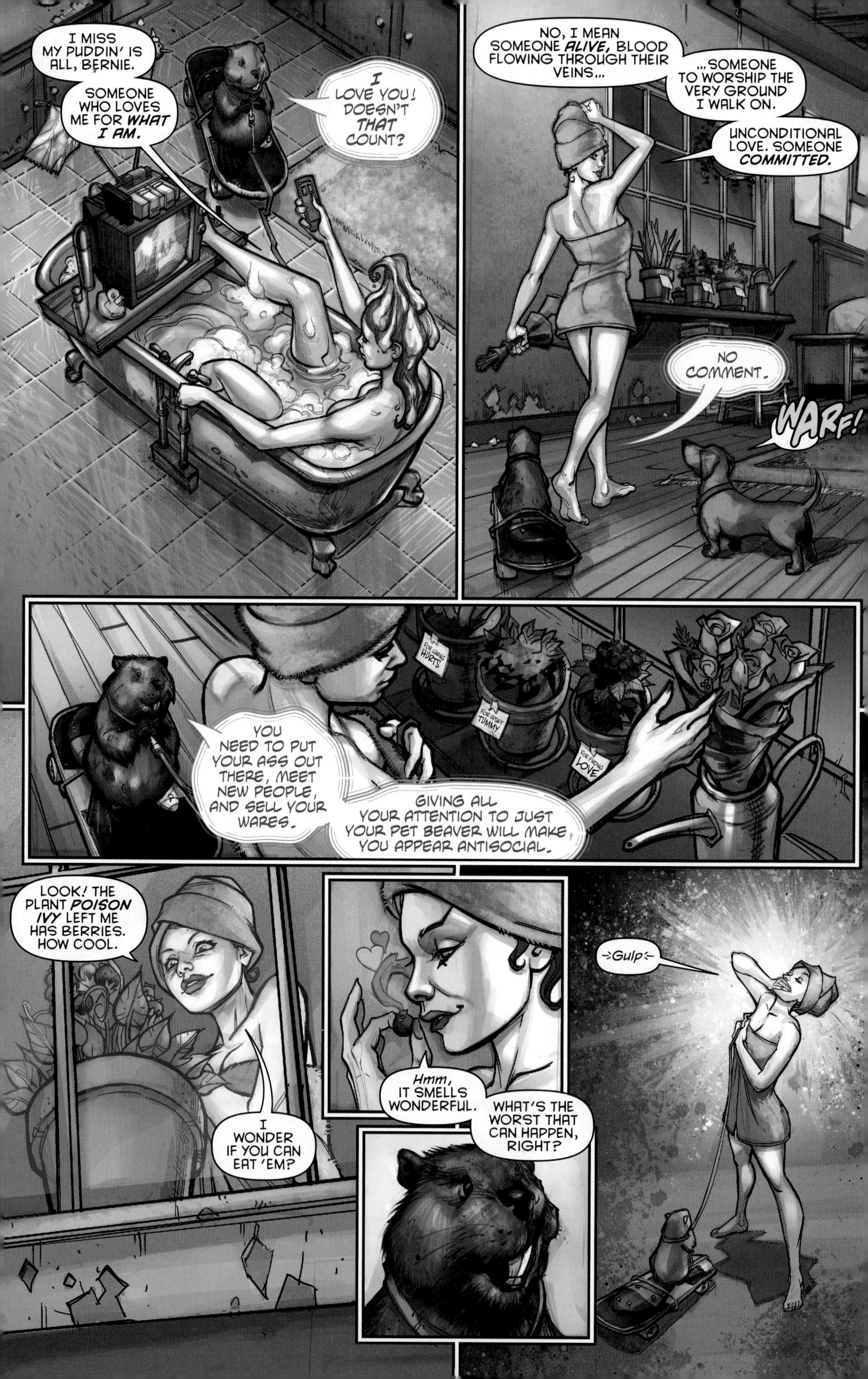
I MISS MY PUDDIN' IS ALL, BERNIE.
SOMEONE WHO LOVES ME FOR WHAT I AM.
I LOVE YOU! DOESN'T THAT COUNT?
NO, I MEAN SOMEONE ALIVE, BLOOD FLOWING THROUGH THEIR VEINS...
...SOMEONE TO WORSHIP THE VERY GROUND I WALK ON.
UNCONDITIONAL LOVE. SOMEONE COMMITTED.
NO COMMENT.
WARF!
FOR CURING HURTS
FOR UPSET TUMMY
FOR FINDING LOVE
YOU NEED TO PUT YOUR ASS OUT THERE, MEET NEW PEOPLE, AND SELL YOUR WARES.
GIVING ALL YOUR ATTENTION TO JUST YOUR PET BEAVER WILL MAKE YOU APPEAR ANTISOCIAL.
LOOK! THE PLANT POISON IVY LEFT ME HAS BERRIES. HOW COOL.
I WONDER IF YOU CAN EAT 'EM?
Hmm, IT SMELLS WONDERFUL.
WHAT'S THE WORST THAT CAN HAPPEN, RIGHT?
Gulp

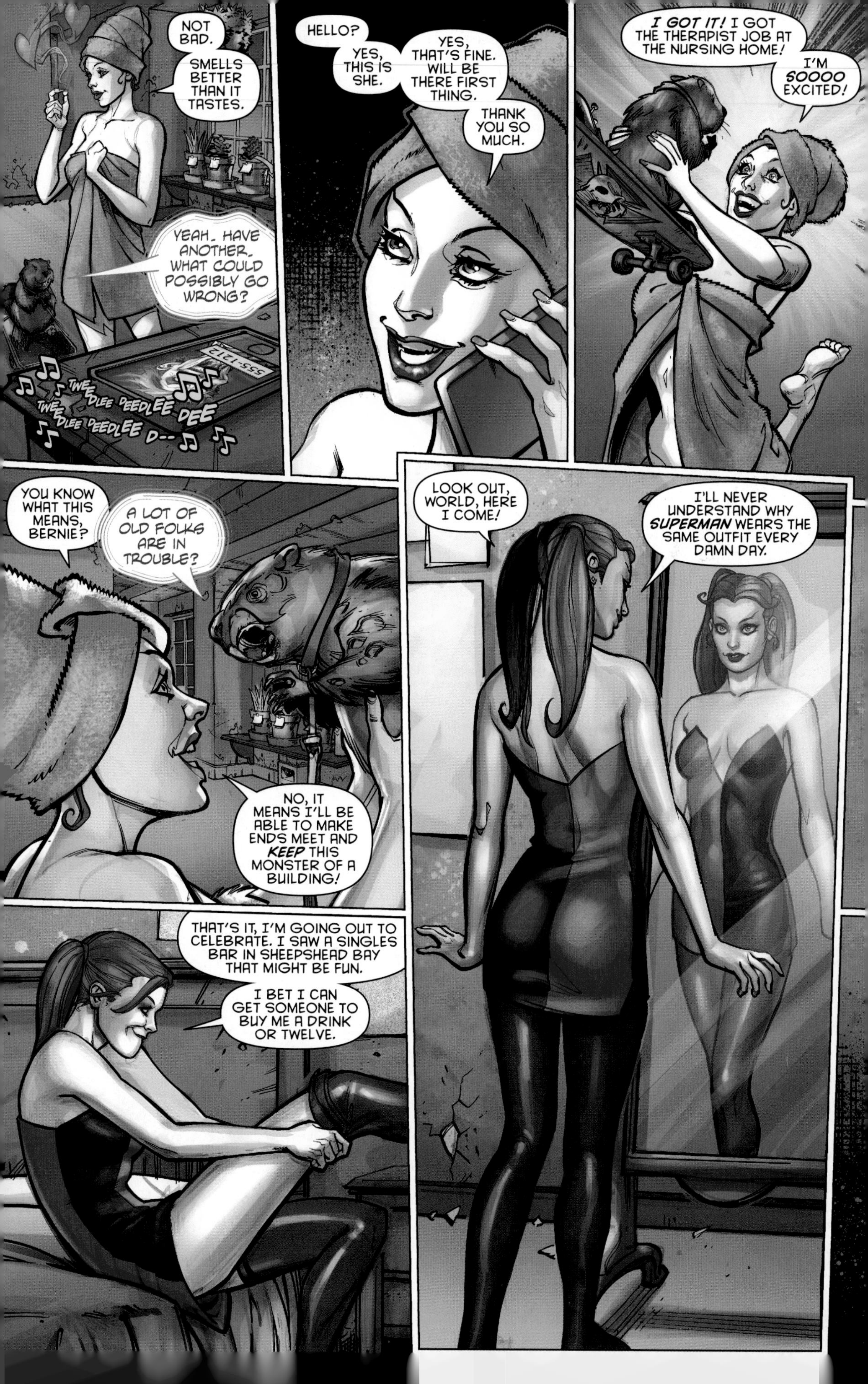

NOT BAD.
SMELLS BETTER THAN IT TASTES.
YEAH. HAVE ANOTHER. WHAT COULD POSSIBLY GO WRONG?
555-1212
TWEEDLEE DEEDLEE DEE
TWEEDLEE DEEDLEE D--
HELLO?
YES, THIS IS SHE.
YES, THAT'S FINE. WILL BE THERE FIRST THING.
THANK YOU SO MUCH.
I GOT IT! I GOT THE THERAPIST JOB AT THE NURSING HOME!
I'M SOOOO EXCITED!
YOU KNOW WHAT THIS MEANS, BERNIE?
A LOT OF OLD FOLKS ARE IN TROUBLE?
NO, IT MEANS I'LL BE ABLE TO MAKE ENDS MEET AND KEEP THIS MONSTER OF A BUILDING!
THAT'S IT, I'M GOING OUT TO CELEBRATE. I SAW A SINGLES BAR IN SHEEPSHEAD BAY THAT MIGHT BE FUN.
I BET I CAN GET SOMEONE TO BUY ME A DRINK OR TWELVE.
LOOK OUT, WORLD, HERE I COME!
I'LL NEVER UNDERSTAND WHY SUPERMAN WEARS THE SAME OUTFIT EVERY DAMN DAY.

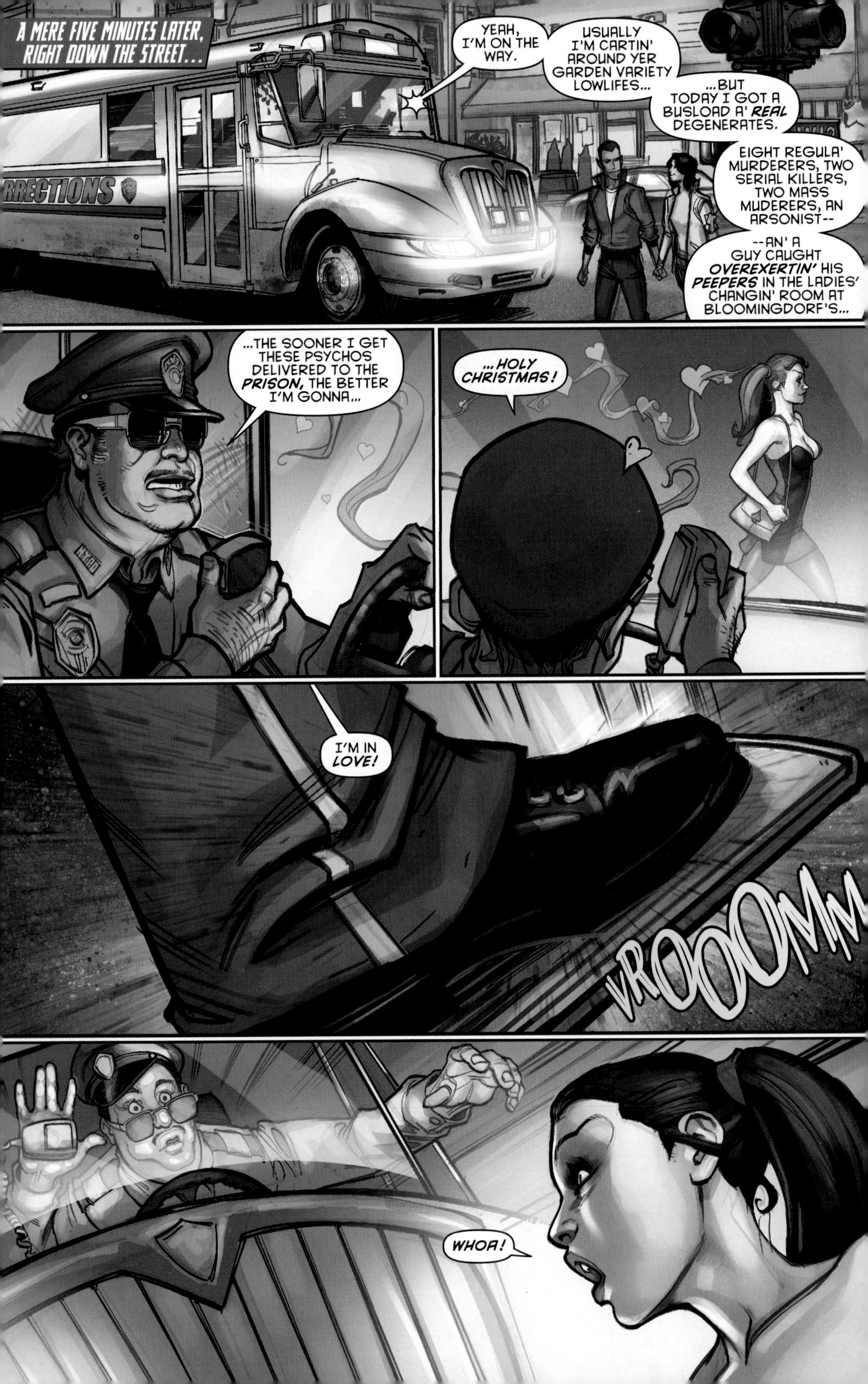
A MERE FIVE MINUTES LATER, RIGHT DOWN THE STREET...
YEAH, I'M ON THE WAY.
USUALLY I'M CARTIN' AROUND YER GARDEN VARIETY LOWLIFES...
...BUT TODAY I GOT A BUSLOAD A' REAL DEGENERATES.
EIGHT REGULA' MURDERERS, TWO SERIAL KILLERS, TWO MASS MUDERERS, AN ARSONIST--
--AN' A GUY CAUGHT OVEREXERTIN' HIS PEEPERS IN THE LADIES' CHANGIN' ROOM AT BLOOMINGDORF'S...
RRECTIONS
...THE SOONER I GET THESE PSYCHOS DELIVERED TO THE PRISON, THE BETTER I'M GONNA...
...HOLY CHRISTMAS!
I'M IN LOVE!
VROOOMM
WHOA!

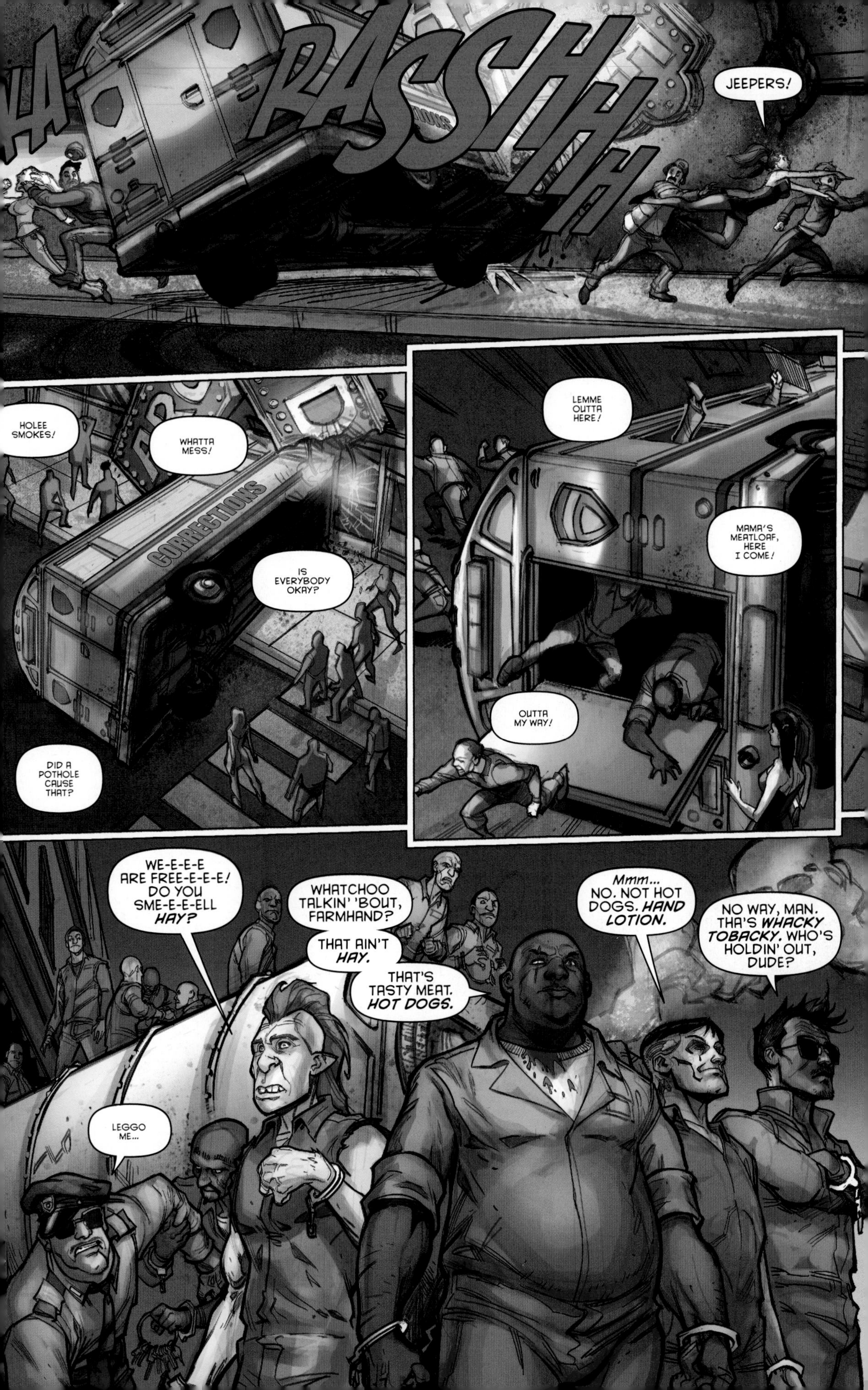

KA-RASSHH
JEEPERS!
HOLEE SMOKES!
WHATTA MESS!
CORRECTIONS
IS EVERYBODY OKAY?
DID A POTHOLE CAUSE THAT?
LEMME OUTTA HERE!
MAMA'S MEATLOAF, HERE I COME!
OUTTA MY WAY!
WE-E-E-E ARE FREE-E-E-E! DO YOU SME-E-E-ELL HAY?
WHATCHOO TALKIN' 'BOUT, FARMHAND?
THAT AIN'T HAY.
THAT'S TASTY MEAT. HOT DOGS.
Mmm... NO. NOT HOT DOGS. HAND LOTION.
NO WAY, MAN. THA'S WHACKY TOBACKY. WHO'S HOLDIN' OUT, DUDE?
LEGGO ME...

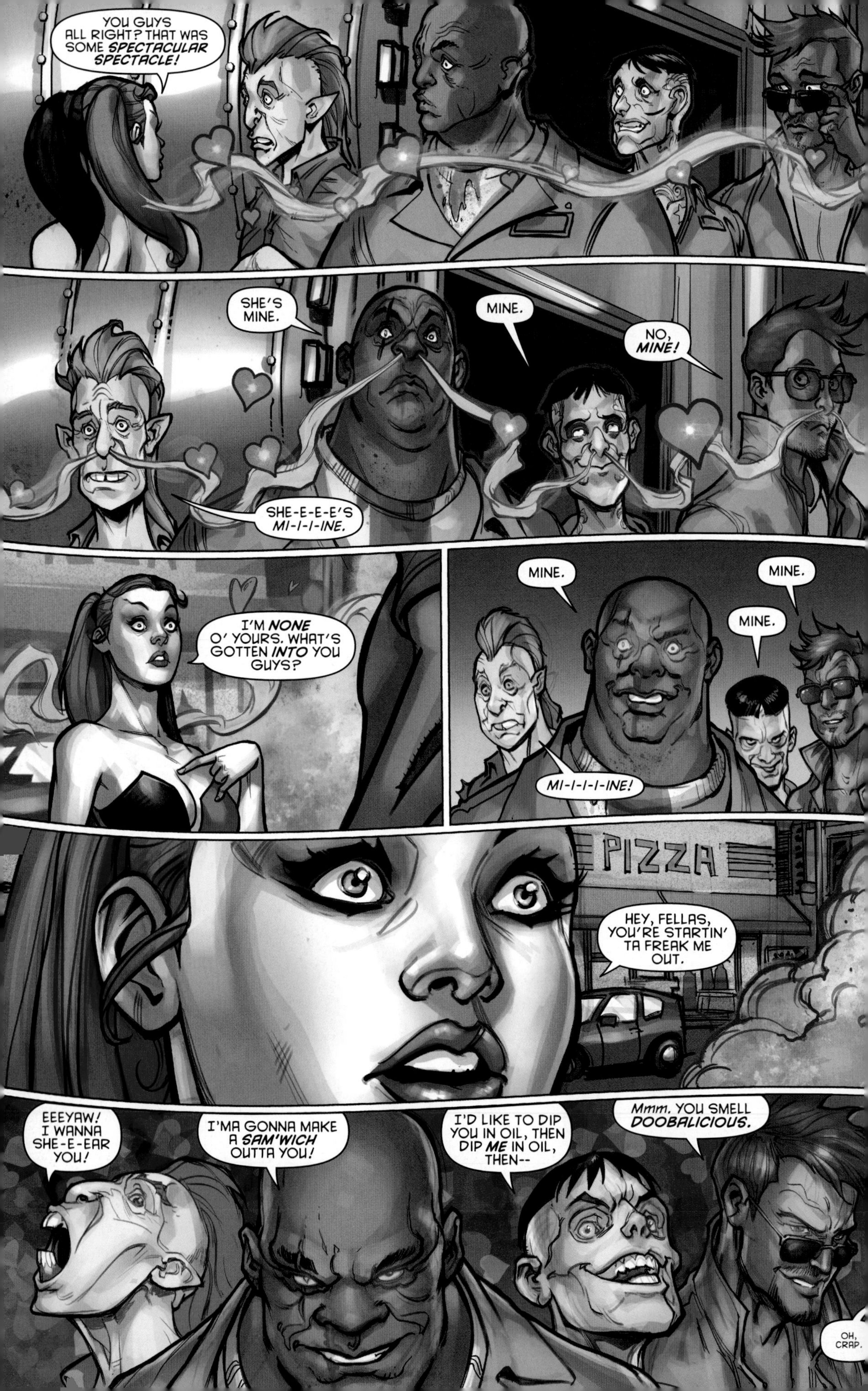
YOU GUYS ALL RIGHT? THAT WAS SOME SPECTACULAR SPECTACLE!
SHE'S MINE.
MINE.
NO, MINE!
SHE-E-E-E'S MI-I-I-INE.
I'M NONE O' YOURS. WHAT'S GOTTEN INTO YOU GUYS?
MINE.
MINE.
MINE.
MI-I-I-I-INE!
PIZZA
HEY, FELLAS, YOU'RE STARTIN' TA FREAK ME OUT.
EEEYAW! I WANNA SHE-E-EAR YOU!
I'MA GONNA MAKE A SAM'WICH OUTTA YOU!
I'D LIKE TO DIP YOU IN OIL, THEN DIP ME IN OIL, THEN--
Mmm. YOU SMELL DOOBALICIOUS.
OH, CRAP.

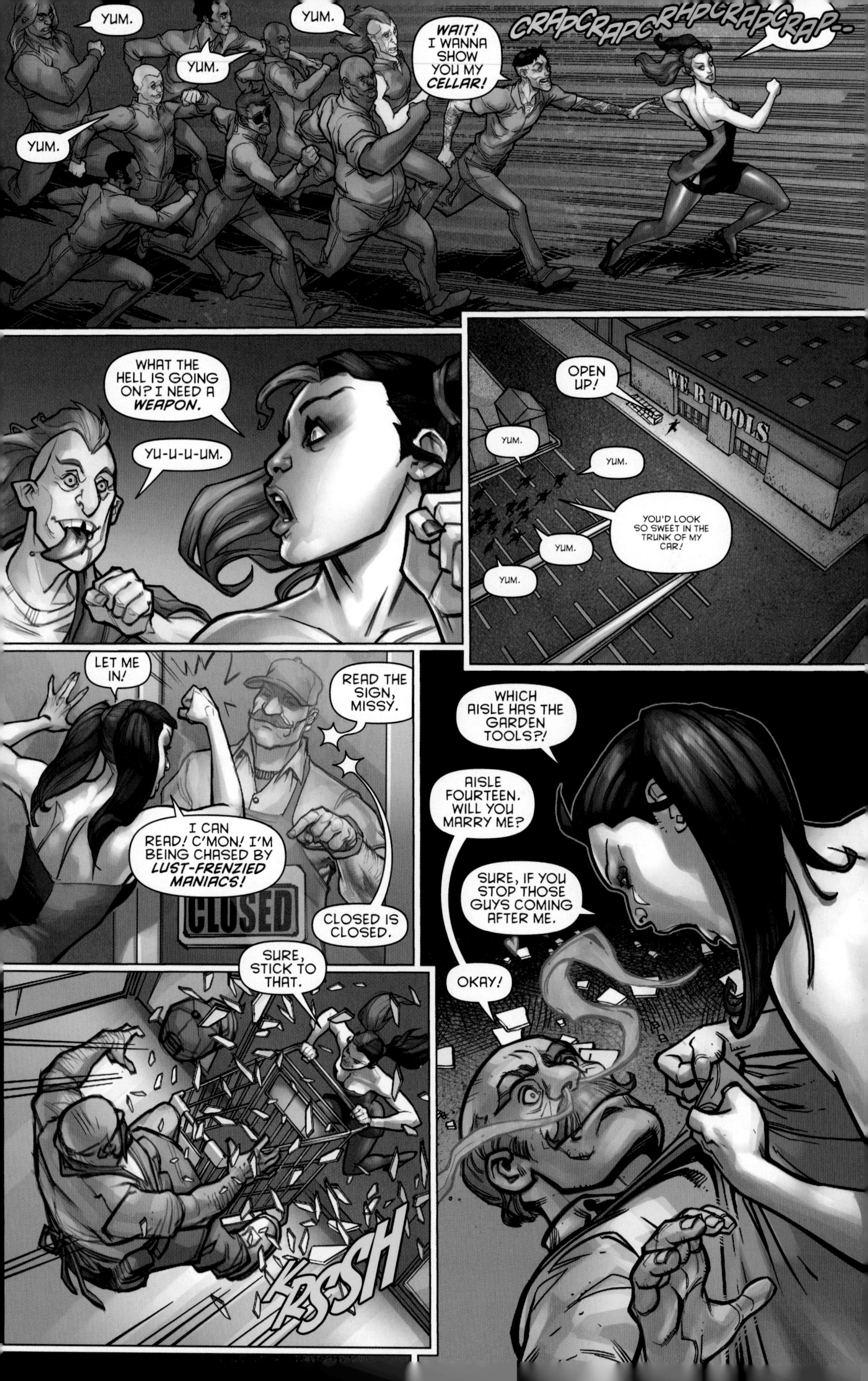
CRAPCRAPCRAPCRAPCRAP..
YUM.
YUM.
YUM.
YUM.
WAIT! I WANNA SHOW YOU MY CELLAR!
WHAT THE HELL IS GOING ON? I NEED A WEAPON.
YU-U-U-UM.
OPEN UP!
W.E.B TOOLS
YUM.
YUM.
YOU'D LOOK SO SWEET IN THE TRUNK OF MY CAR!
YUM.
YUM.
LET ME IN!
READ THE SIGN, MISSY.
I CAN READ! C'MON! I'M BEING CHASED BY LUST-FRENZIED MANIACS!
CLOSED
CLOSED IS CLOSED.
SURE, STICK TO THAT.
KRSSH
WHICH AISLE HAS THE GARDEN TOOLS?!
AISLE FOURTEEN. WILL YOU MARRY ME?
SURE, IF YOU STOP THOSE GUYS COMING AFTER ME.
OKAY!

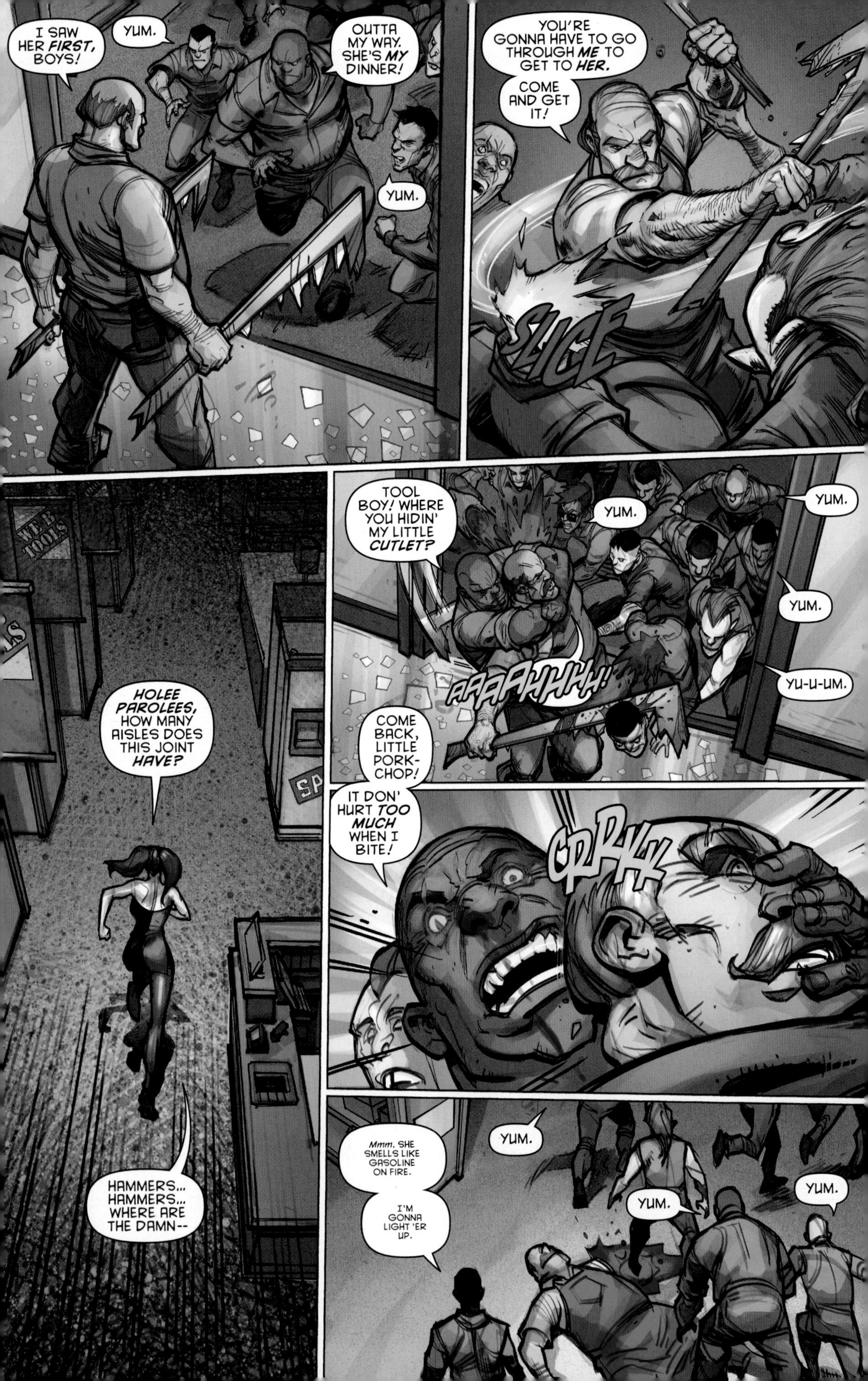
I SAW HER *FIRST*, BOYS!
YUM.
OUTTA MY WAY. SHE'S *MY* DINNER!
YUM.
YOU'RE GONNA HAVE TO GO THROUGH *ME* TO GET TO *HER*.
COME AND GET IT!
SLICE
WE B TOOLS
HOLEE PAROLEES, HOW MANY AISLES DOES THIS JOINT *HAVE*?
HAMMERS... HAMMERS... WHERE ARE THE DAMN--
TOOL BOY! WHERE YOU HIDIN' MY LITTLE *CUTLET?*
YUM.
YUM.
YUM.
YU-U-UM.
AAAAHHHH!
COME BACK, LITTLE PORK-CHOP!
IT DON' HURT *TOO MUCH* WHEN I BITE!
CRRKK
Mmm. SHE SMELLS LIKE GASOLINE ON FIRE.
I'M GONNA LIGHT 'ER UP.
YUM.
YUM.
YUM.

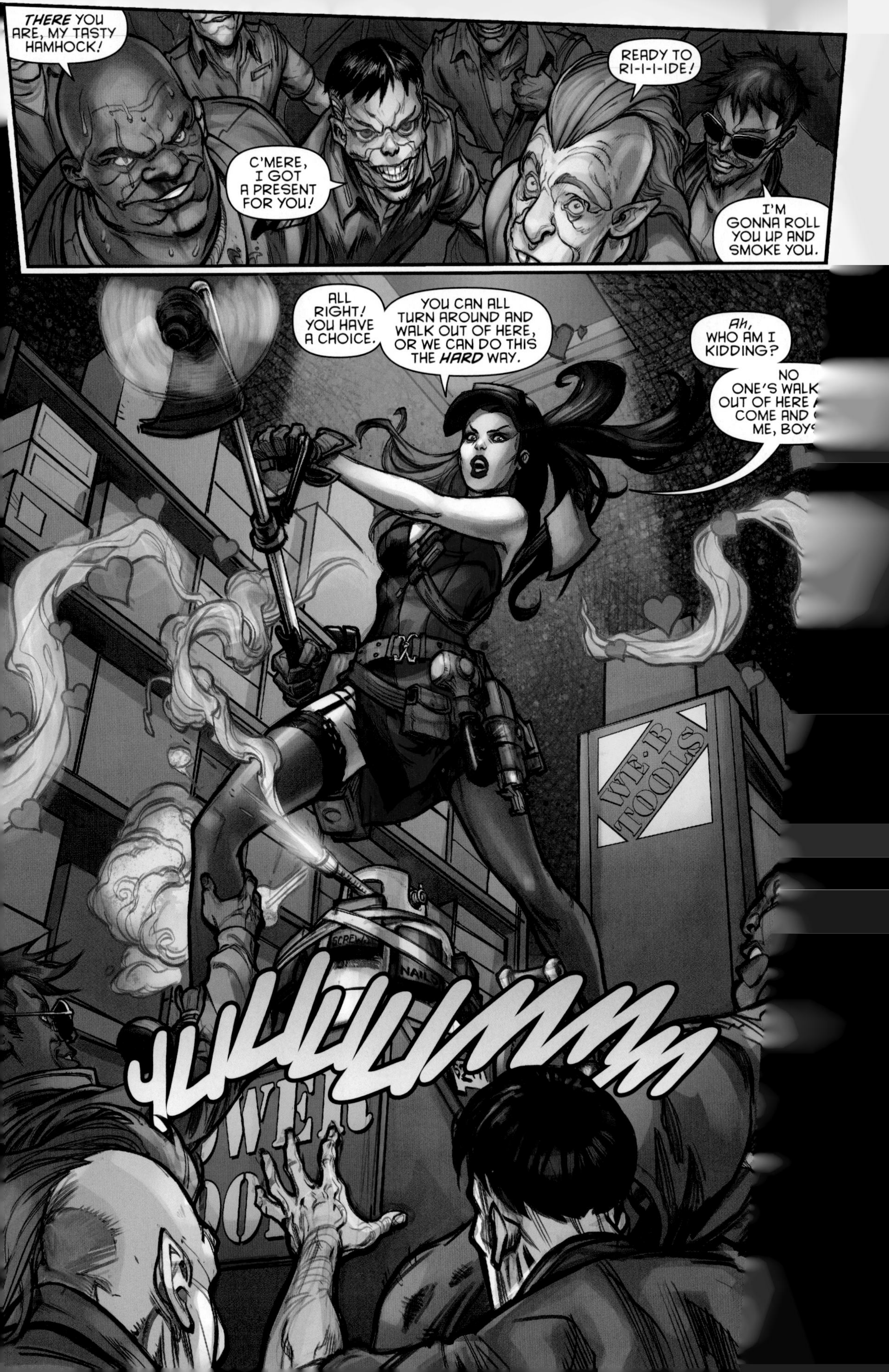
THERE YOU ARE, MY TASTY HAMHOCK!
C'MERE, I GOT A PRESENT FOR YOU!
READY TO RI-I-I-IDE!
I'M GONNA ROLL YOU UP AND SMOKE YOU.
ALL RIGHT! YOU HAVE A CHOICE.
YOU CAN ALL TURN AROUND AND WALK OUT OF HERE, OR WE CAN DO THIS THE *HARD* WAY.
Ah, WHO AM I KIDDING?
NO ONE'S WALK OUT OF HERE COME AND ME, BOYS
WE-B TOOLS

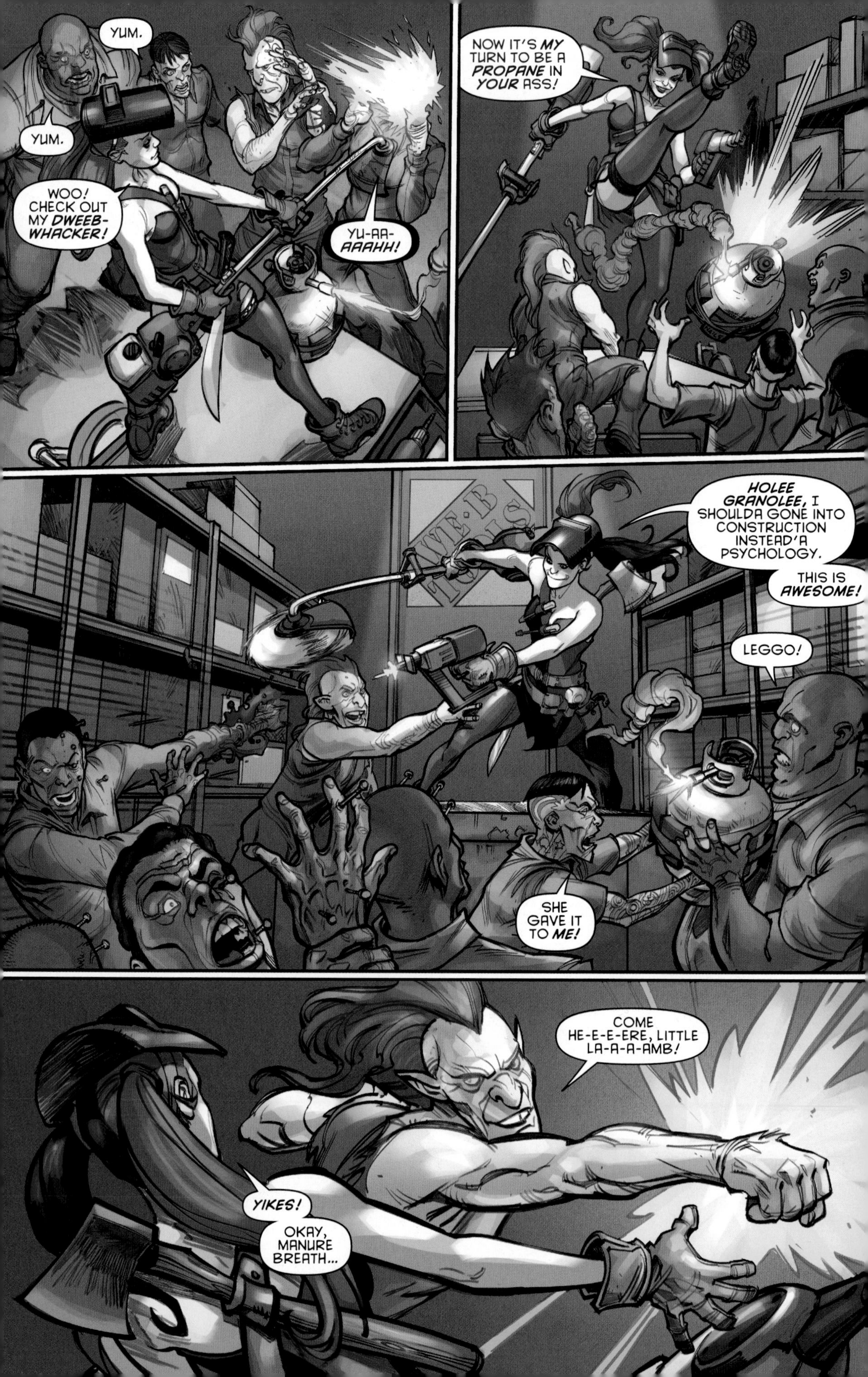
YUM.
YUM.
WOO! CHECK OUT MY *DWEEB-WHACKER!*
YU-AA-*AAAHH!*
NOW IT'S *MY* TURN TO BE A *PROPANE* IN *YOUR* ASS!
HOLEE GRANOLEE, I SHOULDA GONE INTO CONSTRUCTION INSTEAD'A PSYCHOLOGY.
THIS IS *AWESOME!*
LEGGO!
SHE GAVE IT TO *ME!*
COME HE-E-E-ERE, LITTLE LA-A-A-AMB!
YIKES!
OKAY, MANURE BREATH...

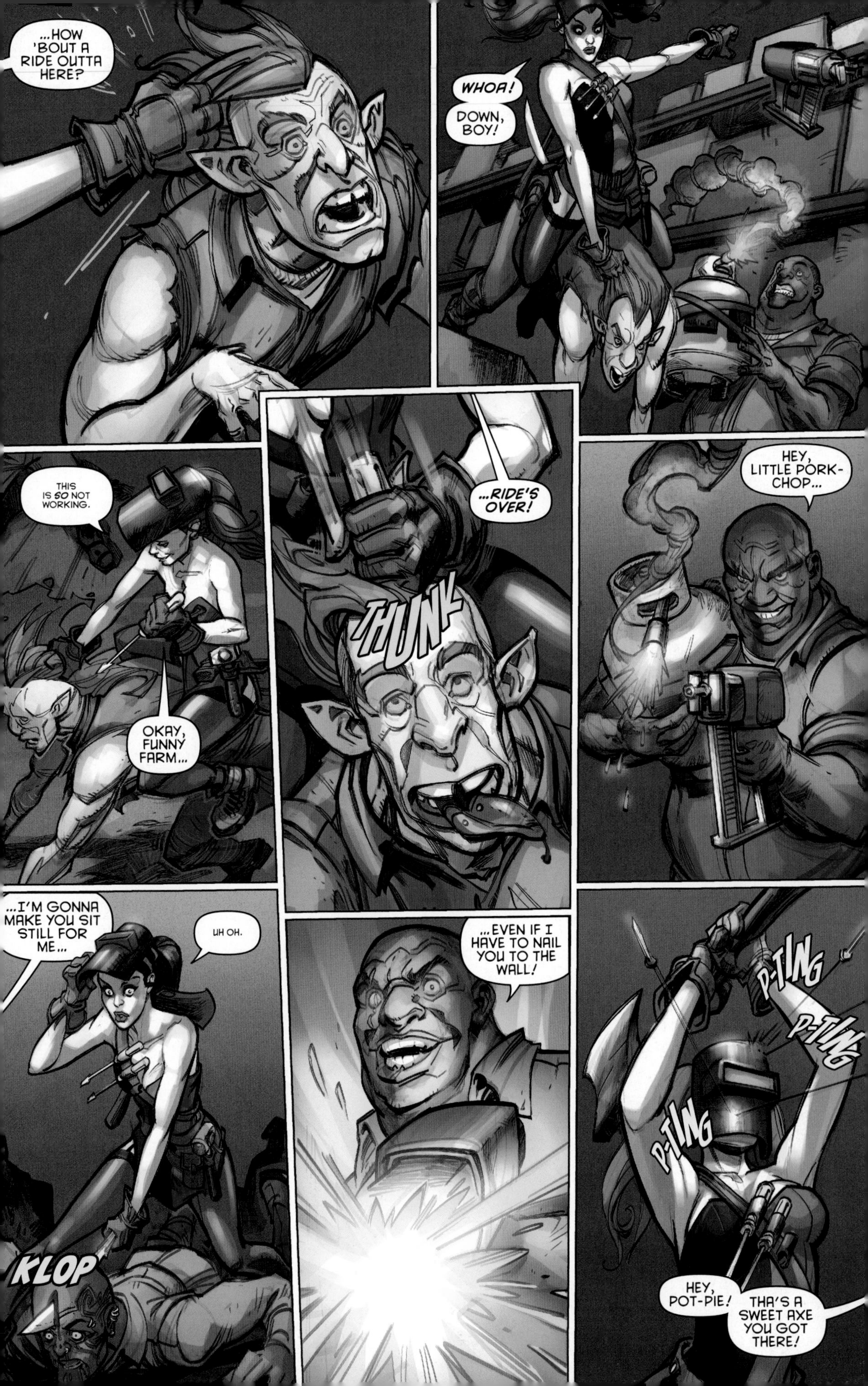
...HOW 'BOUT A RIDE OUTTA HERE?
WHOA!
DOWN, BOY!
THIS IS SO NOT WORKING.
OKAY, FUNNY FARM...
...RIDE'S OVER!
THUNK
HEY, LITTLE PORK-CHOP...
...I'M GONNA MAKE YOU SIT STILL FOR ME...
UH OH.
KLOP
...EVEN IF I HAVE TO NAIL YOU TO THE WALL!
P-TING
P-TING
P-TING
HEY, POT-PIE!
THA'S A SWEET AXE YOU GOT THERE!

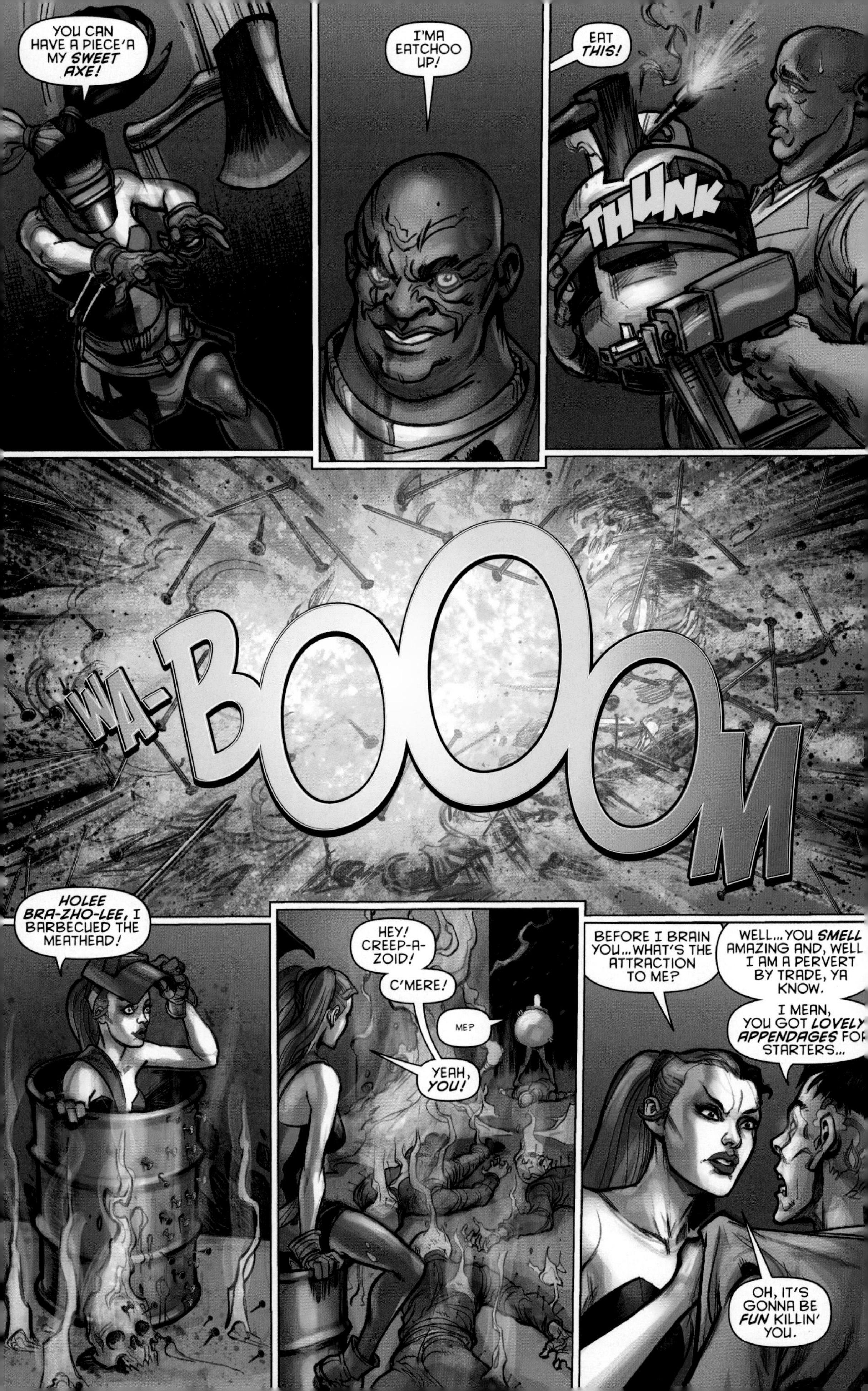

YOU CAN HAVE A PIECE'A MY *SWEET AXE!*
I'MA EATCHOO UP!
EAT *THIS!*
THUNK
WA-BOOOM
HOLEE BRA-ZHO-LEE, I BARBECUED THE MEATHEAD!
HEY! CREEP-A-ZOID!
C'MERE!
ME?
YEAH, *YOU!*
BEFORE I BRAIN YOU...WHAT'S THE ATTRACTION TO ME?
WELL...YOU *SMELL* AMAZING AND, WELL I AM A PERVERT BY TRADE, YA KNOW.
I MEAN, YOU GOT *LOVELY APPENDAGES* FOR STARTERS...
OH, IT'S GONNA BE *FUN* KILLIN' YOU.

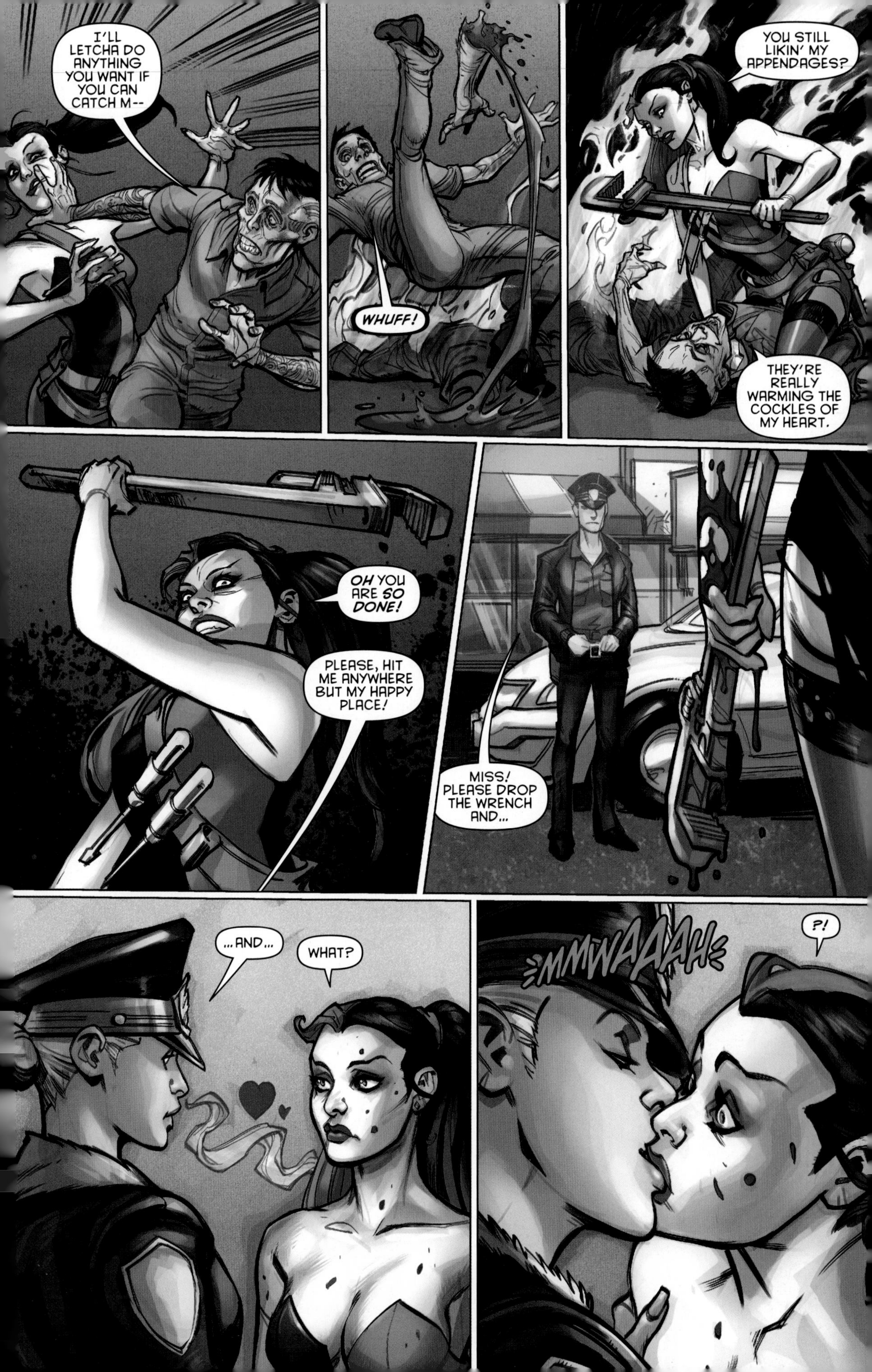
I'LL LETCHA DO ANYTHING YOU WANT IF YOU CAN CATCH M--
WHUFF!
YOU STILL LIKIN' MY APPENDAGES?
THEY'RE REALLY WARMING THE COCKLES OF MY HEART.
OH YOU ARE SO DONE!
PLEASE, HIT ME ANYWHERE BUT MY HAPPY PLACE!
MISS! PLEASE DROP THE WRENCH AND...
...AND...
WHAT?
MMWAAAH
?!

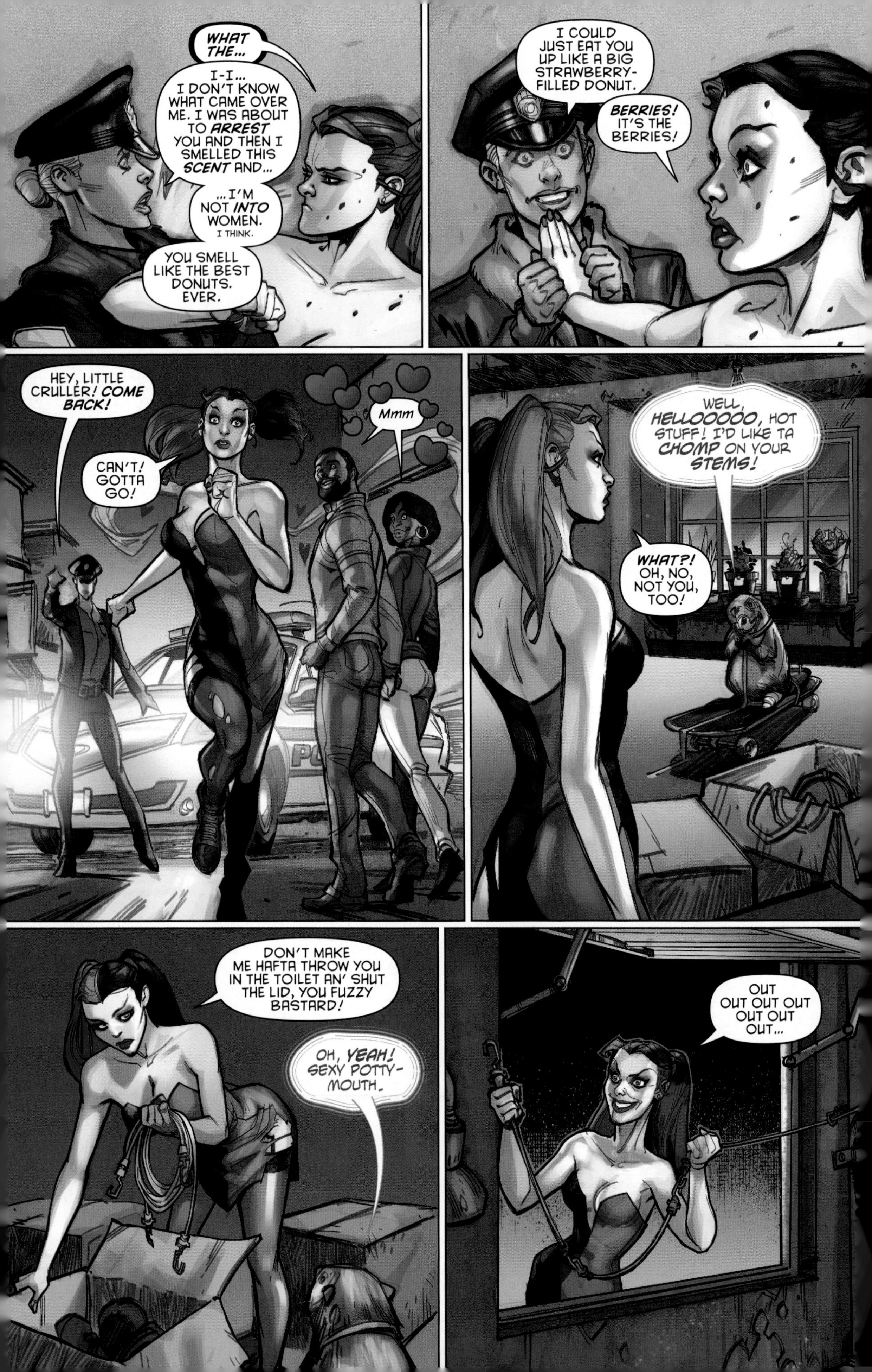
WHAT THE...
I-I... I DON'T KNOW WHAT CAME OVER ME. I WAS ABOUT TO ARREST YOU AND THEN I SMELLED THIS SCENT AND...
...I'M NOT INTO WOMEN. I THINK.
YOU SMELL LIKE THE BEST DONUTS. EVER.
I COULD JUST EAT YOU UP LIKE A BIG STRAWBERRY-FILLED DONUT.
BERRIES! IT'S THE BERRIES!
HEY, LITTLE CRULLER! COME BACK!
CAN'T! GOTTA GO!
Mmm
WELL, HELLOOOOO, HOT STUFF! I'D LIKE TA CHOMP ON YOUR STEMS!
WHAT?! OH, NO, NOT YOU, TOO!
DON'T MAKE ME HAFTA THROW YOU IN THE TOILET AN' SHUT THE LID, YOU FUZZY BASTARD!
OH, YEAH! SEXY POTTY-MOUTH.
OUT OUT OUT OUT OUT OUT OUT...

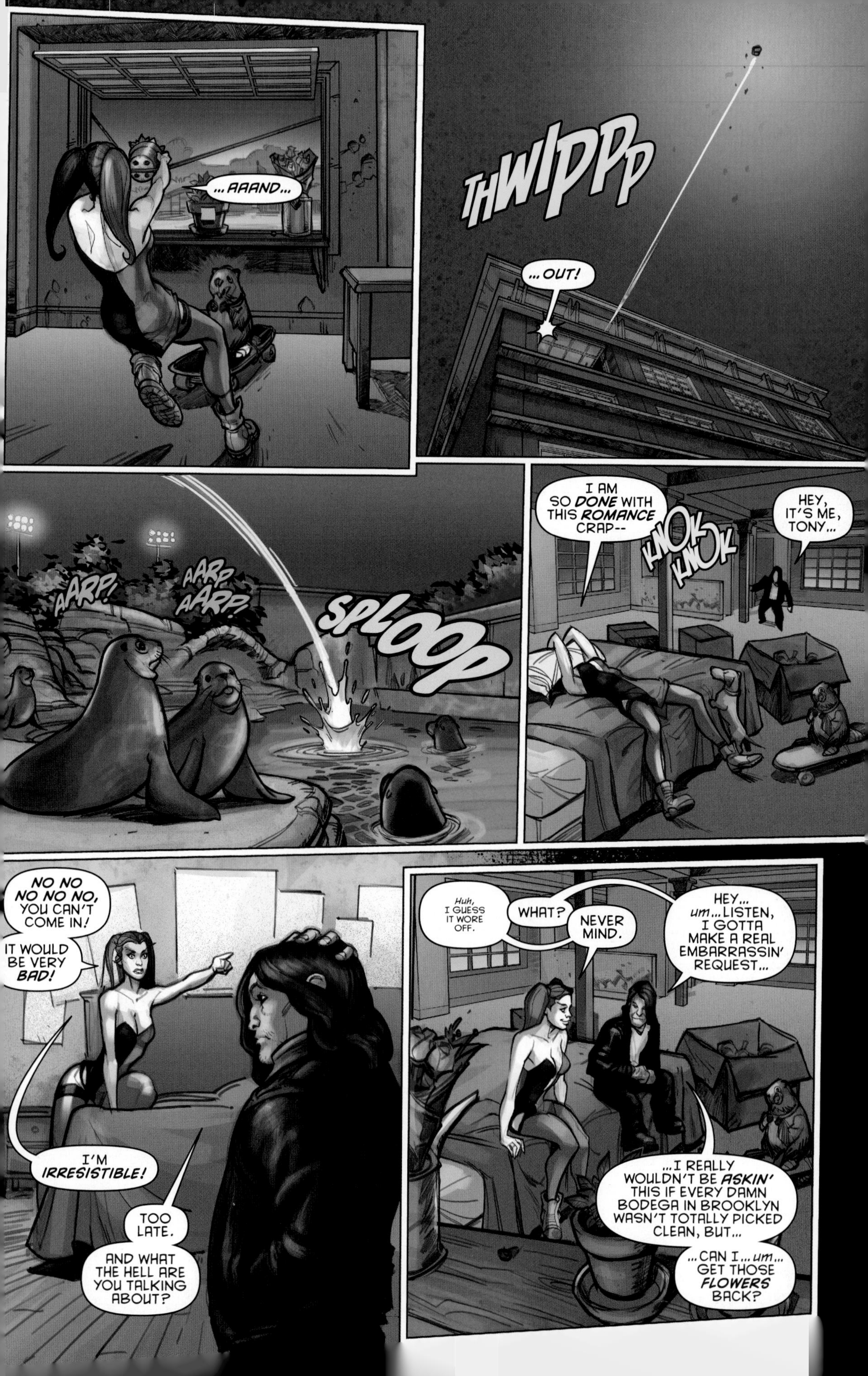
...AAAND...
THWIPPP
...OUT!
AARP!
AARP AARP
SPLOOP
I AM SO DONE WITH THIS ROMANCE CRAP--
KNOK KNOK
HEY, IT'S ME, TONY...
NO NO NO NO NO, YOU CAN'T COME IN!
IT WOULD BE VERY BAD!
I'M IRRESISTIBLE!
TOO LATE.
AND WHAT THE HELL ARE YOU TALKING ABOUT?
Huh, I GUESS IT WORE OFF.
WHAT?
NEVER MIND.
HEY... um... LISTEN, I GOTTA MAKE A REAL EMBARRASSIN' REQUEST...
...I REALLY WOULDN'T BE ASKIN' THIS IF EVERY DAMN BODEGA IN BROOKLYN WASN'T TOTALLY PICKED CLEAN, BUT...
...CAN I... um... GET THOSE FLOWERS BACK?

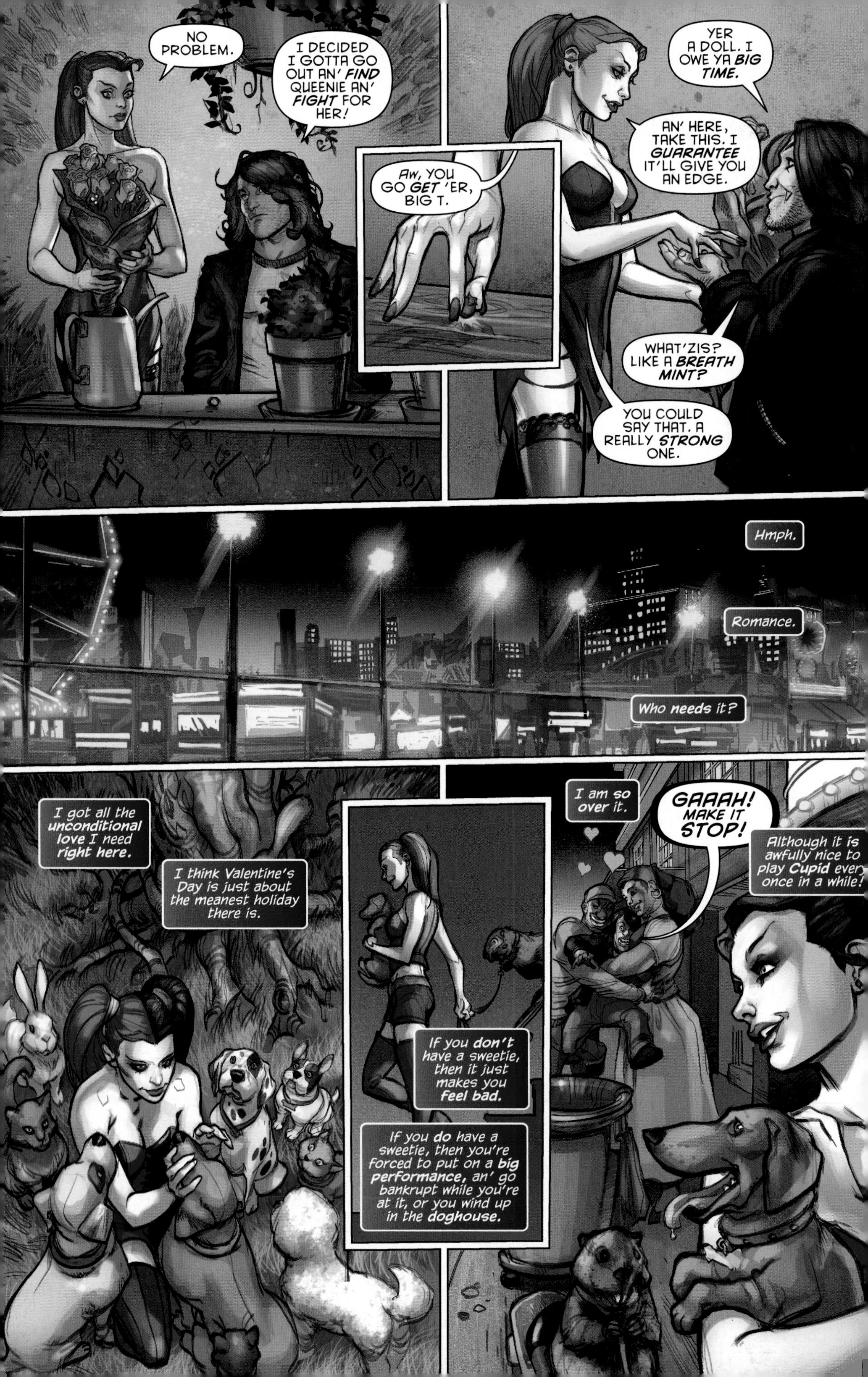
NO PROBLEM.
I DECIDED I GOTTA GO OUT AN' FIND QUEENIE AN' FIGHT FOR HER!
AW, YOU GO GET 'ER, BIG T.
YER A DOLL. I OWE YA BIG TIME.
AN' HERE, TAKE THIS. I GUARANTEE IT'LL GIVE YOU AN EDGE.
WHAT'ZIS? LIKE A BREATH MINT?
YOU COULD SAY THAT. A REALLY STRONG ONE.
Hmph.
Romance.
Who needs it?
I got all the unconditional love I need right here.
I think Valentine's Day is just about the meanest holiday there is.
If you don't have a sweetie, then it just makes you feel bad.
If you do have a sweetie, then you're forced to put on a big performance, an' go bankrupt while you're at it, or you wind up in the doghouse.
I am so over it.
GAAAH! MAKE IT STOP!
Although it is awfully nice to play Cupid every once in a while!

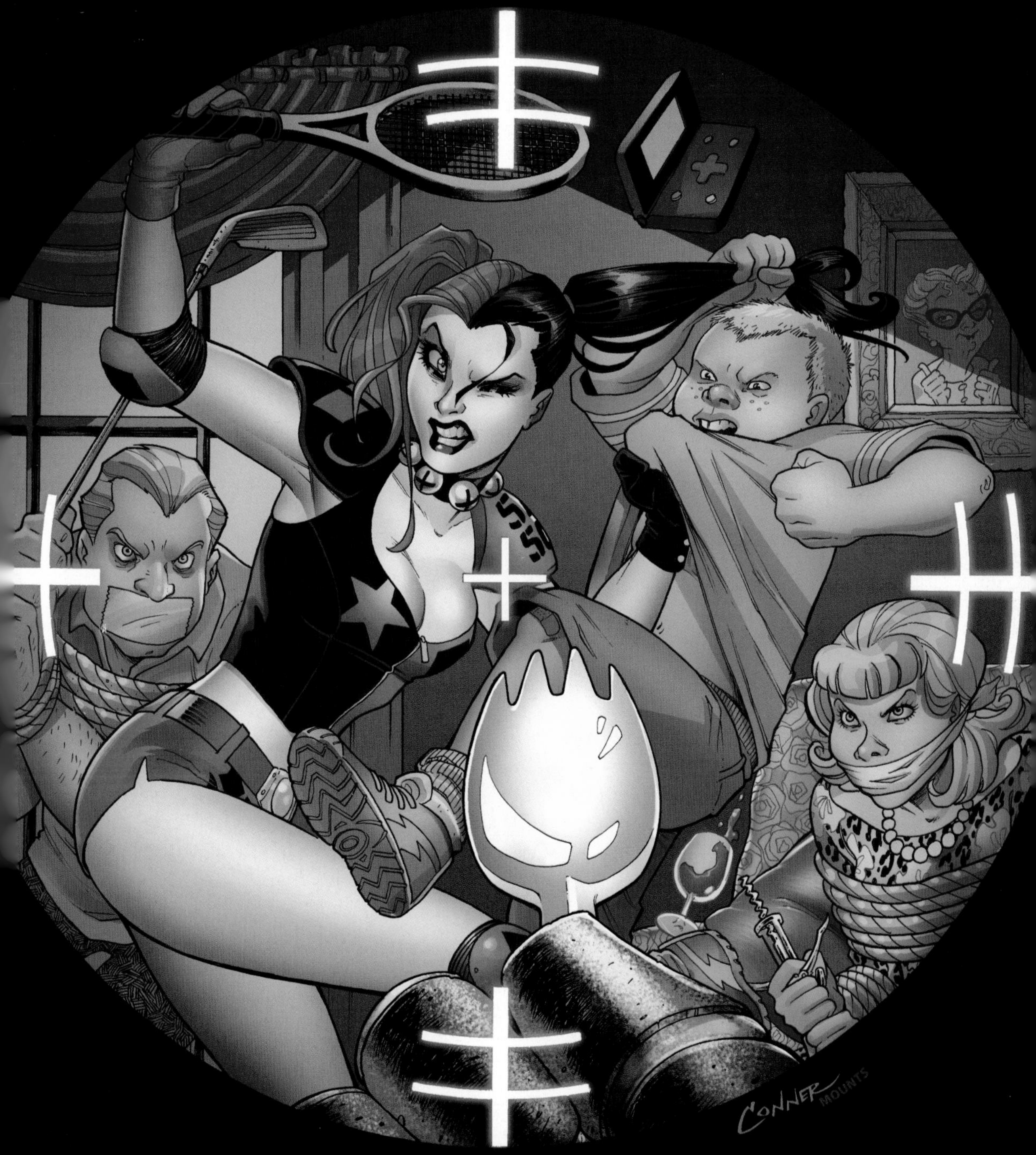
CONNER
MOUNTS

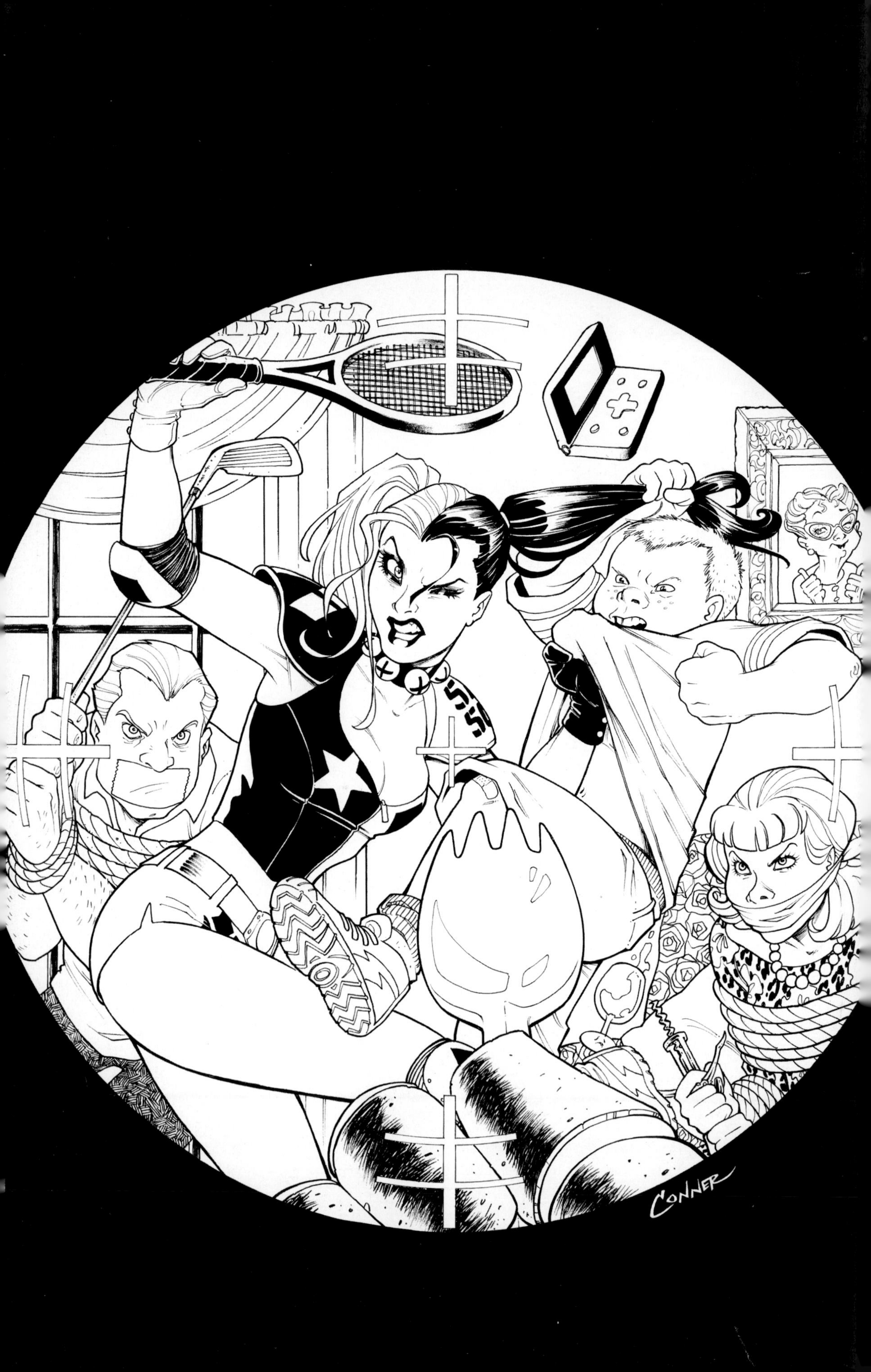
CONNER

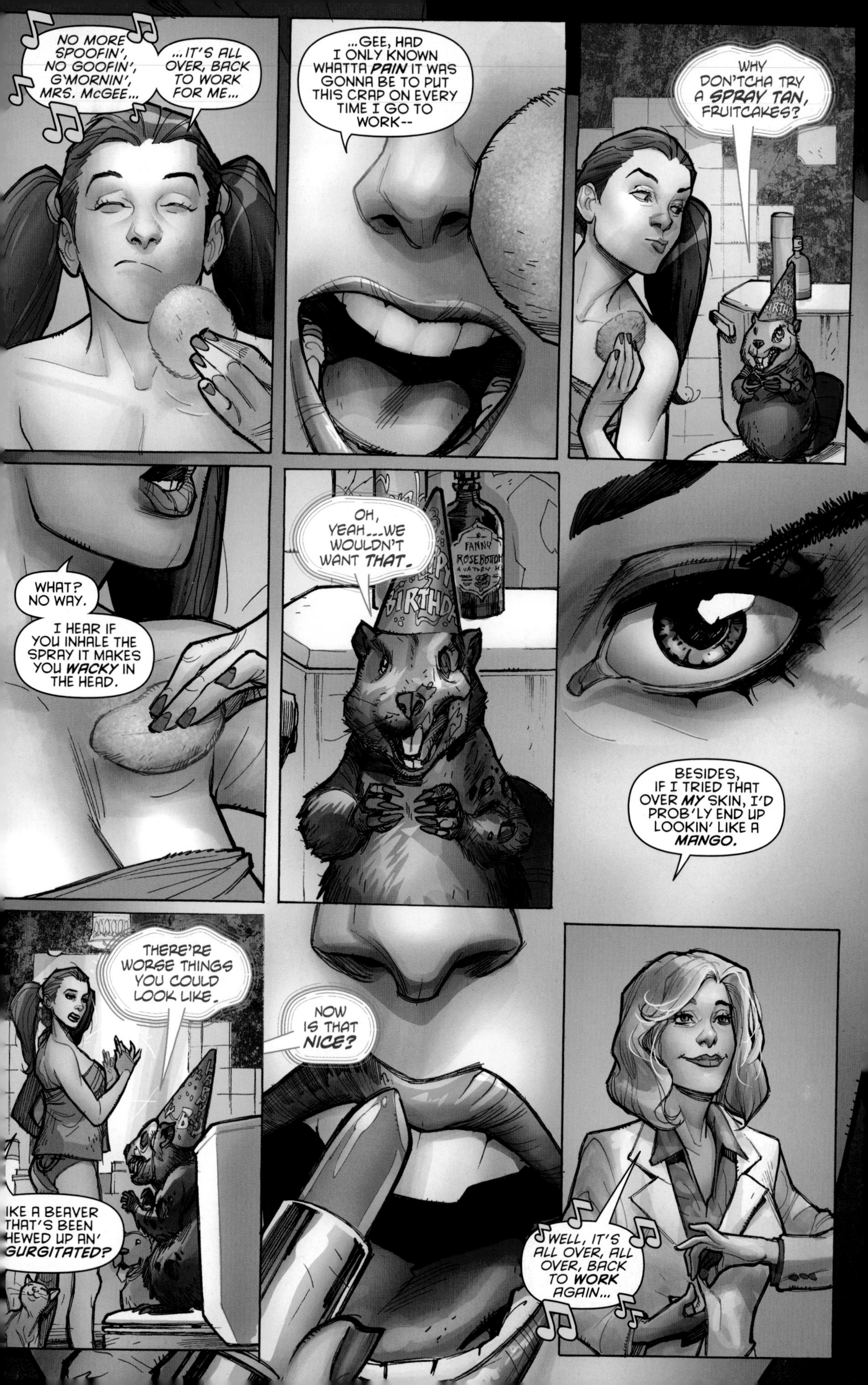
NO MORE SPOOFIN', NO GOOFIN', G'MORNIN', MRS. McGEE...
...IT'S ALL OVER, BACK TO WORK FOR ME...
...GEE, HAD I ONLY KNOWN WHATTA PAIN IT WAS GONNA BE TO PUT THIS CRAP ON EVERY TIME I GO TO WORK--
WHY DON'TCHA TRY A SPRAY TAN, FRUITCAKES?
HAPPY BIRTHDAY
WHAT? NO WAY.
I HEAR IF YOU INHALE THE SPRAY IT MAKES YOU WACKY IN THE HEAD.
OH, YEAH...WE WOULDN'T WANT THAT.
FANNY ROSEBOTTOM
BESIDES, IF I TRIED THAT OVER MY SKIN, I'D PROB'LY END UP LOOKIN' LIKE A MANGO.
THERE'RE WORSE THINGS YOU COULD LOOK LIKE.
NOW IS THAT NICE?
IKE A BEAVER THAT'S BEEN HEWED UP AN' GURGITATED?
WELL, IT'S ALL OVER, ALL OVER, BACK TO WORK AGAIN...

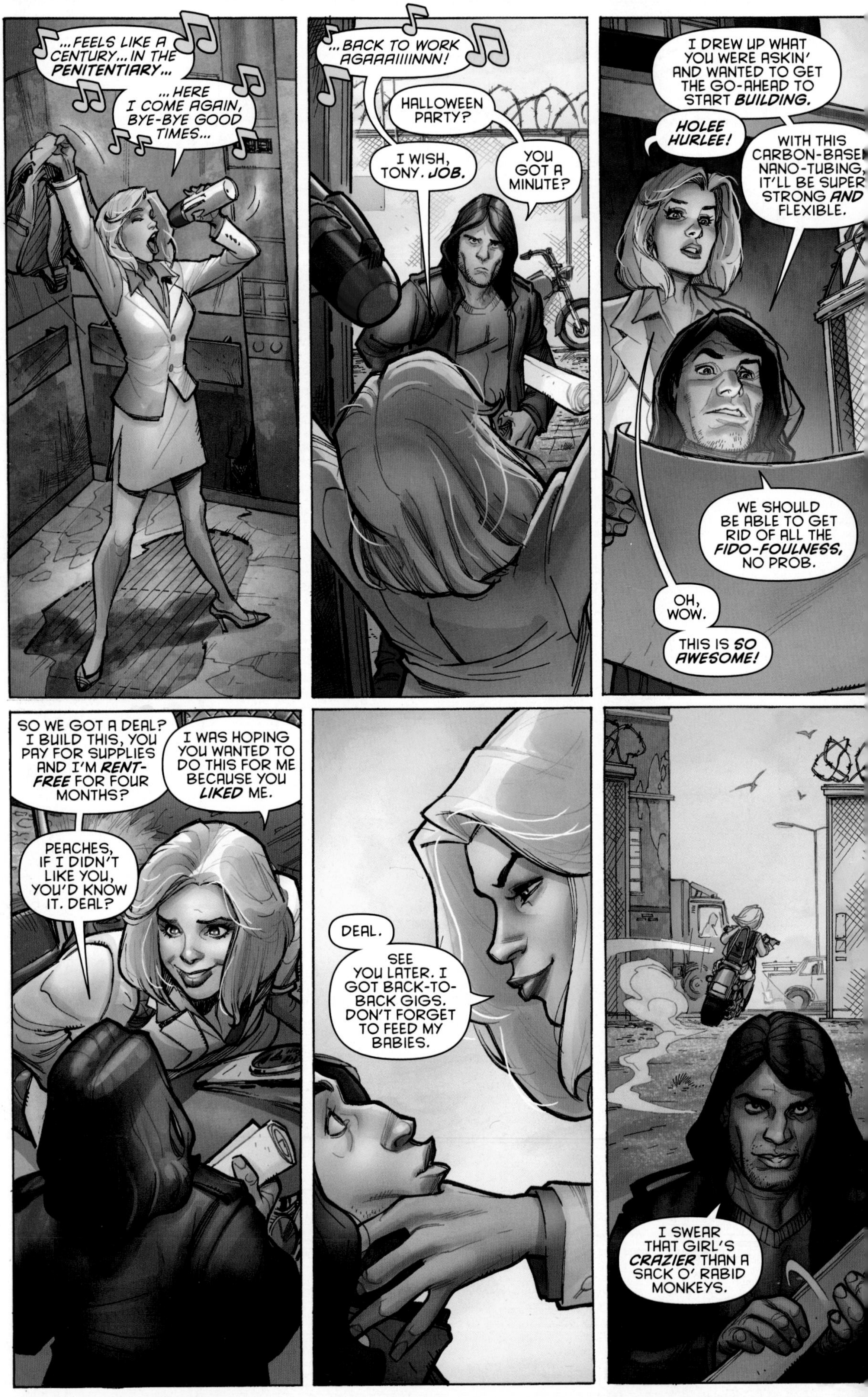
...FEELS LIKE A CENTURY... IN THE PENITENTIARY...
...HERE I COME AGAIN, BYE-BYE GOOD TIMES...
...BACK TO WORK AGAAAIIIINNN!
HALLOWEEN PARTY?
I WISH, TONY. JOB.
YOU GOT A MINUTE?
I DREW UP WHAT YOU WERE ASKIN' AND WANTED TO GET THE GO-AHEAD TO START BUILDING.
HOLEE HURLEE!
WITH THIS CARBON-BASE NANO-TUBING, IT'LL BE SUPER STRONG AND FLEXIBLE.
WE SHOULD BE ABLE TO GET RID OF ALL THE FIDO-FOULNESS, NO PROB.
OH, WOW.
THIS IS SO AWESOME!
SO WE GOT A DEAL? I BUILD THIS, YOU PAY FOR SUPPLIES AND I'M RENT-FREE FOR FOUR MONTHS?
I WAS HOPING YOU WANTED TO DO THIS FOR ME BECAUSE YOU LIKED ME.
PEACHES, IF I DIDN'T LIKE YOU, YOU'D KNOW IT. DEAL?
DEAL.
SEE YOU LATER. I GOT BACK-TO-BACK GIGS. DON'T FORGET TO FEED MY BABIES.
I SWEAR THAT GIRL'S CRAZIER THAN A SACK O' RABID MONKEYS.

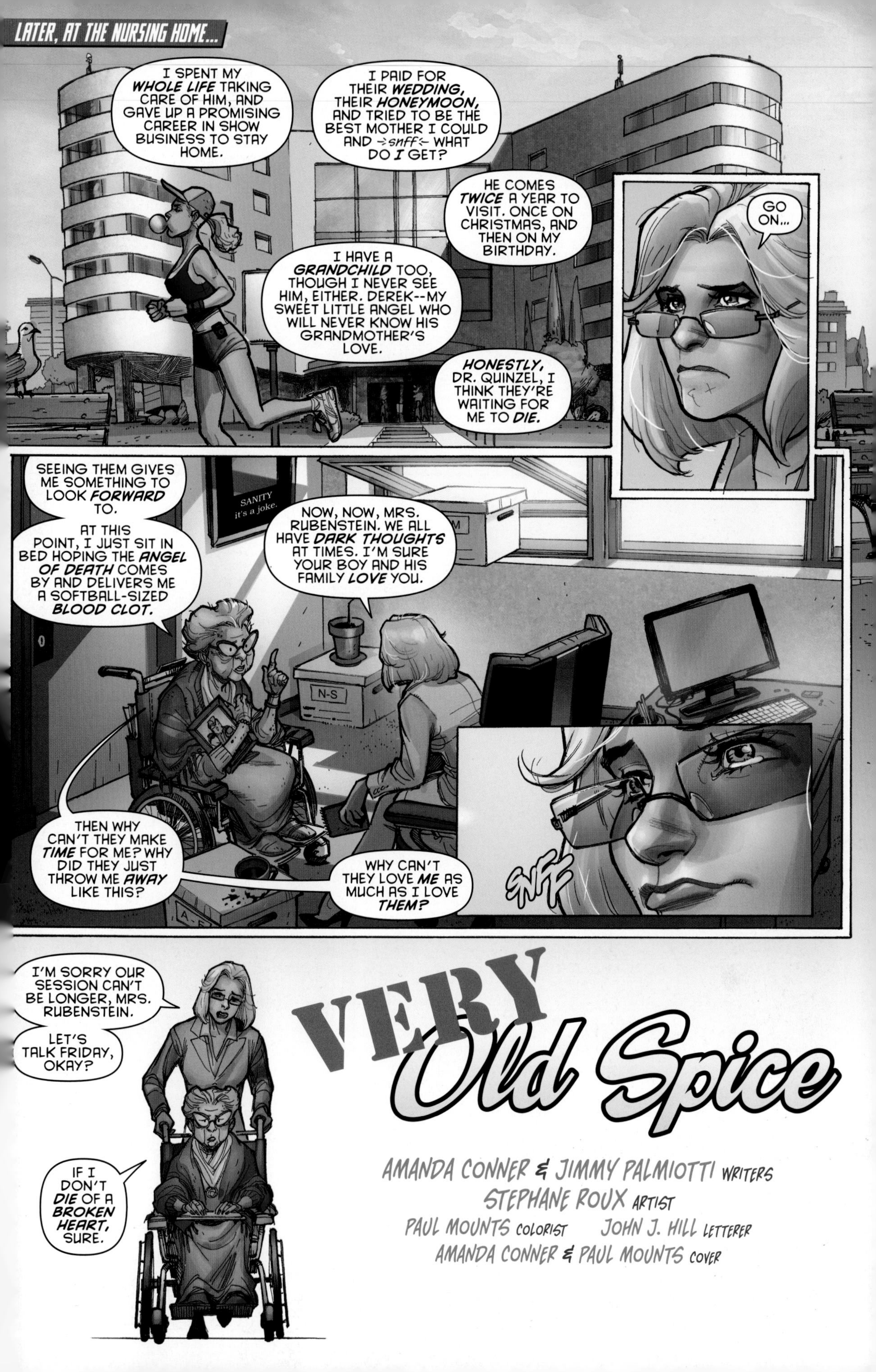
LATER, AT THE NURSING HOME...
I SPENT MY WHOLE LIFE TAKING CARE OF HIM, AND GAVE UP A PROMISING CAREER IN SHOW BUSINESS TO STAY HOME.
I PAID FOR THEIR WEDDING, THEIR HONEYMOON, AND TRIED TO BE THE BEST MOTHER I COULD AND -snff- WHAT DO I GET?
HE COMES TWICE A YEAR TO VISIT. ONCE ON CHRISTMAS, AND THEN ON MY BIRTHDAY.
I HAVE A GRANDCHILD TOO, THOUGH I NEVER SEE HIM, EITHER. DEREK--MY SWEET LITTLE ANGEL WHO WILL NEVER KNOW HIS GRANDMOTHER'S LOVE.
HONESTLY, DR. QUINZEL, I THINK THEY'RE WAITING FOR ME TO DIE.
GO ON...
SEEING THEM GIVES ME SOMETHING TO LOOK FORWARD TO.
AT THIS POINT, I JUST SIT IN BED HOPING THE ANGEL OF DEATH COMES BY AND DELIVERS ME A SOFTBALL-SIZED BLOOD CLOT.
SANITY it's a joke.
NOW, NOW, MRS. RUBENSTEIN. WE ALL HAVE DARK THOUGHTS AT TIMES. I'M SURE YOUR BOY AND HIS FAMILY LOVE YOU.
N-S
THEN WHY CAN'T THEY MAKE TIME FOR ME? WHY DID THEY JUST THROW ME AWAY LIKE THIS?
WHY CAN'T THEY LOVE ME AS MUCH AS I LOVE THEM?
SNFF
I'M SORRY OUR SESSION CAN'T BE LONGER, MRS. RUBENSTEIN.
LET'S TALK FRIDAY, OKAY?
IF I DON'T DIE OF A BROKEN HEART, SURE.
VERY Old Spice
AMANDA CONNER & JIMMY PALMIOTTI WRITERS
STEPHANE ROUX ARTIST
PAUL MOUNTS COLORIST JOHN J. HILL LETTERER
AMANDA CONNER & PAUL MOUNTS COVER

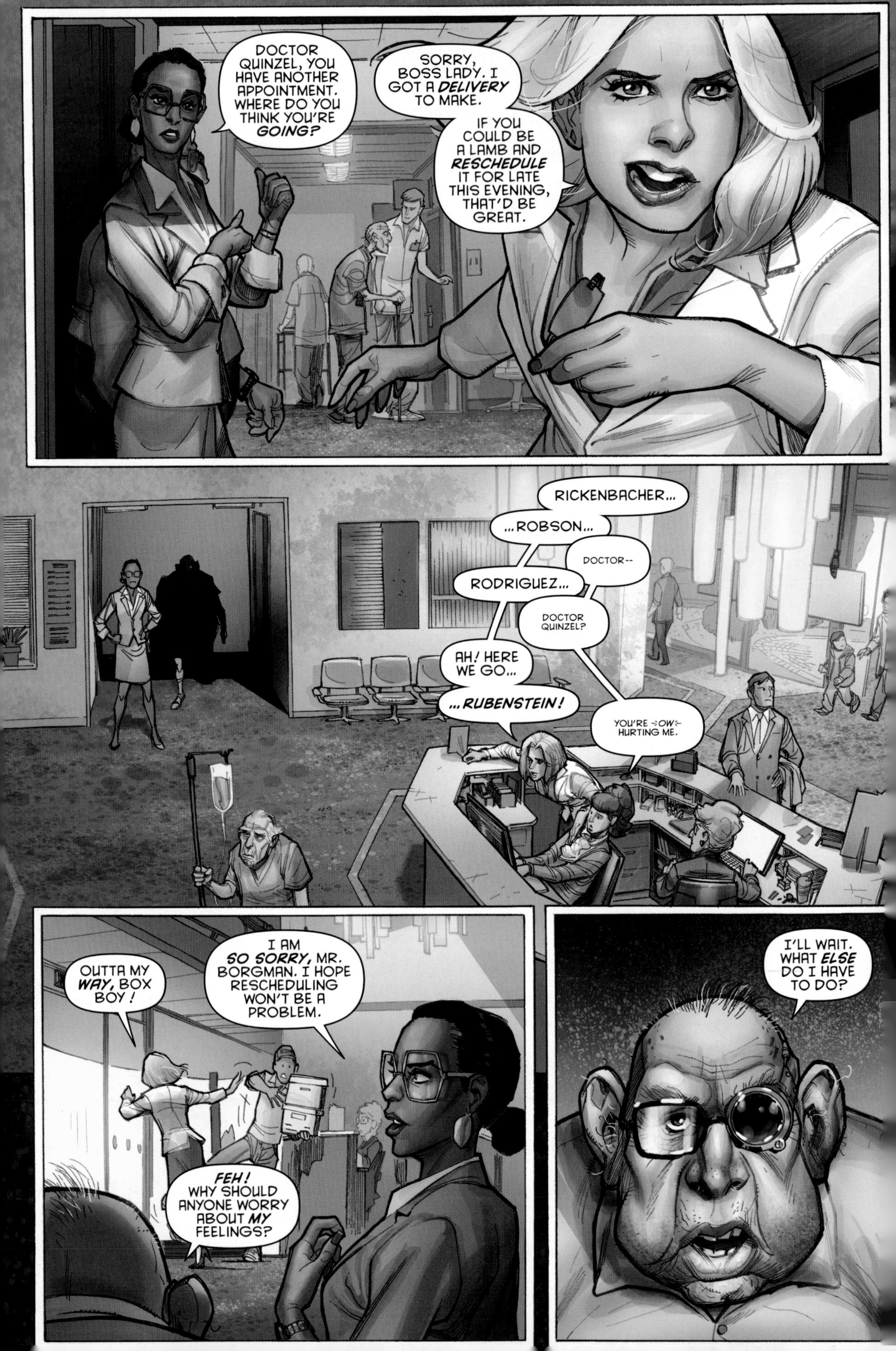
DOCTOR QUINZEL, YOU HAVE ANOTHER APPOINTMENT. WHERE DO YOU THINK YOU'RE GOING?
SORRY, BOSS LADY. I GOT A DELIVERY TO MAKE.
IF YOU COULD BE A LAMB AND RESCHEDULE IT FOR LATE THIS EVENING, THAT'D BE GREAT.
RICKENBACHER...
...ROBSON...
DOCTOR--
RODRIGUEZ...
DOCTOR QUINZEL?
AH! HERE WE GO...
...RUBENSTEIN!
YOU'RE =OW= HURTING ME.
OUTTA MY WAY, BOX BOY!
I AM SO SORRY, MR. BORGMAN. I HOPE RESCHEDULING WON'T BE A PROBLEM.
FEH! WHY SHOULD ANYONE WORRY ABOUT MY FEELINGS?
I'LL WAIT. WHAT ELSE DO I HAVE TO DO?

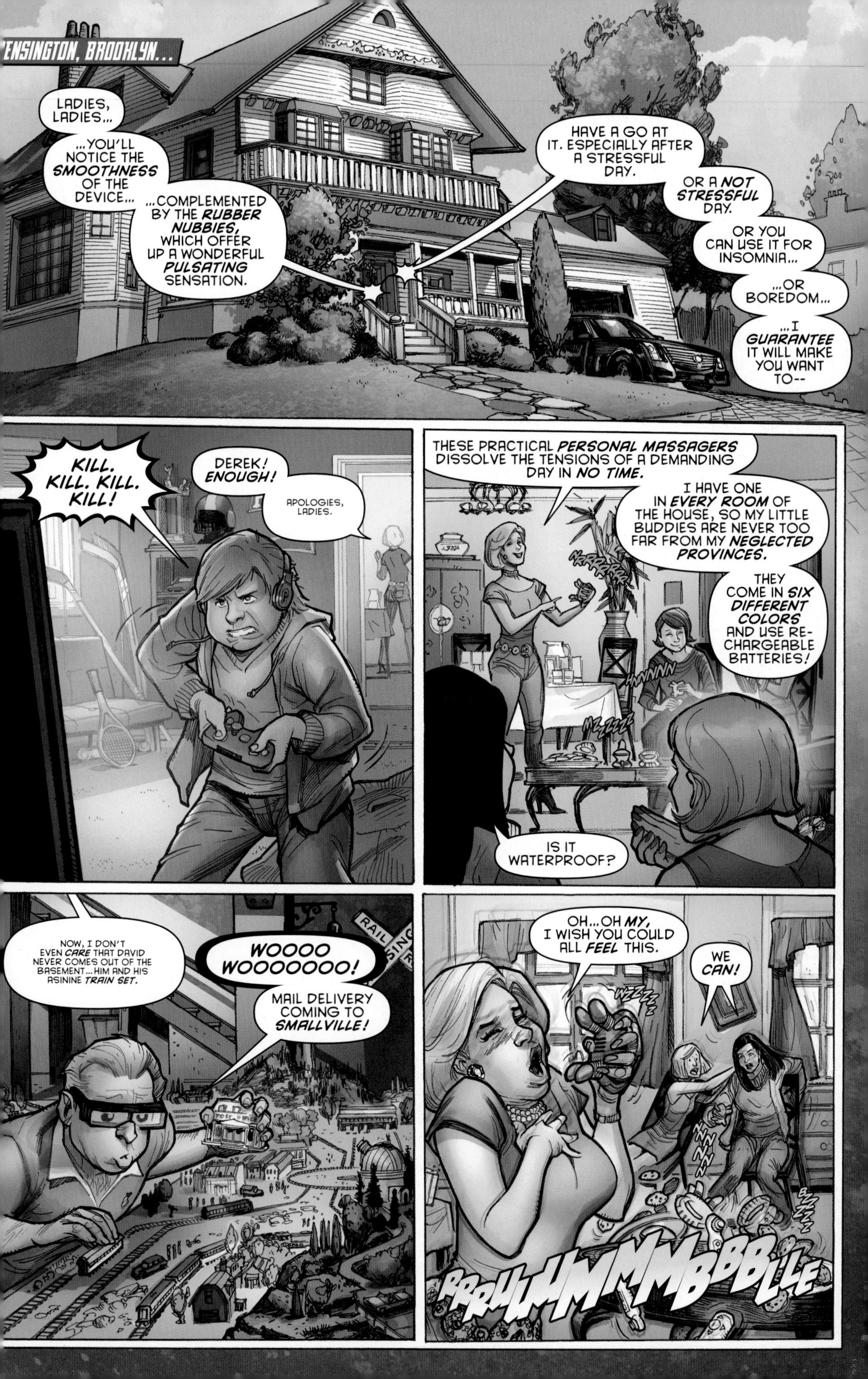
ENSINGTON, BROOKLYN...
LADIES, LADIES...
...YOU'LL NOTICE THE SMOOTHNESS OF THE DEVICE...
...COMPLEMENTED BY THE RUBBER NUBBIES, WHICH OFFER UP A WONDERFUL PULSATING SENSATION.
HAVE A GO AT IT. ESPECIALLY AFTER A STRESSFUL DAY.
OR A NOT STRESSFUL DAY.
OR YOU CAN USE IT FOR INSOMNIA...
...OR BOREDOM...
...I GUARANTEE IT WILL MAKE YOU WANT TO--
KILL. KILL. KILL. KILL!
DEREK! ENOUGH!
APOLOGIES, LADIES.
THESE PRACTICAL PERSONAL MASSAGERS DISSOLVE THE TENSIONS OF A DEMANDING DAY IN NO TIME.
I HAVE ONE IN EVERY ROOM OF THE HOUSE, SO MY LITTLE BUDDIES ARE NEVER TOO FAR FROM MY NEGLECTED PROVINCES.
THEY COME IN SIX DIFFERENT COLORS AND USE RE-CHARGEABLE BATTERIES!
IS IT WATERPROOF?
NOW, I DON'T EVEN CARE THAT DAVID NEVER COMES OUT OF THE BASEMENT...HIM AND HIS ASININE TRAIN SET.
WOOOO WOOOOOOO!
MAIL DELIVERY COMING TO SMALLVILLE!
RAIL
OH...OH MY, I WISH YOU COULD ALL FEEL THIS.
WE CAN!
PRRRUUMMMMBBBLLE

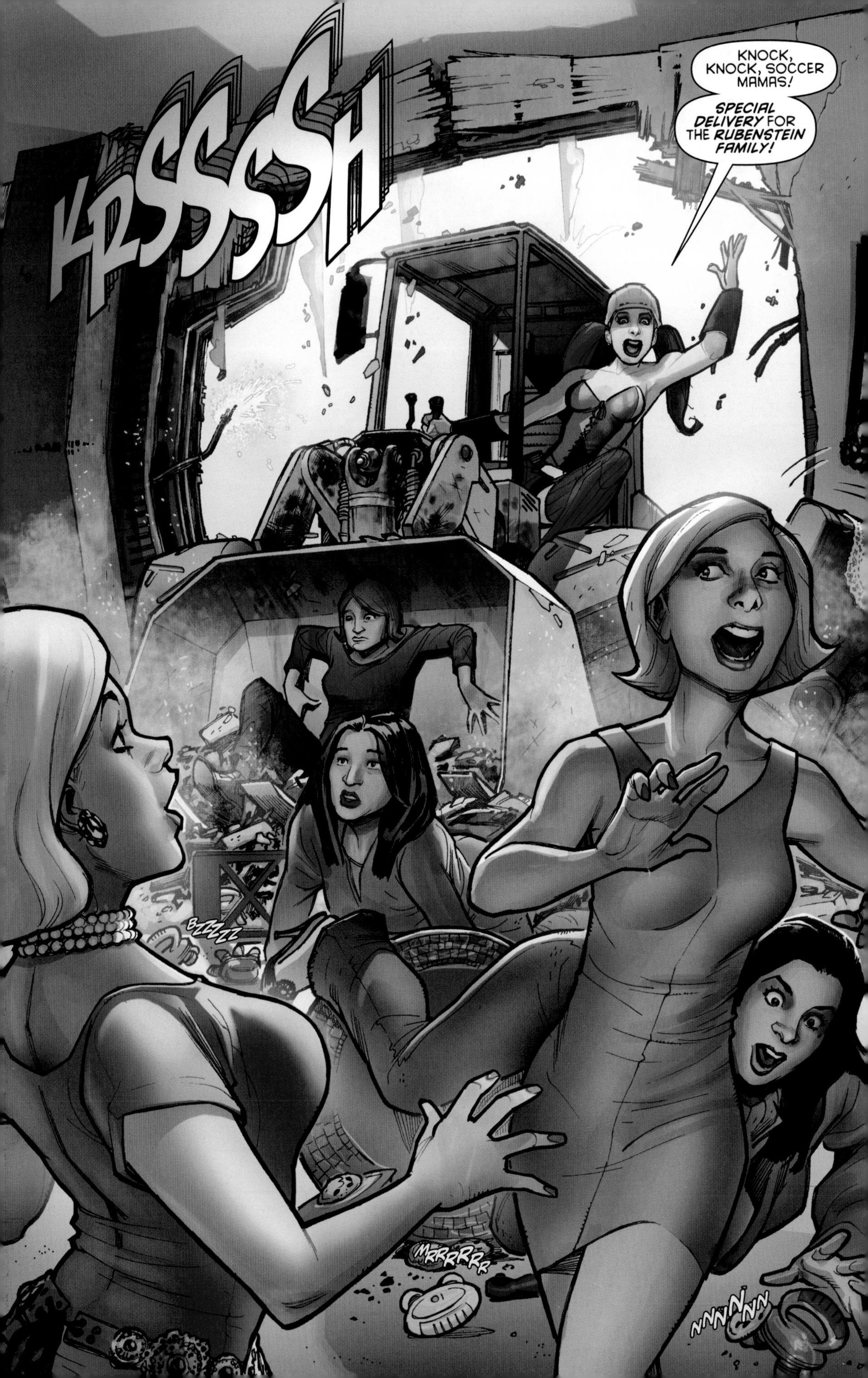
KRSSSSH
KNOCK, KNOCK, SOCCER MAMAS!
SPECIAL DELIVERY FOR THE RUBENSTEIN FAMILY!
BZZZZZZ
MRRRRRR
NNNNNN

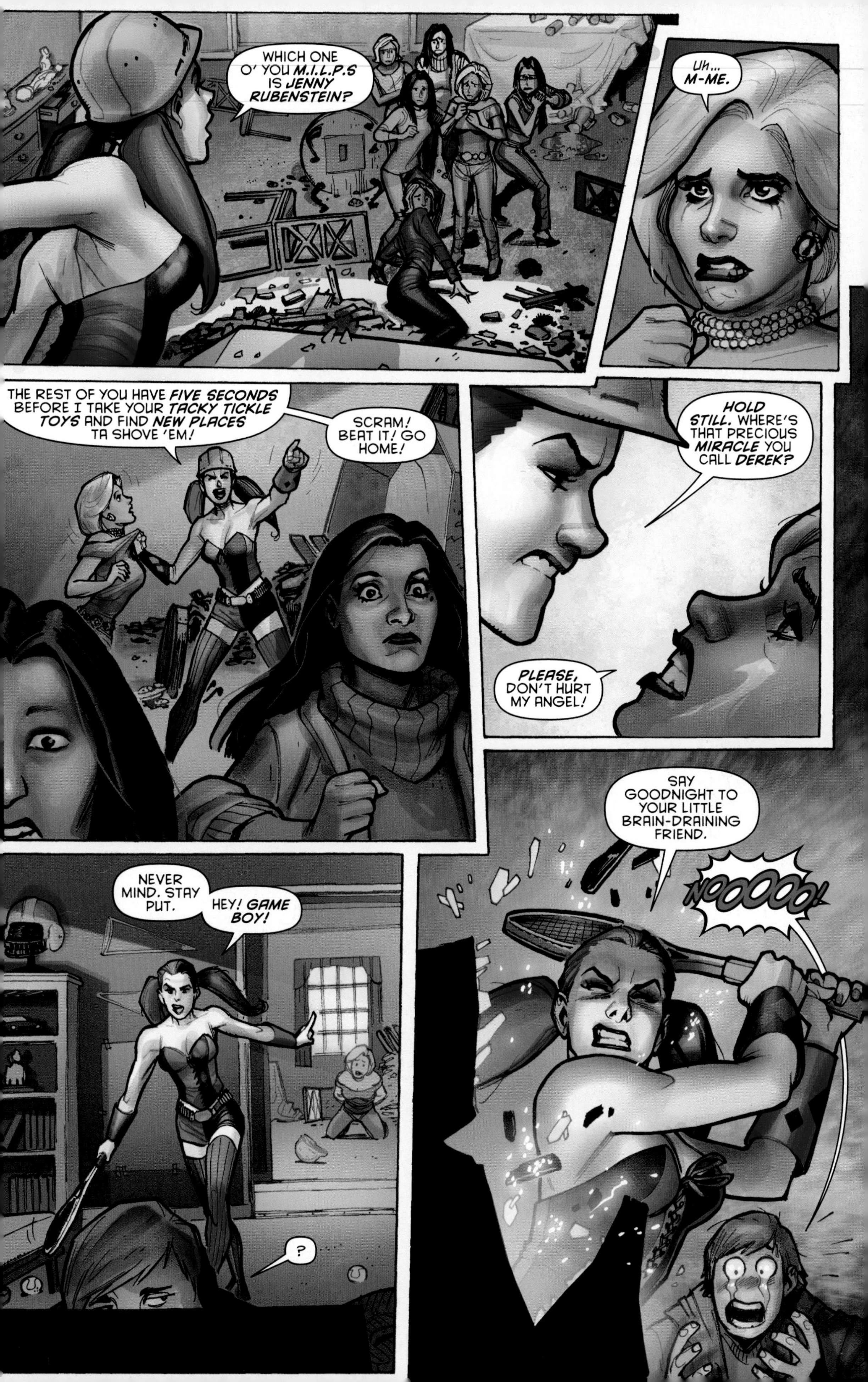
WHICH ONE O' YOU M.I.L.P.S IS JENNY RUBENSTEIN?
Uh... M-ME.
THE REST OF YOU HAVE FIVE SECONDS BEFORE I TAKE YOUR TACKY TICKLE TOYS AND FIND NEW PLACES TA SHOVE 'EM!
SCRAM! BEAT IT! GO HOME!
HOLD STILL. WHERE'S THAT PRECIOUS MIRACLE YOU CALL DEREK?
PLEASE, DON'T HURT MY ANGEL!
NEVER MIND. STAY PUT.
HEY! GAME BOY!
?
SAY GOODNIGHT TO YOUR LITTLE BRAIN-DRAINING FRIEND.
NOOOOO!

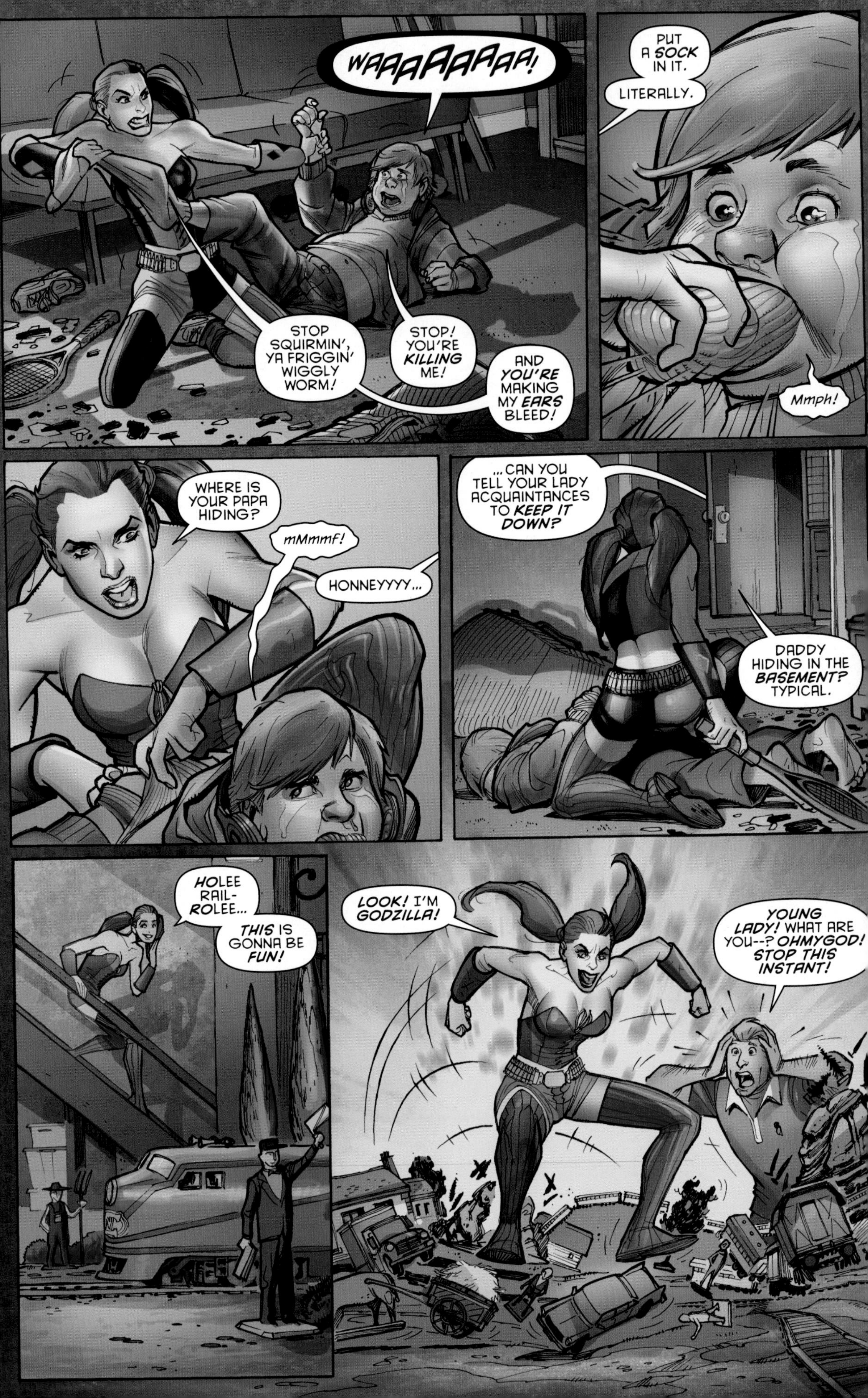
WAAAAAAAA!
STOP SQUIRMIN', YA FRIGGIN' WIGGLY WORM!
STOP! YOU'RE KILLING ME!
AND YOU'RE MAKING MY EARS BLEED!
PUT A SOCK IN IT.
LITERALLY.
Mmph!
WHERE IS YOUR PAPA HIDING?
mMmmf!
HONNEYYYY...
...CAN YOU TELL YOUR LADY ACQUAINTANCES TO KEEP IT DOWN?
DADDY HIDING IN THE BASEMENT? TYPICAL.
HOLEE RAIL-ROLEE...
THIS IS GONNA BE FUN!
LOOK! I'M GODZILLA!
YOUNG LADY! WHAT ARE YOU--? OHMYGOD! STOP THIS INSTANT!

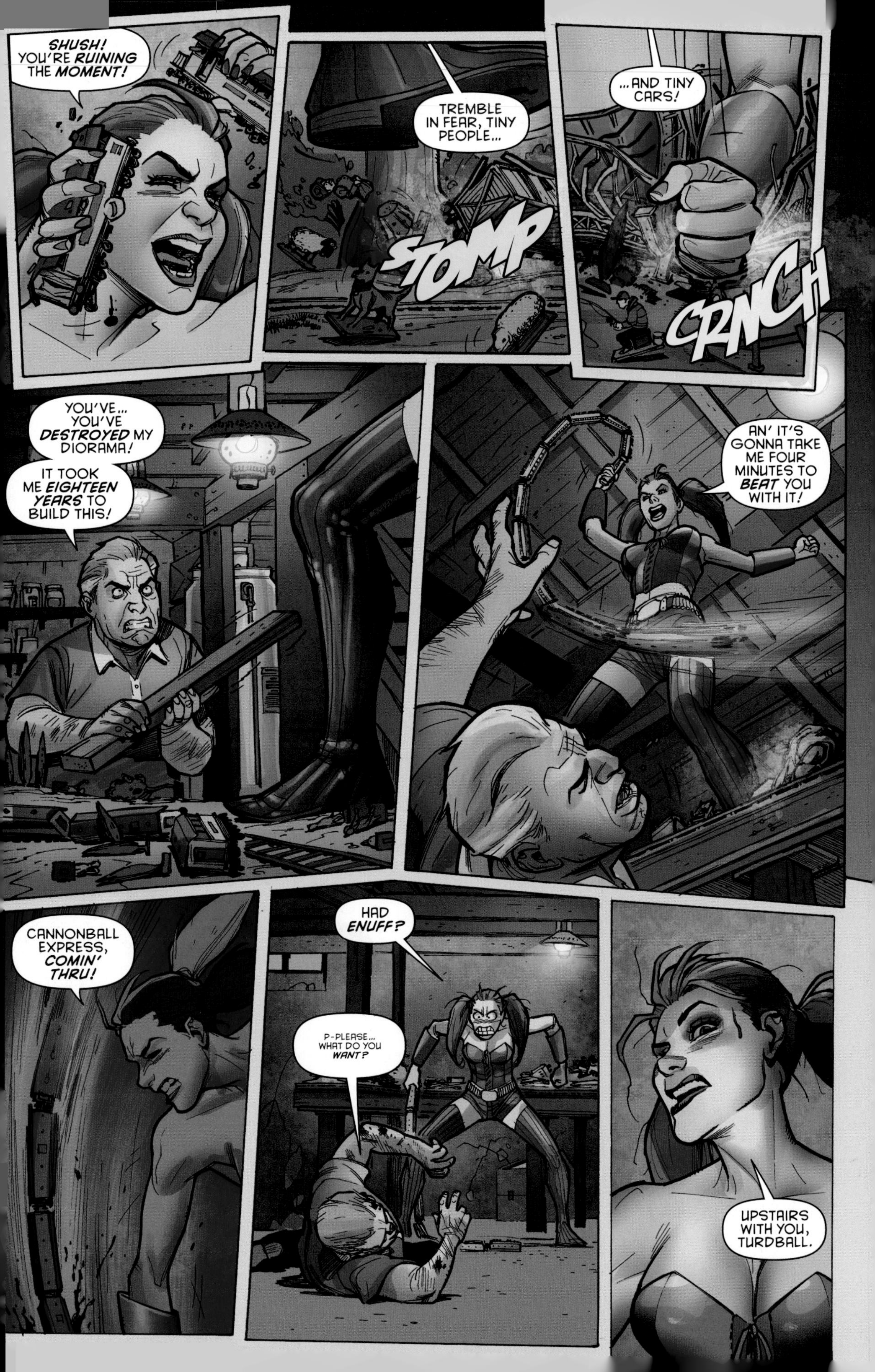
SHUSH! YOU'RE RUINING THE MOMENT!
TREMBLE IN FEAR, TINY PEOPLE...
STOMP
...AND TINY CARS!
CRNCH
YOU'VE... YOU'VE DESTROYED MY DIORAMA!
IT TOOK ME EIGHTEEN YEARS TO BUILD THIS!
AN' IT'S GONNA TAKE ME FOUR MINUTES TO BEAT YOU WITH IT!
CANNONBALL EXPRESS, COMIN' THRU!
HAD ENUFF?
P-PLEASE... WHAT DO YOU WANT?
UPSTAIRS WITH YOU, TURDBALL.

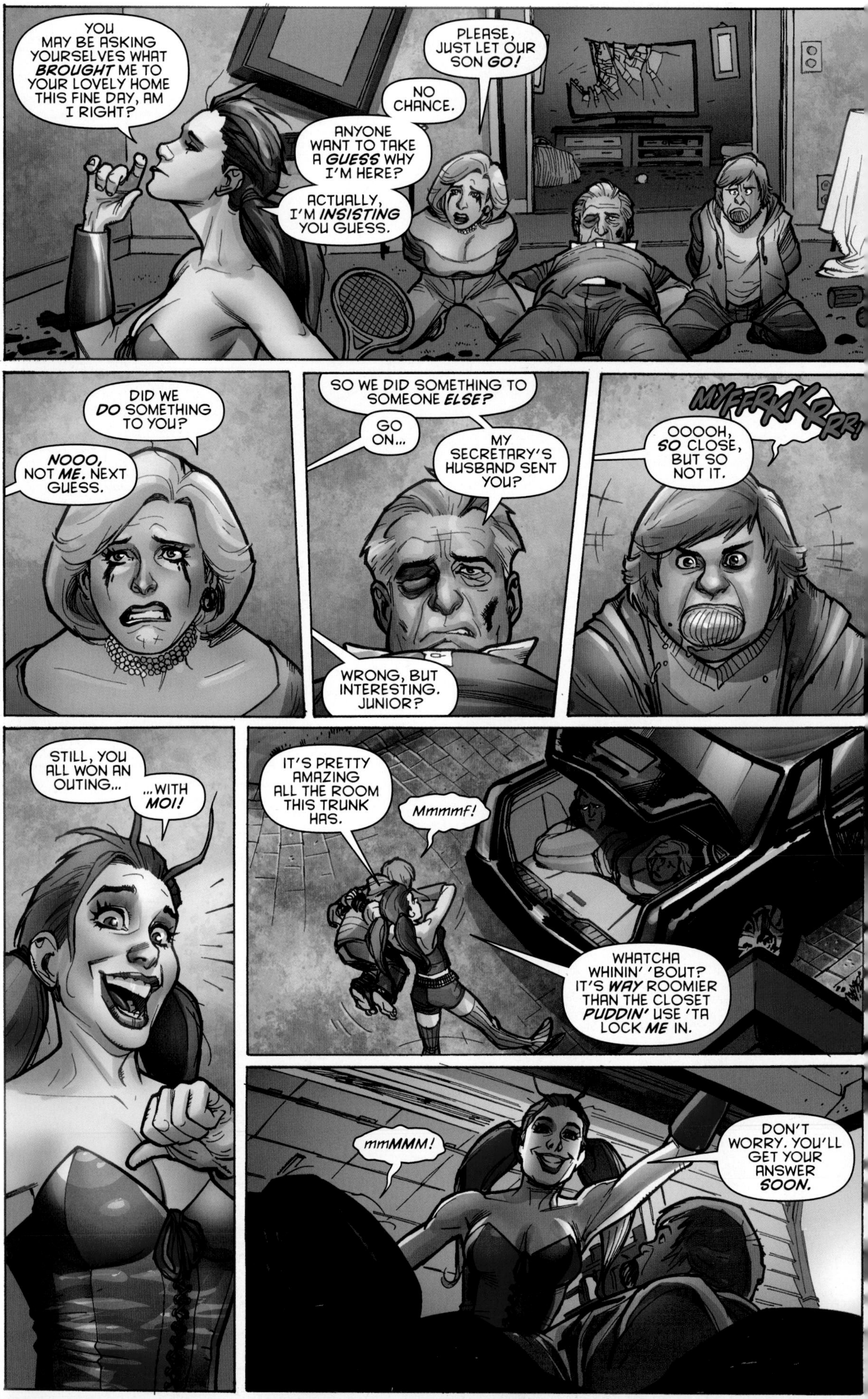

YOU MAY BE ASKING YOURSELVES WHAT BROUGHT ME TO YOUR LOVELY HOME THIS FINE DAY, AM I RIGHT?
PLEASE, JUST LET OUR SON GO!
NO CHANCE.
ANYONE WANT TO TAKE A GUESS WHY I'M HERE?
ACTUALLY, I'M INSISTING YOU GUESS.
DID WE DO SOMETHING TO YOU?
NOOO, NOT ME. NEXT GUESS.
SO WE DID SOMETHING TO SOMEONE ELSE?
GO ON...
MY SECRETARY'S HUSBAND SENT YOU?
WRONG, BUT INTERESTING. JUNIOR?
MYFFRKKRRR!
OOOOH, SO CLOSE, BUT SO NOT IT.
STILL, YOU ALL WON AN OUTING...
...WITH MOI!
IT'S PRETTY AMAZING ALL THE ROOM THIS TRUNK HAS.
Mmmmf!
WHATCHA WHININ' 'BOUT? IT'S WAY ROOMIER THAN THE CLOSET PUDDIN' USE 'TA LOCK ME IN.
mmMMM!
DON'T WORRY. YOU'LL GET YOUR ANSWER SOON.

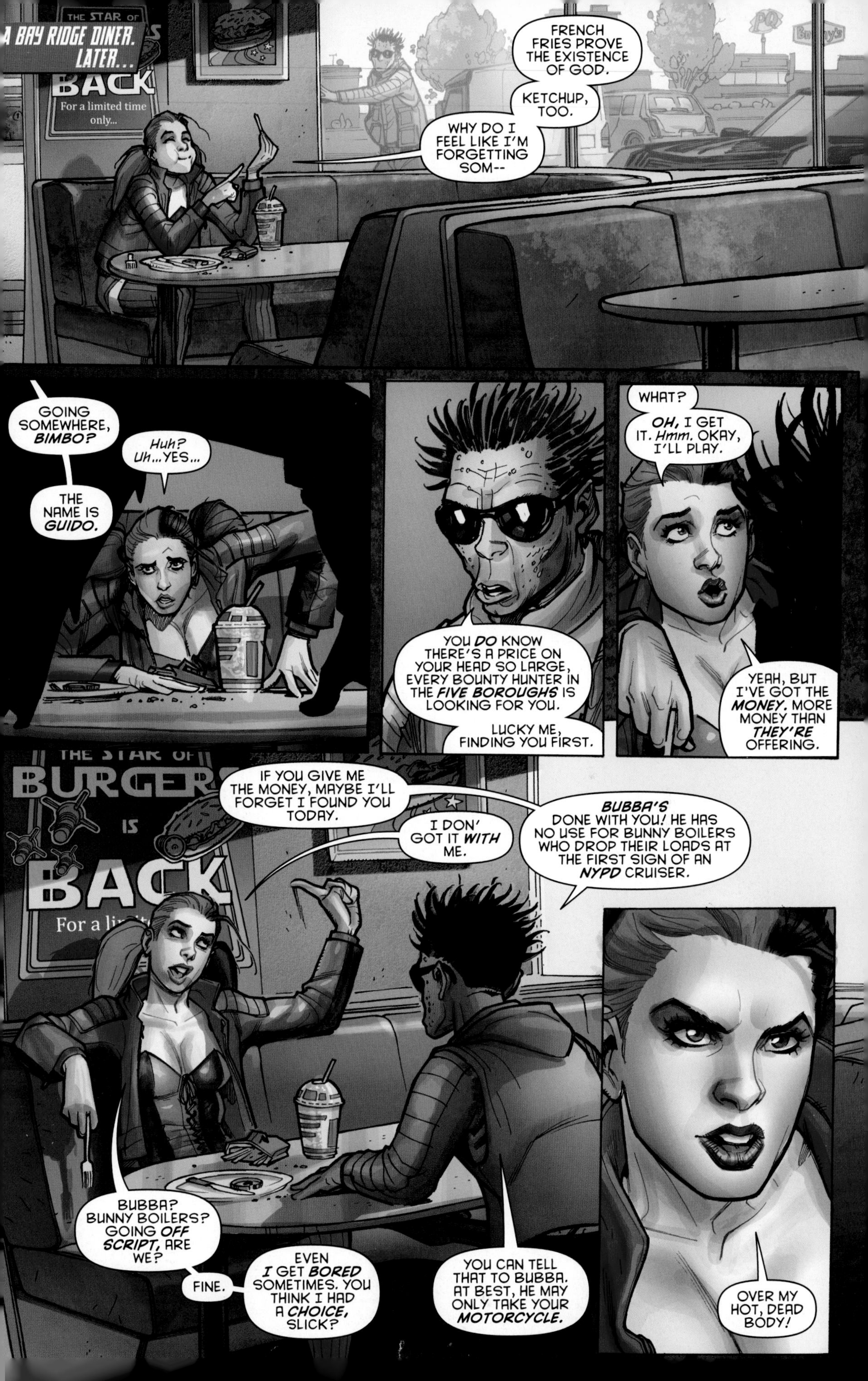

A BAY RIDGE DINER. LATER...
THE STAR OF
BACK
For a limited time only...
FRENCH FRIES PROVE THE EXISTENCE OF GOD.
KETCHUP, TOO.
WHY DO I FEEL LIKE I'M FORGETTING SOM--
GOING SOMEWHERE, BIMBO?
Huh? Uh...YES...
THE NAME IS GUIDO.
YOU DO KNOW THERE'S A PRICE ON YOUR HEAD SO LARGE, EVERY BOUNTY HUNTER IN THE FIVE BOROUGHS IS LOOKING FOR YOU.
LUCKY ME, FINDING YOU FIRST.
WHAT?
OH, I GET IT. Hmm. OKAY, I'LL PLAY.
YEAH, BUT I'VE GOT THE MONEY. MORE MONEY THAN THEY'RE OFFERING.
THE STAR OF
BURGERS
IS
BACK
For a li
IF YOU GIVE ME THE MONEY, MAYBE I'LL FORGET I FOUND YOU TODAY.
I DON' GOT IT WITH ME.
BUBBA'S DONE WITH YOU! HE HAS NO USE FOR BUNNY BOILERS WHO DROP THEIR LOADS AT THE FIRST SIGN OF AN NYPD CRUISER.
BUBBA? BUNNY BOILERS? GOING OFF SCRIPT, ARE WE?
FINE.
EVEN I GET BORED SOMETIMES. YOU THINK I HAD A CHOICE, SLICK?
YOU CAN TELL THAT TO BUBBA. AT BEST, HE MAY ONLY TAKE YOUR MOTORCYCLE.
OVER MY HOT, DEAD BODY!

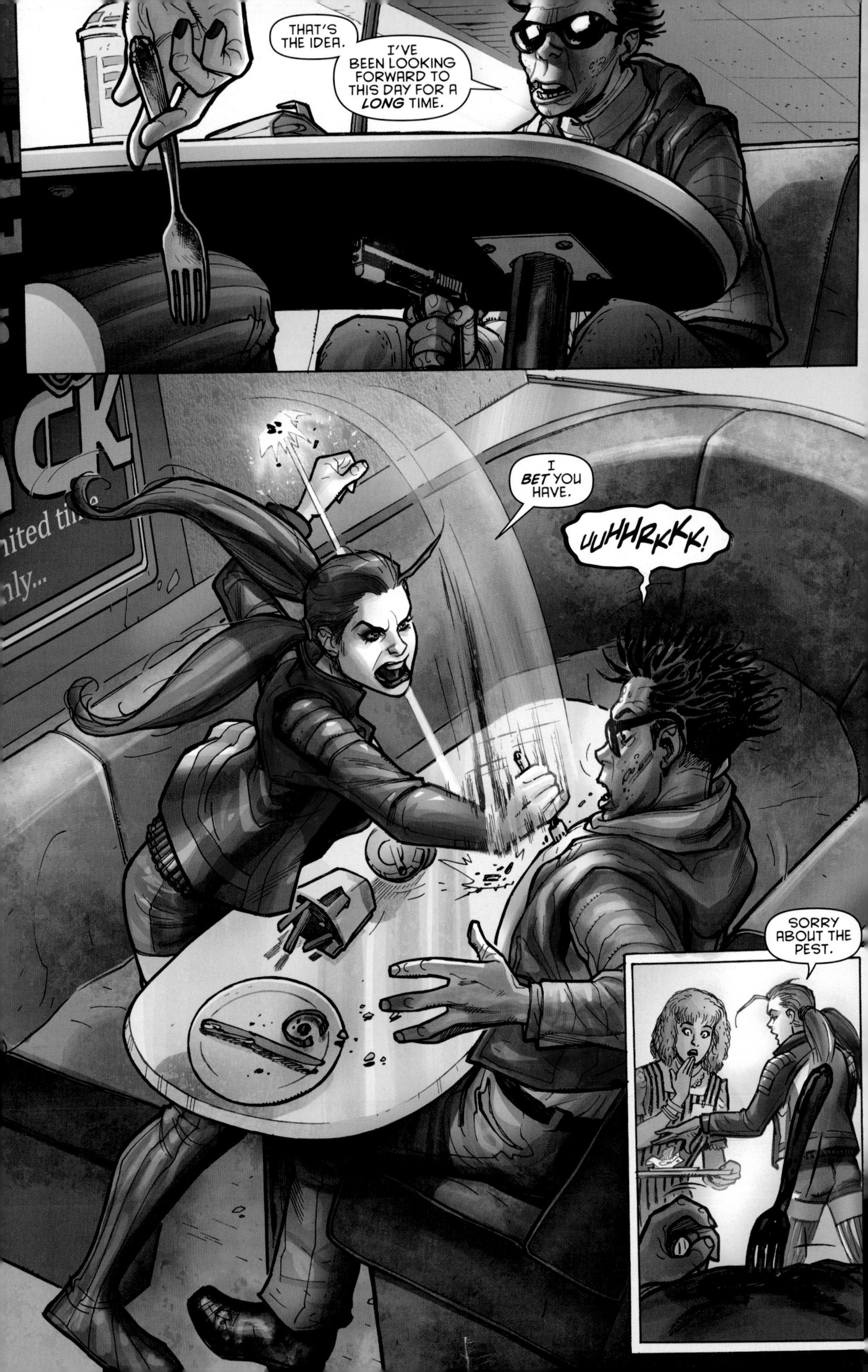
THAT'S THE IDEA.
I'VE BEEN LOOKING FORWARD TO THIS DAY FOR A *LONG* TIME.
I *BET* YOU HAVE.
UUHHRKKK!
SORRY ABOUT THE PEST.

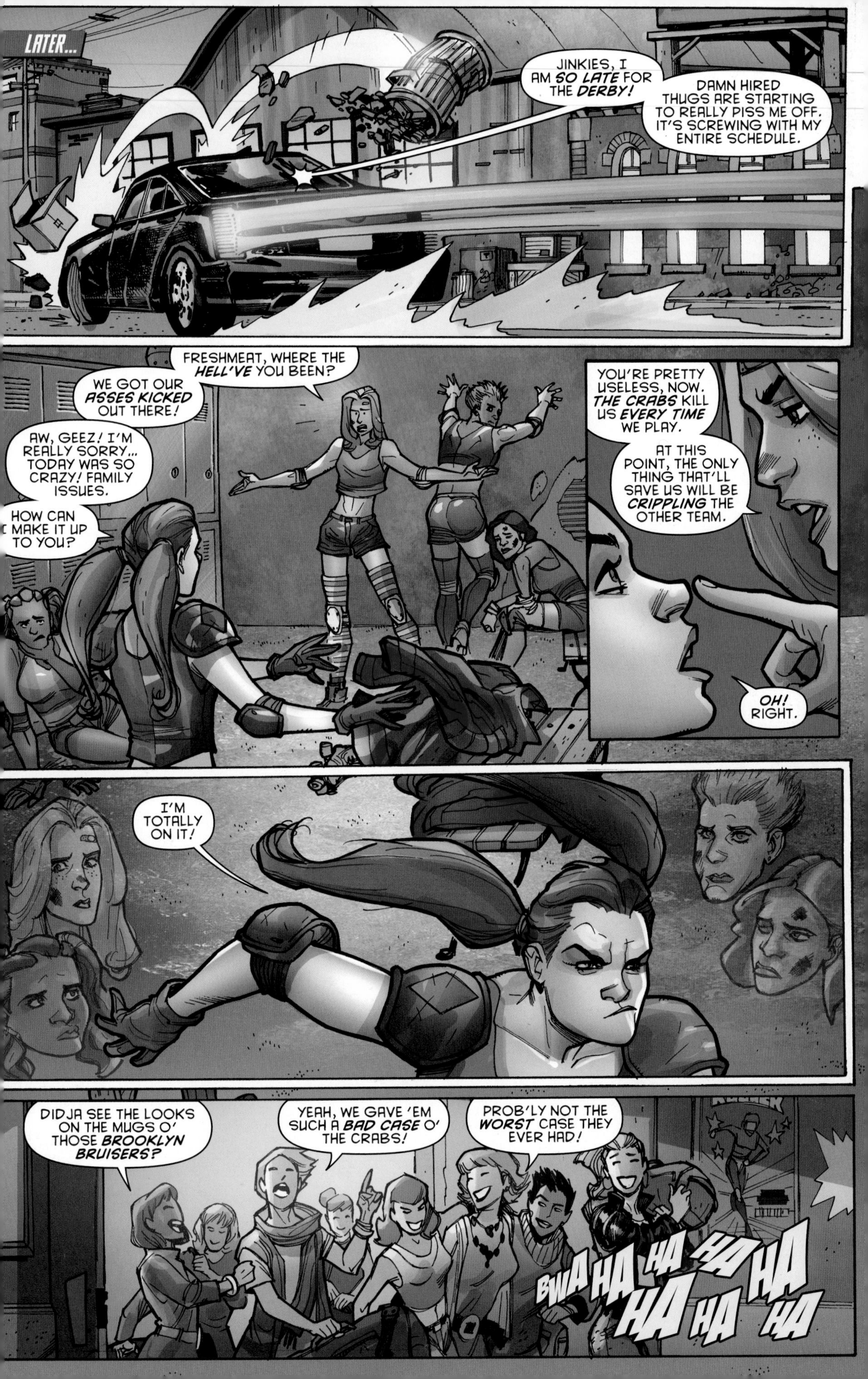

LATER...
JINKIES, I AM SO LATE FOR THE DERBY!
DAMN HIRED THUGS ARE STARTING TO REALLY PISS ME OFF. IT'S SCREWING WITH MY ENTIRE SCHEDULE.
FRESHMEAT, WHERE THE HELL'VE YOU BEEN?
WE GOT OUR ASSES KICKED OUT THERE!
AW, GEEZ! I'M REALLY SORRY... TODAY WAS SO CRAZY! FAMILY ISSUES.
HOW CAN I MAKE IT UP TO YOU?
YOU'RE PRETTY USELESS, NOW. THE CRABS KILL US EVERY TIME WE PLAY.
AT THIS POINT, THE ONLY THING THAT'LL SAVE US WILL BE CRIPPLING THE OTHER TEAM.
OH! RIGHT.
I'M TOTALLY ON IT!
DIDJA SEE THE LOOKS ON THE MUGS O' THOSE BROOKLYN BRUISERS?
YEAH, WE GAVE 'EM SUCH A BAD CASE O' THE CRABS!
PROB'LY NOT THE WORST CASE THEY EVER HAD!
BWAHA HA HA HA HA HA HA HA HA

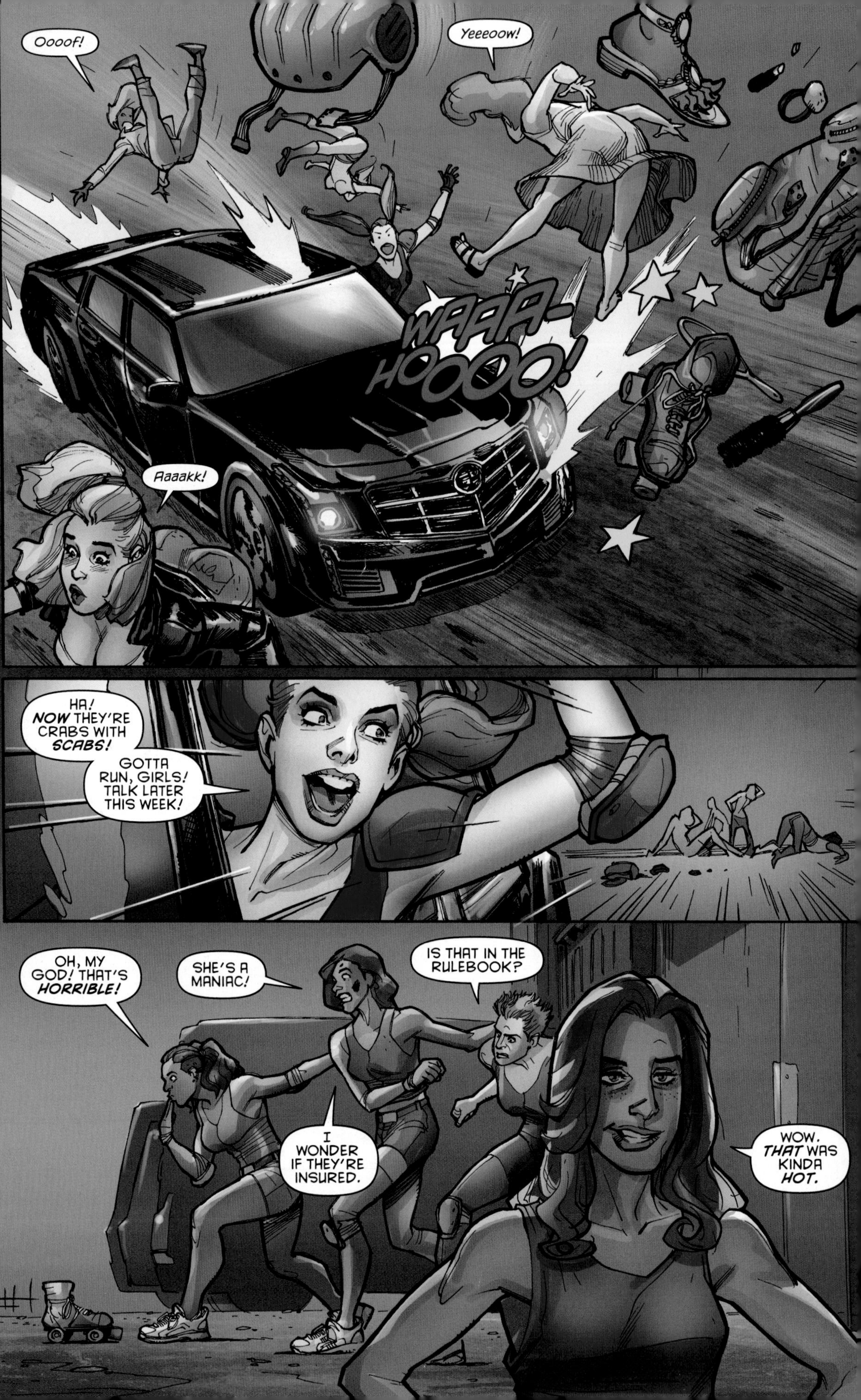
Ooooof!
Yeeeoow!
WAAA-HOOOO!
Aaaakk!
HA! NOW THEY'RE CRABS WITH SCABS!
GOTTA RUN, GIRLS! TALK LATER THIS WEEK!
OH, MY GOD! THAT'S HORRIBLE!
SHE'S A MANIAC!
IS THAT IN THE RULEBOOK?
I WONDER IF THEY'RE INSURED.
WOW. THAT WAS KINDA HOT.

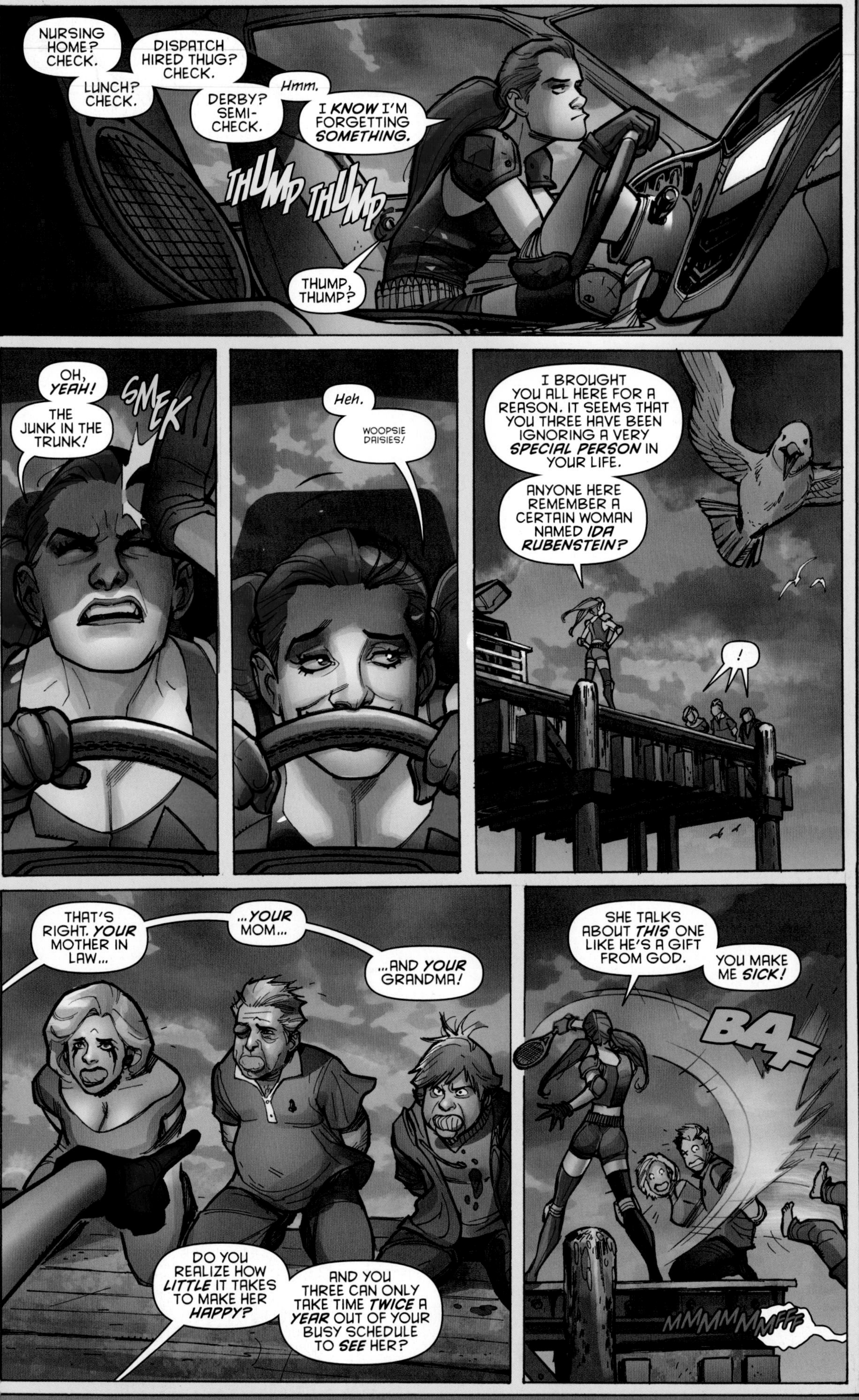

NURSING HOME? CHECK.
LUNCH? CHECK.
DISPATCH HIRED THUG? CHECK.
DERBY? SEMI-CHECK.
Hmm.
I KNOW I'M FORGETTING SOMETHING.
THUMP THUMP
THUMP, THUMP?
OH, YEAH!
THE JUNK IN THE TRUNK!
SMEK
Heh.
WOOPSIE DAISIES!
I BROUGHT YOU ALL HERE FOR A REASON. IT SEEMS THAT YOU THREE HAVE BEEN IGNORING A VERY SPECIAL PERSON IN YOUR LIFE.
ANYONE HERE REMEMBER A CERTAIN WOMAN NAMED IDA RUBENSTEIN?
!
THAT'S RIGHT. YOUR MOTHER IN LAW...
...YOUR MOM...
...AND YOUR GRANDMA!
DO YOU REALIZE HOW LITTLE IT TAKES TO MAKE HER HAPPY?
AND YOU THREE CAN ONLY TAKE TIME TWICE A YEAR OUT OF YOUR BUSY SCHEDULE TO SEE HER?
SHE TALKS ABOUT THIS ONE LIKE HE'S A GIFT FROM GOD.
YOU MAKE ME SICK!
BAF
MMMMMMMFFF

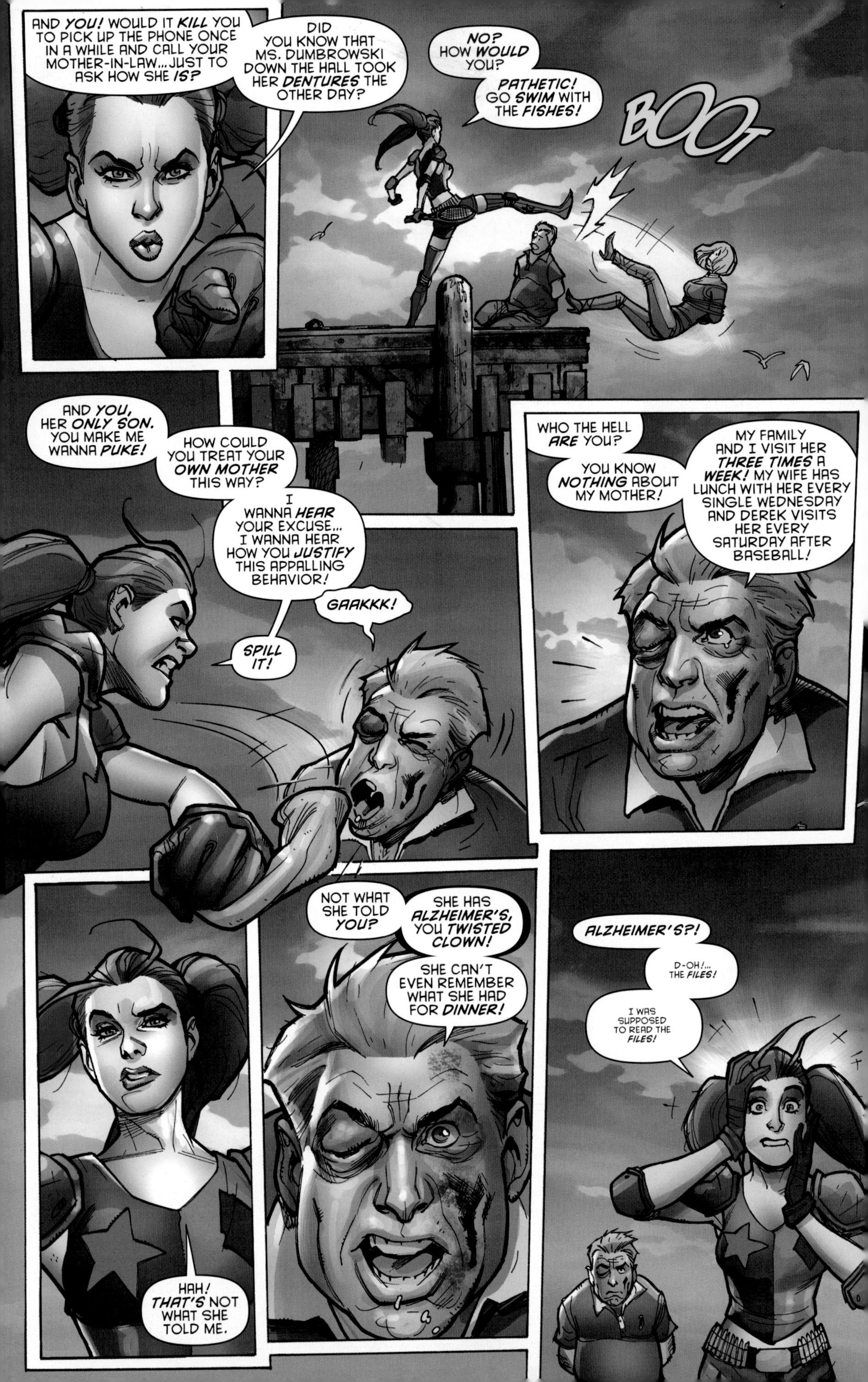
AND YOU! WOULD IT KILL YOU TO PICK UP THE PHONE ONCE IN A WHILE AND CALL YOUR MOTHER-IN-LAW...JUST TO ASK HOW SHE IS?
DID YOU KNOW THAT MS. DUMBROWSKI DOWN THE HALL TOOK HER DENTURES THE OTHER DAY?
NO? HOW WOULD YOU?
PATHETIC! GO SWIM WITH THE FISHES!
BOOT
AND YOU, HER ONLY SON. YOU MAKE ME WANNA PUKE!
HOW COULD YOU TREAT YOUR OWN MOTHER THIS WAY?
I WANNA HEAR YOUR EXCUSE... I WANNA HEAR HOW YOU JUSTIFY THIS APPALLING BEHAVIOR!
SPILL IT!
GAAKKK!
WHO THE HELL ARE YOU?
YOU KNOW NOTHING ABOUT MY MOTHER!
MY FAMILY AND I VISIT HER THREE TIMES A WEEK! MY WIFE HAS LUNCH WITH HER EVERY SINGLE WEDNESDAY AND DEREK VISITS HER EVERY SATURDAY AFTER BASEBALL!
HAH! THAT'S NOT WHAT SHE TOLD ME.
NOT WHAT SHE TOLD YOU?
SHE HAS ALZHEIMER'S, YOU TWISTED CLOWN!
SHE CAN'T EVEN REMEMBER WHAT SHE HAD FOR DINNER!
ALZHEIMER'S?!
D-OH!... THE FILES!
I WAS SUPPOSED TO READ THE FILES!

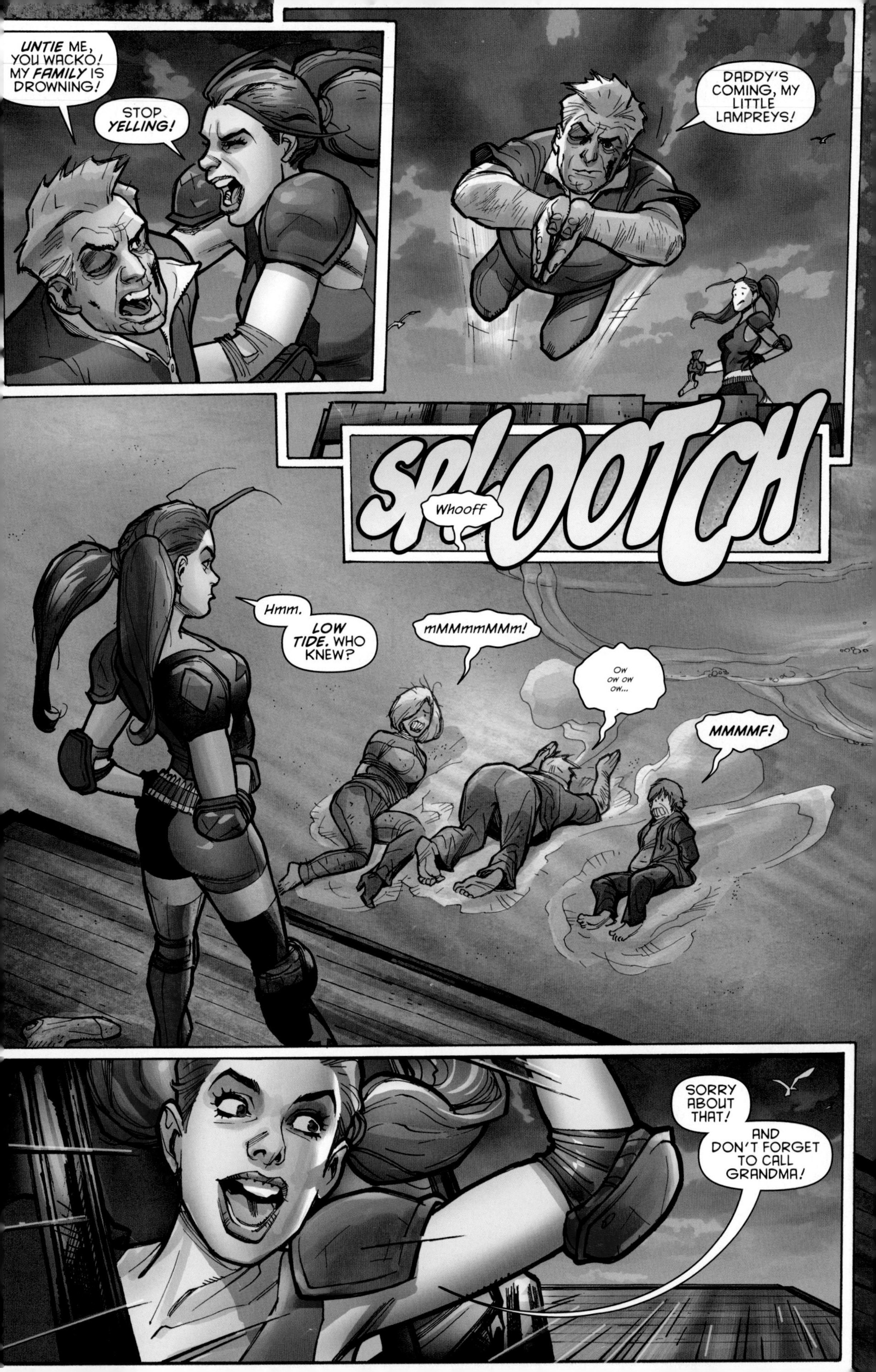
UNTIE ME, YOU WACKO! MY FAMILY IS DROWNING!
STOP YELLING!
DADDY'S COMING, MY LITTLE LAMPREYS!
SPLOOTCH
Whooff
Hmm. LOW TIDE. WHO KNEW?
mMMmmMMm!
Ow ow ow ow...
MMMMF!
SORRY ABOUT THAT!
AND DON'T FORGET TO CALL GRANDMA!

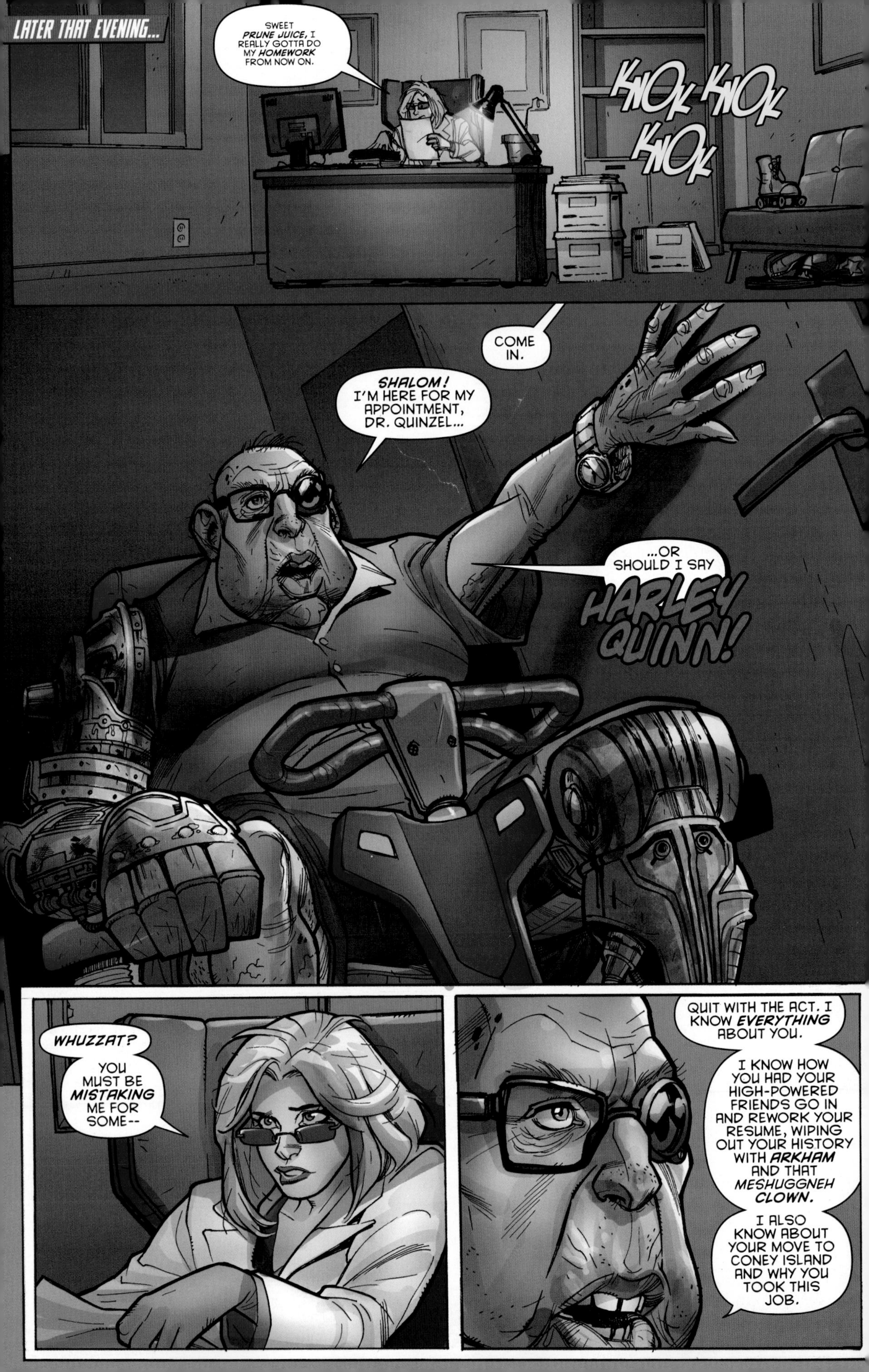
LATER THAT EVENING...
SWEET PRUNE JUICE, I REALLY GOTTA DO MY HOMEWORK FROM NOW ON.
KNOK KNOK KNOK
COME IN.
SHALOM! I'M HERE FOR MY APPOINTMENT, DR. QUINZEL...
...OR SHOULD I SAY HARLEY QUINN!
WHUZZAT?
YOU MUST BE MISTAKING ME FOR SOME--
QUIT WITH THE ACT. I KNOW EVERYTHING ABOUT YOU.
I KNOW HOW YOU HAD YOUR HIGH-POWERED FRIENDS GO IN AND REWORK YOUR RESUME, WIPING OUT YOUR HISTORY WITH ARKHAM AND THAT MESHUGGNEH CLOWN.
I ALSO KNOW ABOUT YOUR MOVE TO CONEY ISLAND AND WHY YOU TOOK THIS JOB.

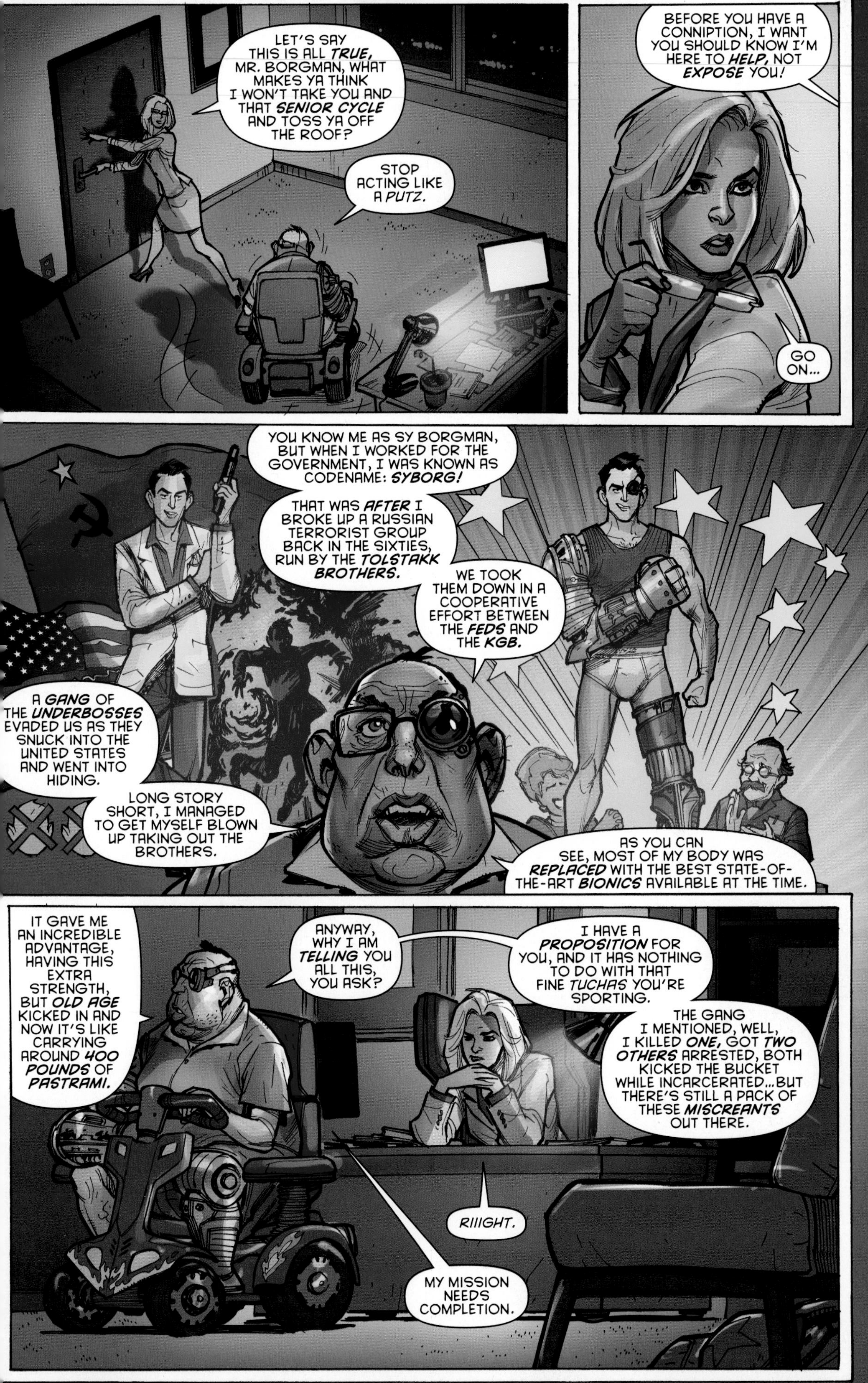
LET'S SAY THIS IS ALL TRUE, MR. BORGMAN, WHAT MAKES YA THINK I WON'T TAKE YOU AND THAT SENIOR CYCLE AND TOSS YA OFF THE ROOF?
STOP ACTING LIKE A PUTZ.
BEFORE YOU HAVE A CONNIPTION, I WANT YOU SHOULD KNOW I'M HERE TO HELP, NOT EXPOSE YOU!
GO ON...
YOU KNOW ME AS SY BORGMAN, BUT WHEN I WORKED FOR THE GOVERNMENT, I WAS KNOWN AS CODENAME: SYBORG!
THAT WAS AFTER I BROKE UP A RUSSIAN TERRORIST GROUP BACK IN THE SIXTIES, RUN BY THE TOLSTAKK BROTHERS.
WE TOOK THEM DOWN IN A COOPERATIVE EFFORT BETWEEN THE FEDS AND THE KGB.
A GANG OF THE UNDERBOSSES EVADED US AS THEY SNUCK INTO THE UNITED STATES AND WENT INTO HIDING.
LONG STORY SHORT, I MANAGED TO GET MYSELF BLOWN UP TAKING OUT THE BROTHERS.
AS YOU CAN SEE, MOST OF MY BODY WAS REPLACED WITH THE BEST STATE-OF-THE-ART BIONICS AVAILABLE AT THE TIME.
IT GAVE ME AN INCREDIBLE ADVANTAGE, HAVING THIS EXTRA STRENGTH, BUT OLD AGE KICKED IN AND NOW IT'S LIKE CARRYING AROUND 400 POUNDS OF PASTRAMI.
ANYWAY, WHY I AM TELLING YOU ALL THIS, YOU ASK?
I HAVE A PROPOSITION FOR YOU, AND IT HAS NOTHING TO DO WITH THAT FINE TUCHAS YOU'RE SPORTING.
THE GANG I MENTIONED, WELL, I KILLED ONE, GOT TWO OTHERS ARRESTED, BOTH KICKED THE BUCKET WHILE INCARCERATED...BUT THERE'S STILL A PACK OF THESE MISCREANTS OUT THERE.
RIIIGHT.
MY MISSION NEEDS COMPLETION.

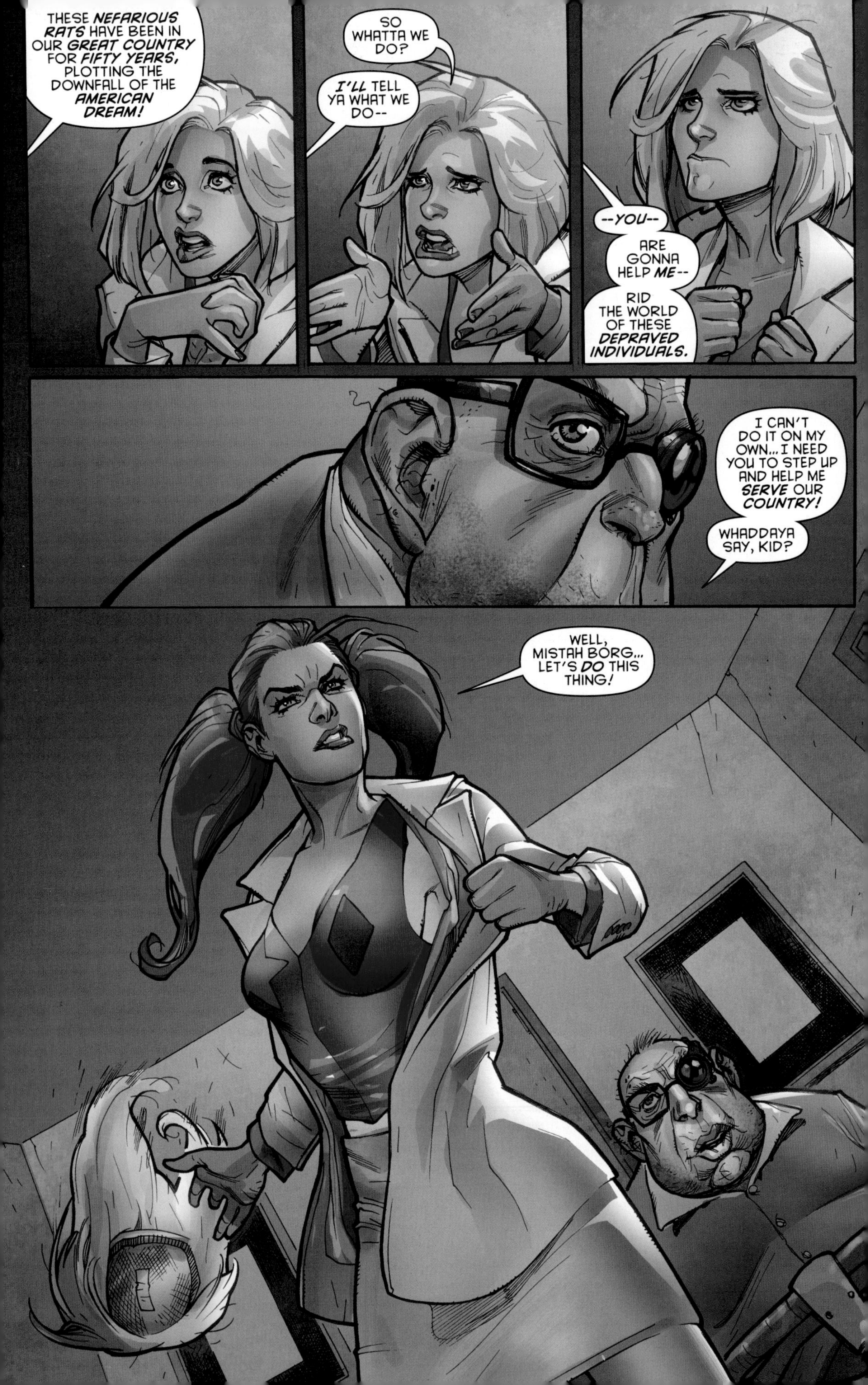
THESE NEFARIOUS RATS HAVE BEEN IN OUR GREAT COUNTRY FOR FIFTY YEARS, PLOTTING THE DOWNFALL OF THE AMERICAN DREAM!
SO WHATTA WE DO?
I'LL TELL YA WHAT WE DO--
--YOU--
ARE GONNA HELP ME--
RID THE WORLD OF THESE DEPRAVED INDIVIDUALS.
I CAN'T DO IT ON MY OWN... I NEED YOU TO STEP UP AND HELP ME SERVE OUR COUNTRY!
WHADDAYA SAY, KID?
WELL, MISTAH BORG... LET'S DO THIS THING!

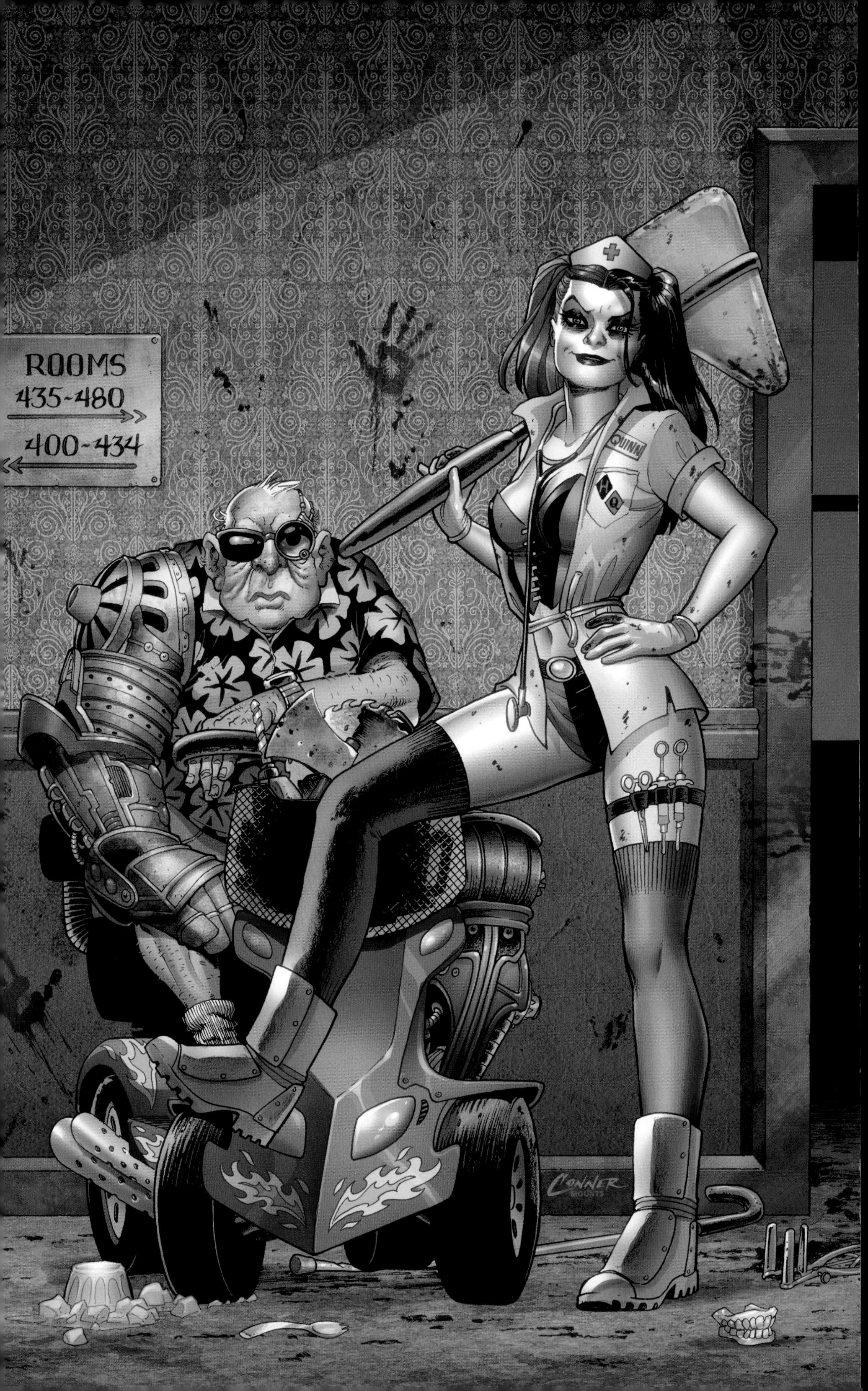
ROOMS
435-480
400-434
QUINN
HQ
CONNER
MOUNTS

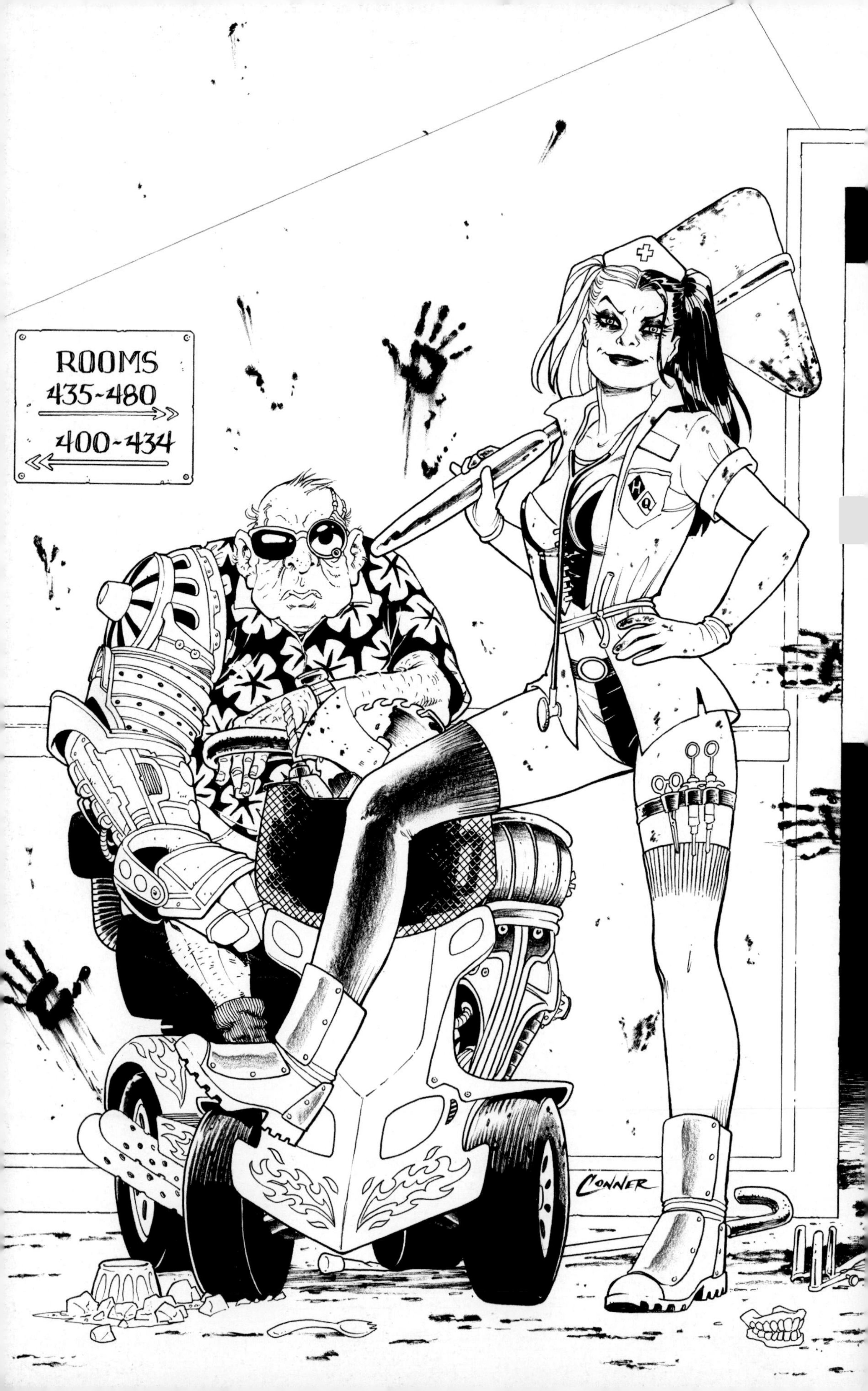
ROOMS
435-480
400-434
CONNER

THE HUNT FOR RED OCTOGENARIANS

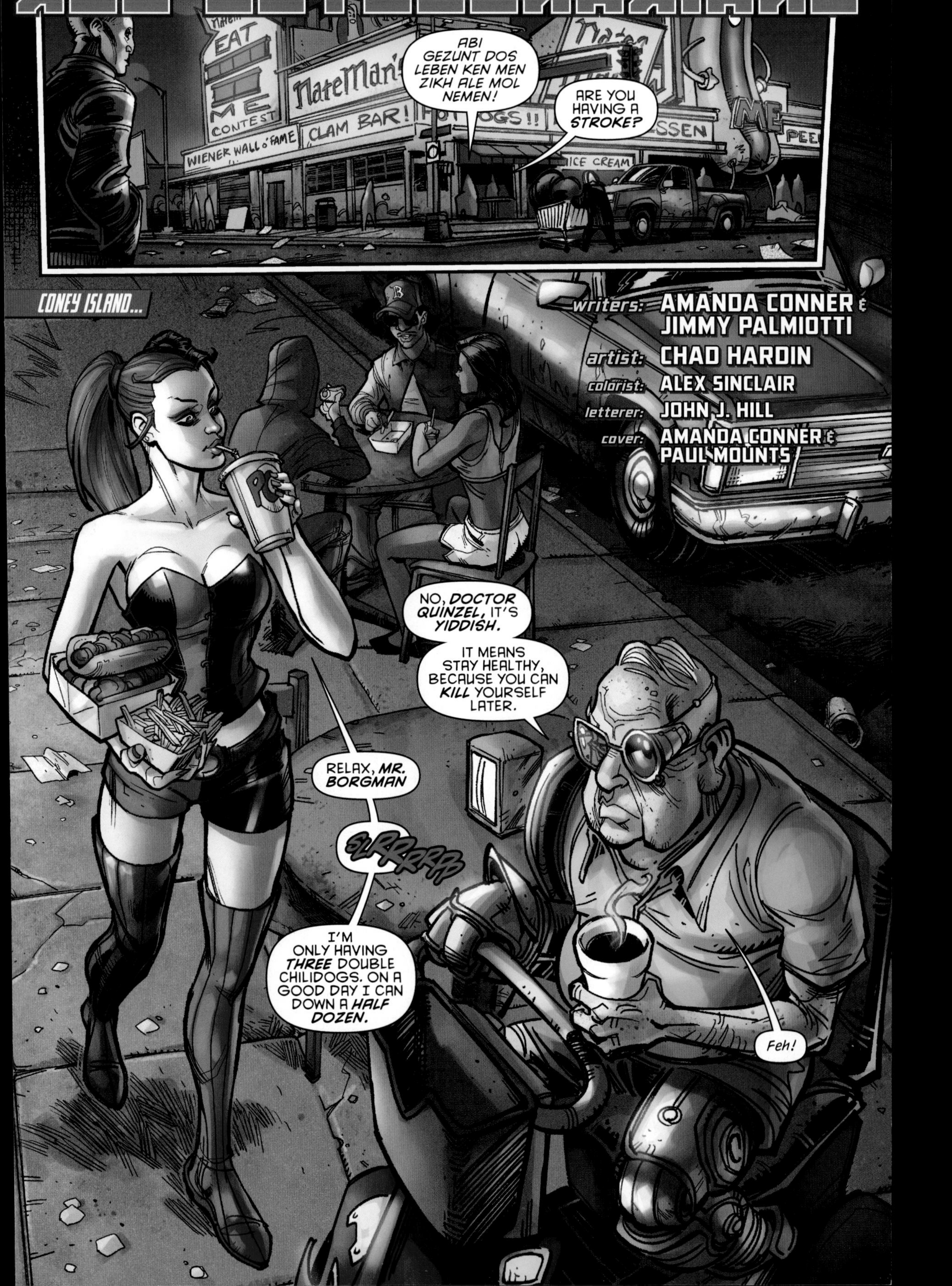

ABI GEZUNT DOS LEBEN KEN MEN ZIKH ALE MOL NEMEN!
ARE YOU HAVING A STROKE?
CONEY ISLAND...
writers: AMANDA CONNER & JIMMY PALMIOTTI
artist: CHAD HARDIN
colorist: ALEX SINCLAIR
letterer: JOHN J. HILL
cover: AMANDA CONNER & PAUL MOUNTS
NO, DOCTOR QUINZEL, IT'S YIDDISH.
IT MEANS STAY HEALTHY, BECAUSE YOU CAN KILL YOURSELF LATER.
RELAX, MR. BORGMAN
SLURRRRRB
I'M ONLY HAVING THREE DOUBLE CHILIDOGS. ON A GOOD DAY I CAN DOWN A HALF DOZEN.
Feh!

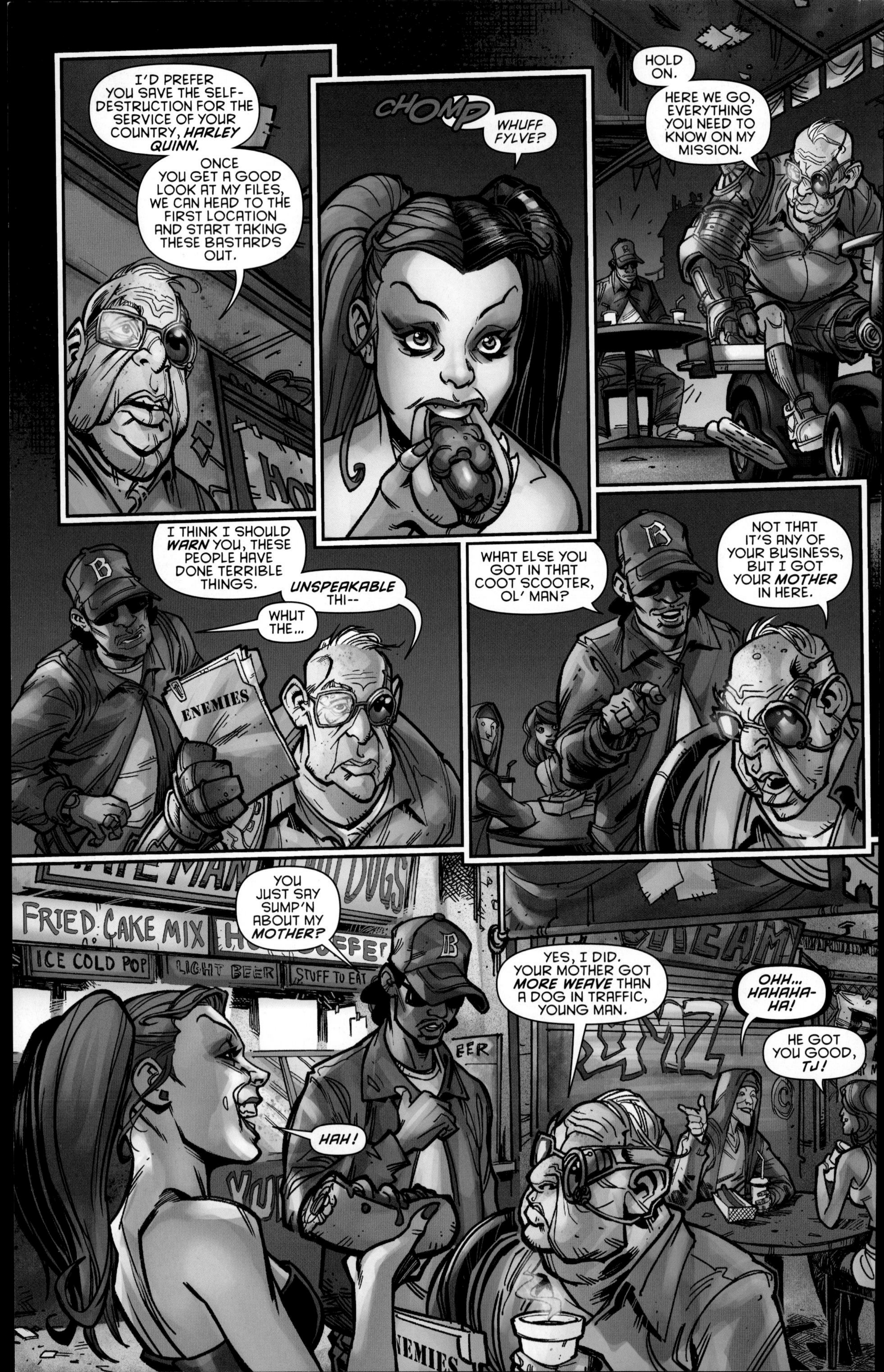

I'D PREFER YOU SAVE THE SELF-DESTRUCTION FOR THE SERVICE OF YOUR COUNTRY, HARLEY QUINN.
ONCE YOU GET A GOOD LOOK AT MY FILES, WE CAN HEAD TO THE FIRST LOCATION AND START TAKING THESE BASTARDS OUT.
CHOMP
WHUFF FYLVE?
HOLD ON.
HERE WE GO, EVERYTHING YOU NEED TO KNOW ON MY MISSION.
I THINK I SHOULD WARN YOU, THESE PEOPLE HAVE DONE TERRIBLE THINGS.
UNSPEAKABLE THI--
WHUT THE...
ENEMIES
WHAT ELSE YOU GOT IN THAT COOT SCOOTER, OL' MAN?
NOT THAT IT'S ANY OF YOUR BUSINESS, BUT I GOT YOUR MOTHER IN HERE.
HOT DOGS
FRIED CAKE MIX
ICE COLD POP
LIGHT BEER
STUFF TO EAT
YOU JUST SAY SUMP'N ABOUT MY MOTHER?
YES, I DID. YOUR MOTHER GOT MORE WEAVE THAN A DOG IN TRAFFIC, YOUNG MAN.
OHH... HAHAHA-HA!
HE GOT YOU GOOD, TJ!
HAH!
NEMIES

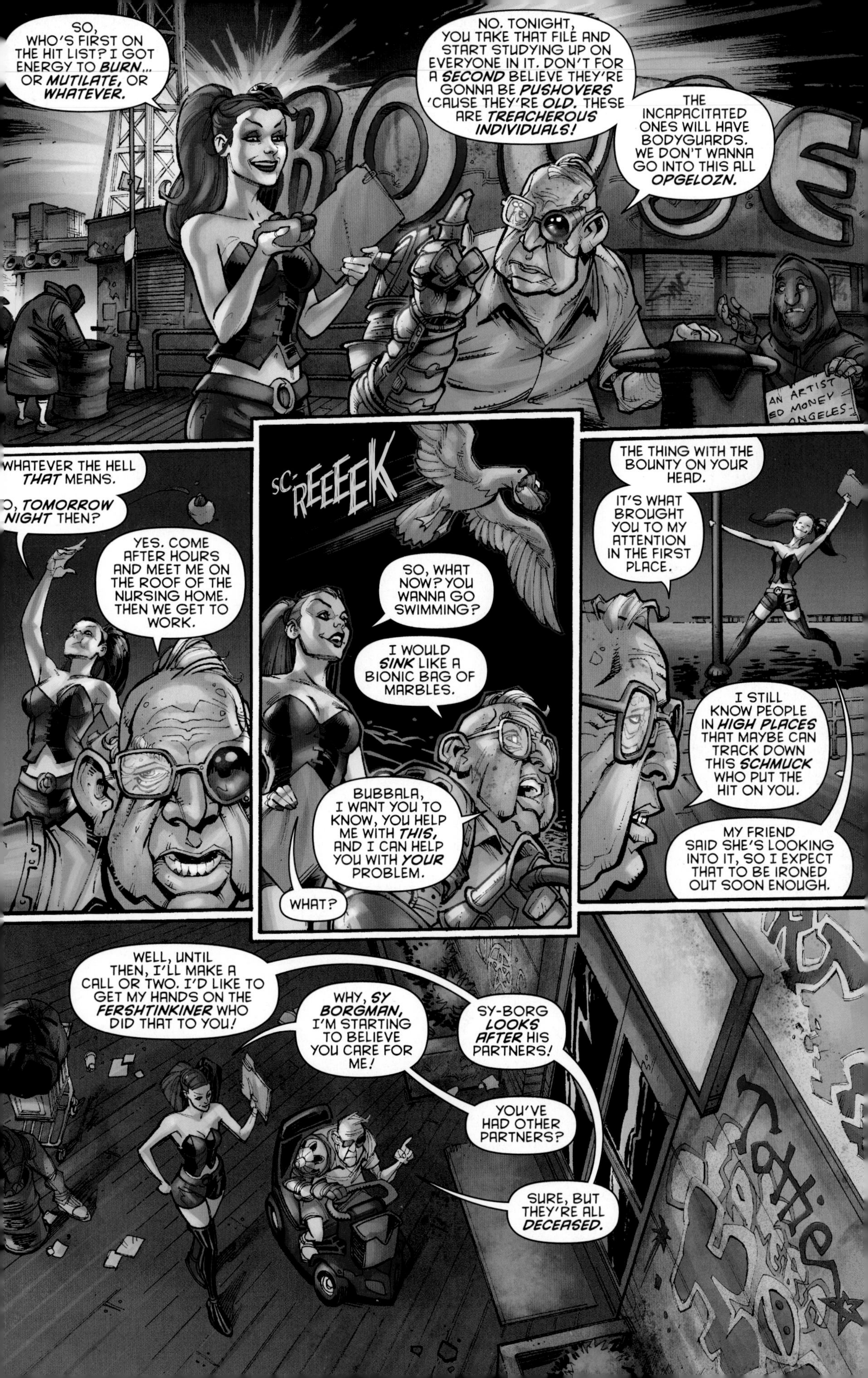

SO, WHO'S FIRST ON THE HIT LIST? I GOT ENERGY TO *BURN*... OR *MUTILATE*, OR *WHATEVER.*
NO. TONIGHT, YOU TAKE THAT FILE AND START STUDYING UP ON EVERYONE IN IT. DON'T FOR A *SECOND* BELIEVE THEY'RE GONNA BE *PUSHOVERS* 'CAUSE THEY'RE *OLD.* THESE ARE *TREACHEROUS INDIVIDUALS!*
THE INCAPACITATED ONES WILL HAVE BODYGUARDS. WE DON'T WANNA GO INTO THIS ALL *OPGELOZN.*
AN ARTIST
ED MONEY
ANGELES
WHATEVER THE HELL *THAT* MEANS.
O, *TOMORROW NIGHT* THEN?
YES. COME AFTER HOURS AND MEET ME ON THE ROOF OF THE NURSING HOME. THEN WE GET TO WORK.
SC-REEEEK
SO, WHAT NOW? YOU WANNA GO SWIMMING?
I WOULD *SINK* LIKE A BIONIC BAG OF MARBLES.
BUBBALA, I WANT YOU TO KNOW, YOU HELP ME WITH *THIS,* AND I CAN HELP YOU WITH *YOUR* PROBLEM.
WHAT?
THE THING WITH THE BOUNTY ON YOUR HEAD.
IT'S WHAT BROUGHT YOU TO MY ATTENTION IN THE FIRST PLACE.
I STILL KNOW PEOPLE IN *HIGH PLACES* THAT MAYBE CAN TRACK DOWN THIS *SCHMUCK* WHO PUT THE HIT ON YOU.
MY FRIEND SAID SHE'S LOOKING INTO IT, SO I EXPECT THAT TO BE IRONED OUT SOON ENOUGH.
WELL, UNTIL THEN, I'LL MAKE A CALL OR TWO. I'D LIKE TO GET MY HANDS ON THE *FERSHTINKINER* WHO DID THAT TO YOU!
WHY, *SY BORGMAN,* I'M STARTING TO BELIEVE YOU CARE FOR ME!
SY-BORG *LOOKS AFTER* HIS PARTNERS!
YOU'VE HAD OTHER PARTNERS?
SURE, BUT THEY'RE ALL *DECEASED.*

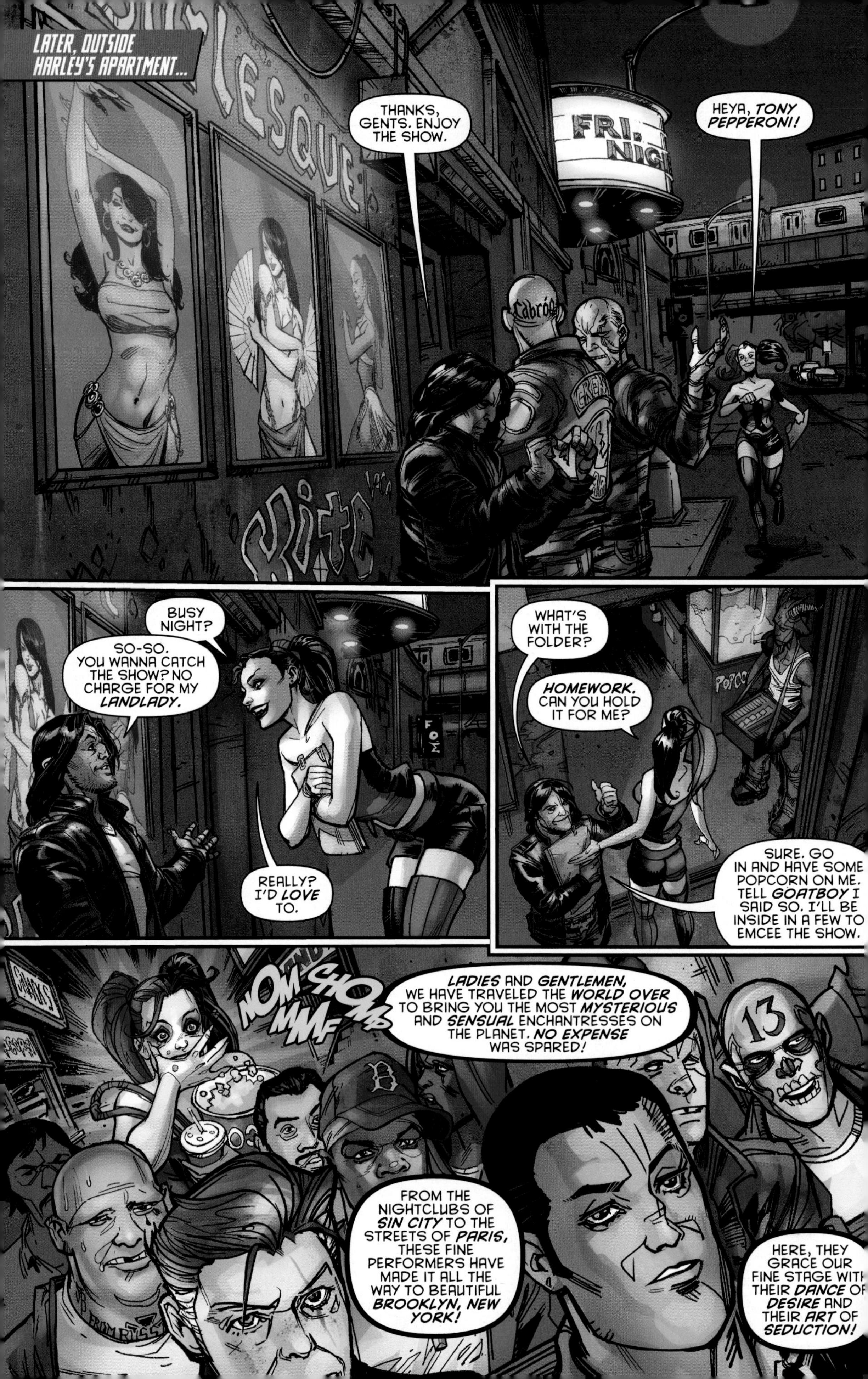
LATER, OUTSIDE HARLEY'S APARTMENT...
THANKS, GENTS. ENJOY THE SHOW.
HEYA, TONY PEPPERONI!
BUSY NIGHT?
SO-SO. YOU WANNA CATCH THE SHOW? NO CHARGE FOR MY LANDLADY.
REALLY? I'D LOVE TO.
WHAT'S WITH THE FOLDER?
HOMEWORK. CAN YOU HOLD IT FOR ME?
SURE. GO IN AND HAVE SOME POPCORN ON ME. TELL GOATBOY I SAID SO. I'LL BE INSIDE IN A FEW TO EMCEE THE SHOW.
NOM CHOMP MMF
LADIES AND GENTLEMEN, WE HAVE TRAVELED THE WORLD OVER TO BRING YOU THE MOST MYSTERIOUS AND SENSUAL ENCHANTRESSES ON THE PLANET. NO EXPENSE WAS SPARED!
FROM THE NIGHTCLUBS OF SIN CITY TO THE STREETS OF PARIS, THESE FINE PERFORMERS HAVE MADE IT ALL THE WAY TO BEAUTIFUL BROOKLYN, NEW YORK!
HERE, THEY GRACE OUR FINE STAGE WITH THEIR DANCE OF DESIRE AND THEIR ART OF SEDUCTION!

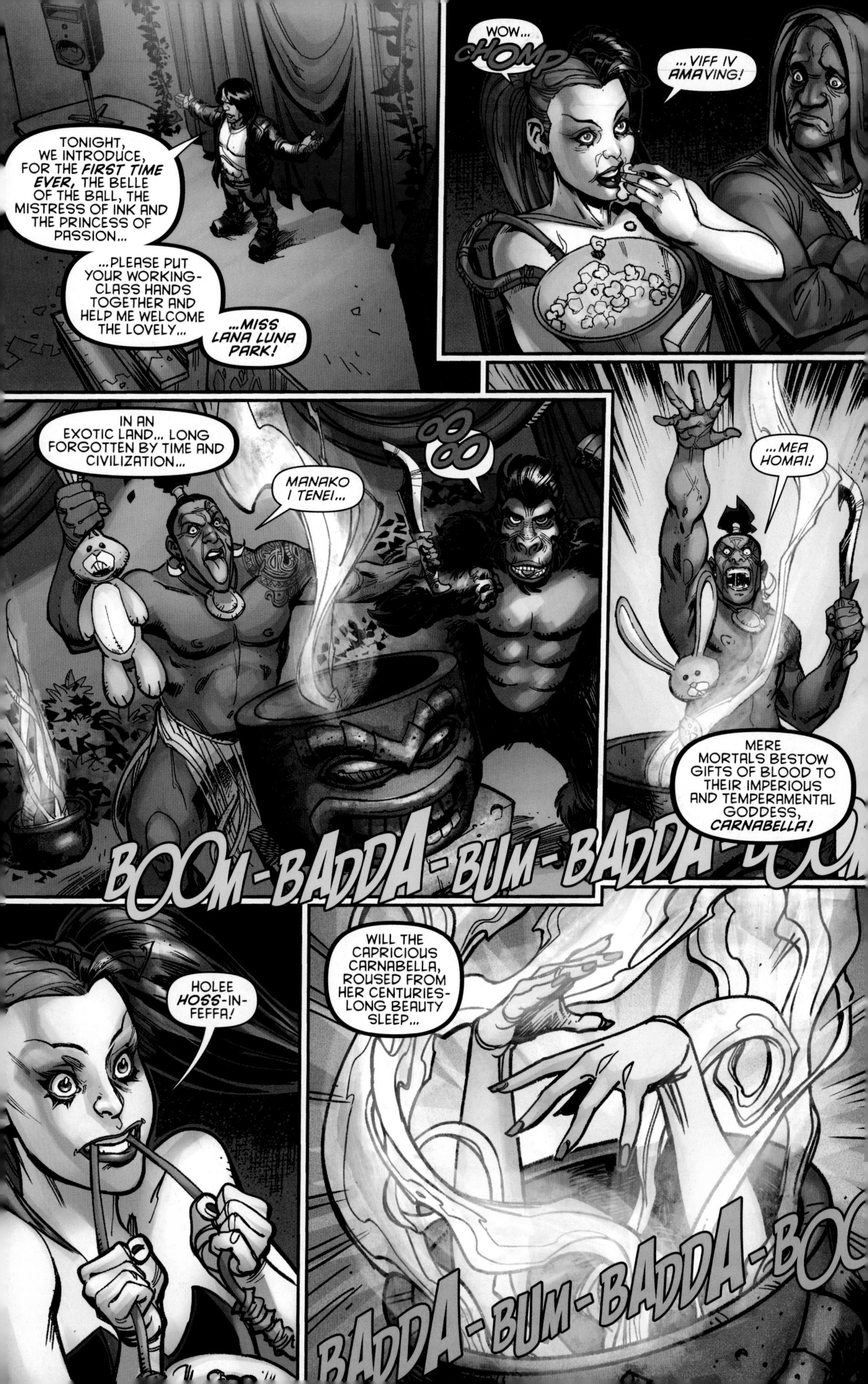

TONIGHT, WE INTRODUCE, FOR THE FIRST TIME EVER, THE BELLE OF THE BALL, THE MISTRESS OF INK AND THE PRINCESS OF PASSION...
...PLEASE PUT YOUR WORKING-CLASS HANDS TOGETHER AND HELP ME WELCOME THE LOVELY...
...MISS LANA LUNA PARK!
WOW...
CHOMP
...VIFF IV AMAVING!
IN AN EXOTIC LAND... LONG FORGOTTEN BY TIME AND CIVILIZATION...
MANAKO I TENEI...
...MEA HOMAI!
MERE MORTALS BESTOW GIFTS OF BLOOD TO THEIR IMPERIOUS AND TEMPERAMENTAL GODDESS, CARNABELLA!
BOOM-BADDA-BUM-BADDA-
HOLEE HOSS-IN-FEFFA!
WILL THE CAPRICIOUS CARNABELLA, ROUSED FROM HER CENTURIES-LONG BEAUTY SLEEP...
BADDA-BUM-BADDA-

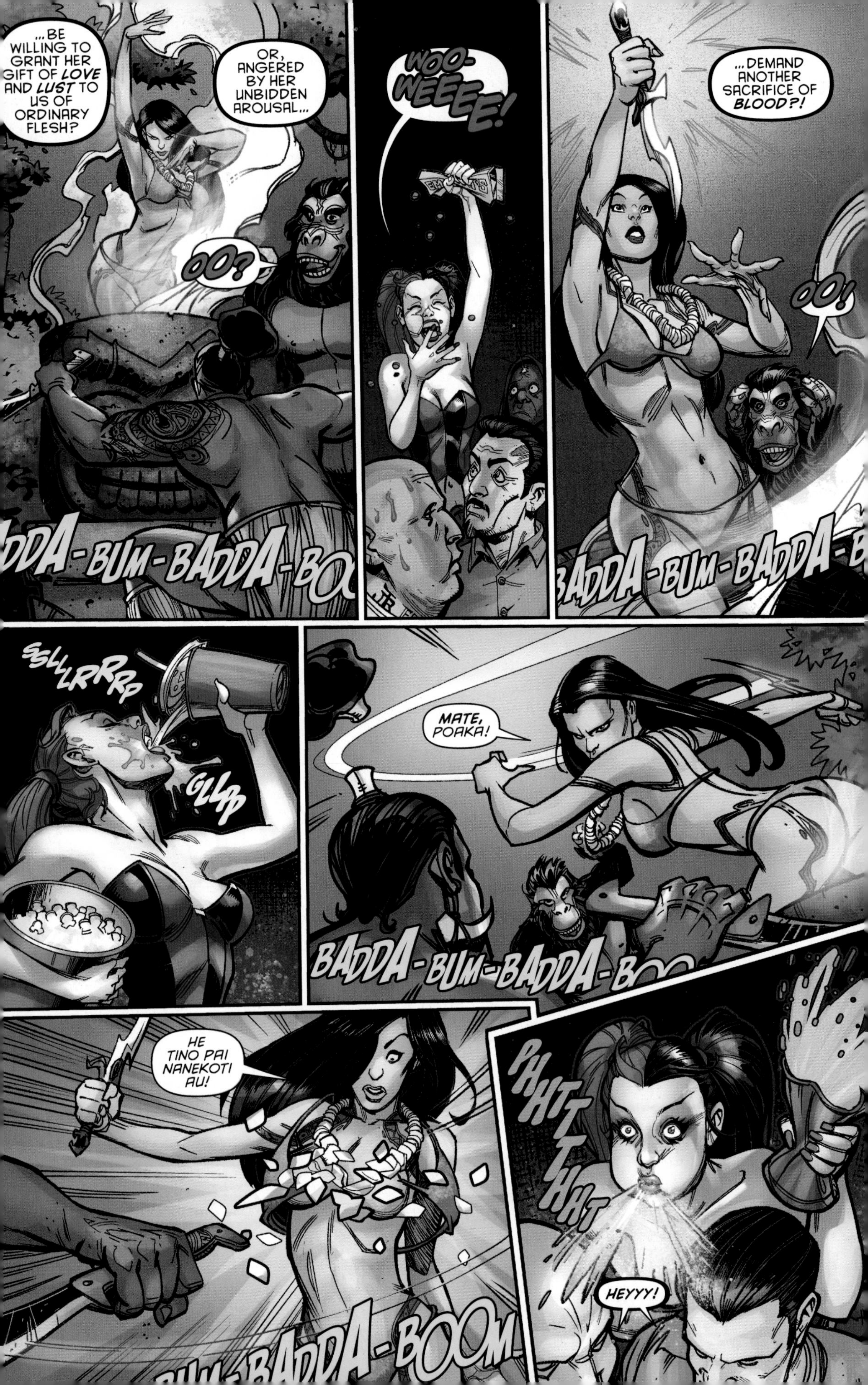
...BE WILLING TO GRANT HER GIFT OF LOVE AND LUST TO US OF ORDINARY FLESH?
OR, ANGERED BY HER UNBIDDEN AROUSAL...
OO?
BADDA-BUM-BADDA-BOO
WOO-WEEEEE!
...DEMAND ANOTHER SACRIFICE OF BLOOD?!
OO!
BADDA-BUM-BADDA-B
SSLLLRRRP
GLLP
MATE, POAKA!
BADDA-BUM-BADDA-BOO
HE TINO PAI NANEKOTI AU!
BUM-BADDA-BOOM
PHHTTTHHT
HEYYY!

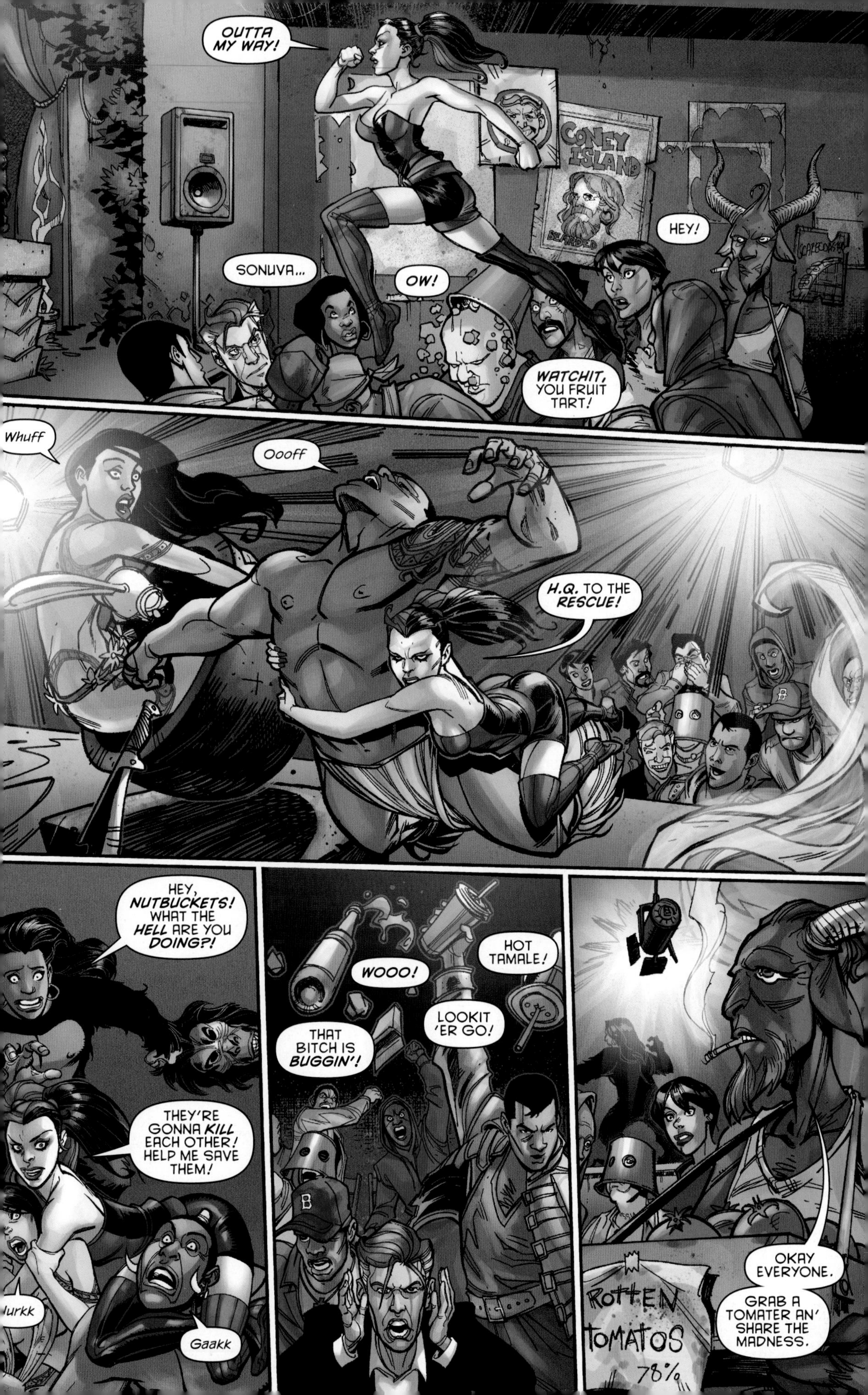

OUTTA MY WAY!
CONEY ISLAND
BEARDED
HEY!
SONUVA...
OW!
WATCHIT, YOU FRUIT TART!
Whuff
Oooff
H.Q. TO THE RESCUE!
HEY, NUTBUCKETS! WHAT THE HELL ARE YOU DOING?!
THEY'RE GONNA KILL EACH OTHER! HELP ME SAVE THEM!
Gaakk
WOOO!
HOT TAMALE!
LOOKIT 'ER GO!
THAT BITCH IS BUGGIN'!
OKAY EVERYONE.
GRAB A TOMATER AN' SHARE THE MADNESS.
ROTTEN TOMATOS
78%

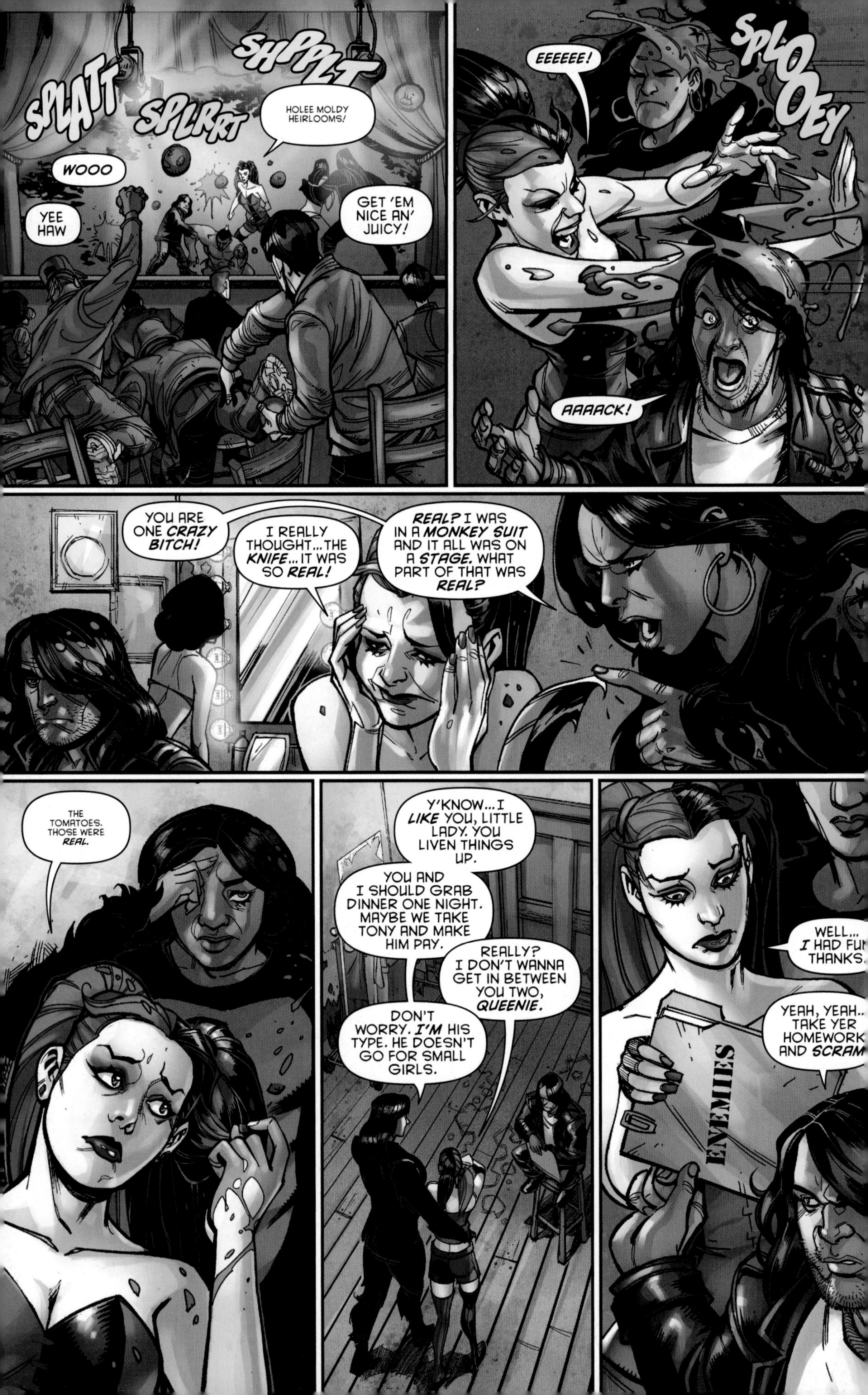
SPLATT
SPLRRRT
SHPPLT
HOLEE MOLDY HEIRLOOMS!
WOOO
YEE HAW
GET 'EM NICE AN' JUICY!
EEEEEE!
SPLOOEY
AAAACK!
YOU ARE ONE CRAZY BITCH!
I REALLY THOUGHT... THE KNIFE... IT WAS SO REAL!
REAL? I WAS IN A MONKEY SUIT AND IT ALL WAS ON A STAGE. WHAT PART OF THAT WAS REAL?
THE TOMATOES. THOSE WERE REAL.
Y'KNOW... I LIKE YOU, LITTLE LADY. YOU LIVEN THINGS UP.
YOU AND I SHOULD GRAB DINNER ONE NIGHT. MAYBE WE TAKE TONY AND MAKE HIM PAY.
REALLY? I DON'T WANNA GET IN BETWEEN YOU TWO, QUEENIE.
DON'T WORRY. I'M HIS TYPE. HE DOESN'T GO FOR SMALL GIRLS.
WELL... I HAD FUN THANKS.
YEAH, YEAH... TAKE YER HOMEWORK AND SCRAM
ENEMIES

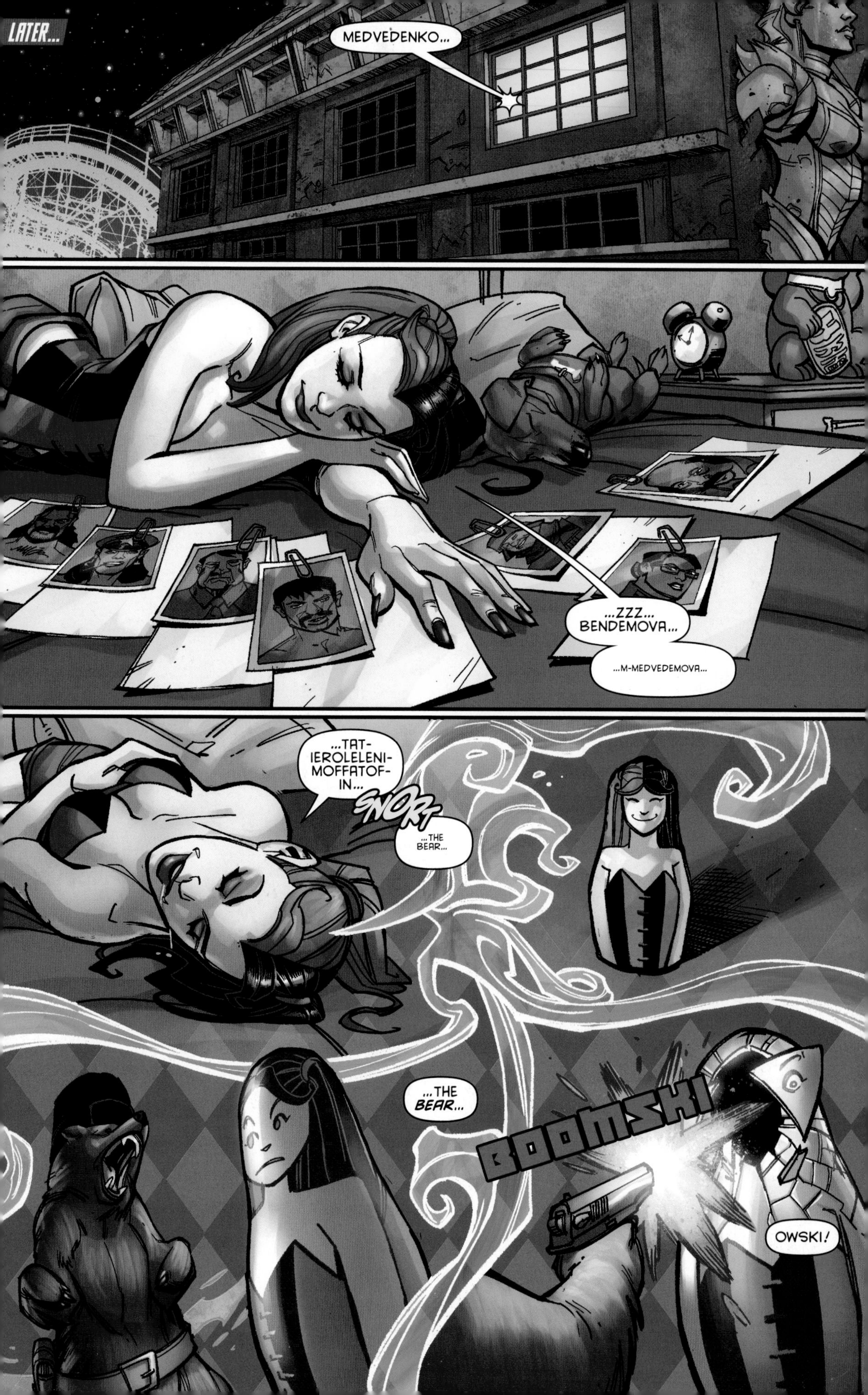
LATER...
MEDVEDENKO...
...ZZZ... BENDEMOVA...
...M-MEDVEDEMOVA...
...TAT-IEROLELENI-MOFFATOF-IN...
SNORT
...THE BEAR...
...THE BEAR...
BOOMSKI
OWSKI!

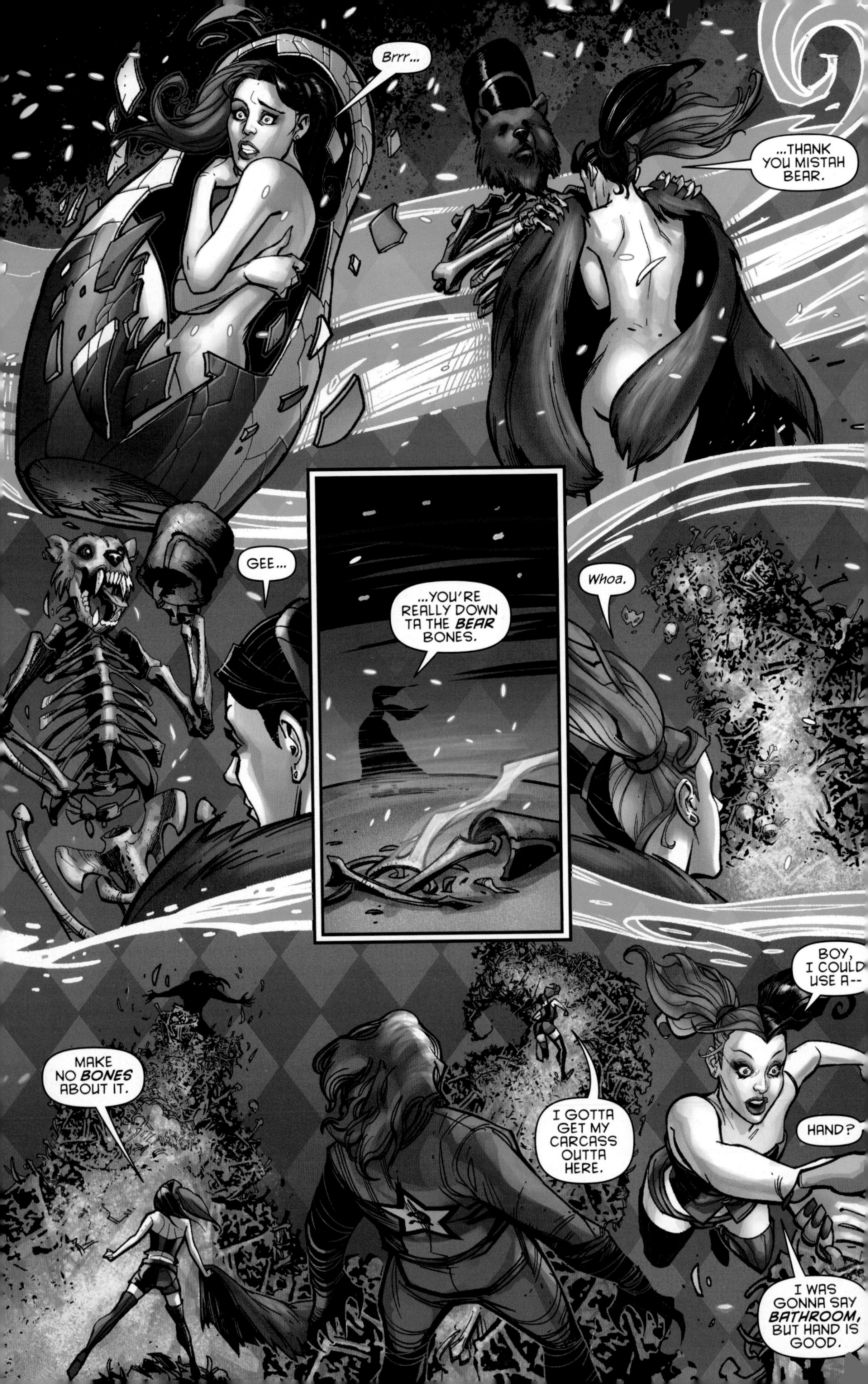
Brrr...
...THANK YOU MISTAH BEAR.
GEE...
...YOU'RE REALLY DOWN TA THE *BEAR* BONES.
Whoa.
MAKE NO *BONES* ABOUT IT.
I GOTTA GET MY CARCASS OUTTA HERE.
BOY, I COULD USE A--
HAND?
I WAS GONNA SAY *BATHROOM,* BUT HAND IS GOOD.

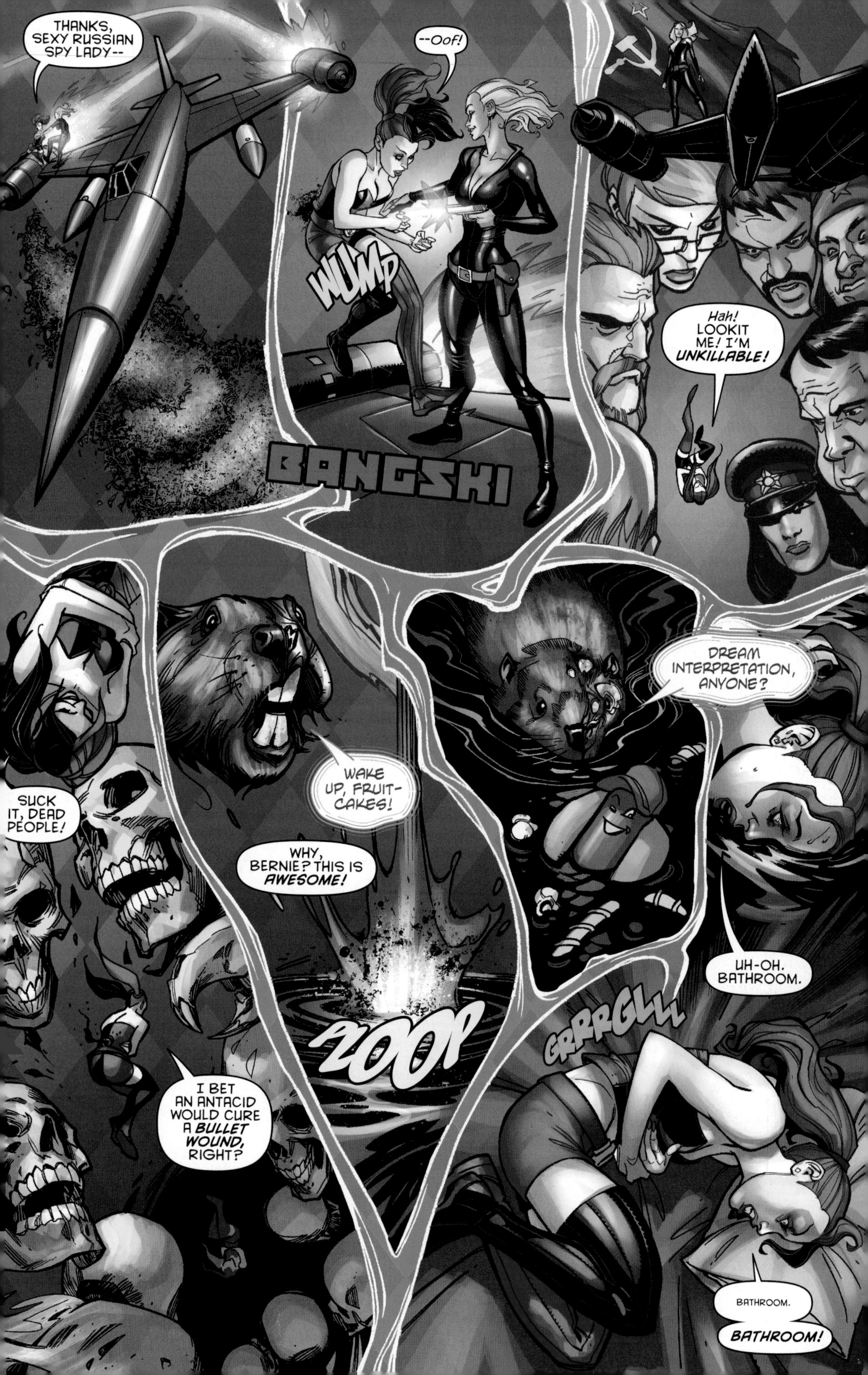
THANKS, SEXY RUSSIAN SPY LADY--
--Oof!
WUMP
BANGSKI
Hah! LOOKIT ME! I'M UNKILLABLE!
WAKE UP, FRUIT-CAKES!
WHY, BERNIE? THIS IS AWESOME!
DREAM INTERPRETATION, ANYONE?
SUCK IT, DEAD PEOPLE!
ZOOP
UH-OH. BATHROOM.
GRRRGLLL
I BET AN ANTACID WOULD CURE A BULLET WOUND, RIGHT?
BATHROOM.
BATHROOM!

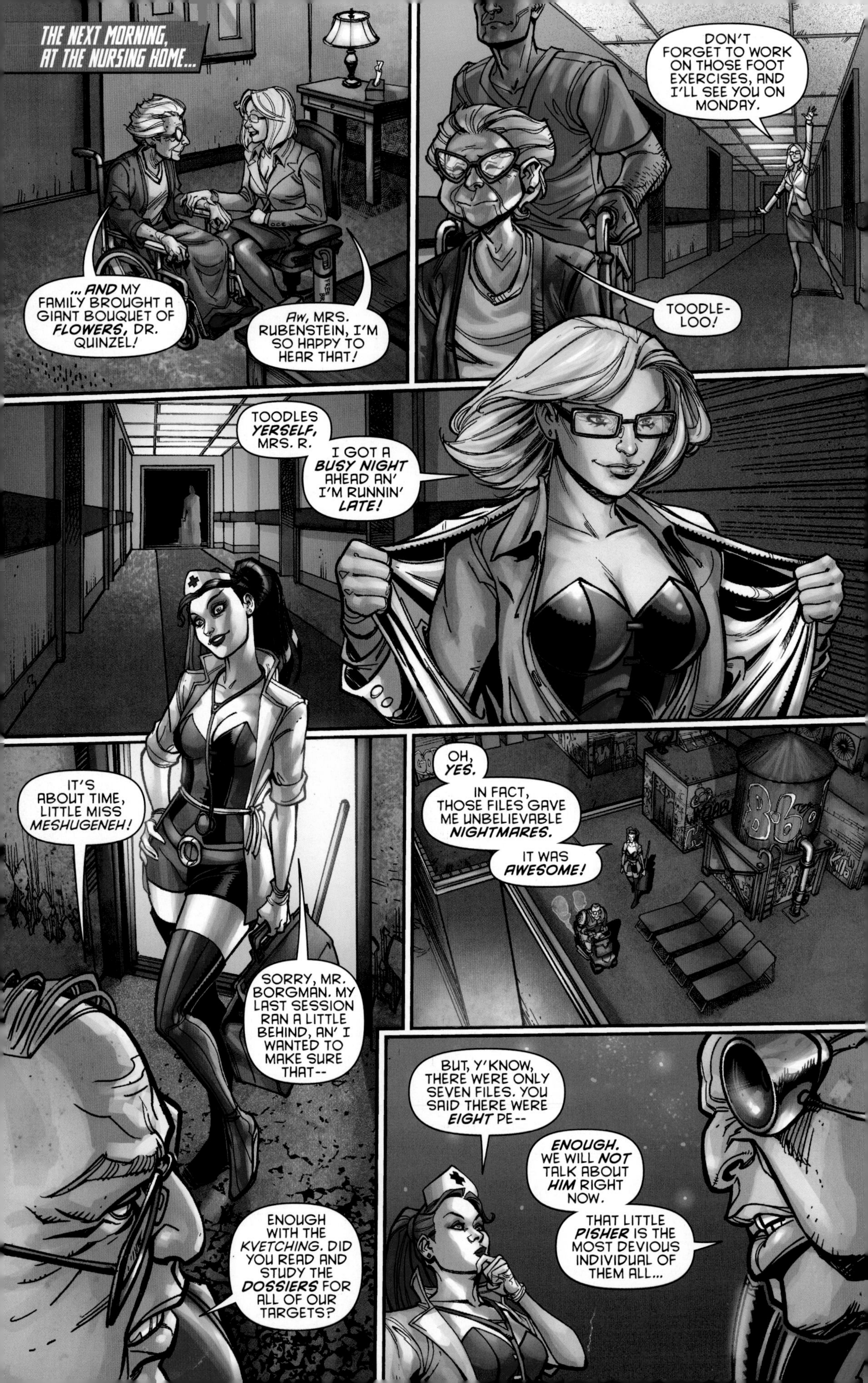
THE NEXT MORNING, AT THE NURSING HOME...
...AND MY FAMILY BROUGHT A GIANT BOUQUET OF FLOWERS, DR. QUINZEL!
AW, MRS. RUBENSTEIN, I'M SO HAPPY TO HEAR THAT!
DON'T FORGET TO WORK ON THOSE FOOT EXERCISES, AND I'LL SEE YOU ON MONDAY.
TOODLE-LOO!
TOODLES YERSELF, MRS. R.
I GOT A BUSY NIGHT AHEAD AN' I'M RUNNIN' LATE!
IT'S ABOUT TIME, LITTLE MISS MESHUGENEH!
SORRY, MR. BORGMAN. MY LAST SESSION RAN A LITTLE BEHIND, AN' I WANTED TO MAKE SURE THAT--
ENOUGH WITH THE KVETCHING. DID YOU READ AND STUDY THE DOSSIERS FOR ALL OF OUR TARGETS?
OH, YES.
IN FACT, THOSE FILES GAVE ME UNBELIEVABLE NIGHTMARES.
IT WAS AWESOME!
BUT, Y'KNOW, THERE WERE ONLY SEVEN FILES. YOU SAID THERE WERE EIGHT PE--
ENOUGH. WE WILL NOT TALK ABOUT HIM RIGHT NOW.
THAT LITTLE PISHER IS THE MOST DEVIOUS INDIVIDUAL OF THEM ALL...

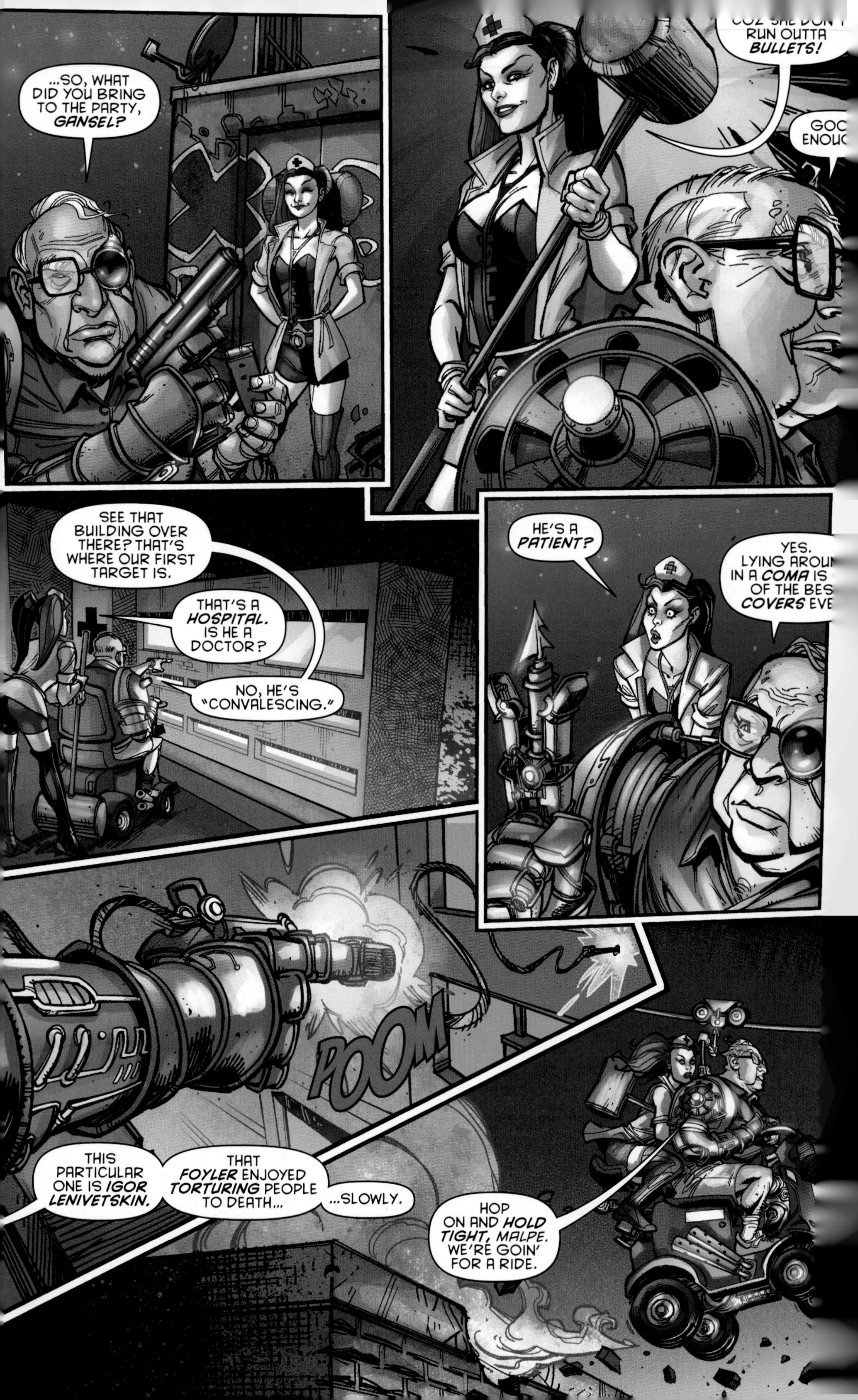
...SO, WHAT DID YOU BRING TO THE PARTY, GANSEL?
RUN OUTTA BULLETS!
GOO ENOUG
SEE THAT BUILDING OVER THERE? THAT'S WHERE OUR FIRST TARGET IS.
THAT'S A HOSPITAL. IS HE A DOCTOR?
NO, HE'S "CONVALESCING."
HE'S A PATIENT?
YES. LYING AROU IN A COMA IS OF THE BES COVERS EVE
POOM
THIS PARTICULAR ONE IS IGOR LENIVETSKIN.
THAT FOYLER ENJOYED TORTURING PEOPLE TO DEATH...
...SLOWLY.
HOP ON AND HOLD TIGHT, MALPE. WE'RE GOIN' FOR A RIDE.

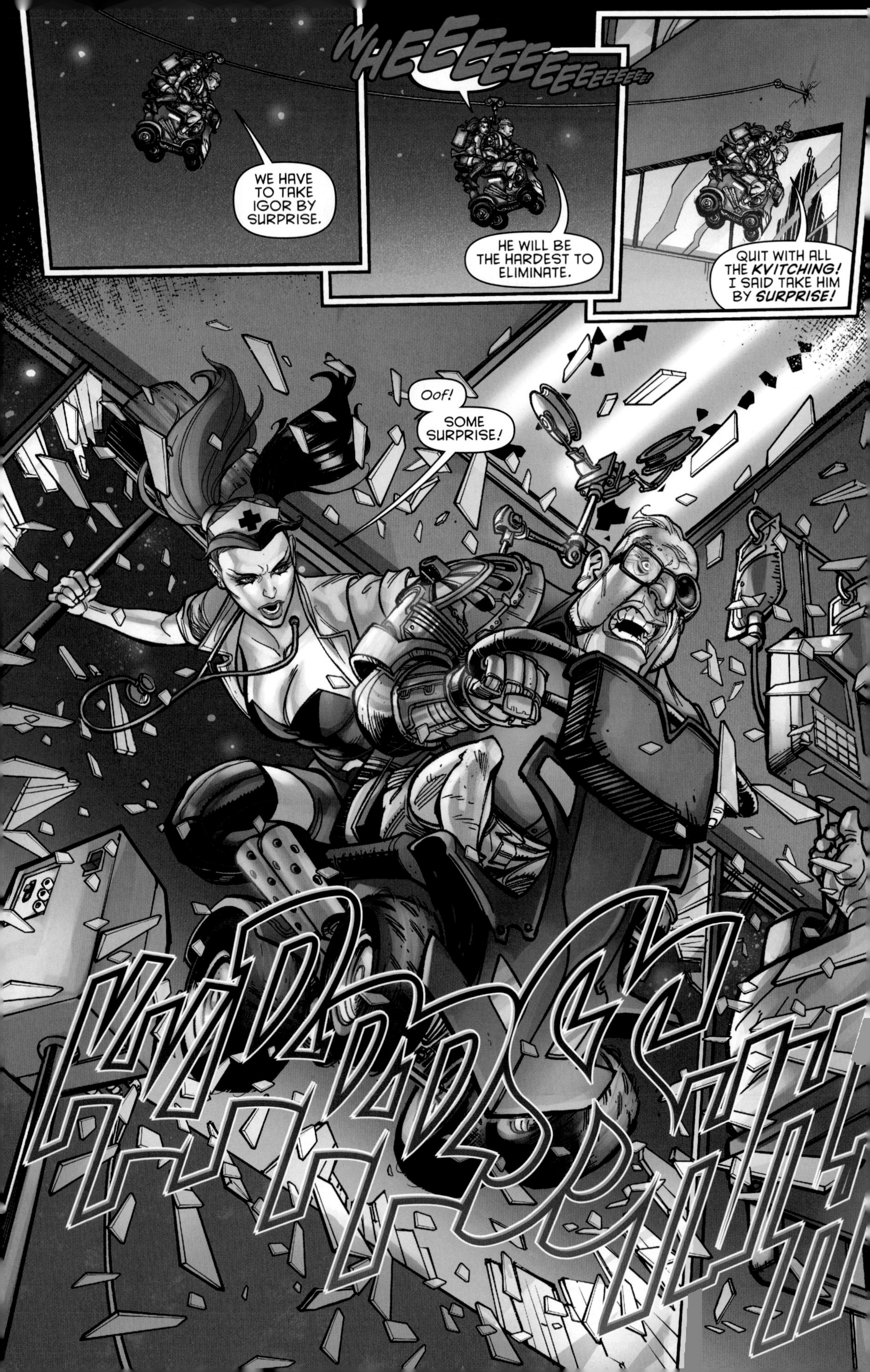
WHEEEEEEEEEEEEE!
WE HAVE TO TAKE IGOR BY SURPRISE.
HE WILL BE THE HARDEST TO ELIMINATE.
QUIT WITH ALL THE KVITCHING! I SAID TAKE HIM BY SURPRISE!
Oof!
SOME SURPRISE!
KRASSHHH

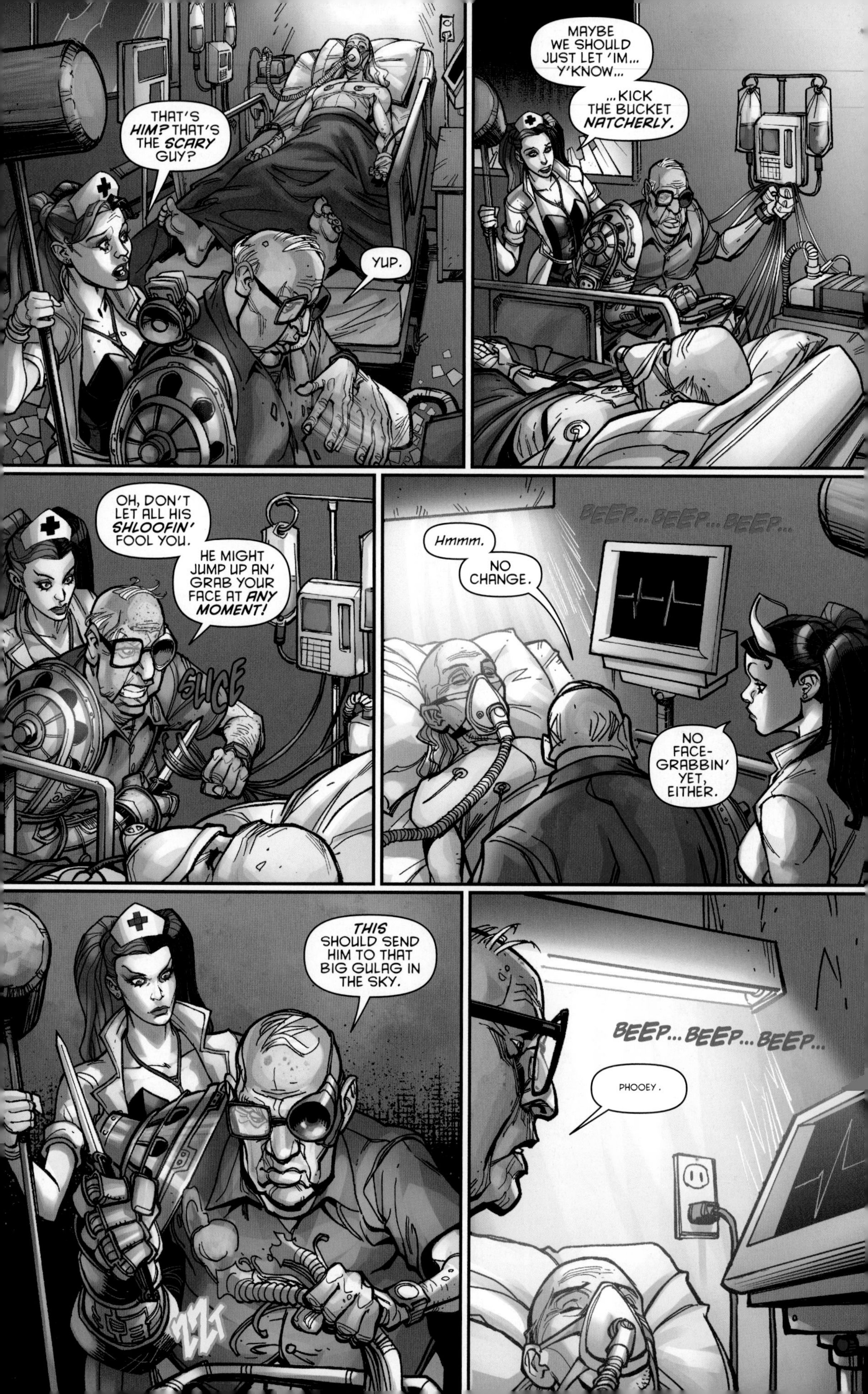
THAT'S *HIM?* THAT'S THE *SCARY* GUY?
YUP.
MAYBE WE SHOULD JUST LET 'IM... Y'KNOW...
...KICK THE BUCKET *NATCHERLY.*
OH, DON'T LET ALL HIS *SHLOOFIN'* FOOL YOU.
HE MIGHT JUMP UP AN' GRAB YOUR FACE AT *ANY MOMENT!*
SLICE
BEEP...BEEP...BEEP...
Hmmm.
NO CHANGE.
NO FACE-GRABBIN' YET, EITHER.
THIS SHOULD SEND HIM TO THAT BIG GULAG IN THE SKY.
ZZZT
BEEP...BEEP...BEEP...
PHOOEY.

MAYBE *THIS'LL* TAKE CARE OF THE *MAMZER*.

ZOT

COME ON, YOU DUMB *ALTE-COCKA!*

SMEK

~Sigh~

BEEP... BEEP...

WILL YOU *DIE* ALREADY, YOU *SONOVA*--?!

GIMME THAT!

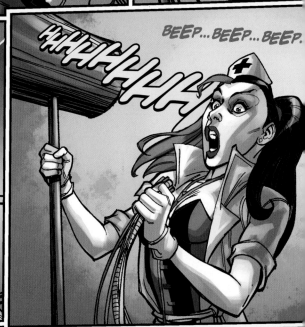

HHHHHHHH

BEEP...BEEP...BEEP.

BEEP...BE--

PHHHHHHHT

JINKIES!

OY!

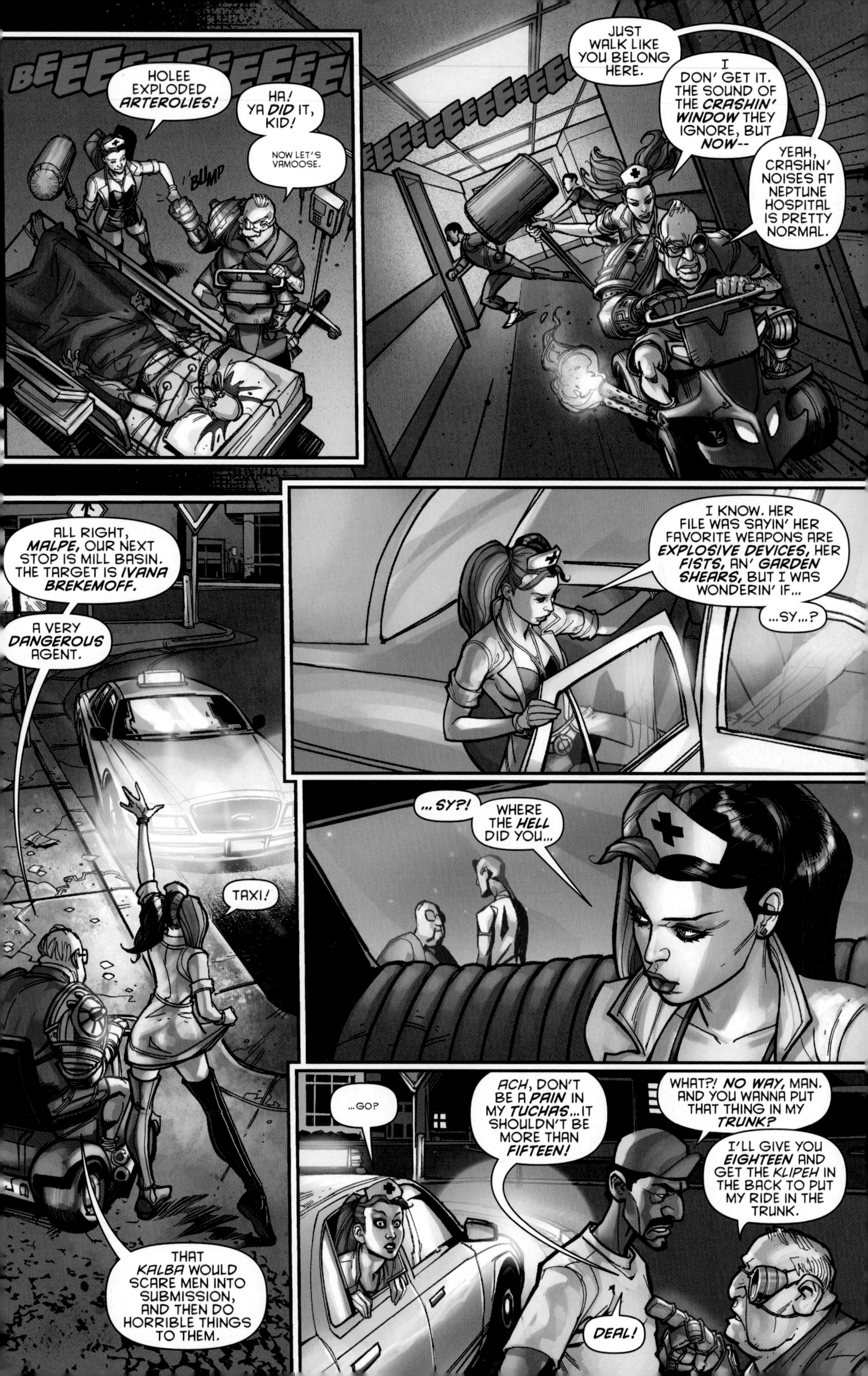
BEEEEEEEEEEEE
HOLEE EXPLODED ARTEROLIES!
HA! YA DID IT, KID!
NOW LET'S VAMOOSE.
BUMP
EEEEEEEEEEEEE
JUST WALK LIKE YOU BELONG HERE.
I DON' GET IT. THE SOUND OF THE CRASHIN' WINDOW THEY IGNORE, BUT NOW--
YEAH, CRASHIN' NOISES AT NEPTUNE HOSPITAL IS PRETTY NORMAL.
ALL RIGHT, MALPE, OUR NEXT STOP IS MILL BASIN. THE TARGET IS IVANA BREKEMOFF.
A VERY DANGEROUS AGENT.
TAXI!
THAT KALBA WOULD SCARE MEN INTO SUBMISSION, AND THEN DO HORRIBLE THINGS TO THEM.
I KNOW. HER FILE WAS SAYIN' HER FAVORITE WEAPONS ARE EXPLOSIVE DEVICES, HER FISTS, AN' GARDEN SHEARS, BUT I WAS WONDERIN' IF...
...SY...?
...SY?!
WHERE THE HELL DID YOU...
...GO?
ACH, DON'T BE A PAIN IN MY TUCHAS...IT SHOULDN'T BE MORE THAN FIFTEEN!
WHAT?! NO WAY, MAN. AND YOU WANNA PUT THAT THING IN MY TRUNK?
I'LL GIVE YOU EIGHTEEN AND GET THE KLIPEH IN THE BACK TO PUT MY RIDE IN THE TRUNK.
DEAL!

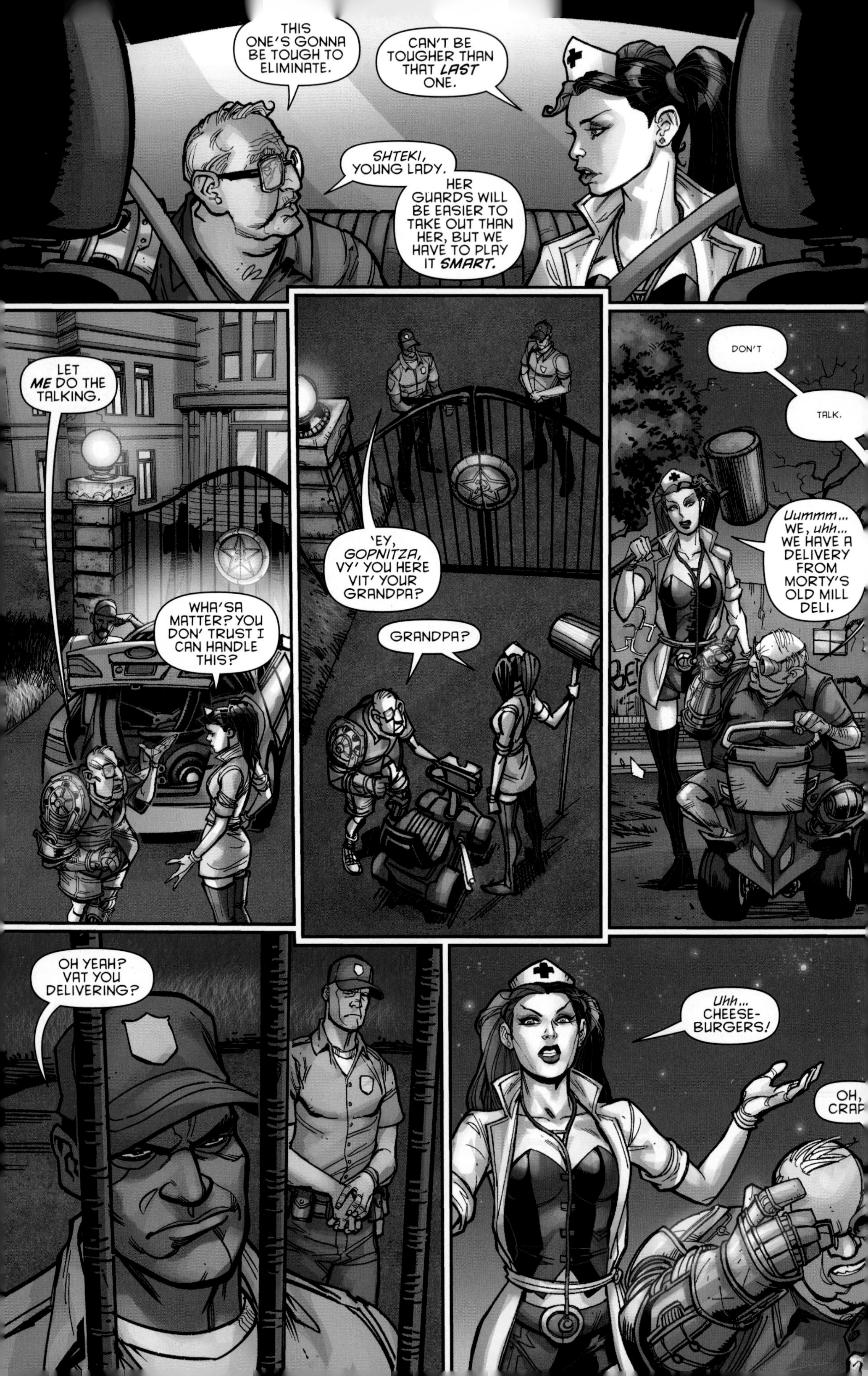

THIS ONE'S GONNA BE TOUGH TO ELIMINATE.
CAN'T BE TOUGHER THAN THAT *LAST* ONE.
SHTEKI, YOUNG LADY.
HER GUARDS WILL BE EASIER TO TAKE OUT THAN HER, BUT WE HAVE TO PLAY IT *SMART.*
LET *ME* DO THE TALKING.
WHA'SA MATTER? YOU DON' TRUST I CAN HANDLE THIS?
'EY, *GOPNITZA,* VY' YOU HERE VIT' YOUR GRANDPA?
GRANDPA?
DON'T
TALK.
Uummm... WE, *uhh...* WE HAVE A DELIVERY FROM MORTY'S OLD MILL DELI.
OH YEAH? VAT YOU DELIVERING?
Uhh... CHEESE-BURGERS!
OH, CRAP

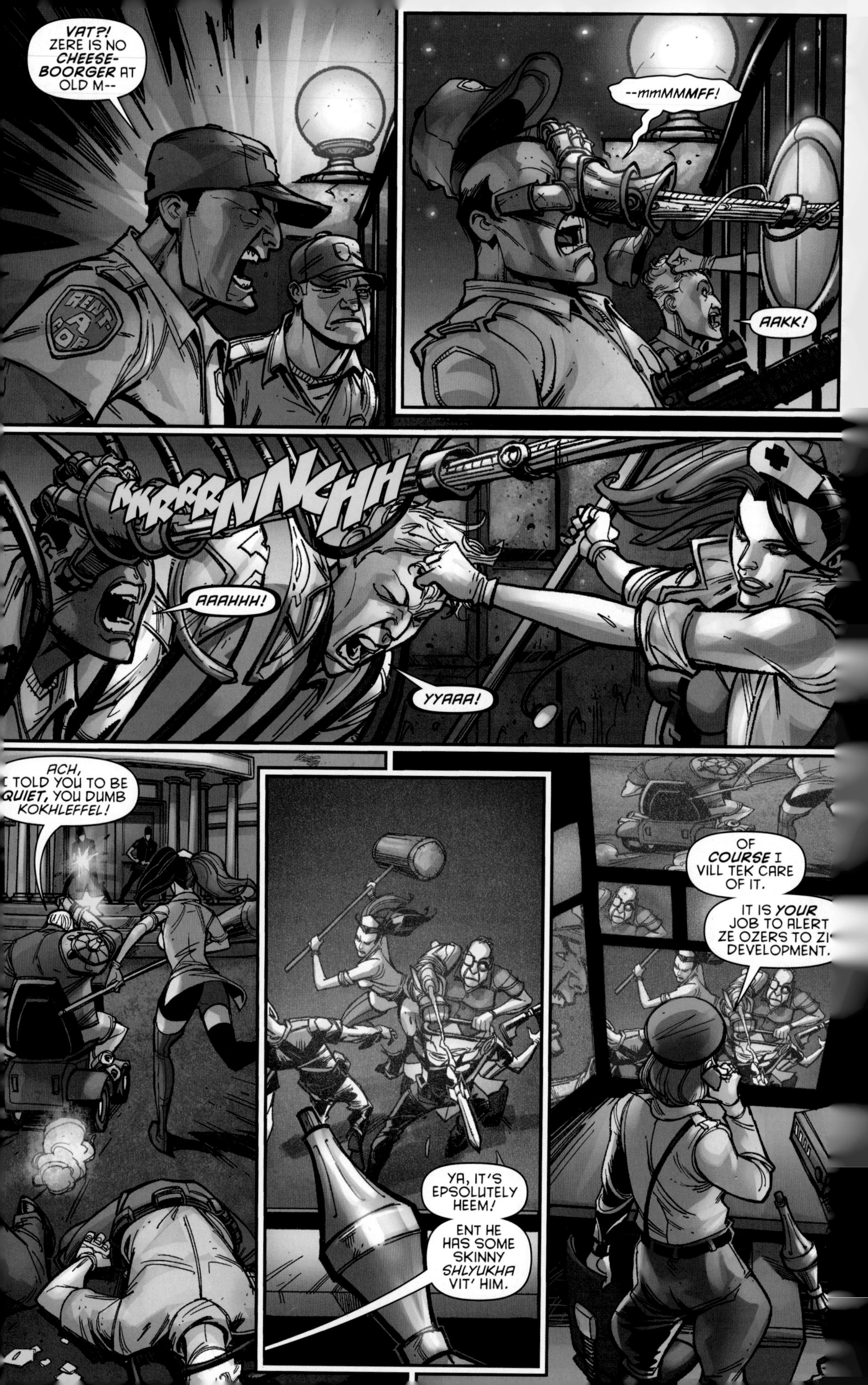
VAT?! ZERE IS NO CHEESE-BOORGER AT OLD M--
--mmMMMFF!
AAKK!
MMRRRRNNNCHH
AAAHHH!
YYAAA!
ACH, I TOLD YOU TO BE QUIET, YOU DUMB KOKHLEFFEL!
YA, IT'S EPSOLUTELY HEEM!
ENT HE HAS SOME SKINNY SHLYUKHA VIT' HIM.
OF COURSE I VILL TEK CARE OF IT.
IT IS YOUR JOB TO ALERT ZE OZERS TO ZI DEVELOPMENT.

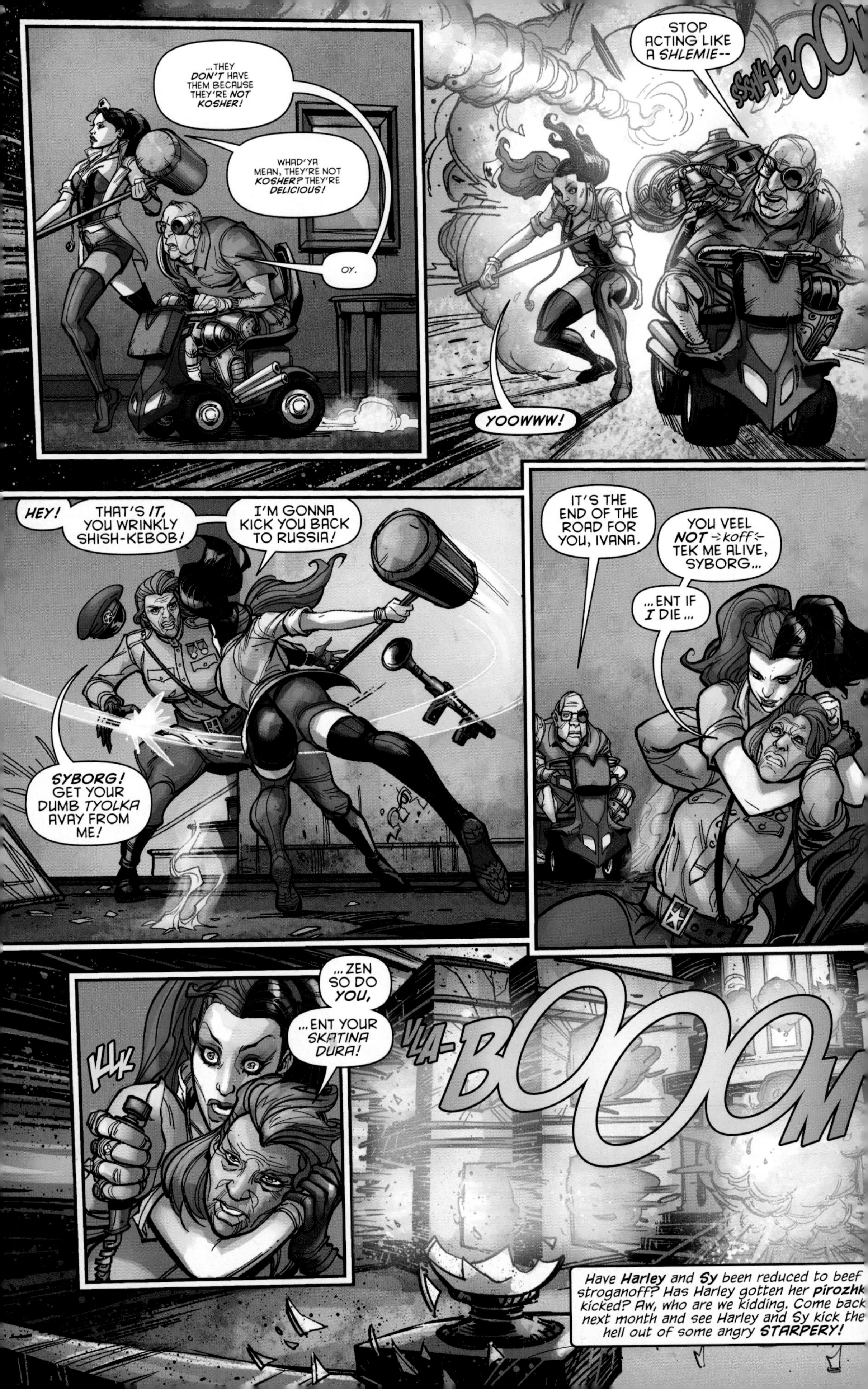
...THEY DON'T HAVE THEM BECAUSE THEY'RE NOT KOSHER!
WHAD'YA MEAN, THEY'RE NOT KOSHER? THEY'RE DELICIOUS!
OY.
STOP ACTING LIKE A SHLEMIE--
$SHA-BOOM
YOOWWW!
HEY!
THAT'S IT, YOU WRINKLY SHISH-KEBOB!
I'M GONNA KICK YOU BACK TO RUSSIA!
SYBORG! GET YOUR DUMB TYOLKA AVAY FROM ME!
IT'S THE END OF THE ROAD FOR YOU, IVANA.
YOU VEEL NOT ->koff<- TEK ME ALIVE, SYBORG...
...ENT IF I DIE...
...ZEN SO DO YOU,
...ENT YOUR SKATINA DURA!
KLIK
VLA-BOOOM
Have Harley and Sy been reduced to beef stroganoff? Has Harley gotten her pirozhk kicked? Aw, who are we kidding. Come back next month and see Harley and Sy kick the hell out of some angry STARPERY!

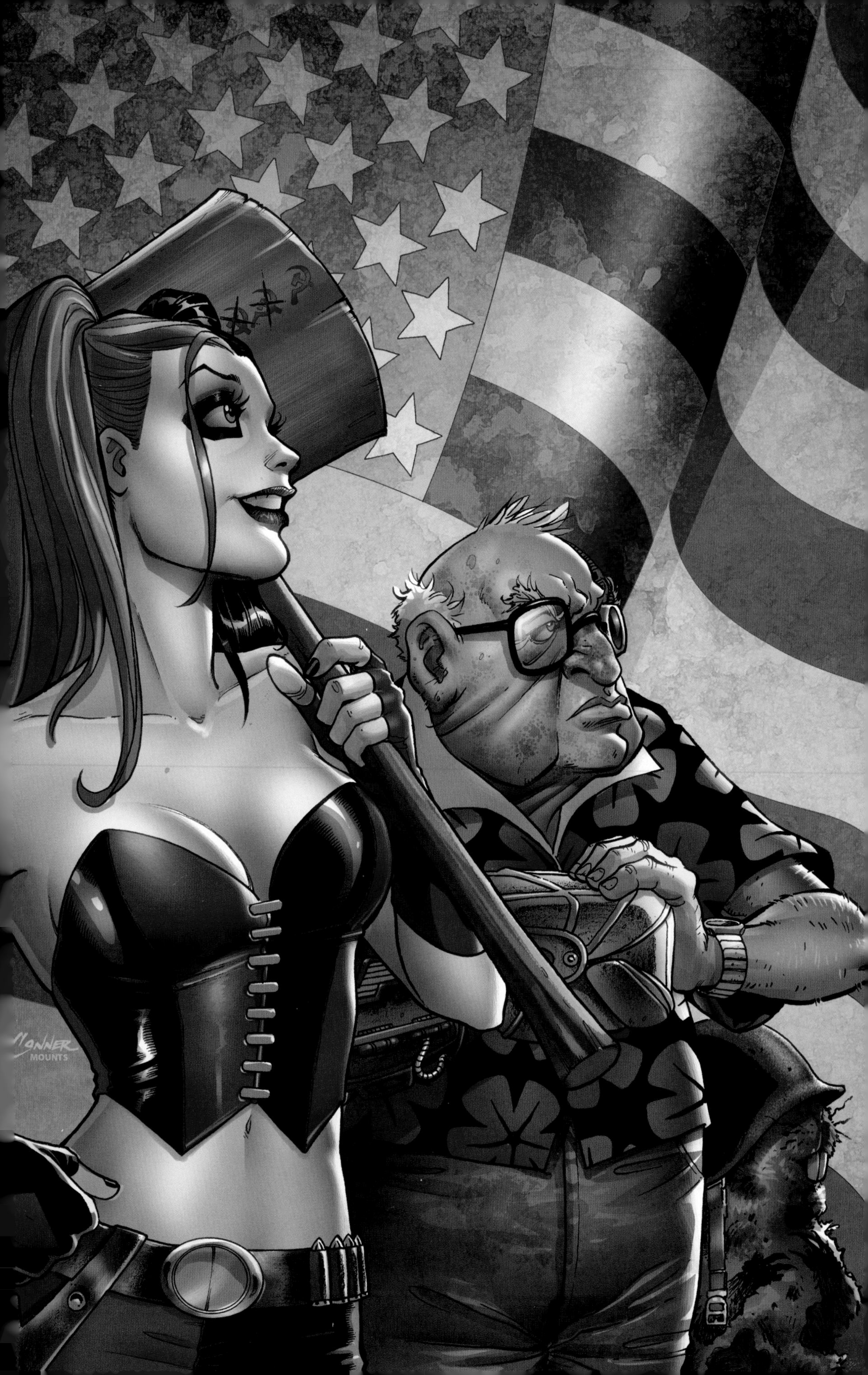
MOUNTS

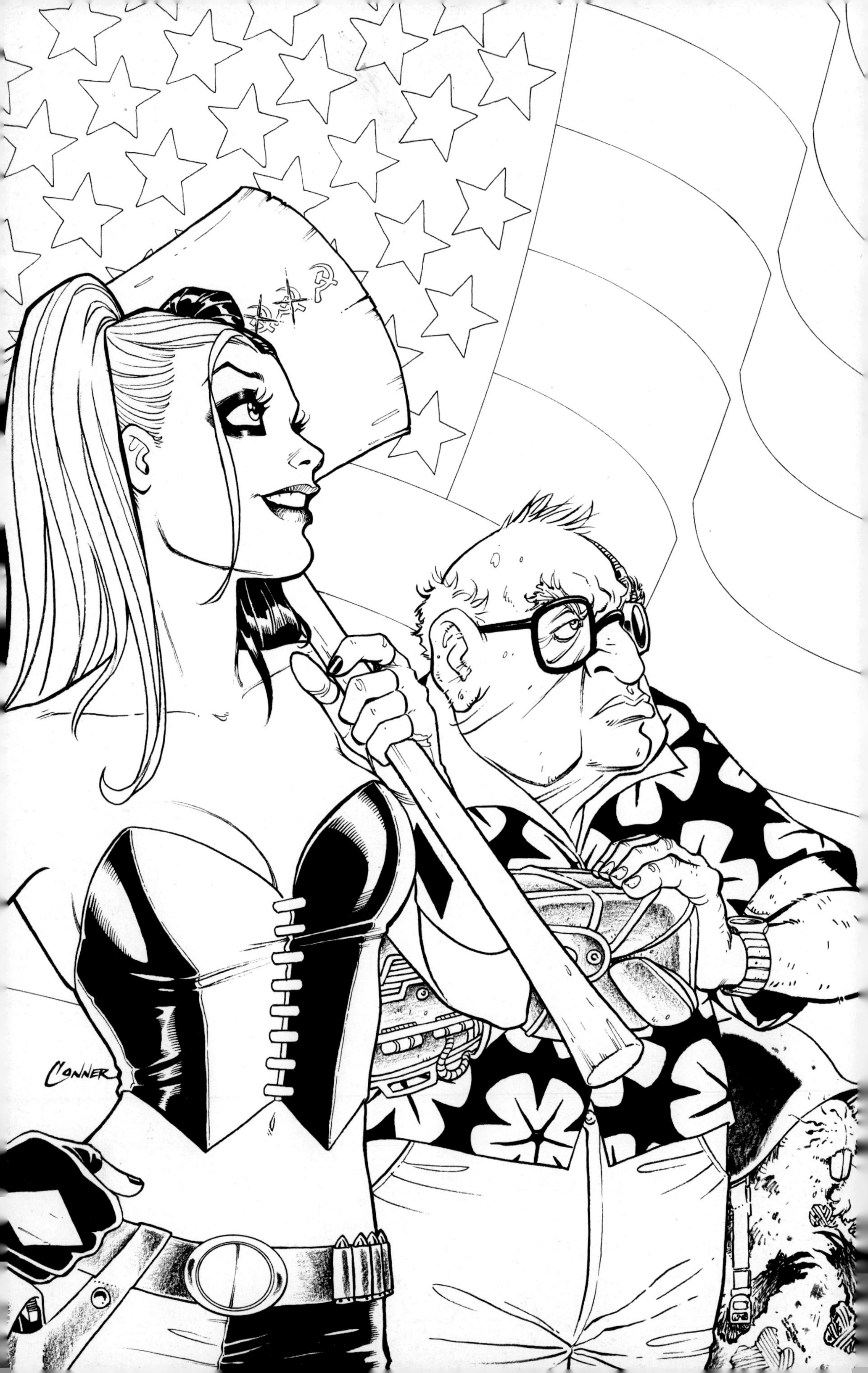
CONNER

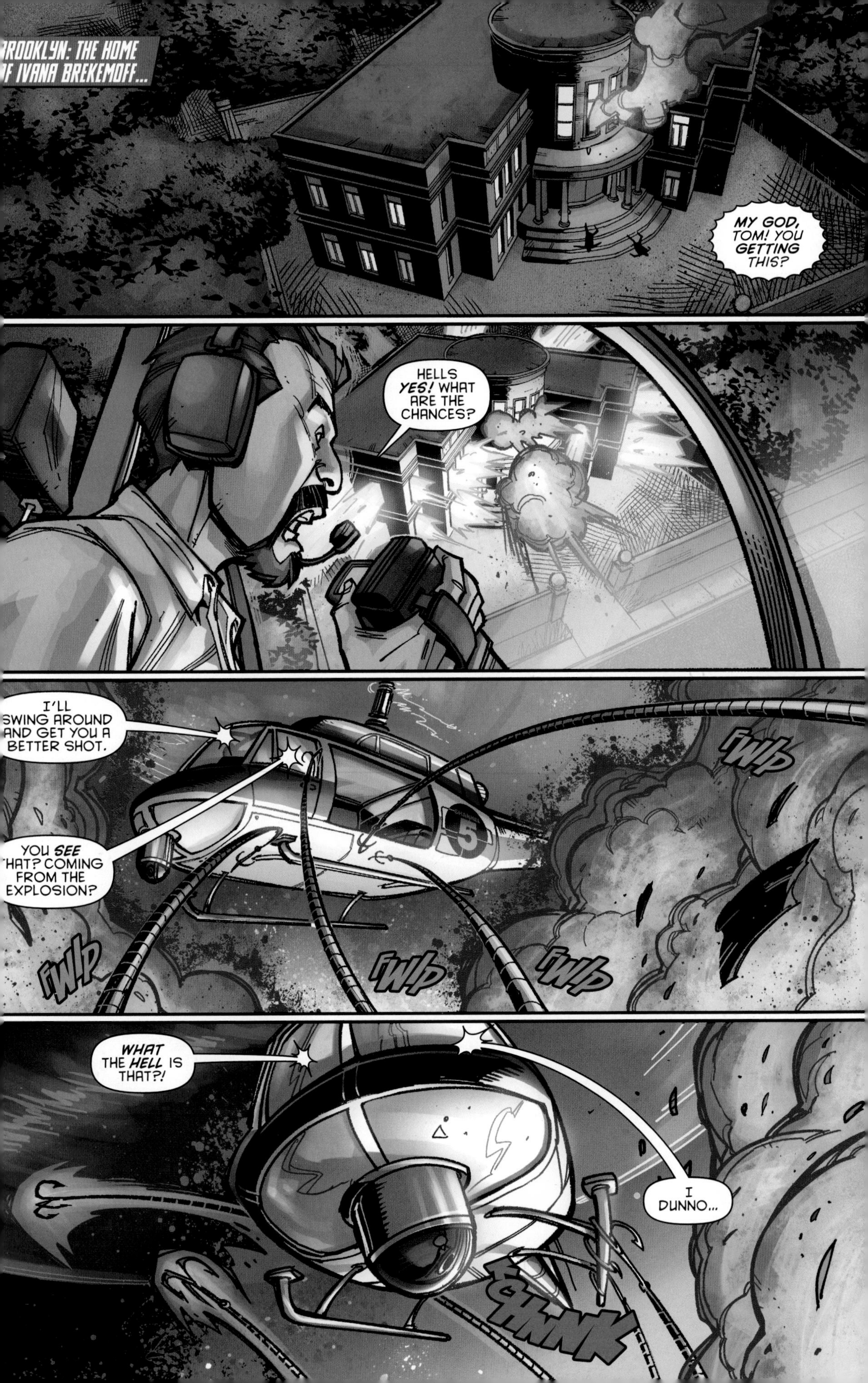
BROOKLYN: THE HOME OF IVANA BREKEMOFF...
MY GOD, TOM! YOU GETTING THIS?
HELLS YES! WHAT ARE THE CHANCES?
I'LL SWING AROUND AND GET YOU A BETTER SHOT.
YOU SEE THAT? COMING FROM THE EXPLOSION?
CHANNEL 5
FWIP
FWIP
FWIP
FWIP
WHAT THE HELL IS THAT?!
I DUNNO...
KCHNNK

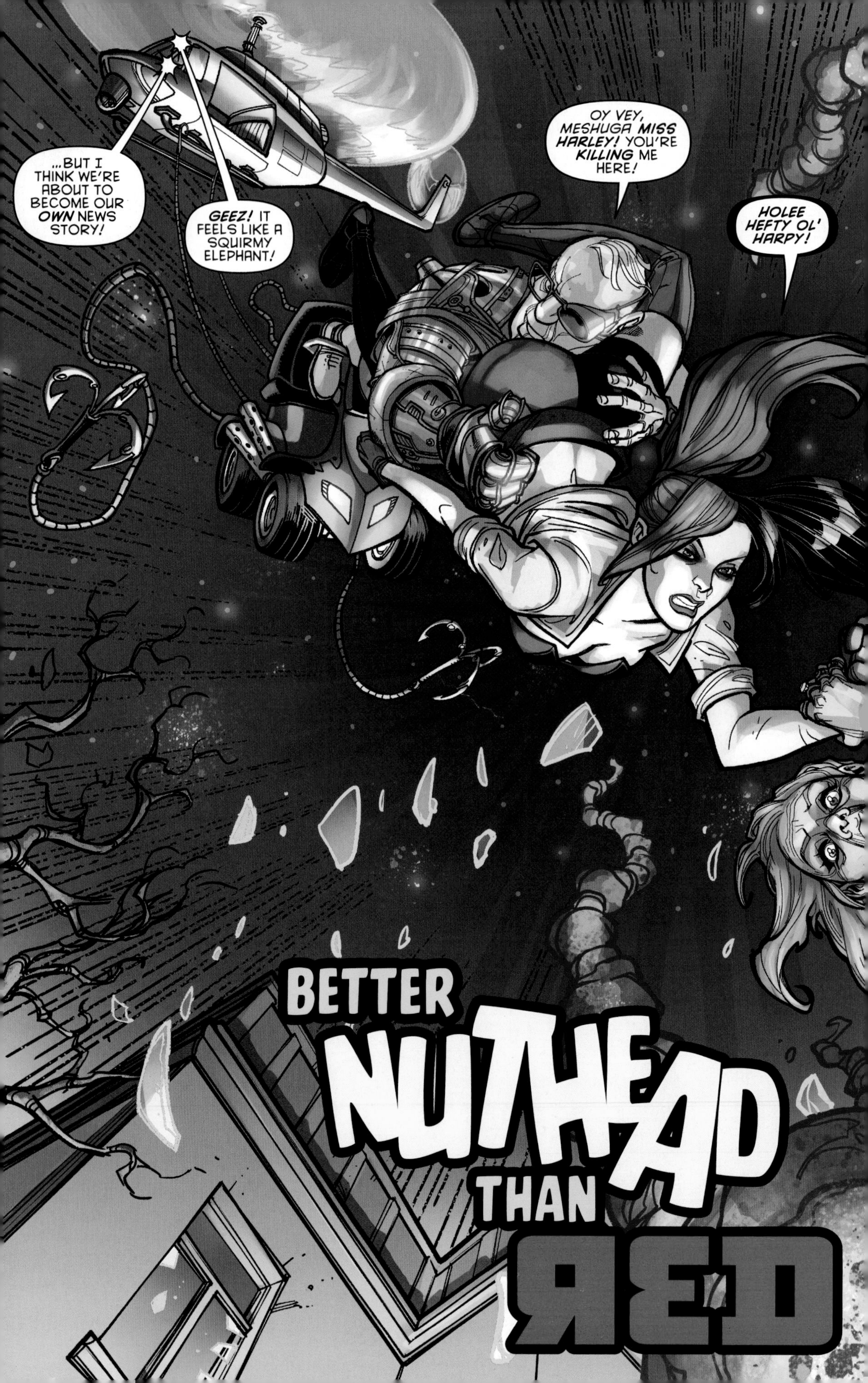

...BUT I THINK WE'RE ABOUT TO BECOME OUR OWN NEWS STORY!
GEEZ! IT FEELS LIKE A SQUIRMY ELEPHANT!
OY VEY, MESHUGA MISS HARLEY! YOU'RE KILLING ME HERE!
HOLEE HEFTY OL' HARPY!
BETTER NUTHEAD THAN RED

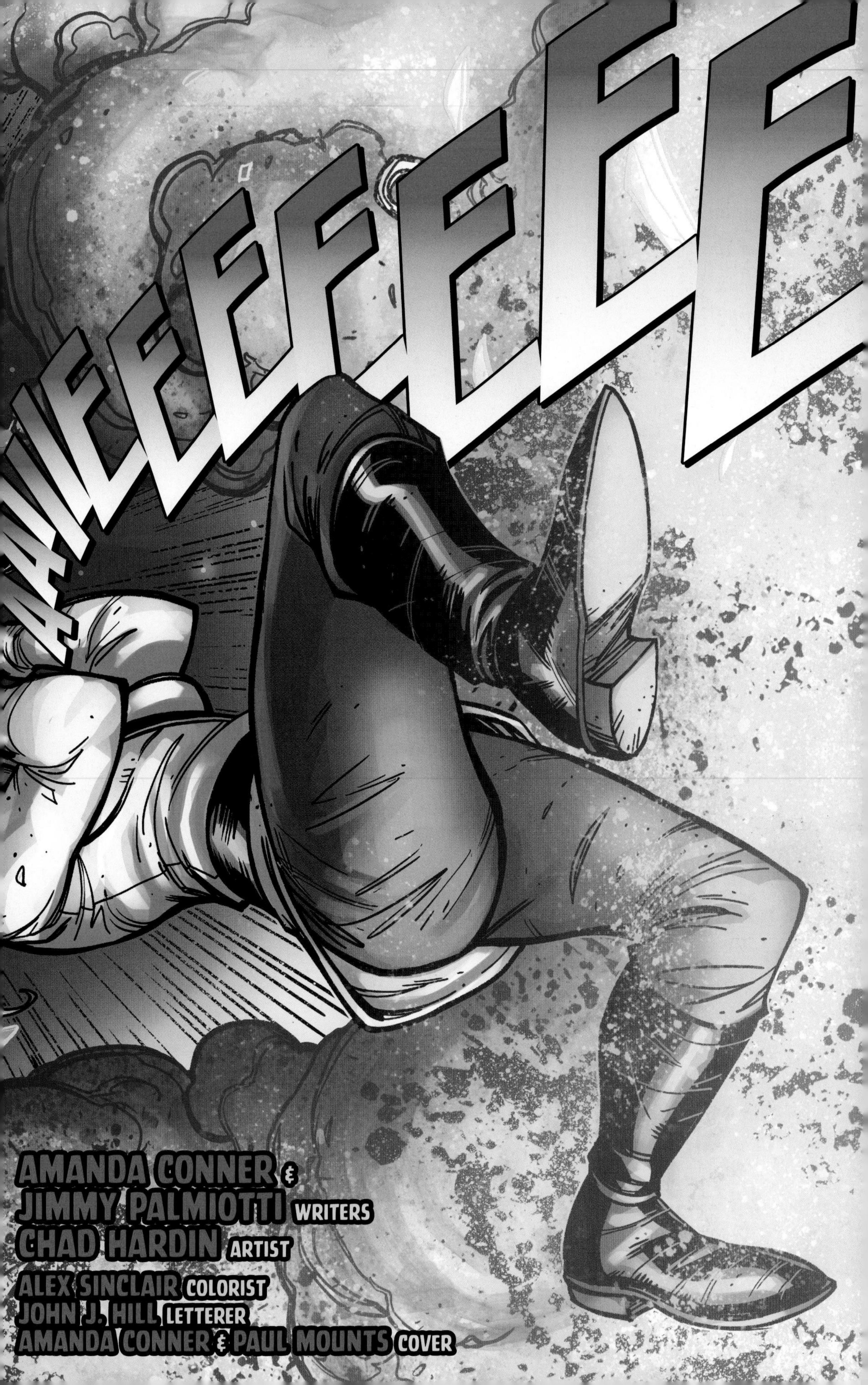
AAIEEEEEEE
AMANDA CONNER & JIMMY PALMIOTTI WRITERS
CHAD HARDIN ARTIST
ALEX SINCLAIR COLORIST
JOHN J. HILL LETTERER
AMANDA CONNER & PAUL MOUNTS COVER

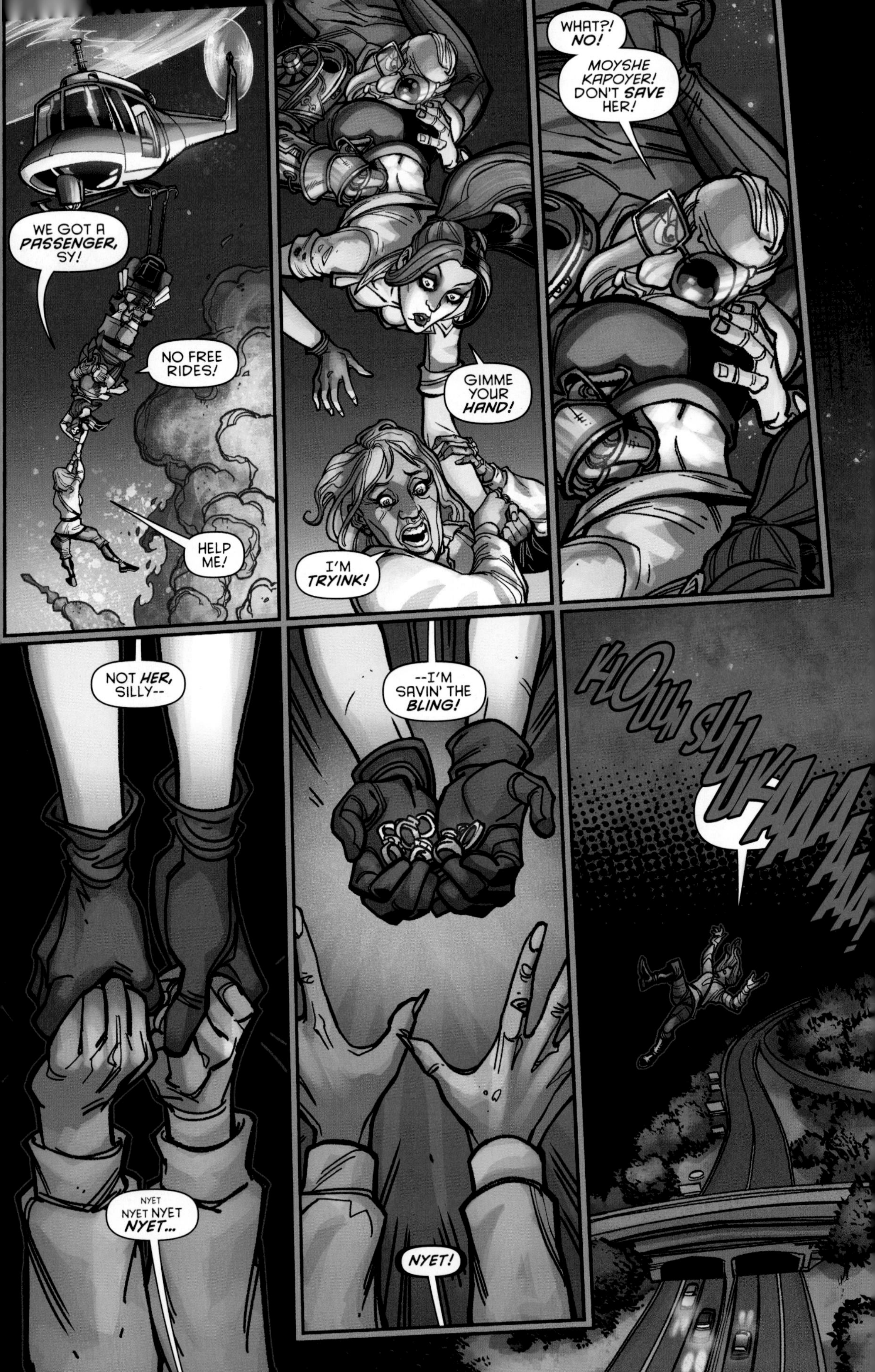
WE GOT A PASSENGER, SY!
NO FREE RIDES!
HELP ME!
GIMME YOUR HAND!
I'M TRYINK!
WHAT?! NO!
MOYSHE KAPOYER! DON'T SAVE HER!
NOT HER, SILLY--
NYET NYET NYET NYET...
--I'M SAVIN' THE BLING!
NYET!
FLOW SUUUHAAAAAA

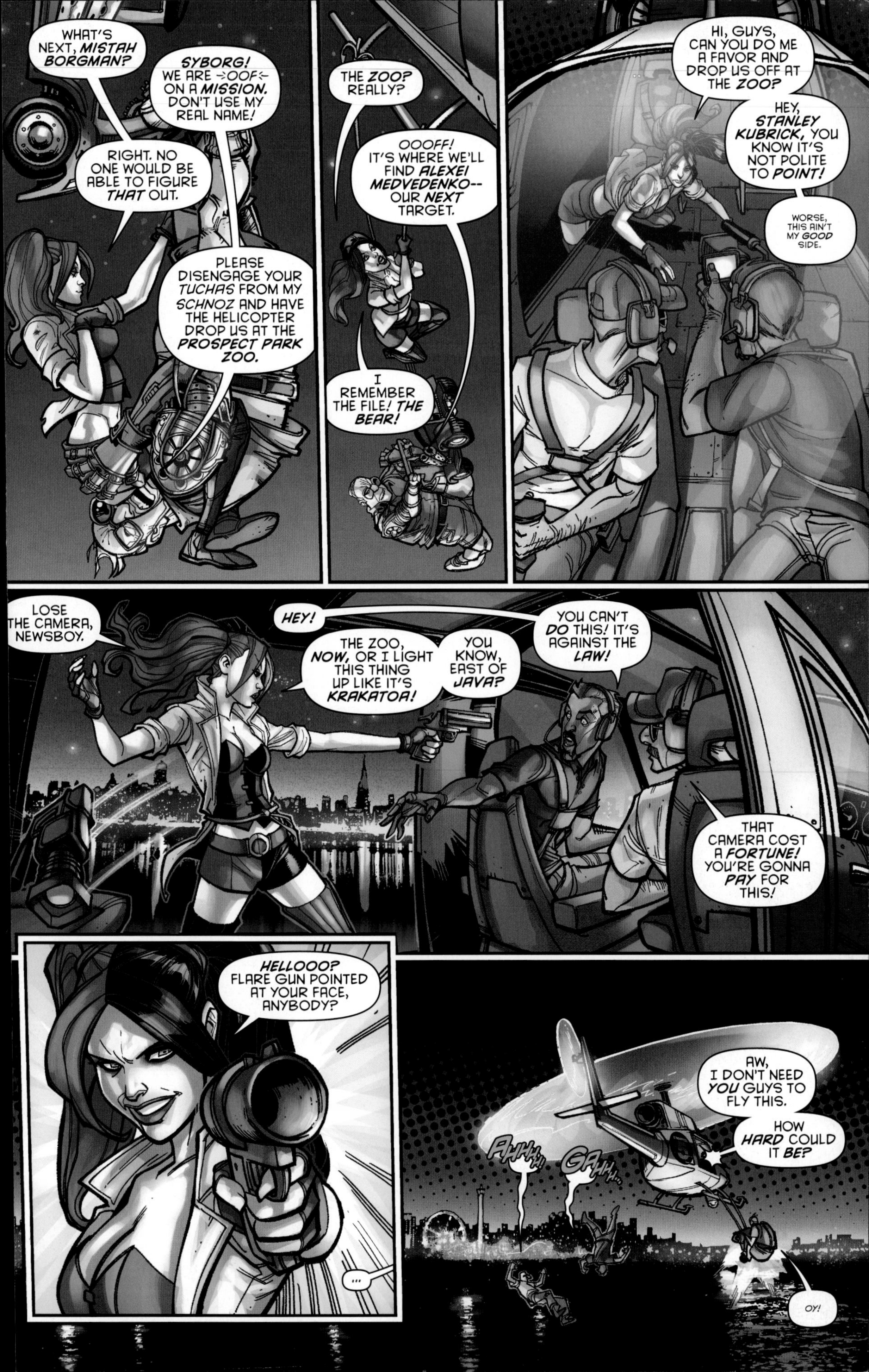
WHAT'S NEXT, MISTAH BORGMAN?
SYBORG! WE ARE →OOF← ON A MISSION. DON'T USE MY REAL NAME!
RIGHT. NO ONE WOULD BE ABLE TO FIGURE THAT OUT.
PLEASE DISENGAGE YOUR TUCHAS FROM MY SCHNOZ AND HAVE THE HELICOPTER DROP US AT THE PROSPECT PARK ZOO.
THE ZOO? REALLY?
OOOFF! IT'S WHERE WE'LL FIND ALEXEI MEDVEDENKO-- OUR NEXT TARGET.
I REMEMBER THE FILE! THE BEAR!
HI, GUYS, CAN YOU DO ME A FAVOR AND DROP US OFF AT THE ZOO?
HEY, STANLEY KUBRICK, YOU KNOW IT'S NOT POLITE TO POINT!
WORSE, THIS AIN'T MY GOOD SIDE.
LOSE THE CAMERA, NEWSBOY.
HEY!
THE ZOO, NOW, OR I LIGHT THIS THING UP LIKE IT'S KRAKATOA!
YOU KNOW, EAST OF JAVA?
YOU CAN'T DO THIS! IT'S AGAINST THE LAW!
THAT CAMERA COST A FORTUNE! YOU'RE GONNA PAY FOR THIS!
HELLOOO? FLARE GUN POINTED AT YOUR FACE, ANYBODY?
...
AW, I DON'T NEED YOU GUYS TO FLY THIS.
HOW HARD COULD IT BE?
AHHHH!!
GAHH...
OY!

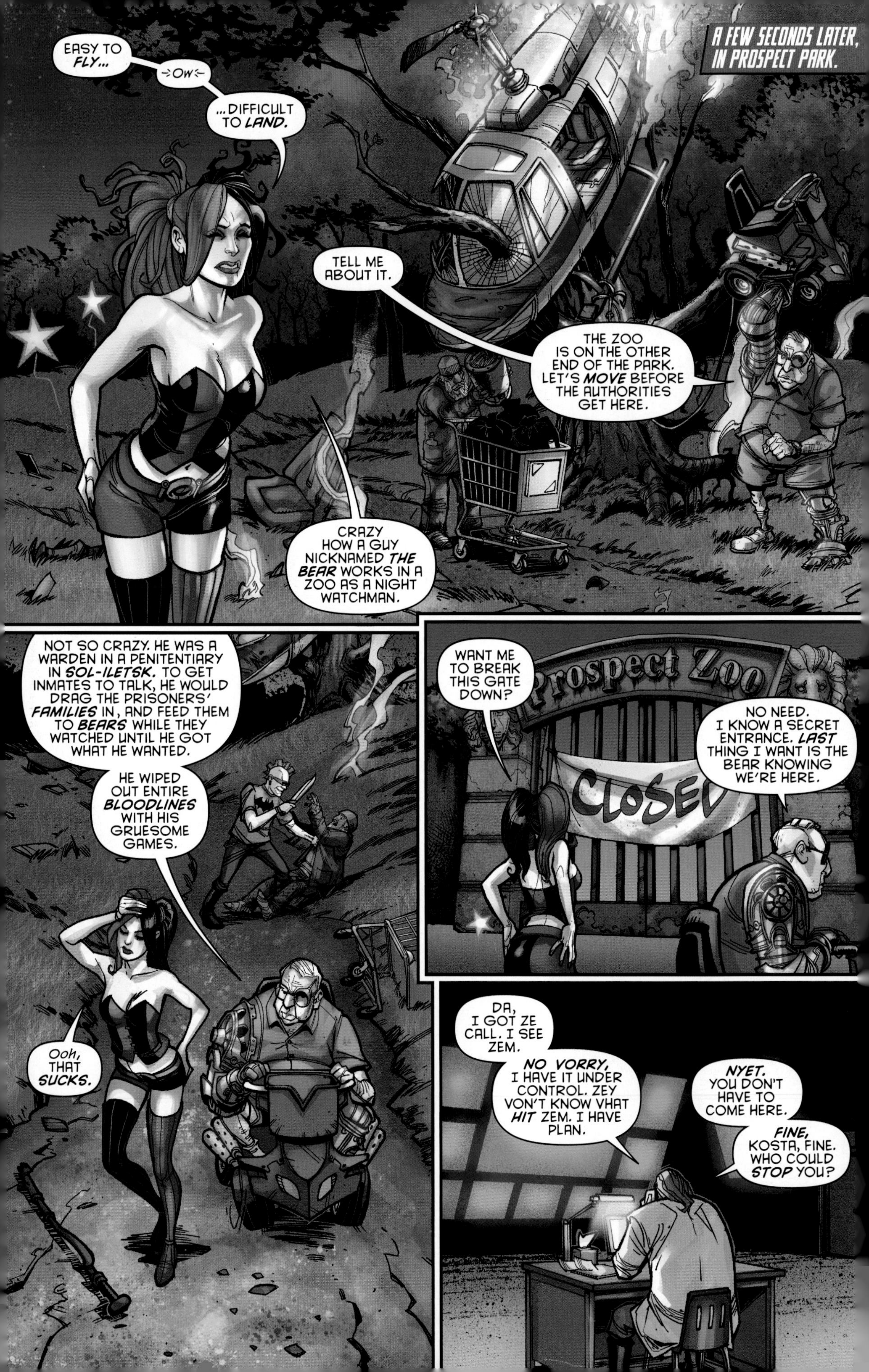

A FEW SECONDS LATER, IN PROSPECT PARK.
EASY TO FLY...
OW
...DIFFICULT TO LAND.
TELL ME ABOUT IT.
THE ZOO IS ON THE OTHER END OF THE PARK. LET'S MOVE BEFORE THE AUTHORITIES GET HERE.
CRAZY HOW A GUY NICKNAMED THE BEAR WORKS IN A ZOO AS A NIGHT WATCHMAN.
NOT SO CRAZY. HE WAS A WARDEN IN A PENITENTIARY IN SOL-ILETSK. TO GET INMATES TO TALK, HE WOULD DRAG THE PRISONERS' FAMILIES IN, AND FEED THEM TO BEARS WHILE THEY WATCHED UNTIL HE GOT WHAT HE WANTED.
HE WIPED OUT ENTIRE BLOODLINES WITH HIS GRUESOME GAMES.
Ooh, THAT SUCKS.
Prospect Zoo
WANT ME TO BREAK THIS GATE DOWN?
CLOSED
NO NEED. I KNOW A SECRET ENTRANCE. LAST THING I WANT IS THE BEAR KNOWING WE'RE HERE.
DA, I GOT ZE CALL. I SEE ZEM.
NO VORRY, I HAVE IT UNDER CONTROL. ZEY VON'T KNOW VHAT HIT ZEM. I HAVE PLAN.
NYET. YOU DON'T HAVE TO COME HERE.
FINE, KOSTA, FINE. WHO COULD STOP YOU?

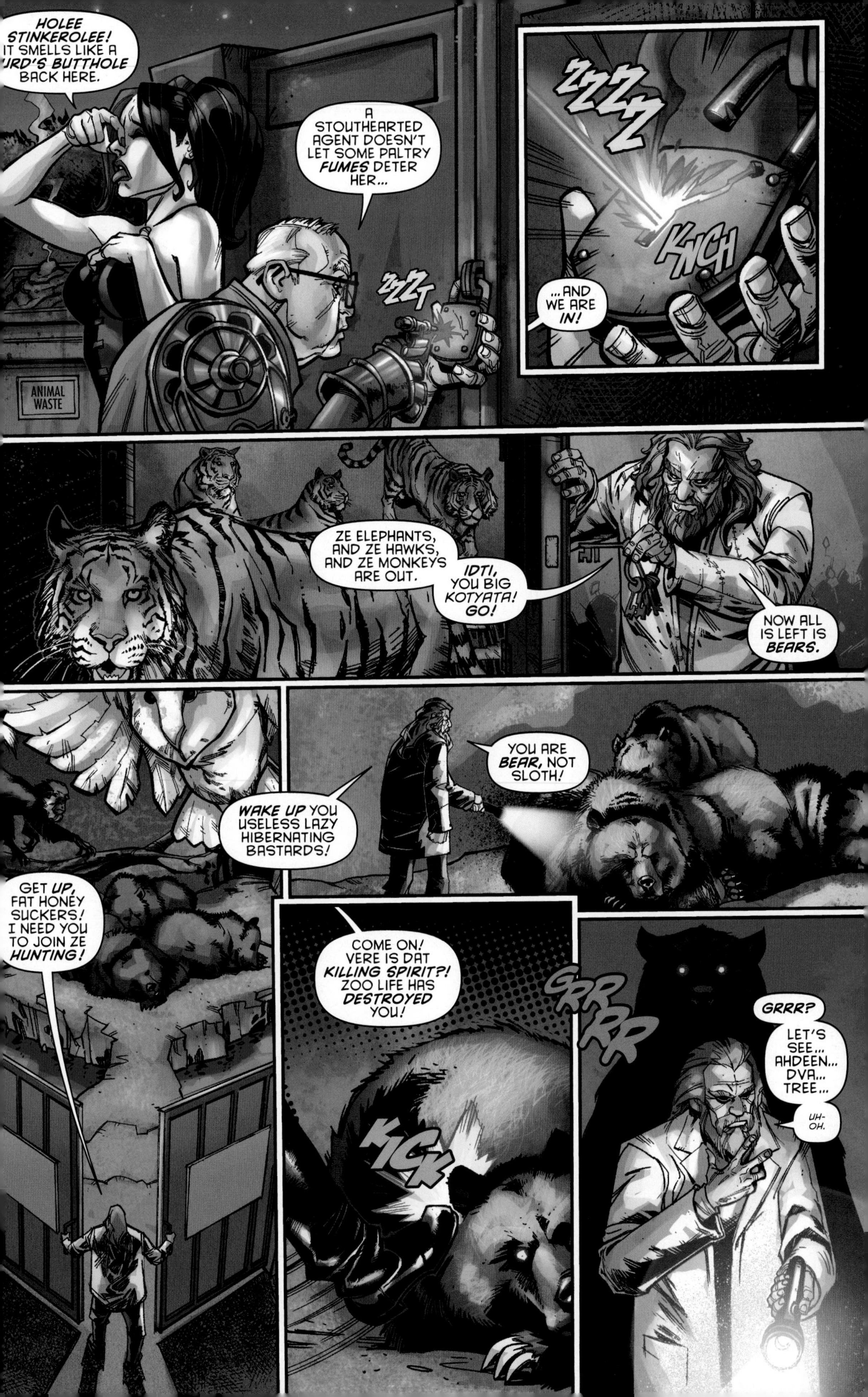
HOLEE STINKEROLEE! IT SMELLS LIKE A URD'S BUTTHOLE BACK HERE.
A STOUTHEARTED AGENT DOESN'T LET SOME PALTRY FUMES DETER HER...
ANIMAL WASTE
ZZZT
ZZZZ
KNCH
...AND WE ARE IN!
ZE ELEPHANTS, AND ZE HAWKS, AND ZE MONKEYS ARE OUT.
IDTI, YOU BIG KOTYATA! GO!
NOW ALL IS LEFT IS BEARS.
WAKE UP YOU USELESS LAZY HIBERNATING BASTARDS!
YOU ARE BEAR, NOT SLOTH!
GET UP, FAT HONEY SUCKERS! I NEED YOU TO JOIN ZE HUNTING!
COME ON! VERE IS DAT KILLING SPIRIT?! ZOO LIFE HAS DESTROYED YOU!
KICK
GRRRRR
GRRR? LET'S SEE... AHDEEN... DVA... TREE...
UH-OH.

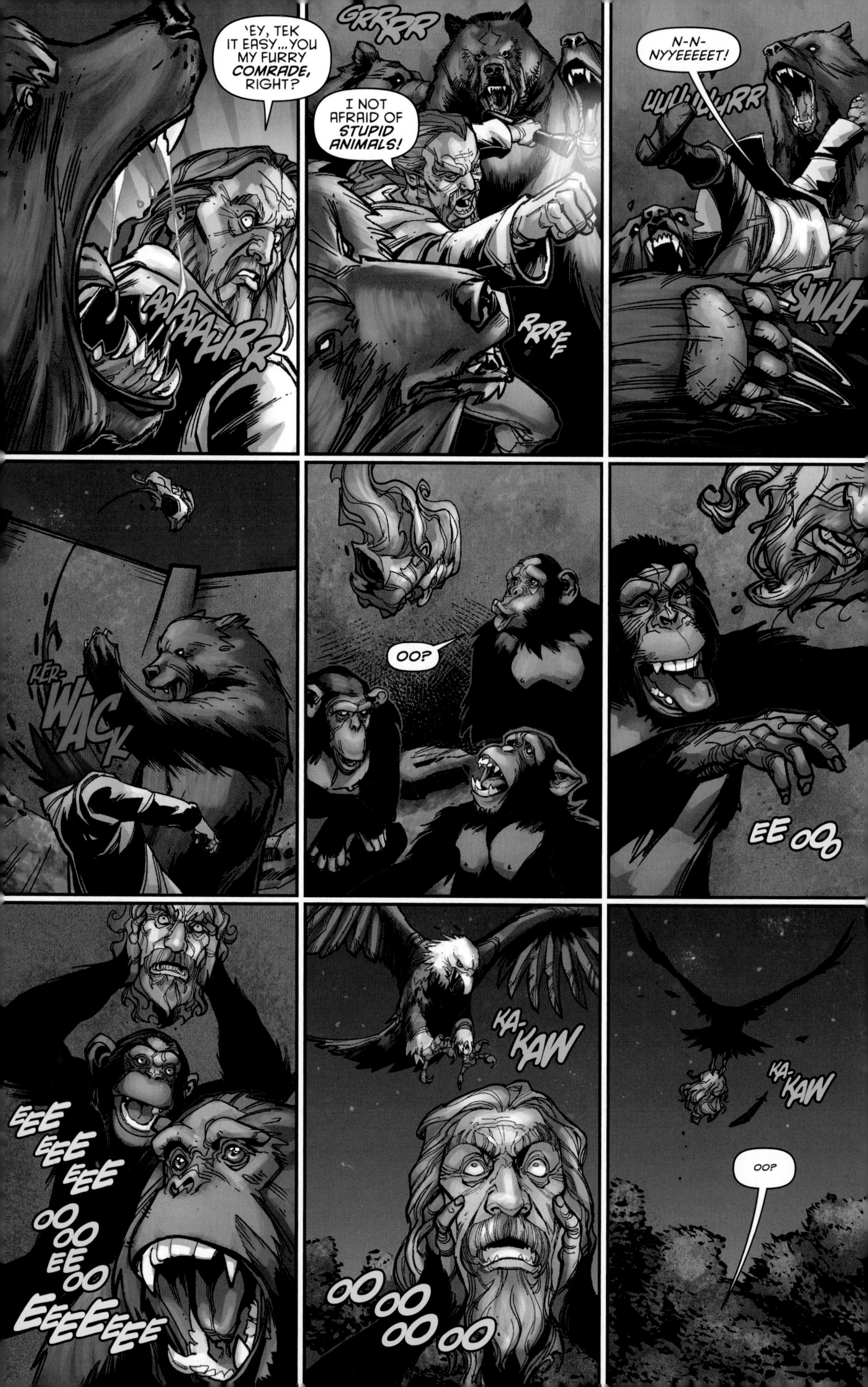
'EY, TEK IT EASY...YOU MY FURRY COMRADE, RIGHT?
AAAAAAURR
GRRRR
I NOT AFRAID OF STUPID ANIMALS!
RRRF
N-N-NYYEEEEET!
UUUUURR
SWAT
KER-WACK
OO?
EE OOO
EEE EEE EEE OOOO EEOO EEEEEEEE
KA-KAW
OOOO OOOO
KA-KAW
OO?

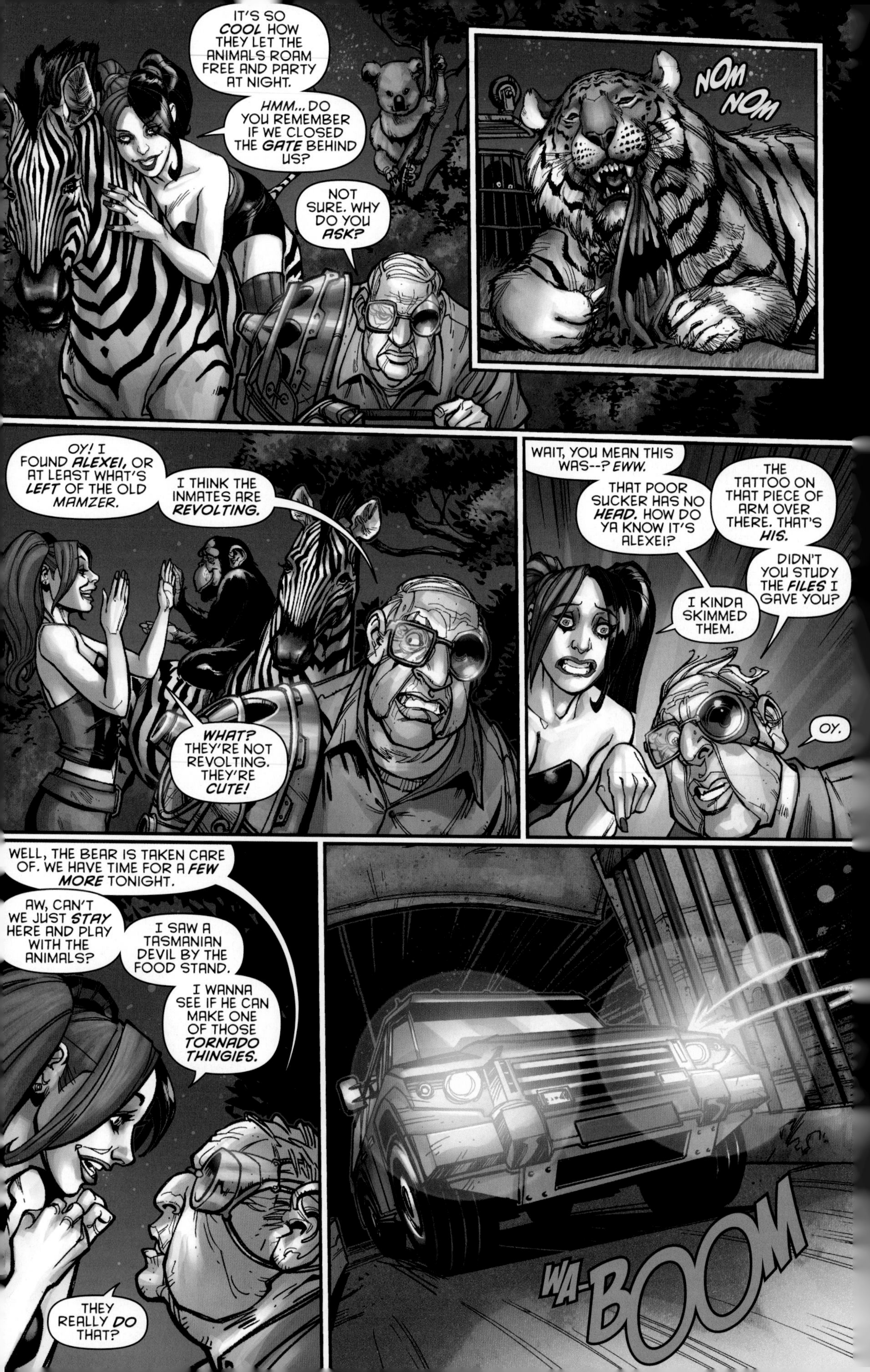
IT'S SO COOL HOW THEY LET THE ANIMALS ROAM FREE AND PARTY AT NIGHT.
HMM... DO YOU REMEMBER IF WE CLOSED THE GATE BEHIND US?
NOT SURE. WHY DO YOU ASK?
NOM NOM
OY! I FOUND ALEXEI, OR AT LEAST WHAT'S LEFT OF THE OLD MAMZER.
I THINK THE INMATES ARE REVOLTING.
WHAT? THEY'RE NOT REVOLTING. THEY'RE CUTE!
WAIT, YOU MEAN THIS WAS--? EWW.
THAT POOR SUCKER HAS NO HEAD. HOW DO YA KNOW IT'S ALEXEI?
THE TATTOO ON THAT PIECE OF ARM OVER THERE. THAT'S HIS.
DIDN'T YOU STUDY THE FILES I GAVE YOU?
I KINDA SKIMMED THEM.
OY.
WELL, THE BEAR IS TAKEN CARE OF. WE HAVE TIME FOR A FEW MORE TONIGHT.
AW, CAN'T WE JUST STAY HERE AND PLAY WITH THE ANIMALS?
I SAW A TASMANIAN DEVIL BY THE FOOD STAND.
I WANNA SEE IF HE CAN MAKE ONE OF THOSE TORNADO THINGIES.
THEY REALLY DO THAT?
WA-BOOM

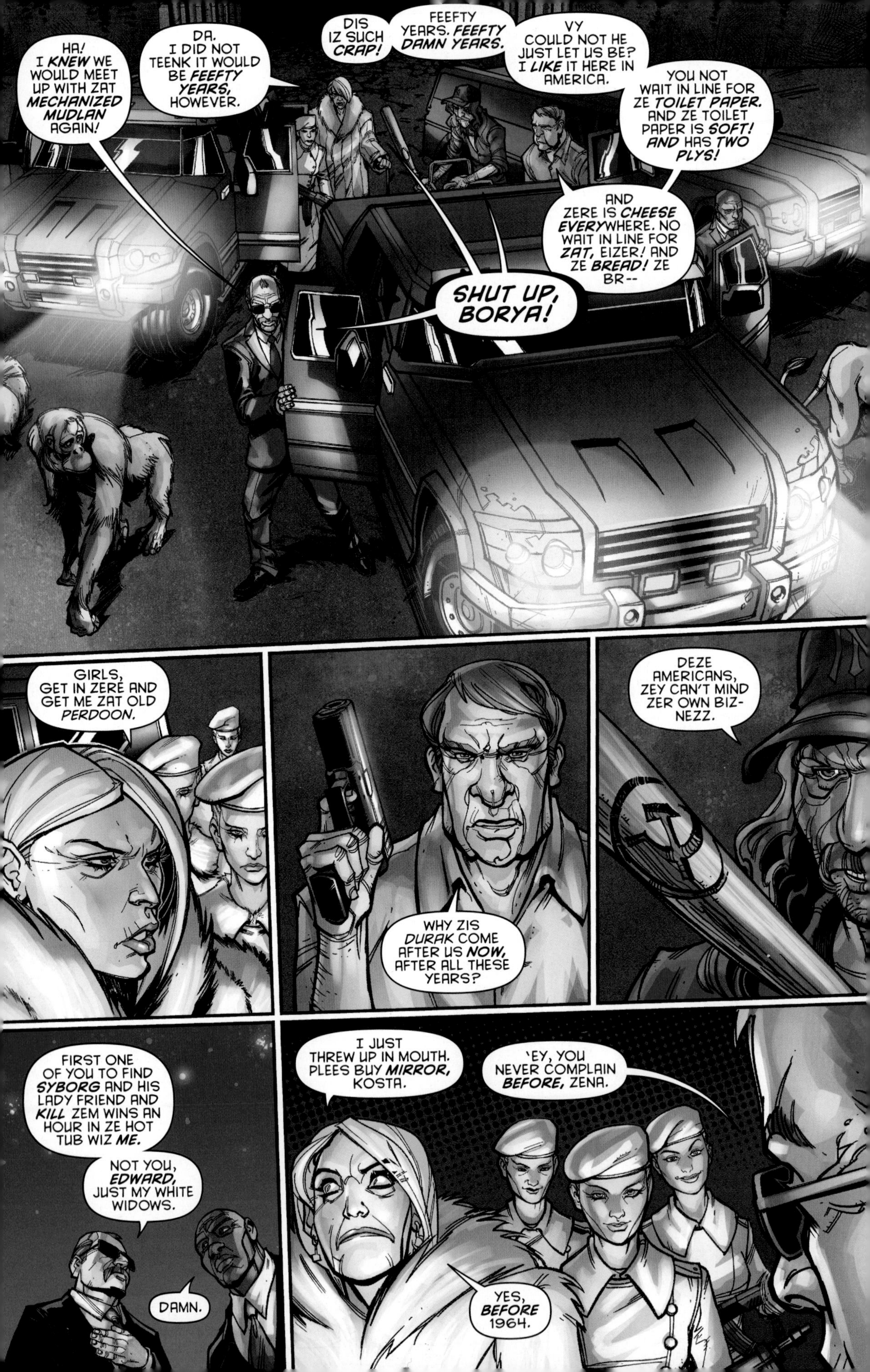

HA! I KNEW WE WOULD MEET UP WITH ZAT MECHANIZED MUDLAN AGAIN!
DA. I DID NOT TEENK IT WOULD BE FEEFTY YEARS, HOWEVER.
DIS IZ SUCH CRAP!
FEEFTY YEARS. FEEFTY DAMN YEARS.
VY COULD NOT HE JUST LET US BE? I LIKE IT HERE IN AMERICA.
YOU NOT WAIT IN LINE FOR ZE TOILET PAPER. AND ZE TOILET PAPER IS SOFT! AND HAS TWO PLYS!
AND ZERE IS CHEESE EVERYWHERE. NO WAIT IN LINE FOR ZAT, EIZER! AND ZE BREAD! ZE BR--
SHUT UP, BORYA!
GIRLS, GET IN ZERE AND GET ME ZAT OLD PERDOON.
WHY ZIS DURAK COME AFTER US NOW, AFTER ALL THESE YEARS?
DEZE AMERICANS, ZEY CAN'T MIND ZER OWN BIZ-NEZZ.
FIRST ONE OF YOU TO FIND SYBORG AND HIS LADY FRIEND AND KILL ZEM WINS AN HOUR IN ZE HOT TUB WIZ ME.
NOT YOU, EDWARD, JUST MY WHITE WIDOWS.
DAMN.
I JUST THREW UP IN MOUTH. PLEES BUY MIRROR, KOSTA.
'EY, YOU NEVER COMPLAIN BEFORE, ZENA.
YES, BEFORE 1964.

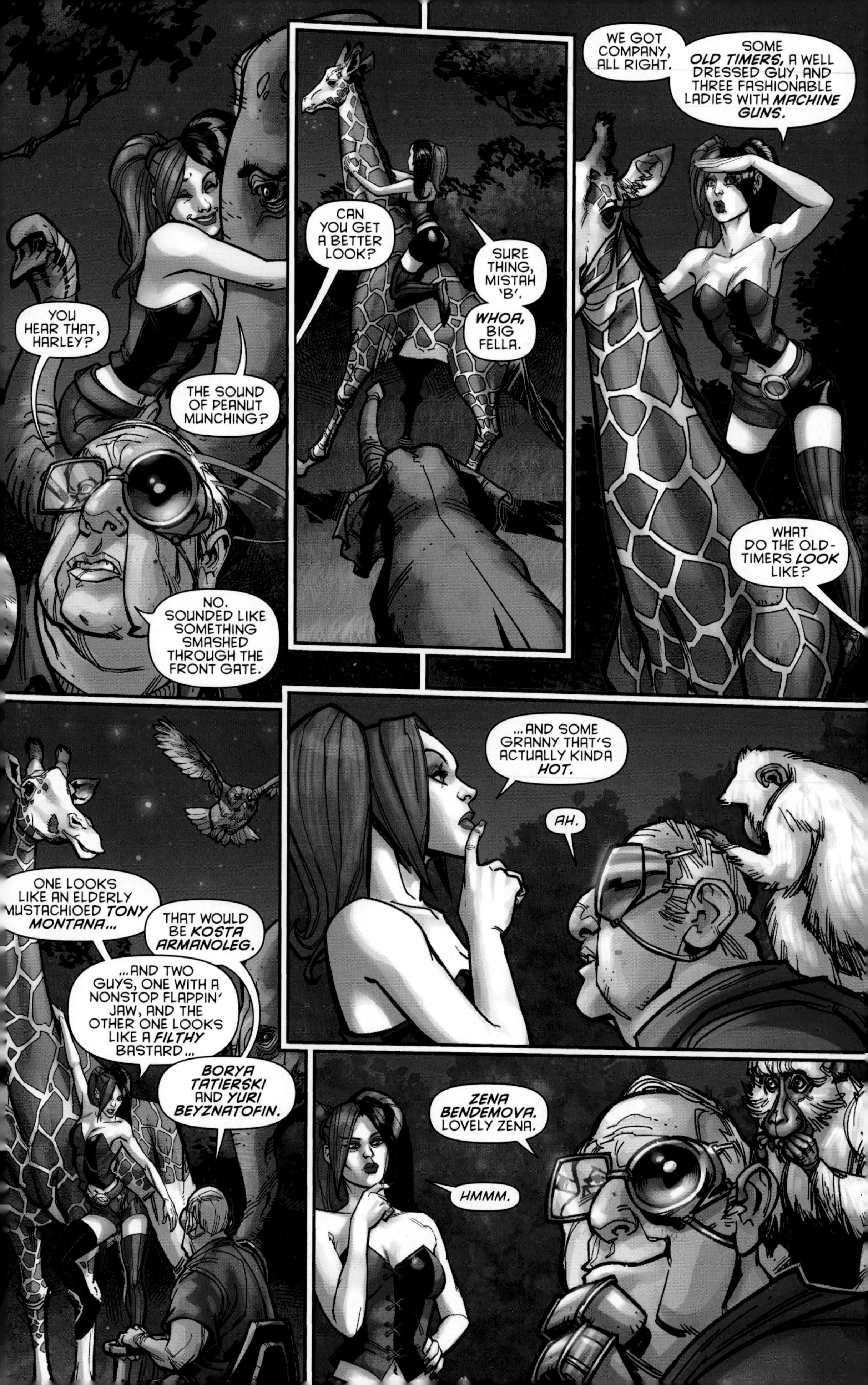
YOU HEAR THAT, HARLEY?
THE SOUND OF PEANUT MUNCHING?
NO. SOUNDED LIKE SOMETHING SMASHED THROUGH THE FRONT GATE.
CAN YOU GET A BETTER LOOK?
SURE THING, MISTAH 'B'.
WHOA, BIG FELLA.
WE GOT COMPANY, ALL RIGHT.
SOME OLD TIMERS, A WELL DRESSED GUY, AND THREE FASHIONABLE LADIES WITH MACHINE GUNS.
WHAT DO THE OLD-TIMERS LOOK LIKE?
ONE LOOKS LIKE AN ELDERLY MUSTACHIOED TONY MONTANA...
THAT WOULD BE KOSTA ARMANOLEG.
...AND TWO GUYS, ONE WITH A NONSTOP FLAPPIN' JAW, AND THE OTHER ONE LOOKS LIKE A FILTHY BASTARD...
BORYA TATIERSKI AND YURI BEYZNATOFIN.
...AND SOME GRANNY THAT'S ACTUALLY KINDA HOT.
AH.
ZENA BENDEMOVA. LOVELY ZENA.
HMMM.

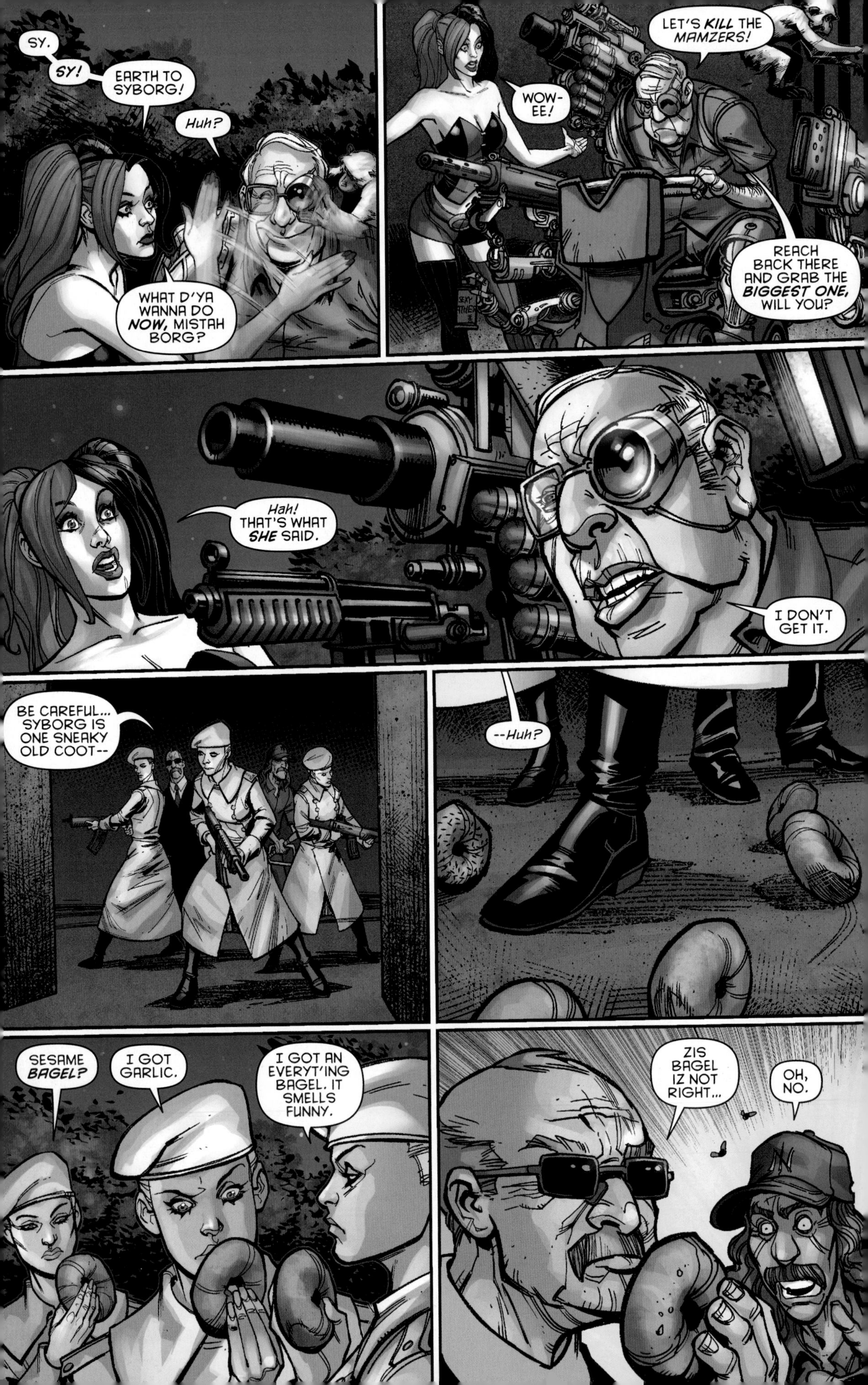
SY.
SY!
EARTH TO SYBORG!
Huh?
WHAT D'YA WANNA DO NOW, MISTAH BORG?
LET'S KILL THE MAMZERS!
WOW-EE!
REACH BACK THERE AND GRAB THE BIGGEST ONE, WILL YOU?
Hah! THAT'S WHAT SHE SAID.
I DON'T GET IT.
BE CAREFUL... SYBORG IS ONE SNEAKY OLD COOT--
--Huh?
SESAME BAGEL?
I GOT GARLIC.
I GOT AN EVERYT'ING BAGEL. IT SMELLS FUNNY.
ZIS BAGEL IZ NOT RIGHT...
OH, NO.

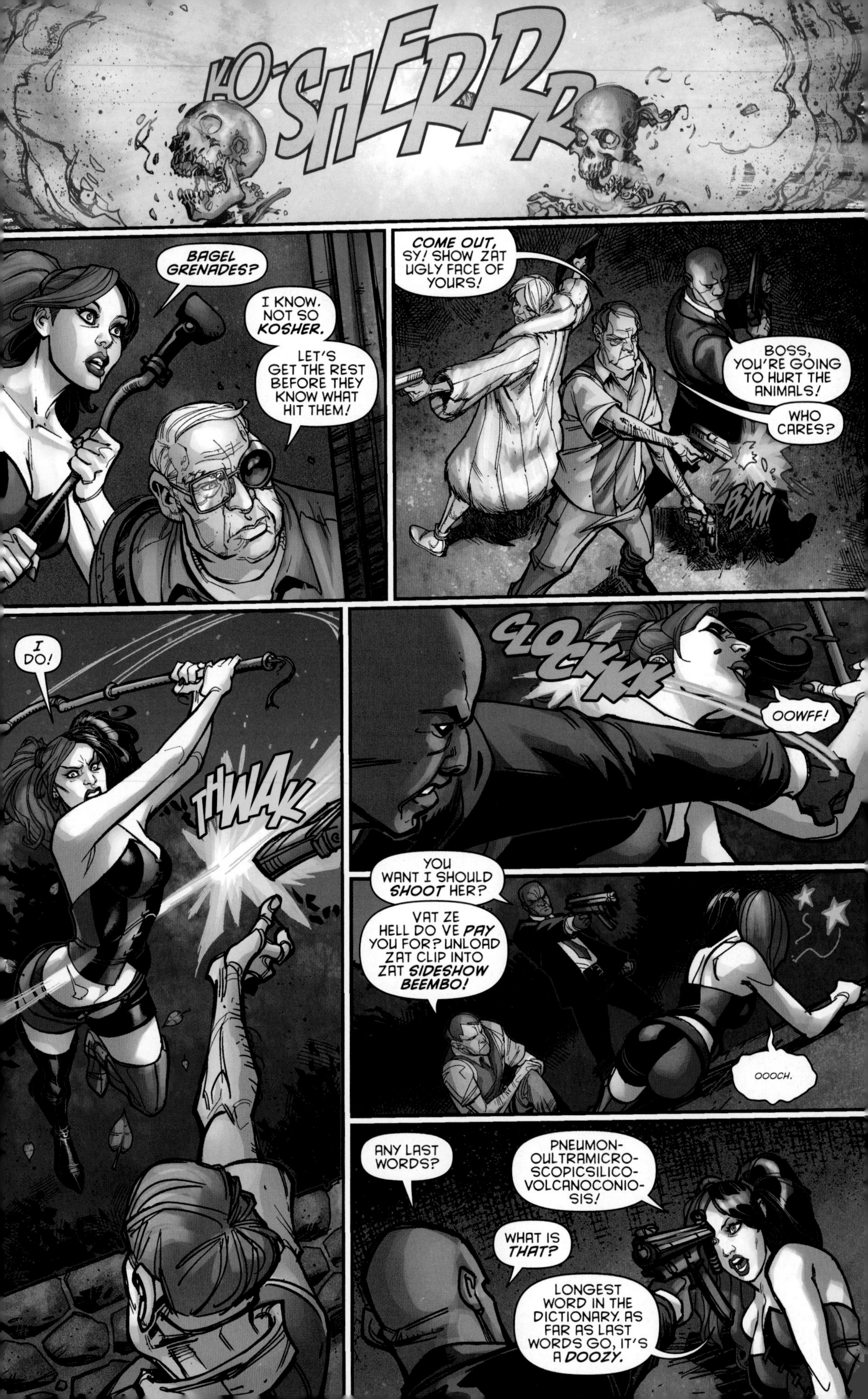
KO-SHERRR
BAGEL GRENADES?
I KNOW. NOT SO KOSHER.
LET'S GET THE REST BEFORE THEY KNOW WHAT HIT THEM!
COME OUT, SY! SHOW ZAT UGLY FACE OF YOURS!
BOSS, YOU'RE GOING TO HURT THE ANIMALS!
WHO CARES?
BLAM
I DO!
THWAK
CLOCKKK
OOWFF!
YOU WANT I SHOULD SHOOT HER?
VAT ZE HELL DO VE PAY YOU FOR? UNLOAD ZAT CLIP INTO ZAT SIDESHOW BEEMBO!
OOOCH.
ANY LAST WORDS?
PNEUMONOULTRAMICROSCOPICSILICOVOLCANOCONIOSIS!
WHAT IS THAT?
LONGEST WORD IN THE DICTIONARY. AS FAR AS LAST WORDS GO, IT'S A DOOZY.

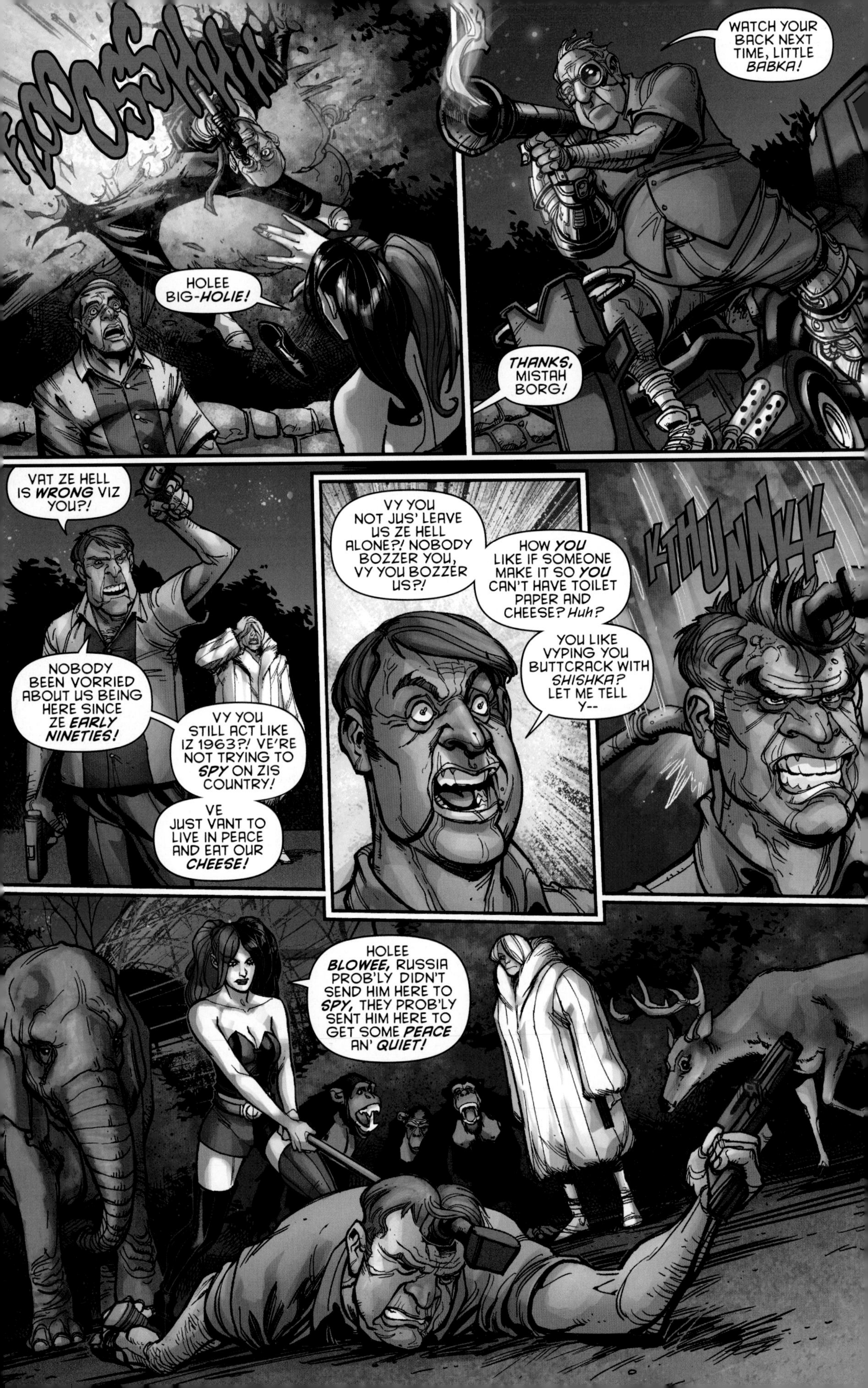
FOOOSHHH!
HOLEE BIG-HOLIE!
WATCH YOUR BACK NEXT TIME, LITTLE BABKA!
THANKS, MISTAH BORG!
VAT ZE HELL IS WRONG VIZ YOU?!
NOBODY BEEN VORRIED ABOUT US BEING HERE SINCE ZE EARLY NINETIES!
VY YOU STILL ACT LIKE IZ 1963?! VE'RE NOT TRYING TO SPY ON ZIS COUNTRY!
VE JUST VANT TO LIVE IN PEACE AND EAT OUR CHEESE!
VY YOU NOT JUS' LEAVE US ZE HELL ALONE?! NOBODY BOZZER YOU, VY YOU BOZZER US?!
HOW YOU LIKE IF SOMEONE MAKE IT SO YOU CAN'T HAVE TOILET PAPER AND CHEESE? Huh?
YOU LIKE VYPING YOU BUTTCRACK WITH SHISHKA? LET ME TELL Y--
KTHUNNK
HOLEE BLOWEE, RUSSIA PROB'LY DIDN'T SEND HIM HERE TO SPY, THEY PROB'LY SENT HIM HERE TO GET SOME PEACE AN' QUIET!

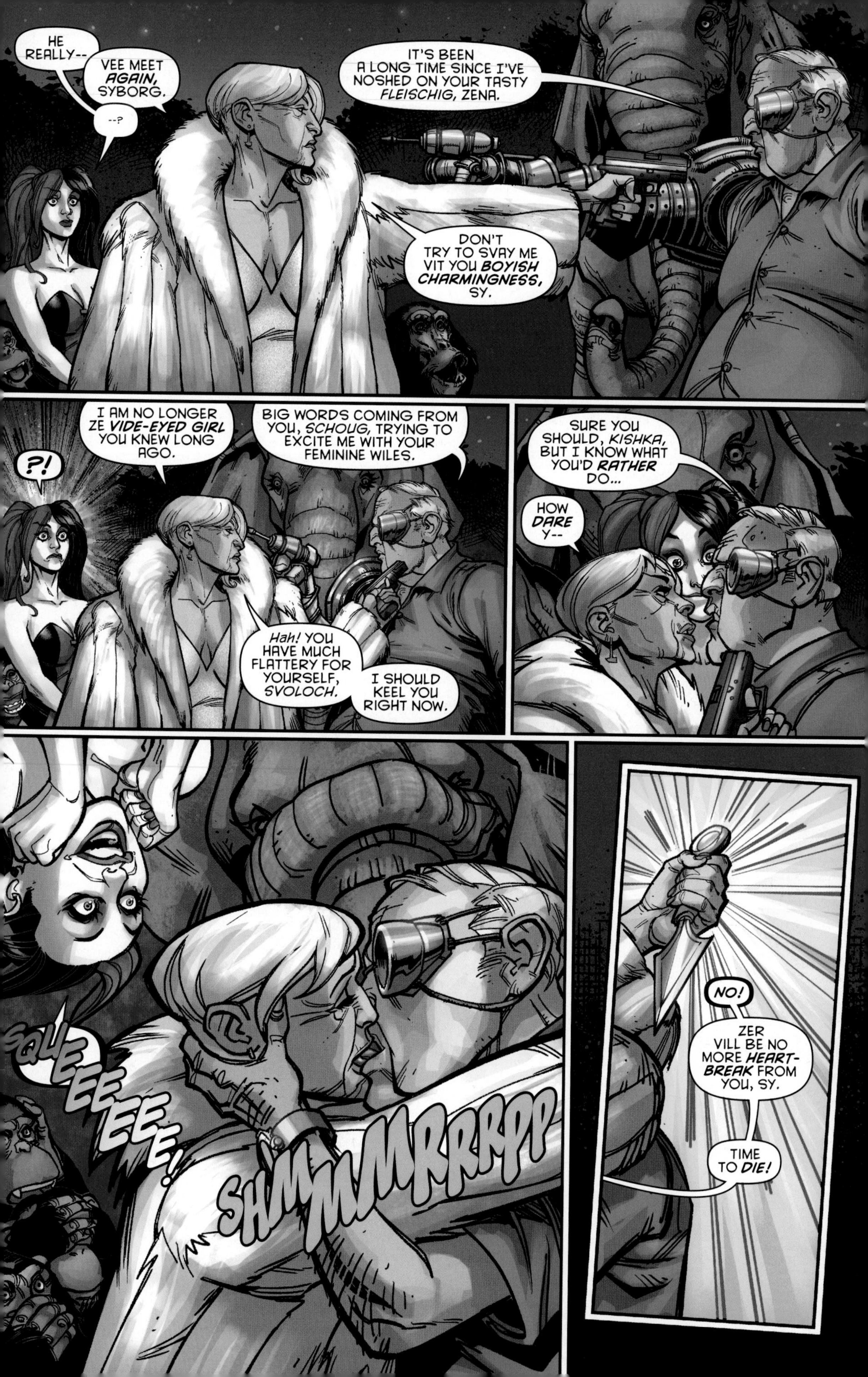
HE REALLY--
VEE MEET AGAIN, SYBORG.
--?
IT'S BEEN A LONG TIME SINCE I'VE NOSHED ON YOUR TASTY FLEISCHIG, ZENA.
DON'T TRY TO SVAY ME VIT YOU BOYISH CHARMINGNESS, SY.
?!
I AM NO LONGER ZE VIDE-EYED GIRL YOU KNEW LONG AGO.
BIG WORDS COMING FROM YOU, SCHOUG, TRYING TO EXCITE ME WITH YOUR FEMININE WILES.
Hah! YOU HAVE MUCH FLATTERY FOR YOURSELF, SVOLOCH.
I SHOULD KEEL YOU RIGHT NOW.
SURE YOU SHOULD, KISHKA, BUT I KNOW WHAT YOU'D RATHER DO...
HOW DARE Y--
SQUEEEEEEEE!
SHMMMRRRPP
NO!
ZER VILL BE NO MORE HEART-BREAK FROM YOU, SY.
TIME TO DIE!

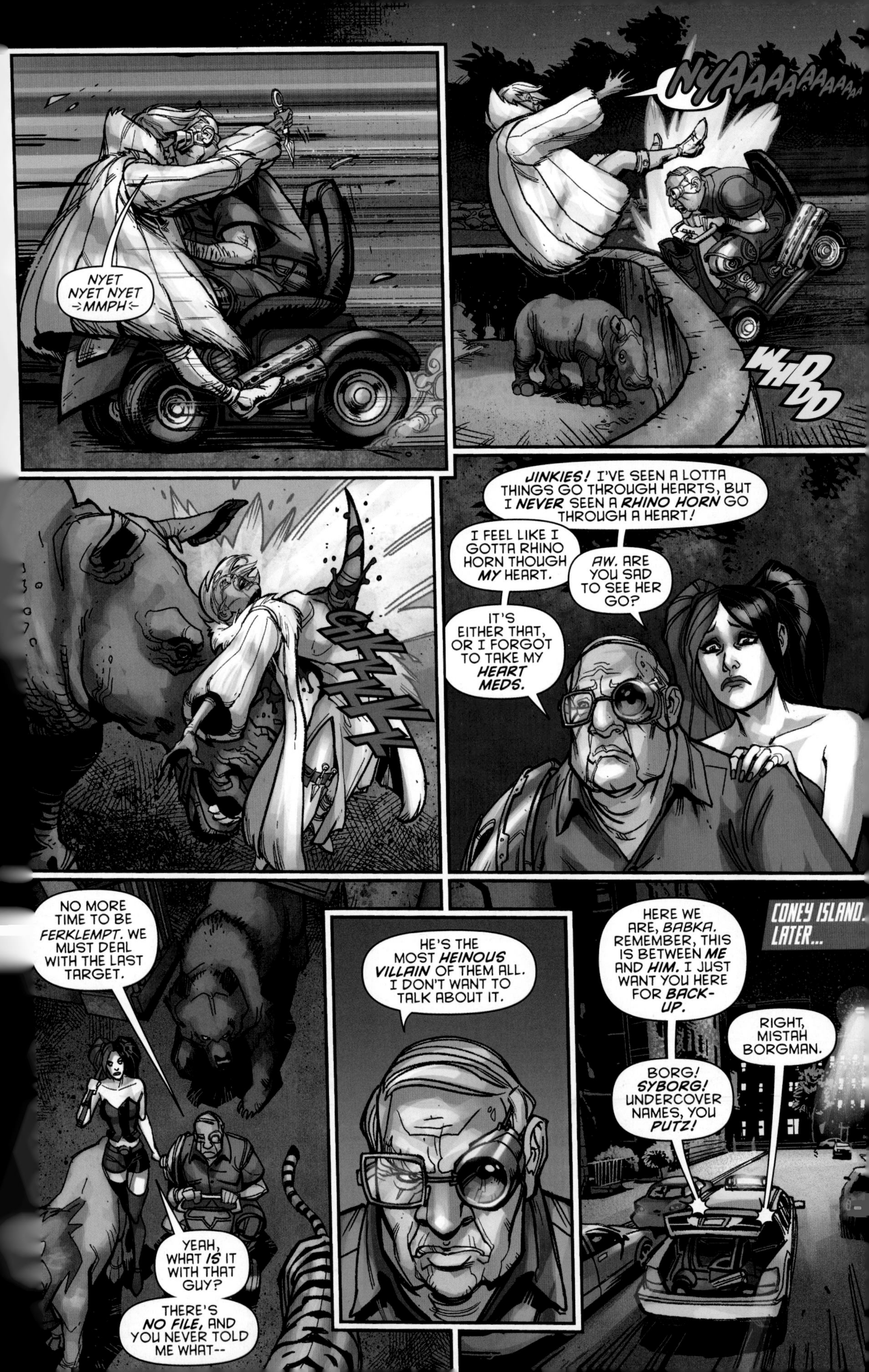
NYET NYET NYET MMPH
NYAAAAAAAAAAA
WHDDD
GHHHH
JINKIES! I'VE SEEN A LOTTA THINGS GO THROUGH HEARTS, BUT I NEVER SEEN A RHINO HORN GO THROUGH A HEART!
AW. ARE YOU SAD TO SEE HER GO?
I FEEL LIKE I GOTTA RHINO HORN THOUGH MY HEART.
IT'S EITHER THAT, OR I FORGOT TO TAKE MY HEART MEDS.
NO MORE TIME TO BE FERKLEMPT. WE MUST DEAL WITH THE LAST TARGET.
YEAH, WHAT IS IT WITH THAT GUY?
THERE'S NO FILE, AND YOU NEVER TOLD ME WHAT--
HE'S THE MOST HEINOUS VILLAIN OF THEM ALL. I DON'T WANT TO TALK ABOUT IT.
CONEY ISLAND. LATER...
HERE WE ARE, BABKA. REMEMBER, THIS IS BETWEEN ME AND HIM. I JUST WANT YOU HERE FOR BACK-UP.
RIGHT, MISTAH BORGMAN.
BORG! SYBORG! UNDERCOVER NAMES, YOU PUTZ!

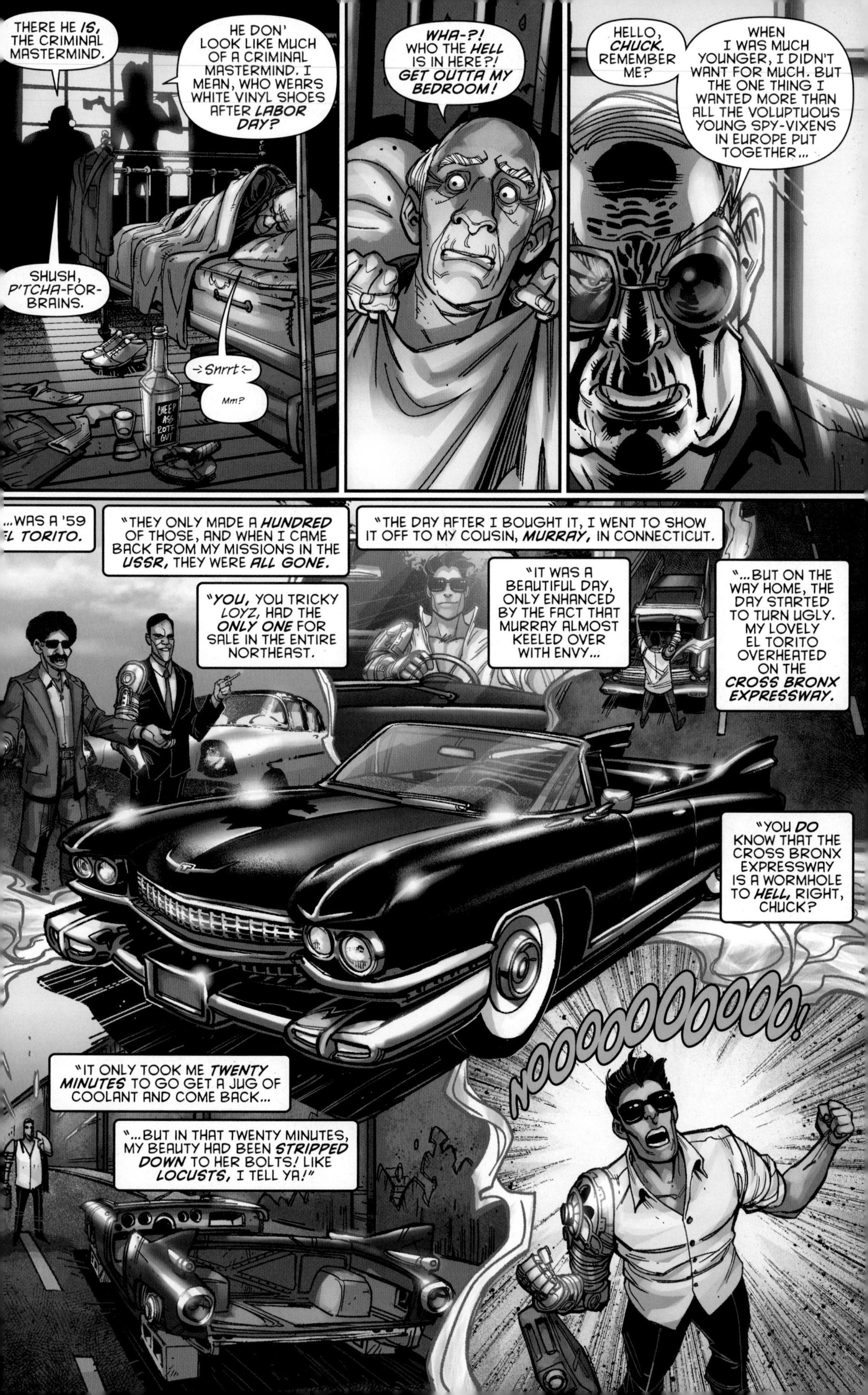
THERE HE IS, THE CRIMINAL MASTERMIND.
HE DON' LOOK LIKE MUCH OF A CRIMINAL MASTERMIND. I MEAN, WHO WEARS WHITE VINYL SHOES AFTER LABOR DAY?
SHUSH, P'TCHA-FOR-BRAINS.
Snrrt
Mm?
CHEEP ASS ROTT GUT
WHA-?! WHO THE HELL IS IN HERE?! GET OUTTA MY BEDROOM!
HELLO, CHUCK. REMEMBER ME?
WHEN I WAS MUCH YOUNGER, I DIDN'T WANT FOR MUCH. BUT THE ONE THING I WANTED MORE THAN ALL THE VOLUPTUOUS YOUNG SPY-VIXENS IN EUROPE PUT TOGETHER...
...WAS A '59 EL TORITO.
"THEY ONLY MADE A HUNDRED OF THOSE, AND WHEN I CAME BACK FROM MY MISSIONS IN THE USSR, THEY WERE ALL GONE.
"YOU, YOU TRICKY LOYZ, HAD THE ONLY ONE FOR SALE IN THE ENTIRE NORTHEAST.
"THE DAY AFTER I BOUGHT IT, I WENT TO SHOW IT OFF TO MY COUSIN, MURRAY, IN CONNECTICUT.
"IT WAS A BEAUTIFUL DAY, ONLY ENHANCED BY THE FACT THAT MURRAY ALMOST KEELED OVER WITH ENVY...
"...BUT ON THE WAY HOME, THE DAY STARTED TO TURN UGLY. MY LOVELY EL TORITO OVERHEATED ON THE CROSS BRONX EXPRESSWAY.
"YOU DO KNOW THAT THE CROSS BRONX EXPRESSWAY IS A WORMHOLE TO HELL, RIGHT, CHUCK?
"IT ONLY TOOK ME TWENTY MINUTES TO GO GET A JUG OF COOLANT AND COME BACK...
"...BUT IN THAT TWENTY MINUTES, MY BEAUTY HAD BEEN STRIPPED DOWN TO HER BOLTS! LIKE LOCUSTS, I TELL YA!"
NOOOOOOOOOOOo!

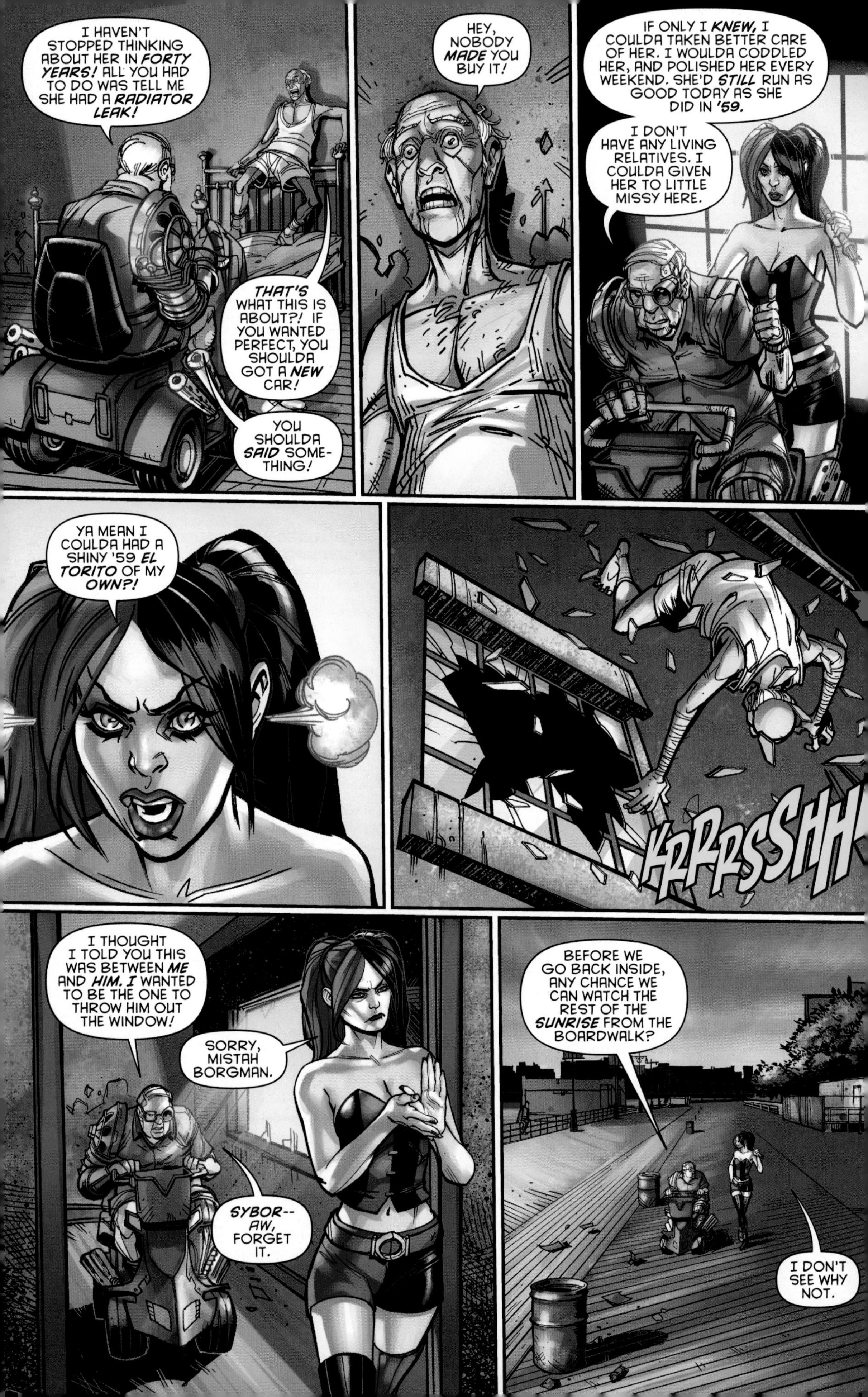
I HAVEN'T STOPPED THINKING ABOUT HER IN FORTY YEARS! ALL YOU HAD TO DO WAS TELL ME SHE HAD A RADIATOR LEAK!
THAT'S WHAT THIS IS ABOUT?! IF YOU WANTED PERFECT, YOU SHOULDA GOT A NEW CAR!
YOU SHOULDA SAID SOME-THING!
HEY, NOBODY MADE YOU BUY IT!
IF ONLY I KNEW, I COULDA TAKEN BETTER CARE OF HER. I WOULDA CODDLED HER, AND POLISHED HER EVERY WEEKEND. SHE'D STILL RUN AS GOOD TODAY AS SHE DID IN '59.
I DON'T HAVE ANY LIVING RELATIVES. I COULDA GIVEN HER TO LITTLE MISSY HERE.
YA MEAN I COULDA HAD A SHINY '59 EL TORITO OF MY OWN?!
KRRRSSHH
I THOUGHT I TOLD YOU THIS WAS BETWEEN ME AND HIM. I WANTED TO BE THE ONE TO THROW HIM OUT THE WINDOW!
SORRY, MISTAH BORGMAN.
SYBOR-- AW, FORGET IT.
BEFORE WE GO BACK INSIDE, ANY CHANCE WE CAN WATCH THE REST OF THE SUNRISE FROM THE BOARDWALK?
I DON'T SEE WHY NOT.

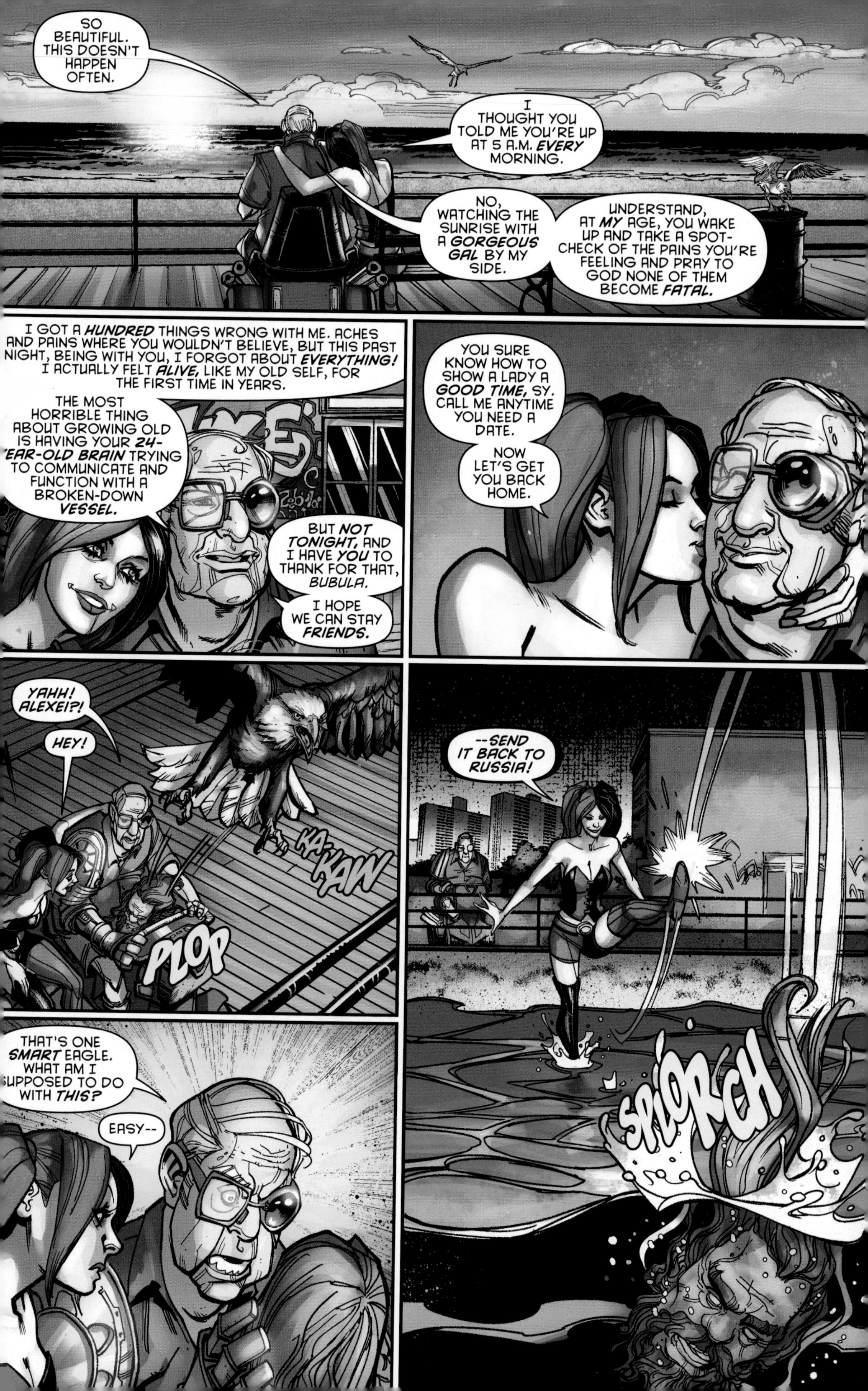

SO BEAUTIFUL. THIS DOESN'T HAPPEN OFTEN.
I THOUGHT YOU TOLD ME YOU'RE UP AT 5 A.M. EVERY MORNING.
NO, WATCHING THE SUNRISE WITH A GORGEOUS GAL BY MY SIDE.
UNDERSTAND, AT MY AGE, YOU WAKE UP AND TAKE A SPOT-CHECK OF THE PAINS YOU'RE FEELING AND PRAY TO GOD NONE OF THEM BECOME FATAL.
I GOT A HUNDRED THINGS WRONG WITH ME. ACHES AND PAINS WHERE YOU WOULDN'T BELIEVE, BUT THIS PAST NIGHT, BEING WITH YOU, I FORGOT ABOUT EVERYTHING! I ACTUALLY FELT ALIVE, LIKE MY OLD SELF, FOR THE FIRST TIME IN YEARS.
THE MOST HORRIBLE THING ABOUT GROWING OLD IS HAVING YOUR 24-YEAR-OLD BRAIN TRYING TO COMMUNICATE AND FUNCTION WITH A BROKEN-DOWN VESSEL.
BUT NOT TONIGHT, AND I HAVE YOU TO THANK FOR THAT, BUBULA.
I HOPE WE CAN STAY FRIENDS.
YOU SURE KNOW HOW TO SHOW A LADY A GOOD TIME, SY. CALL ME ANYTIME YOU NEED A DATE.
NOW LET'S GET YOU BACK HOME.
YAHH! ALEXEI?!
HEY!
KA-KAW
PLOP
--SEND IT BACK TO RUSSIA!
THAT'S ONE SMART EAGLE. WHAT AM I SUPPOSED TO DO WITH THIS?
EASY--
SPLORCH

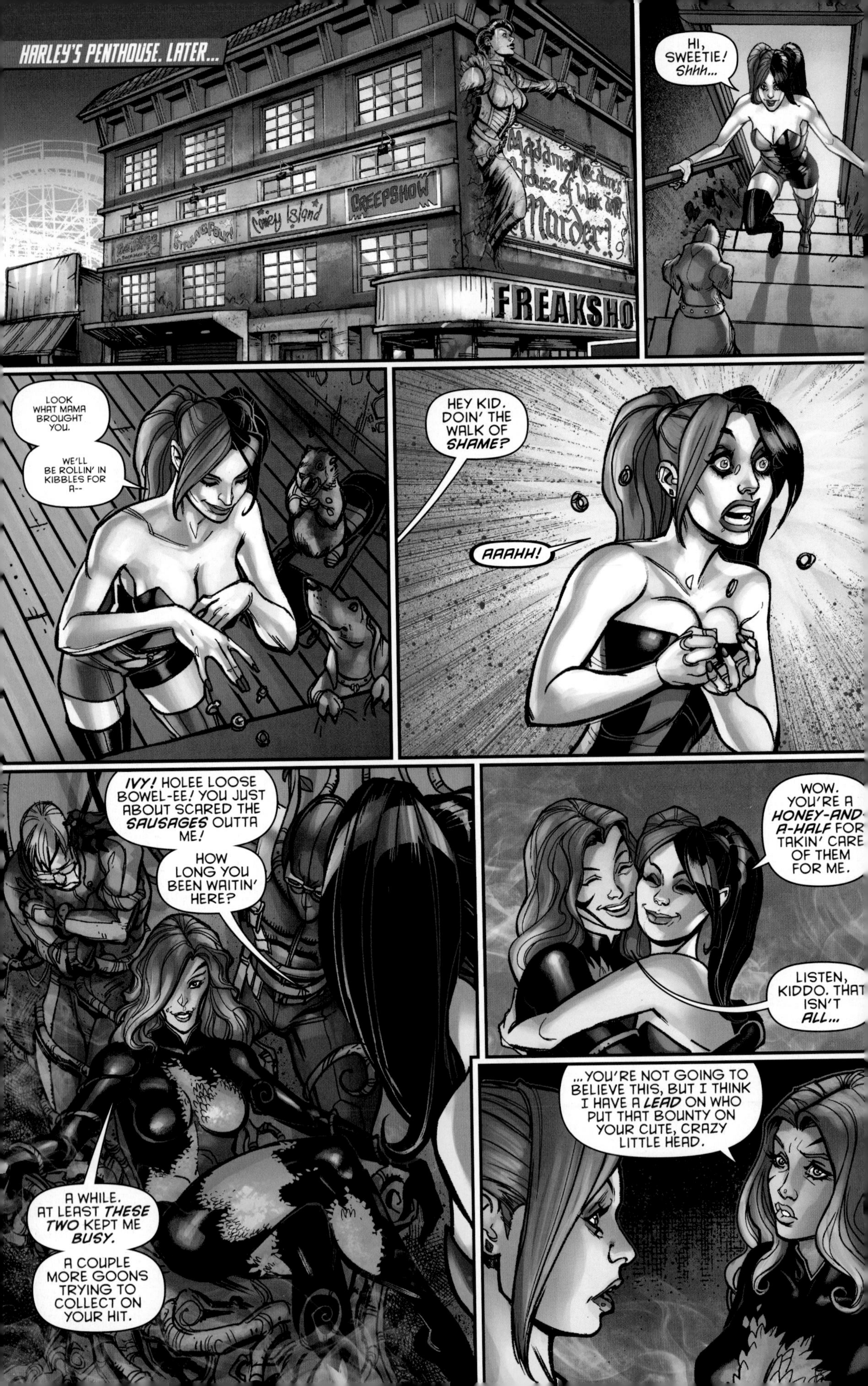

HARLEY'S PENTHOUSE. LATER...
Madame Macabre's House of Wax and Murder!
CREEPSHOW
Coney Island
FREAKSHO
HI, SWEETIE! Shhh...
LOOK WHAT MAMA BROUGHT YOU.
WE'LL BE ROLLIN' IN KIBBLES FOR A--
HEY KID. DOIN' THE WALK OF SHAME?
AAAHH!
IVY! HOLEE LOOSE BOWEL-EE! YOU JUST ABOUT SCARED THE SAUSAGES OUTTA ME!
HOW LONG YOU BEEN WAITIN' HERE?
A WHILE. AT LEAST THESE TWO KEPT ME BUSY.
A COUPLE MORE GOONS TRYING TO COLLECT ON YOUR HIT.
WOW. YOU'RE A HONEY-AND-A-HALF FOR TAKIN' CARE OF THEM FOR ME.
LISTEN, KIDDO. THAT ISN'T ALL...
...YOU'RE NOT GOING TO BELIEVE THIS, BUT I THINK I HAVE A LEAD ON WHO PUT THAT BOUNTY ON YOUR CUTE, CRAZY LITTLE HEAD.

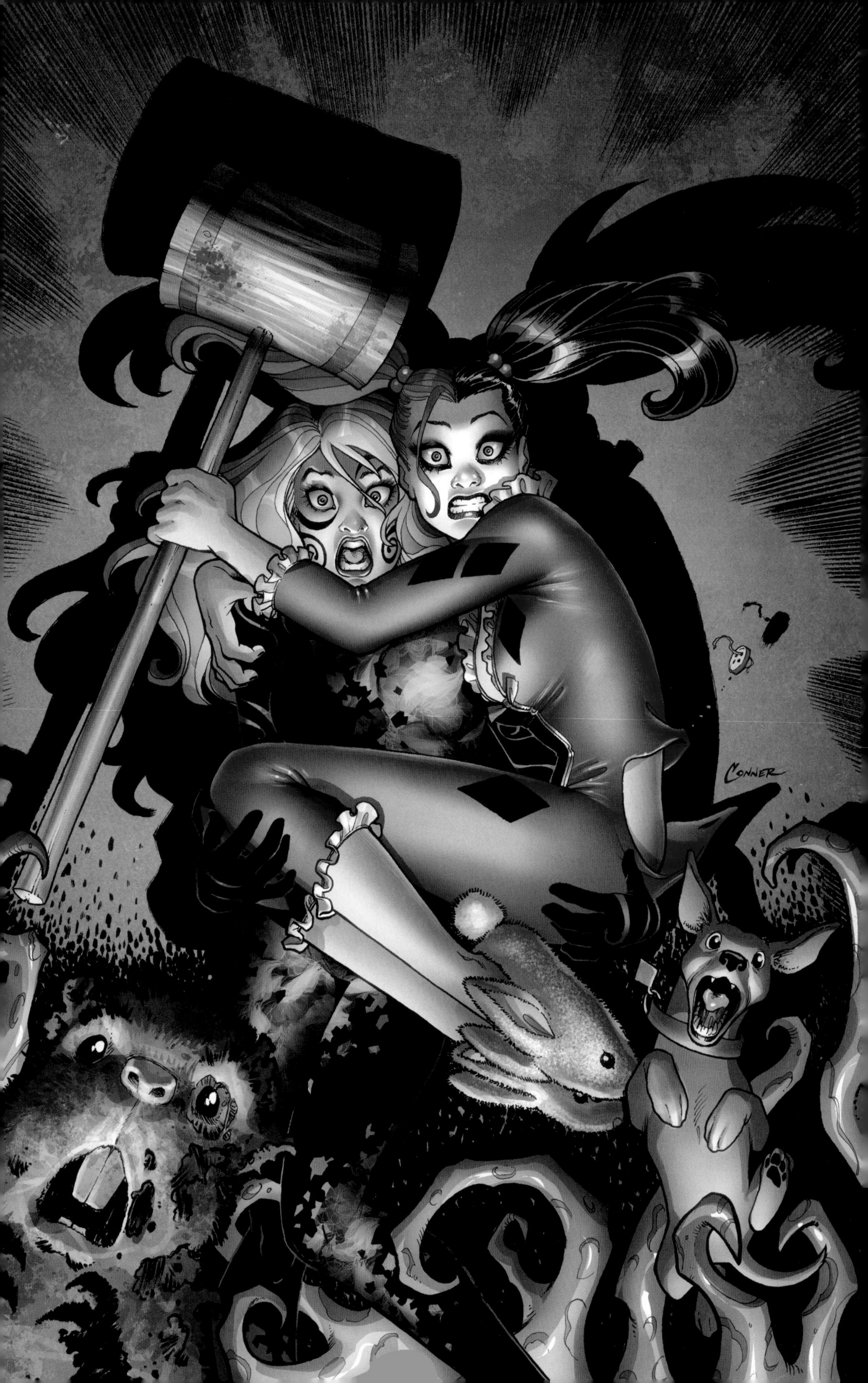
CONNER

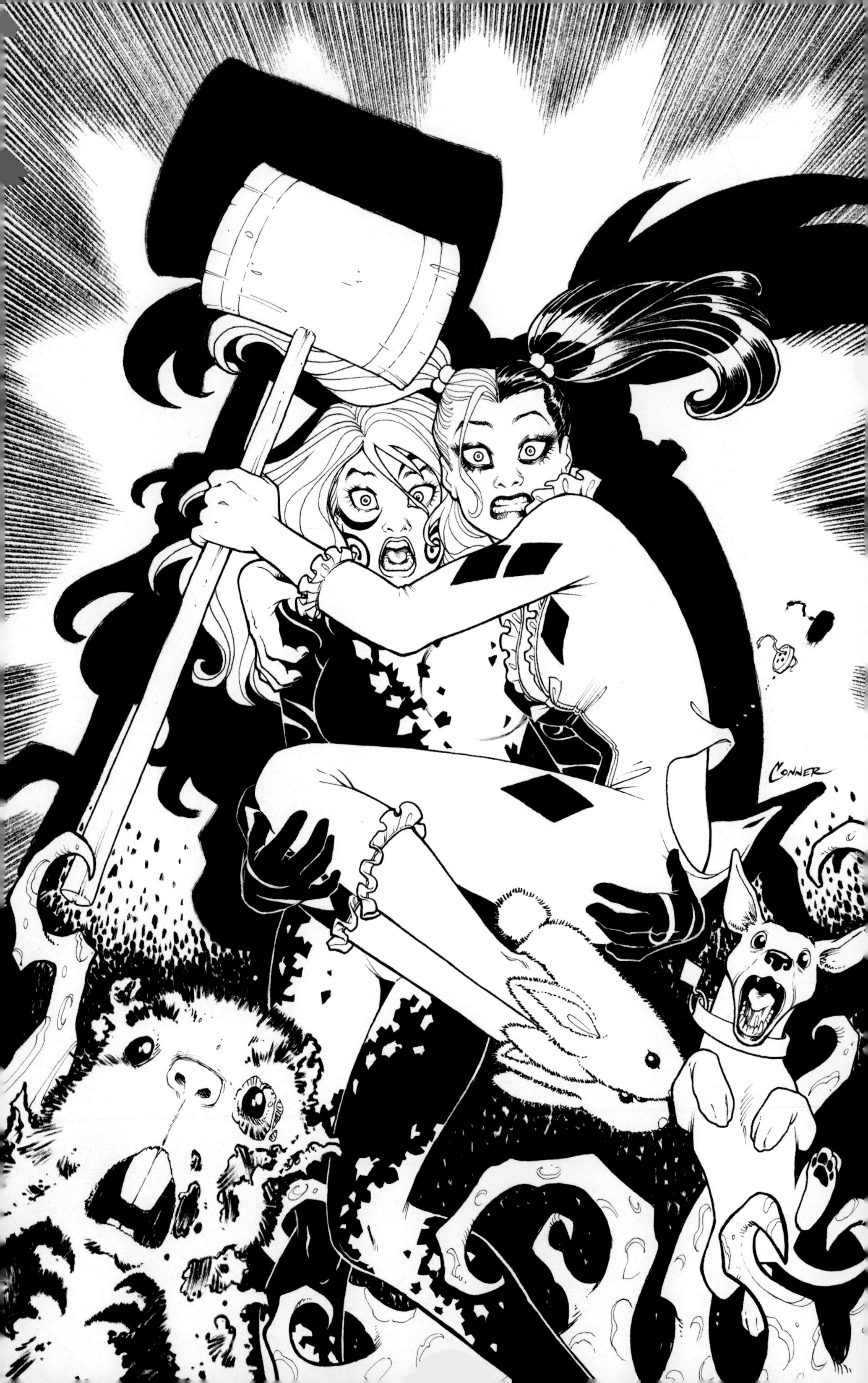
CONNER

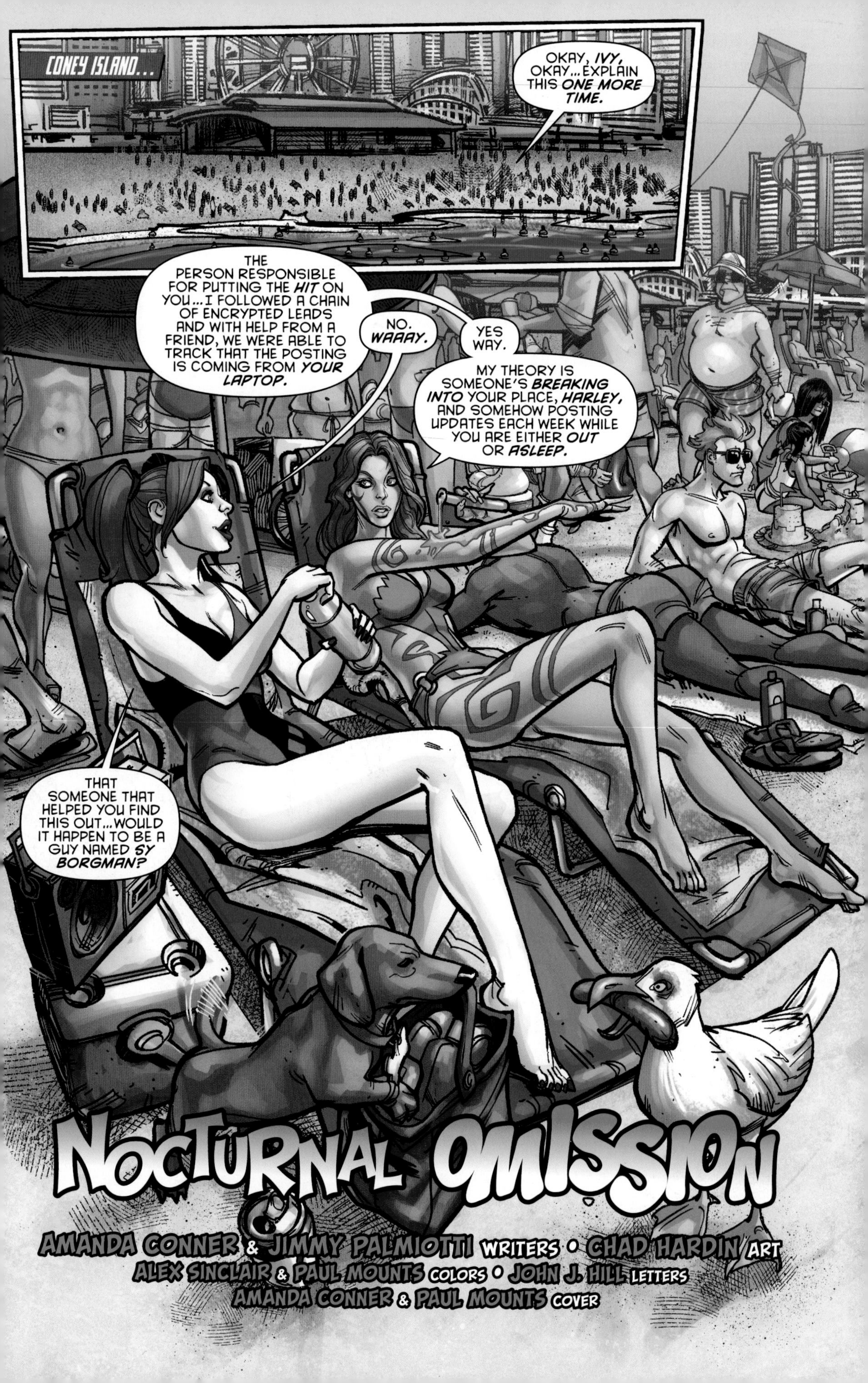
CONEY ISLAND...
OKAY, IVY, OKAY...EXPLAIN THIS ONE MORE TIME.
THE PERSON RESPONSIBLE FOR PUTTING THE HIT ON YOU...I FOLLOWED A CHAIN OF ENCRYPTED LEADS AND WITH HELP FROM A FRIEND, WE WERE ABLE TO TRACK THAT THE POSTING IS COMING FROM YOUR LAPTOP.
NO. WAAAY.
YES WAY.
MY THEORY IS SOMEONE'S BREAKING INTO YOUR PLACE, HARLEY, AND SOMEHOW POSTING UPDATES EACH WEEK WHILE YOU ARE EITHER OUT OR ASLEEP.
THAT SOMEONE THAT HELPED YOU FIND THIS OUT...WOULD IT HAPPEN TO BE A GUY NAMED SY BORGMAN?
NOCTURNAL OMISSION
AMANDA CONNER & JIMMY PALMIOTTI WRITERS • CHAD HARDIN ART
ALEX SINCLAIR & PAUL MOUNTS COLORS • JOHN J. HILL LETTERS
AMANDA CONNER & PAUL MOUNTS COVER

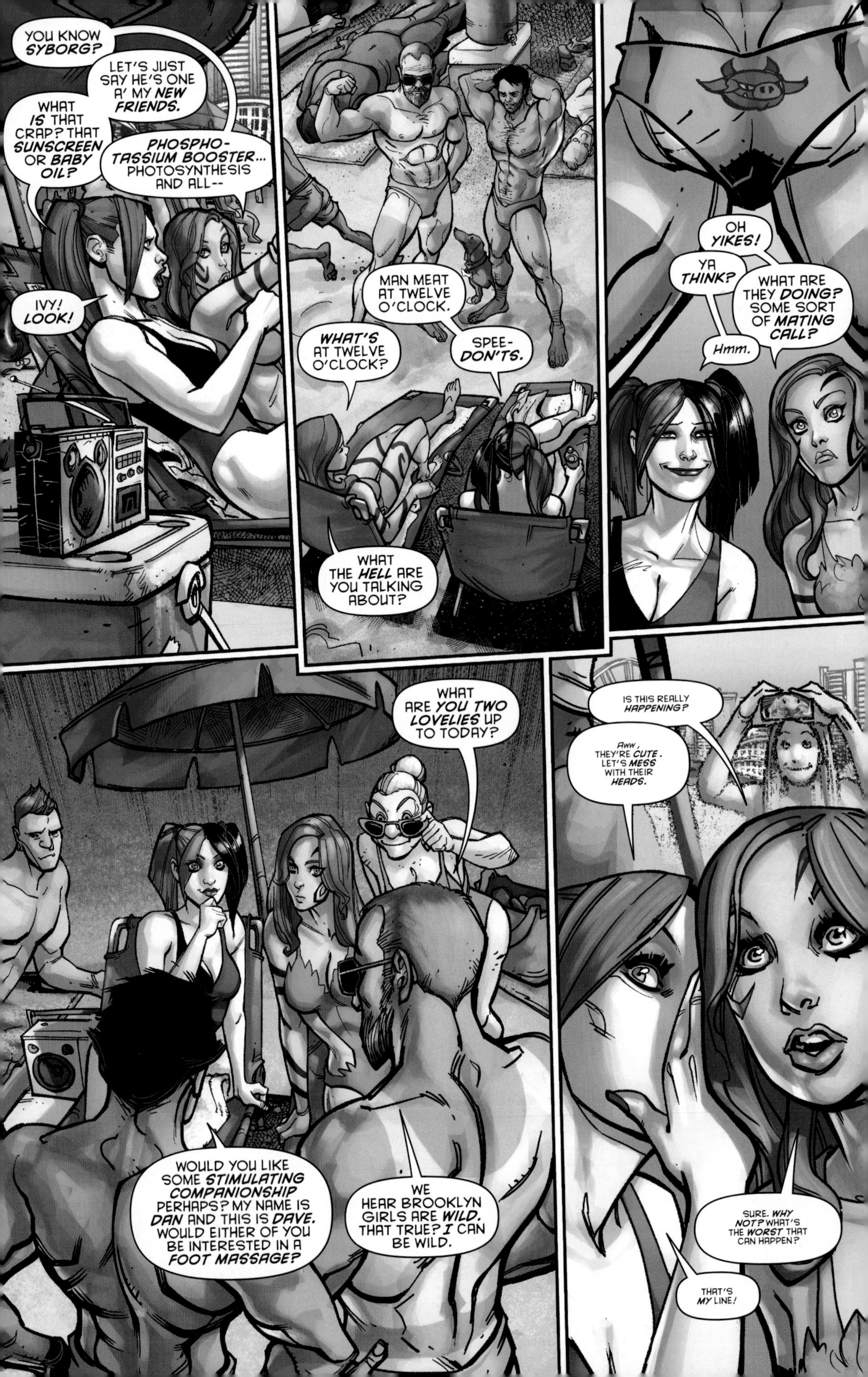
YOU KNOW SYBORG?
LET'S JUST SAY HE'S ONE A' MY NEW FRIENDS.
WHAT IS THAT CRAP? THAT SUNSCREEN OR BABY OIL?
PHOSPHO-TASSIUM BOOSTER... PHOTOSYNTHESIS AND ALL--
IVY! LOOK!
MAN MEAT AT TWELVE O'CLOCK.
WHAT'S AT TWELVE O'CLOCK?
SPEE-DON'TS.
WHAT THE HELL ARE YOU TALKING ABOUT?
OH YIKES!
YA THINK?
WHAT ARE THEY DOING? SOME SORT OF MATING CALL?
Hmm.
WHAT ARE YOU TWO LOVELIES UP TO TODAY?
WOULD YOU LIKE SOME STIMULATING COMPANIONSHIP PERHAPS? MY NAME IS DAN AND THIS IS DAVE. WOULD EITHER OF YOU BE INTERESTED IN A FOOT MASSAGE?
WE HEAR BROOKLYN GIRLS ARE WILD. THAT TRUE? I CAN BE WILD.
IS THIS REALLY HAPPENING?
Aww, THEY'RE CUTE. LET'S MESS WITH THEIR HEADS.
SURE. WHY NOT? WHAT'S THE WORST THAT CAN HAPPEN?
THAT'S MY LINE!

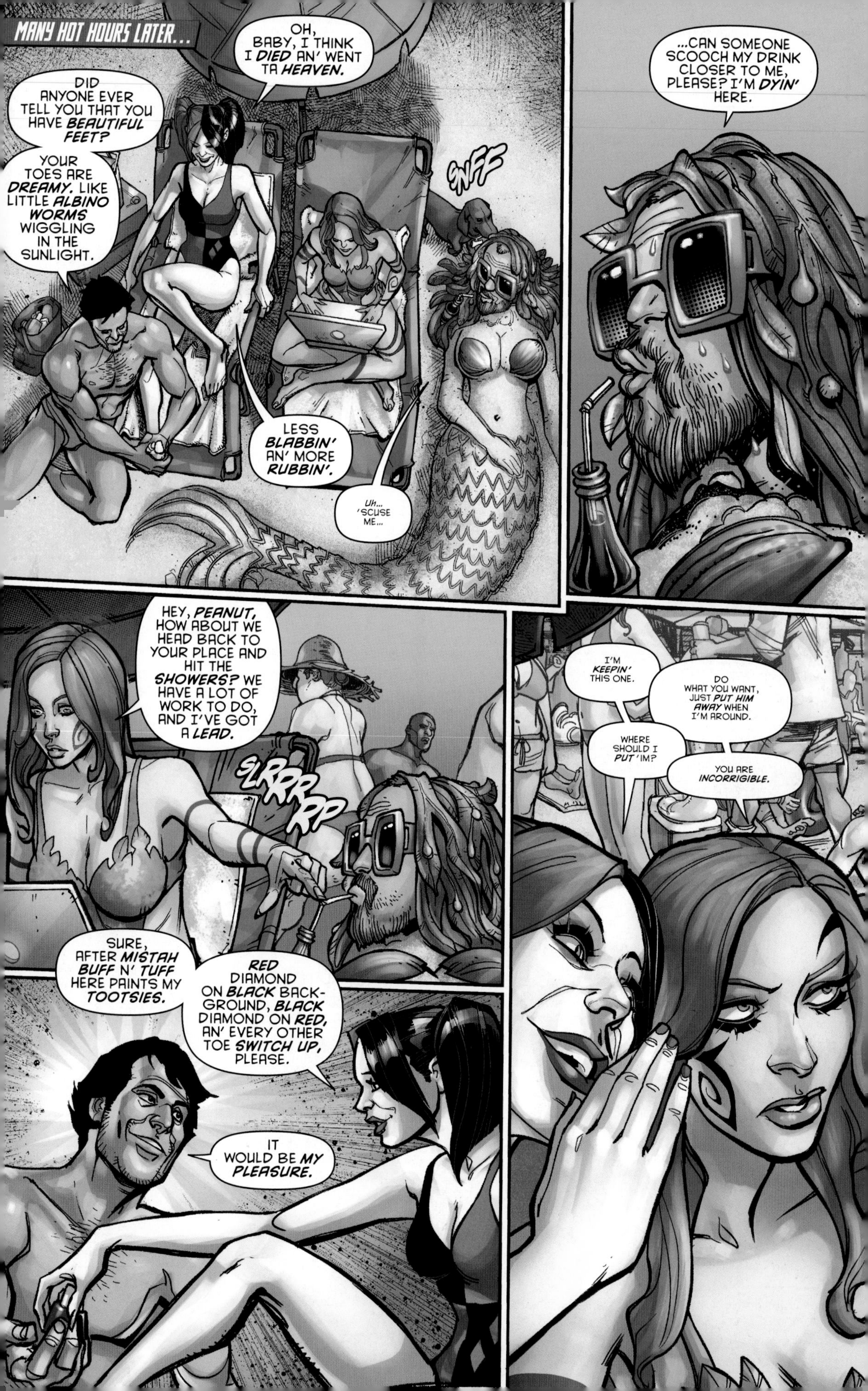
MANY HOT HOURS LATER...
DID ANYONE EVER TELL YOU THAT YOU HAVE BEAUTIFUL FEET?
YOUR TOES ARE DREAMY. LIKE LITTLE ALBINO WORMS WIGGLING IN THE SUNLIGHT.
OH, BABY, I THINK I DIED AN' WENT TA HEAVEN.
SNFF
LESS BLABBIN' AN' MORE RUBBIN'.
UH... 'SCUSE ME...
...CAN SOMEONE SCOOCH MY DRINK CLOSER TO ME, PLEASE? I'M DYIN' HERE.
HEY, PEANUT, HOW ABOUT WE HEAD BACK TO YOUR PLACE AND HIT THE SHOWERS? WE HAVE A LOT OF WORK TO DO, AND I'VE GOT A LEAD.
SLRRRRP
SURE, AFTER MISTAH BUFF N' TUFF HERE PAINTS MY TOOTSIES.
RED DIAMOND ON BLACK BACK-GROUND, BLACK DIAMOND ON RED, AN' EVERY OTHER TOE SWITCH UP, PLEASE.
IT WOULD BE MY PLEASURE.
I'M KEEPIN' THIS ONE.
DO WHAT YOU WANT, JUST PUT HIM AWAY WHEN I'M AROUND.
WHERE SHOULD I PUT 'IM?
YOU ARE INCORRIGIBLE.

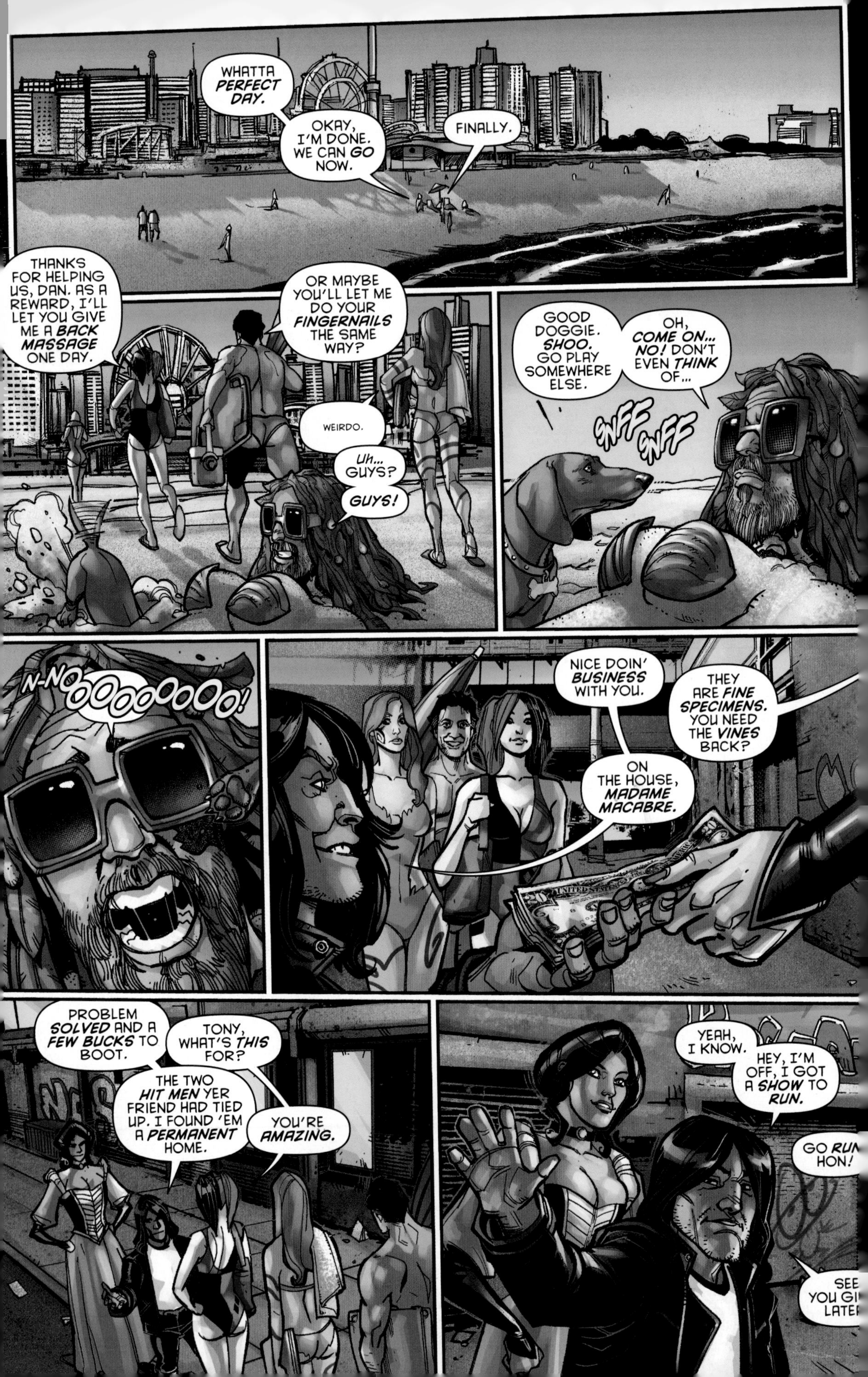

WHATTA PERFECT DAY.
OKAY, I'M DONE. WE CAN GO NOW.
FINALLY.
THANKS FOR HELPING US, DAN. AS A REWARD, I'LL LET YOU GIVE ME A BACK MASSAGE ONE DAY.
OR MAYBE YOU'LL LET ME DO YOUR FINGERNAILS THE SAME WAY?
WEIRDO.
Uh... GUYS?
GUYS!
GOOD DOGGIE. SHOO. GO PLAY SOMEWHERE ELSE.
OH, COME ON... NO! DON'T EVEN THINK OF...
SNFF SNFF
N-NOOOOOOOOOOO!
NICE DOIN' BUSINESS WITH YOU.
THEY ARE FINE SPECIMENS. YOU NEED THE VINES BACK?
ON THE HOUSE, MADAME MACABRE.
PROBLEM SOLVED AND A FEW BUCKS TO BOOT.
TONY, WHAT'S THIS FOR?
THE TWO HIT MEN YER FRIEND HAD TIED UP. I FOUND 'EM A PERMANENT HOME.
YOU'RE AMAZING.
YEAH, I KNOW.
HEY, I'M OFF, I GOT A SHOW TO RUN.
GO RUN HON!
SEE YOU GI LATER

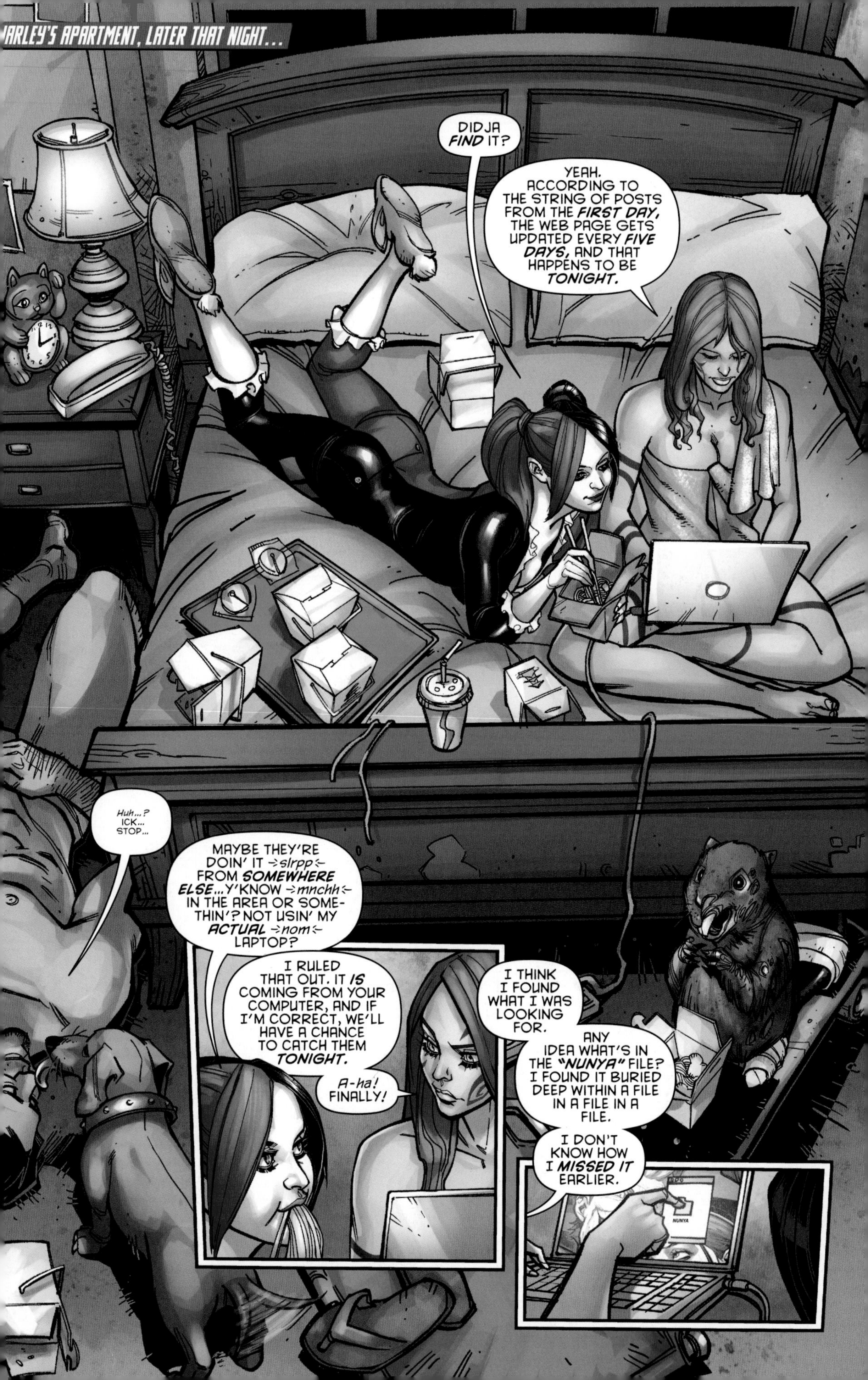
ARLEY'S APARTMENT, LATER THAT NIGHT...
DIDJA FIND IT?
YEAH. ACCORDING TO THE STRING OF POSTS FROM THE FIRST DAY, THE WEB PAGE GETS UPDATED EVERY FIVE DAYS, AND THAT HAPPENS TO BE TONIGHT.
Huh...? ICK... STOP...
MAYBE THEY'RE DOIN' IT ⇒slrpp⇐ FROM SOMEWHERE ELSE...Y'KNOW ⇒mnchh⇐ IN THE AREA OR SOMETHIN'? NOT USIN' MY ACTUAL ⇒nom⇐ LAPTOP?
I RULED THAT OUT. IT IS COMING FROM YOUR COMPUTER, AND IF I'M CORRECT, WE'LL HAVE A CHANCE TO CATCH THEM TONIGHT.
A-ha! FINALLY!
I THINK I FOUND WHAT I WAS LOOKING FOR.
ANY IDEA WHAT'S IN THE "NUNYA" FILE? I FOUND IT BURIED DEEP WITHIN A FILE IN A FILE IN A FILE.
I DON'T KNOW HOW I MISSED IT EARLIER.
NUNYA

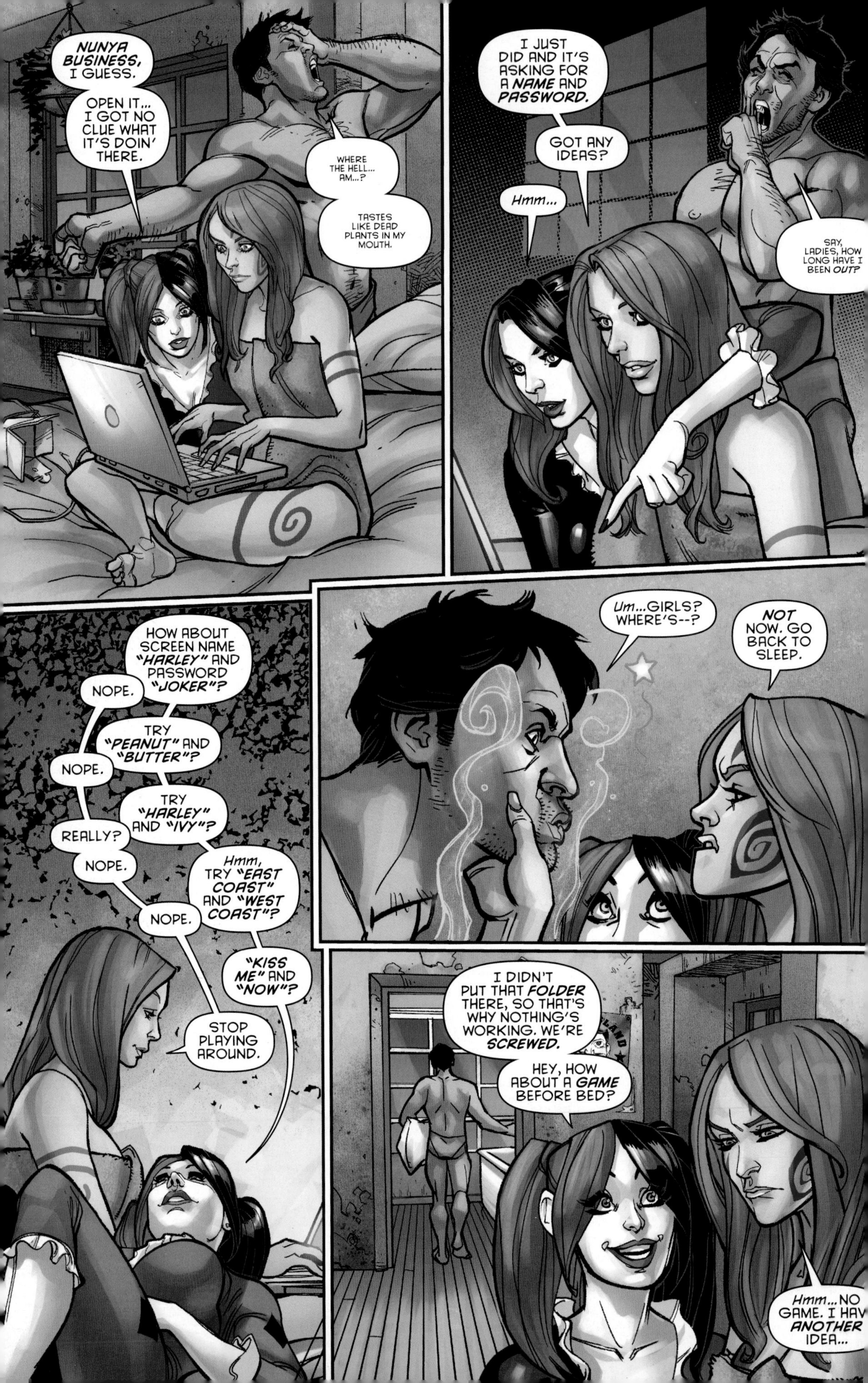
NUNYA BUSINESS, I GUESS.
OPEN IT... I GOT NO CLUE WHAT IT'S DOIN' THERE.
WHERE THE HELL... AM...?
TASTES LIKE DEAD PLANTS IN MY MOUTH.
I JUST DID AND IT'S ASKING FOR A NAME AND PASSWORD.
GOT ANY IDEAS?
Hmm...
SAY, LADIES, HOW LONG HAVE I BEEN OUT?
HOW ABOUT SCREEN NAME "HARLEY" AND PASSWORD "JOKER"?
NOPE.
TRY "PEANUT" AND "BUTTER"?
NOPE.
TRY "HARLEY" AND "IVY"?
REALLY?
NOPE.
Hmm, TRY "EAST COAST" AND "WEST COAST"?
NOPE.
"KISS ME" AND "NOW"?
STOP PLAYING AROUND.
Um...GIRLS? WHERE'S--?
NOT NOW. GO BACK TO SLEEP.
I DIDN'T PUT THAT FOLDER THERE, SO THAT'S WHY NOTHING'S WORKING. WE'RE SCREWED.
HEY, HOW ABOUT A GAME BEFORE BED?
Hmm... NO GAME. I HAV ANOTHER IDEA...

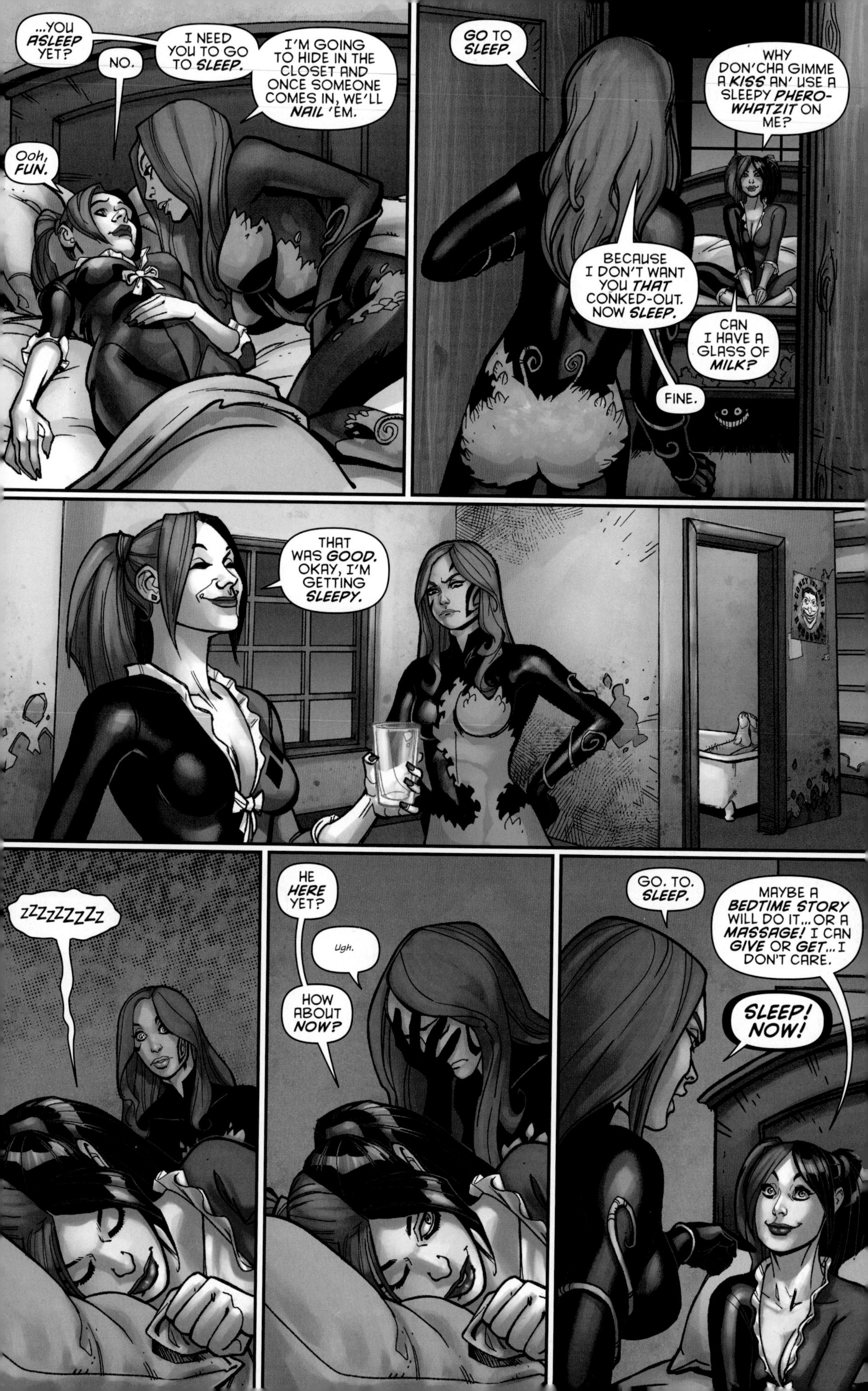
...YOU ASLEEP YET?
NO.
I NEED YOU TO GO TO SLEEP.
I'M GOING TO HIDE IN THE CLOSET AND ONCE SOMEONE COMES IN, WE'LL NAIL 'EM.
Ooh, FUN.
GO TO SLEEP.
WHY DON'CHA GIMME A KISS AN' USE A SLEEPY PHERO-WHATZIT ON ME?
BECAUSE I DON'T WANT YOU THAT CONKED-OUT. NOW SLEEP.
CAN I HAVE A GLASS OF MILK?
FINE.
THAT WAS GOOD. OKAY, I'M GETTING SLEEPY.
ZZZZZZZZZ
HE HERE YET?
Ugh.
HOW ABOUT NOW?
GO. TO. SLEEP.
MAYBE A BEDTIME STORY WILL DO IT... OR A MASSAGE! I CAN GIVE OR GET... I DON'T CARE.
SLEEP! NOW!

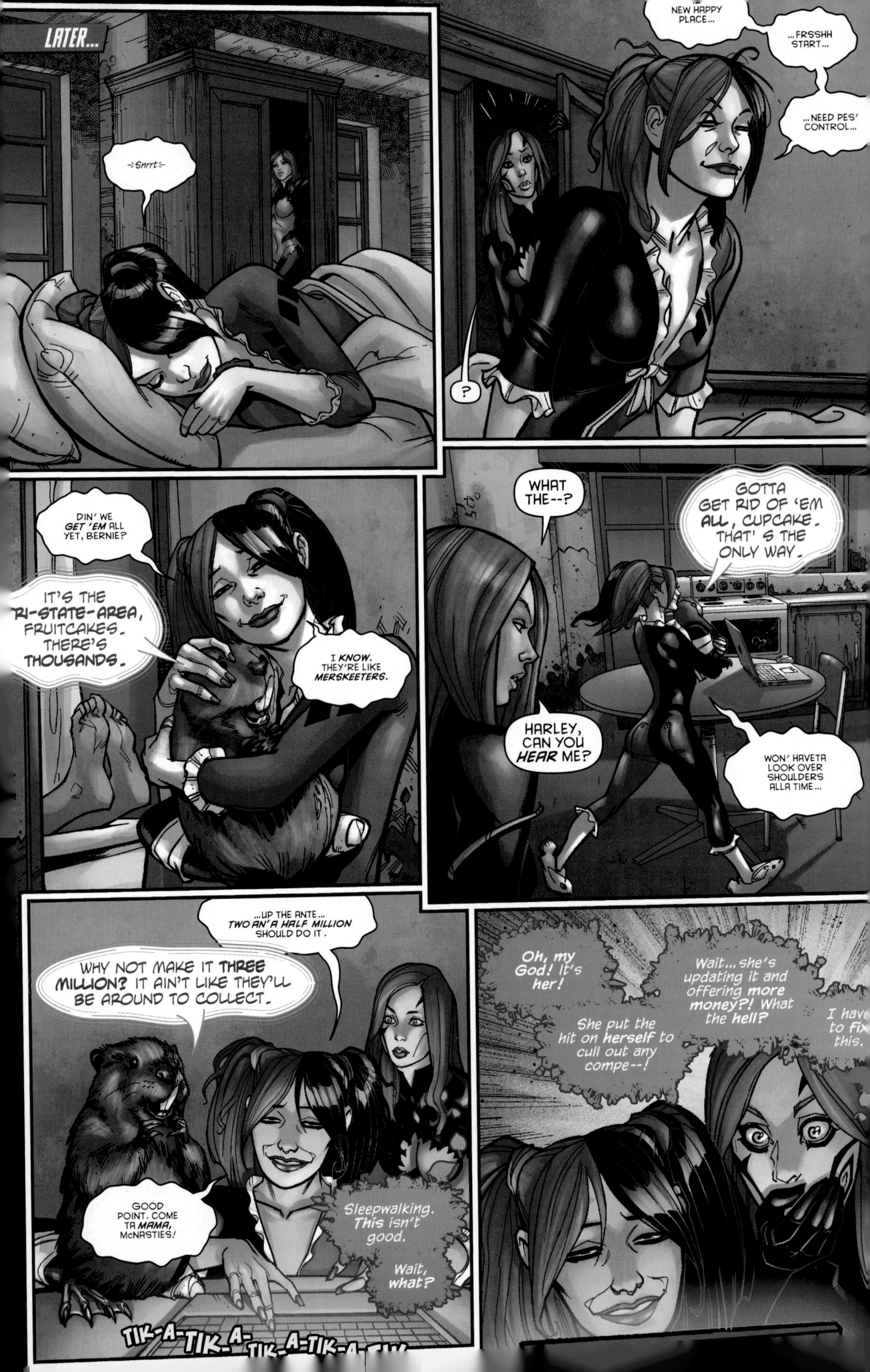
LATER...
Snrrt
NEW HAPPY PLACE...
...FRSSHH START...
...NEED PES' CONTROL...
?
DIN' WE GET 'EM ALL YET, BERNIE?
IT'S THE RI-STATE-AREA, FRUITCAKES. THERE'S THOUSANDS.
I KNOW. THEY'RE LIKE MERSKEETERS.
WHAT THE--?
GOTTA GET RID OF 'EM ALL, CUPCAKE. THAT'S THE ONLY WAY.
HARLEY, CAN YOU HEAR ME?
WON' HAVETA LOOK OVER SHOULDERS ALLA TIME...
...UP THE ANTE... TWO AN' A HALF MILLION SHOULD DO IT.
WHY NOT MAKE IT THREE MILLION? IT AIN'T LIKE THEY'LL BE AROUND TO COLLECT.
GOOD POINT. COME TA MAMA, McNASTIES!
Sleepwalking. This isn't good.
Wait, what?
TIK-A-TIK-A-TIK-A-TIK-A-TIK
Oh, my God! It's her!
She put the hit on herself to cull out any compe--!
Wait... she's updating it and offering more money?! What the hell?
I hav to fix this.

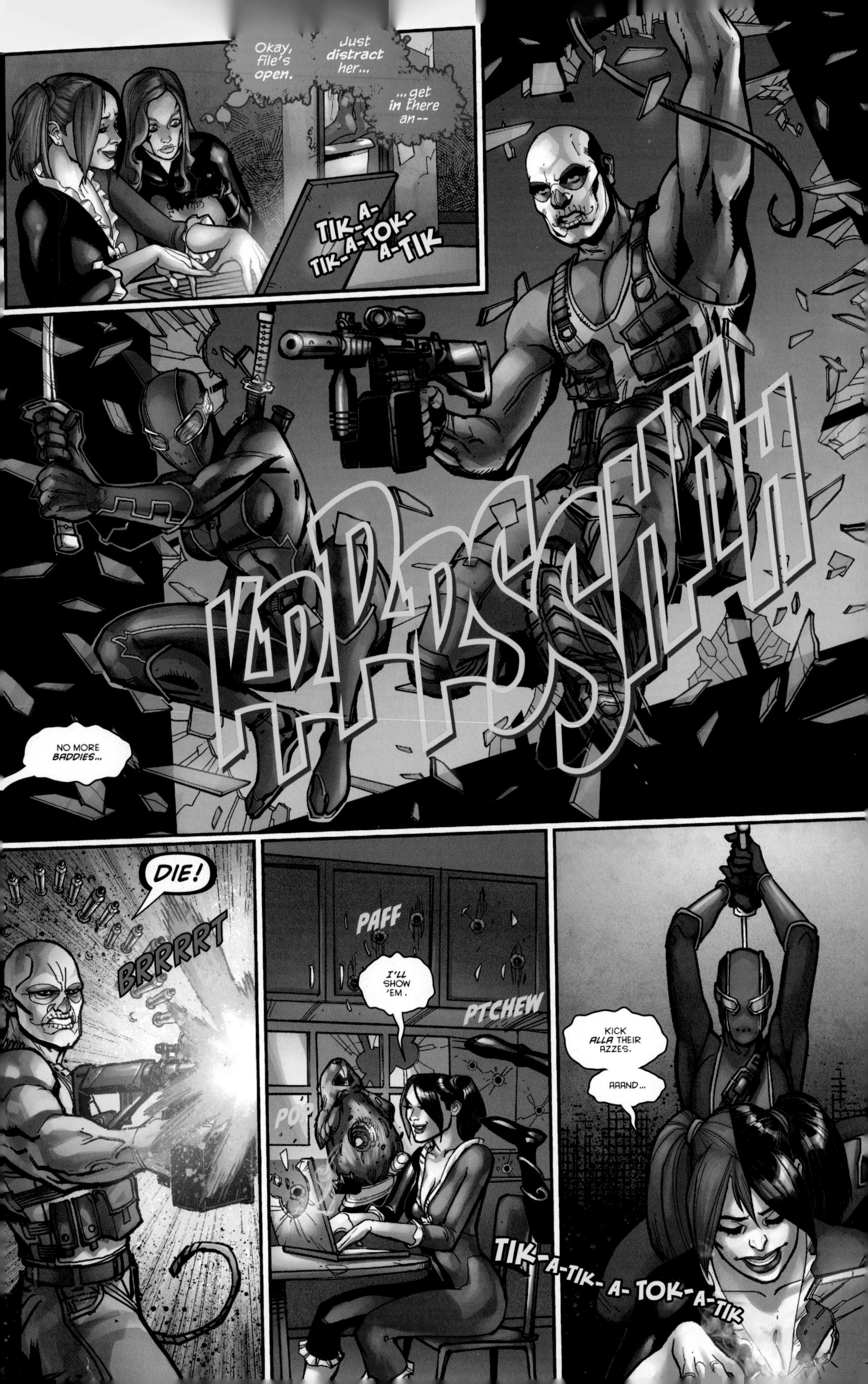
Okay, file's open.
Just distract her...
...get in there an--
TIK-A-TIK-A-TOK-A-TIK
KRASSHH
NO MORE BADDIES...
DIE!
BRRRRT
PAFF
I'LL SHOW 'EM.
PTCHEW
POP
KICK ALLA THEIR AZZES.
AAAND...
TIK-A-TIK-A-TOK-A-TIK

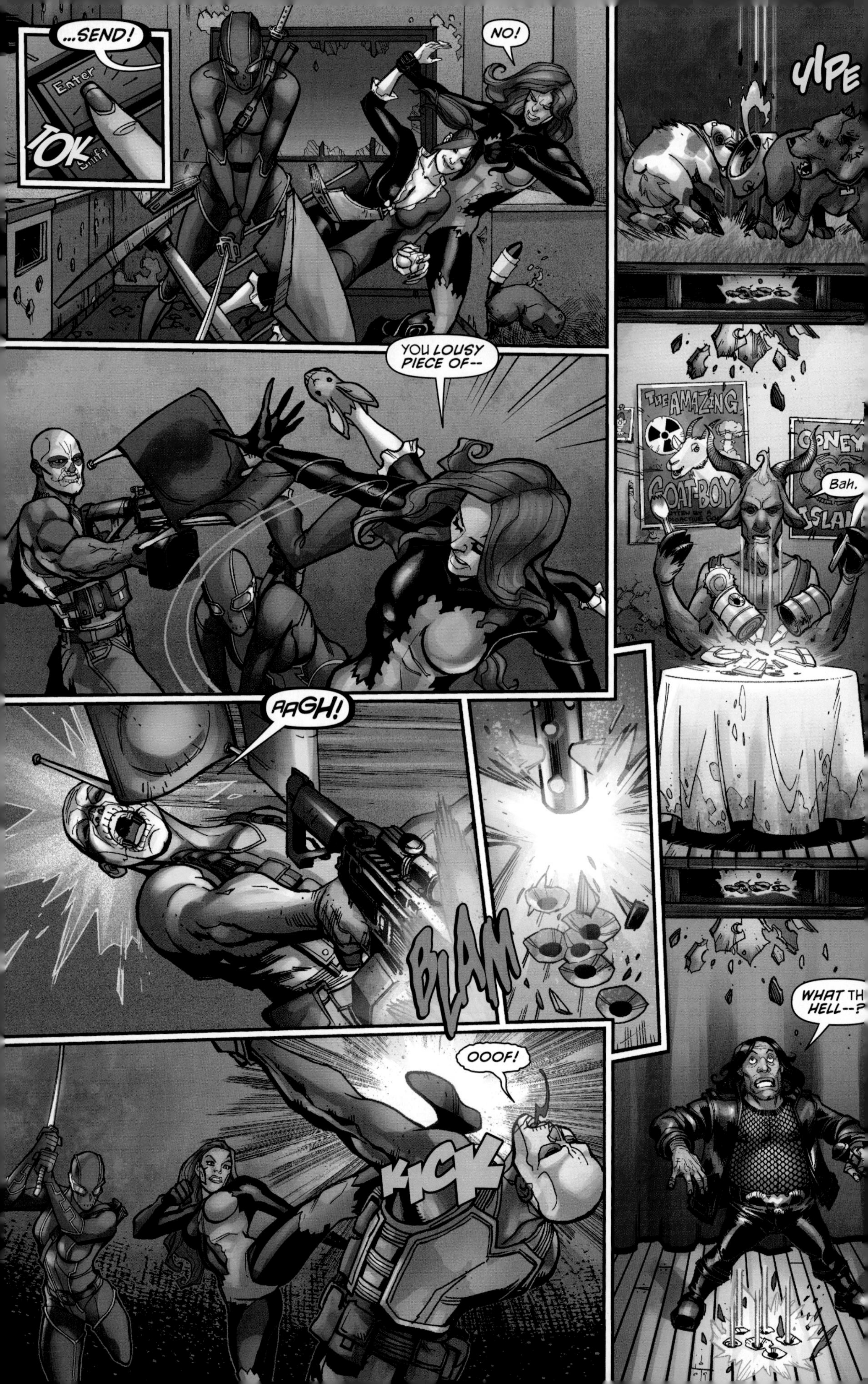

...SEND!
Enter
TOK
NO!
YOU LOUSY PIECE OF--
AAGH!
BLAM
OOOF!
KICK
YIPE
THE AMAZING
GOAT-BOY
Bah.
WHAT TH HELL--?

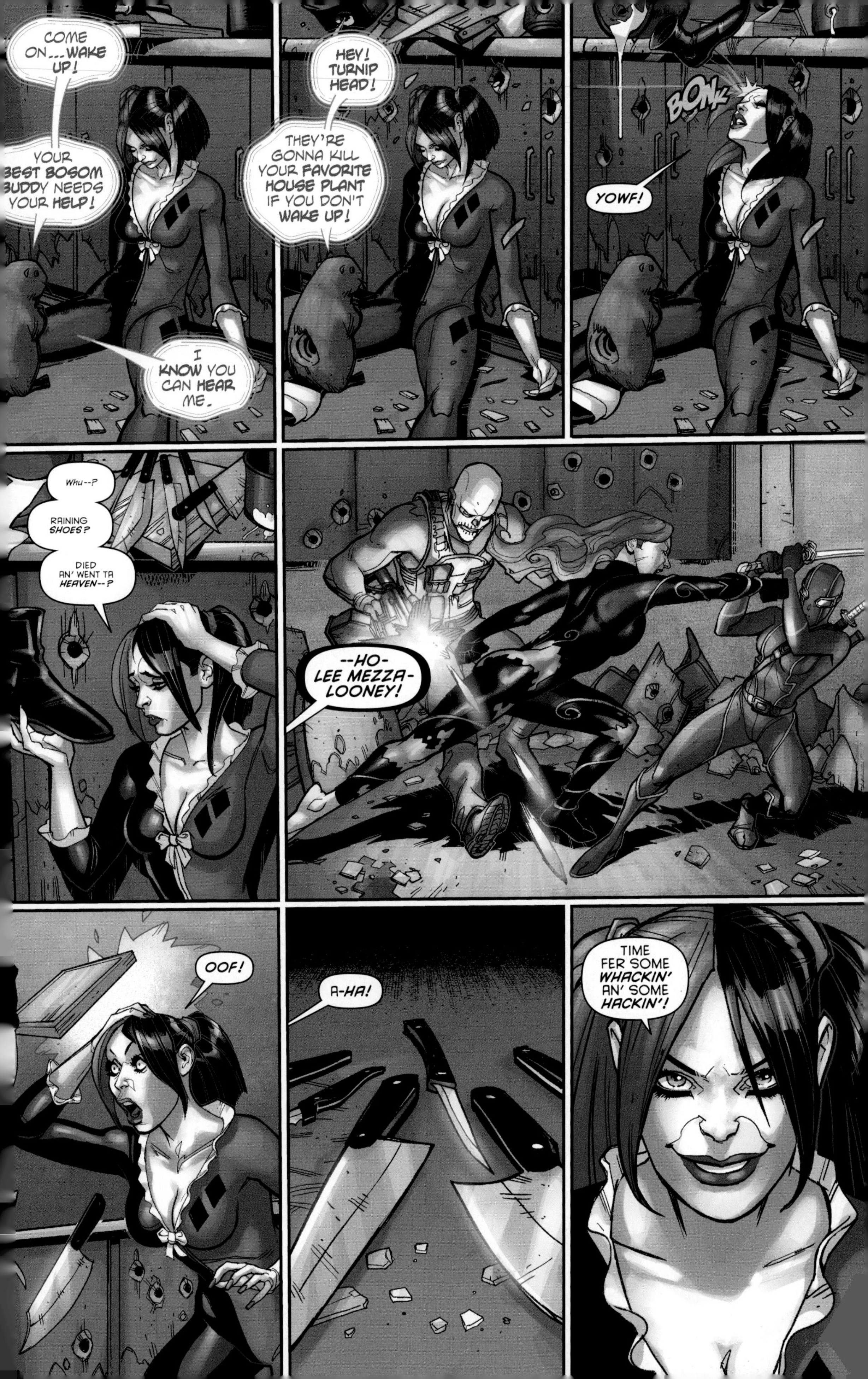
COME ON...WAKE UP!
YOUR BEST BOSOM BUDDY NEEDS YOUR HELP!
I KNOW YOU CAN HEAR ME.
HEY! TURNIP HEAD!
THEY'RE GONNA KILL YOUR FAVORITE HOUSE PLANT IF YOU DON'T WAKE UP!
BONK
YOWF!
Whu--?
RAINING SHOES?
DIED AN' WENT TA HEAVEN--?
--HO-LEE MEZZA-LOONEY!
OOF!
A-HA!
TIME FER SOME WHACKIN' AN' SOME HACKIN'!

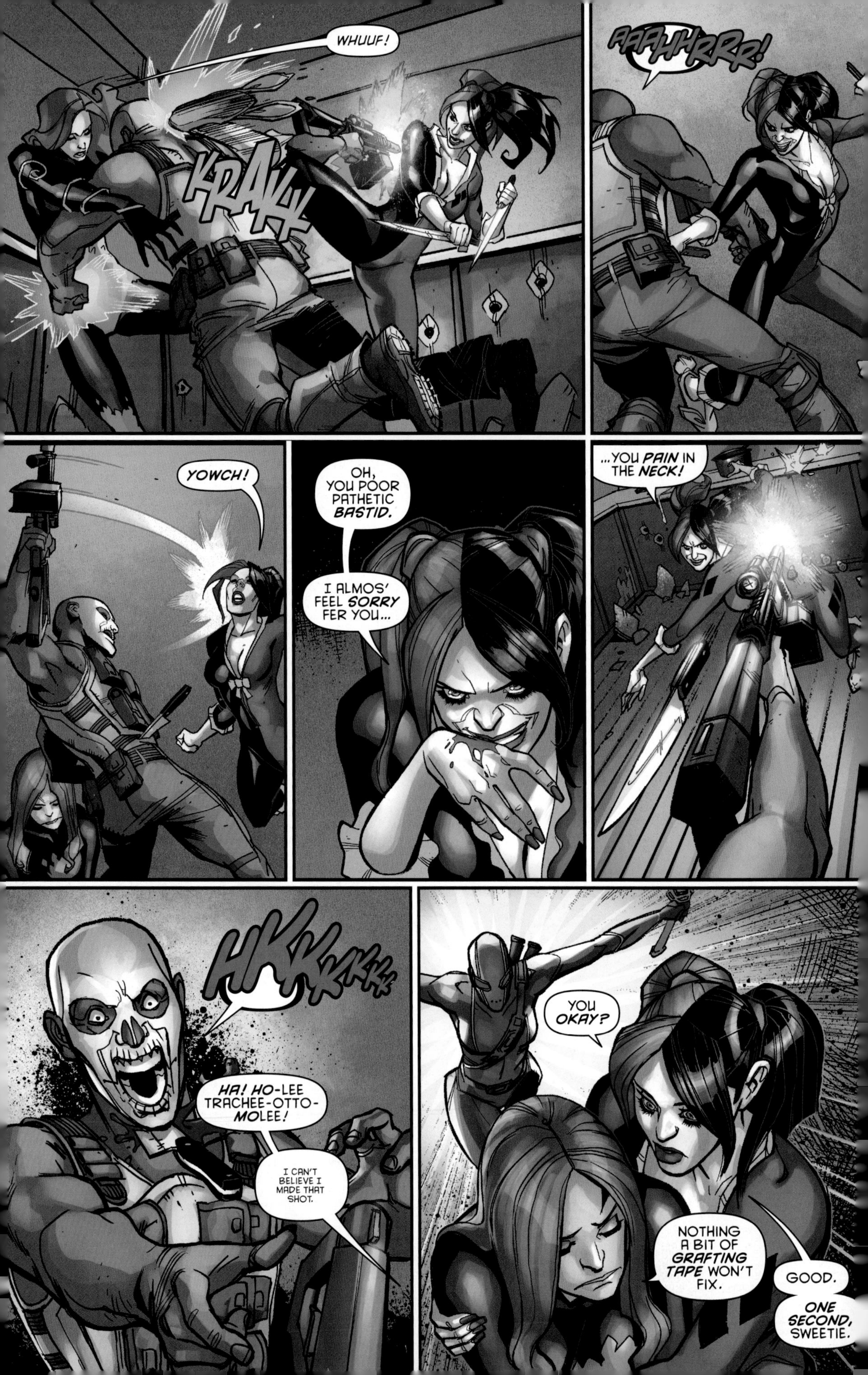
WHUUF!
KRAKK
AAAHHRRR!
YOWCH!
OH, YOU POOR PATHETIC BASTID.
I ALMOS' FEEL SORRY FER YOU...
...YOU PAIN IN THE NECK!
HKKKKKK
HA! HO-LEE TRACHEE-OTTO-MOLEE!
I CAN'T BELIEVE I MADE THAT SHOT.
YOU OKAY?
NOTHING A BIT OF GRAFTING TAPE WON'T FIX.
GOOD.
ONE SECOND, SWEETIE.

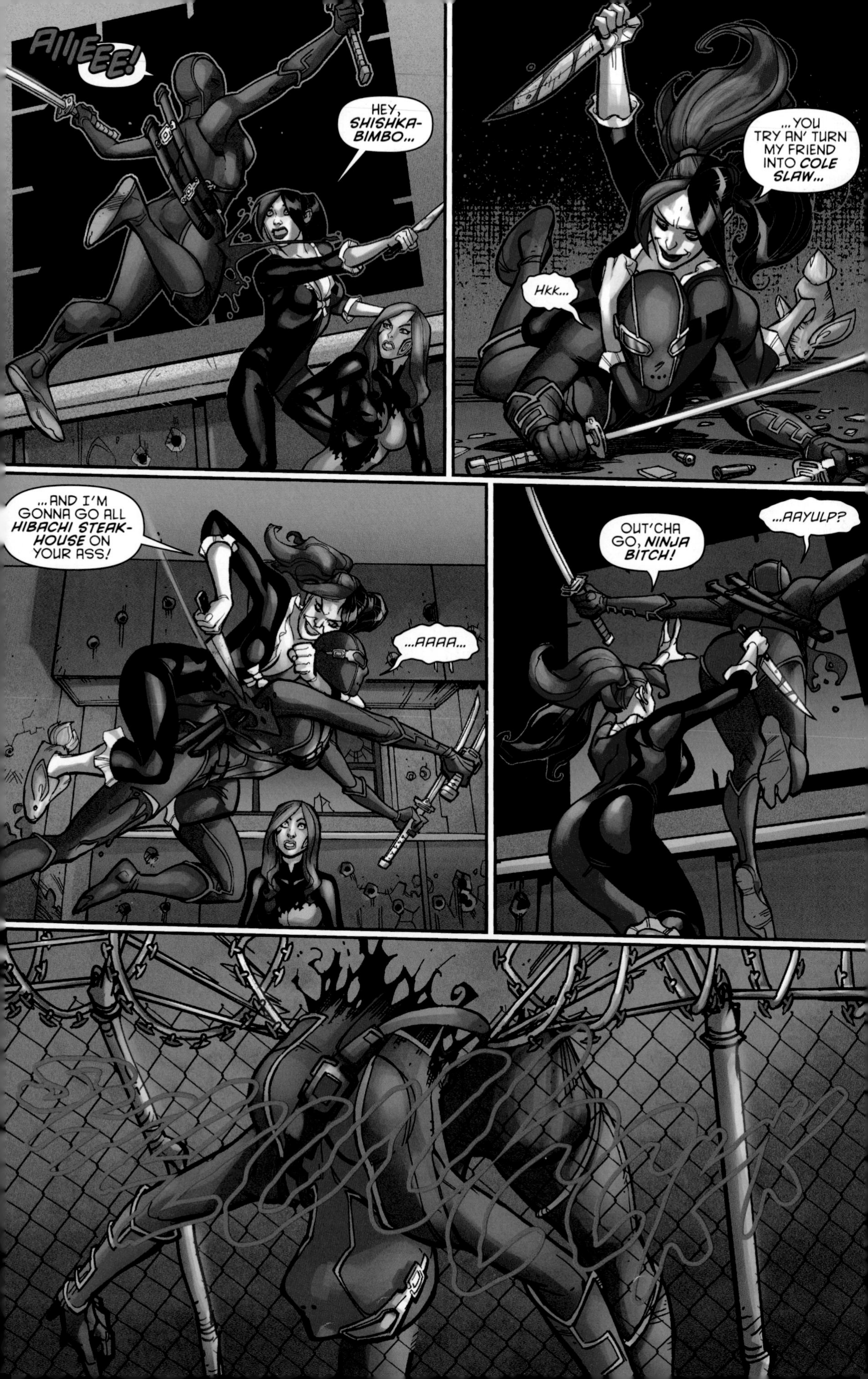
AIIIEEE!
HEY, SHISHKA-BIMBO...
...YOU TRY AN' TURN MY FRIEND INTO COLE SLAW...
HKK...
...AND I'M GONNA GO ALL HIBACHI STEAK-HOUSE ON YOUR ASS!
...AAAA...
OUT'CHA GO, NINJA BITCH!
...AAYULP?

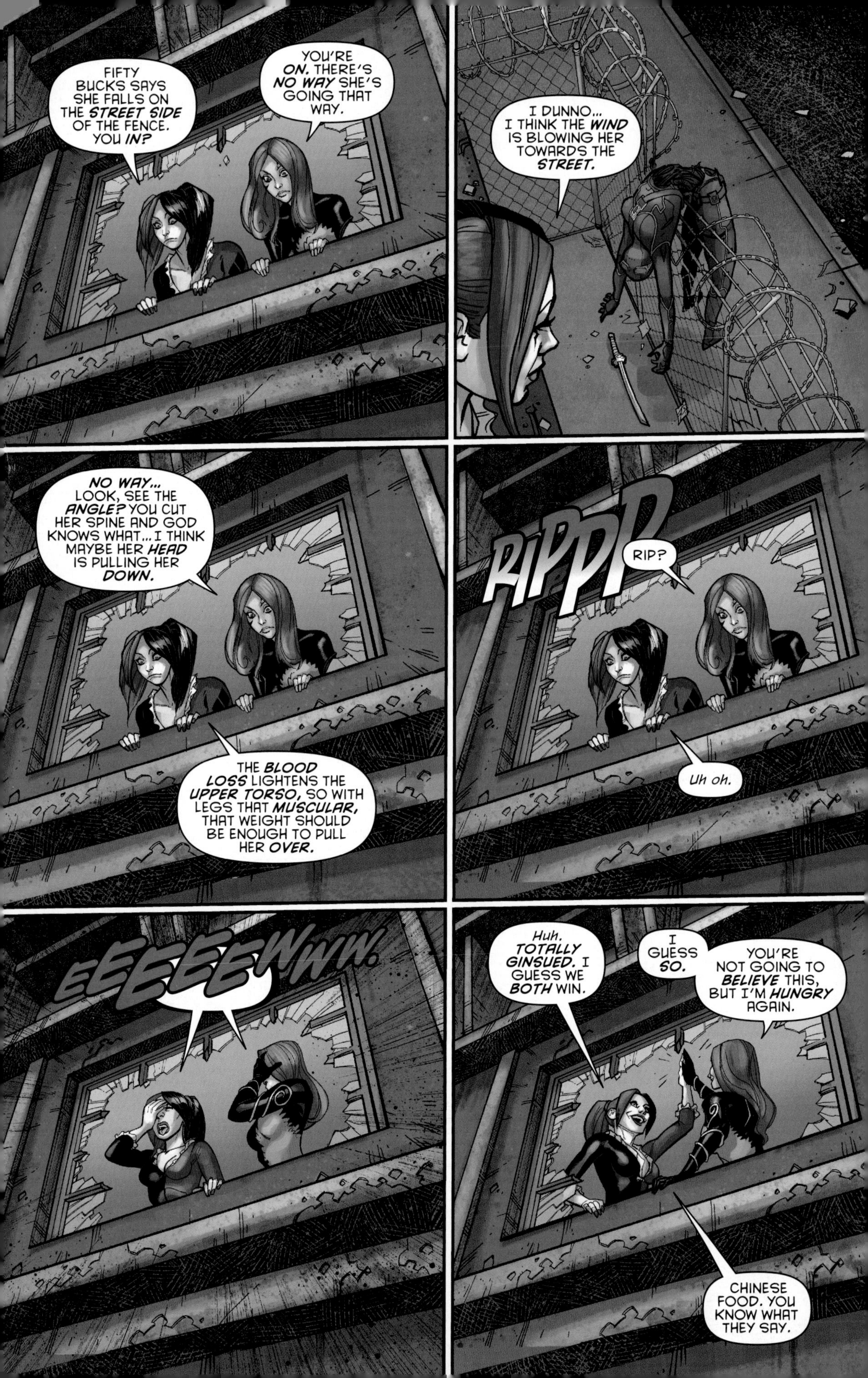
FIFTY BUCKS SAYS SHE FALLS ON THE STREET SIDE OF THE FENCE. YOU IN?
YOU'RE ON. THERE'S NO WAY SHE'S GOING THAT WAY.
I DUNNO... I THINK THE WIND IS BLOWING HER TOWARDS THE STREET.
NO WAY... LOOK, SEE THE ANGLE? YOU CUT HER SPINE AND GOD KNOWS WHAT... I THINK MAYBE HER HEAD IS PULLING HER DOWN.
THE BLOOD LOSS LIGHTENS THE UPPER TORSO, SO WITH LEGS THAT MUSCULAR, THAT WEIGHT SHOULD BE ENOUGH TO PULL HER OVER.
RIPPP
RIP?
Uh oh.
EEEEEWWW.
Huh. TOTALLY GINSUED. I GUESS WE BOTH WIN.
I GUESS SO.
YOU'RE NOT GOING TO BELIEVE THIS, BUT I'M HUNGRY AGAIN.
CHINESE FOOD. YOU KNOW WHAT THEY SAY.

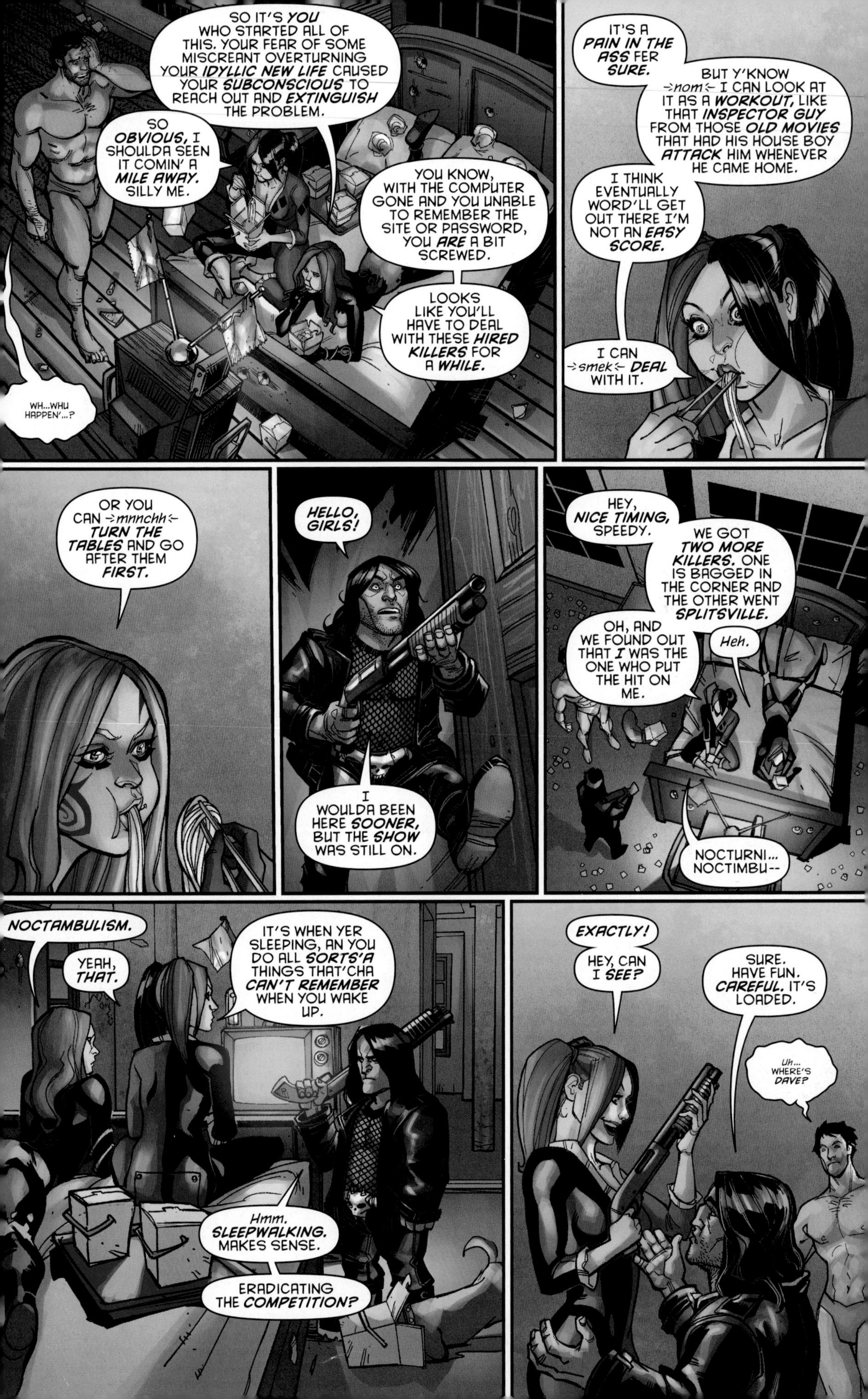
SO IT'S YOU WHO STARTED ALL OF THIS. YOUR FEAR OF SOME MISCREANT OVERTURNING YOUR IDYLLIC NEW LIFE CAUSED YOUR SUBCONSCIOUS TO REACH OUT AND EXTINGUISH THE PROBLEM.
SO OBVIOUS, I SHOULDA SEEN IT COMIN' A MILE AWAY. SILLY ME.
YOU KNOW, WITH THE COMPUTER GONE AND YOU UNABLE TO REMEMBER THE SITE OR PASSWORD, YOU ARE A BIT SCREWED.
LOOKS LIKE YOU'LL HAVE TO DEAL WITH THESE HIRED KILLERS FOR A WHILE.
WH...WHU HAPPEN'...?
IT'S A PAIN IN THE ASS FER SURE.
BUT Y'KNOW ->nom<- I CAN LOOK AT IT AS A WORKOUT, LIKE THAT INSPECTOR GUY FROM THOSE OLD MOVIES THAT HAD HIS HOUSE BOY ATTACK HIM WHENEVER HE CAME HOME.
I THINK EVENTUALLY WORD'LL GET OUT THERE I'M NOT AN EASY SCORE.
I CAN ->smek<- DEAL WITH IT.
OR YOU CAN ->mnnchh<- TURN THE TABLES AND GO AFTER THEM FIRST.
HELLO, GIRLS!
I WOULDA BEEN HERE SOONER, BUT THE SHOW WAS STILL ON.
HEY, NICE TIMING, SPEEDY.
WE GOT TWO MORE KILLERS. ONE IS BAGGED IN THE CORNER AND THE OTHER WENT SPLITSVILLE.
OH, AND WE FOUND OUT THAT I WAS THE ONE WHO PUT THE HIT ON ME.
Heh.
NOCTURNI... NOCTIMBU--
NOCTAMBULISM.
YEAH, THAT.
IT'S WHEN YER SLEEPING, AN YOU DO ALL SORTS'A THINGS THAT'CHA CAN'T REMEMBER WHEN YOU WAKE UP.
Hmm. SLEEPWALKING. MAKES SENSE.
ERADICATING THE COMPETITION?
EXACTLY!
HEY, CAN I SEE?
SURE. HAVE FUN. CAREFUL. IT'S LOADED.
Uh... WHERE'S DAVE?

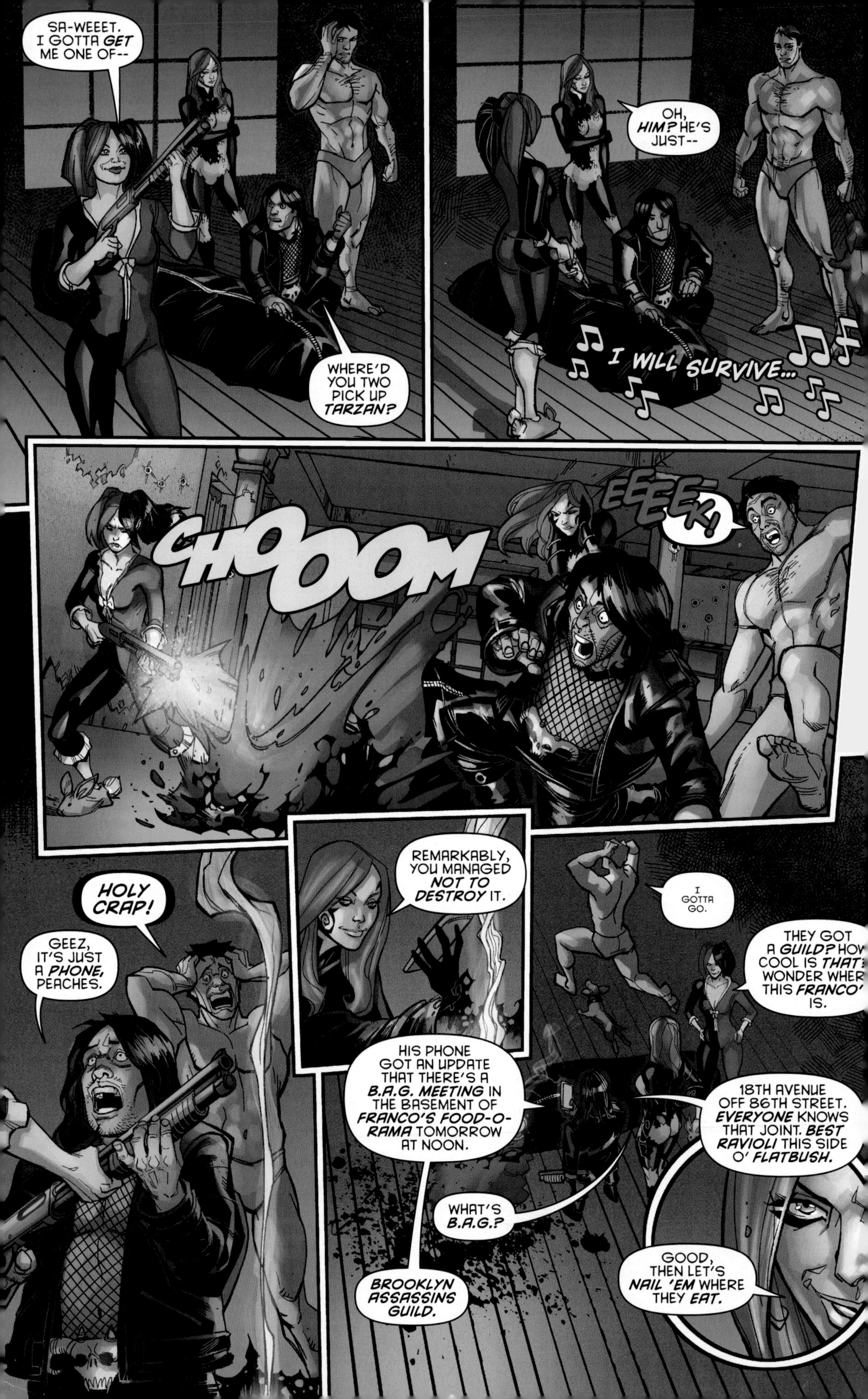
SA-WEEET. I GOTTA GET ME ONE OF--
WHERE'D YOU TWO PICK UP TARZAN?
OH, HIM? HE'S JUST--
I WILL SURVIVE...
CHOOOM
EEEEEK!
HOLY CRAP!
GEEZ, IT'S JUST A PHONE, PEACHES.
REMARKABLY, YOU MANAGED NOT TO DESTROY IT.
I GOTTA GO.
THEY GOT A GUILD? HOW COOL IS THAT? WONDER WHERE THIS FRANCO'S IS.
HIS PHONE GOT AN UPDATE THAT THERE'S A B.A.G. MEETING IN THE BASEMENT OF FRANCO'S FOOD-O-RAMA TOMORROW AT NOON.
18TH AVENUE OFF 86TH STREET. EVERYONE KNOWS THAT JOINT. BEST RAVIOLI THIS SIDE O' FLATBUSH.
WHAT'S B.A.G.?
BROOKLYN ASSASSINS GUILD.
GOOD, THEN LET'S NAIL 'EM WHERE THEY EAT.

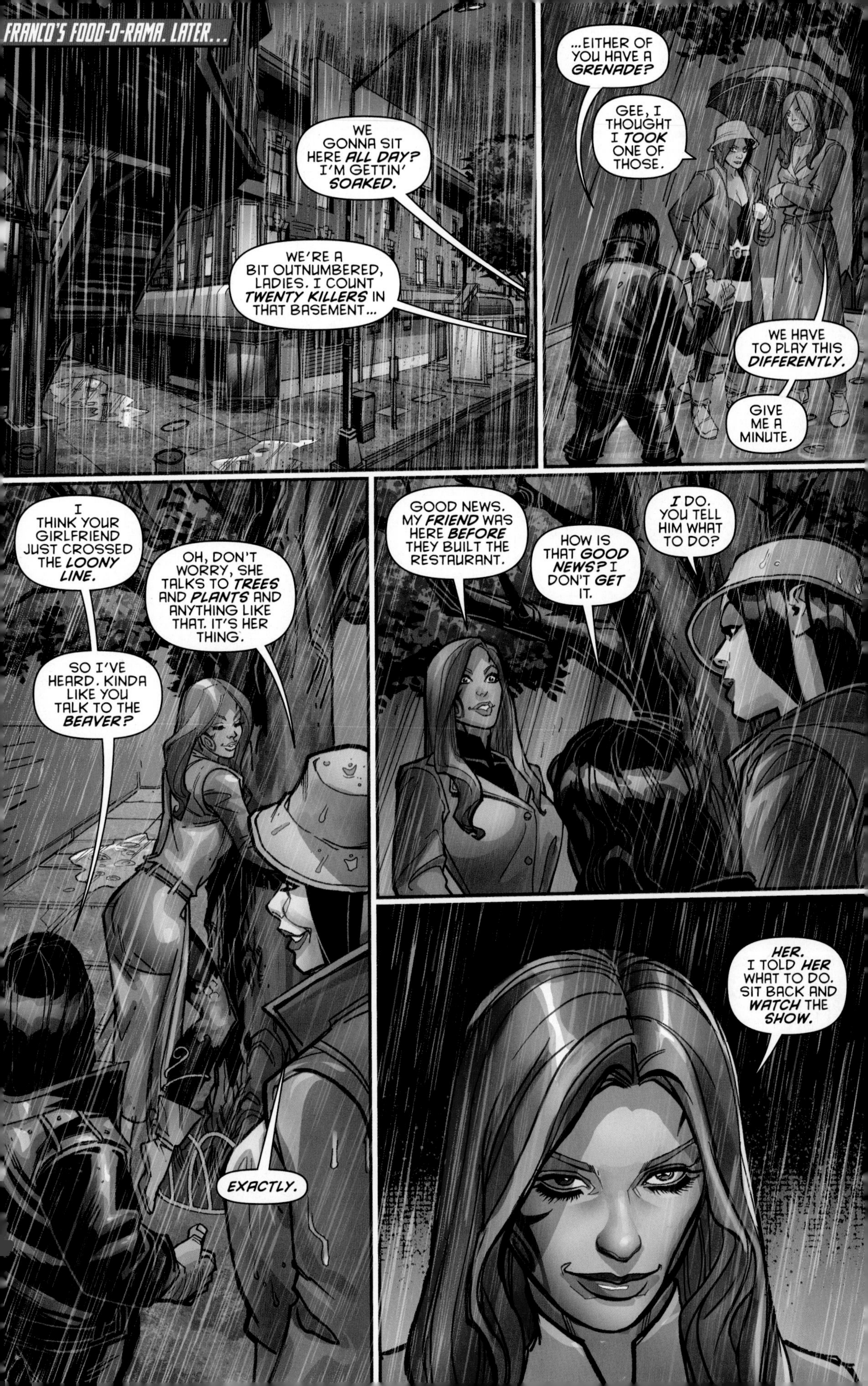
FRANCO'S FOOD-O-RAMA. LATER...
WE GONNA SIT HERE ALL DAY? I'M GETTIN' SOAKED.
WE'RE A BIT OUTNUMBERED, LADIES. I COUNT TWENTY KILLERS IN THAT BASEMENT...
...EITHER OF YOU HAVE A GRENADE?
GEE, I THOUGHT I TOOK ONE OF THOSE.
WE HAVE TO PLAY THIS DIFFERENTLY.
GIVE ME A MINUTE.
I THINK YOUR GIRLFRIEND JUST CROSSED THE LOONY LINE.
OH, DON'T WORRY, SHE TALKS TO TREES AND PLANTS AND ANYTHING LIKE THAT. IT'S HER THING.
SO I'VE HEARD. KINDA LIKE YOU TALK TO THE BEAVER?
EXACTLY.
GOOD NEWS. MY FRIEND WAS HERE BEFORE THEY BUILT THE RESTAURANT.
HOW IS THAT GOOD NEWS? I DON'T GET IT.
I DO. YOU TELL HIM WHAT TO DO?
HER. I TOLD HER WHAT TO DO. SIT BACK AND WATCH THE SHOW.

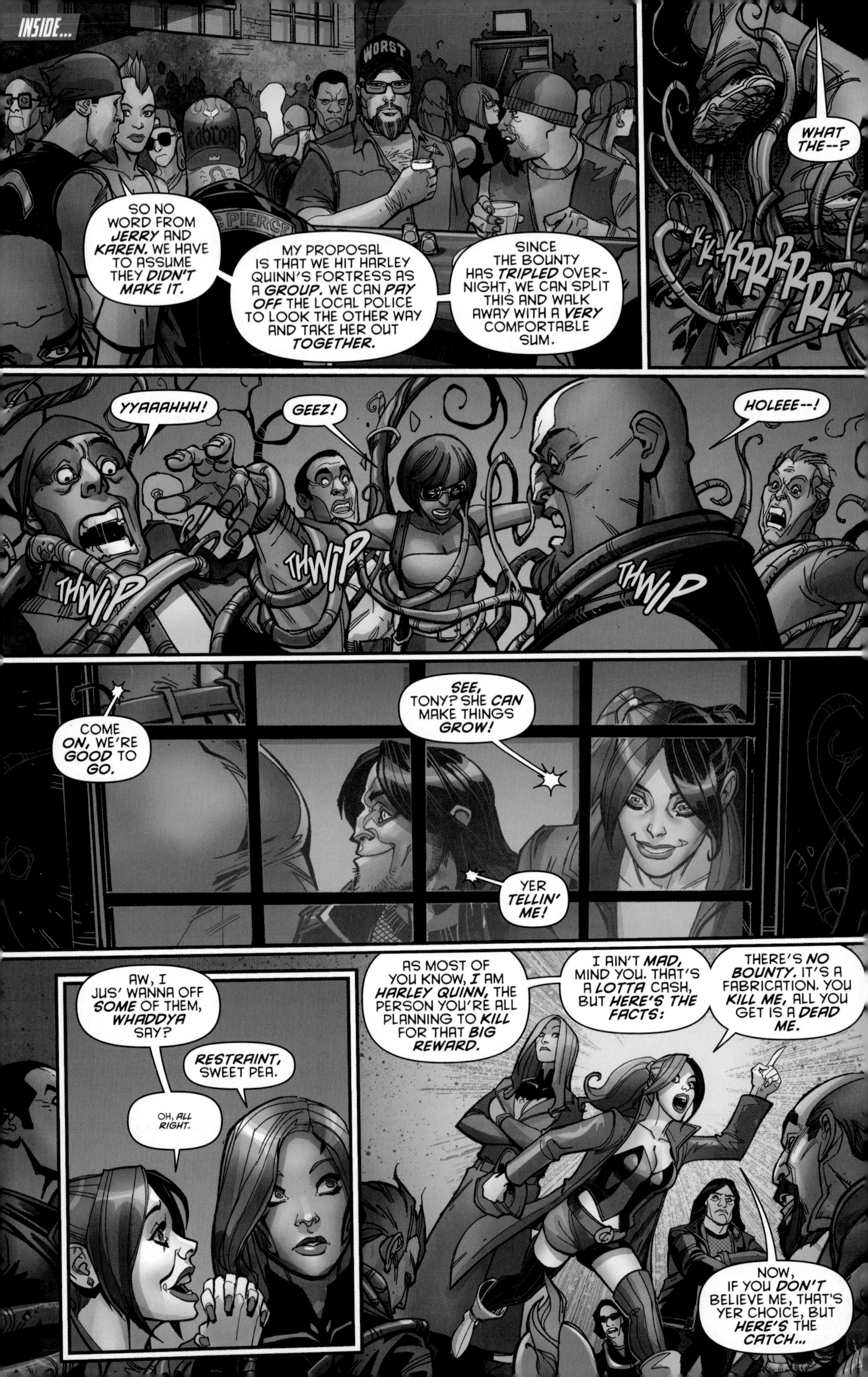
INSIDE...
WORST
SO NO WORD FROM JERRY AND KAREN. WE HAVE TO ASSUME THEY DIDN'T MAKE IT.
MY PROPOSAL IS THAT WE HIT HARLEY QUINN'S FORTRESS AS A GROUP. WE CAN PAY OFF THE LOCAL POLICE TO LOOK THE OTHER WAY AND TAKE HER OUT TOGETHER.
SINCE THE BOUNTY HAS TRIPLED OVER-NIGHT, WE CAN SPLIT THIS AND WALK AWAY WITH A VERY COMFORTABLE SUM.
WHAT THE--?
KK-KRRRRRRK
YYAAAHHH!
GEEZ!
HOLEEE--!
THWIP
THWIP
THWIP
COME ON, WE'RE GOOD TO GO.
SEE, TONY? SHE CAN MAKE THINGS GROW!
YER TELLIN' ME!
AW, I JUS' WANNA OFF SOME OF THEM, WHADDYA SAY?
RESTRAINT, SWEET PEA.
OH, ALL RIGHT.
AS MOST OF YOU KNOW, I AM HARLEY QUINN, THE PERSON YOU'RE ALL PLANNING TO KILL FOR THAT BIG REWARD.
I AIN'T MAD, MIND YOU. THAT'S A LOTTA CASH, BUT HERE'S THE FACTS:
THERE'S NO BOUNTY. IT'S A FABRICATION. YOU KILL ME, ALL YOU GET IS A DEAD ME.
NOW, IF YOU DON'T BELIEVE ME, THAT'S YER CHOICE, BUT HERE'S THE CATCH...

...MY ASSOCIATE WILL BE COLLECTING ALL YOUR WALLETS AND INFORMATION.

I SEE OR HEAR A *PEEP* FROM ANY OF YOU JACKHOLES, NOT ONLY WILL I *COME AFTER* YOU, BUT I'LL TAKE OUT YER *FAMILIES*, JUST FOR THE *FUN* OF IT. AM I BEING *CLEAR ENOUGH?*

PRETTY CLEAR.

ALL IN FAVOR OF *LEAVING ME ALONE* AND GOING BACK TO YOUR LIVES, SAY *"AYE"!*

AYE!

AYE!

AYE!

PHOOEY!

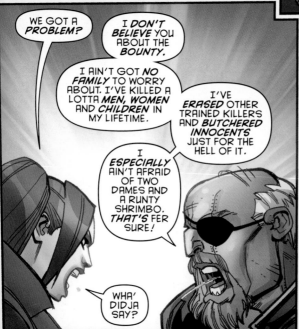

WE GOT A *PROBLEM?*

I *DON'T BELIEVE* YOU ABOUT THE *BOUNTY.*

I AIN'T GOT *NO FAMILY* TO WORRY ABOUT. I'VE KILLED A *LOTTA MEN, WOMEN* AND *CHILDREN* IN MY LIFETIME.

I'VE *ERASED* OTHER TRAINED KILLERS AND *BUTCHERED INNOCENTS* JUST FOR THE HELL OF IT.

I *ESPECIALLY AIN'T AFRAID* OF TWO DAMES AND A RUNTY SHRIMBO. *THAT'S* FER SURE!

WHA' DIDJA SAY?

HE HAS A *POINT,* HARLEY.

THERE'S *NO WAY* TO PROVE YOU PUT UP THE *BOUNTY* AND HE HAS *NO FAMILY,* SO NO *THREAT...*

BUT I *DEFINITELY* HAVE A SOLUTION WHAT'LL *WORK OUT* FER *ALL* OF US.

YOU SAY YOU *AIN'T AFRAID* OF A RUNTY SHRIMBO, *RIGHT?*

ESPECIALLY ONE THAT LOOKS LIKE *YOU,* LITTLE MAN.

BLAM

HE WAS RIGHT-- HE *WOULDA* BEEN A PROBLEM.

PROBLEM *SOLVED.*

ANYONE *ELSE* HAVE AN ISSUE, LEMME KNOW *NOW.*

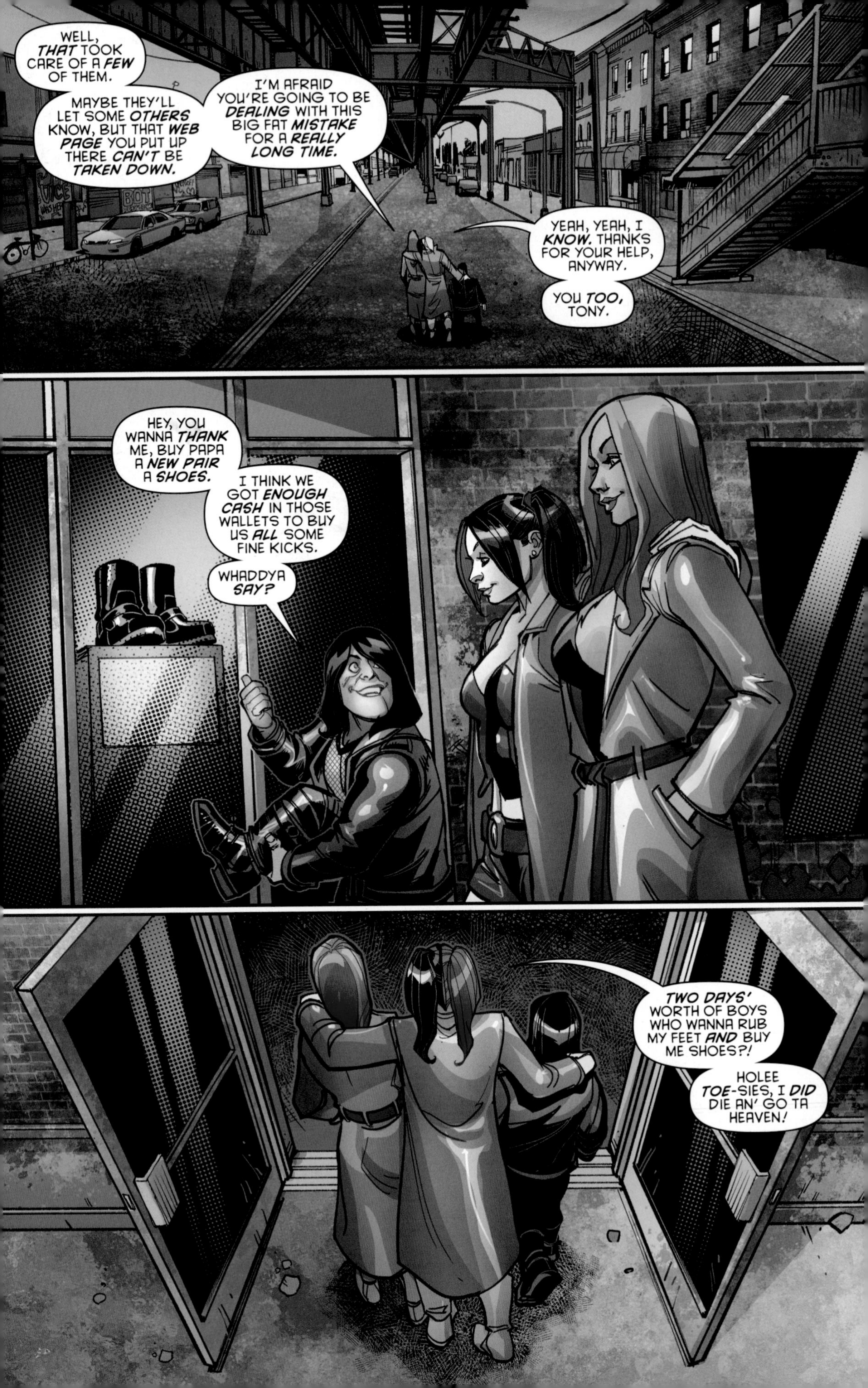
WELL, THAT TOOK CARE OF A FEW OF THEM.
MAYBE THEY'LL LET SOME OTHERS KNOW, BUT THAT WEB PAGE YOU PUT UP THERE CAN'T BE TAKEN DOWN.
I'M AFRAID YOU'RE GOING TO BE DEALING WITH THIS BIG FAT MISTAKE FOR A REALLY LONG TIME.
YEAH, YEAH, I KNOW. THANKS FOR YOUR HELP, ANYWAY.
YOU TOO, TONY.
HEY, YOU WANNA THANK ME, BUY PAPA A NEW PAIR A SHOES.
I THINK WE GOT ENOUGH CASH IN THOSE WALLETS TO BUY US ALL SOME FINE KICKS.
WHADDYA SAY?
TWO DAYS' WORTH OF BOYS WHO WANNA RUB MY FEET AND BUY ME SHOES?!
HOLEE TOE-SIES, I DID DIE AN' GO TA HEAVEN!

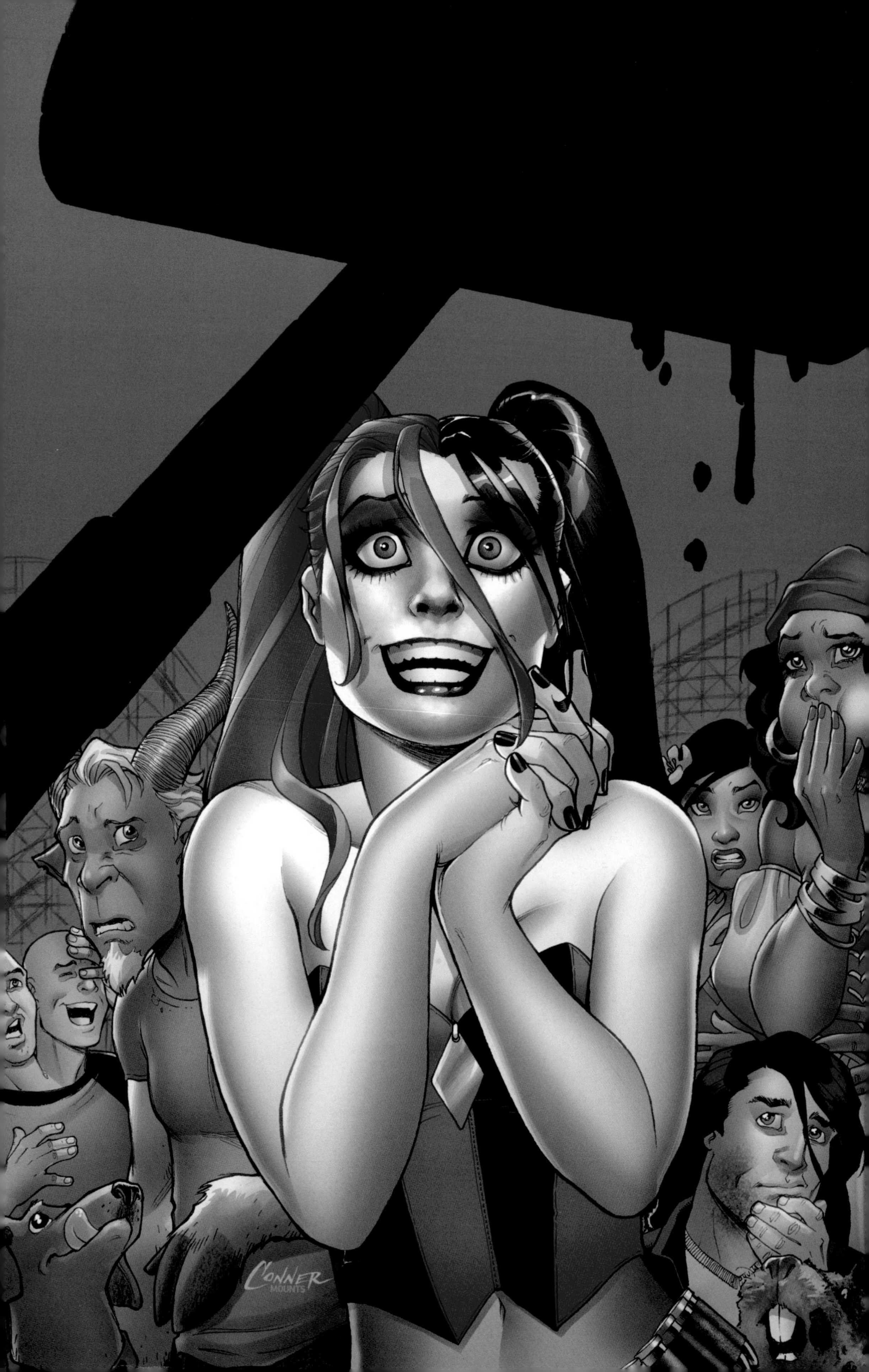
CONNER
MOUNTS

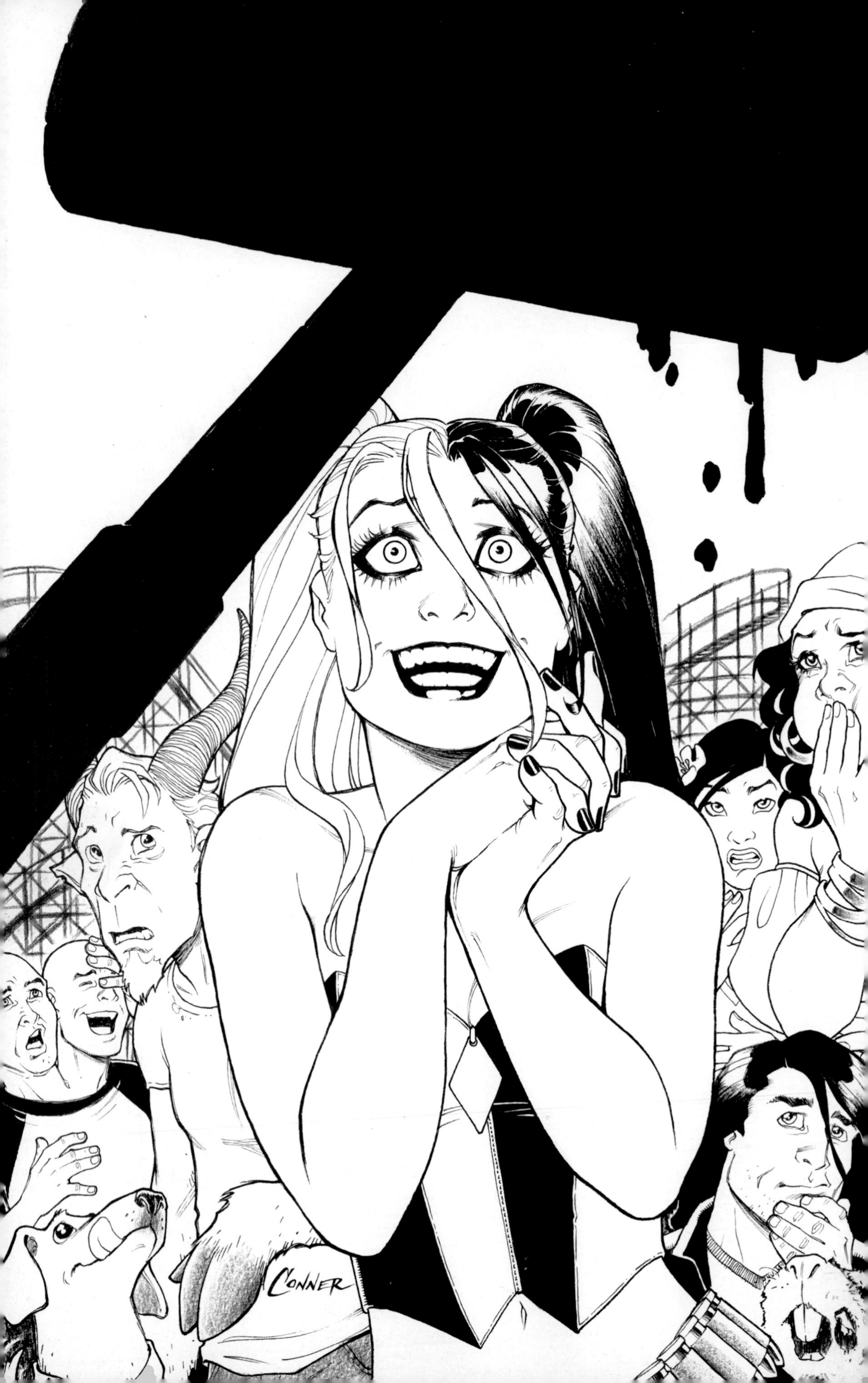
CONNER

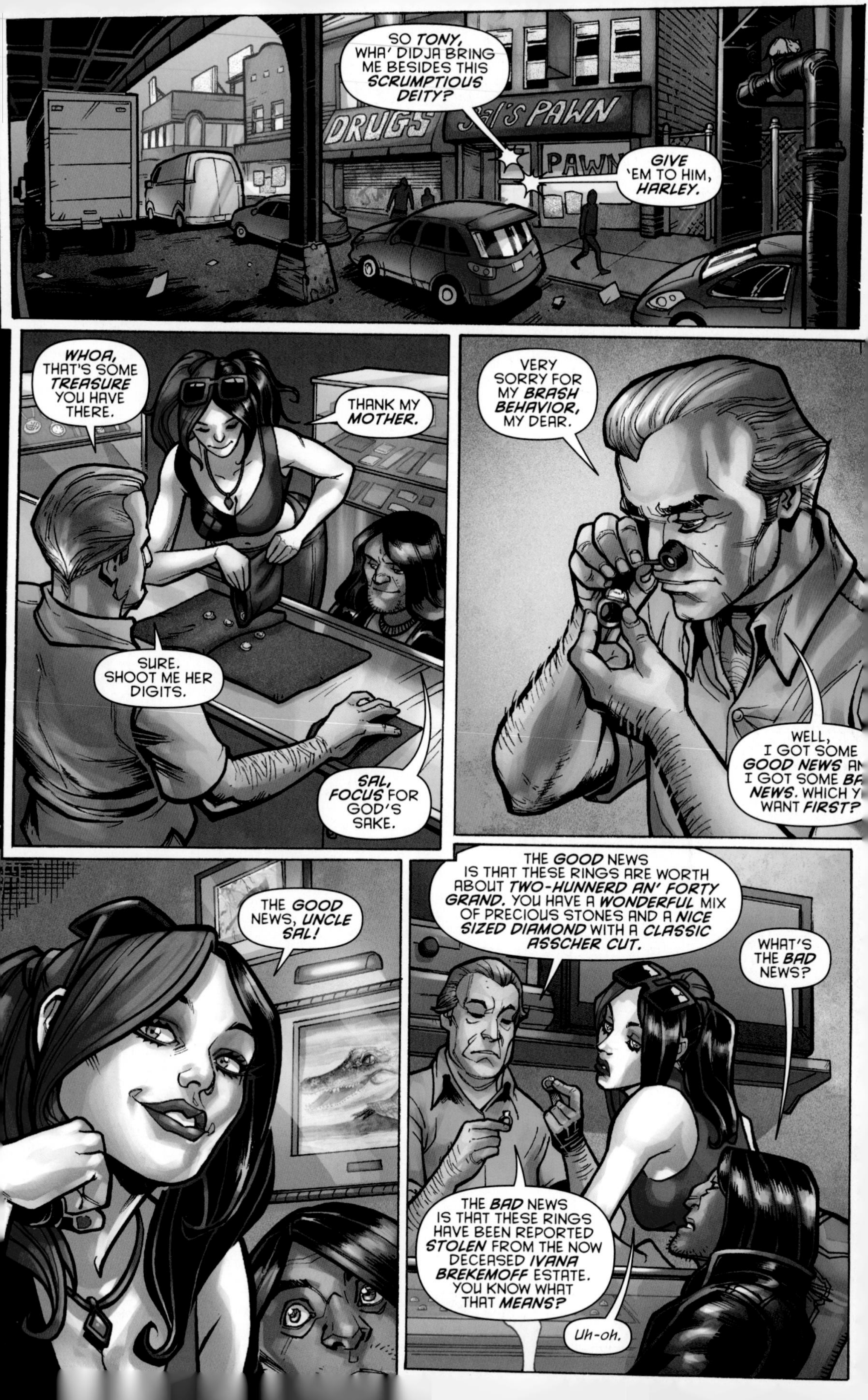

DRUGS
SAL'S PAWN
PAWN
SO TONY, WHA' DIDJA BRING ME BESIDES THIS SCRUMPTIOUS DEITY?
GIVE 'EM TO HIM, HARLEY.
WHOA, THAT'S SOME TREASURE YOU HAVE THERE.
THANK MY MOTHER.
SURE. SHOOT ME HER DIGITS.
SAL, FOCUS FOR GOD'S SAKE.
VERY SORRY FOR MY BRASH BEHAVIOR, MY DEAR.
WELL, I GOT SOME GOOD NEWS AN
I GOT SOME BA
NEWS. WHICH Y
WANT FIRST?
THE GOOD NEWS, UNCLE SAL!
THE GOOD NEWS IS THAT THESE RINGS ARE WORTH ABOUT TWO-HUNNERD AN' FORTY GRAND. YOU HAVE A WONDERFUL MIX OF PRECIOUS STONES AND A NICE SIZED DIAMOND WITH A CLASSIC ASSCHER CUT.
WHAT'S THE BAD NEWS?
THE BAD NEWS IS THAT THESE RINGS HAVE BEEN REPORTED STOLEN FROM THE NOW DECEASED IVANA BREKEMOFF ESTATE. YOU KNOW WHAT THAT MEANS?
Uh-oh.

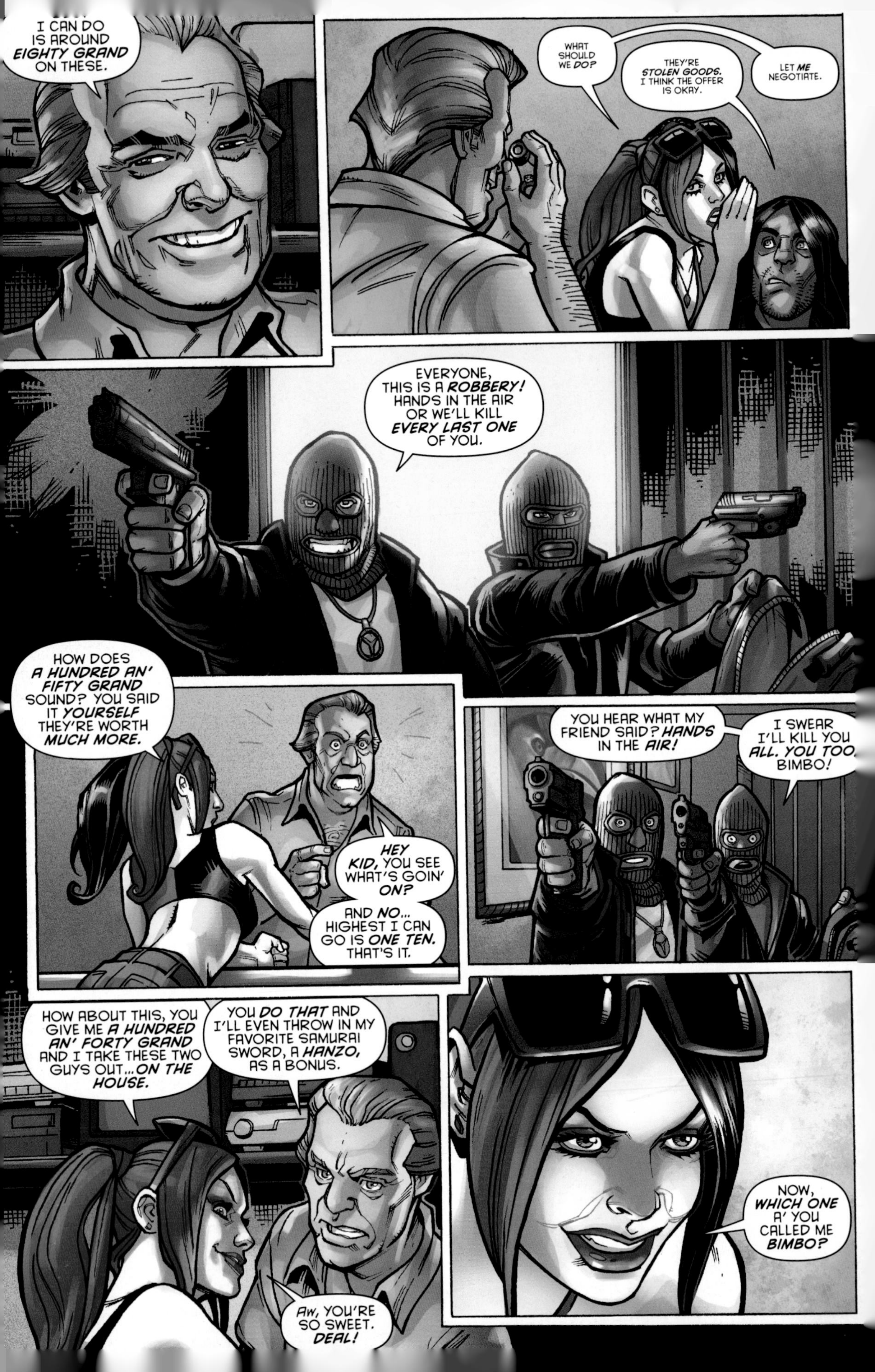
I CAN DO IS AROUND EIGHTY GRAND ON THESE.
WHAT SHOULD WE DO?
THEY'RE STOLEN GOODS. I THINK THE OFFER IS OKAY.
LET ME NEGOTIATE.
EVERYONE, THIS IS A ROBBERY! HANDS IN THE AIR OR WE'LL KILL EVERY LAST ONE OF YOU.
HOW DOES A HUNDRED AN' FIFTY GRAND SOUND? YOU SAID IT YOURSELF THEY'RE WORTH MUCH MORE.
HEY KID, YOU SEE WHAT'S GOIN' ON?
AND NO... HIGHEST I CAN GO IS ONE TEN. THAT'S IT.
YOU HEAR WHAT MY FRIEND SAID? HANDS IN THE AIR!
I SWEAR I'LL KILL YOU ALL. YOU TOO, BIMBO!
HOW ABOUT THIS, YOU GIVE ME A HUNDRED AN' FORTY GRAND AND I TAKE THESE TWO GUYS OUT...ON THE HOUSE.
YOU DO THAT AND I'LL EVEN THROW IN MY FAVORITE SAMURAI SWORD, A HANZO, AS A BONUS.
AW, YOU'RE SO SWEET. DEAL!
NOW, WHICH ONE A' YOU CALLED ME BIMBO?

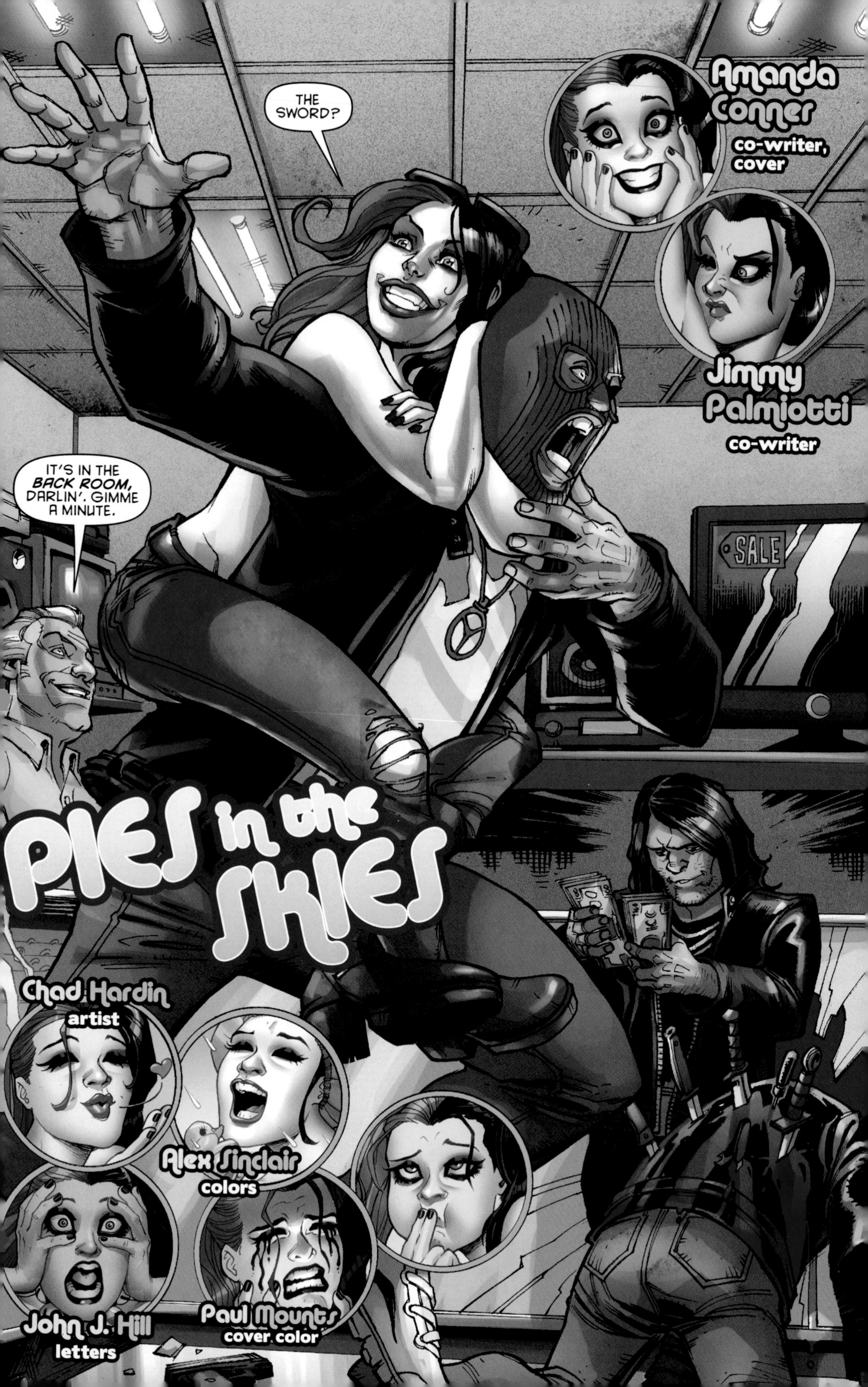
THE SWORD?
IT'S IN THE BACK ROOM, DARLIN'. GIMME A MINUTE.
SALE
Amanda Conner co-writer, cover
Jimmy Palmiotti co-writer
PIES in the SKIES
Chad Hardin artist
Alex Sinclair colors
John J. Hill letters
Paul Mounts cover color

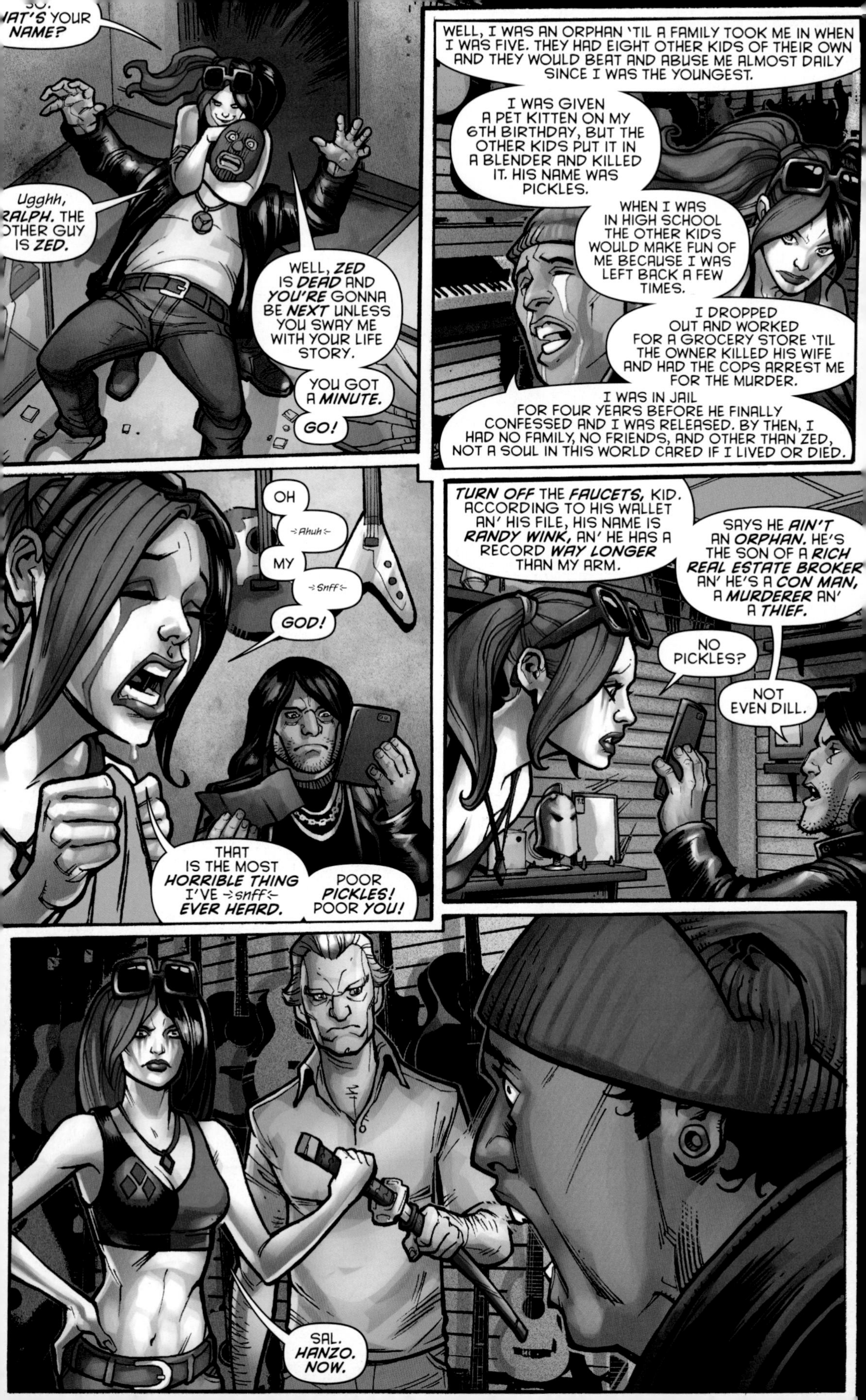

...AT'S YOUR NAME?
Ugghh, ...RALPH. THE OTHER GUY IS ZED.
WELL, ZED IS DEAD AND YOU'RE GONNA BE NEXT UNLESS YOU SWAY ME WITH YOUR LIFE STORY.
YOU GOT A MINUTE.
GO!
WELL, I WAS AN ORPHAN 'TIL A FAMILY TOOK ME IN WHEN I WAS FIVE. THEY HAD EIGHT OTHER KIDS OF THEIR OWN AND THEY WOULD BEAT AND ABUSE ME ALMOST DAILY SINCE I WAS THE YOUNGEST.
I WAS GIVEN A PET KITTEN ON MY 6TH BIRTHDAY, BUT THE OTHER KIDS PUT IT IN A BLENDER AND KILLED IT. HIS NAME WAS PICKLES.
WHEN I WAS IN HIGH SCHOOL THE OTHER KIDS WOULD MAKE FUN OF ME BECAUSE I WAS LEFT BACK A FEW TIMES.
I DROPPED OUT AND WORKED FOR A GROCERY STORE 'TIL THE OWNER KILLED HIS WIFE AND HAD THE COPS ARREST ME FOR THE MURDER.
I WAS IN JAIL FOR FOUR YEARS BEFORE HE FINALLY CONFESSED AND I WAS RELEASED. BY THEN, I HAD NO FAMILY, NO FRIENDS, AND OTHER THAN ZED, NOT A SOUL IN THIS WORLD CARED IF I LIVED OR DIED.
OH
Ahuh
MY
Snff
GOD!
THAT IS THE MOST HORRIBLE THING I'VE snff EVER HEARD.
POOR PICKLES! POOR YOU!
TURN OFF THE FAUCETS, KID. ACCORDING TO HIS WALLET AN' HIS FILE, HIS NAME IS RANDY WINK, AN' HE HAS A RECORD WAY LONGER THAN MY ARM.
SAYS HE AIN'T AN ORPHAN. HE'S THE SON OF A RICH REAL ESTATE BROKER AN' HE'S A CON MAN, A MURDERER AN' A THIEF.
NO PICKLES?
NOT EVEN DILL.
SAL. HANZO. NOW.

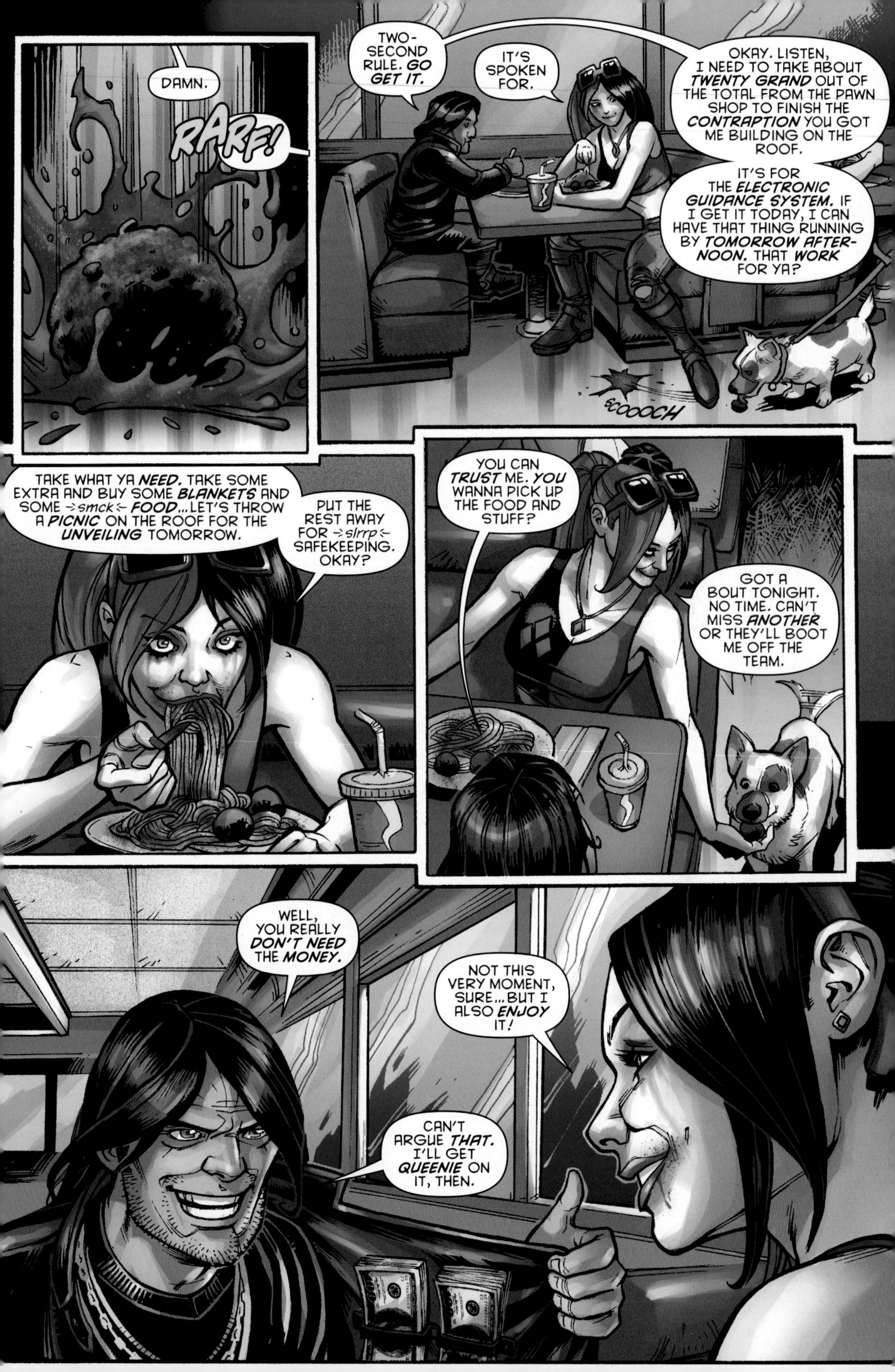

DAMN.
RARF!
TWO-SECOND RULE. GO GET IT.
IT'S SPOKEN FOR.
OKAY. LISTEN, I NEED TO TAKE ABOUT TWENTY GRAND OUT OF THE TOTAL FROM THE PAWN SHOP TO FINISH THE CONTRAPTION YOU GOT ME BUILDING ON THE ROOF.
IT'S FOR THE ELECTRONIC GUIDANCE SYSTEM. IF I GET IT TODAY, I CAN HAVE THAT THING RUNNING BY TOMORROW AFTER-NOON. THAT WORK FOR YA?
SCOOOCH
TAKE WHAT YA NEED. TAKE SOME EXTRA AND BUY SOME BLANKETS AND SOME -smck- FOOD...LET'S THROW A PICNIC ON THE ROOF FOR THE UNVEILING TOMORROW.
PUT THE REST AWAY FOR -slrrp- SAFEKEEPING. OKAY?
YOU CAN TRUST ME. YOU WANNA PICK UP THE FOOD AND STUFF?
GOT A BOUT TONIGHT. NO TIME. CAN'T MISS ANOTHER OR THEY'LL BOOT ME OFF THE TEAM.
WELL, YOU REALLY DON'T NEED THE MONEY.
NOT THIS VERY MOMENT, SURE...BUT I ALSO ENJOY IT!
CAN'T ARGUE THAT. I'LL GET QUEENIE ON IT, THEN.

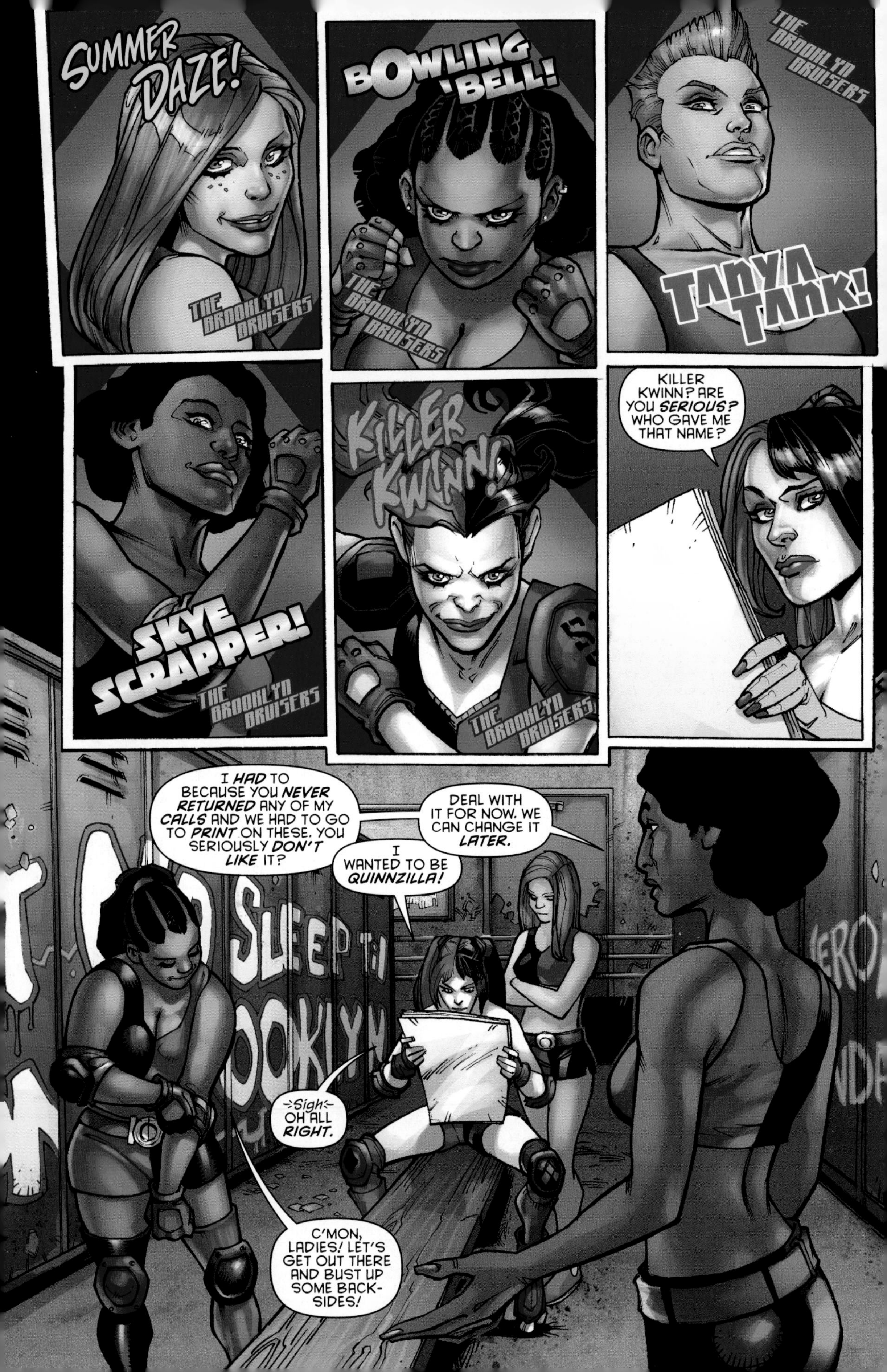
SUMMER DAZE!
THE BROOKLYN BRUISERS
BOWLING 'BELL!
THE BROOKLYN BRUISERS
THE BROOKLYN BRUISERS
TANYA TANK!
SKYE SCRAPPER!
THE BROOKLYN BRUISERS
KILLER KWINN!
THE BROOKLYN BRUISERS
KILLER KWINN? ARE YOU SERIOUS? WHO GAVE ME THAT NAME?
I HAD TO BECAUSE YOU NEVER RETURNED ANY OF MY CALLS AND WE HAD TO GO TO PRINT ON THESE. YOU SERIOUSLY DON'T LIKE IT?
I WANTED TO BE QUINNZILLA!
DEAL WITH IT FOR NOW. WE CAN CHANGE IT LATER.
Sigh OH ALL RIGHT.
C'MON, LADIES! LET'S GET OUT THERE AND BUST UP SOME BACK-SIDES!

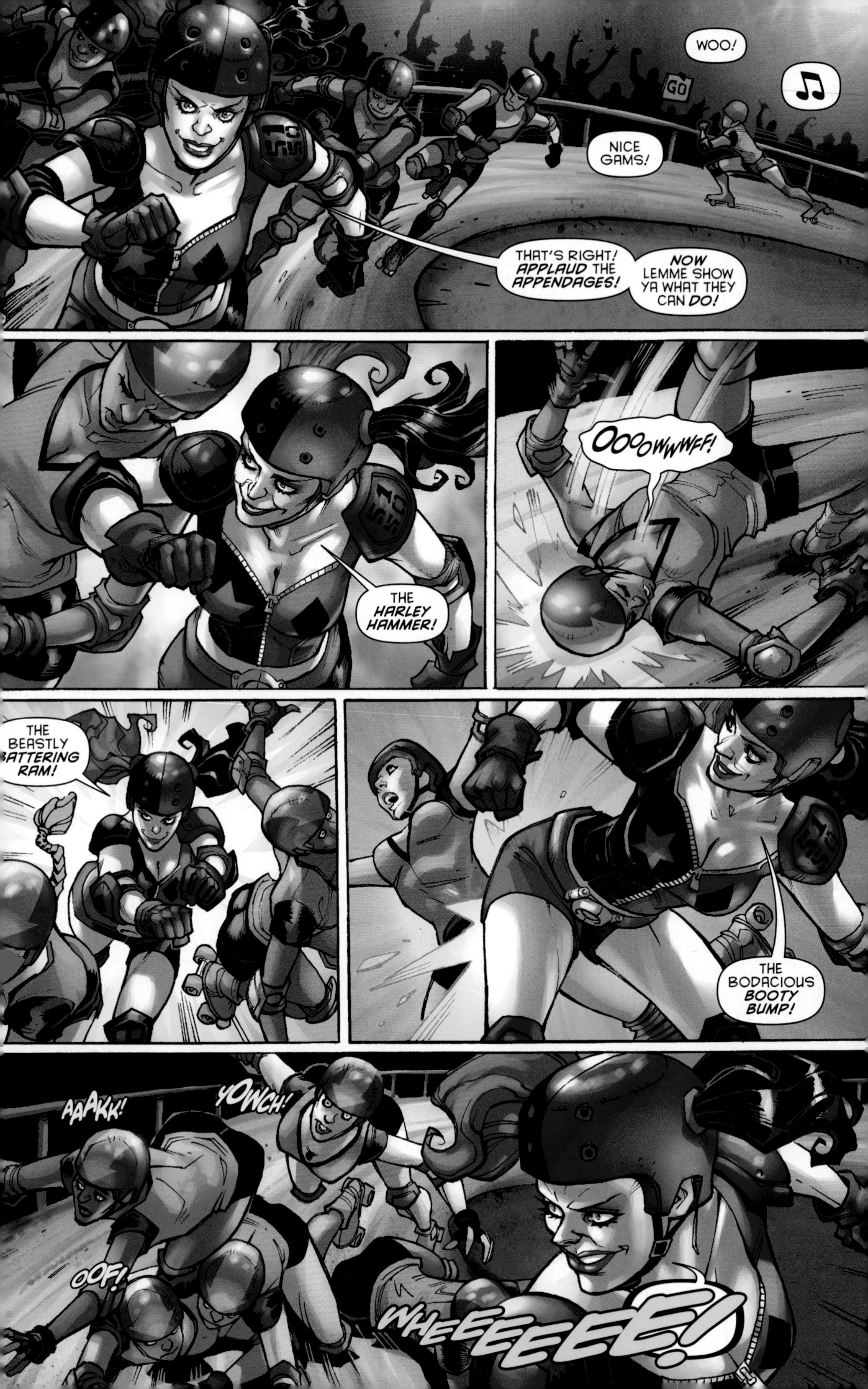
WOO!
♫
NICE GAMS!
GO
THAT'S RIGHT! APPLAUD THE APPENDAGES!
NOW LEMME SHOW YA WHAT THEY CAN DO!
THE HARLEY HAMMER!
OOOOWWWFF!
THE BEASTLY BATTERING RAM!
THE BODACIOUS BOOTY BUMP!
AAAKK!
YOWCH!
OOF!
WHEEEEEEEE!

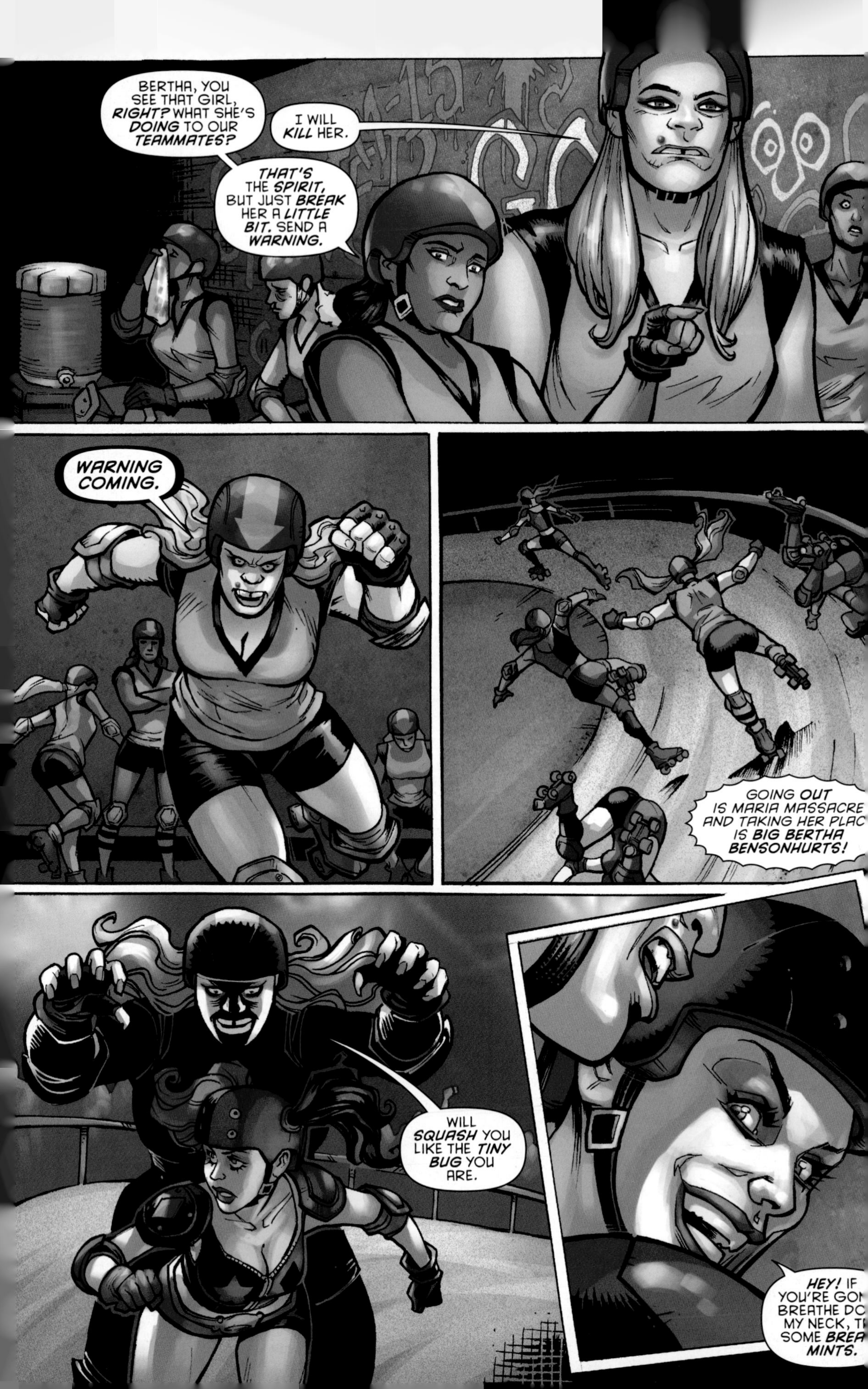
BERTHA, YOU SEE THAT GIRL, RIGHT? WHAT SHE'S DOING TO OUR TEAMMATES?
I WILL KILL HER.
THAT'S THE SPIRIT, BUT JUST BREAK HER A LITTLE BIT. SEND A WARNING.
WARNING COMING.
GOING OUT IS MARIA MASSACRE AND TAKING HER PLAC IS BIG BERTHA BENSONHURTS!
WILL SQUASH YOU LIKE THE TINY BUG YOU ARE.
HEY! IF YOU'RE GO BREATHE DO MY NECK, T SOME BREA MINTS.

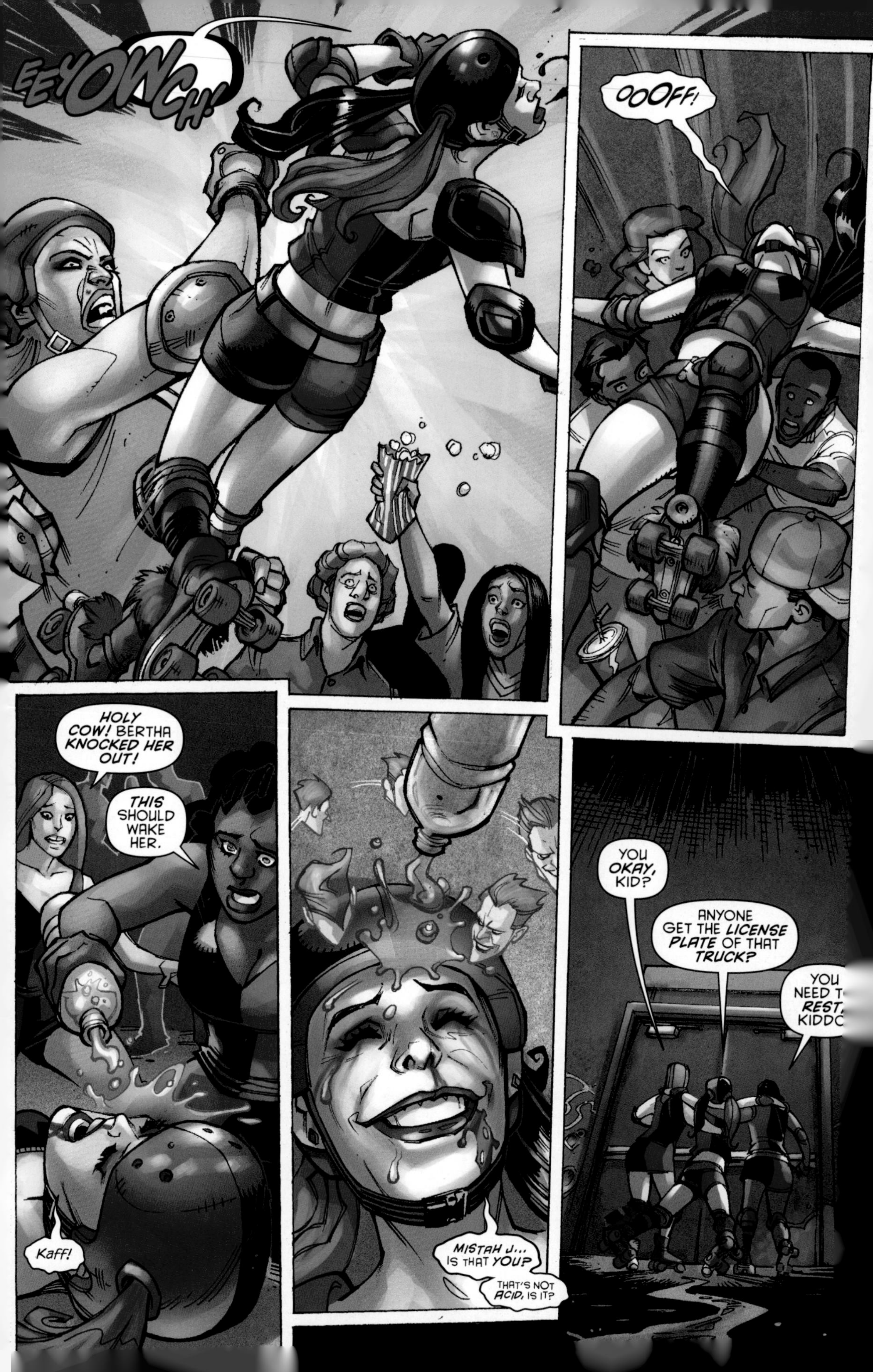
EEYOWNCH!
OOOFF!
HOLY COW! BERTHA KNOCKED HER OUT!
THIS SHOULD WAKE HER.
Kaff!
MISTAH J... IS THAT YOU?
THAT'S NOT ACID, IS IT?
YOU OKAY, KID?
ANYONE GET THE LICENSE PLATE OF THAT TRUCK?
YOU NEED T REST, KIDDO

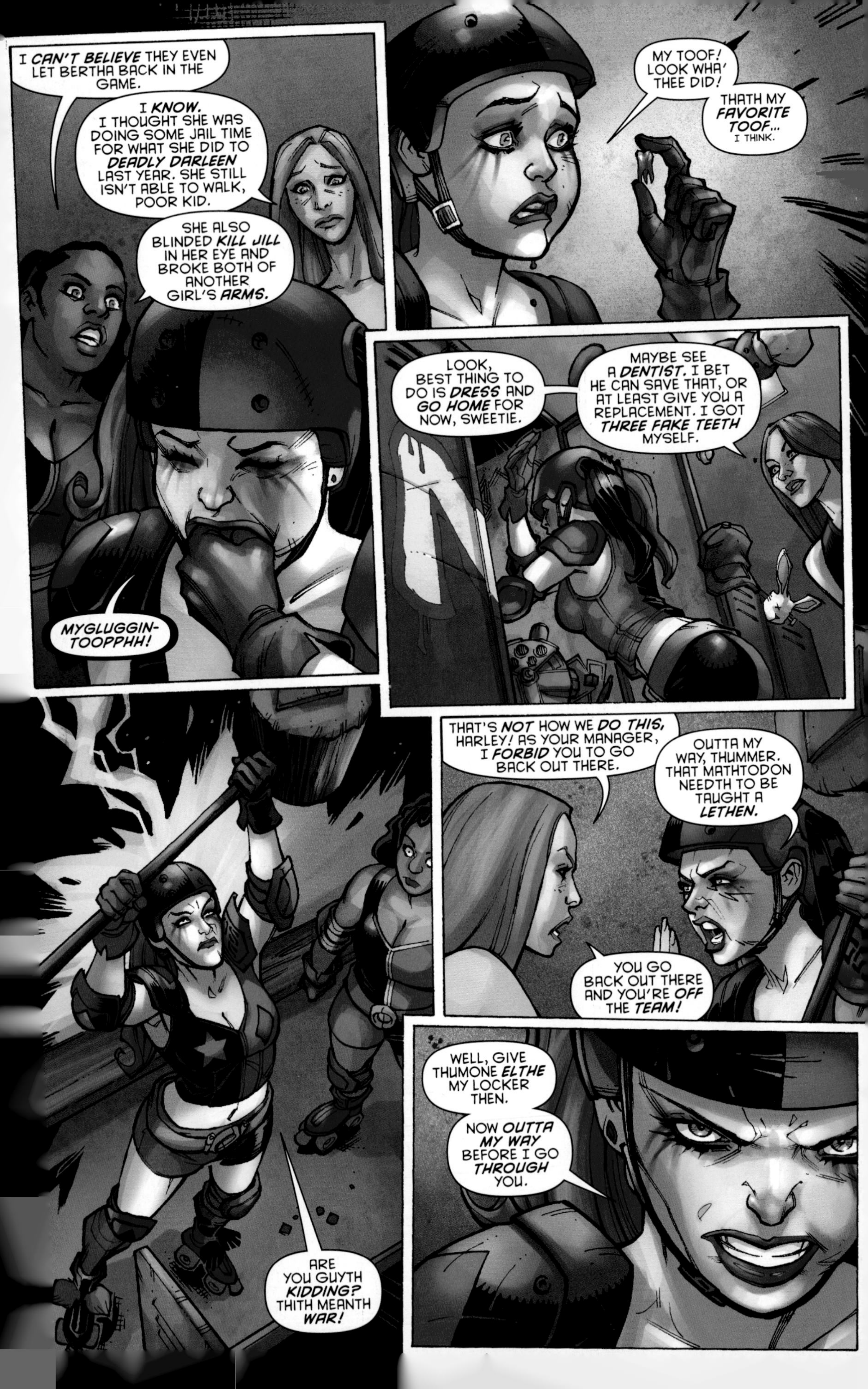
I CAN'T BELIEVE THEY EVEN LET BERTHA BACK IN THE GAME.
I KNOW. I THOUGHT SHE WAS DOING SOME JAIL TIME FOR WHAT SHE DID TO DEADLY DARLEEN LAST YEAR. SHE STILL ISN'T ABLE TO WALK, POOR KID.
SHE ALSO BLINDED KILL JILL IN HER EYE AND BROKE BOTH OF ANOTHER GIRL'S ARMS.
MYGLUGGIN-TOOPPHH!
MY TOOF! LOOK WHA' THEE DID!
THATH MY FAVORITE TOOF... I THINK.
LOOK, BEST THING TO DO IS DRESS AND GO HOME FOR NOW, SWEETIE.
MAYBE SEE A DENTIST. I BET HE CAN SAVE THAT, OR AT LEAST GIVE YOU A REPLACEMENT. I GOT THREE FAKE TEETH MYSELF.
ARE YOU GUYTH KIDDING? THITH MEANTH WAR!
THAT'S NOT HOW WE DO THIS, HARLEY! AS YOUR MANAGER, I FORBID YOU TO GO BACK OUT THERE.
OUTTA MY WAY, THUMMER. THAT MATHTODON NEEDTH TO BE TAUGHT A LETHEN.
YOU GO BACK OUT THERE AND YOU'RE OFF THE TEAM!
WELL, GIVE THUMONE ELTHE MY LOCKER THEN.
NOW OUTTA MY WAY BEFORE I GO THROUGH YOU.

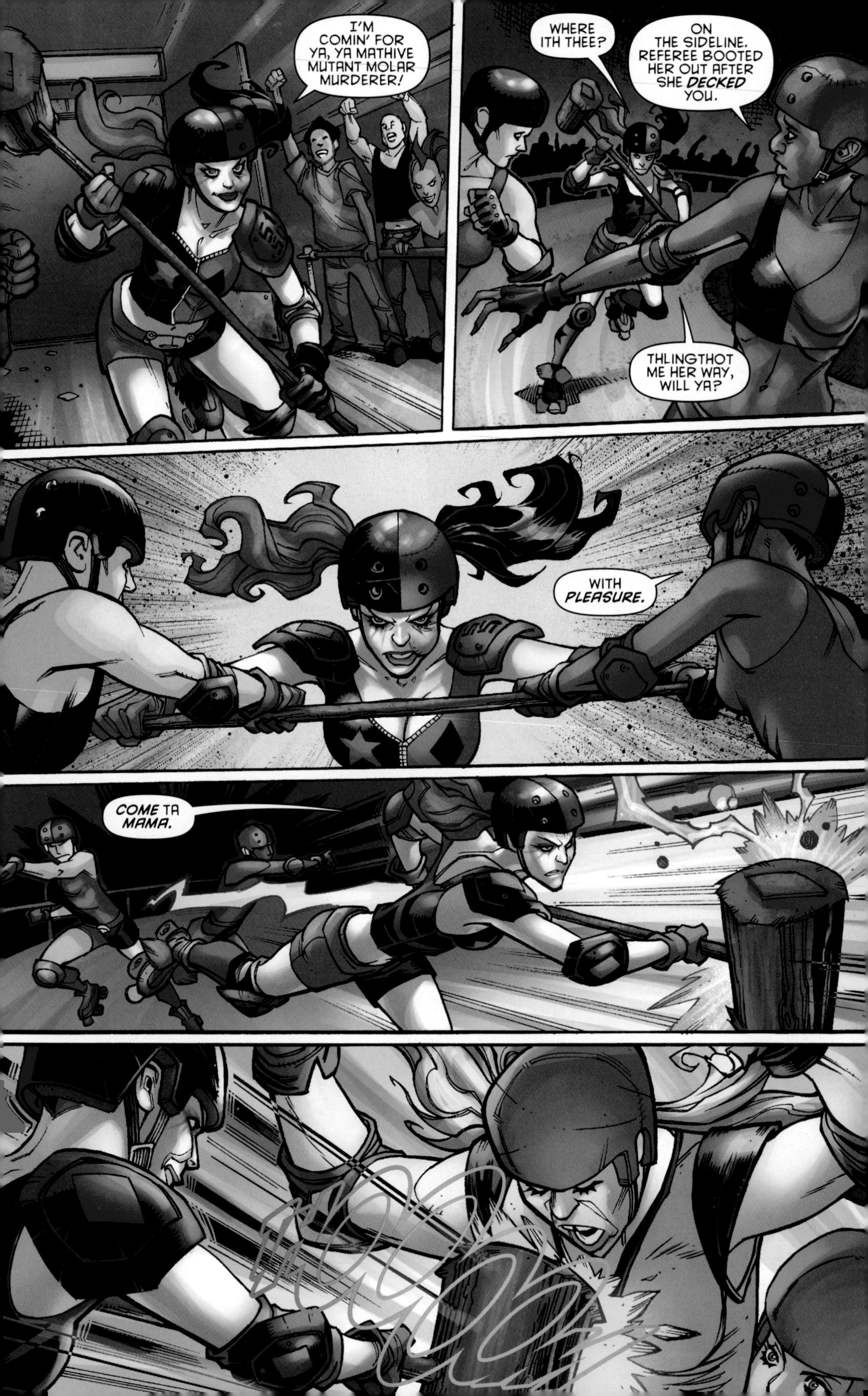
I'M COMIN' FOR YA, YA MATHIVE MUTANT MOLAR MURDERER!
WHERE ITH THEE?
ON THE SIDELINE. REFEREE BOOTED HER OUT AFTER SHE DECKED YOU.
THLINGTHOT ME HER WAY, WILL YA?
WITH PLEASURE.
COME TA MAMA.

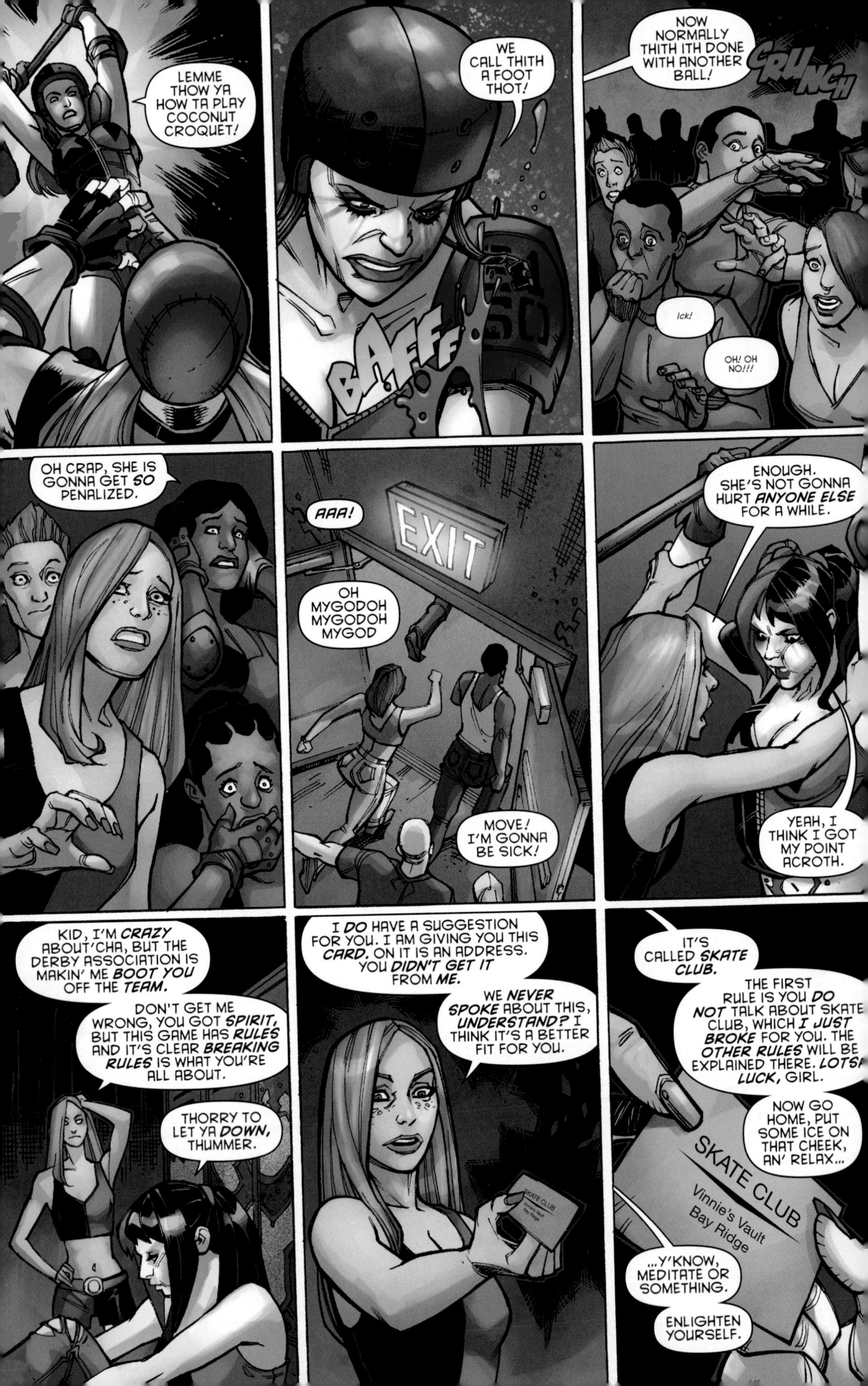
LEMME THOW YA HOW TA PLAY COCONUT CROQUET!
WE CALL THITH A FOOT THOT!
BAFFF
NOW NORMALLY THITH ITH DONE WITH ANOTHER BALL!
CRUNCH
Ick!
OH! OH NO!!!
OH CRAP, SHE IS GONNA GET SO PENALIZED.
AAA!
EXIT
OH MYGODOH MYGODOH MYGOD
MOVE! I'M GONNA BE SICK!
ENOUGH. SHE'S NOT GONNA HURT ANYONE ELSE FOR A WHILE.
YEAH, I THINK I GOT MY POINT ACROTH.
KID, I'M CRAZY ABOUT'CHA, BUT THE DERBY ASSOCIATION IS MAKIN' ME BOOT YOU OFF THE TEAM.
DON'T GET ME WRONG, YOU GOT SPIRIT, BUT THIS GAME HAS RULES AND IT'S CLEAR BREAKING RULES IS WHAT YOU'RE ALL ABOUT.
THORRY TO LET YA DOWN, THUMMER.
I DO HAVE A SUGGESTION FOR YOU. I AM GIVING YOU THIS CARD. ON IT IS AN ADDRESS. YOU DIDN'T GET IT FROM ME.
WE NEVER SPOKE ABOUT THIS, UNDERSTAND? I THINK IT'S A BETTER FIT FOR YOU.
IT'S CALLED SKATE CLUB.
THE FIRST RULE IS YOU DO NOT TALK ABOUT SKATE CLUB, WHICH I JUST BROKE FOR YOU. THE OTHER RULES WILL BE EXPLAINED THERE. LOTSH LUCK, GIRL.
NOW GO HOME, PUT SOME ICE ON THAT CHEEK, AN' RELAX...
SKATE CLUB
Vinnie's Vault
Bay Ridge
...Y'KNOW, MEDITATE OR SOMETHING.
ENLIGHTEN YOURSELF.

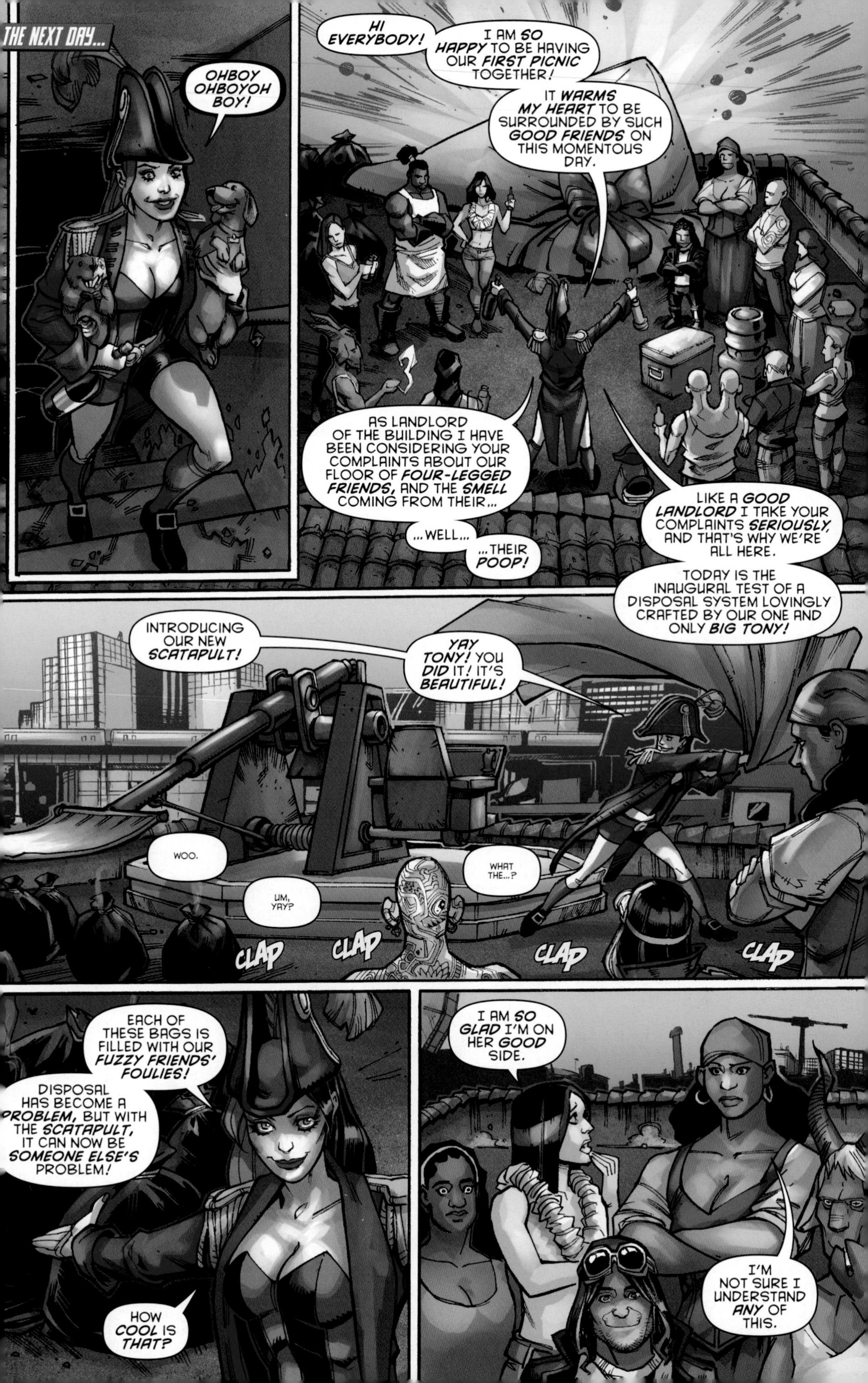
THE NEXT DAY...
OHBOY OHBOYOH BOY!
HI EVERYBODY!
I AM SO HAPPY TO BE HAVING OUR FIRST PICNIC TOGETHER!
IT WARMS MY HEART TO BE SURROUNDED BY SUCH GOOD FRIENDS ON THIS MOMENTOUS DAY.
AS LANDLORD OF THE BUILDING I HAVE BEEN CONSIDERING YOUR COMPLAINTS ABOUT OUR FLOOR OF FOUR-LEGGED FRIENDS, AND THE SMELL COMING FROM THEIR...
...WELL...
...THEIR POOP!
LIKE A GOOD LANDLORD I TAKE YOUR COMPLAINTS SERIOUSLY, AND THAT'S WHY WE'RE ALL HERE.
TODAY IS THE INAUGURAL TEST OF A DISPOSAL SYSTEM LOVINGLY CRAFTED BY OUR ONE AND ONLY BIG TONY!
INTRODUCING OUR NEW SCATAPULT!
YAY TONY! YOU DID IT! IT'S BEAUTIFUL!
WOO.
UM, YAY?
WHAT THE...?
CLAP
CLAP
CLAP
CLAP
EACH OF THESE BAGS IS FILLED WITH OUR FUZZY FRIENDS' FOULIES!
DISPOSAL HAS BECOME A PROBLEM, BUT WITH THE SCATAPULT, IT CAN NOW BE SOMEONE ELSE'S PROBLEM!
HOW COOL IS THAT?
I AM SO GLAD I'M ON HER GOOD SIDE.
I'M NOT SURE I UNDERSTAND ANY OF THIS.

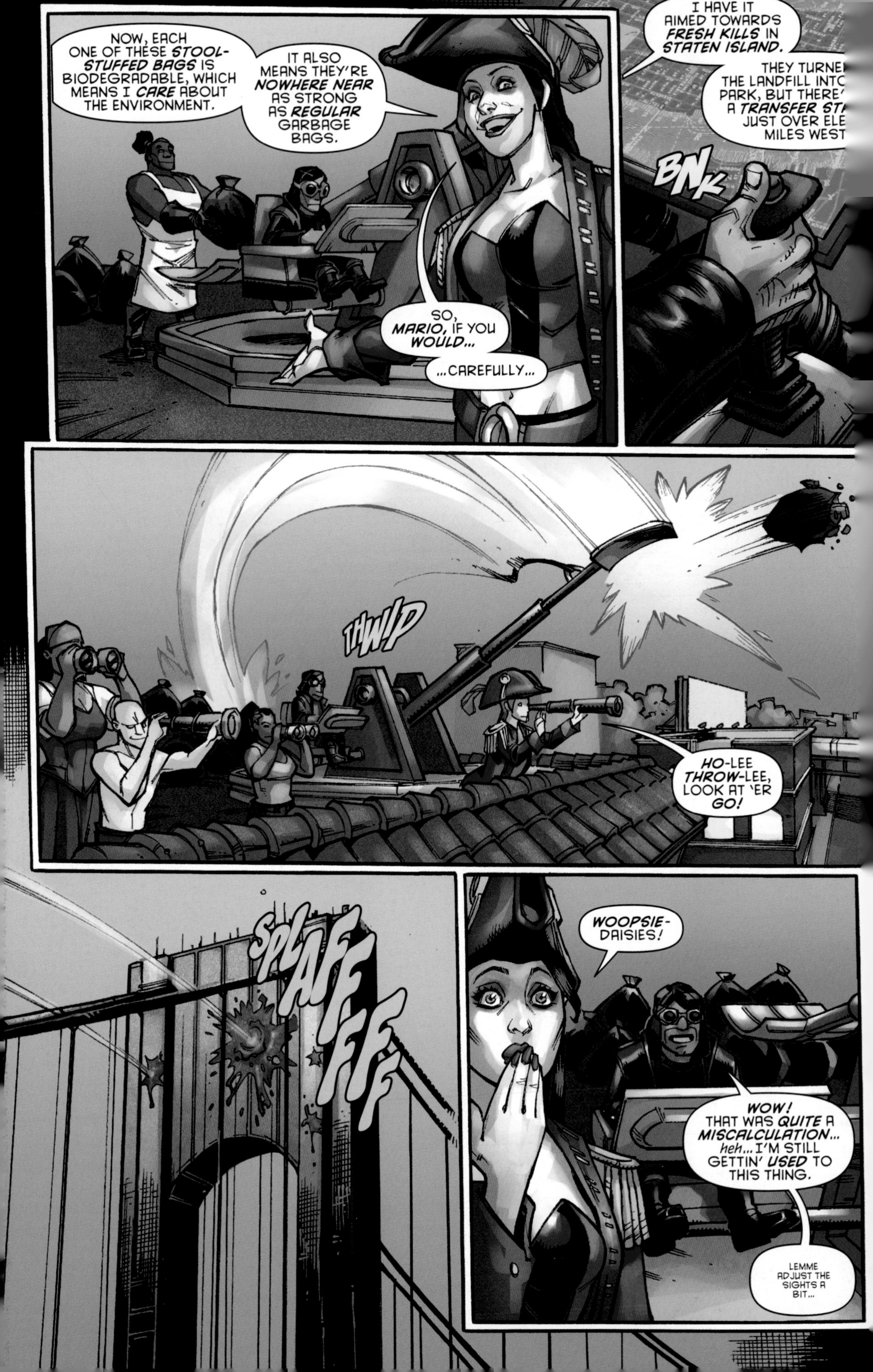

NOW, EACH ONE OF THESE STOOL-STUFFED BAGS IS BIODEGRADABLE, WHICH MEANS I CARE ABOUT THE ENVIRONMENT.
IT ALSO MEANS THEY'RE NOWHERE NEAR AS STRONG AS REGULAR GARBAGE BAGS.
SO, MARIO, IF YOU WOULD...
...CAREFULLY...
I HAVE IT AIMED TOWARDS FRESH KILLS IN STATEN ISLAND.
BNK
THWIP
HO-LEE THROW-LEE, LOOK AT 'ER GO!
SPLAFFFFF
WOOPSIE-DAISIES!
WOW! THAT WAS QUITE A MISCALCULATION... heh... I'M STILL GETTIN' USED TO THIS THING.
LEMME ADJUST THE SIGHTS A BIT...

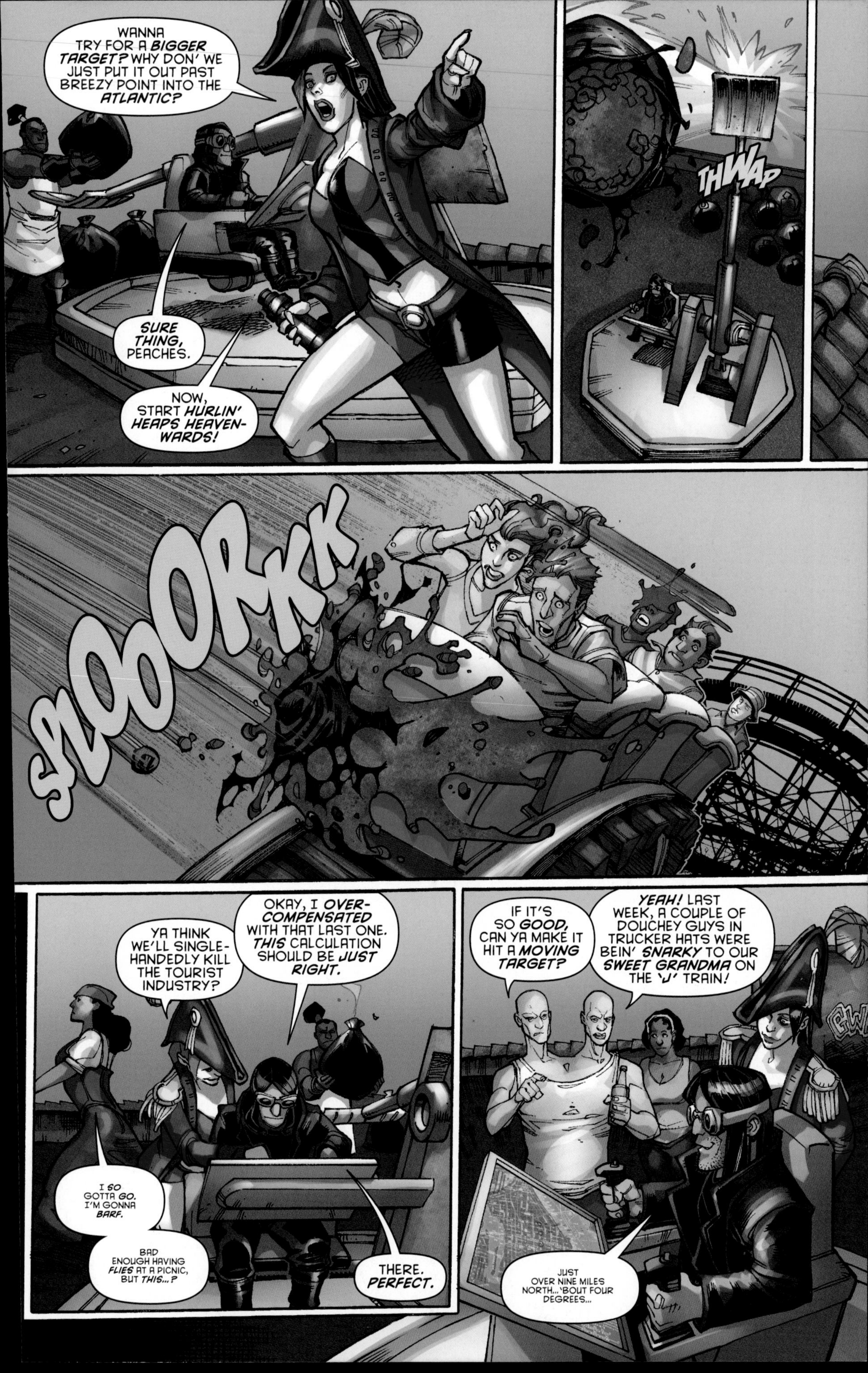
WANNA TRY FOR A BIGGER TARGET? WHY DON' WE JUST PUT IT OUT PAST BREEZY POINT INTO THE ATLANTIC?
SURE THING, PEACHES.
NOW, START HURLIN' HEAPS HEAVEN-WARDS!
THWAP
SPLOORKK
YA THINK WE'LL SINGLE-HANDEDLY KILL THE TOURIST INDUSTRY?
OKAY, I OVER-COMPENSATED WITH THAT LAST ONE. THIS CALCULATION SHOULD BE JUST RIGHT.
I SO GOTTA GO. I'M GONNA BARF.
BAD ENOUGH HAVING FLIES AT A PICNIC, BUT THIS...?
THERE. PERFECT.
IF IT'S SO GOOD, CAN YA MAKE IT HIT A MOVING TARGET?
YEAH! LAST WEEK, A COUPLE OF DOUCHEY GUYS IN TRUCKER HATS WERE BEIN' SNARKY TO OUR SWEET GRANDMA ON THE 'J' TRAIN!
JUST OVER NINE MILES NORTH... 'BOUT FOUR DEGREES...

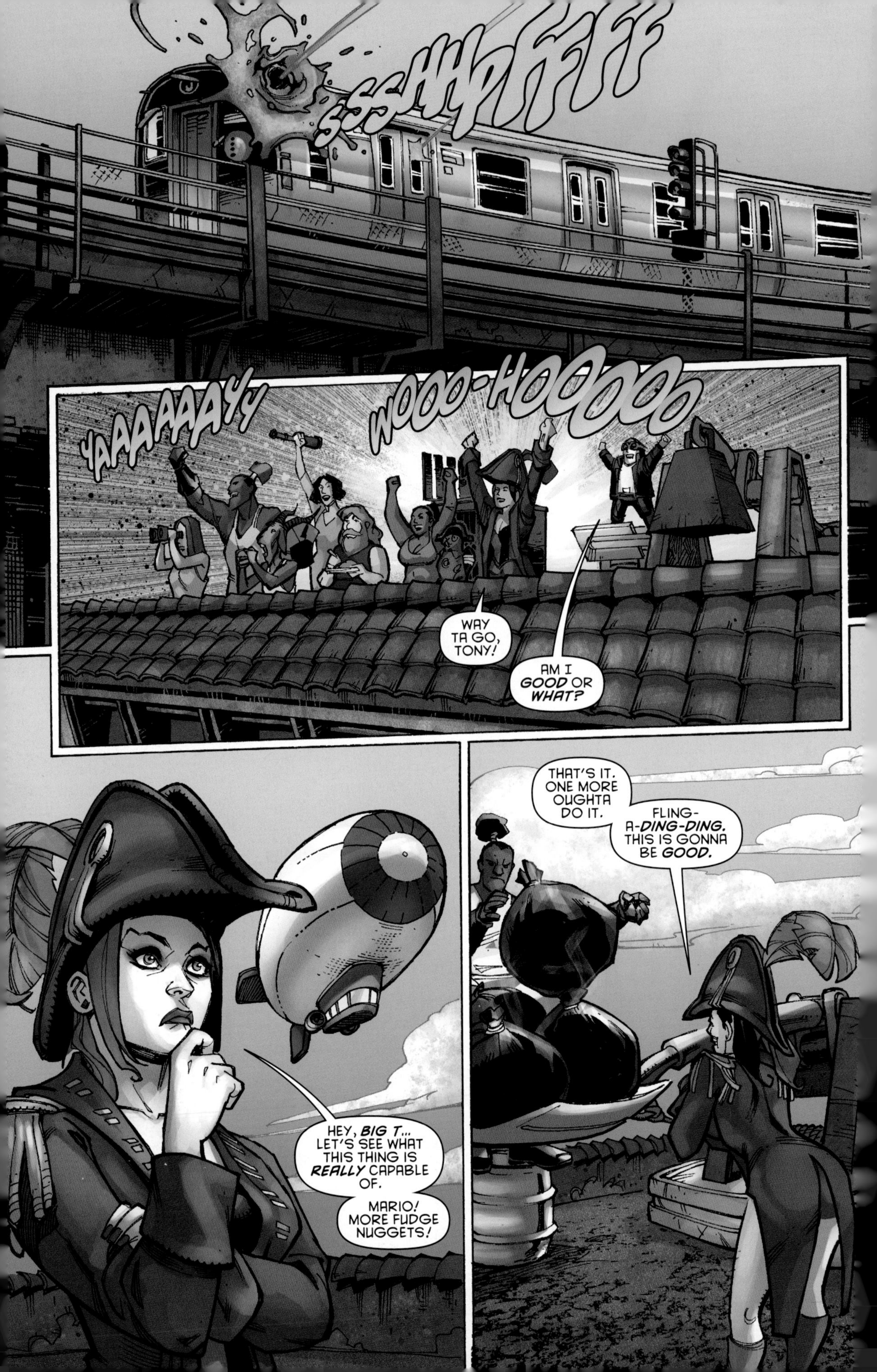
SSSHHPFFFFF
YAAAAAAYYY
WOOO-HOOOOOOO
WAY TA GO, TONY!
AM I GOOD OR WHAT?
HEY, BIG T... LET'S SEE WHAT THIS THING IS REALLY CAPABLE OF.
MARIO! MORE FUDGE NUGGETS!
THAT'S IT. ONE MORE OUGHTA DO IT.
FLING-A-DING-DING. THIS IS GONNA BE GOOD.

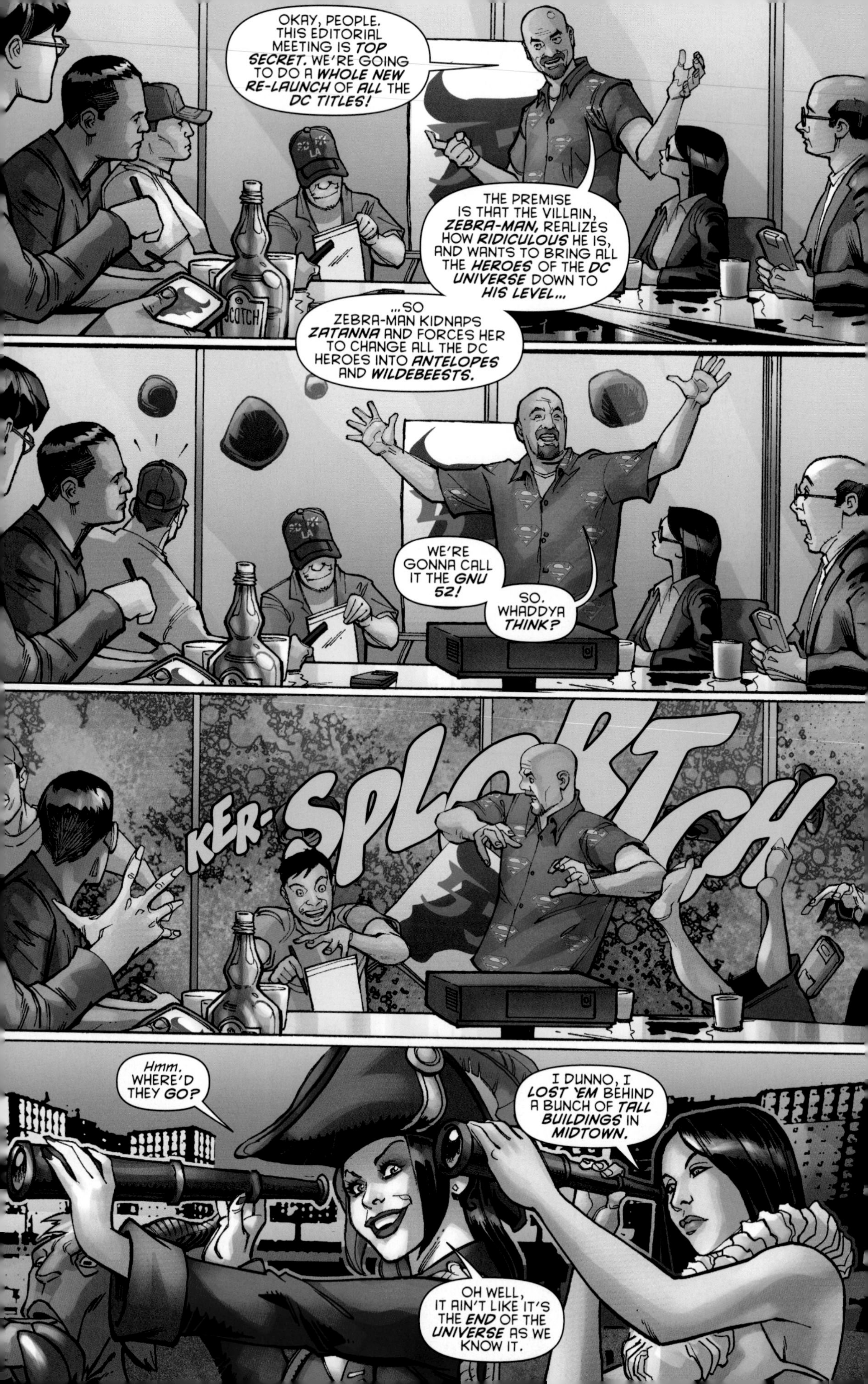
OKAY, PEOPLE. THIS EDITORIAL MEETING IS TOP SECRET. WE'RE GOING TO DO A WHOLE NEW RE-LAUNCH OF ALL THE DC TITLES!
THE PREMISE IS THAT THE VILLAIN, ZEBRA-MAN, REALIZES HOW RIDICULOUS HE IS, AND WANTS TO BRING ALL THE HEROES OF THE DC UNIVERSE DOWN TO HIS LEVEL...
...SO ZEBRA-MAN KIDNAPS ZATANNA AND FORCES HER TO CHANGE ALL THE DC HEROES INTO ANTELOPES AND WILDEBEESTS.
SCOTCH
WE'RE GONNA CALL IT THE GNU 52!
SO. WHADDYA THINK?
KER-SPLORTCH
Hmm. WHERE'D THEY GO?
I DUNNO, I LOST 'EM BEHIND A BUNCH OF TALL BUILDINGS IN MIDTOWN.
OH WELL, IT AIN'T LIKE IT'S THE END OF THE UNIVERSE AS WE KNOW IT.

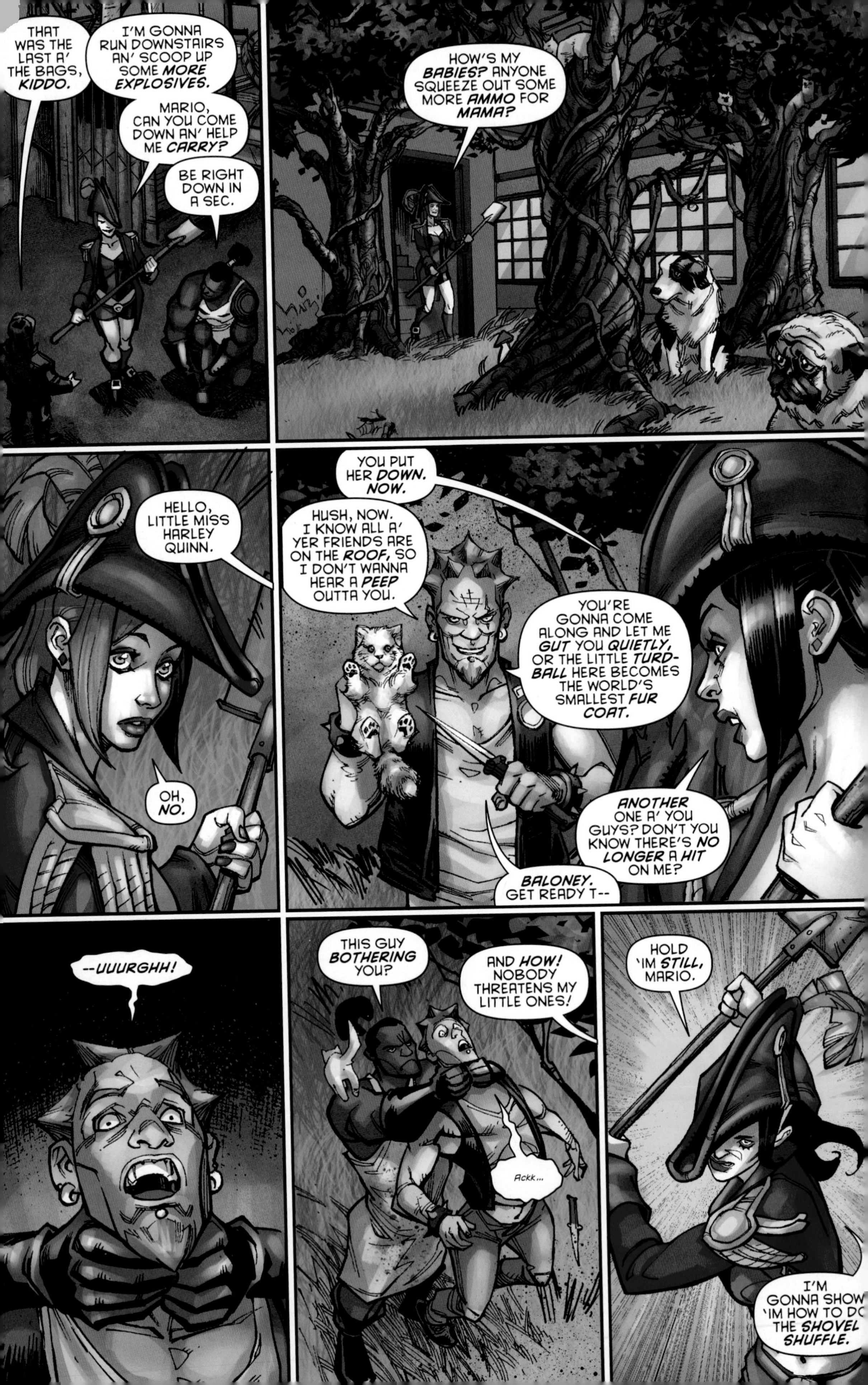
THAT WAS THE LAST A' THE BAGS, KIDDO.
I'M GONNA RUN DOWNSTAIRS AN' SCOOP UP SOME MORE EXPLOSIVES.
MARIO, CAN YOU COME DOWN AN' HELP ME CARRY?
BE RIGHT DOWN IN A SEC.
HOW'S MY BABIES? ANYONE SQUEEZE OUT SOME MORE AMMO FOR MAMA?
HELLO, LITTLE MISS HARLEY QUINN.
OH, NO.
YOU PUT HER DOWN. NOW.
HUSH, NOW. I KNOW ALL A' YER FRIENDS ARE ON THE ROOF, SO I DON'T WANNA HEAR A PEEP OUTTA YOU.
YOU'RE GONNA COME ALONG AND LET ME GUT YOU QUIETLY, OR THE LITTLE TURD-BALL HERE BECOMES THE WORLD'S SMALLEST FUR COAT.
ANOTHER ONE A' YOU GUYS? DON'T YOU KNOW THERE'S NO LONGER A HIT ON ME?
BALONEY. GET READY T--
--UUURGHH!
THIS GUY BOTHERING YOU?
AND HOW! NOBODY THREATENS MY LITTLE ONES!
Ackk...
HOLD 'IM STILL, MARIO.
I'M GONNA SHOW 'IM HOW TO DO THE SHOVEL SHUFFLE.

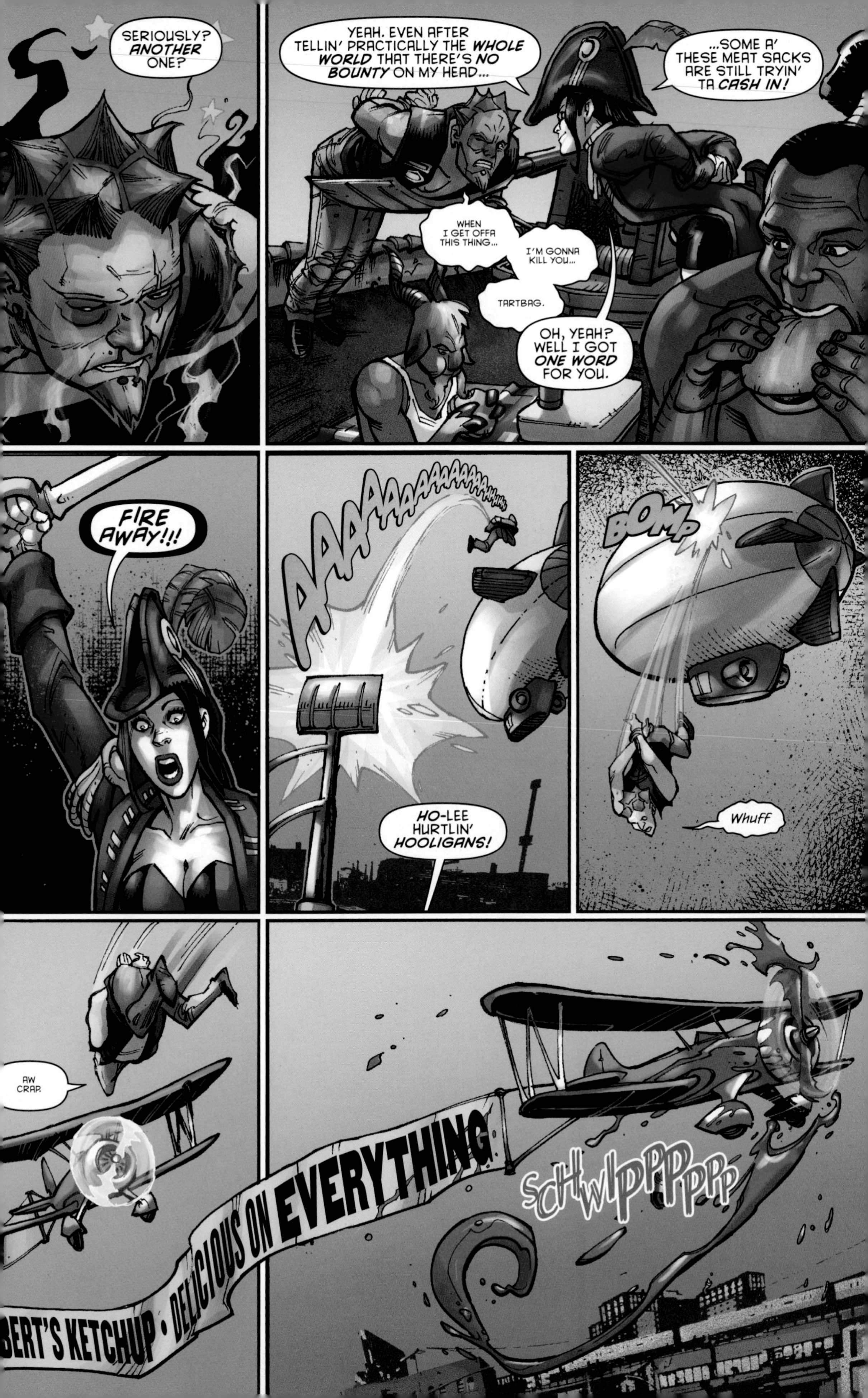
SERIOUSLY? ANOTHER ONE?
YEAH. EVEN AFTER TELLIN' PRACTICALLY THE WHOLE WORLD THAT THERE'S NO BOUNTY ON MY HEAD...
...SOME A' THESE MEAT SACKS ARE STILL TRYIN' TA CASH IN!
WHEN I GET OFFA THIS THING...
I'M GONNA KILL YOU...
TARTBAG.
OH, YEAH? WELL I GOT ONE WORD FOR YOU.
FIRE AWAY!!!
AAAAAAAAAAAAAAAAAAA
HO-LEE HURTLIN' HOOLIGANS!
BOMP
Whuff
AW CRAP.
BERT'S KETCHUP • DELICIOUS ON EVERYTHING
SCHWIPPPPPP

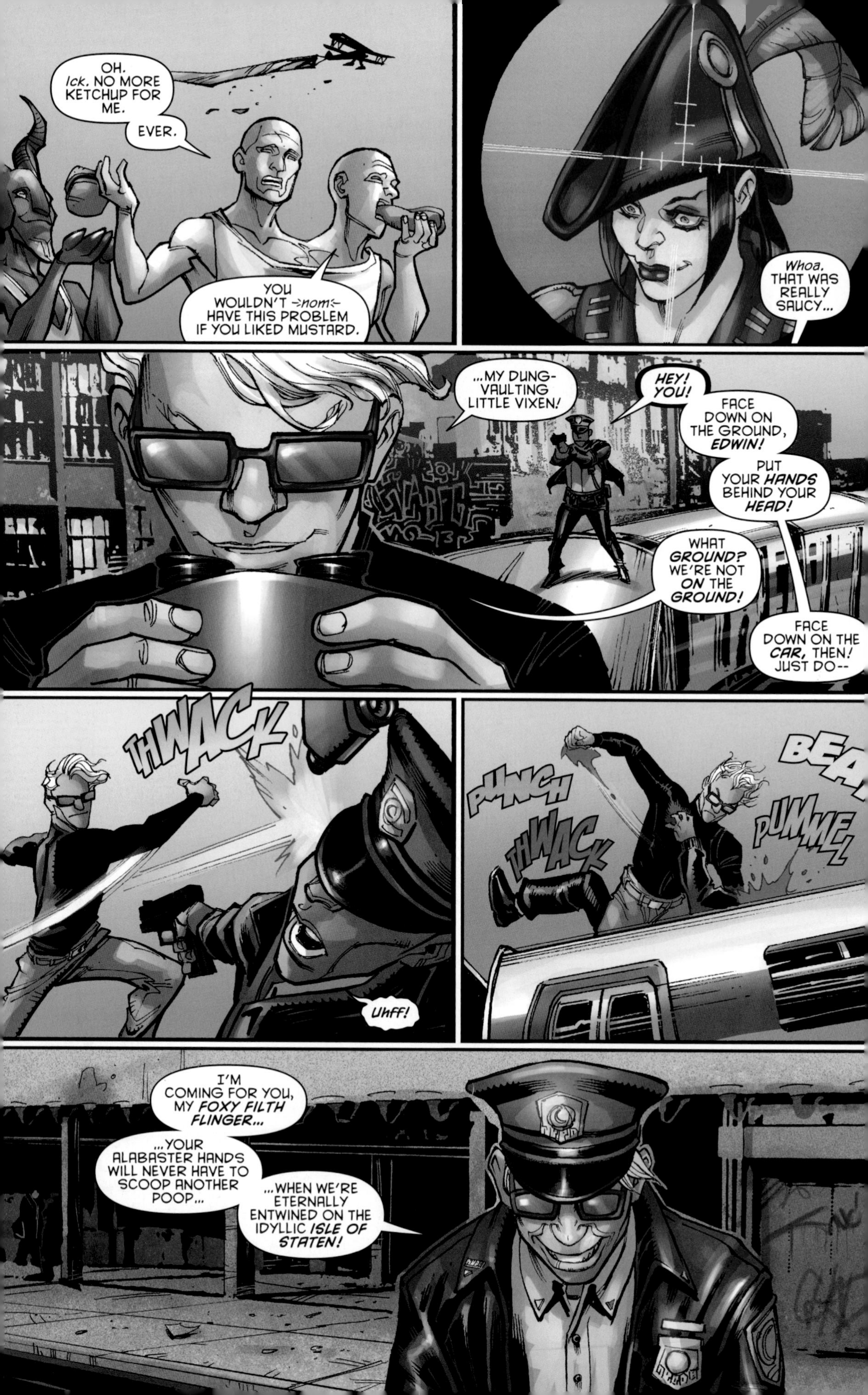

OH. *Ick.* NO MORE KETCHUP FOR ME.
EVER.
YOU WOULDN'T ~nom~ HAVE THIS PROBLEM IF YOU LIKED MUSTARD.
Whoa. THAT WAS REALLY SAUCY...
...MY DUNG-VAULTING LITTLE VIXEN!
HEY! YOU!
FACE DOWN ON THE GROUND, EDWIN!
PUT YOUR HANDS BEHIND YOUR HEAD!
WHAT GROUND? WE'RE NOT ON THE GROUND!
FACE DOWN ON THE CAR, THEN! JUST DO--
THWACK
Uhff!
PUNCH
THWACK
PUMMEL
I'M COMING FOR YOU, MY FOXY FILTH FLINGER...
...YOUR ALABASTER HANDS WILL NEVER HAVE TO SCOOP ANOTHER POOP...
...WHEN WE'RE ETERNALLY ENTWINED ON THE IDYLLIC ISLE OF STATEN!

Harley Quinn #0 Variant Cover by Stephane Roux

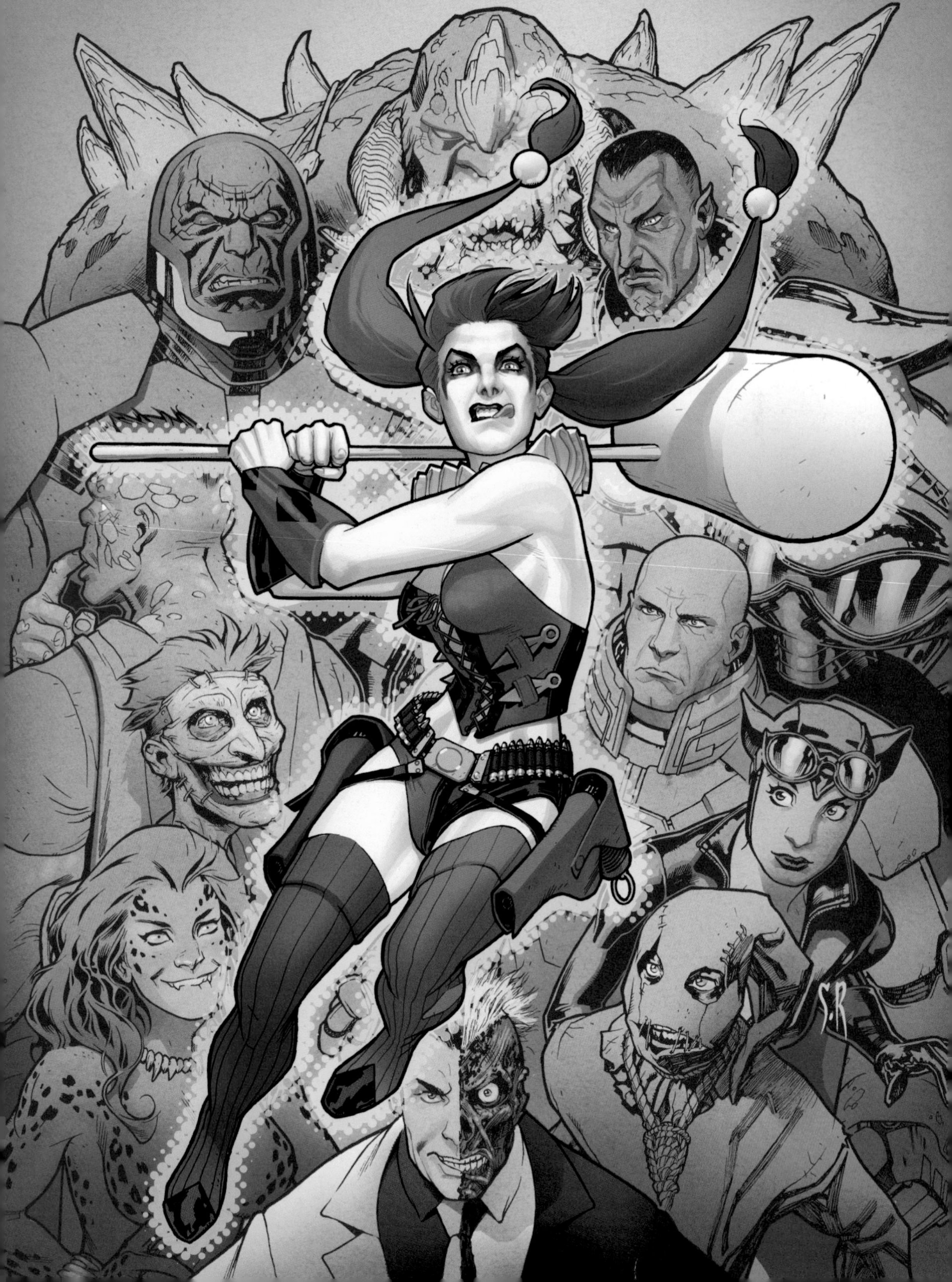

Harley Quinn #1 Variant Cover by Adam Hughes

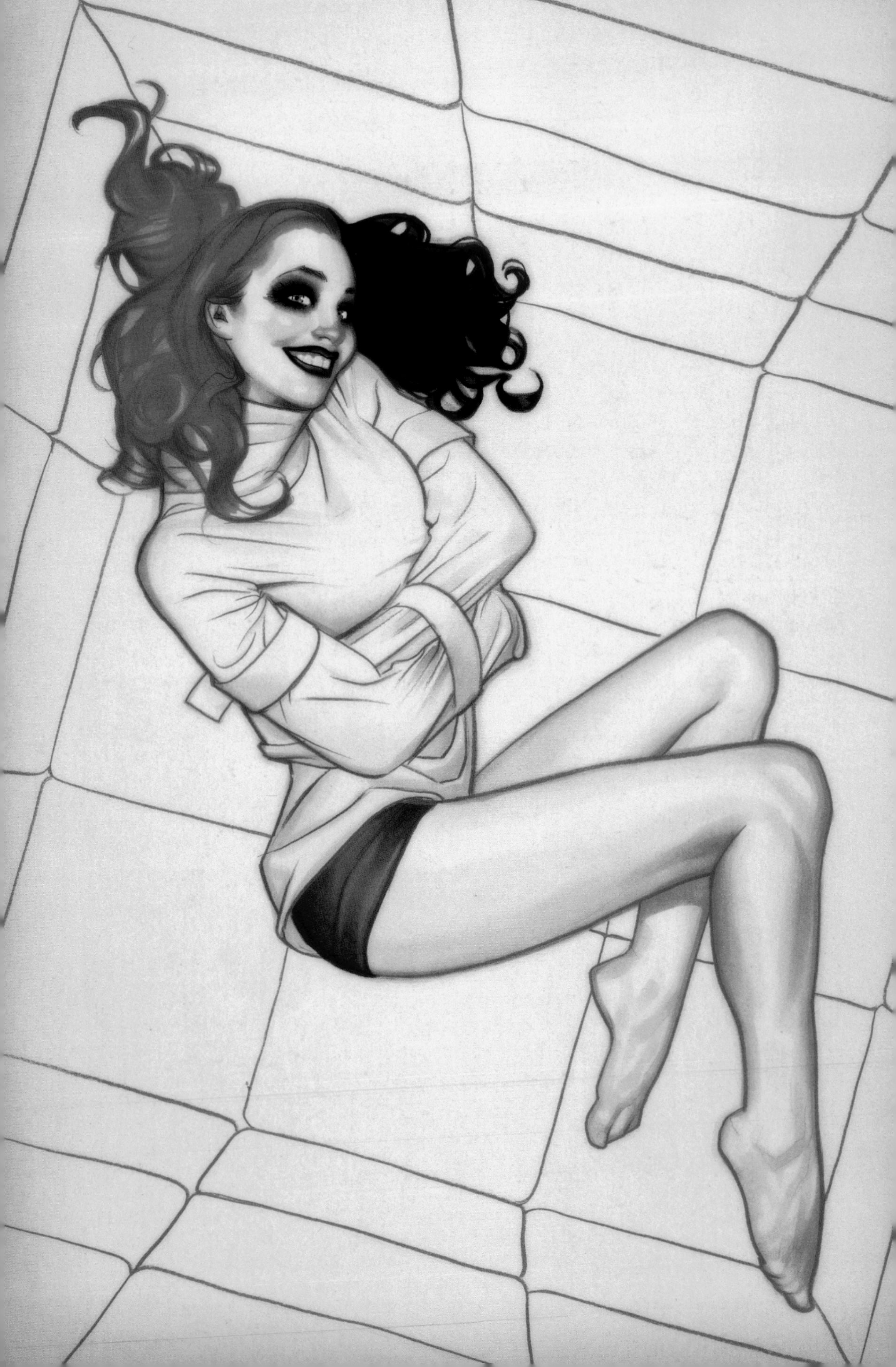

Harley Quinn #1 2nd Printing Cover by
Amanda Conner and Paul Mounts

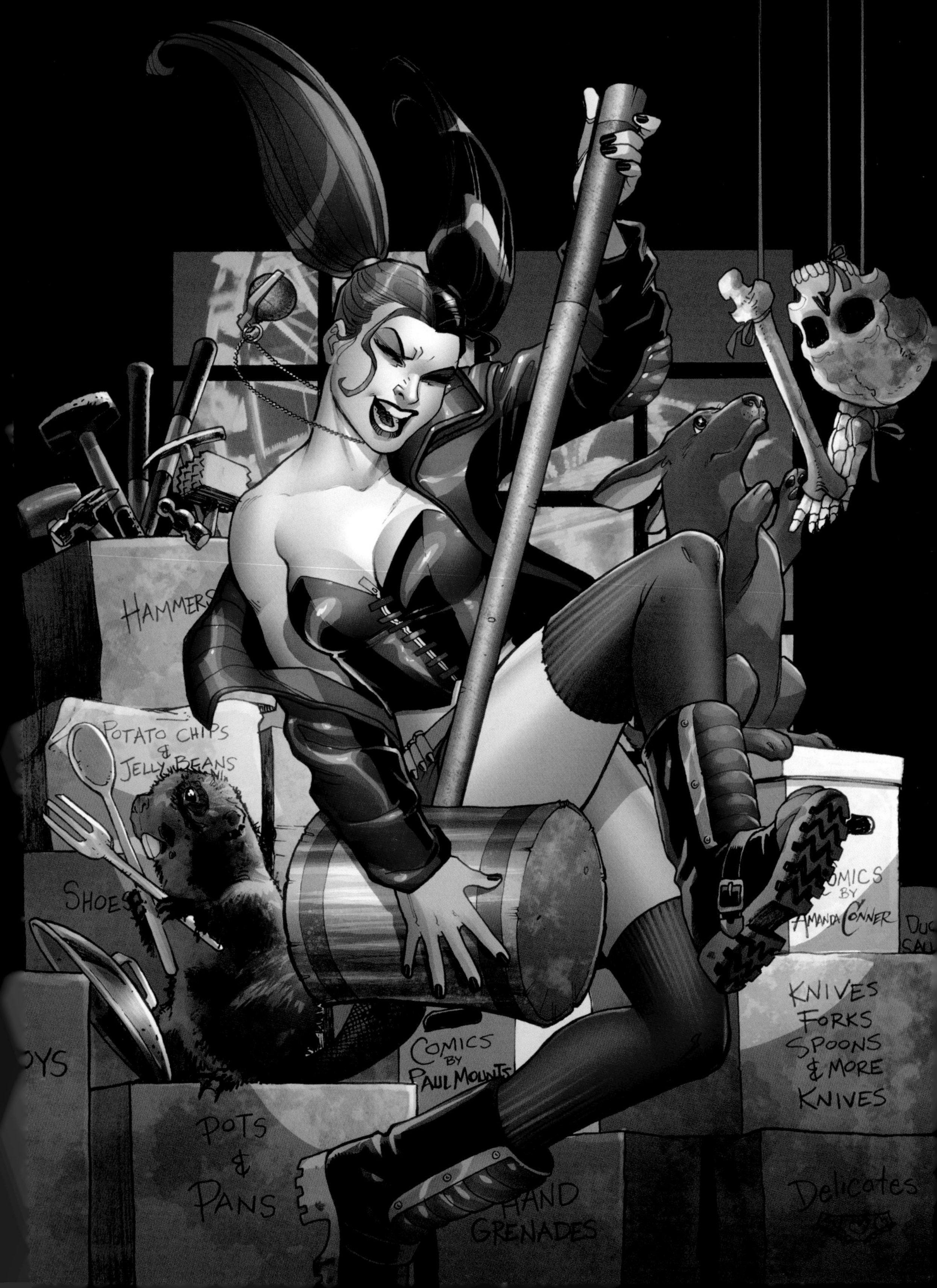
HAMMERS
POTATO CHIPS & JELLY BEANS
SHOES
COMICS BY AMANDA CONNER
KNIVES FORKS SPOONS & MORE KNIVES
COMICS BY PAUL MOUNTS
POTS & PANS
HAND GRENADES
Delicates

Harley Quinn #1 3rd Printing Cover by Pop Mahn

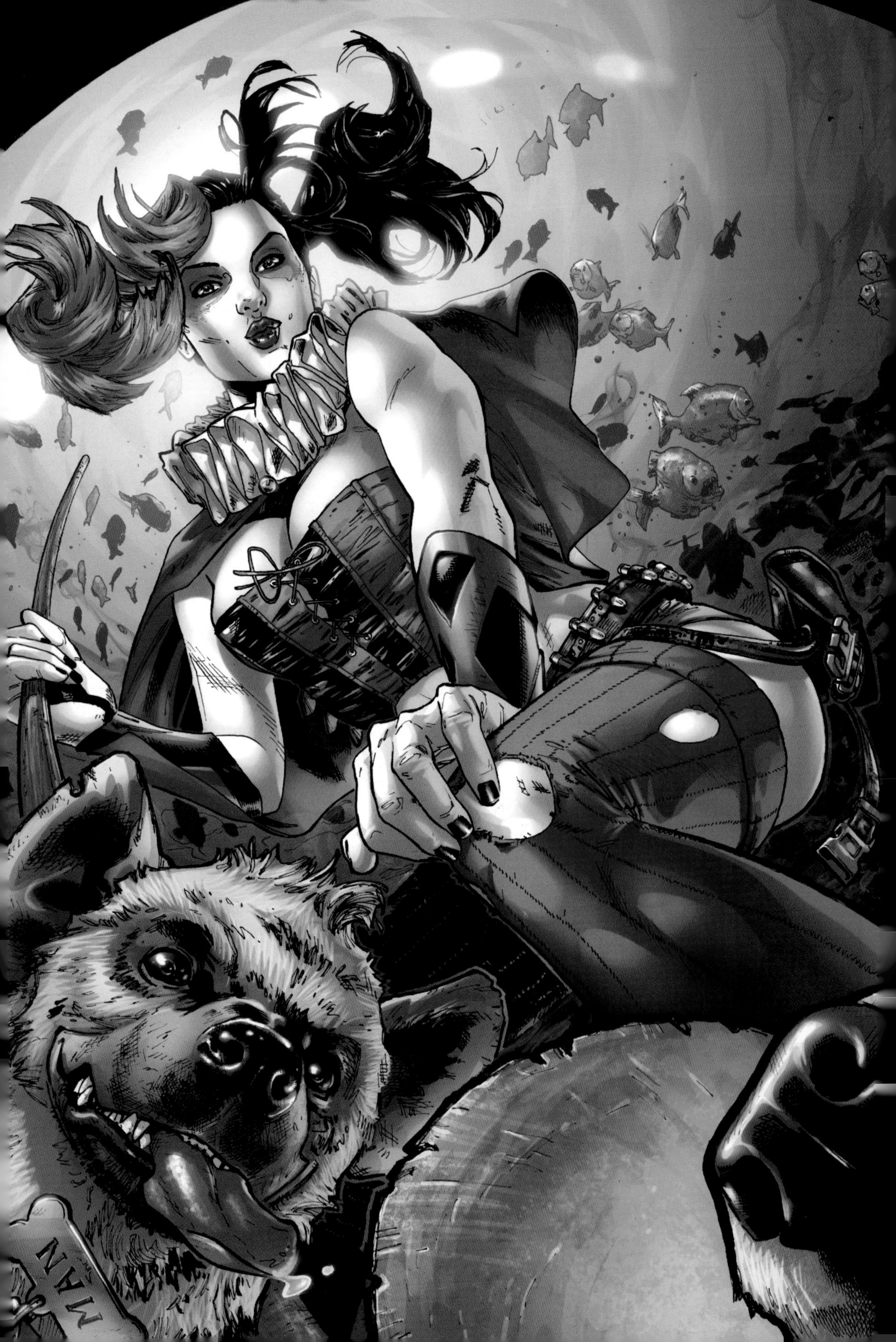
MAN

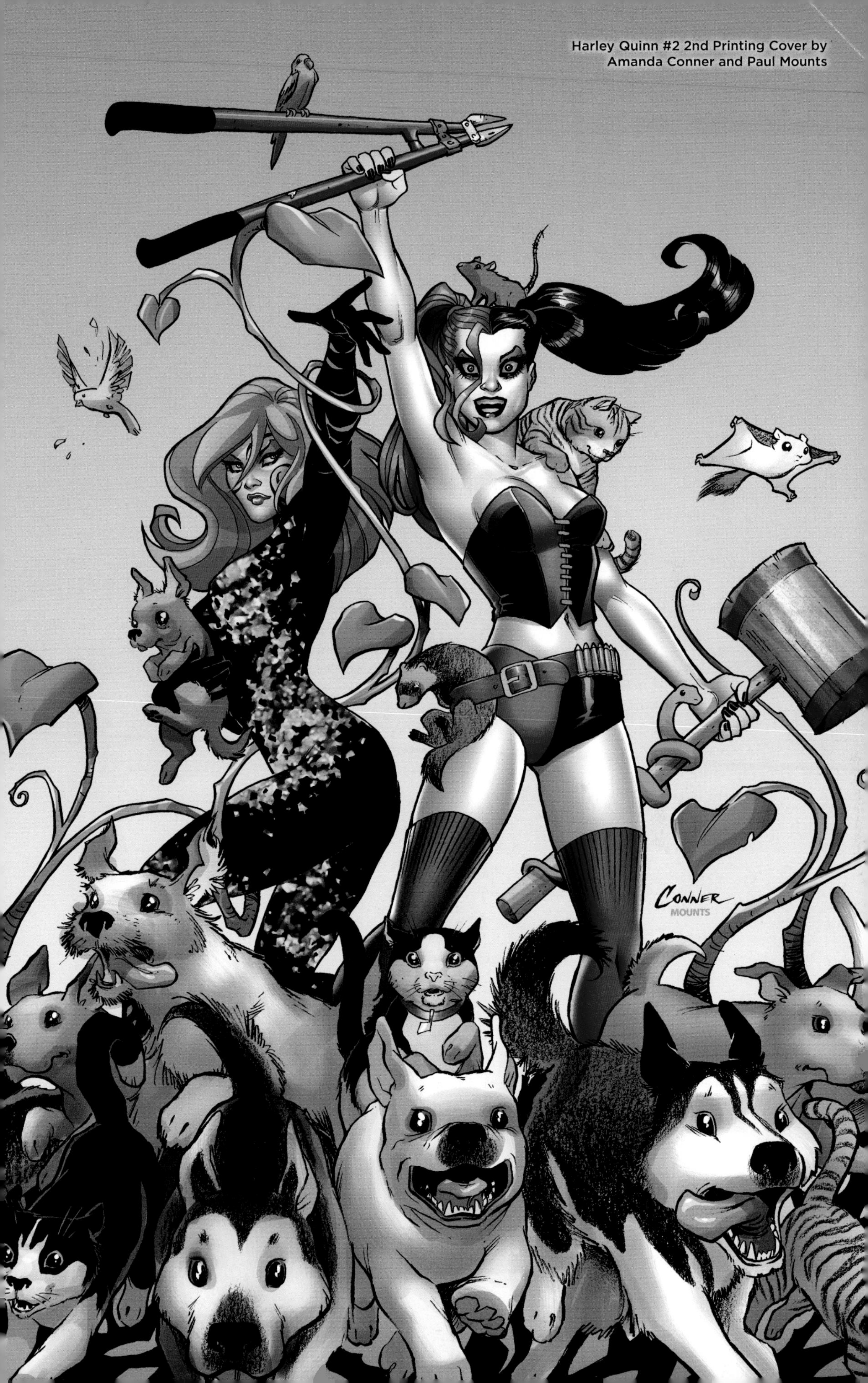
CONNER
MOUNTS

Harley Quinn #2 2nd Printing Cover by Amanda Conner and Paul Mounts

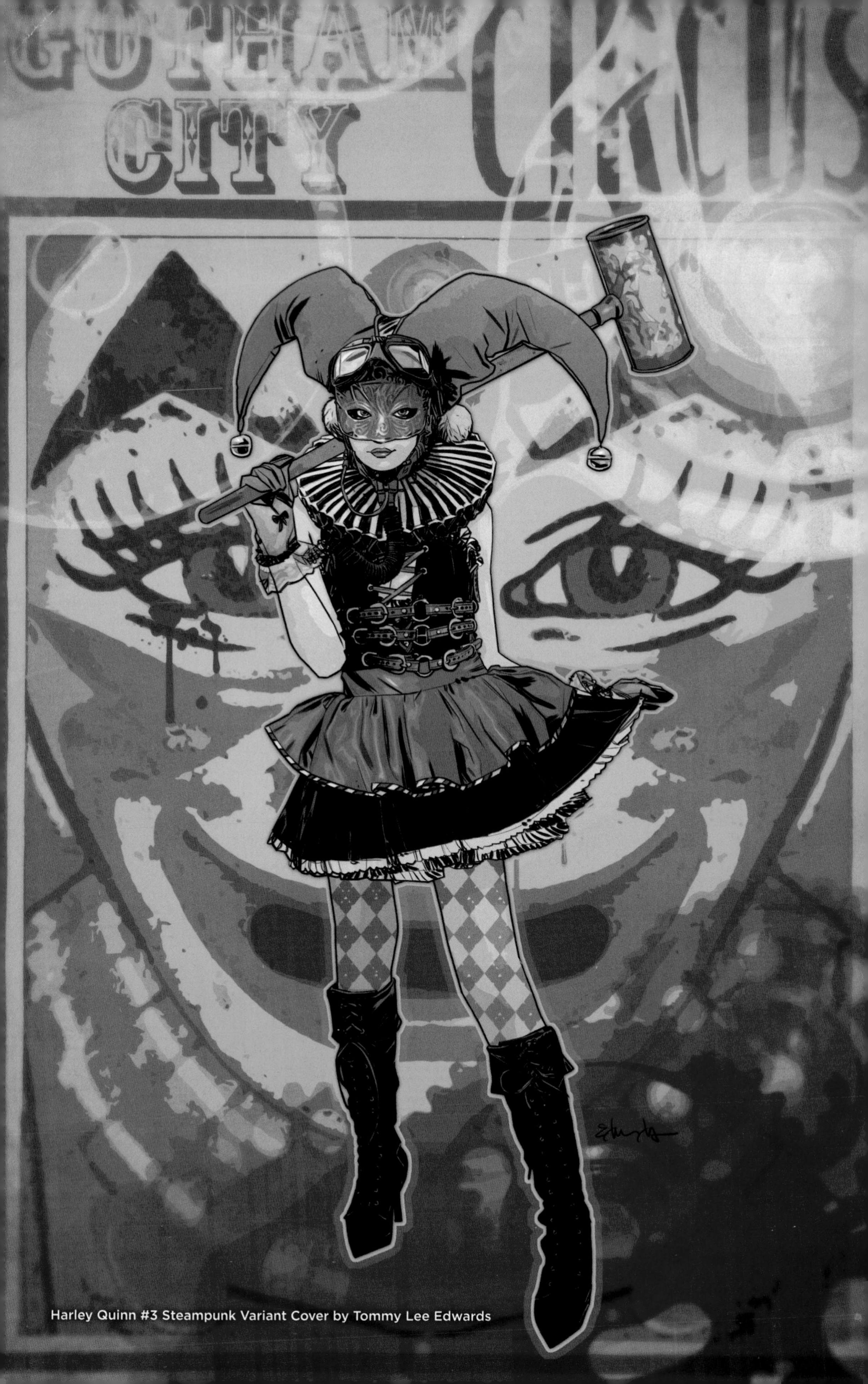
GOTHAM CITY
CIRCUS

Harley Quinn #3 Steampunk Variant Cover by Tommy Lee Edwards

Harley Quinn #4 Robot Chicken Variant Cover by RC Stoodios

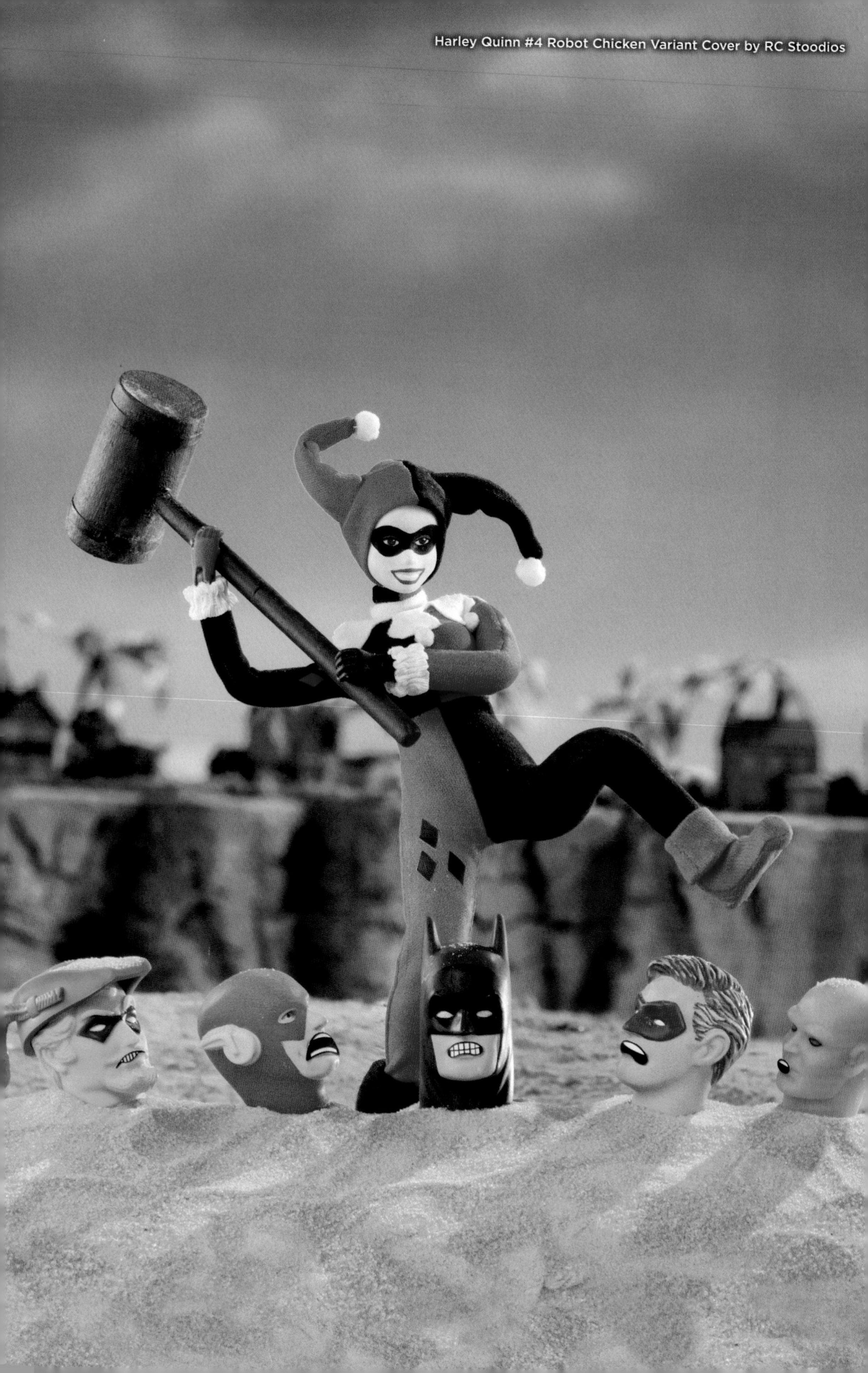

Harley Quinn #5 MAD Variant Cover by Sergio Aragones and Tom Luth

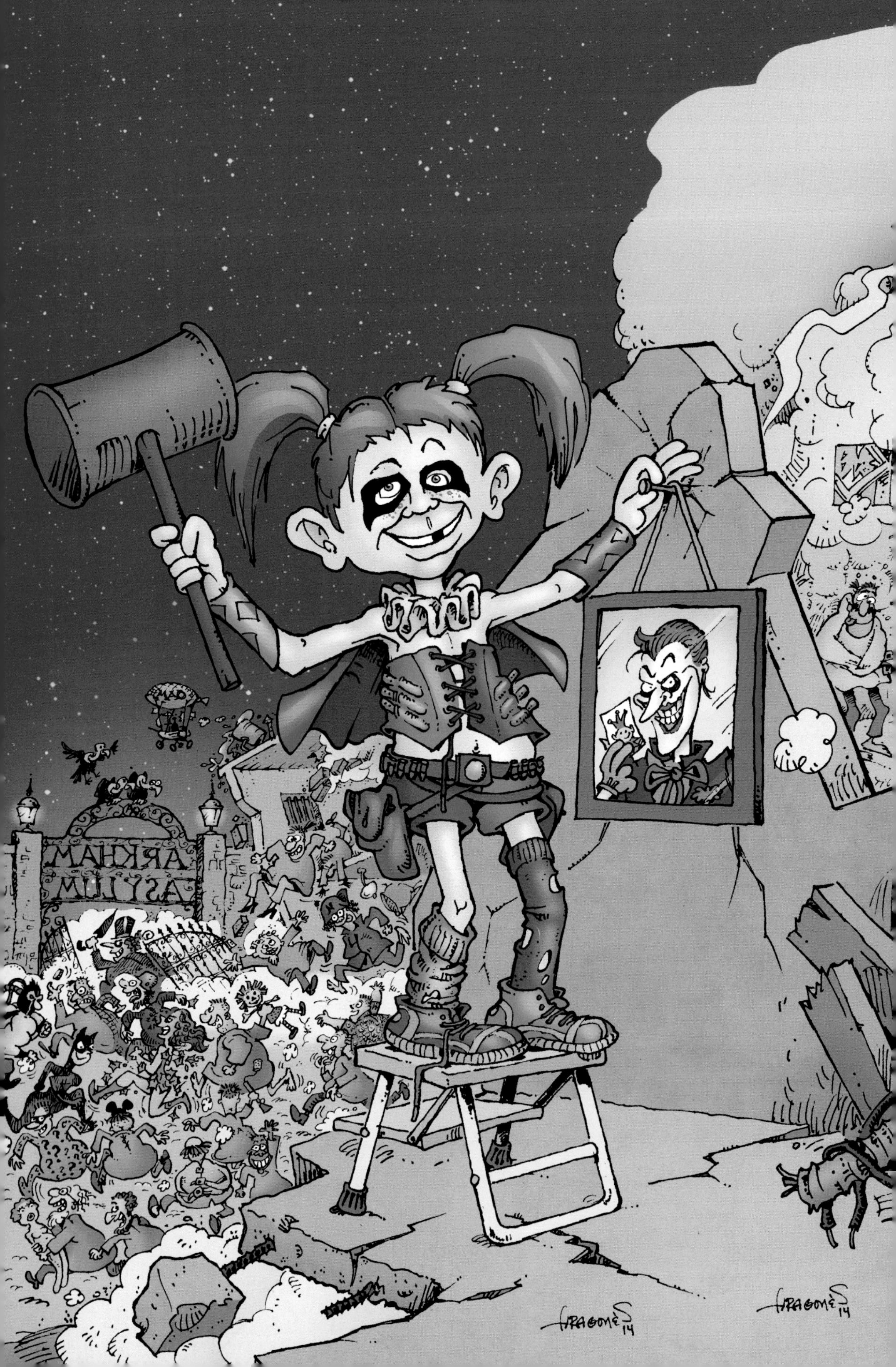
MAD
ARKHAM
ASYLUM
ARAGONÉS 14
ARAGONÉS 14

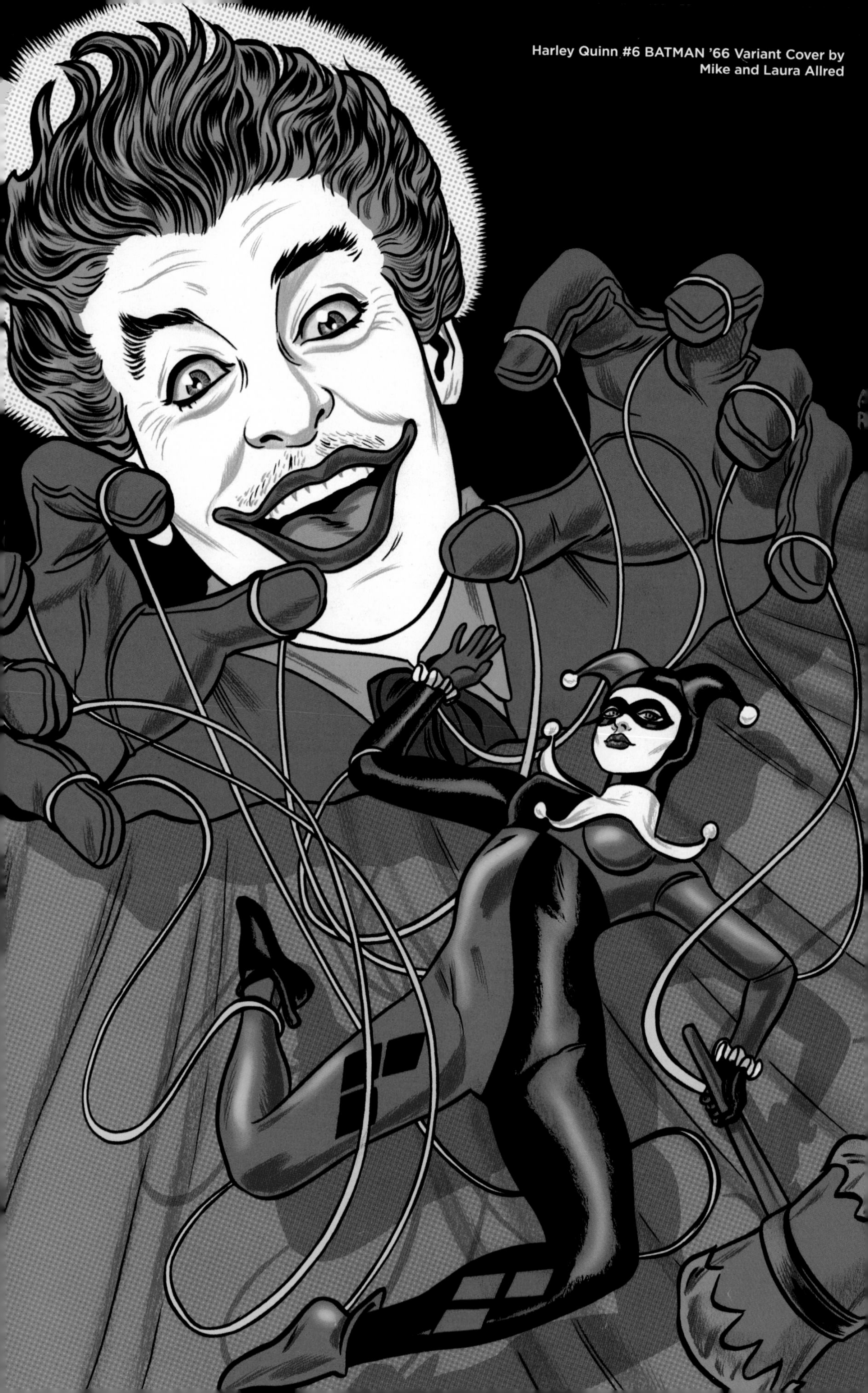

Harley Quinn #6 BATMAN '66 Variant Cover by
Mike and Laura Allred

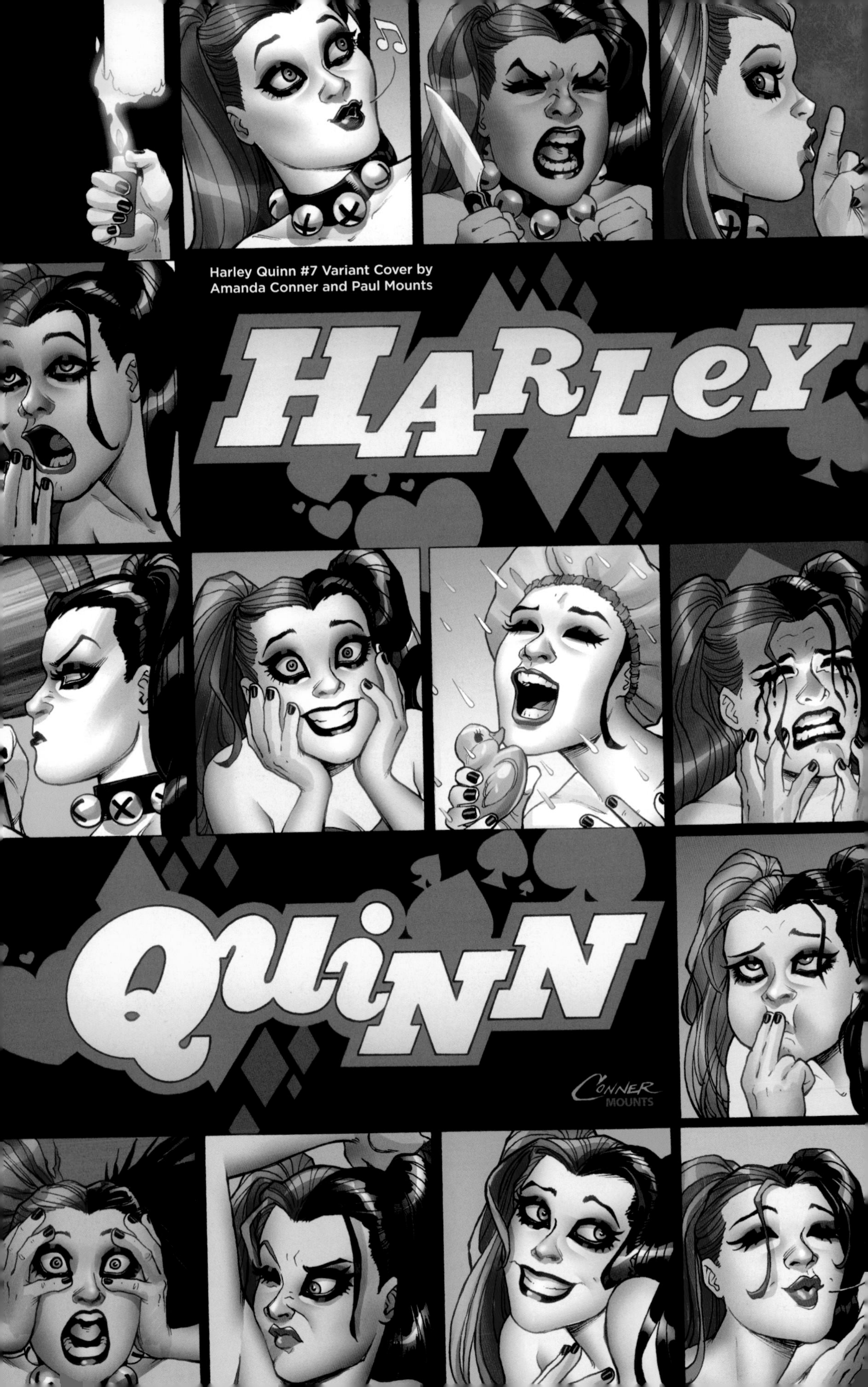
HARLEY
QUINN
CONNER
MOUNTS
Harley Quinn #7 Variant Cover by
Amanda Conner and Paul Mounts

Harley Quinn #7 Bombshell Variant Cover by Ant Lucia

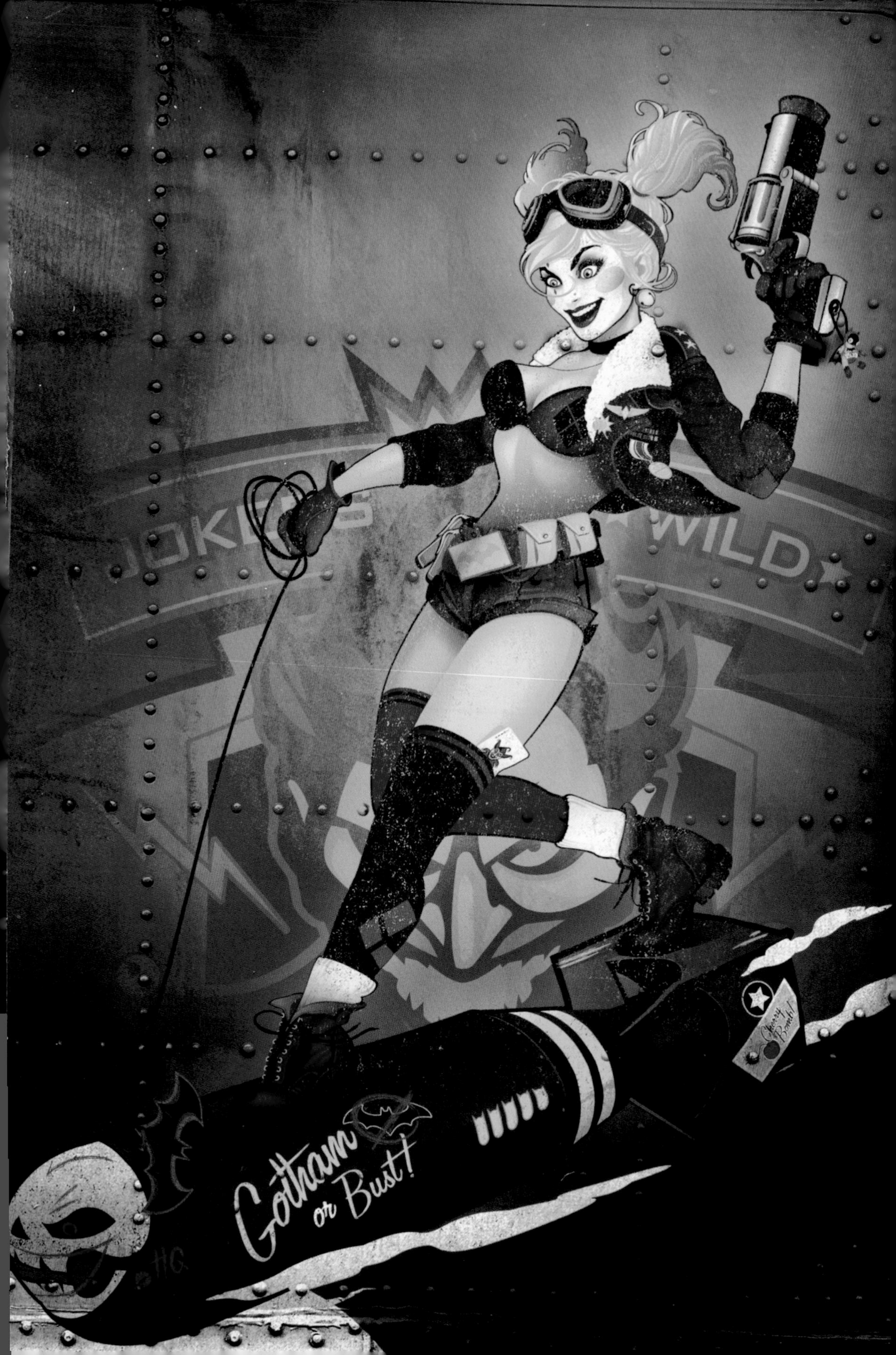
JOKERS WILD
Gotham or Bust!
Cherry Bomb!

Harley Quinn #8 Variant Cover by Dan Panosian

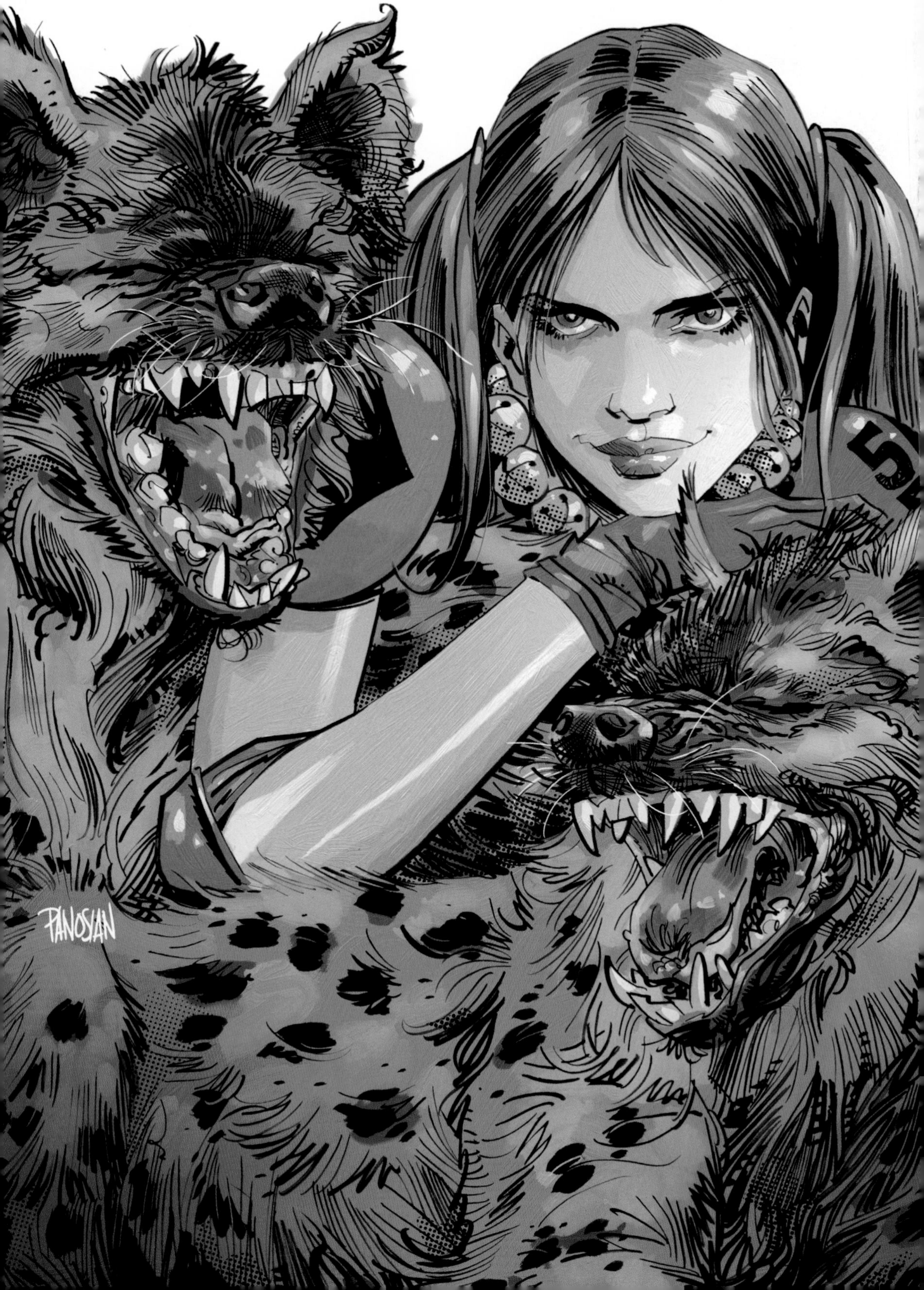
PANOSYAN

Harley Quinn #8 Batman 75th Anniversary
Variant Cover by Dave Johnson

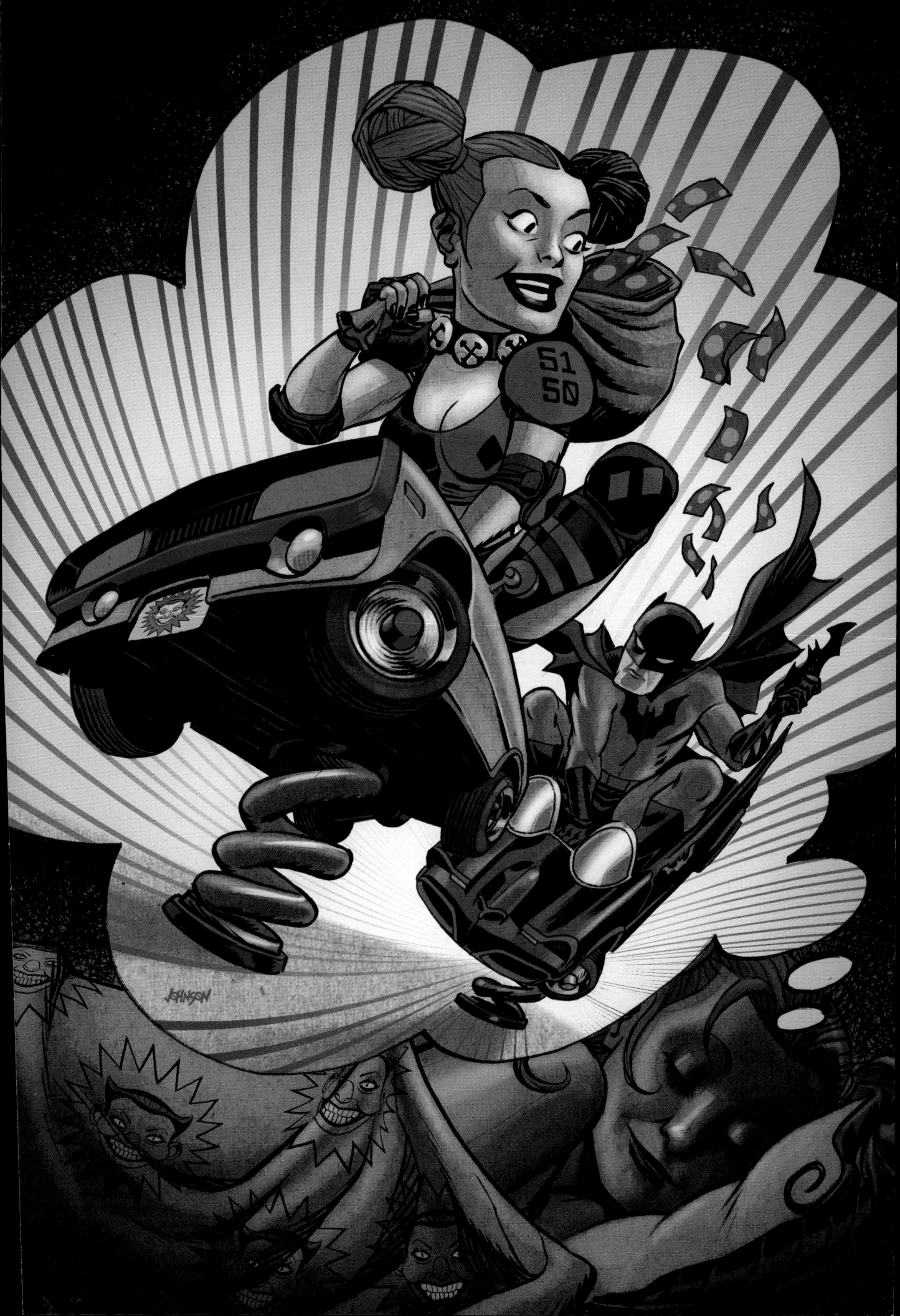
51
50
JOHNSON

Harley Quinn #0 Director's Cut Cover by Amanda Conner and Paul Mounts

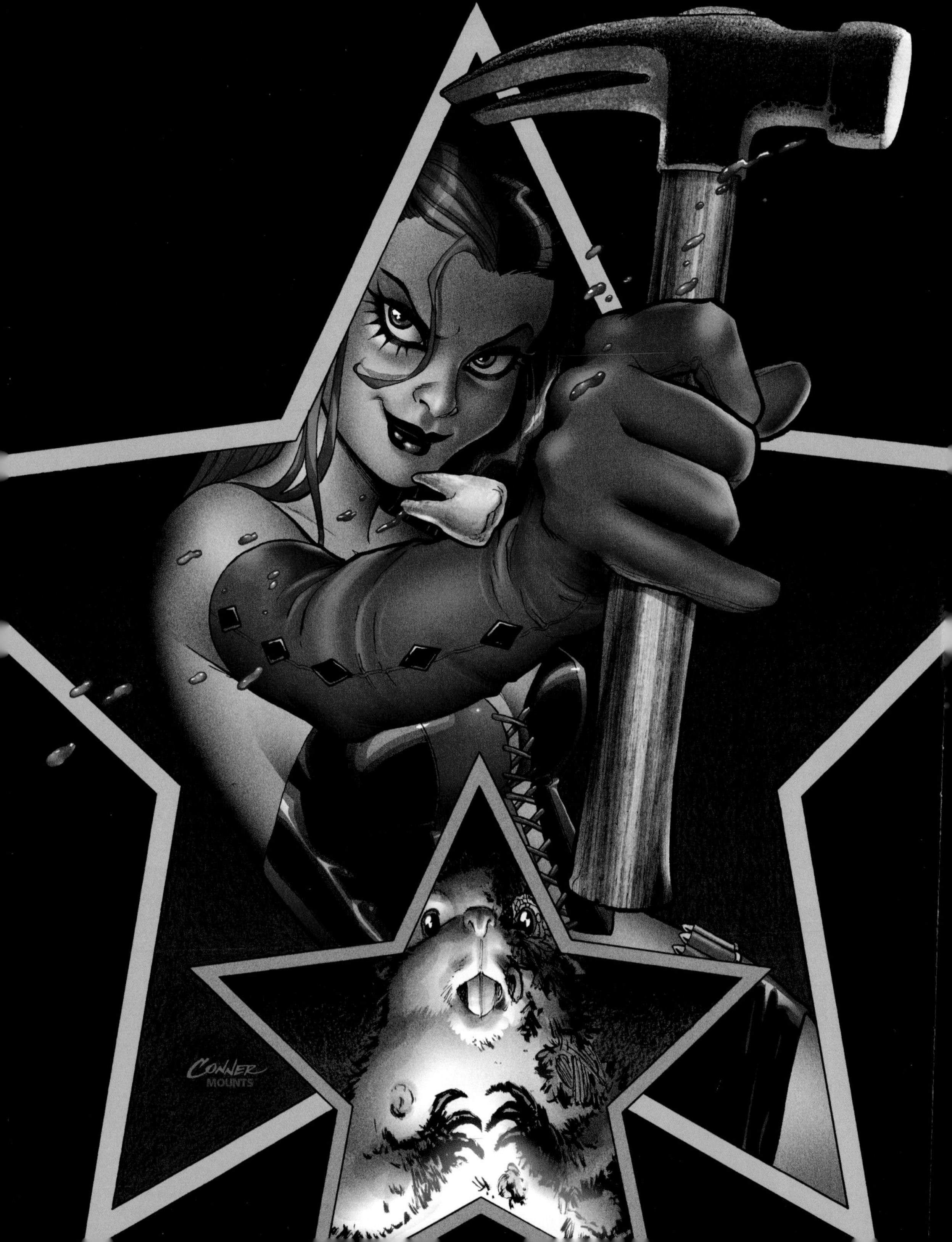
CONNER
MOUNTS

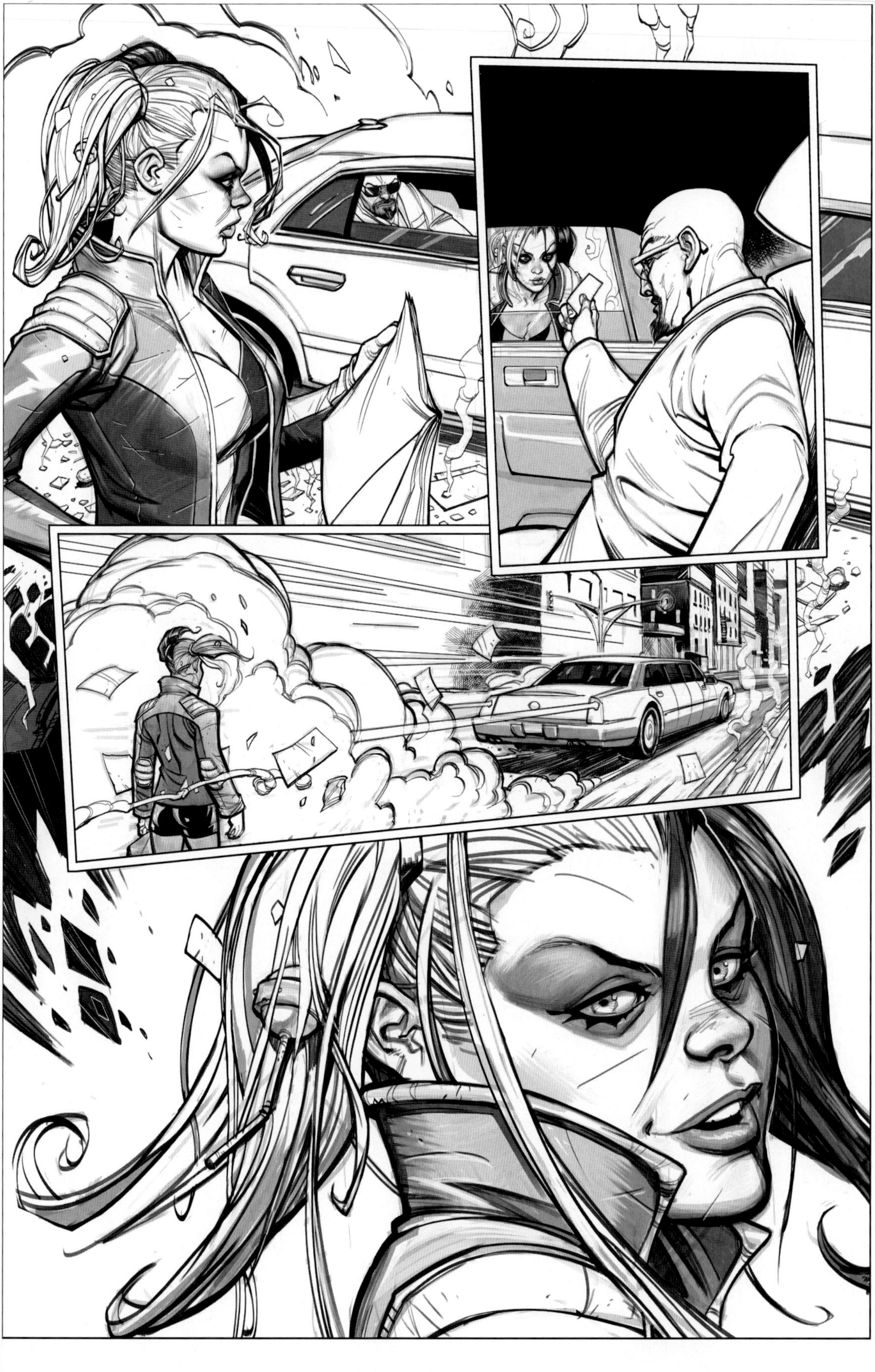

PENCILLER
INKER
PAGE#
TITLE
ISSUE #
MONTH
INTERIORS
DOUBLE PAGE SPREAD: CUT AS SHOWN, ABUT PAGE EDGES. TAPE ON BACK. DO NOT OVERLAP

PENCILLER
INKER
PAGE#
TITLE
ISSUE #
MONTH
INTERIORS
DOUBLE PAGE SPREAD: CUT AS SHOWN, ABUT PAGE EDGES. TAPE ON BACK. DO NOT OVERLAP

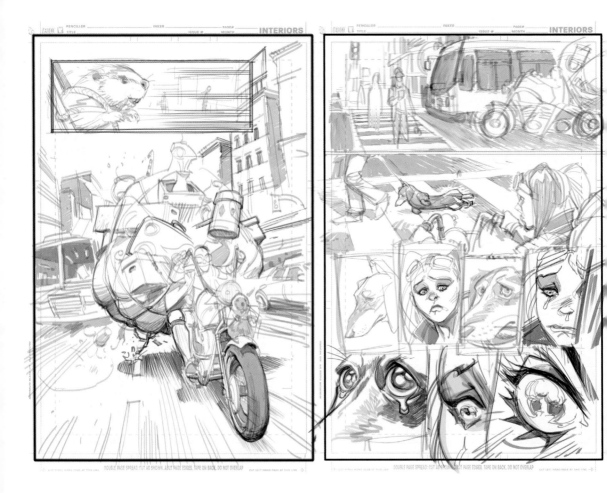

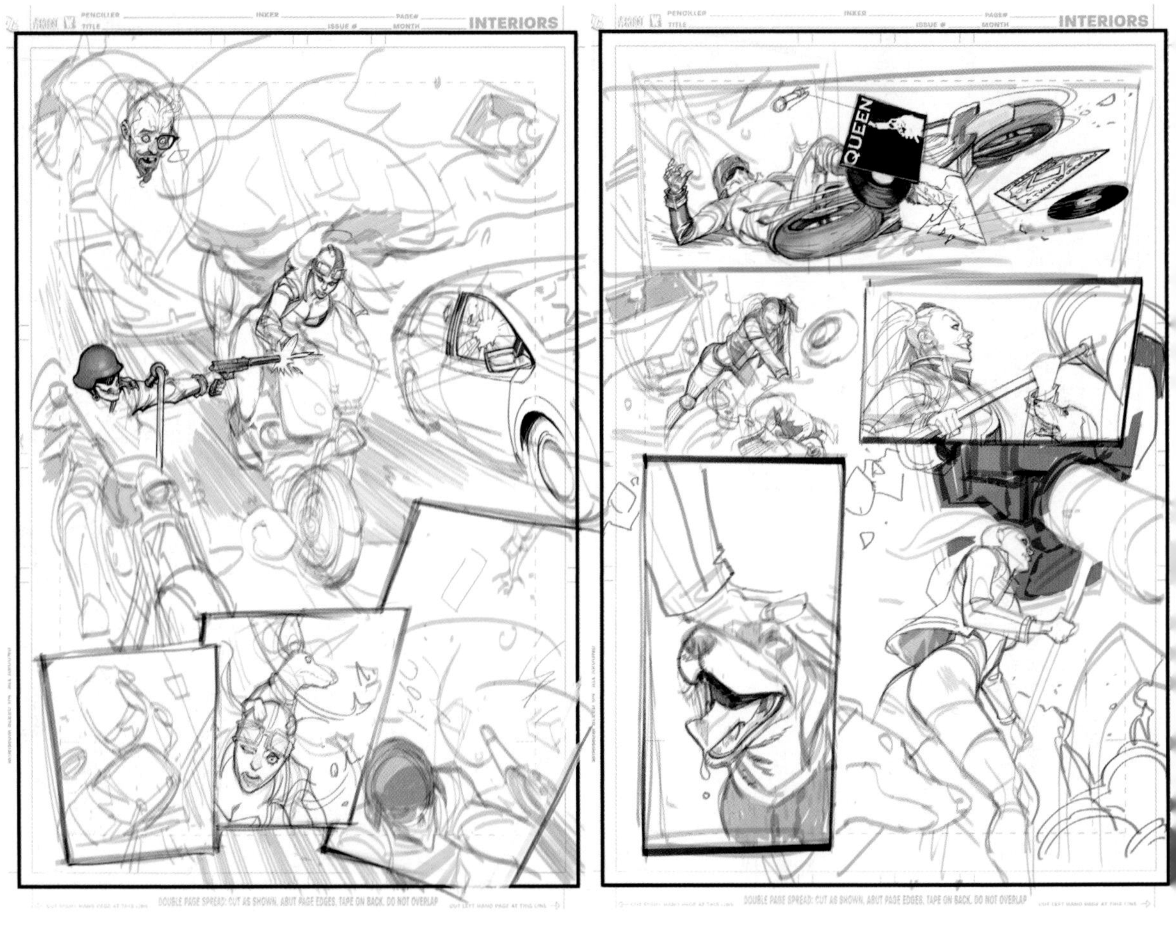
PENCILLER
INKER
PAGE#
TITLE
ISSUE #
MONTH
INTERIORS
QUEEN
DOUBLE PAGE SPREAD: CUT AS SHOWN, ABUT PAGE EDGES, TAPE ON BACK. DO NOT OVERLAP

PENCILLER INKER PAGE# **INTERIORS**
TITLE ISSUE # MONTH

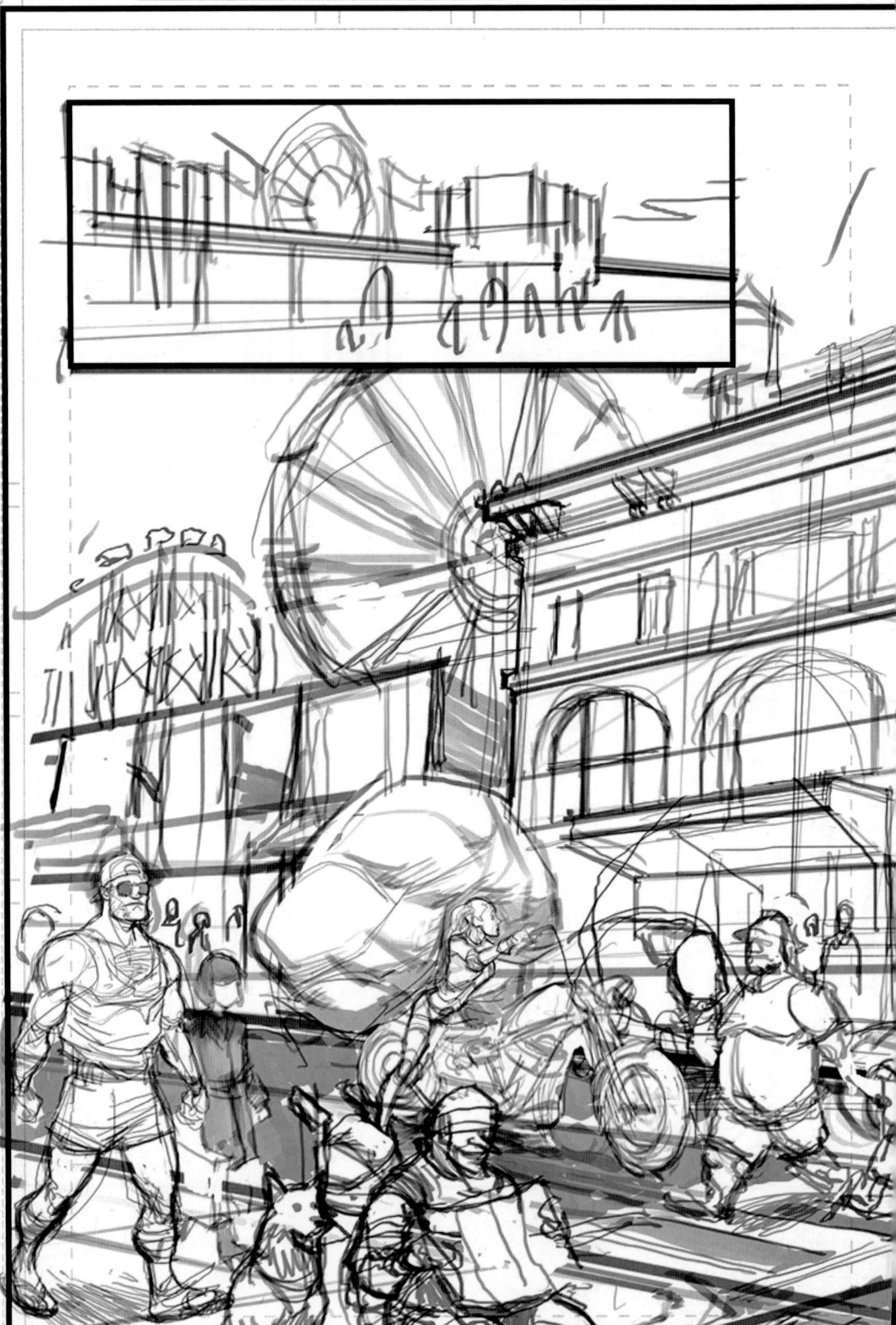

MINIMUM BLEED 1/4" ALL AROUND

CUT RIGHT-HAND PAGE AT THIS LINE — DOUBLE PAGE SPREAD: CUT AS SHOWN, ABUT PAGE EDGES, TAPE ON BACK, DO NOT OVERLAP — CUT LEFT HAND PAGE AT THIS LINE

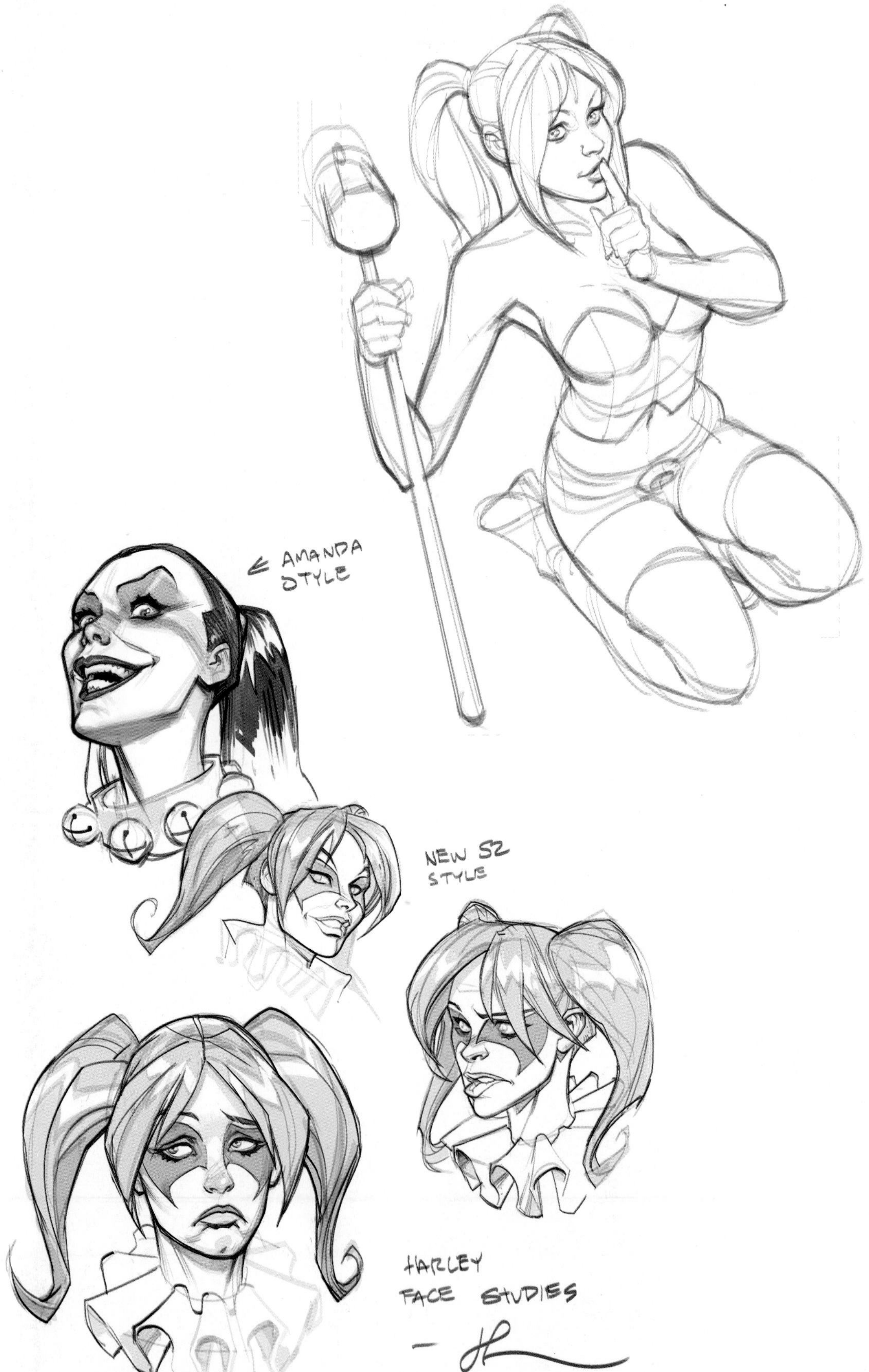
← AMANDA STYLE
NEW 52 STYLE
HARLEY FACE STUDIES